Principles of the Carriage of (

Principles of the Carriage of Goods by Sea offers students studying this topic as part of their LLM or LLB course an accessible, comprehensive overview of the subject from a leading expert in the field. Written specifically with students in mind, concentrating on principles, and tailored to common law coverage, this title presents all the essential topics and is supported by the following useful pedagogy:

- Line Diagrams: illustrating the relationships between parties so that this may be understood at a glance; also, where appropriate, time lines
- Case Studies: looking at topical matters such as piracy, and problematic areas of law such as reachable on arrival clauses and the carriage of bulk oil by sea
- Sample Problem Questions: problem questions and suggestions to help students to prepare for assessment
- Annotated Appendices: concise appendix of the most important legislation and international conventions, with useful annotation from the author that explains these and puts them in context

Paul Todd is Professor of Commercial and Maritime Law at the University of Southampton. He has been teaching law for almost 40 years, and has written a wide range of publications in international trade law and carriage of goods by sea.

Principles of the Carriage of Goods by Sea

Paul Todd

Routledge
Taylor & Francis Group

LONDON AND NEW YORK

First published 2016
by Routledge
2 Park Square, Milton Park, Abingdon, Oxon, OX14 4RN

and by Routledge
711 Third Avenue, New York, NY 10017

Routledge is an imprint of the Taylor & Francis Group, an Informa business

© 2016 Paul Todd

British Library Cataloguing-in-Publication Data
A catalogue record for this book is available from the British Library

Library of Congress Cataloging-in-Publication Data
Todd, Paul, 1954–
    Principles of the carriage of goods by sea / Paul Todd.
        pages cm
    Includes bibliographical references and index.
    1. Maritime law. I. Title.
    K1160.T63 2016
    343.09'62—dc23
    2015016220

ISBN: 978-0-415-74374-7 (hbk)
ISBN: 978-0-415-74373-0 (pbk)
ISBN: 978-1-315-81349-3 (ebk)

Typeset in Joanna
by Apex CoVantage, LLC

Outline Contents

Detailed Contents

Preface

This is a book on principles, of the English law of carriage of goods by sea, and it is aimed at students of the subject.

There are other books on carriage of goods by sea. Some are large reference books, very comprehensive and authoritative, aimed primarily at practitioners, or perhaps at students at the dissertation stage. I have nothing against these books. They do what they set out to do very well, are authorities in the sense that they are cited in court, and no doubt influence the development of the law. I think it is fair to say, though, that they are not very useful for teaching students. Indeed, they often seem to assume that their readers already know about the subject under discussion.

This book is not like that. It is not intended to be used primarily as a reference book, or as an authority to be cited in court. It is intended to be used to teach students the principles of the law of carriage of goods by sea. It assumes no prior knowledge of either law of practice of carriage of goods by sea. It is helpful if you know how English law works, and can handle cases and statutes. It also helps if you have prior knowledge of the English law of contract, though there are two chapters devoted to general legal principles, which attempt to offer at least some explanation.

Much of carriage of goods by sea is contract-based, and so we are looking at a specialist application of the general law of contract. Absolutely central, and forming the backbone of the book, are charterparties and bills of lading. Not all of the book is about contract. The bill of lading has properties that go beyond the carriage contract. There is some legislation we need to consider, based on international conventions. It is also important to be aware of the bailment relationship that underpins carriage (to the extent that it is not modified by contract), to the torts of negligence and conversion, and to the principles upon which defences work.

It is important to appreciate that carriage is not carried out in a vacuum, but is part of a wider transaction. To understand how various relationships intermesh is an important part of the subject. All of this is the stuff of this book. We also take a little space to consider carriage in the modern world, and where it might go in the near future.

This is a book on the English law of carriage. That might seem parochial, but contracts all over the world are made subject to English law, and English law also forms the basis of the law of (particularly) Commonwealth countries. It is therefore a subject that has a genuinely worldwide application. Though there is some legislation, the subject is based very largely on cases, and I make no apologies for making the cases central to the text. With one exception (in the first chapter), I try to use cases as authorities, and not (as some writers seem to treat them) merely examples. The cases make the law, and there would not be a lot we could say in their absence.

I have had some difficulty keeping the book down to a reasonable length, and have had to be fairly ruthless about the limits of the subject. Conflict of laws and dispute resolution no doubt have an important role to play in practice, but they are not specific to carriage of goods by sea and are therefore omitted from this book. Some of the books have voluminous appendices, but all the legislation and main standard forms are freely available on the Internet, so I have kept appendices short. I have also not devoted a great deal of space to the Rotterdam Rules. There are many good ideas in the Rotterdam Rules, and some countries, for example the People's Republic of China, have (I understand) incorporated parts of them into their domestic legislation. Perhaps this is the future of this set of Rules, to be cherry-picked, and for the best bits to be adopted. There seems no rush to adopt them *in toto* internationally, still less any desire to incorporate them into English law. This book therefore discusses the Rotterdam Rules, but as a liability regime, to contrast it with the Hague-Visby Rules, which *are* part of English law. It is also possible, of course, that various parts of Rotterdam will appear in bills of lading and charterparties that come before the English courts, much as we still see cases on the Hague Rules, though they were superseded in UK law almost 40 years ago.

At the end of each chapter is a chapter of questions, and links to online questions, which I hope will provoke thought. There is also a (very short) chapter of suggestions for further reading, though really, for further reading, you could do a lot worse than starting with the footnotes.

Stylistically, parties to actions are almost always companies, legally people rather than things, and are "he" or "him". Ships, of course, are female, whether Lloyd's agrees or not. Nothing should be read into this, other than convention.

As far as I can, I have stated the law as of 13 August 2015.

Acknowledgments

Writing is a solitary business, involving hours and hours in front of the computer. So first I would like to give thanks to my wife, Lena, for putting up with my reclusiveness, and the moodiness that writing can engender. I would also like to thank her for discussing with me much of the material I have included in this book, though carriage of goods by sea is by no means her specialist area.

It is no doubt possible to write a book such as this without being attached to a university, but my being part of the Law School at the University of Southampton made it very much easier, principally in providing access to legal databases, and to the Institute of Maritime Law library. As Internet sources (such as BAILII) expand, it should eventually become possible to study law for nothing, but writing a book in 2015 would have been much more expensive had I not been attached to a university.

I have written this book myself, and any mistakes are mine. I have not, as far as I am aware, used (without appropriate attribution) any material that belongs to anyone else.

Table of Cases

Statutes

Part 1

Introduction to carriage of goods by sea

Chapter 1

Introduction, Bills of lading and charterparties

Chapter Contents

1.1 Layout of the book

The substantive part of this book divides into four parts. Part 1 introduces the subject, and considers issues (including general legal principles) that relate to all types of carriage. Part 2 is on the voyage charter, and Part 3 on the time charterparty. Part 4 considers the very different issues that arise from bills of lading (and other contracts for the carriage of goods by sea).

This is intended to be a book for learning as well as reference. At the end of each chapter are self-assessment questions, and ideas about the issues raised.

1.2 Introduction: distinction between charterparties and bills of lading

Traditionally, there are two main instruments used in the carriage of goods by sea, the charterparty and the bill of lading. Though both are absolutely central to any study of this subject, they are fundamentally different types of instrument. In very general terms, charterparties relate to the ship and bills of lading to the cargo.

A charterparty is (nearly always) a contract for the use of an entire vessel. It is used by shippers of large quantities of cargo, and by people who intend to trade as carriers in their own right but without purchasing a ship, either by sub-chartering, or by carrying merchants' cargo for payment of freight. A charterparty might also be used by a purchaser or seller of cargo, who needs a particular type of vessel. A charterparty provides the charterer with a ship and (unless by demise) the services of the crew. Though it does not relate (directly at least) to cargo, both time and voyage charters usually envisage the carriage of goods, and are therefore, I suggest, properly categorised as contracts for the carriage of goods by sea. By contrast, a demise charterparty, which is in effect a chattel lease of a ship, and has no service element, is not.[1]

A bill of lading relates to goods shipped (or at least received for shipment).[2] It may be issued to a shipper of a single item, or a small amount of cargo insufficient to fill the ship, in which case the bill of lading will relate to that specific consignment. But charterers of vessels who ship their own cargo will usually also take bills of lading for the cargo they load, even if the cargo fills the ship, to enable them to resell on the voyage. (Bulk dry-cargoes are often split among several buyers, whereas tanker cargoes as usually traded in their entirety.) Consequently, the goods described in a bill of lading may or may not fill the vessel. A bill of lading contract is a contract for the carriage of goods, however, and is not a contract for the use of a ship.

More interestingly from a legal viewpoint, a charterparty is itself a contract, not merely evidence of a contract, whereas (at least in the hands of a shipper) a bill of lading usually merely evidences a contract. This is an important distinction, which we examine in chapter 15.[3] A charterer may well also hold a bill of lading, either as shipper or subsequent holder, and there can be an issue if charterparty and bill of lading terms differ.

A charterparty is a contract of carriage between shipowner and charterer[4] and, unlike a bill of lading, it is not a transferable document. It does not directly create contractual relationships with anyone other than shipowner and charterer. There will often be sub-charterparties, but these will be separate contracts in their own right. Conversely, a bill of lading can transfer contractual rights and liabilities to subsequent holders as it is itself transferred.

---

1 Demise and time charters share many terms; their similarities and differences are covered in chapter 10.
2 See further chapter 14 on this distinction.
3 See section [15.1.3].
4 Or disponent owner – see section [1.9].

A bill of lading, then, is evidence of a contract for the carriage of goods, but it is also much more than that. It is the document that enables the goods to be traded at sea, which can transfer rights of property and possession, and contractual rights and liabilities as against carriers. Unlike a charterparty its terms are usually regulated to some extent by law. It is fundamentally a different beast from a charterparty. It is described in Part 4 of the book, beginning at chapter 14.

1.3 Types of charterparty

There are three main types of charterparty, voyage, time and demise. An important point, though, is that charterparties are contracts whose terms are almost entirely unregulated. Almost all aspects of charterparties can be altered by the parties, if so desired. This is, therefore, the starting point, but the evolution of charterparties was driven by the trading parties. It was not (and is not) dictated by the law. So nothing here is set in stone.

Time and demise varieties are both period charters, the demise form being the older.[5] The demise charter is a demise of the ship alone, and there is no service element. (It is also often described as a bareboat charterparty.) The charterer provides his own crew, and uses the vessel as he wishes (subject to trading limits in the charterparty). Demise charterparties are rarely used these days, apart from for pleasure craft (where if a holidaymaker is qualified as a yacht skipper,[6] he or she can charter a yacht, providing his or her own crew), and for ship finance. In the latter case the financier is the shipowner, the demise form being used because the financier does not wish to be involved in the day-to-day operation of the vessel. Finance charterparties are often for lengthy terms, with a purchase option on the payment of the last month's hire – in effect this is a hire-purchase agreement.[7]

The demise charter is really a contract for the hire of a ship, rather than a contract for the carriage of goods by sea. We will therefore not devote much space to demise charters, but you need to be aware of them, because there is a demise charterparty in the background in some of the cases we study.[8] There are similarities between time and demise charters, the time charterparty deriving many of its terms from the earlier demise form, and there are demise charterparty cases that are also authorities for the time form.[9] We will also examine some of the differences between demise and time charters, drawing a contrast in order the better to understand the time charter.[10]

The overwhelming majority of charterparty coverage in this book, however, is to the time and the voyage charterparty. As its name implies, a voyage charter is usually taken for the duration of a voyage, and a time charter for a period of time, generally sufficient for several voyages to be undertaken. However, this is an over-simplification. A voyage charter may also be taken for a period (for example, two years) of consecutive voyages,[11] and a time charter can be used for a single trip.[12] So this is not the basis of the distinction between the two types.

---

5 Time charters do not seem to have been used widely until towards the end of the nineteenth century, when steamships were beginning to replace sail, even for long ocean voyages: see section [10.1].

6 A commercial rather than legal requirement.

7 Eg, Barecon 2001, Part IV of which provides for a hire-purchase option. See further section [10.2].

8 Eg, *Candlewood Navigation Corp Ltd v Mitsui OSK Lines Ltd (The Mineral Transporter)* [1986] AC 1, in section [10.7] (where the vessel was demise chartered and then time chartered back to the owner).

9 Eg, *Gator Shipping Corp v Trans-Asiatic Oil Ltd SA (The Odenfeld)* [1978] 2 Lloyd's Rep 357, in section [11.3.1].

10 See generally chapter 10, and in particular sections [10.5]; [10.8].

11 Eg, *Suisse Atlantique Société d'Armement Maritime SA v NV Rotterdamsche Kolen Centrale* [1967] 1 AC 361; *Navigazione Alta Italia SpA v Svenska Petroleum AB (The Nai Matteini)* [1988] 1 Lloyd's Rep 452 (two years and 13 years respectively). These cases are considered at sections [5.6] and [15.2.3], and the consecutive voyage charter generally at [5.5].

12 Eg, *Ocean Tramp Tankers Corp v V/O Sovfracht (The Eugenia)* [1964] 2 QB 226, in section [2.12]; *Marbienes Compania Naviera SA v Ferrostaal AG (The Democritos)* [1976] 2 Lloyd's Rep 149 in section [10.4]. In the latter case the charterparty was expressed to be of duration "about 4 to 6 months", but ". . . for a trip via Port or Ports via the Pacific". Though it was envisaged to be for a single voyage, it was held to be a time charter.

The fundamental difference between the two is as to the risk of delay. In a voyage charter, it is the shipowner who bears the risk of delay. In a time charter, it is the charterer.[13]

Under a voyage charterparty, the shipowner is paid freight, the calculation of which does not depend on the length of the voyage. If there is delay on the voyage, or in the loading and discharge, then (as a starting point – subject to any contrary terms) it is the shipowner who bears that risk. In a time charter by contrast, hire is payable per day or month, whatever use is made of the vessel, and so the cost of any delay is borne by the charterer.

Another (related) difference between the two types is that, with a voyage charter, the charterer can more easily calculate his costs, since the freight paid is (subject to any contrary terms) unaffected by chance events causing delay. Conversely, for a time charterparty, it is the shipowner who can more easily calculate his costs, since the hire paid is (again, subject to contrary terms) likewise unaffected by events causing delay,[14] and because the duration of the charterparty is also approximately fixed.[15]

1.4 More on voyage charter terms

So, under a voyage charterparty (which is an older variety than its time counterpart), freight is paid by the charterer for the carriage of his goods for a voyage. The amount of freight payable can be agreed as a lump sum, but more usually it depends on the quantity of cargo carried. It does not depend on the time the voyage takes.

Thus it is the shipowner,[16] not the charterer, who bears the cost of any delay.[17] If the voyage takes longer than expected, the shipowner bears the cost: he cannot claim any extra freight from the charterer to compensate for the delay, nor can he make use of the vessel for that period to earn freight elsewhere. Conversely, if the voyage takes less time than expected, the shipowner gains, because the freight is not thereby reduced, and the shipowner can make profitable use of the time gained by employing the vessel elsewhere. This is, as we have seen, fundamentally the distinction between voyage and time charterparties. In time charterparties, since hire is paid on the period for which the vessel is used, independently of how many voyages are completed and how much cargo is carried, it is the charterer who bears the risk of delay.

It may be that one reason why the voyage charter is a much older form of agreement than its time counterpart is that in the days of sail, the speed of a voyage was crucially dependent on the industry and skill of the master and crew. Charterers would have been reluctant to pay on a period basis, when the duration of the voyage could so easily have been extended by master and crew provided by the shipowner. Today, of course, this is less likely to be a factor, and time charterers are probably sufficiently protected by the obligation on the owner to make reasonable despatch on the voyage. By comparison with the sea voyage, delays at loading and discharge (because even now more uncertain) have taken on a greater importance today.

Thus, whereas (as we will see in chapter 10) time charterparties contain hire clauses, voyage charters make provision for freight. Since (unless – rarely – lumpsum freight is agreed) the amount of freight depends on the quantity of cargo loaded,[18] in order to safeguard the freight earned by the owner, the charterer will typically be under an obligation to load a full and complete cargo. Dead-freight is payable as damages, if the charterers are in breach of this obligation.

---

13 See also observations in *Hyundai Merchant Marine Co Ltd v Furnace Withy (Australia) Pty (The Doric Pride)* [2006] 2 Lloyd's Rep 175, in section [10.4].

14 There will, of course, be contrary terms, principally laytime and demurrage provisions in a voyage charter, and off-hire provision in a time charter.

15 See chapter 11 on the period of the charterparty.

16 Or disponent owner: see section [1.9].

17 At least to the extent that delay risks are not altered by the terms of the contract.

18 On lumpsum freight see section [7.3].

All voyage charters would therefore be expected to make provision for freight, for the charterers to load a full and complete cargo, and for deadfreight. None of these terms would be appropriate in a time (or demise) charterparty.

Other terms that are universally included in voyage (but only voyage) charters relate to laytime and demurrage.[19] Clearly, since they are working for a fixed freight, shipowners under a voyage charterparty would like the voyage to be completed as quickly as possible. The speed of the loading and discharging process may well be controlled by the charterer, however, for example if the cargo is not yet available for shipment when the vessel arrives at the loading port, or (since congestion is often an issue) if the charterers have a choice of loading and/or discharge ports. Yet delay at this stage is to the shipowner's detriment, because it means that his ship is tied up for longer earning the same freight for the voyage.[20] All voyage charterparties, therefore, have clauses stipulating how quickly the cargo must be loaded and discharged.

It is the function of laytime and demurrage clauses to encourage the charterer to delay as little as possible in loading and discharging the cargo. Disputes about laytime and demurrage are among the most common in the law of charterparties, and we devote two chapters of the book to them.[21]

The laytime is the time in which (after a valid notice of readiness has been tendered) the charterer is allowed to load and/or discharge.[22] If he exceeds the laytime allowed, demurrage becomes payable at the agreed demurrage rate.[23] If, on the other hand, the charterer discharges the cargo before the expiry of the laytime, the owner may be required to pay the charterer a reward known as "despatch money" for every day saved.[24] However, whereas laytime and demurrage provisions are universally made in voyage charters, universal provision is not made for despatch money, although it is certainly not unusual.[25] Like laytime and demurrage, of course, despatch money is appropriate only in voyage, as opposed to time charters.

We will see that demurrage is liquidated damages for the charterer's breach of contract in failing to complete the handling of the cargo within the laytime.[26] Laytime is paid for within the freight and, if there were no stipulation, a reasonable laytime would be implied.[27] Demurrage provisions, though in practice universal, are not necessary to the operation of a voyage charter and, if absent, would not be implied.[28] If there were no stipulation for payment of demurrage, damages would be awarded for detention of the vessel, if the charterer exceeded the laytime. The damages (which would be ordinary damages for breach of contract, and would be at large – in other words, not fixed) would be based on the freight the shipowner could have earned elsewhere for the period of the delay. Especially on a rising freight market this would typically be higher than a demurrage rate, although the owner would have to prove loss. In practice, really to make matters simpler, demurrage is universally agreed, but there is sometimes a limit to the number of days on demurrage, in which case damages at large, for detention, will be awarded for longer delays.[29] We will also see in chapters 8 and 9 other situations where damages for detention might be payable, as opposed to demurrage.[30]

Freight, laytime and demurrage provisions are fundamental to voyage charterparties, and will be found only in voyage charterparties, or contracts that are related to them (eg, the contract of

---

19 See chapters 8 and 9.
20 See further section [8.1].
21 Chapters 8 and 9.
22 As we will see in section [8.9], there is sometimes separate provision for laytime at loading and discharging, and sometimes a single provision covering both.
23 Sometimes a scale is agreed (eg, Worldscale for tankers): see further section [1.10].
24 See, eg, the description in *The General Capinpin* in section [9.1].
25 See further section [9.1].
26 See section [9.1].
27 See section [8.1].
28 See further section [9.1].
29 Eg, cl. 7 of pre-1994 versions of Gencon, which provided for 10 running days on demurrage. See further section [9.2].
30 See section [8.7].

affreightment and the consecutive voyage charter, considered in chapter 5). You would not see laytime and demurrage provisions in a time charterparty.[31]

Under a contract of affreightment, a related form of agreement that we examine in chapter 5, the shipowner agrees to move a tonnage of cargo over a period, and is not necessarily restricted to a single ship. Under all normal voyage and time charters, however, the ship is stipulated, and cannot be substituted. Voyage charters will therefore contain terms relating to the ship. Some of these, for example relating to her present position, and estimated readiness to load time, are dealt with fully in chapter 6, on the approach voyage. There will also be descriptive terms, though typically fewer than in a time charter, where charterers are more critically concerned with the speed and fuel consumption capabilities of the vessel. On the other hand, voyage charterers need to know the capacity of the vessel, her suitability to carry their cargo, her classification, and perhaps her flag, and one would expect to find warranties about these in a voyage charter.

There are also terms that are not generally appropriate for inclusion in a voyage charter. Since it is in the interests of the owner to hurry, there is not normally any need for a voyage charterparty to stipulate (eg) the speed of the vessel. Most voyage charterparties do not in fact contain such a stipulation, unlike time charterparties, which invariably do.[32]

1.5 More on time charterparty terms

A time charterparty is a contract (between shipowners and charterers) for the use of a ship, owned by the shipowners, and the services of its master and crew. Many of the complexities of a time charterparty are caused by the entitlement of the charterers to give orders to the master, who is engaged by and on behalf of the shipowners, and is also responsible for the safety of the ship. The relationship between owners and charterers is much more complex than in the earlier demise variant, where the charterers engage their own master and crew, and also operate the ship. These complexities are discussed fully in chapter 13, but the service element to a time charterparty also has a bearing on some of the discussion in chapter 12 (on withdrawal for non-payment of hire).

Although initially the terminology was unsettled,[33] the consideration moving from the charterers is the payment of what is now universally termed hire. Hire is paid on a period basis, whatever use the charterer make of the vessel. Delay therefore costs the charterers money, because they continue to pay hire in any event, whereas the shipowners are entitled to the same rate of hire, however much the vessel is delayed, and so (as we have seen) the starting point is that it is the charterers who bear the delay risk. There will be a hire clause, including a withdrawal provision,[34] conferring upon the owners the right to withdraw the vessel for non-payment of hire.

But just as voyage charters protect owners against the voyage being lengthened by the charterers, so time charters contain terms to guard against voyages being lengthened by owners, for example speed clauses (which are not necessary and not usually included in a voyage charter),[35] or off-hire clauses (which suspend payments of hire) where there is a defect in the machinery, or some other reason why the vessel cannot be used, or at least fully used.[36] Time charterers also typically pay

---

31 Indeed, Lloyd J observed in *Care Shipping Corp v Latin American Shipping Corp (The Cebu)* [1983] QB 1005, commenting on the rapid recent growth of the trip-time charterparty: "No doubt the time charter trip has many advantages over the voyage charter. For one thing it avoids the hideous complexities of demurrage". On the "hideous complexities", see chapter 9. On *The Cebu*, see further [12.1.8].

32 As we will see in section [5.2], there are speed clauses in some voyage charters, but their role is different from that in time charters.

33 See section [12.1].

34 Withdrawal for late payment of hire is discussed in section [12.1.2].

35 On speed clauses see section [10.3].

36 See further section [12.3].

for bunker fuel, and there are fuel consumption warranties, and statements as to how much bunker fuel is on board. You would not expect to see any of these clauses in a voyage charterparty.

Anything to do with hire, including off-hire and withdrawal provisions for non, late or under-payment, indeed the stuff of chapter 12, would be entirely inapposite in a voyage charterparty. So too, generally speaking, would anything to do with the period of the charterparty, the stuff of chapter 11, since the period of a voyage charterparty is normally determined simply by the length of the voyage. This is not a distinction that is set in stone, however, since the period of a trip-time charterparty is also determined by the length of the voyage,[37] and both contracts of affreightment and consecutive voyage charterparties in chapter 5, neither of which is a true period charter, often do state a period.[38]

On the other hand, since under a time charter it is in the interest of the charterer to hurry, there is no need for laytime and demurrage provisions. Whereas all voyage (and consecutive voyage) charterparties contain laytime and demurrage clauses, they are never found in time (or demise) forms. Usually, on the other hand, there will be an off-hire clause to prevent hire continuing to be payable when the ship is unusable to the charterer due to (eg) repairs.[39]

As with a voyage charterparty, but not a contract of affreightment, a time charter relates to a particular vessel.

1.6 Terms that are common to both types of charterparty

Voyage charters share a number of terms with their time counterparts. Arbitration and jurisdiction clauses are equally appropriate in any type of charterparty. Obligations regarding care of the cargo may be dealt with by charterparty term, whether the charterparty is on a voyage or time basis.

There are other clauses that, though they might be used in both varieties, are used differently, or are more common in one than the other. The cesser clauses in chapter 7 do not appear to be very common at all today, but in so far that they are used at all, are probably more common in voyage than time charters.[40] All charterparties in reality have a war clause, but voyage and time variants typically differ, primarily because of the (usually) longer term of time charters, and also because time charterers usually have a greater choice as to where to trade the vessel.[41] Time charters nearly always have an express safe port and/or safe berth warranty.[42] These can sometimes be found in voyage charters also, but are less common, again because voyage charterers typically have less choice as to trading routes. Either type of charterparty can contain a lien clause, but again they are used differently as between the two types of charter. All these are dealt with more fully in the appropriate part of the book.[43]

As we will see in Part 3 of the book, time charterers, who are often trading the vessel rather than simply shipping their own cargo, can give orders to the master as to the employment of the vessel (essentially where she should go, and what she should load), and also as to the issue of bills of lading. The consequences of following such orders can create additional risks for shipowners, and perhaps incur them in liability to third parties. Consequently, time charterparties often have bill of lading and indemnity, or wider employment and indemnity clauses, which provide for this, but

---

37 See sections [1.7]; [10.4].
38 See sections [5.5]–[5.7].
39 See further [12.3].
40 See section [7.9].
41 For time charter war clauses see section [13.10].
42 See section [13.9].
43 For liens compare section [7.9] with [12.1.8].

also for charterers to indemnify owners against potential costs and liabilities.[44] Such clauses are also sometimes seen in voyage charterparties, but are less common, probably because voyage charterers are more often shipping their own cargo (and are therefore entitled to bills of lading as shippers), and because they typically have a narrower choice (if any) of route, than their time counterparts.

1.7 Erosion of the distinction?

We should remember that charterparties are contracts the terms of which are largely unregulated. Neither the three main types of charterparty, nor any of their terms, are therefore set in stone. Time and voyage charterparties have evolved as an instrument to satisfy the needs of the parties, but their form is their servant and not their master.[45] Indeed, the time form itself evolved (into its modern form probably around 125 years ago) from the earlier demise charter.

Consequently, we have charterparties that are in a sense hybrids. We have trip-time charterparties, which though for a single voyage, are in time form.[46] We have charterparties for a period, but for a series of consecutive voyages.[47] (In the former the risk of delay is on the charterers, in the latter the owners, so to that extent at least they conform to the fundamental distinction between time and voyage charterparties.) We will see in chapter 5 speed terms creeping into voyage charters, and in chapter 11 final voyage clauses eroding the idea of a fixed period in time charterparties. If the parties do not care for the traditional rigid categories, they can change them.[48]

1.8 Does the distinction matter?

Given that almost all aspects of charterparties can be altered by the parties, the question has to be asked – why does the distinction matter? The law does not dictate that a time charter must contain these provisions, a voyage charter those provisions. Anything goes, in principle, subject only to the general contractual requirements of offer, acceptance, consideration, etc. The varieties of charterparty in use today exist because the parties find them convenient, and not because of any dictat from the courts.[49]

Nonetheless, there are cases which turn on the categorisation.[50] Moreover, however detailed the charterparty may be, it can never provide for every contingency. What the parties do not provide, the courts must fill in. The courts are of course entitled, in so doing, to look at whether the charterparty is described as time or voyage. The categorisation is relevant to a determination of the parties' intentions – it is part, if you like, of the factual matrix.

We see this, for example, in the well-known case of *The Johanna Oldendorff*,[51] the subject of a case study on carriage contract terms in chapter 22.[52] Here the parties used a port charterparty, which, as we will see in chapter 8, is a type of voyage charterparty. Of course the parties are free to alter the

---

44 See sections [13.2]–[13.8].

45 See section [1.3].

46 See further section [10.4].

47 See further section [5.5]. Cf. the charterparty in *The Democritos* [1976] 2 Lloyd's Rep 149, which was neither clearly a time nor a voyage charter, though it was eventually categorised by the Court of Appeal as a trip-time charter.

48 See sections [5.2]; [11.6].

49 The same is true of FOB and CIF sale contracts; the role of the courts is to interpret the intentions of the parties, not to lay down rules as to what they should contain.

50 Eg, *The Democritos* [1976] 2 Lloyd's Rep 149 and *The Eugenia* [1964] 2 QB 226, in section [10.4]; *Baumwoll Manufactur von Carl Scheibler v Christopher Furness* [1893] AC 8, in section [10.8].

51 Oldendorff (EL) & Co GmbH v Tradax Export SA (*The Johanna Oldendorff*) [1974] AC 479, also in section [8.5].

52 See section [22.2].

basic port charterparty, and frequently do so,[53] but in determining the issue (which was ultimately as to when laytime started to run), Lord Diplock used the classification of the charterparty as a guide for filling in the detailed terms, where the parties have said nothing to the contrary. The classification is the starting point, and will determine the issue if there is nothing else.

We see something similar with an interpretation of a final voyage clause (which can allow charterers to extend the period of a time charterparty) in chapter 11. In The Peonia,[54] Bingham LJ refused to adopt a very wide interpretation, as the charterers argued, on the grounds that (in his view) it would "disturb in . . . a radical manner the ordinary rule whereby risk of delay under a time charter-party (in the absence of breach by the owner) falls on the charterer".[55] Here, then, the classification is being used to constrain the interpretation of an ambiguous term. Even so, Bingham LJ accepted that "clear and compelling language" could have even that effect, and indeed in The World Renown a different clause was interpreted in precisely the manner rejected in The Peonia.[56]

The Democritos and The Doric Pride both concerned trip-time charters.[57] In The Democritus, once the contract was classified as a time charter then the issue whether the charterers were entitled to send her on her last voyage was determined in accordance with the time charterparty principles discussed in chapter 11. These principles have no application to voyage charters, and so the classification of the charterparty as a time charterparty was important to the decision. In The Doric Pride, an off-hire clause was interpreted in the light of the usual division of responsibilities in a time charter, and in The Saldanha also, Gross J refused to interpret an off-hire clause so as to interfere with what he saw as "the allocation of the risk of delay under a typical time charterparty".[58] In all these cases, the contract was interpreted in the light of what was typical within the particular type of charter.

Ultimately, however, there is nothing fundamental about the distinction between voyage and time charterparties. The distinction is a matter of commercial convenience. The law does not lay down that you have to have one type or the other, and there are hybrids, or clauses that do not fit well the traditional classification. Some voyage forms contain speed clauses. Some time forms (as we have also seen) include last voyage clauses, which (by giving charterers leeway as to the duration of the charterparty) make it more difficult for shipowners exactly to calculate their costs. The charterparty in any case evolves over time, to suit the needs of the commercial parties.

Nonetheless, the basic distinction between voyage and time forms has been around now for well over a century, and in general seems to accord with what the commercial parties want.

1.9 Sub-charterparties

If the charterparty is the head charterparty, the shipowner will be party to it, but in most time and voyage charterparties the charterer has the right to create a sub-charter,[59] and indeed it is not uncommon for the sub-charterer to continue the process by creating a further sub-charter. Sub-charters may be created for various reasons, a common one being a time charterer hoping to use one profitably to trade. We will come across a number of cases in this book where sub charterparties have been

---

53 Eg, section [8.8].
54 *Hyundai Merchant Marine Co Ltd v Gesuri Chartering Co Ltd (The Peonia)* [1991] 1 Lloyd's Rep 100.
55 [1991] 1 Lloyd's Rep 100, 117. See further section [11.6] for detailed discussion of the particular term.
56 *Chiswell Shipping Ltd v National Iranian Tanker Co (The World Symphony and The World Renown)* [1992] 2 Lloyd's Rep 115, also considered at section [11.6].
57 See further section [10.4].
58 See sections [12.3.1] and [12.3.6]: the off-hire clause was interpreted to be consistent with the traditional allocation of responsibilities for time charter – matters pertaining to the vessel were for the owners.
59 Though not usually demise charters: see section [10.5] for the main differences between time and demise charters.

created. There is no reason why head and sub-charterparties should have similar terms, or even be of the same type; indeed, as we will see in chapter 15, often they are not.[60]

Sub-charters are no different in principle from any other charterparty, except that because the owner under the sub-charter is the charterer under the head charter, he is referred to as "disponent owner", to distinguish him from the shipowner under the head charter. Thus, the parties to the head charter will be the shipowner and head charterer, those to the sub-charter the head charterer (as disponent owner) and sub-charterer. The following diagram illustrates:

Owner --- head charter ---- charterer

disponent owner ---- sub charter --- sub-charterer

In this book, since the same principles are generally applicable to all charterparties, whether or not the shipowner himself is party, the parties to all charterparties will be referred to simply as "shipowner" and "charterer" throughout.[61]

1.10 Standard forms

Nearly all charterparties are on standard forms, of which there are perhaps several dozen commonly used. We will look at the interpretation of standard forms as a case study.[62] We will also see in the next chapter that, though a bill of lading cannot perform all of its functions unless it is in writing, no formalities are required for a valid charterparty. A charterparty can be handwritten or even oral. Many charterparties are in fact made with the minimum of formality, but in the expectation that they will be reduced to writing later.[63] However, the eventual written contract will almost always be based on one of the many standard forms commonly in use, though very often with typed or written amendments.

The standard form charterparties are important because many disputes (probably the majority) on charterparties ultimately turn on the construction of the standard form used. As we will see, however, amendments to standard forms are more likely to give rise to legal dispute,[64] because the charterparty must be interpreted as a whole,[65] and because where any standard form is amended, the courts give greater weight to the amendments than to the unamended part of the form.[66]

There are many voyage forms, fewer time and demise, though in reality we come across a small number again and again. There are differences between trades, and for different types of ship. The most fundamental distinction, however, at least for time and voyage forms, is between dry-cargo and tanker. Though there are obvious differences between the trades and the vessels, it is the nature of the market that predominantly determines these differences. The dry-cargo market favours pro-shipowner forms, the tanker market pro-charterer. In almost every clause is this distinction apparent.

---

60 Also sections [15.2.3]; see also *The Mineral Transporter* in section [10.7].

61 This is not uncommon usage: eg, *The Doric Pride* [2006] 2 Lloyd's Rep 175, [1] (Rix LJ) (a decision on off-hire considered in section [12.3.5]). Also *Gard Marine & Energy Ltd v China National Chartering Co Ltd (The Ocean Victory)* [2014] 1 Lloyd's Rep 14, [17] (Teare J), rvsd CA: [2015] 1 Lloyd's Rep 381.

62 Sections [22.2]–[22.3].

63 Eg, *Partenreederei M/S Heidberg v Grosvenor Grain and Feed Co Ltd (The Heidberg)* [1994] 2 Lloyd's Rep 287; *Welex AG v Rosa Maritime Ltd (The Epsilon Rosa)* [2003] 2 Lloyd's Rep 509, both of which are considered in detail in section [15.2.3]. See also generally section [2.2] on the requirements for the formation of charterparties.

64 Eg, *The Johanna Oldendorff* [1974] AC 479, in sections [8.5]; [22.2].

65 Eg, *Nereide SpA di Navigazione v Bulk Oil International (The Laura Prima)* [1982] 1 Lloyd's Rep 1: see further sections [22.3].

66 *Glynn v Margetson & Co* [1893] AC 1, considered further in sections [4.4.4]; [22.2].

1.10.1 Standard form charters: dry cargo

In the dry-cargo market the shipowner usually enjoys the greater bargaining strength, and the terms of dry-cargo forms tend to reflect this. The older forms, in particular, favour shipowners, and though there have been attempts to draft more pro-charterer forms,[67] they have not gained acceptance in a pro-shipowner market.

The most commonly used voyage form is probably BIMCO's Gencon.[68] This is an old charter (revised in 1922, 1976 and 1994), intended for general use for dry cargo ("for trades where no approved form is in force"). In common with the older standard forms Gencon's terms favour the shipowner as against the charterer. The most commonly used time charter forms for dry-cargoes are Baltime 1939 and the New York Produce Exchange charterparty (usually referred to as "NYPE"). Baltime, last revised in 2001, is also an old pro-shipowner form (dating originally as far back as 1912), and is essentially the Gencon of time charterparties. NYPE (though originally dating back to November 1913) is marginally more modern, and to an extent favours the charterer, although only to the extent commensurate with a largely pro-owner market.

Possibly in consequence of the age of Gencon and Baltime, neither incorporates the Hague or Hague-Visby Rules, or any part of those Rules. As we will see later in the book, the Hague (and later Hague-Visby) Rules protect cargo-owners, but whereas they are compulsorily written into bills of lading, there is no requirement for them to be written into charterparties.[69] Both Gencon and Baltime have terms that are more favourable to owners than the Hague or Hague-Visby regimes. As we will see it is by no means clear that shipowners gain from this, though the latest revision of Gencon protects them quite well. This whole issue is examined further in chapter 18.

Though the standard forms are periodically, albeit infrequently, revised, trading parties are often very conservative, preferring to stick with what they know. Hence, NYPE 1946 remains widely in use, the later revisions in 1981 and 1993 not having gained widespread acceptance. (It will be interesting to see whether the revision currently under consideration – in 2015 does any better.)[70] Of course the old forms are not always suitable as they stand, and are frequently amended – the so-called rider syndrome. Given the problems that amendments can cause, the rider syndrome is rightly derided, and attempts have been made to draft forms allowing choices, to try to discourage it.[71] An example is Multiform 1982/1986, a multi-purpose voyage form drafted by the Federation of National Associations of Ship Brokers and Agents (FONASBA). It tends, however, to favour the charterer in a pro-shipowner market, and has not gained acceptance.

There can be problems of interpretation, where the old forms are simply inapplicable to the modern situation. A case that is cited, simply because it is an interesting example, is *The Sounion*,[72] a Court of Appeal interpretation of the NYPE 46 grates and stoves clause. Clause 20 of the 1946 form provides that:

---

67 Eg, Norgrain 89; Multiform 1982/1986. The former is the North American Grain Charterparty 1973, as amended May 1989, which can be found at https://www.bimco.org/~/media/Chartering/Document_Samples/Voyage_Charter_Parties/Sample_Copy_NORGRAIN_89.ashx.

68 BIMCO is the Baltic and International Maritime Council, an organisation that represents shipowners.

69 See generally chapter 18.

70 There is text and a commentary at https://www.bimco.org/~/media/News/2014/NYPE_93_v_NYPE_2014_comparison.ashx.

71 The revisions to NYPE (which have not gained market acceptance) were motivated partly by a desire to deal with the "rider syndrome", where old forms are used with many added (and not always well-drafted) additions, and partly by a desire to bring the form up to date and improve its structure. In some respects, if anything, the form has become more pro-shipowner since 1946.

72 *Summit Investment Inc v British Steel Corp (The Sounion)* [1987] 1 Lloyd's Rep 230. It is not generally a good reason for citing a case that it is a good example. Cases are authorities, not examples, but I make an exception here – because I think it is quite an interesting example.

"Fuel used by the vessel while off hire, also for cooking, condensing water, or for grates and stoves to be agreed as to quantity, and the cost of replacing same to be allowed by owners."

This clause had its origins in the original (1913) version of NYPE. At that time vessels were generally coal powered, whereas lighting for the crew was by paraffin. The coal was purchased by the charterers and the paraffin by the owners. If coal was also used for domestic cooking and heating, for example in grates and stoves, the shipowners would pay for the coal so used. Clause 20 provides for this, and its effect is (or rather was, when grates and stoves were still in use) that fuel used for the domestic consumption of the crew is paid for by the shipowner.

By 1979, when the charterparty in The Sounion was entered into, grates and stoves were no longer in use (indeed, they were going out of use even by 1946), yet as Lord Donaldson MR observed:[73]

"Today very many ships are motor driven and, even when they are not, steam is raised using oil fuel instead of coal. Accordingly a ship equipped with either a 'grate' or a 'stove' must be a great rarity. Nevertheless, despite revision in 1921, 1931 and 1946, the New York Produce Exchange form obstinately continues to refer to 'grates and stoves' and we have been called upon to construe the phrase."

In The Sounion, the 1946 form (which remember dated from 1913) was the most up-to-date version of NYPE. It has now been superseded, but parties continue to use the 1946 form today. It is quite likely that the "grates and stoves" clause is still widely used.

Lord Donaldson continued with the observation that oil is used to power the vessels, and for electricity for the comfort of the crew, but that electricity today is used for far more than just cooking and keeping warm.

A literal interpretation of cl. 20 would have rendered it nugatory, but neither shipowners nor charterers argued for that, at any rate by the time the case reached the Court of Appeal. The question was whether the shipowners should pay for all fuel used for domestic consumption or only that used for cooking and heating. The Court of Appeal, purporting to adopt a purposive interpretation,[74] took the view that the pattern of the charter was clear, that the owners were obliged to provide and pay for the crew (this was, after all, a time charterparty) – and that they should pay for all fuel used for their domestic consumption.

NYPE was revised again in 1981 and 1993, and "grates and stoves" are no longer mentioned. The 1981 drafting requires the charterers to provide all fuel "except as otherwise agreed", and NYPE 1993 makes no provision at all for crew consumption. But the parties continue to use 1946 in preference to 1981 or 1993. The Sounion is cited, simply as an example of a cautionary tale.

The layout of standard forms can affect the construction of the charterparty.[75] Older standard forms were single documents with gaps to be filled in, eg, for the name of the parties, length of charter and rate of hire (if a time charterparty), or freight and voyage details (if a voyage charterparty), details of the ship, and so on. Later forms, from about the 1970s onwards, are often divided into two parts: Part I consisting of gaps or boxes to be filled in, and Part II the standard terms. (The

---

73 [1987] 1 Lloyd's Rep 230, 231.

74 Lloyd LJ began his judgment ([1987] 1 Lloyd's Rep 230, 235): "If ever a case were designed to separate the purposive sheep from the literalist goats this is it." However, both constructions are purposive, since a literal construction would have simply emasculated the clause – so the issue really was to determine the purpose. See further on construction section [22.2].

75 See section [2.4].

latest revisions of Gencon and Baltime adopt a box format, and division into Parts I and II.) The advantage of this layout is that if the parties do not intend to vary the standard terms, only Part I needs to be filled in and posted around, Part II terms being incorporated by reference. (Of course, division into parts is only worthwhile, however, if the parties are content to adopt the standard terms without alteration, whereas in reality this rarely occurs.)

On questions of construction,[76] we will see in chapter 2 that typed or written amendments to the standard forms prevail where there is a conflict over the standard terms themselves, because of the assumption that the parties have addressed their minds more directly to them. For the same reason, where there is a division into Parts I and II, the provisions of Part I prevail, because they have to be specifically filled in, whereas Part II is merely adopted wholesale.

1.10.2 Standard form charters: tankers

Tanker charterparties have their own standard forms, partly because of the different problems associated with tanker carriage, but also to reflect the relatively stronger bargaining power of tanker charterers. Most of the major oil companies have their own forms (eg, Shellvoy 6, BPVOY 4, Shelltime 4, BPTIME 3).

Of course the tanker forms reflect the different physical characteristics of tankers, as for example with loading and discharge provisions.[77] Also, characteristics peculiar to liquid cargo, and in particular the difficulties of shipowners enforcing liens against such cargo,[78] lead to freight generally being made payable later under the standard tanker voyage forms than under their dry-cargo counterparts.[79]

We are not interested, in this book, in the characteristics of oil cargoes. For the lawyer, the most significant difference, reflecting a different market, is a marked pro-charterer bias, at any rate by comparison with Gencon and Baltime. The responsibilities of the shipowner regarding seaworthiness and care of the cargo are typically defined by reference to the Hague or Hague-Visby Rules,[80] rather than less generously to the charterers, as in Gencon and Baltime. As we will see throughout the book, we can see the difference in bias in nearly every clause.[81] The duties of the parties are generally better defined, to help lessen costly disputes. The charterparties are divided, and in BPVOY4 there is an explicit provision that Part I prevails. There is an attempt to avoid the rider syndrome by allowing the use of additional clauses, for use for example with Shellvoy 6. The additional clauses allow the agreement to be adjusted, for example, to deal with local conditions in various parts of the world.

There have also been initiatives to draft alternative forms, principally by INTERTANKO (the International Association of Independent Tanker Owners). Not surprisingly, INTERTANKO forms tend to be pro-shipowner, and have not found favour in a pro-charterer market. They are, however, well thought out, and worthy of study for that reason alone, in spite of their limited market uptake.

Intertankvoy 76, replaced by Tankervoy 87, was intended for tanker owners who had no forms of their own.[82] It was intended to replace the "London Form", which was traditionally used but regarded as outmoded, and is based largely on other oil forms, especially Exxonvoy 69 and Shellvoy 3

---

76 Ibid.

77 Obviously, crude oil washing and cargo heating provisions would not be relevant to dry-cargo.

78 See section [7.9].

79 See section [8.7].

80 See chapter 18.

81 See (eg) section [8.5] (freight); [12.3.2] (off-hire).

82 A full draft can be found at https://www.bimco.org/~/media/Chartering/Document_Samples/Voyage_Charter_Parties/Sample_Copy_TANKERVOY_87.ashx.

(precursor to the current Shellvoy 6).[83] It is tightly drafted "(for example Tankervoy cl. 8 - a clause which originated in Intertankvoy 76 - was drafted to avoid the uncertainties of "the arrived ship" question).[84]

Intertanktime 80 is the time equivalent of Tankervoy 87. The INTERTANKO forms, like the latest revisions of Baltime and Gencon, are split into two parts, Part I being filled in and Part II consisting of the standard terms.

1.11 Charterparties and markets

There are many disputes that can be understood only in the light of market conditions. Freight (and consequently hire) rates fluctuate, sometimes extensively and rapidly. Just by way of example, these were the actual Worldscale freight rates in *The Elena D'Amico*:[85]

March 1973.	WS 132,
August 1973.	WS 310,
November 1973.	WS 638,
March 1974.	WS 287,
August 1974.	WS 127,
November 1974.	WS 192.

There is obviously here, over a period of just a few months, a spectacular (almost five-fold) rise followed by almost as spectacular a fall.

The oil market in 1973 and 1974 was no doubt atypical, following as it did the Yom Kippur war in October 1973 and the consequent OPEC embargo, which gave rise to chaos in oil markets. Goff J observed that the extent but not fact of the fluctuation was admitted to be unusual,[86] but a shipowner who had entered a long-term charterparty in March 1973 would be very tempted to get out of it, if he could, and refix the vessel in November, whereas the charterer who time chartered in November 1973 would be anxious to get out of the charterparty, and obtain alternative tonnage in August 1974. As we will see in chapter 2, the charterers in *The Elena d'Amico* made a decision not immediately to recharter in March 1973, when the shipowners wrongfully withdrew their vessel from a time charterparty, but instead to delay. They based their decision on a view of the market, presumably predicting a market fall. The decision obviously went badly wrong for them.

Fluctuations as extreme as this are unusual, but this is by no means unique. Most charterparties are concerned with the carriage of commodities, and freight rates follow the fortunes of those commodities, and also world market conditions. In a number of cases in this book, the catastrophic market fall at the end of 2008, clearly tied into global recession, was a major factor in the dispute.[87] The Baltic Dry Index, a commodities freight index that began life in 1985 at 1,000 points, reached an all-time high of 11,793 in May 2008, but by November of that year had crashed to just 663, a

---

83 We examine the unfortunate saga of Exxonvoy 69 when considering reachable on arrival clauses in section [8.5.1].

84 See section [8.5].

85 *Koch Marine Inc v d'Amica Societa di Navigazione ARL (The Elena d'Amico)* [1980] 1 Lloyd's Rep 75, these rates being set out at 85 (Goff J). We return to *The Elena D'Amico* in section [2.9.2]. Worldscale is a freight index scale, in $ per long ton, based on a notional standard tanker. It is used to allow actual freight rates to be calculated: https://www.worldscale.co.uk/.

86 [1980] 1 Lloyd's Rep 75, 85.

87 Eg, *Kuwait Rocks Co v Amn Bulkcarriers Inc (The Astra)* [2013] 2 Lloyd's Rep 69, discussed fully at section [12.1.6]; *Fulton Shipping Inc of Panama v Globalia Business Travel SAU (The New Flamenco)* [2014] 2 Lloyd's Rep 230 (section [2.9.2]).

fall of 94 per cent in six months. A vessel that had been able to command £100,000 a day in May could have been fixed at just £6,000 a day by the year's end. Since then the index rallied somewhat, reaching as high as 4,661 in 2009, but in early 2015 reached a new all-time low of just 509.[88] Of course charterers who fixed long-term charters in early 2008 would try to get out of these, if they could.

World events affect markets. The closure of the Suez Canal in the 1950s increased voyage lengths and also (consequently) decreased available tonnage, so of course there was a spike in rates, reversed overnight when the canal reopened a few months later. The reopening of Suez was the reason for the large market fall that motivated the events in *Hongkong Fir Shipping Co Ltd v Kawasaki Kisen Kaisha Ltd*,[89] where time charterers argued (unsuccessfully) an entitlement to repudiate the charterparty; rates had fallen catastrophically following the reopening of Suez in 1957, and they wished to obtain alternative cheaper tonnage.[90] The dispute in *The Astra* arose because of the market fall in late 2008, but Flaux J reminds us that:[91]

> ". . . 1920 was a previous occasion when market conditions were akin to those in the period 2008 to 2010 existed (that is a sudden and extreme drop in freight and hire rates from a previous high). Immediately after the First World War, a demand for shipping drove up rates but by early 1920 the market had slumped and freight rates had collapsed."

Even large-scale crashes, such as occurred in 2008, are not unique.

Even in more normal times, there are trade cycles. The supply of tonnage influences freight rates. In slack times older vessels will be scrapped, leading to a shortage when the market picks up, as shipbuilding will inevitably lag behind demand. In good times newbuildings, once started, might be impossible to stop, leading to a glut when the market falls, until scrappings bring the situation back into balance. Particularly for longer term charters, there is often a considerable percentage rise or fall over the term, just because of normal cycles. In *The Laconia* the rates had risen (in just over three months) from a contract rate of $3.10 per ton to $5.59 per ton, when the shipowners understandably grasped the opportunity given them by the charterers, to withdraw the vessel and refix her elsewhere.[92] There was nothing particularly unusual about the market at this time.

Many of the cases in this book can only be understood in the light of the market fluctuations that motivate the disputes.

1.12 Following chapters

The next three chapters continue with an introduction to carriage of goods by sea, but are more in the way of the legal principles underpinning the subject.

---

88 A chart of the first 30 years of the Baltic Dry Index, from 1985 until January 2015, can be found at http://www.zerohedge.com/sites/default/files/images/user3303/imageroot/2015/01-overflow/20150129_BDIY.jpg. It is not flat! By contrast with dry cargo, VLCC rates appear quite buoyant, perhaps because vessels are being used for storage during current low oil prices, creating a shortage of tonnage: http://www.koenig-cie.de/en/content/vlcc-200000-320000-tdw.

89 [1962] 2 QB 26, Salmon J observed that this was why the charterers were anxious to get out of the charter; see further sections [2.5]; [2.6].

90 *Hongkong Fir Shipping Co Ltd v Kawasaki Kisen Kaisha Ltd* [1962] 2 QB 26, discussed in sections [2.5]; [2.6].

91 *The Astra* [2013] 2 Lloyd's Rep 69, [54]. *The Astra* is an important case on late payment of time charter hire considered in section [12.1.7].

92 *Mardorf Peach & Co Ltd v Attika Sea Carriers Corp of Liberia (The Laconia)* [1977] AC 850 (HL), discussed in section [12.1.2].

1.13 Questions

At the end of each chapter are questions that are intended to be thought-provoking, so that if you work through them, you will have a better understanding of the subject than before. (That, at least, is the idea.)

These questions are about the differences between the types of charterparty, and between dry-cargo and tanker forms. Ideally you should look at some of the standard forms, to which there are links in chapter 23, but you should in any case be able to work out the answers, on the basis of what you already know, from reading this chapter.

These questions have clear answers, but those in the remainder of the book, depending as they do on case analysis, generally do not.

Question 1.1

Suppose you were to see the following clause. Would you expect it to be in a voyage or a time charterparty?

> "The vessel shall perform the ballast passage with utmost despatch and the laden passage at . . . knots weather and safe navigation permitting at a consumption of . . . tonnes of Fueloil (state grade. . . .) per day.
>
> Charterers shall have the option to instruct the vessel to increase speed with Charterers reimbursing Owners for the additional bunkers consumed, at replacement cost."

Comment

The answer might surprise you. You really need to have a look at some charterparty forms. They are most easily found on the Internet, and there are links in the further reading, chapter 23. Alternatively, you can find standard forms easily enough, just using a Google search. This is from a Shell form, so compare Shellvoy 6 and Shelltime 4.

You expect to see speed and fuel consumption clauses in time charterparties, but clauses like this are also appearing in voyage charters – probably for considerations of efficient loading and discharge. This is, of course, a voyage clause. Nonetheless, most voyage charters do not need, and do not have, speed and fuel consumption warranties.

Cf. for a time clause, you might also have a look at BPTIME3, cl. 18 (again, you can find links to the standard forms at the end of chapter 23). The time clauses are rather more comprehensive, as you might expect.

Question 1.2

Would you say that the following clause is from a tanker or dry-cargo charterparty?

> "Freight shall be earned concurrently with delivery of cargo at the nominated discharging port or ports and shall be paid by Charterers to Owners without any deductions, . . . in United States Dollars at the rate(s) specified . . . on the gross bill of lading quantity as furnished by the shipper . . ., upon receipt by Charterers of notice of completion of final discharge of cargo, . . ."

Comment

I am sure you have worked this out. Freight is not earned until delivery, so this is a pro-charterer provision. It is in fact from the same (Shell) form as in the previous question, this time cl. 5.

Freight is nearly always payable on delivery in tanker charters, and usually in advance in dry-cargo charters. However, the dry-cargo forms do not all speak with one voice, with many allowing the parties to choose either advance or delivered freight.[93]

Question 1.3

Here are clauses, one from Baltime and one from BPTIME3. Which do you suppose is which?

"The Vessel shall be employed in lawful trades for the carriage of lawful merchandise only between safe ports or places where the Vessel can safely lie always afloat within the limits stated in Box 17 . . . ."

Here is the second clause:

". . . Before instructing Owners to direct the Vessel to any port, Charterers shall exercise due diligence to ascertain the safety of such port, but Charterers do not warrant the safety of any port and shall be under no liability in respect thereof except for loss or damage caused by Charterers' failure to exercise due diligence."

Comment

Again, ideally, you should find Baltime and BPTIME3 on the Internet. As before, there are links in chapter 23, or you can simply find them using Google.

But in any case, you know that tanker forms tend to favour charterers, dry-cargo shipowners. The first clause makes clear that the vessel can only be employed between safe ports, the implication being that charterers would be in breach in ordering her to an unsafe port. Under the second clause, the charterers undertake virtually no responsibility at all. So there is your answer.

The second (safe port) clause is also qualified by a due diligence provision, common in tanker, but not dry-cargo forms.[94]

Question 1.4

One of these clauses is from Baltime, one from STB TIME (an American tanker time charterparty, also called ASBA II). Again, which is which?

"The Owner warrants that the Vessel is capable of maintaining and shall maintain throughout the period of this Charter Party on all sea passages from Seabuoy to Seabuoy a guaranteed average speed under all weather conditions of . . . knots in a laden condition and . . . knots in ballast (speed will be determined by taking the total miles at sea divided by the total hours at sea as shown in the log books excluding stops at sea and any sea passage covered by an off-hire calculation) on a guaranteed daily consumption of . . . tons (of 2,240 lbs.) of Diesel / Bunker C / High Viscosity Fuel Oil maximum . . . seconds Redwood No.1 at 100 degrees F. for main engine, and . . . tons (of 2,240 lbs.) of Diesel for auxiliaries for propulsion."

Here is the second clause:

"Speed capability in knots (abt.) . . . on a consumption in tons (abt.) of . . . ."

---

93 See further section [7.5].
94 See generally section [13.9] for the safe port obligation.

Comment

Asba II can be found at the Shipping Forum website.

All you really need to know is that speed and performance clauses in tanker time charterparties tend to be a lot more detailed than in dry-cargo, probably again reflecting charterers' desire for properly enforceable undertakings on the part of owners. Note the vagueness of the second clause – what is the shipowner really warranting? By comparison, note the detail in the first clause. This is a much more precise form of warranty, which the charterer could more easily enforce. So, there again, is your answer. The first is the tanker clause, the second dry-cargo.

Question 1.5

Now for a comparison between two withdrawal clauses, one from NYPE 1946 (cl. 5), one from Beepeetime 2 (cl. 13):[95]

> "Payment of said hire to be made in New York in cash in United States Currency, semi-monthly in advance, and for the last half month or part of same the approximate amount of hire, and should same not cover the actual time, hire is to be paid for the balance day by day, as it becomes due, if so required by Owners, unless bank guarantee or deposit is made by the Charterers, otherwise failing the punctual and regular payment of the hire, or bank guarantee, or on any breach of this Charter Party, the Owners shall be at liberty to withdraw the vessel from the service of the Charterers, without prejudice to any claim they (the Owners) may otherwise have on the Charterers."

Here is the second clause:

> "In the event of such payment not being made on the due date, Owners shall notify Charterers whereupon Charterers shall make payment of the amount due within seven days of receipt of notification from Owners, failing which Owners shall have the right to withdraw the vessel from the service of Charterers, without prejudice to any claim Owners may otherwise have on Charterers under this charter."

Comment

Again, you need to know that dry-cargo forms favour shipowners, and of course NYPE 1946 is the most widely used dry-cargo time form. By contrast, the now superseded Beepeetime 2 was one of the most pro-charterer forms, in a pro-charterer market. The first clause allows the owners immediately to withdraw the vessel. The second is a much more pro-charterer anti-technicality clause (giving a seven-day grace period). So it is obvious that it is the second, which is the tanker form.

NYPE itself has moved on. NYPE 93 (cl. 11) has an anti-technicality provision (called a "grace period"), as does the revised version of NYPE, currently under consideration (search Google for NYPE 2014 and go to the BIMCO site). However, it is the 1946 (not 1993) form which remains in widespread use. In any case, the grace period under the proposed new NYPE form is a lot shorter than the seven days in Beepeetime 2.

BP has also moved on, and you might look at the even more comprehensive provision in BPTIME3 (cl. 8.4).

---

95 On withdrawal for late payment of hire, see generally section [12.1].

Question 1.6

Again two time charter (off-hire) clauses, from Baltime (cl. 11) and Beepeetime 2 (cl. 23):[96]

> "In the event of drydocking or other necessary measures to maintain the efficiency of the Vessel, deficiency of men or Owners' stores, breakdown of machinery, damage to hull or other accident, either hindering or preventing the working of the Vessel and continuing for more than twenty-four consecutive hours, no hire to be paid in respect of any time lost thereby during the period in which the Vessel is unable to perform the service immediately required. Any hire paid in advance to be adjusted accordingly."

Here is the second clause:

> "All periods of off-hire shall run from the commencement of loss of time . . . until the vessel is in a fully efficient state to resume her service . . . ."

Comment

These are off-hire clauses, the first of which is a "net loss of time" and the second a "period off-hire" clause. The "net loss of time" clause obviously favours the owners. The difference is obvious if you think about a vessel that is capable of discharging at half speed. The first clause penalises shipowners only for the time lost, which will not of course be the entire discharge period.

From what you already know, you would not expect a dry-cargo charter to be period off-hire, and so you should be able to work out that the period off-hire clause is in the tanker form. So the second is Beepeetime 2.

Actually, period off-hire clauses are far from universal, even in the tanker market. Beepeetime 2 was one of the more pro-charterer tanker forms (certainly more so than Shelltime 4). That is partly why I have chosen it. The off-hire wording in BPTIME 3 differs from that of Beepeetime 2, and it may be that the market turned towards shipowners between the drafting of the forms.

Interestingly, the older Baltime clauses (eg, the 1920 revision) used period off-hire wording – maybe the dry-cargo market has turned towards shipowners over the last century or so.[97]

---

96 On off-hire, see generally section [12.3].

97 Eg, *Tynedale Steam Shipping Co Ltd v Anglo-Soviet Shipping Co Ltd (The Hordern)* (1936) 54 Ll L Rep 341, in section [12.3.4].

Chapter 2

Carriage and the general law of contract

Chapter Contents

2.1 Introduction

In this chapter and the next, a number of general principles of law are considered, which underpin all varieties of carriage of goods by sea.

Much of the law of carriage is a particular application of the general law of contract, there being no special law of carriage contracts, as such. This chapter therefore touches on the formation of carriage contracts (terms being the subject of a case study in chapter 22),[1] the extent to which contracts can affect non-parties to them, and (probably the main source of disputes in carriage contracts) termination and breach. It is not possible to cover the general law of contract in detail in a single chapter, and most students of carriage of goods by sea have already studied contract. This chapter therefore concentrates on those aspects of the law that are particularly important for this book.[2]

Chapter 3 concludes consideration of general legal principles, beginning with non-contractual actions. There is also consideration of the extent to which principles of good faith and equity affect carriage. It is important to appreciate that carriage is part of a more general system of law.

Chapter 3 will begin with a discussion of the law of bailment. A bailment arises when one person voluntarily takes possession of the property of another, and particularly if it is a bailment for reward, the bailee comes under stringent duties to care for and return the property. Bailment is the underlying basis of all carriage of goods and, if there were no contract, there would remain a bailment. Today, bailment duties have been so modified by contractual provision as to be largely redundant, but nonetheless there are circumstances where they remain relevant.

2.2 Contract formation

For a bill of lading to perform its functions as a document of title, as described in chapter 20, it needs to be in writing and signed on behalf of the carrier. *Leduc & Co v Ward* implies that, at any rate where the action is not between carrier and the original shipper, contractual terms in the bill of lading must be in writing to be enforceable.[3]

No such formality requirements apply to charterparties. A charterparty can be oral, though it is arguable that only written terms from a charterparty can be incorporated into a bill of lading.[4] In reality, most charterparties are based on standard forms. It is, however, common for fixtures to be made without formality, for example by phone, email or telex, in the expectation that the form will follow later. An example of this was the second charterparty entered into in *The Heidberg*.[5] This was a voyage charterparty, arranged hurriedly (because the charterers needed a ship at short notice) by telephone, and later followed up by a recap telex. There was never any doubt that this was an enforceable charterparty (though one of the issues in the case was whether it was possible to incorporate into a bill of lading terms from what was still, at the time of the issue of the bill, an oral charterparty). An arbitration clause in any contract, however, will be enforceable only if in writing.[6]

---

1 See section [22.2].

2 Those who want more depth on the general law of contract should consult a book such as Peel, *Treitel on the Law of Contract*, 13th ed (2011), Sweet & Maxwell (new edition expected 2015), or McKendrick, *Contract Law*, 11th ed (2015), Palgrave Macmillan.

3 (1888) 20 QBD 475: see [15.1.4].

4 *Partenreederei M/S Heidberg v Grosvenor Grain and Feed Co Ltd (The Heidberg)* [1994] 2 Lloyd's Rep 287, discussed in section [15.2.3].

5 [1994] 2 Lloyd's Rep 287.

6 Arbitration Act 1996, s. 5.

Even an oral fixture will usually be agreed on the basis on a standard form, that in *The Heidberg*, for example, being on the basis of an amended version of the Continent Grain Charterparty 1990 (Synacomex 90). It was also assumed that the form would eventually be drawn up and signed. Some of the modern charterparty forms go further; BPVOY4 (in cl. 48.1) envisages that:

> "Unless otherwise specifically requested by either Owners or Charterers, no formal char-terparty shall be prepared or signed. The terms and conditions of the Charter shall be evi-denced by a recap fixture telex ('Recap Fixture Telex') . . . ."

Of course it is known that BPVOY4 is the form on which the charterparty is to be based, even if no formal charterparty is ever entered into.[7]

It is also common, especially for long-term fixtures, for details of future performance to be left to be determined later. Sometimes (as with BPVOY4) it will be known which form will be used, but matters may be less formal, and agreement may not have been reached on all aspects of the charterparty. The courts are not the destroyers of bargains and, as long as the parties have reached agreement, and intend that agreement to be enforceable, they are prepared to enforce contracts with the minimum of detail needed to make them work, implying any terms that need to be filled in.[8] However, all this assumes that the parties have concluded an agreement, and that they clearly intend to be bound. If they are still feeling their way towards agreement, then there is no contract. While they do not need to have agreed every detail before we can conclude that they intend to be bound, if their conduct is consistent with unfinished negotiations then there will be no contract. If the parties leave something to be later agreed by themselves, there is no contract.

To say that an agreement is subject to something does not necessarily imply that agreement has not yet been reached. For example, an agreement to hold a fete, subject to the weather, could in principle be binding. So could a sale, subject to survey. Good weather, and a satisfactory survey, are simply conditions precedent to the agreement operating. There are, however, terms of art that have a known meaning. Phrases like "subject to contract" are known to negate an intention to be bound,[9] and in general if the parties expressly make the contract "subject to" something that is not yet agreed, the courts will infer a lack of agreement at this stage, even if the terms yet to be agreed are not fundamental.

In the present context, the starting point is often taken to be *The Solholt*, where Staughton J said (of a contract for the sale of a ship) that:[10]

> "She is described as having on that day been 'fixed subject to details'. That means that the main terms were agreed, but until the subsidiary terms and the details had also been agreed no contract existed."

This was *obiter*, because shortly afterwards "the details of the . . . charter-party were agreed and that became a concluded contract", and in any case the dispute was not about that contract.[11] Staughton J's view has gained widespread acceptance, however. If the parties expressly use

---

7 See *Falkonera Shipping Co v Arcadia Energy Pte Ltd (The Falkonera)* [2014] 2 Lloyd's Rep 406, where there was a recap telex but the charter was never signed. No issue was raised as to the validity of the charterparty.

8 Eg, *Hillas and Co Ltd v Arcos Ltd* (1932) 43 Ll L Rep 359, but cf. if even fundamental terms are too ambiguous to be resolved: *Scammell v Ouston* [1941] AC 251 (impossible to resolve price term in contract for the sale of goods). But had no price been agreed at all, the buyer would have been required to pay a reasonable price: Sale of Goods Act 1979, s. 8(2).

9 *Chillingworth v Esche* [1924] 1 Ch 97 (CA).

10 *Sotiros Shipping Inc v Sameiet Solholt (The Solholt)* [1981] 2 Lloyd's Rep 574, 576, affd [1983] 1 Lloyd's Rep 605.

11 The *ratio* of *The Solholt* is on mitigation. On mitigation generally, see section [2.9.2].

terminology such as "subject to details", which clearly indicates an intention not yet to be bound, the courts will give effect to that intention.[12] Otherwise, only the minimum detail is required.

2.3 Terms and their construction

The issue of terms and their construction is dealt with as a separate case study in chapter 22.[13] To know the content of charterparties and bills of lading is fundamental to the law of carriage of goods by sea.

Briefly, we consider two issues there. First, when terms can be implied. It might be thought that charterparties are sufficiently detailed, and tightly drafted, for there to be no need for implication of terms; but this is not the case, and would probably never be the case, however detailed the form. In *Attorney General of Belize v Belize Telecom Ltd*,[14] the Privy Council's advice was to relax the rules and, if the case finds favour, we need to consider its effect on carriage contracts. The second issue is the construction of terms. This time we have the Supreme Court decision in *Rainy Sky SA v Kookmin Bank*,[15] which makes general statements which are certain to have an effect on the construction of contractual terms. Again, we need to consider the implications of this important decision for carriage of goods by sea.

However, this will be left to the case study in chapter 22.

2.4 Privity of contract

This section is about the extent to which contracts affect non-parties to them. It is important because a carriage contract typically has just two parties (for example a charterparty will be a contract just between the shipowner – or disponent owner – and the charterer), but there are many people involved in a carriage transaction, who might wish to benefit from its terms, or who ought really to be bound by its terms. If the carriage is on the terms of the Hague-Visby Rules,[16] it helps to extend their protection to servants, agents and independent contractors employed or engaged by the contracting carrier, and ideally parties other than the original shipper should be bound. Unfortunately, the privity doctrine puts difficulties in the way of this, except to the extent that it has been altered by statute.

Because privity figures large elsewhere in the book, I will say here only that the doctrine states that someone who is not party to a contract cannot (in his own right) enforce benefits under that contract, nor can he have burdens from that contract imposed upon him.

Privity of contract is a principle that seems to be peculiar to English law, and to systems of law derived from English law. It can create significant problems, and fully two chapters of the book (chapters 16 and 17) are devoted to it. Though the emphasis in section [10.6] (on time

---

12 Eg, *Mmecen SA v Inter Ro-Ro SA (The Samah and Lina V)* [1981] 1 Lloyd's Rep 40; *The Nissos Samos* [1985] 1 Lloyd's Rep 378, *Granit SA v Benship International Inc* [1994] 1 Lloyd's Rep 526 (where in the absence of the words "subject to details" a contract was held to have been concluded); *Ignazio Messina & Co v Polskie Linie Oceaniczne* [1995] 2 Lloyd's Rep 566; *Star Steamship Society v Beogradska Plovidba (The Junior K)* [1988] 2 Lloyd's Rep 583; *CPC Consolidated Pool Carriers GmbH v CTM Cia Transmediterranea SA (The CPC Gallia)* [1994] 1 Lloyd's Rep 68; *Thoresen & Co (Bangkok) Ltd v Fathom Marine Co* [2004] 1 Lloyd's Rep 622 (where the issue was whether the parties had in fact contracted "subject details").

13 See section [22.2].

14 [2009] 1 WLR 1988, criticised Davies, "Recent developments in the law of implied terms" [2010] LMCLQ 140.

15 [2011] 1 WLR 2900.

16 On which see chapter 18.

charterparties and third parties) is on property, it can also be said that if there were no privity doctrine, the problems there would not arise.

The principle relating to burdens is very old. For benefits, the principle has been restated in the House of Lords in *Dunlop Pneumatic Tyre Co Ltd v Selfridge & Co Ltd*,[17] *Beswick v Beswick*, and in a carriage context in *Midland Silicones Ltd v Scruttons Ltd*.[18] We will see that there has been some relaxation in respect of benefits in the Contract (Rights of Third Parties) Act 1999, which though it does not fully apply to carriage contracts, can certainly affect the issues in chapter 17.[19]

Among the problems caused by the privity doctrine are the enforcement of international conventions, where those responsible for their drafting do not understand, or at any rate do not take into account, the way in which English law works. Often the intention is to allow the convention to extend to anyone involved in the carriage operation, but the lack of success in this respect is firmly demonstrated for the Hague-Visby Rules in *The Captain Gregos*.[20]

2.5 Market variations and remedies

An understanding of how market variations impact on carriage contracts, the substance of the remainder of this chapter, is absolutely central to an understanding of carriage of goods by sea. We have already seen, in chapter 1, how freight and hire markets fluctuate:[21] some market variation is almost inevitable with a long-term time charterparty, because hire rates are volatile.[22] Even with shorter term fixtures, there will be variations, albeit usually less dramatic.

Whatever the legal issues the cases actually turn on, it is market fluctuations that are, in reality, behind many of the disputes in this book. As market rates rise and fall, one of the parties will turn out to have made a good, and the other a bad, bargain. Thus, for example, if a charterparty is fixed when rates are low, the charterer has made a good, and the shipowner a bad, bargain – the converse is obviously true if it is fixed when rates are high. The party who has made a bad bargain will want to get out of it, if he can. Since markets rarely remain static for long, this is the (usually unstated) motivation behind many disputes. Disputes are often quite unmeritorious, in the sense that the reason given for terminating is an excuse, not the genuine reason, but as we will see in chapter 3, there is generally no requirement to act in good faith in performing commercial contracts.[23]

Of course there can be other (more meritorious?) reasons why one party may wish to repudiate. Suppose, for example, a time charterer was genuinely unable to pay hire, or had even gone bankrupt. In that event the only useful remedy available to a shipowner, even on a falling market, is withdrawal of the vessel.[24] Such cases would appear to be the exception, rather than the rule, however.

The effect of a market fluctuation is to make the bargain worse for one of the parties. If market rates drop, the charterer has made a bad bargain. He will be able to earn less freight, whether by sub-charter or bill of lading contract, and he will be locked into a hire rate which will exceed his earnings. If we were able to terminate the charterparty, he could hire replacement tonnage at the new (lower) market rate. Conversely, of course, if rates rise, the shipowner is locked into a hire

---

17 [1915] AC 847, mentioned in *Port Line Ltd v Ben Line Steamers Ltd* [1958] 2 QB 146, a case considered in detail in section [10.6].
18 Respectively [1968] AC 58 and [1962] AC 446. We consider *Midland Silicones* in depth in section [17.2.1].
19 Eg, section [17.2.1].
20 *Compania Portorafti Commerciale SA v Ultramar Panama Inc (The Captain Gregos)* [1990] 1 Lloyd's Rep 310. See further section [17.3].
21 Section [1.5].
22 See section [1.11].
23 See section [3.5].
24 We see a withdrawal on a falling market, for example, in *Kuwait Rocks Co v Amn Bulkcarriers Inc (The Astra)* [2013] 2 Lloyd's Rep 69, in section [12.1.6].

rate that is lower than he could obtain by terminating the charterparty and refixing at the new (higher) rate.

We will see in this book many instances of this. In *The Laconia*,[25] market rates had risen by some 80 per cent since the (time) charterparty was concluded, and of course the owners wished to end it, so that they could refix the vessel at the new rate, rather than continue the charter at the old. They were held validly to have invoked the withdrawal clause, and this was the issue in the case, but the motivation was no doubt to end the charterparty for any reason. Sometimes the motivations are stated explicitly,[26] but more usually they are unstated. Conversely, in *Hongkong Fir Shipping Co Ltd v Kawasaki Kisen Kaisha Ltd*,[27] discussed in detail in the next section, the charterers claimed (unsuccessfully as we will see) the right to repudiate the charterparty, on a falling market. By six months into a two-year time charter, the report tells us that there had been a "catastrophic fall" in market rates (this was the summer of 1957, when the Suez Canal reopened).[28] Had the charterers succeeded in their argument, this would have allowed them to charter another vessel at the new (much lower) market rates, rather than to have remained committed for the remaining 18 months, at the much higher charter rate.

Sometimes it is possible to avoid market constraints without ending the charterparty. There are, for example, ways of avoiding the demurrage regime, which we will examine in chapters 8 and 9. These will also be motivated by market considerations, market freight rates – on which damages at large for detention would be based – having risen above the demurrage rate, which is a rate of compensation agreed in the charterparty.[29] Another possibility is that a charterer who had made a good bargain would prefer to extend the charterparty for as long as possible. In chapter 11 we examine time charter redelivery cases,[30] in most of which the charterers are attempting to prolong the charterparty, market rates having risen above charter hire rates.

Nonetheless, most of the disputes are attempts by one party to terminate. Sometimes the charterparty itself will give either or both parties the right to end it, for example the charterer's right to cancel, or the shipowner's to withdraw the vessel.[31] Often these rights are qualified, and hedged around with restrictions.[32] A cancelling clause does nothing other than create a right to cancel, for example for late delivery of the vessel. But it neither creates, nor necessarily implies, a breach of contract by the shipowner. The shipowner who delivers late may be in breach of contract but, if so, the breach is independent of the cancelling clause. Similarly, a withdrawal clause creates no breach of contract, though it is often triggered by a breach, such as late or non-payment of time charter hire. Its effect may be to alter the nature of the term, in that example to make late payment a breach of condition.[33]

If no right to terminate is given by the charterparty itself, the breach may justify termination – this is the subject of the next section. Not all breaches of contract entitle the innocent party to repudiate, and if one party repudiates when he is not entitled to do so, the other party (even though in breach of contract) may himself sue for wrongful repudiation. This was the actual result of the *Hongkong Fir* case (in the next section): the shipowner succeeded in an action against the charterer for wrongful

---

25　Mardorf Peach & Co Ltd v Attic Sea Carriers Corp of Liberia (The Laconia) [1977] AC 850, in section [12.1.2]. The rise was quite rapid, as the charterparty had only been made only just over three months earlier.

26　Eg, Awilco A/S v Fulvia SpA di Navigazione (The Chikuma) [1980] 2 Lloyd's Rep 409, 411 (Lord Denning MR), in section [12.1.1], another case where shipowners withdrew on a rising market (rvsd [1981] 1 WLR 314).

27　[1962] 2 QB 26.

28　[1962] 2 QB 26, 39, and see section [3.5].

29　Explicitly stated in Inverkip SS Co Ltd v Bunge & Co [1917] 2 KB 198, 200, in section [9.1].

30　Section [11.5].

31　For cancelling clauses see sections [7.2] and [11.2]; for withdrawal clauses section [12.1.2]. There may (or may not) be breaches of contract, apart from the clause, giving a right to damages and (perhaps) repudiation. On why an innocent party might wish to repudiate as well as withdraw, see (eg) The Astra at [12.1.7].

32　See section [12.1.4].

33　See [12.1.6], and in particular commentary on Afovos Shipping Co SA v R. Pagnam & F. Lli (The Afovos) [1983] 1 WLR 195 and The Astra [2013] 2 Lloyd's Rep 69.

repudiation, even though he had provided a vessel that was unseaworthy. It is obviously important to know, therefore, which breaches give rise to a right to withdraw or cancel, which to repudiate, and which give rise to a right to damages only.

2.6 Conditions, warranties and innominate terms

This section is about breach of which contractual terms allows the other party to repudiate (get out of) the contract. Note that repudiation is in addition to any damages action he might have.

2.6.1 Categories of term, and relevance of seriousness of breach

Whether a breach by one party justifies the other in electing to repudiate depends on the categorisation of the term broken, and if it is an innominate (or intermediate) term, the effect of the breach.

There are also some breaches for which, on ordinary contractual principles, the innocent party may repudiate, thereby bringing the contract to an end, whether or not the charterparty (or other contract) expressly so provides.[34]

Historically, contractual terms have been divided into two main categories, conditions and warranties. Lord Denning MR described the distinction as follows:[35]

> "... if the promisor broke a *condition* in *any* respect, however slight, it gave the other party a right to be quit of his future obligations and to sue for damages: ... If the promisor broke a *warranty* in *any* respect, however serious, the other party was not quit of his future obligations. He had to perform them. His only remedy was to sue for damages."

He went on to observe that this categorisation was adopted in the Sale of Goods Act 1893,[36] but it is certainly not limited to sales of goods. On this classification, whether the injured party can repudiate is determined solely on the categorisation of the term broken, and not at all on the effect of the breach. A condition is a term for breach of which, however slight, the injured party has the right to treat the contract as repudiated. The other main category of term is the warranty, for breach of which the injured party can only claim damages, but not (according to Lord Denning MR) a right to repudiate.

There are certainly some advantages in having everything depend on the categorisation of the term, as opposed to the consequences of its breach, especially if this approach is combined with a reluctance to imply conditions; such a system provides the parties with certainty and, at least in theory, causes no injustice, because the parties can stipulate for any term to be a condition, should they so desire.[37] On the other hand, to have to make explicit provision for every conceivably serious breach would make drafting very convoluted. For carriage contracts, and especially voyage charter-parties, it has been recognised that many terms do not fall comfortably into such a categorisation. The consequences of a breach can vary from the insignificant to the very serious, often depending on a time element. If the matter can be remedied quickly, it is not serious; if there will be a sub-stantial delay, then it is.

In *Hongkong Fir Shipping Co Ltd v Kawasaki Kisen Kaisha Ltd*, reported in 1962,[38] the Court of Appeal explicitly recognised that there is a third category of term, where the right to repudiate depends

---

34 The principles here apply to all contracts, including all contracts of carriage, and not just to charterparties.

35 *Maredelanto Compania Naviera SA v Bergbau-Handel GmbH (The Mihalis Angelos)* [1971] 1 QB 164, 193 (Lord Denning's emphasis).

36 Re-enacted with amendments in Sale of Goods Act 1979: see s. 11(3).

37 As pointed out, for example, by Cleasby B in his dissenting judgment in *Jackson v Union Marine Insurance Co Ltd* (1874–5) LR 10 CP 125. The majority view is considered in section [6.6].

38 [1962] 2 QB 26.

on the effect of the breach. Before we examine *Hongkong Fir* in detail, we should note that it was the culmination of a century or so of case law, in which the courts had been moving in this direction. The effect of the breach was the crucial factor in *Stanton v Richardson*, fully 90 years before *Hongkong Fir*.[39] An effect of breach analysis was adopted by Devlin J in *Universal Cargo Carriers Corp v Citati*,[40] considering when the shipowner was entitled to repudiate, where the charterer had broken the contract by exceeding the laytime. Finally, as we will see, the very definition of a condition depended on it being an important term, which could itself depend on the likely effect of it being broken. It is probably fair to say that *Hongkong Fir* formalised what the courts had been leaning towards for decades.

Hongkong Fir Shipping Co Ltd v Kawasaki Kisen Kaisha Ltd concerned a two-year time charter, but the vessel was unseaworthy when delivered, and remained so for the first six months or so. Her machinery was in reasonably good condition, but because of the age of the vessel, needed to be maintained by an experienced engine room staff. In reality the chief engineer was an inefficient alcoholic, and the engine room complement insufficient. The vessel kept breaking down and (after about six months) the charterers purported to repudiate the charterparty. The issue was whether the charterers (motivated a market that had fallen catastrophically) were justified in repudiating.[41] (The vessel was made seaworthy about three months after the charterers purported to repudiate.)

The Court of Appeal, though accepting that the incompetence of the crew rendered the vessel unseaworthy when handed over,[42] held that the charterers were not entitled to repudiate, and that the shipowners were therefore entitled to damages for wrongful repudiation. As we will see in chapter 4, the obligation to provide a seaworthy vessel is (not surprisingly perhaps) regarded as fundamental; it is difficult to contract out of, and a shipowner in breach cannot rely on excepted perils in the carriage contract.[43] However, in *Hongkong Fir* it was held not to be a condition, because the consequences of breach were not always serious; they can vary from the very trivial to the catastrophic. As Sellers LJ observed:[44]

"It would be unthinkable that all the relatively trivial matters which have been held to be unseaworthiness could be regarded as conditions of the contract or conditions precedent to a charterer's liability and justify in themselves a cancellation or refusal to perform on the part of the charterer."

Upjohn LJ gave as examples of the very trivial, that:[45]

". . . if a nail is missing from one of the timbers of a wooden vessel or if proper medical supplies or two anchors are not on board at the time of sailing, the owners are in breach of the seaworthiness stipulation".

At the other end of the scale are the catastrophic instances we will come across in other chapters.[46] The wide range in seriousness of the breach was perhaps the main reason for not regarding the obligation as a condition.

Both Sellers and Upjohn LJJ thought, founding themselves partly on the authorities cited here, that even if a breach is not of a condition, if it is sufficiently serious as to frustrate the objects of

---

39 (1874) LR 9 CP 390, on appeal from (1872) LR 7 CP 421. See further sections [4.2.11]; [6.6].

40 [1957] 2 QB 401.

41 On the motivations see further section [3.5].

42 On the seaworthiness obligation generally, see section [4.2].

43 See section [4.2].

44 [1962] 2 QB 26, 56.

45 [1962] 2 QB 26, 64.

46 Eg, *Mediterranean Freight Services Ltd v BP Oil International Ltd (The Fiona)* [1994] 2 Lloyd's Rep 506 (section [4.6.2]); *Primetrade AG v Ythan Ltd (The Ythan)* [2006] 1 Lloyd's Rep 457 (section [16.6]).

the adventure, then that will allow the innocent party the option to repudiate. Salmon J had held the breach in the case itself to be insufficiently serious, and the Court of Appeal was not prepared to interfere with that finding. Diplock LJ reached the same result, but on the basis that there is a third type of term, which is neither a condition nor a warranty. Only if the breach of such a term is sufficiently serious that it "goes to the root of" the contract can the innocent party repudiate. The test is alternatively stated as whether the breach is sufficiently serious that it frustrates the adventure, and this is also the modern meaning of the term "fundamental breach" of contract.[47] If the breach is insufficiently serious, the innocent party is limited to a claim for damages alone. This is a far more stringent test than one of "reasonableness", so that a breach can be unreasonable without being serious enough to frustrate the adventure.

There is no difference in substance between the three Court of Appeal judgments in Hongkong Fir, but Diplock LJ's tripartite classification is now common currency. He did not name this third category of term in Hongkong Fir itself, which may explain why, in later cases, it is often described as an "innominate" term.[48] Whereas with a breach of condition the consequences of the breach are irrelevant to the right of the injured party to repudiate, for breach of an innominate term they are of paramount importance. It might be said that (to the extent to which it applies) Hongkong Fir substituted for the classification of the term, an approach based on the gravity of the breach, to the question whether repudiation was justified. As we have seen, the charterers in the case itself were unable to show that the consequences of the particular breach were sufficiently serious to allow them to repudiate the charterparty.

2.6.2 Conditions after Hongkong Fir

Hongkong Fir either represents a change in emphasis towards giving greater weight to the consequences of the breach, or is simply a culmination in a range of authorities that were already heading in that direction. But the case has not replaced the condition with the innominate term, and all three judges in the Court of Appeal recognised that the parties may have reason to categorise some contractual terms as conditions. We now know that many terms, and particularly time terms in international sale contracts, continue to be conditions.[49]

A few years after Hongkong Fir, the Court of Appeal held in The Mihalis Angelos that the expected readiness clause in a voyage charterparty was a condition,[50] and that this was unaffected by anything in Hongkong Fir. At first instance, Mocatta J had taken the view that in the absence of well-established authority in relation to expected readiness clauses in charters, "I think I should apply the reasoning in the Hongkong Fir case".[51] The view taken in the Court of Appeal was essentially that Hongkong Fir had stated, rather than altered, the law that there was authority that the expected readiness clause was a condition, at least in an FOB sale contract (where the buyers have to provide a ship to take the goods), and that there was no good ground for distinguishing between sale and carriage contracts.[52]

So, given that conditions continue to survive, we need to be able to identify them. There are not chains of carriage contracts, as there are of international sale contracts, and the certainty imperatives

---

47 The usage, for example, in Photo Production Ltd v Securicor Transport Ltd [1980] AC 827, 849 (Lord Diplock).

48 The slightly more informative "intermediate" term is also used. Neither is used in Hongkong Fir itself; both are used in Soon Hua Seng Co Ltd v Glencore Grain Ltd [1996] 1 Lloyd's Rep 398; "innominate term" is used in Torvald Klaveness A/S v Arni Maritime Corp (The Gregos) [1994] 1 WLR 1465. There seems to be no conventional usage.

49 On the survival of conditions post Hongkong Fir, see Bunge Corp, New York v Tradax Export SA, Panama [1981] 1 WLR 711.

50 Maredelanto Compania Naviera SA v Bergbau-Handel GmbH (The Mihalis Angelos) [1971] 1 QB 164. We consider The Mihalis Angelos in detail at section [6.3].

51 [1971] 1 QB 164, 176. (The first instance decision is reported at the same place as the CA.)

52 Eg, [1971] 1 QB 164, 194 (Lord Denning MR) and cases therein cited.

from the international sale case of *Bunge Corp, New York v Tradax Export SA, Panama*[53] do not apply with such force in carriage contracts. There is, in carriage contracts, no equivalent to the implied conditions in the Sale of Goods Act 1979, ss. 12–15. Charterparties contain relatively few conditions, but *The Mihalis Angelos* tells us that there are some. As we will see in chapter 5, some statements as to the ship are conditions.[54] Also, even the slightest deviation by the shipowner allows a voyage charterer to repudiate the charter, or a cargo-owner to repudiate the bill of lading contract.[55]

Nonetheless, it remains the case that most terms of charterparties and other carriage contracts are probably innominate terms. Even time terms are often innominate terms, and to this extent, sale and carriage contracts tend to diverge.[56] We have already seen that the duty of a voyage charterer to load and discharge the vessel within the allotted laytime. If he does not do so, the shipowner cannot immediately withdraw the vessel, otherwise demurrage provisions might never apply, but if the charterer takes so long as to frustrate the adventure, then the shipowner may withdraw.[57]

So how do you tell whether a term is a condition? If the parties expressly state that a term is a condition the courts will generally give effect to that. This was made clear in *Hongkong Fir* itself.[58] It is rare for charterparties explicitly to make terms conditions, but BPVOY4 makes it "a condition of this Charter that the responses in the BP Shipping Questionnaire are correct as at the date hereof". The courts would almost certainly give effect to this designation.

We will see in chapter 6 that statements in voyage charters relating to the likely arrival time, such as the present position of vessel, and the expected readiness statement, are treated as conditions.[59] We will see in chapter 12 that punctual payment of time charterparty hire has recently been held to be a condition.[60] On the other hand, for a voyage charterer to exceed the laytime is definitely not a breach of condition,[61] and we have already seen that the obligation to provide a seaworthy vessel is not a condition.

In chapter 6 we will consider in greater detail *Bentsen v Taylor*,[62] where the Court of Appeal held a statement in a voyage charter that the ship was about to sail was a condition. Bowen LJ said that in order to determine whether a term was a condition, even where explicit provision had not been made:[63]

". . . one of the first things you would look to is, to what extent the accuracy of the statement – the truth of what is promised – would be likely to affect the substance and foundation of the adventure which the contract is intended to carry out . . .".

He continued, that it would depend:

". . . not the *effect* of the breach which has in fact taken place, but the effect likely to be produced on the foundation of the adventure by any such breach of that portion of the contract".

---

53 [1981] 1 WLR 711.

54 Section [5.4].

55 Section [4.4].

56 Eg, *Torvald Klaveness A/S v Arni Maritime Corp (The Gregos)* [1994] 1 WLR 1465, in section [11.5]. Cf. *Kuwait Rocks Co v Amn Bulkcarriers Inc (The Astra)* [2013] 2 Lloyd's Rep 69, in section [12.1.6], if it is correct.

57 See above, section [2.1], and see also section [9.4]. See also *ERG Raffinerie Mediterranee SpA v Chevron USA Inc (The Luxmar)* [2007] 2 Lloyd's Rep 542, where we can see the contrast between sale and carriage contracts.

58 Eg, [1962] 2 QB 26, 69–70 (Diplock LJ). Cf. *L Schuler AG v Wickman Machine Tool Sales Ltd* [1974] AC 235, where the House of Lords held that the word "condition" would not be given that meaning if such a construction produced a result so unreasonable that the parties could not have intended it. *Schuler* should probably best be seen as a rare exceptional case. See further [5.4].

59 Section [6.3].

60 Section [12.1.6].

61 Section [9.7].

62 [1893] 2 QB 274, and see section [6.3].

63 *Bentsen v Taylor, Sons & Co* [1893] 2 QB 274, 281. On *Bentsen v Taylor*, see further section [6.5].

In other words, unlike *Hongkong Fir* itself, where the issue depended on the actual breach in the particular case, a term will be a condition if breach would *generally* be likely to go to the foundation of the adventure. In *Hongkong Fir* itself, Diplock LJ's test (for a condition) was that:[64]

> "... it can be predicated that every breach of such an undertaking must give rise to an event which will deprive the party not in default of substantially the whole benefit which it was intended that he should obtain from the contract ...".

This appears similar to Bowen LJ's test, though possibly slightly more difficult to satisfy.

In *The Seaflower*,[65] the Court of Appeal held the requirements of a "majors approval clause" to be a condition of a time charterparty, though it was not stated to be a condition. Though the case adds little to the above tests, the authorities, including *Bentsen v Taylor*,[66] were fully reviewed, and the importance of loss of approval was regarded as significant.

2.6.3 Effect of repudiation

Assuming that a breach has occurred that allows the injured party to repudiate, he can elect whether to do so, or instead to keep the contract alive (or in other words "affirm" the contract). If he has made a bad bargain he will usually wish to repudiate, but might be reluctant otherwise, unless there are serious doubts about the ability of the other party to perform. He must make the election quickly, and affirmation may be inferred from his conduct. If he elects to repudiate, from that moment both parties are relieved from any further performance of what Lord Diplock described in *Photo Production Ltd v Securicor Transport Ltd* as the primary obligations under the contract.[67] The primary obligations are really the performance obligations. The "secondary obligation on the part of the contract breaker ... to pay monetary compensation to the other party for the loss sustained by him in consequence of the breach" remains, so even if he repudiates the injured party may sue for damages. There are other parts of the contract that can also survive an election to repudiate, for example arbitration clauses,[68] and possibly time bars, but the performance obligations of both parties come to an end on repudiation. Note, however, that, in principle at least, all terms of the contract remain alive prior to the election to repudiate.[69] This includes contractual exemptions, and we elaborate on this below.[70]

If the innocent party affirms, thereby keeping the contract alive, all the contractual terms remain in force. *The Simona* in chapter 6 is an instance of this, where the shipowner's election to affirm rather than repudiate allowed the charterers later to cancel, the cancelling clause remaining in force.[71] The injured party retains, of course, the right to sue for damages for the breach.

2.7 Anticipatory breach

It must be clear from the foregoing section that whether a breach is repudiatory often has a time element. As we have seen, for example, a charterer cannot repudiate merely because the vessel is

---

64 [1962] 2 QB 26, 69.
65 BS & N Ltd (BVI) v Micado Shipping Ltd (Malta) (The Seaflower) [2001] 1 Lloyd's Rep 341, a "majors approval clause" requiring written evidence of approvals from "Major Oil Companies".
66 [2001] 1 Lloyd's Rep 341, [40] (Waller LJ).
67 [1980] AC 827, 849.
68 Heyman v Darwins Ltd [1942] AC 356.
69 See further section [4.4].
70 Section [2.10].
71 Fercometal SARL v Meditteranean Shipping Co SA (The Simona) [1989] AC 788, considered further in sections [6.2]; [11.2].

unseaworthy, but he can do so if she cannot be made seaworthy within a frustrating time. For a charterer to exceed the laytime does not allow the shipowner to repudiate the charter but, if he does not provide a cargo within a frustrating time, the shipowner can sail away.

It is not necessary for the injured party to wait, before repudiating, until a breach of an innominate term has become so serious as to frustrate the adventure. The contractual doctrine of anticipatory breach allows him to repudiate earlier, but this can be risky, because if it turns out that he was not entitled to do so, he may be sued for wrongful repudiation by the other party.

The criteria were stated by Lord Porter in *Heyman v Darwins Ltd*,[72] and have been applied in a number of the cases cited in this book, for example by Devlin J in *Universal Cargo Carriers Corpn v Citati*,[73] by Lord Wilberforce in *The Nanfri*,[74] and recently by Flaux J in *The Astra*.[75] There are essentially two types of anticipatory breach, renunciation or impossibility of performance. *The Nanfri* and *The Astra* are instances of the former, *Universal Cargo Carriers Corpn v Citati* of the latter.

Renunciation is a refusal to perform, or to perform other than in a manner "such as to deprive the [innocent party] of substantially the whole benefit which it was the intention of the parties that the [innocent party] should obtain from the further performance of [its] own contractual undertakings".[76] This is essentially the same root of contract test that was used in *Hongkong Fir* itself. The refusal may be expressed or inferred from conduct. In *The Nanfri* the shipowners informed the time charterers that the masters of the three ships under dispute were being instructed "to withdraw all direct or implied authority to charterer or its agents to sign bills of lading", and not to sign any freight pre-paid bill. They did indeed so instruct the masters, and this was held to amount to a renunciation of the time charter, since it would have substantially deprived the charterers of virtually the whole benefit of the charterparty. In *The Astra*, the time charterers were held to have renounced the charterparty by threatening bankruptcy unless the owners agreed to a substantial reduction in the rate of hire.[77]

In the case of impossibility, it is clear from *Universal Cargo Carriers Corpn v Citati* that it must be inevitable that the tendered performance will involve either a breach sufficiently serious as to frustrate the adventure. This is a wholly objective test, and does not depend at all on what the innocent party thought. The innocent party can rely on the guilty party's inability to perform even if he (the innocent party) was not aware of it, or did not even suspect it, at the time of repudiation.

In *The Afovos*,[78] Lord Diplock took the view that the anticipatory breach doctrine works only for root of contract breaches, which he also describes as fundamental breaches. There is no equivalent for breaches of conditions, still less to a situation that is certain to (but has not yet) give risen to a right to withdraw from or cancel a charterparty, unless of course that situation will also give rise to a fundamental breach of contract.

2.8 Affirmation by the innocent party

Generally speaking, an innocent party does not have to accept a repudiatory breach by the other party as bringing an end to the contract. He can elect instead to keep the contract alive. If it were

---

72 [1942] AC 356, 397.

73 [1957] 2 QB 401 (see section [9.7]).

74 *Federal Commerce and Navigation Co Ltd v Molena Alpha Inc (The Nanfri)* [1979] AC 757, 778–9, also discussed (in this context) in section [12.1.5].

75 *The Astra* [2013] 2 Lloyd's Rep 69, also discussed (in this context) in section [12.1.5].

76 [1979] AC 757, 779 (Lord Wilberforce), adopting *Hongkong Fir Shipping Co Ltd v Kawasaki Kisen Kaisha Ltd* [1962] 2 QB 26, 72 (Diplock LJ). Later, Lord Wilberforce observes simply that there is a "common principle that, to amount to repudiation a breach must go to the root of the contract", so a renunciation must amount to a refusal which goes to the root of the contract.

77 [2013] 2 Lloyd's Rep 69, [23] *et seq*, and see section [12.1.6].

78 [1983] 1 Lloyd's Rep 335, and see section [12.1.4].

otherwise, a person would need only to commit a serious breach of contract unilaterally to renounce his contractual obligations and, in principle, perhaps, this should not be allowed.

The leading UK authority is the House of Lords decision in *White and Carter (Councils) Ltd v McGregor*.[79] A contract was concluded allowing the appellants to display advertisements on plates on their dustbins, advertising the respondents' garage, for three years. On the very day the contract was made, the respondents tried to back out, but the appellants refused to allow them to do so. The appellants carried the advertisements for the full three years and sued successfully for the agreed price. Note that this was an action for the price and not for damages. Had it been an action for damages, the appellants would have been required (on principles discussed below)[80] to mitigate their losses, by finding alternative custom. Even in that event, the starting point would still have been the price, less such profits as had been made, or should reasonably have been made, over the period. (Thus, the appellants would still have been able to keep the benefit of their bargain, had rates fallen.)

The respondents argued that the appellants should have treated the respondents' breach as bringing the contract to an end. This would have restricted them to a damages action. Instead, the appellants had simply gone on carrying the advertisements, and made no attempt to mitigate. The respondents argued that the award should have been reduced by the amount the appellants could reasonably have received for the hire of the advertising space to someone else.

The respondents' argument was rejected, albeit by a bare majority, but subsequent decisions further establish the *White and Carter* principle. By keeping the contract alive, however unreasonably, and suing not for damages but for the agreed price, the appellants were able to avoid any difficulties over mitigation. Lord Reid said that the law did not require a person only to enforce his contractual rights in a reasonable way, being persuaded partly by certainty arguments.[81] So the reasonableness or otherwise of the innocent party's choice is not relevant.

Nonetheless, Lord Reid placed some limits on the operation of the principle, and though these limitations appear in his speech alone, they have been adopted in later cases, and almost certainly represent a correct statement of the law. First, it must be possible for the innocent party to continue to perform without the co-operation of the other party.[82] Secondly, even if the innocent party can continue to perform without the co-operation of the guilty party, he must also have a "legitimate interest, financial or otherwise, in performing the contract rather than claiming damages".[83] Unfortunately there is little elaboration on what "legitimate interest" might mean in this context. We return to this issue in chapter 11.[84]

It might be thought that the first limitation would generally rule out the operation of *White and Carter* in carriage cases, since carriage contracts (other than demise charterparties) have a service element; they are not like placing advertisements on bins, which requires no co-operation at all from the customer. The principle has, however, been applied where a time charterer has redelivered the vessel early on a falling market, and there are cases where the shipowner has successfully claimed hire (without the need to mitigate) for the remainder of the charter period. A shipowner does not require the co-operation of a time charterer to perform (though no doubt the charterer requires the co-operation of the shipowner). The authorities, on how the principle applies to time charters, are considered in chapter 11.[85]

---

79 [1962] AC 413, and see section [11.3].
80 Section [2.9.2].
81 [1962] AC 413, 430.
82 [1962] AC 413, 429, cited in *The Aquafaith* [2012] 2 Lloyd's Rep 61, [5].
83 [1962] AC 413, 431, cited in *The Aquafaith* [2012] 2 Lloyd's Rep 61, [6].
84 Section [11.3.1], where the case is discussed in a time charterparty context.
85 Section [11.3.1].

2.9 Damages revisited

2.9.1 General principles

We have already seen that damages in contract compensate the injured party. They protect expectation losses, the starting point being that the innocent party should be put, as far as possible, into the position he would have been in, had the contract been properly performed. Suppose, for example, a ship has been time chartered at a hire rate that is above the current market rate (ie, the market has fallen). Suppose further that the charterer redelivers early, in breach of contract. The breach has deprived the shipowner of his expectation, which is continued hire, at the contract rate. Damages will compensate him for that, the starting point being hire for the remaining contractual period, less hire or freight actually earned over the period. This will put him into the same financial position as if the contract had been properly performed.

Importantly, however, damages are not intended to do anything more than compensate. In recent cases "the compensatory principle" has sometimes been prayed in aid, but on its own it does not get us very far. We need to know for precisely what losses damages for breach of contract will compensate.

It is well established that, where the main loss has been caused by market fluctuation, the starting point for damages will be the difference between contract and current market rates. So, for example, if a ship on time charter is wrongly withdrawn from service by the shipowner, the charterer will be compensated for the costs of chartering a substitute. If the market has risen, the starting point will be the difference between the new market hire, and the lower contract hire rate. On a falling market, of course, the charterers may be able to obtain a substitute more cheaply and suffer no loss at all. In that event, they will not be entitled to more than nominal damages.

The calculation is not always that simple. Most breaches cause consequential losses. There will, at least, for example, be expenses associated with making alternative arrangements. Consequential losses are recoverable, subject to the ordinary contractual principles of remoteness of damage. Deriving from *Hadley v Baxendale*, these principles were stated by Alderson B as follows:[86]

> "Where two parties have made a contract which one of them has broken, the damages which the other party ought to receive in respect of such breach of contract should be such as may fairly and reasonably be considered either arising naturally, ie, according to the usual course of things, from such breach of contract itself, or such as may reasonably be supposed to have been in the contemplation of both parties, at the time they made the contract, as the probable result of the breach of it."

The main point of this is that if the claimant is likely to suffer a special loss, such as an unusually lucrative sub-charter, which is outside the normal contemplation of the defendant, the defendant will not be liable unless it was disclosed, prior to the making of the contract. Then it can be taken into account, either by adjusting the contractual terms, or by refusing to enter into the contract in the first place. It is a just way to ensure open dealing in contractual negotiations. It is contrasted with indemnities in chapter 13.[87]

These principles were applied in *The Heron II*,[88] where a ship's late arrival at the discharge port caused the cargo-owners to lose their market, and they were held entitled to recover in respect of

---

86 (1854) 9 Exch 341.
87 Section [13.6].
88 *Koufos v C. Czarnikow Ltd (The Heron II)* [1969] 1 AC 350.

this.[89] The case therefore suggests there might be damages for delay, whether or not the contract explicitly so provides.[90]

2.9.2 Mitigation

Damages are also subject to the principles of mitigation. For our purposes, the injured party must take all reasonable steps to mitigate the loss to him consequent upon the defendant's wrong, not in the sense that there is an actionable duty, but in that he "cannot recover damages for any such loss which he could thus have avoided but has failed, through unreasonable action or inaction, to avoid. Put shortly, the claimant cannot recover for avoidable loss". The other side of the coin is that, "where the claimant does take steps to mitigate the loss to him consequent upon the defendant's wrong and these steps are successful, the defendant is entitled to the benefit accruing from the claimant's action and is liable only for the loss as lessened . . . [put] shortly, the claimant cannot recover for avoided loss".[91]

The "avoidable loss" principle requires the claimant to take all reasonable steps in mitigation. It is also necessary to establish a causal link between the breach and the loss, and this may amount to the same thing; the claimant who fails to take reasonable steps to mitigate can also be regarded as having, to that extent, caused his own loss. Whether the test is formulated in terms of mitigation or causation, however, it is not enough simply to establish that what the claimant has done is reasonable, from a business viewpoint. The requirement is to take *all* reasonable steps in mitigation. In chapter 1 we saw the extraordinary market fluctuations in *The Elena d'Amico*.[92] In that case, the vessel was in need of substantial repairs, and the owners withdrew her from service. This was in March 1973, when the market was low. The charterers, it appears, expected the market to fall still further, and did not immediately charter in replacement tonnage. In the event, the market rose significantly, as we saw in chapter 1, and the charterers claimed entitlement to the profits they would have earned, had the owners not wrongfully withdrawn the vessel. Goff J held that their decision not immediately to charter in a replacement was independent of the wrong, and was not therefore caused by it. The charterers were held, in effect, to have caused their own loss. The charterers had, however, acted reasonably, and had simply forecast the market incorrectly. They were nonetheless disentitled from claiming in respect of this consequential loss.

The "avoided loss" principle is that if the claimant does mitigate, and hence reduces his loss, the contract-breaker is entitled to the benefit of that mitigation. There must be a causative relationship, however, between the breach and the act that reduces the loss. In *The New Flamenco*,[93] time charterers wrongfully redelivered the vessel two years early in late 2007. At that time the market was good and the owners were able to sell the vessel at a good price. Two years later, with the world deep in recession, the market value of the vessel would have been much lower. The charterers claimed the difference in mitigation of loss. After fully analysing the authorities, Popplewell J refused to accept that the "avoided loss" principle required the benefit to be of the same kind as the loss claimed, but held that it must be possible to say that the benefit was causally related to the breach. He did not think that the decision to sell the vessel was sufficiently closely related – after all, the shipowners could have sold the vessel, irrespective of whether the charterparty had been terminated.

---

89 See also *Geogas SA v Trammo Gas Ltd (The Baleares)* [1993] 1 Lloyd's Rep 215, for recovery of a market loss. See further on this case section [6.6].

90 The Hamburg and Rotterdam Rules do, but Hague-Visby does not: see further sections [21.4]; [21.5].

91 The quotes are from *Fulton Shipping Inc of Panama v Globalia Business Travel SAU (The New Flamenco)* [2014] 2 Lloyd's Rep 230, [18], quoting the current edition of McGregor on *Damages* (19th ed (2014), Sweet & Maxwell), [7.004]–[7.006]. These statements of law are uncontroversial.

92 *Koch Marine Inc v d'Amica Societa di Navigazione ARL (The Elena d'Amico)* [1980] 1 Lloyd's Rep 75, and see section [1.11].

93 [2014] 2 Lloyd's Rep 230, noted [2014] LMCLQ 482.

2.9.3 Other limits to damages

Apart from causation, remoteness and mitigation, there can be other limits on contractual damages. The two that are most interesting instances are, first, the analysis, in terms of the risks each party has agreed to bear, in the House of Lords in *The Achilleas*.[94] The second is the compensatory principle, a development by the House of Lords in *The Golden Victory*,[95] of a principle that has embryonic roots in *The Mihalis Angelos*. These developments are considered in detail in the appropriate part of the book.[96]

In determining the losses flowing from a breach of contract, an assessment needs to be made of what would have happened, but for the breach. In *The Mihalis Angelos*, as we have seen, the charterers were held entitled to repudiate the charterparty because of a breach of condition by the owners. The owners had broken the expected readiness to load clause, having stated a date that they could not reasonably believe to be true, when they stated it. The vessel was engaged on a previous fixture and, based on her speed, likely discharge time and also delay for an inspection, there was no reasonable prospect of her arriving in time to load the charterers' cargo by the expected readiness date. The charterers (who for unconnected reasons had no cargo) were therefore held entitled to repudiate the charter for breach of condition, although the cancelling date had not arrived. Presumably because the decision was only a few years after *Hongkong Fir*, however, the Court of Appeal also considered the position, were they wrong on the condition issue, in other words, on the assumption that the charterers had wrongfully repudiated. Even on this assumption the shipowners were entitled to no damages, because the charterers would certainly have cancelled, once the cancelling date arrived. This is an application of the "compensatory principle", later to be accorded House of Lords authority in *The Golden Victory*; but the same result could also be reached on an assumption of performance least beneficial to the owners.[97]

2.9.4 Penalties

Contractual damages are intended to be compensatory and not penal. Their function is not to deter breach, nor to provide the injured party with a windfall, in the event of a breach. It is quite acceptable for a contract to have a liquidated damages clause, fixing the damages payable in the event of a breach and, indeed, this is precisely what demurrage clauses do in voyage charters.[98] A liquidated damages clause must, however, be a genuine pre-estimate of damage. By contrast, a penalty clause, which is not a genuine pre-estimate but is intended to deter breach, is unenforceable. We see the application of this in *The Paragon* in chapter 11,[99] and in *The Astra* in chapter 12 a penalty clause argument failed.[100] It is probably because penalty clauses are unenforceable that demurrage is usually fixed in line with market rates prevailing at the time the charterparty was entered into. As we will see in chapter 9, demurrage will not therefore fully compensate the shipowner on a rising market (because market rates will then have risen above the demurrage rate),[101] and in chapters 8 and 9 we see devices that shipowners can use to avoid the demurrage regime.[102]

---

94 *Transfield Shipping Inc v Mercator Shipping Inc (The Achilleas)* [2009] 1 AC 61, fully discussed in section [11.5.2].
95 *Golden Strait Corp v Nippon Yusen Kubisha Kaisha (The Golden Victory)* [2007] 2 AC 353.
96 Section [11.5.2] (*Achilleas*); [11.3.2] (*Golden Victory*).
97 See section [11.4], but there is also some discussion in the reachable on arrival cases in section [22.3].
98 See chapter 9.
99 Section [11.5.2].
100 Section [12.1.7].
101 Section [9.1].
102 See also reachable on arrival clauses in section [22.3].

2.10 Repudiation and exemption clauses

In some of the older cases, the view was taken that, if one party commits a sufficiently serious breach of the contract of carriage, this renders the contract void *ab initio*. He cannot therefore rely on any exemption clauses that would otherwise protect him, or on any other terms of the carriage contract that are to his benefit.

There is a logic to this view. In order to benefit from contractual exceptions the party relying on them must be performing the contract. This has sometimes been expressed as "the four corners rule", and is clearly related to what was ultimately an abortive attempt by the courts to develop a substantive doctrine of fundamental breach of contract.[103] In particular, a deviating carrier has been regarded as embarking on an entirely different voyage, and hence not entitled to the exceptions apposite for that voyage.[104] In recent years, however, the courts have resiled from treating "the four corners rule" as a rule of law, perhaps being more attracted by the principle that the parties should be free to agree any contractual terms, including exceptions, and that these should continue to govern, until one party commits a breach sufficiently serious as to allow the other party to repudiate. The deviation cases themselves might be seen as exceptional,[105] but probably the better view is that even they are consistent with the general law of contract.[106]

The consequences of serious breaches of contract were clarified by the House of Lords in *Photo Production v Securicor*.[107] However, even for some time prior to that decision, arguments that a serious breach could render the contract void *ab initio* had not found favour, except perhaps in deviation cases. Thus, for example, the charterers failed in an argument in *Kish v Taylor* that a shipowner who had rendered his vessel unseaworthy (by overloading) could not (because his breach had rendered the contract void *ab initio*) claim deadfreight to which he was otherwise entitled under the charterparty. They also failed in an argument that he could not later deviate from the agreed route, although at common law this was a justifiable deviation (because it was to save life).[108]

In the light of *Photo Production* we can say that if the breach is one that gives rise only to a remedy in damages, then there are no further consequences whatever. The contract survives in its entirety, and the contract-breaker can continue to rely on any clauses in the charterparty (or other contract) from which he benefits.

If the breach is such as to allow repudiation by the innocent party,[109] then, as we have seen, he may elect either to repudiate or to affirm the contract. If the innocent party affirms, then every term of the contract remains enforceable. Each party may continue to rely on any term he wishes, though the innocent party can claim damages in respect of the breach of contract that has occurred. If, however, a repudiatory breach is committed *and* the innocent party elects to treat the breach as bringing the contract to an end, then, from that moment, only the secondary obligations (to pay damages) remain effective. From that moment, both parties are relieved of performance of their primary obligations. Though it is not entirely clear from *Photo Production* itself, it seems that exemption clauses and limits to liability are also ineffective in respect of anything following a valid repudiation.[110] But the

---

103 On "four corners" see the cases cited in *Suisse Atlantique Societe D'Armement Maritime SA v NV Rotterdamsche Kolen Centrale* [1967] AC 361, 412 (Hodson), 424 (Upjohn), 434 (Wilberforce).

104 See in particular the discussion of *Joseph Thorley Ltd v Orchis SS Co* [1907] 1 KB 243 and *Internationale Guano en Superphosphaat-Werken v Robert Macandrew & Co* [1909] 2 KB 360 in section [4.4].

105 Eg, *Photo Production Ltd v Securicor Transport Ltd* [1980] AC 827, 845 (Wilberforce), but cf. *Kenya Railways v Antares Co Pte Ltd (The Antares Nos. 1 and 2)* [1987] 1 Lloyd's Rep 424, 430 (Lloyd LJ); *Daewoo Heavy Industries Ltd v Klipriver Shipping Ltd (The Kapitan Petko Voivoda)* [2003] 2 Lloyd's Rep 1, [14] (Longmore LJ).

106 We return to the controversy about deviation in section [4.4].

107 [1980] AC 827. See above, section [2.6.3].

108 *Kish (JE) v Charles Taylor & Sons* [1912] AC 604, discussed at section [4.2.11]. On justified deviation see section [4.4.3].

109 On the principles in section [2.6].

110 Not however arbitration clauses: *Heyman v Darwins Ltd* [1942] AC 356, and perhaps not time bars.

contract is not rendered void *ab initio*. Only from the time of repudiation do contractual terms cease to apply. The contract-breaker can still rely on exemption clauses, and other clauses protecting him, covering the period of time up to the breach, and those covering the breach itself.

Suppose, then, the shipowner commits a repudiatory breach, and the charterer elects to repudiate the charter. If the charterer's cargo is still on board (for example if the repudiation occurs during the voyage), and if it is *subsequently* damaged the shipowner will be unable to rely on any clauses in the charterparty that would otherwise have protected him. This is a possible explanation of some of the deviation cases, at any rate where the deviation precedes the loss, although deviation still presents some special problems.[111] We also see, in chapter 9, how shipowners remain locked into the demurrage rate, which is often lower than damages for delay would otherwise be, unless the delay is so long as to amount to a repudiatory breach, and the owners elect to repudiate.[112]

Whatever the position for deviation, it is now clear that a contract-breaker does not lose benefits to which he would otherwise be entitled under the charter merely because he is in breach of the charterparty, even if the breach is a serious one.

2.11 Construction and serious breaches

Though neither the doctrine of fundamental breach, nor the related "four corners" rule, allow the innocent party to avoid exceptions as a matter of law, there remain principles of construction. Thus exceptions may still be construed not to apply to serious breaches, or to particular breaches. The leading authority, which we will come across often in this book, is *Glynn v Margetson*,[113] which is authority for the proposition that a clause will not (in the absence of very clear words) be interpreted so as to allow one party to frustrate the main objects and intents of the contract. One application of this principle is in making it very difficult to exempt liability for delivery without production of an original bill of lading, since where a bill of lading is issued, it is fundamental that the carrier has agreed to deliver, only against its production.[114]

2.12 Frustration of a contract of carriage

In this section, we see that the frustration doctrine effectively destroys the bargain made by the parties. It can also have extreme, arbitrary and sometimes unfair consequences. So it is rarely invoked. But sometimes unforeseen events occur, which would make it unjust to hold the parties to their bargain, and it is to prevent this injustice that the doctrine has been developed. We will see that it has been described as a multi-faceted doctrine, that it is rarely invoked, and that it is based on justice.

The contractual doctrine of frustration can apply to charterparties and other contracts for the carriage of goods by sea, albeit that it does so only fairly rarely. If a contract is frustrated, then subject to the Law Reform (Frustrated Contracts) Act 1943,[115] the general position is that both parties are discharged from any further obligations under it. Given that the courts prefer to give effect to rather than destroy freely-made bargains,[116] it is no surprise that the frustration doctrine is very narrow. It applies only where an event occurs that was unforeseen by the parties when the contract was made,

---

111 Eg, *Thorley (Joseph) Ltd v Orchis SS Co* [1907] 1 KB 660, but there remains a problem with *Internationale Guano en Superphosphaat-Werken v Robert Macandrew & Co* [1909] 2 KB 360, where the loss came first. Both cases are discussed in section [4.4.2].

112 See sections [9.7] and [9.8].

113 [1893] AC 351, and see especially section [4.4.4].

114 See section [20.5].

115 On which see section [2.12.1].

116 Eg, section [2.2].

and that is sufficiently serious to undermine the whole basis upon which the contract was to be performed. Lord Radcliffe said in *Davis Contractors Ltd v Fareham Urban District Council* that:[117]

> "frustration occurs whenever the law recognises that without default of either party a contractual obligation has become incapable of being performed because the circumstances in which performance is called for would render it a thing radically different from that which was undertaken by the contract . . . It was not this that I promised to do . . . ."

Note the requirement for a radical difference from that which was undertaken. It seems now to be accepted that the frustrating event must "go to the root of the contract", the same test as that for repudiation considered above.[118] An event that renders further performance impossible can frustrate it,[119] as can supervening illegality,[120] but it is not enough for the contract simply to have become more difficult or more expensive for one of the parties.[121]

The frustrating event must also not have been something not brought about by the fault of either party. Otherwise there is simply a breach of contract, not a frustration.[122] In *The Hannah Blumenthal*,[123] Lord Brandon restated the radical difference requirement, but also emphasised that the change is extraneous to the contract, and that it "must have occurred without the fault or the default of either party to the contract". Thus if a shipowner owns more than one vessel, and one is destroyed, or cannot be legally used, the shipowner will not be able to claim frustration of the contract, if he allocated that ship, rather than another.[124]

Cases on frustration essentially fill out these principles. It has been emphasised that the doctrine is based on justice (which is why it applies so narrowly). The circumstances must have changed sufficiently to make it unjust to hold the parties to their original bargain. The application of the doctrine has also been said to require a multi-factorial approach, including consideration of the terms of the contract, its matrix or context, the parties' knowledge, expectations, assumptions and contemplations.[125] Consequently, it is quite difficult to state, in advance of litigation, whether a contract is frustrated.

A case where the doctrine was applied was *Joseph Constantine Steamship Line Ltd v Imperial Smelting Corporation Ltd*,[126] where a voyage charterparty was frustrated by the destruction of the vessel, without fault being proved on the part of either of the parties. Before loading the cargo, the vessel was destroyed by an explosion that was not proved to have been due to any breach of contract on the part of the shipowners. In a claim by the charterers for damages for failure to load a cargo, the House of Lords held the charterparty to have been frustrated. (This is an impossibility case – remember that a voyage charterparty is for a particular vessel.) The main issue was as to burden of proof: the owners did not have to prove lack of fault.

Of course the parties can (as ever) make their own provision, and often do, in the shape of force majeure clauses, which discharge the parties from their obligations in the case of defined events.

---

117 [1956] AC 696, 729.

118 See section [2.6.1].

119 *Comptoir d'Achat et de Vente Du Boerenbond Belge S/A v Luis de Ridder Limitada (The Julia)* [1949] AC 293.

120 *Fibrosa Spolka Akcyjna v Fairbairn Lawson Combe Barbour Ltd* [1943] AC 32.

121 See further section [2.12.3].

122 This was essentially the argument in *Kodros Shipping Corp v Empresa Cubana de Fletes (The Evia (No. 2))* [1983] 1 AC 736, in section [13.9].

123 *Paal Wilson and Co v Partenreederei Hannah Blumenthal (The Hannah Blumenthal)* [1983] 1 AC 854.

124 *Maritime National Fish Ltd v Ocean Trawlers Ltd* [1935] AC 524 (illegality); *The Super Servant Two* [1990] 1 Lloyd's Rep 1: specialist vessel sank but the other one could have been used. In neither case was the contract frustrated, since the shipowner could have allocated another vessel. In an FOB sale context: *The Mary Nour* [2008] 2 Lloyd's Rep 526.

125 *Edwinton Commercial Corporation v Tsavliris Russ (Worldwide Salvage & Towage) Ltd (The Sea Angel)* [2007] 2 Lloyd's Rep 517, [111].

126 [1942] AC 154.

2.12.1 Law Reform (Frustrated Contracts) Act 1943

If a contract is frustrated, then (subject to the Law Reform (Frustrated Contracts) Act 1943) both parties are discharged from any further obligations under it, whether performance of duties or payment of money (eg, voyage charterparty freight or time charterparty hire). Payments that have been made cannot generally be recovered, however, and payment that became due before the frustrating event remain due, even if they have not yet been paid. Thus the shipowner can claim advance freight if the contract is frustrated after payment has become due, even if it has not already been paid.[127] The only exception allowed by the common law is where consideration for the payment has *totally* failed, in which case the money paid can be recovered. This can only occur where there had been no performance under the carriage contract at all. It would not allow recovery of advance freight already paid if, for example, the vessel were lost at sea, since the contract would already have been partly performed, or prevent it being payable if it had not already been paid, in spite of payment having by then become due.[128]

The position has been altered by the Law Reform (Frustrated Contracts) Act 1943, to those contracts to which it applies. The most important sections of this statute provide that even sums that had already become payable at the time of frustration cannot be claimed by the other party. Also, any sums actually paid are recoverable, without the requirement for a total failure of consideration.[129] However, s. 2(5) provides that:

"This Act shall not apply —

(a) to any charter party, except a time charterparty or a charterparty by way of demise, or to any contract (other than a charterparty) for the carriage of goods by sea; . . ."

Voyage charterparties and bill of lading contracts continue to be governed by the common law, therefore, though the Act applies to period (including trip-time) charters.

2.12.2 Requisition and entrapment

This section and the next look at particular applications of the doctrine, but we need to guard against too close an inspection of the particular facts, and in particular (in this section) of lengths of time, or proportions of length of requisition or entrapment with the length of unexpired charterparty. Ultimately, the cases turn on the general principles described at the start of section [2.12].[130]

Many of the cases where the doctrine has been invoked concern time charterparties, where the vessel has been requisitioned, or where she is trapped by the outbreak of a war. For example, in *Bank Line Ltd v Arthur Capel and Co*,[131] a 12-month time charterparty was held frustrated by the House of Lords when the vessel was requisitioned before delivery, during World War I. In *The Wenjiang*,[132] the Court of Appeal held that a time charterparty had been frustrated when the vessel was trapped in the Shatt-al-Arab waterway at the outbreak of the Iran–Iraq conflict of that period.[133] Requisition or entrapment will only frustrate a time charterparty if it is of such a length as to frustrate the

---

127 See sections [7.4]; [7.6].

128 Bank of Boston Connecticut v European Grain and Shipping Ltd (The Dominique) [1989] 1 AC 1056, in sections [7.4]; [7.6].

129 See s. 1(2) and (3), discussed in BP Exploration Co (Libya) Ltd v Hunt (No. 2) [1979] 1 WLR 783; the rationale is essentially restitutionary, to prevent unjust enrichment rationale. Partial failure of consideration is enough to recover money under s. 1(2).

130 Edwinton Commercial Corporation v Tsavliris Russ (Worldwide Salvage & Towage) Ltd (The Sea Angel) [2007] 2 Lloyd's Rep 517 (where a very short charterparty was not determined by a very lengthy detention).

131 [1919] AC 435.

132 International Sea Tankers Inc v Hemisphere Shipping Co Ltd (The Wenjiang (No. 2)) [1983] 1 Lloyd's Rep 400.

133 Also The Evia (No. 2) [1983] 1 AC 736, in section [13.9].

adventure. In *Bank Line Ltd v Arthur Capel & Co*,[134] the vessel was requisitioned for five months, and the effect would have been to postpone delivery for five months (from April to September). Under the terms of the particular agreement the charterparty would accordingly have been 5 months later, but would still have run for 12 months. The House of Lords took the view that a September to September charterparty was a completely different adventure from an April to April charter. A case on the other side of the line, where the doctrine was not invoked, was *Port Line Ltd v Ben Line Steamers Ltd*,[135] where the period of requisition was relatively short (the vessel was requisitioned for a period of three months, out of a 30-month charterparty, with 17 months still to run). This case is dealt with in greater detail in chapter 10.[136]

Though Diplock J was certainly influenced by the likelihood that the requisition would last for substantially less than the remaining period of the charterparty,[137] too much emphasis should not be placed on such proportions of time; a multi-factorial approach is adopted, and whether an adventure is frustrated will depend on the adventure. In *The Sea Angel*,[138] a vessel with a very short period to run on the charterparty was detained because of a refusal to issue a certificate that was a prerequisite to port clearance. Though the detention would have been of some considerable length, it was ultimately amenable to negotiation. Rix LJ distinguished the requisition cases on the grounds that requisition could not be rectified, and could not be altered by negotiation.[139] So factors other than ratios of times are important.

2.12.3 Frustration and delay

It would be very unusual for a voyage of trip-time charterparty to be frustrated by mere delay, or an increase in the length of the voyage, and consequently its expense to one of the parties. Many of the recent cases have concerned the closures of the Suez Canal in 1956 and 1967, because of the consequent increase in the length of voyages. It was in the interests of the party bearing the risk of delay to claim frustration, but the only case where a frustration argument succeeded was *The Massalia*,[140] where the length of the voyage was approximately doubled. However, the contract was interpreted as requiring passage through Suez, and Pearson J's judgment was not regarded as being of general application, when the House of Lords considered the matter a few years later, in *Tsakiroglou & Co Ltd v Noblee Thorl GmbH*.[141] There the claim was that a CIF contract, rather than a charterparty or carriage contract, was frustrated. As in *The Massalia*, the effect of the closure was approximately to double the length of the voyage, and also its freight cost to the shippers, but the House of Lords refused to hold the CIF contract frustrated. In the view of the House, the voyage via the Cape was not made fundamentally different from a voyage via Suez, although it was, of course, considerably more expensive. Of course, the situation is slightly different with a CIF sale contract, because the freight element was a much smaller part of the total consideration. No disapproval was expressed of *The Massalia*, and in the earlier case Pearson J had thought that sale and carriage contracts should be treated differently.

In *The Eugenia*,[142] the Court of Appeal refused to accept the claim of trip-time charterers (who of course bore the delay risk) that the closure of the canal (and consequent entrapment of the vessel)

---

134 [1919] AC 435.
135 [1958] 2 QB 146.
136 See section [10.6].
137 [1958] 2 QB 146, 162.
138 [2007] 2 Lloyd's Rep 517.
139 [2007] 2 Lloyd's Rep 517, [118].
140 *Société Franco Tunisienne D'Armement v Sidermar SPA (The Massalia)* [1961] 2 QB 278.
141 [1962] AC 93.
142 *Ocean Tramp Tankers Corp v V/O Sovfracht (The Eugenia)* [1964] 2 QB 226; note that Lord Denning MR did not think that foreseeability would necessarily prevent frustration of the charterparty. See further section [10.4].

frustrated the charterparty. The position was complicated by the fact that the charterers sailed into the canal, although it was obviously dangerous, and anti-aircraft guns were in action at the time. Consequently, the vessel was trapped for some three months by the closure. The charterers could not rely on the entrapment as frustrating the charter, since their decision to sail into the canal was, in the circumstances, in breach of the war clause in the charterparty. They were forced to argue, therefore, that the closure of the canal would have frustrated the adventure even had they not sailed into the canal. The Court of Appeal, which was unimpressed by this hypothetical argument, held that there would have been no frustration in that event. The length of the voyage would have only been increased from 108 days to 138 days by the closure,[143] and the cargo (of metal goods) would not have been adversely affected by the delay. The closure of the canal was therefore not sufficiently serious to frustrate the adventure, its only effect being that the charterers (on whom, of course, since this was a time charterparty, the risk of delay was placed) would have had to pay an extra 30 days' hire. *The Massalia* was overruled, and Lord Denning MR could see no reason to distinguish between sale and carriage contracts.

The Commercial Court in *The Captain George K* also considered the doctrine in relation to the closure of the canal, but this time as the result of the Arab–Israeli war in 1967.[144] This time the charterparty was on a voyage basis, and the shipowners bore the risk of delay. It was therefore in their interests to claim frustration. The closure did not occur until the vessel had almost reached the entrance to the canal, and she therefore had to sail right back up the Mediterranean. This virtually doubled the length of the voyage from 9,700 miles to 18,400 miles,[145] but even so the Commercial Court refused to invoke the doctrine (with some reluctance, Mocatta J feeling that he was bound by *The Eugenia*).

Though there is in these cases some difference of judicial opinion, they perhaps reflect a view that charterparties (and other shipping contracts) provide for the risk of delay to be on one or other party, and only in extreme circumstances will these provisions be displaced. Whether an adventure is frustrated depends, of course, on the nature of the adventure, and perhaps different results would have obtained if, for example, the goods were perishable.

2.13 Question

A two-year time charterparty provides that the vessel is to be "capable of about 15 kts". In fact she is capable of only 12 kts. Half way through the first voyage, the charter market plummets, and the charterers inform the shipowners that they repudiate the charterparty. The pears on board (belonging to the charterers) deteriorate because of the increased length of the voyage, and the charterers sue, claiming to avoid the Hague-Visby Rules package limitations (which are incorporated into the charterparty).

Advise the charterers. Does it make a difference at what time on the voyage the deterioration occurred?

Would your answer be different if the charterparty also provided that as a condition of the contract all instruments on the vessel must be in perfect working order (the bridge is fitted with duplicates of all instruments, and one of the engine speed indicators flickers wildly)?

---

143 This depends on what constituted the adventure. Cargo was to be carried from the Black Sea to India via Suez, but the vessel was delivered at Genoa. These were the periods for the whole voyage from Genoa to India. The proportions would have been somewhat different, had the cargo-carrying stage only been considered (56 days as against 26).

144 *Palmco Shipping Inc v Continental Ore Corp (The Captain George K)* [1970] 2 Lloyd's Rep 21.

145 The voyage, from Mexico to India, would have been only 12,100 miles, had the vessel proceeded directly via the Cape.

Comment

First, a general comment. Where cases are being interpreted you cannot expect to find clear answers, as you might for a code. The best you can hope for is to find arguments that are likely to succeed if the matter is litigated. In this quest, you will know that the backing of weighty authorities increases the likelihood of an argument's success. So, the objective is to seek good arguments, not clear answers.

Turning to this particular question, it concerns partly the categorisation of terms, when a term is a condition and, if it is not, what is needed for there to be a frustrating breach. You should look back at section [2.6] for the tests for categorisation, and at repudiation for breach of an innominate term.

There is also the issue of the effect of the breach (and repudiation, if valid) on the package limitation (also discussed in section [2.6]). For present purposes, you do not really need to know the details of the package limitation, but, if you are interested, the Hague-Visby Rules are the subject of chapter 18.

Chapter 3

Other legal principles underpinning carriage of goods by sea

Chapter Contents

3.1 Introduction

This chapter continues to look at general principles of law. The law of carriage is not just about contracts, and we begin by considering the role of bailment, and tort actions. These may be secondary to contract, but the law of carriage is incomplete without discussion of them. We then look at principles of equity, and good faith, which have been largely (but not entirely) excluded from commercial and maritime law fields. We end the chapter with discussion of which party has agreed to bear the risk of an event occurring. Analysis of risk is relatively new in carriage by sea, but it has now been adopted in a number of areas, and appears to be more than a passing fad. Whether repackaging questions in risk terms makes any real difference may perhaps be open to doubt, but the development is one that we cannot ignore.

3.2 Bailment

Bailment is the underlying relationship between a shipper of cargo and a carrier, the shipper being bailor and the carrier bailee. A bailment arises when one person voluntarily takes possession of the property of another, and particularly if it is a bailment for reward, the bailee comes under stringent duties to care for and return the property. It is obvious that a sea carrier is (at the very least) in the position of a bailee for reward (the cargo-owner being the bailor),[1] and, if there were nothing else, there would still be a bailment.

In past centuries, bailment was central to the law of carriage of goods by sea, to a far greater extent than today. Nowadays, and for at least the last 150 years or so, bailment duties have been so heavily modified by carriage contract terms that bailment has been relegated to a background role. Nonetheless, the underlying bailment relationship continues to underpin the law of carriage in the ways described in the next section. We will also see, later in the book, that there are common law liens, for freight and general average, which have their origins in bailment.[2]

3.2.1 Principles of bailment

Like anybody else who voluntarily takes care of the property of someone else, a sea carrier becomes bailee of that property, and, on the assumption that he is carrying it for reward, he owes the duties of a bailee for reward.[3] As such, in the absence of a contractual provision to the contrary, he is under a duty to take reasonable care to keep the goods safe, to deliver them in the condition in which he took them, or to show that any damage was not caused by his neglect or default. As Lord Denning MR observed in *Morris v CW Martin & Sons*:[4]

> "If the goods are lost or damaged, whilst they are in [the bailee's] possession, he is liable unless he can show – and the burden is on him to show – that the loss or damage occurred without any neglect or default or misconduct of himself or of any of the servants to whom he delegated his duty."

He will also be liable for breach of bailment if he fails to deliver the goods, or misdelivers them.

---

1 As we will see in the following section, a shipowner may well owe the even stricter duties of a common carrier, particularly after the contract has been validly repudiated following his breach, as in section [4.4].

2 See section [7.9].

3 He might also be a common carrier, but this does not appear ever to have been actually decided. The cases are annotated in *Dockray, Cases and Materials on the Carriage of Goods by Sea*, 3rd ed (2004), Cavendish, ch. 2.

4 [1966] 1 QB 716, 726.

Note that it is for the bailee to disprove fault, not for the bailor to prove it.

Historically, common carriers were (and are) subject to stricter duties. It is not clear whether, historically, shipowners were truly common carriers, because a common (or public) carrier undertook to carry for anyone who asked him,[5] but they seem to have been treated as such, whether they were really common carriers or not.[6] There is also authority that (even today) a deviating carrier is treated as (at best) a common carrier.[7] A common carrier can only prove absence of fault by showing that any damage had been caused by one of the common law excepted perils:[8]

1.   Act of God, or
2.   of the King's (or Queen's) enemies.

He would also not be liable if the loss or damage was caused by an inherent vice of the goods, but of course he would not then have caused the loss.[9]

These are rather narrow exceptions, but (if the shipowner was treated as a common carrier) were, in the absence of contractual provision, the only ways of disproving fault. Of course the duties of a common carrier (or bailee for reward) are always modified, in practice, by the terms of the carriage contract, for example by increasing the range of excepted perils. The modifications are usually so extensive as (it might be thought) to render the underlying bailment redundant, but it remains important for the following reasons:

1.   Bailment continues to influence the burden of proof in cargo claims. The cargo-owner must, of course, prove damage, but the burden then shifts to the carrier to bring himself within an excepted peril.[10] This remains true even today, in the era of the Hague-Visby Rules (on which see further chapter 18).[11]
2.   Bailment is the relationship that remains, between carrier and cargo-owner, where there is no enforceable contract, for example after a carriage contract has been frustrated or validly repudiated.[12]
3.   The same is true in the absence of any contract at all between the parties, for example where contractual rights have been divested by the Carriage of Goods by Sea Act 1992.[13]
4.   The same is true if the vessel is withdrawn from service, for example under a time charter-party withdrawal clause, when cargo remains on board.[14]
5.   If the carrier remains in possession after the Hague or Hague-Visby Rules regimes cease to apply, then he will remain a bailee, and entitled to the common law excepted perils.[15]
6.   Bailment is the basis of some of the fundamental implied carriage obligations, such as the duty of a carrier to provide a seaworthy vessel, and not to deviate from the agreed or customary route.[16]

---

5   Eg, *Ingate v Christie* (1850) 3 C & K 61 (Alderson B).
6   Eg, *Liver Alkali v Johnson* (1874) LR 9 Ex 338 (Brett J – his brethren all thought the defendant was a common carrier there though); cf. *Nugent v Smith* (1876) 1 CPD 423 (Cockburn CJ). The authorities are not conclusive.
7   *Thorley v Orchis; Hain.* The authorities suggest that this is the best the carrier can expect, but the authorities differ on whether he is entitled to freight for carrying the goods to their destination.
8   See, eg, Lord Wright's observations in *Paterson Steamships Ltd v Canadian Co-Operative Wheat Producers Ltd* [1934] AC 538, 545. *Coggs v Barnard* (1703) 2 Ld Raym 918.
9   *Greenshields v Stephens* [1908] AC 431; *Gould v South Eastern and Chatham Rly* [1920] 2 KB 136 (Atkin LJ).
10 See further section [4.2.10].
11 See section [18.3.4]; the structure of Hague-Visby makes some changes to the bailment analysis, however.
12 As, for example, with the deviation authorities discussed in section [4.4].
13 As (exceptionally) in *East West Corpn v DKBS AF 1912 A/S* [2003] QB 1509 (see further section [16.6.1]).
14 Eg, *ENE Kos 1 Ltd v Petroleo Brasileiro SA (The Kos) (No 2)* [2012] 2 AC 164; see section [12.1.2].
15 As in *The MSC Amsterdam* [2007] 2 Lloyd's Rep 622, in section [18.6.3].
16 See also further sections [4.2] and [4.4].

As carriers became able, using their superior bargaining power, to write increasingly wide exceptions into carriage contracts, from the bailment relationship were derived fundamental legal obligations, to provide a ship that was seaworthy at the start of the voyage, and not negligently to cause harm to the goods. As Lord Wright observed in *Paterson Steamships Ltd v Canadian Co-Operative Wheat Producers Ltd*, at common law the carrier:[17]

> "was absolutely responsible for delivering in like order and condition at the destination the goods bailed to him for carriage. He could avoid liability for loss or damage only by showing that the loss was due to the act of God or the King's enemies. But it became the practice for the carrier to stipulate that for loss due to various specified contingencies or perils he should not be liable: the list of these specific excepted perils grew as time went on. That practice, however, brought into view two separate aspects of the sea carrier's duty which it had not been material to consider when his obligation to deliver was treated as absolute. It was recognized that his overriding obligations might be analysed into a special duty to exercise due care and skill in relation to the carriage of the goods and a special duty to furnish a ship that was fit for the adventure at its inception. These have been described as fundamental undertakings, or implied obligations."

These obligations, "to exercise due care and skill in relation to the carriage of the goods and a special duty to furnish a ship that was fit for the adventure at its inception", were (and indeed remain) fundamental in two senses. First, the clearest words are needed to exclude them. In *Smith, Hogg v Black Sea and Baltic General Insurance*, Lord Wright said:[18]

> "... when the practice of having express exceptions limiting that obligation became common, it was laid down that there were fundamental obligations, which were not affected by the specific exceptions, unless that was made clear by express words".

Secondly, if loss is caused by a breach of one of these obligations, the carrier is unable to rely on excepted perils, according to Lord Wright, even if the loss is also partly caused by an excepted peril.[19] For seaworthiness, this remains the case today, even under the Hague-Visby Rules, though Hague-Visby treats want of due care differently.[20]

3.2.2 Burden of proof

If there were no contract, the liability of the shipowner would be absolute, subject only to the common law excepted perils, which in a bailment action the shipowner would have to prove. That is the starting position and, if the shipowner wants to rely on contractual excepted perils, it is for him to establish his entitlement. In other words, once the cargo-owner has proved loss, the burden shifts to the carrier to bring himself within an excepted peril.

We have seen that, if the cargo-owner can breach the "duty to exercise due care and skill in relation to the carriage of the goods" or the "duty to furnish a ship that was fit for the adventure at its inception", the carrier will be unable to rely on an excepted peril, but in *The Glendarroch* this was treated "as an exception upon the exceptions",[21] so that the burden of proof shifted to the

---

17 [1934] AC 538, 544 (PC).
18 [1940] AC 997, 1004. See also *Nelson v Nelson* [1908] AC 16 (on negligence).
19 [1940] AC 997, 1005. See further section [4.2.8].
20 See section [18.3.2].
21 [1894] P 226, 231 (Esher). The case is also authority, *obiter*, that the burden is on the carrier to bring himself within the excepted peril in the first place: at 230–1. A new trial was ordered in *The Glendarroch*.

cargo-owner at this stage. In other words, if an excepted peril is established, it is for the cargo-owner to prove negligence or unseaworthiness.

Burdens of proof can be important where no there is other evidence, and if The Glendarroch is correct we end up with the following position at common law:

1. Cargo-owner shows damage;
2. Carrier shows excepted peril;
3. Cargo-owner shows breach of fundamental obligation (negligence in The Glendarroch itself), which, if proved, prevents the carrier from relying on an excepted peril (perils of the seas in The Glendarroch itself).

It has, however, been argued that the burden of proof should remain on the carrier at stage 3, because this is consistent with the underlying bailment.[22] The authorities (which are not strong) suggest otherwise, however.

We will see in chapter 18 that the Hague and Hague-Visby Rules add an additional hurdle where unseaworthiness is shown, in that the shipowners will not be liable if they can show no want of due diligence. We will see that the burden is on the carriers at this stage. Negligence is treated differently, and in any case burdens of proof do not appear to mirror exactly those at common law.[23]

3.2.3 Rights of common carriers and bailees for reward

At common law, even a common carrier was entitled to a reasonable freight, and to a common law lien for freight and general average. Though in reality contractual freight is always agreed, recourse may be needed to the common law position where the original contract cannot be performed,[24] or where the contract has been discharged by frustration or breach.[25] If the shipowner delivers the cargo he may still be entitled to freight.[26] Further, though generally speaking, "English law does not allow a general right of recovery for benefits conferred on others or expenses incurred in the course of conferring them",[27] the shipowner after the contract has been terminated may be entitled to expenses as a bailee until the cargo is delivered.[28]

Common law liens for freight and general average remain important (though again they are usually in reality supplemented by contractual liens),[29] and their release can also form the basis of a new contract, implied between the carrier and the cargo-owner.[30]

3.2.4 Bailment on terms

This is quite a different application of bailment principles, and is described in chapter 17 as a device to avoid the privity of contract doctrine.[31] It can be used to protect sub-carriers, for example in a multimodal transport operation. Conceptually, it binds the head-bailor to the terms of the

---

22 Ezeoke, *Allocating onus of proof in sea cargo claims: the contest of conflicting principles* [2001] LMCLQ 261.

23 Section [18.3.4].

24 Eg, *Cargo ex Argos* (1872) LR 5 PC 134, in section [7.2]. The basis is probably *quantum meruit*.

25 For frustration see *Société Franco Tunisienne d'Armement v Sidermar SpA (The Massalia)* [1961] 2 QB 278. However, the actual decision, that the contract was frustrated, was overruled in *The Eugenia* [1964] 2 QB 226, in section [2.11].

26 Though the position is unclear for a deviating carrier: see section [4.4.2].

27 *The Kos (No. 2)* [2012] 2 AC 164, [19] (Sumption), citing *Falcke v Scottish Imperial Insurance Co* (1886) 34 Ch D 234, 248 (Bowen LJ).

28 *Ratio of The Kos (No. 2)*.

29 See section [7.9].

30 See further section [16.8].

31 Section [17.4].

sub-bailment, but in reality it can allow the sub-bailee (ie, actual carrier) to enjoy the terms agreed between shipper and head bailor, even though he is not party to the contract that sets up the head bailment. We will consider bailment on terms in chapter 17.

3.3 Tort actions

Though most cases involving both damage to goods and their wrongful delivery will probably be brought in contract, where damage is occasioned negligently there will also be a tort action (in negligence), and where a cargo-owner's title is impugned, there will also be an action in conversion.[32]

When, in relation to bills of lading, the Law Commission were given the opportunity to reform the law,[33] they decided instead to reform only the law of contract. Though the resulting contractual regime is comprehensive, they did not go so far as to make it exhaustive, and tort actions were left entirely alone.

Though the law of carriage is overwhelmingly governed by the law of contract, it remains necessary to be aware of tort actions, which might be additional or alternative to those in contract. In particular, tort actions can be used even when there is no contract between the parties. They can also be used to avoid contractual exemptions, limitations on liability, or even entire statutory regimes. The co-existence of tort and contract actions can create problems of both privity of contract, and potential double liability. We will come across a number of instances in the book where an action in tort is central, or at any rate has been argued to be so.[34]

3.4 Law and equity in carriage

3.4.1 Introduction

Most of commercial and maritime law is common law based, but equity plays a small role, and we therefore need to be aware of it.

Equity is part of English law and that of other English-speaking jurisdictions, but it is not part of continental systems. The reasons for equity lie in ancient history (mostly from around the eleventh to thirteenth centuries), but all that it is necessary to appreciate, for our purposes, is that for reasons connected with protecting feudal rights, the common law of the Middle Ages was rigid and formal.[35] In particular, it placed restrictions on who could own property, and it placed obstacles in the way of its disposal. Feudal lords needed to know the identity of their feudal tenants, to extract feudal dues.[36] Equity developed to mitigate the severity of the common law. It has its origins in land transactions, and though in principle equitable principles can apply to all property, the courts have been reluctant to extend them into commercial and maritime areas, except where the parties have expressly adopted them.[37]

The way in which equity worked historically was not to challenge common law ownership as such. Now (as then) it grants rights to beneficiaries, which are enforceable against the legal owner,

---

32 Respectively, sections [16.9] (negligence); [20.1]; [20.2] (conversion).
33 See chapter 16.
34 Eg, sections [16.9]; [17.2]; [17.3]; [17.4].
35 Eg, Todd & Wilson's *Textbook on Trusts & Equity*, 12th ed (2015), OUP, ch. 1.
36 Most such dues had their value eroded by inflation, but some, such as escheat, remained valuable to lords until the sixteenth century.
37 As for example in the trust receipt, used in bankers' documentary credits: eg, Todd, *Bills of Lading and Bankers' Documentary Credits*, 4th ed (2007), LLP, ch. 4. But for the general reluctance, see below, [3.4.3]–[3.4.4].

or trustee. The beneficiary's equitable rights, now as then, are discretionary, and based on notions of conscience and justice. They do not exist as of right, and can be defeated by his conduct, or for other reasons. Equity is more flexible than the common law, and tempers the rigidity of the common law.

Given the emphasis on certainty that we have already seen many times in this book, it will not surprise readers that the courts have been reluctant to extend equitable principles, which had their origin in title to land, into the fields of maritime or commercial law. Of course if a trust is clearly intended and set up, the courts will give effect to it; but for the most part, equity's role in carriage of goods by sea is on the periphery only.

3.4.2 Equitable notice doctrine

Though equity works by providing rights against an individual, usually the common law owner of property, the rights can be enforced against others, if their conscience is affected. Suppose, for example, we have a trust, where, as we have seen, the legal owner (or trustee) holds the property on behalf of the equitable owner (or beneficiary). Suppose further that the original trustee sells the property. The new owner will also be bound by the trust, unless his conscience is unaffected. This came to mean, and means today, that he will be bound, unless he is a *bona fide* purchaser of the legal title, without notice of the equitable rights (the so-called "equity's darling"). Diagrammatically, we can represent this as follows:[38]

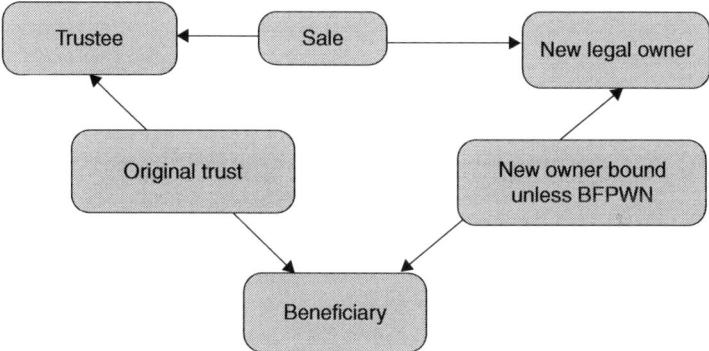

Notice is not limited to actual notice, but includes constructive notice (what the new owner should have discovered, had he looked).[39] It is this aspect of notice that would cause problems were it to be applied too readily in the field of commerce.

The notice doctrine prevailed in land for centuries but, because of the difficulties and expense caused by the notice doctrine in conveying land, has now been almost entirely replaced by a registration system.[40] In principle the notice doctrine continues to operate for property other than land (where there is no equivalent registration system), but where paradoxically the constructive notice doctrine might be regarded as even more of a nuisance. The doctrine applies not only to rights of beneficiaries, who are regarded as equitable owners, but also to other equitable

---

38 "BFPWN" is used here as shorthand for *bona fide* purchaser, for value, of the legal estate (or legal property) without notice.

39 There is a useful discussion in *R Griggs Group Ltd v Evans* [2005] 2 WLR 513, beginning at [37], explaining the conscience basis of the notice doctrine. See also section [10.6].

40 In England, by the Land Registration Act 2002.

rights, that might be regarded as less than full property rights, where the conscience of the third party is affected.[41]

3.4.3 Notice doctrine in maritime commerce

The common law concept of ownership may be rigid and formal, but it has the advantage of certainty, which, as we have seen, is regarded as of some importance in commercial and maritime law. By contrast, the idea of constructive notice is inherently uncertain. While it has a place in land transactions, which typically take many months and where a potential purchaser has the leisure to make extensive enquiries of interests that might affect the land, it is not so suitable for commercial transactions, which are much faster.

The courts have in fact shown themselves reluctant to extend constructive notice to property other than land.[42] One of the earliest cases, where a reluctance was shown towards extending the concept of constructive notice to commerce generally, was *Manchester Trust v Furness*,[43] a case considered in detail in chapter 17.[44] Briefly, the shipowners had entered into a voyage charterparty, which contained a demise clause under which the captain and crew were to be regarded as the agents and servants of the charterers (and hence not the owners) for all purposes. The shipowners were no doubt trying to protect themselves from actions by bill of lading holders in respect of loss of or damage to cargo, but the charterparty contract was of course only between themselves and the charterers.

The charterers fraudulently took the cargo, but, as is often the way with fraudsters, they were not worth suing, so the cargo-owners sued the shipowners, who, but for the demise clause, would on the principles in chapter 17 have been regarded as the contracting carrier. Though the bill of lading holders were not party to the contract into which the demise clause was written, the shipowners argued that they should be bound by it on the constructive notice doctrine. Diagrammatically, we can represent this as follows:[45]

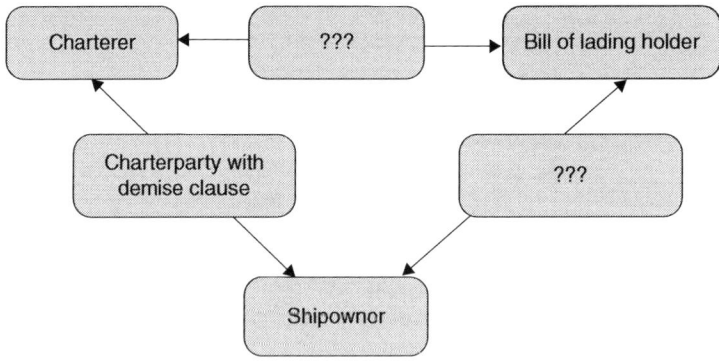

---

41 For example, if a husband, by exercising undue influence over his wife, persuades her to mortgage her half share of the matrimonial home to a bank, the bank will also be tainted by the undue influence, if it has notice of it: *Barclays Bank plc v O'Brien* [1994] 1 AC 180.

42 Eg, *Polly Peck International plc v Nadir* [1992] 2 Lloyd's Rep 238. However, note the analysis of liens in terms of equitable assignment in section [12.1.7].

43 [1895] 2 QB 539.

44 Section [17.1].

45 This diagram has the shipowner at the bottom, to make its shape consistent with the earlier diagram. The issue was whether the shipowner's rights deriving from the charterparty could bind the bill of lading holder, as a third party with constructive notice. It was held that the notice doctrine had no application.

This is similar to the earlier diagram, in that there is an attempt to bind a third party to the transaction, by use of the notice doctrine.

Lindley LJ was unimpressed by the attempt to apply the notice doctrine here. In an extremely well-known and oft-cited passage he said:[46]

". . . as regards the extension of the equitable doctrines of constructive notice to commercial transactions, the Courts have always set their face resolutely against it. The equitable doctrines of constructive notice are common enough in dealing with land and estates, with which the Court is familiar; but there have been repeated protests against the introduction into commercial transactions of anything like an extension of those doctrines, and the protest is founded on perfect good sense. In dealing with estates in land title is everything, and it can be leisurely investigated; in commercial transactions possession is everything and there is no time to investigate title; and if we were to extend the doctrine of constructive notice to commercial transactions we should be doing infinite mischief and paralyzing the trade of the country."

This passage has been cited and approved many times.[47] The main justification is that the relative speed of commercial transactions makes a requirement extensively to investigate third party rights inappropriate.

3.4.4 Reluctance elsewhere to extend equitable principles

We see in this book other instances of a reluctance to introduce equitable principles into this area of law. In chapter 10 we see that time charterers are not accorded equitable property, binding the new owners if the shipowner sells the vessel, in the same way that equitable owners under a trust can,[48] or for that matter an equitable tenant of land. In chapter 12 we see clear and decisive rejection, by the House of Lords, of an argument that time charterers, who pay hire late, should be entitled to equitable relief against forfeiture of the charterparty, in the same way that tenants of land are entitled to such relief, when they pay rent late. Had the argument been accepted, it would have given charterers time to pay, before the shipowners could withdraw the vessel from service.[49]

Both these conclusions are based, to some extent, on the nature of time charterparties, which are in many respects dissimilar to leases of land. But there is also a feeling, expressed in the cases, that charterparties are commercial transactions, between parties dealing at arm's length, and that charterers do not need the protection of the courts, in the way that a tenant of land might.

We can conclude that, though equity has a role in the law of carriage of goods by sea, that role is limited. As we have seen elsewhere in this and preceding chapters, certainty also forms a large part of the argument. Writing extra-judicially, Lord Goff, referring again to time charterparty withdrawal clauses, observes that:[50]

"Equitable relief [against such withdrawals] is really inconsistent with the principle that in commercial transactions parties must, so far as possible, be able to know where they stand, or at least to obtain helpful advice from their lawyers on the basis of which they can act with a reasonable degree of confidence. People who charter ships are not children in arms. If they are inexperienced, they can get the advice of brokers . . . ."

---

46 [1895] 2 QB 539, 545.

47 Eg, *Eagle Trust plc v SBC Securities Ltd* [1993] 1 WLR 484, 504.

48 Section [10.6]. There may be little injustice here in reality, because if the new owner does not perform the charterparty, the original owner remains liable, as the original contracting party.

49 Section [12.1.2].

50 Goff, *Commercial contracts and the Commercial Court* [1984] LMCLQ 382, 392.

It might also be suggested that rejection of uncertainty by English courts is a major reason why English law is so often favoured by the parties, as against foreign systems of law.

For completeness, we might also notice that another area where equity plays a limited role is in refusing to allow parties to enforce contracts, where they have no legitimate interest in so doing.[51]

3.5 Good faith in carriage of goods by sea

Traditionally, with the exception of fiduciaries and contracts of insurance, English contract law does not recognise a duty of good faith, either at the negotiation stage or in the manner in which the contract is performed. There are some chinks showing, however, and it is possible that good faith will play a greater role than heretofore,[52] but as yet the chinks are not large, and good faith looks unlikely to play a major role in carriage of goods by sea.

At the negotiation stage, in *Walford v Miles*, the House of Lords held that there was no duty to negotiate in good faith, Lord Ackner taking the view that such a duty is "inherently repugnant to the adversarial position of the parties when involved in negotiations" and "unworkable in practice".[53]

Even for contracts of insurance, where there is an utmost good faith requirement, the House of Lords held, in *The Star Sea*, that it did not apply during the lead up to litigation.[54] Once we are at that stage, litigation has its own procedural controls for discovery, which supersede even the utmost good faith requirement in insurance contracts. It follows that, even were a good faith doctrine to develop, to play a greater role in carriage of goods by sea, it would be unlikely to apply to the negotiation process, or to the conduct of the parties during litigation.

Apart from those two periods, uncertainty is also a ground for not implying a duty to perform in good faith into the contract itself. There are certainly many cases in this book where the parties are entitled to act in their own interests, with no consideration of whether or not so to act might be regarded as exercising good faith. Good faith simply does not feature in the equation. We need look no further than *The Laconia* in chapter 12,[55] where the shipowners were held entitled to withdraw the vessel from a time charterparty, where the charterers had paid for hire one day late, the banks being closed on a Sunday. There was no suggestion that the owners feared that the charterers would be unable to pay, nor that they had suffered in any way because of the late payment. It was clear that the real reason for the withdrawal was that the market had risen, since the charterparty had been concluded, from $3.10 to $5.59 per ton. The late payment was used purely as a device, but the law allows this.

More generally, it is accepted that if there is a breach of condition or other repudiatory breach of contract, the innocent party's choice whether or not to determine the contract can be based on any reasons he likes. There is no requirement that it be in any way related to the breach, and, again, the motives are often market-based.[56] In *Hongkong Fir*, as we saw in chapter 2,[57] time charterers wished to escape from a two-year fixture. Though the issue *argued* was whether the shipowners had

---

51 Eg, *White and Carter (Councils) Ltd v McGregor* [1962] AC 413, discussed in section [2.8].

52 Eg, *Yam Seng Pte Ltd v International Trade Corp Ltd* [2013] 1 Lloyd's Rep 526 (Leggatt J), distinguished in *Compass v Mid-Essex Hospital Services* [2013] EWCA Civ 200.

53 [1992] AC 128, 138. However, a lock-out clause was held valid in *Pitt v PHH Management* [1994] 1 WLR 327 (in a negotiation for the sale of land, the lock-out clause precluded the vendor from negotiating with other potential purchasers, as long as contracts were exchanged within a fortnight), and there is some authority that a best endeavours undertaking could be valid.

54 *Manifest Shipping Co Ltd v Uni-Polaris Insurance Co Ltd (The Star Sea)* [2003] 1 AC 469.

55 *The Laconia* [1977] AC 850: section [12.1.2].

56 *Bowes v Shand* (1877) 2 App Cas 455, 465 (Hatherley) where CIF buyers were held entitled to reject documents, it being immaterial "no answer . . . that it would be a means by which purchasers without any real cause would frequently obtain an excuse for rejecting contracts when prices had dropped".

57 *Hongkong Fir Shipping Co Ltd v Kawasaki Kisen Kaisha Ltd* [1962] 2 QB 26: see section [2.6].

committed a repudiatory breach of charter, the issue in reality was almost certainly the significant market fall by the time the charterers argued to repudiate (June 1957), following the reopening of the Suez canal. The motive was made clear in Salmon J's judgment at first instance:[58]

> "I appreciate . . . that there was a catastrophic fall in the freight market between February and June, 1957, and that it would only be natural in these circumstances for the charterers to wish to escape from the charterparty if they lawfully may."

Sellers LJ also observed that:[59]

> "During the currency of the charterparty the freight market had fallen steeply . . .".

We saw that the charterers did not succeed in Hongkong Fir, but it was never doubted that, had the term broken been a condition, or had the breach been sufficiently serious to go to the root of the contract, the fact that their motives were market-based would have been immaterial. Indeed, Salmon J continued:

> "I do not think, however, that in considering the issue of frustration the fall in the market can be material."

In Interfoto Picture Library Ltd v Stiletto Visual Programmes Ltd, Bingham LJ observed that whereas:[60]

> "[in] many civil law systems, and perhaps in most legal systems outside the common law world, the law of obligations recognises and enforces an overriding principle that in making and carrying out contracts parties should act in good faith, . . . English law has, characteristically, committed itself to no such overriding principle but has developed piecemeal solutions in response to demonstrated problems of unfairness."

There are situations where good faith may be implied, then, but there is no systematic basis for its application. One such situation is where there is a discretion: the courts might imply that it must be exercised in good faith. In The Product Star (No. 2),[61] a master had (relying on a discretion granted in a war clause) unreasonably refused not to proceed into a war zone.[62] The Court of Appeal held that the discretion of the owners had to be exercised honestly and in good faith, and having regard to the provisions of the contract by which it was conferred (including that the charterers would pay any additional insurance), it was not to be exercised arbitrarily, capriciously or unreasonably. Leggatt LJ said in The Product Star:[63]

> "Where A and B contract with each other to confer a discretion on A, that does not render B subject to A's uninhibited whim. In my judgment, the authorities show that not only must the discretion be exercised honestly and in good faith, but, having regard to the provisions of the contract by which it is conferred, it must not be exercised arbitrarily, capriciously or unreasonably. That entails a proper consideration of the matter after making any necessary

---

58 [1962] 2 QB 26, 39, the first instance judgment being upheld in the CA (reported in the same place).
59 [1962] 2 QB 26, 39.
60 [1989] 1 QB 433, 439.
61 Abu Dhabi National Tanker Co v Product Star Shipping Ltd (The Product Star) (No. 2) [1993] 1 Lloyd's Rep 397, 404 (distinguished in Compass).
62 On time charterparty war clauses generally, see section [13.10].
63 [1993] 1 Lloyd's Rep 397, 404.

inquiries. To these principles, little is added by the concept of fairness: it does no more than describe the result achieved by their application."

It should be observed, however, that in *The Product Star* (No. 2) there had to be some control on the master's discretion *for the war clause to be workable at all*. The case is not authority for a general control of discretions, and indeed it has frequently been distinguished.[64] In particular, in *Compass v Mid-Essex Hospital Services*, Jackson LJ observed that in cases such as *The Product Star* (No. 2):[65]

> ". . . the discretion did not involve a simple decision whether or not to exercise an absolute contractual right. The discretion involved making an assessment or choosing from a range of options, taking into account the interests of both parties. In any contract under which one party is permitted to exercise such a discretion, there is an implied term. The precise formulation of that term has been variously expressed in the authorities. In essence, however, it is that the relevant party will not exercise its discretion in an arbitrary, capricious or irrational manner."

The distinction in *Compass* might not be all that easy to draw, since exercising an absolute contractual right (as in *Compass* itself) also involves a choice. Perhaps the crucial requirement is for "a range of options, taking into account the interests of both parties". However, to this limited extent, but so far at least no further, carriage contracts can be subject to a good faith requirement.

3.6 Risk in carriage of goods by sea

In recent years we have seen the courts taking into consideration the risks each party is supposed to have undertaken. It is not yet entirely clear how this doctrine will work, or what (if anything) it adds to existing jurisprudence. It may do no more than restate, in different words, existing principles, but it is a developing idea, which might become important.

We will see in chapter 13 that indemnities against orders by time charterers as to employment of the vessel, whether express or implied, cannot cover every such order.[66] In *The Island Archon*,[67] time charterers ordered the chartered vessel to Basrah. This order was one which, under the express terms of the charterparty, they were entitled to give, and which the shipowners were bound to obey; Basrah was not an unsafe port, nor outside the charterparty trading limits. Ordinarily, the owners would have been expected to bear the expense of taking the vessel there, and of discharging her. In the particular case, however, they were liable to consignees for alleged short-delivery or damage, under the so-called "Iraqi system", a liability regime that was unique to Iraq.[68] The "Iraqi system" was unknown when the charterparty was entered into, and the Court of Appeal held that the shipowners had not assumed the unique risks associated with discharging in Basrah. They were therefore held entitled to an indemnity. (As we will see in section [13.4], indemnities in respect of normal trading are not normally granted.)

---

64 *The Product Star* (No. 2) was also distinguished, but on another basis, in *The Paiwan Wisdom* [2012] 2 Lloyd's Rep 416, where the vessel was employed outside an area of which the owners would have been aware, when entering the charterparty – also no similar additional insurance provision. See further section [13.10].

65 [2013] EWCA Civ 200, [83], distinguishing *The Product Star* (No. 2).

66 Section [13.4].

67 *Triad Shipping Co v Stellar Chartering & Brokerage Inc (The Island Archon)* [1994] 2 Lloyd's Rep 227. See further section [13.4].

68 See the discussion at section [13.4].

Analysis in terms of assumption of risks was not new in *The Island Archon*, having been introduced, in the context of dangerous cargoes, in *The Athanasia Comninos*.[69] It has since been developed in other contexts in carriage of goods by sea, perhaps most importantly in the highest court in the land, in *The Achilleas* and in *The Kos*.[70] Apart from *The Achilleas*, the analysis has been used to interpret contractual obligations, including (in *The Island Archon*) the extent of an implied term. In *The Achilleas* the analysis was used in a new context, restricting the damages payable by a time charterer who had redelivered the vessel late. The shipowners had thereby lost a profitable fixture, a loss that came within the normal remoteness of damage rules, but that the shipowners failed to recover.[71] The House of Lords held that the basis upon which damages were calculated for late redelivery were well-known, that the charterers had contracted on this basis, and that they were taken to have limited their damages exposure to the usual basis of calculation. They had not undertaken the risk of compensating for other losses. The case, and the basis upon which damages for late redelivery are usually calculated, are considered fully in chapter 11, where it will also be suggested that the approach in *The Achilleas* will only be taken in unusual circumstances.[72]

In other risk cases, charterparty terms have been construed to limit the responsibility of one of the parties, usually the shipowner, to risks that he has agreed to bear. It is to be doubted whether a risk analysis has made any real difference in the construction cases, though it has perhaps clarified the issues. In *The Island Archon* and *The Athanasia Comninos*, what was crucial was what the shipowner knew, or ought to have known, when entering the contract. He could not be taken to have assumed risks of which he was unaware. Though important,[73] this is only one factor, however. It may be that a risk analysis is little more than a restatement of the principle that a shipowner bears the risks of an ordinary expense incurred in the course of navigation,[74] or ordinary incidents of the chartered service.[75] In *The Kos* Lord Sumption said that:[76]

> "[the] owners are not entitled to an indemnity against things for which they are being remunerated by the payment of hire. There is therefore no indemnity in respect of the ordinary risks and costs associated with the performance of the chartered service. The purpose of the indemnity is to protect them against losses arising from risks or costs which they have not expressly or implicitly agreed in the charterparty to bear."

This does little more than restate established principles of charterparty law.

It may, however, be assumed that these ideas will continue to inform the development of this concept, which is, as yet, in its infancy.

3.7 Question

Alan's cargo of sugar reaches the end of the voyage, and is discovered to be damaged by seawater. The sugar is on board a vessel chartered from Zara for the voyage. The vessel is old, and the welding

---

69 *The Athanasia Comninos and The Georges Chr Lemos* [1990] 1 Lloyd's Rep 277: See section [4.6.3].

70 Respectively [2009] 1 AC 61 (discussed in section [11.5]); ENE 1 Kos Ltd v Petroleo Brasileiro SA (The Kos) [2012] 2 AC 164.

71 See sections [2.9.3] (remoteness generally) and [11.5.2] (*Achilleas* in particular).

72 Section [11.5.2].

73 *Action Navigation Inc v Bottigliere di Navigazione SpA (The Kitsa)* [2005] 1 Lloyd's Rep 432, [24]: ". . . if, at the time that the charter-party is concluded, the occurrence and type of loss or expense to the shipowner flowing from the order as to employment of the vessel were unforeseen, then that will be a potent factor in deciding that the loss or expense will fall [on the shipowner]". See further section [13.3].

74 [2005] 1 Lloyd's Rep 432, [27], Aikens J citing *Actis Co Ltd v Sanko Steamship Co Ltd (The Aquacharm)* [1982] 1 WLR 119.

75 [2012] 2 AC 164, [12].

76 [2012] 2 AC 164, [11].

of some of the hull plates has failed (at some time), allowing seawater to get into the cargo holds. Heavy weather has been encountered on the voyage, and the master noticed no leaks when the vessel sailed.

The charterparty incorporates none of the provisions of either the Hague or Hague-Visby Rules. It excludes liability for perils of the seas.

Advise Alan as to any claim he may have against Zara, what will need to be shown and on which party the burden of proof will lie.

Comment

This is a question on the burden of proof, at common law, since neither Hague nor Hague-Visby Rules apply. You should refer back to section [3.2.2]. You need also to be aware (see section [4.2]) that the vessel will be unseaworthy if the plates had failed before the beginning of the voyage, but not if they only failed afterwards, and you can see that the carrier is protected if the damage resulted only from perils of the seas, but not if it was caused by unseaworthiness.

The facts are very similar to those in *The Hellenic Dolphin* in chapter 18, but the Hague Rules applied in *The Hellenic Dolphin*, and Hague Rules burden of proof issues are dealt with there, rather than here.[77]

---

77 [1978] 2 Lloyd's Rep 336, and see section [18.3.4].

Chapter 4

Obligations implied into contracts for the carriage of goods by sea

Chapter Contents

4.1 Introduction

This chapter considers obligations that are implied into carriage contracts generally, whereas later chapters are on specific contracts. We will cover seaworthiness, the obligation to care for the cargo, deviation, the obligation to make reasonable despatch, and the obligation of shippers not to ship dangerous cargo.

Though these obligations are implied, they are also frequently expressly written into carriage contracts. For charterparties at least, they are also (of course) subject to contrary terms in the charterparty. In respect of the first three obligations, however, exempting liability must be done by the clearest of words, and, in respect of bills of lading, there are usually minimum obligations laid down by the law in any event.[1]

4.2 Duty to provide seaworthy vessel

4.2.1 Introduction

Whether or not it is expressed (and usually it is), it is a term implied into all carriage contracts that the carrier will provide a seaworthy vessel.[2] In *Steel v State Line* the Lord Chancellor said of the term implied:[3]

> "that the ship . . . is at the time of its departure reasonably fit for accomplishing the service which the shipowner engages to perform. Reasonably fit to accomplish that service the ship cannot be unless it is seaworthy."

For a voyage charter or bill of lading we can infer that the obligation attaches at the start of the voyage (we will consider later in this section precisely what this means).[4] It does not continue after the voyage has started.

Time charters invariably make express provision, taking effect at the date of delivery. For example, cl. 1 of Baltime, dealing (among other things) with delivery, requires the vessel to be "in every way fitted for ordinary cargo service", and Shelltime 4, cl. 1 provides:

> "At the date of delivery of the vessel under this charter [shall be]
>
> . . .
>
>   (c) tight, staunch, strong, in good order and condition, and in every way fitted for the service, with her machinery, boilers, hull and other equipment (including but not limited to hull stress calculator and radar) in a good and efficient state;
>   . . ."

The content of the Baltime clause was explicitly equated with the seaworthiness obligation in *Hongkong Fir* and *The Madeleine*,[5] as was similar wording in New York Produce Exchange (NYPE) in

---

1 See chapter 18.
2 *Kopitoff v Wilson* (1876) 1 QBD 377. In a charterparty the carrier is the shipowner or disponent owner. For identity of carrier in bill of lading contracts see section [17.1].
3 *Steel v The State Line Steamship Company* (1877–8) LR 3 App Cas 72, 76.
4 See section [4.2.4].
5 *Hongkong Fir Shipping Co Ltd v Kawasaki Kisen Kaisha Ltd* [1962] 2 QB 26; *Cheikh Boutros Selim El-Khoury v Ceylon Shipping Lines Ltd (The Madeleine)* [1967] 2 Lloyd's Rep 224 (both concerning earlier, but for present purposes identical, versions of Baltime).

The Derby,[6] and the Shelltime 4 provision was treated as equivalent to a seaworthiness obligation in The Elli and The Frixos.[7] From this it might also perhaps be inferred that the timing (delivery of the vessel) also accords with what would be implied, in the absence of express provision. This is also consistent with the sentiment from Steel v State Line that the obligation attaches at the start. If so, the seaworthiness obligation in a time charter attaches (and ends) at delivery of the vessel,[8] the shipowners typically being under a separate obligation to maintain her thereafter. If it is argued that because of the ongoing maintenance obligation, it does not matter when the seaworthiness obligation attaches, the content of the obligations may not be the same. More importantly, it is, as we will see, more difficult to exclude the seaworthiness obligation, and the legal consequences of its breach are more serious.[9]

At common law liability for breach of the obligation is strict (though this is tempered by a due diligence qualification where the Hague or Hague-Visby Rules apply).[10] It is a fundamental obligation, deriving from the obligation of the carrier as bailee for reward and, as such, can be contracted out of, only by very clear words.[11] However, as we saw in chapter 2, the seaworthiness term is not a condition,[12] and it does not deprive shipowners of the right to rely on any contractual terms, in the way that deviation might.[13]

4.2.2 Substance of obligation

The obligation is quite broad, so that, as Diplock LJ observed in Hongkong Fir, it "can be broken by the presence of trivial defects easily and rapidly remediable as well as by defects which must inevitably result in a total loss of the vessel".[14] The breadth of the obligation was one of the reasons for regarding the obligation as an innominate term in that case, rather than a condition.

It has been held that it relates to the particular voyage to be undertaken, the test being whether the vessel is reasonably fit to encounter the ordinary perils that might be expected on a voyage at that season. In Kopitoff v Wilson, Field J defined a seaworthy ship as:[15]

> "good, and . . . in a condition to perform the voyage then about to be undertaken".

In McFadden v Blue Star Line, Channel J stated that to be seaworthy a vessel:[16]

> "must have that degree of fitness which an ordinary careful and prudent owner would require his vessel to have at the commencement of her voyage having regard to all the probable circumstances of it".

---

6   Alfred C Toepfer Schiffahrtsgesellschaft GmbH v Tossa Marine Co Ltd (The Derby) [1984] 1 Lloyd's Rep 635 (see section [4.2.2]).

7   Golden Fleece Maritime Inc v St Shipping and Transport Inc (The Elli and The Frixos) [2008] 2 Lloyd's Rep 119.

8   The view taken, eg, in Coghlin, Baker, Kenny, Kimball and Belknap, Time Charters, 7th ed (2014), Taylor & Francis, [8.10], et seq.

9   Sections [4.2.6]–[4.2.9].

10 See section [18.3.3].

11 See section [3.2.1].

12 Section [2.6.1].

13 On deviation, see section [4.4].

14 [1962] 2 QB 26, 71. See further section [2.6.1].

15 (1876) 1 QBD 377, 380. The main argument in Kopitoff was whether the term should be implied, even though the defendants were not common carriers. There is a similar statement as to the scope of the term in Steel v State Line Steamship Co (1877–8) LR 3 App Cas 72, 76.

16 [1905] 1 KB 697, 706. Many similar statements can be found.

The implication is that all the risks of the particular voyage must be taken into account.[17] Moreover, in *Hongkong Fir Shipping Co Ltd v Kawasaki Kisen Kaisha Ltd*,[18] the unseaworthiness concept was extended to inadequate numbers or incompetence of the crew, and there is authority that it also extends to the vessel's tackle or equipment. Inadequate crew training (for fire-fighting equipment) rendered the vessel unseaworthy in *The Eurasian Dream*.[19]

For a ship to be fit to accomplish the service required of her demands also that she complies with legal requirements. If, therefore, in order to sail, the ship requires documentation, she will be unseaworthy in the absence of such documentation. In *The Madeleine*,[20] a de-ratting certificate was required by Calcutta port authorities, without which, under local law, she was not permitted to sail outside India. Roskill J did not think the ship seaworthy until it was obtained.[21] A seaworthy vessel must be capable of operating legally. In *The Elli and The Frixos*,[22] a ship was held by the Court of Appeal not "seaworthy" when she did not comply with the MARPOL (Marine Pollution) double-hull requirement, which had been recently introduced for ships carrying oil products. Longmore LJ began his judgment as follows:[23]

> "Time charters for the carriage of specific cargoes (such as oils or other fuels) traditionally have clauses whereby shipowners undertake that the vessel will, at the time of delivery under the charterparty, be fit to carry those products, that the vessel will be in every way fit for her service and have on board any necessary documents required to enable her to perform the charter service. . . ."

The following paragraph details the MARPOL Convention, and it is clear that compliance with it is part of the vessel's fitness to carry the products. The case was complicated by issues about what the vessel was required to carry under the charterparty, and the precise scope of the MARPOL Convention, but once it had been held that the ship was required to cover products that were covered by the regulations, and that she did not comply with them, she was not "seaworthy".[24] The main importance of the case lies in its approval, at Court of Appeal level, of *The Madeleine*.[25]

The courts have been more reluctant to extend *The Madeleine* beyond legal requirements, and documents required by law. Thus, in *The Derby*,[26] where the lack of an ITF blue card delayed discharge, the Court of Appeal held that a time charter clause requiring the vessel to be "in every way fitted for the service" related to her physical condition, provision and competence of crew, and documents

---

17 I have suggested elsewhere, for example, that "for a voyage that is known to include areas at high risk of piracy, a ship not equipped with hoses and razor wire, or slow or with a low freeboard, could well be unseaworthy at the commencement of the voyage. Similarly if the ship were inadequately manned to put in place precautions against piracy, or if the crew were not properly trained in this regard": Todd, *Charterparties and piracy today* (2014), CreateSpace Independent Publishing Platform, [4.3].

18 [1962] 2 QB 26. The vessel, though old, was not unseaworthy on account of physical defects, but because of her age needed competent engine room crew, which she did not have.

19 *Papera Traders Co Ltd v Hyundai Merchant Marine Co Ltd (The Eurasian Dream)* [2002] 1 Lloyd's Rep 719 (Cresswell J).

20 [1967] 2 Lloyd's Rep 224 (Roskill J).

21 The case concerned express time charter term requirements, which were, however, assumed to be equivalent to an "express warranty of seaworthiness": [1967] 2 Lloyd's Rep 224, 240, basing on *Hongkong Fir Shipping Co Ltd v Kawasaki Kisen Kaisha Ltd* [1962] 2 QB 26.

22 [2008] 2 Lloyd's Rep 119.

23 [2008] 2 Lloyd's Rep 119, [1].

24 It appears that the vessel could lawfully carry crude oil, but not the fuel oil the charterers intended to carry: [2008] 2 Lloyd's Rep 119, [12]. Much of the case is given over to an interpretation of the charterparty. The case was also complicated by a second clause, placing a continuing obligation on the shipowners – this could not of course be part of the seaworthiness obligation. As in *The Madeleine*, the express provision in the charterparty was treated as making express provision for seaworthiness at the outset: eg, [2008] 2 Lloyd's Rep 119, [17] (Longmore LJ).

25 [2008] 2 Lloyd's Rep 119, [18].

26 *Alfred C Toepfer Schiffahrtsgesellschaft GmbH v Tossa Marine Co Ltd (The Derby)* [1984] 1 Lloyd's Rep 325, considered in *The Elli and The Frixos* [2008] 2 Lloyd's Rep 119, [18].

relating to fitness to perform the service the charter required, but did not extend to non-governmental or non-legal documents issued by an "officious body". How far, if at all, the requirements extend beyond legality remains unclear, but Kerr LJ thought probably not at all.[27] Nonetheless, it might be possible to extend the reasoning in *The Madeleine* to matters such as IMO advice for vessels voyaging to or through a particular area, for example a piracy hotspot.

The Madeleine and *The Elli and The Frixos* ultimately concern the characteristics of the vessel herself, albeit relating to documentation, or to legality. What about documentation relating to the *operation* of the ship? *The Kapitan Sakharov* was concerned with Codes and Regulations relating to her operation.[28] There was a fire and an explosion in a container, caused by the shipment of a dangerous cargo, but it was made worse by shipment of a second dangerous cargo (in another container). One of the issues was whether this second shipment put the carrier in breach of Art. III(1) – the Hague Rules incarnation of the seaworthiness obligation. In the view of the Court of Appeal:[29]

> "the stowage of the tank containers of isopentane [the second cargo] under deck clearly contravened SOLAS, IMDG and MOPOG and was not permitted by the technical certificate; the Judge correctly found that the stowage of isopentane below deck rendered *Kapitan Sakharov* unseaworthy".

In *The Kapitan Sakharov*, failure to comply with the Codes appears to have been determinative of unseaworthiness,[30] but since compliance with SOLAS is a legal requirement, this may add little to the discussion. The Codes were not, however, determinative of the Hague Rules additional requirement for a lack of due diligence, though non-compliance was evidence:[31]

> "compliance or otherwise with codes like MOPOG was not necessarily determinative of the issue of due diligence".

From this we may perhaps conclude that though failure to comply with legal requirements may affect a ship's fitness for voyage, and that, otherwise, Codes and Regulations (though not conclusive) are relevant as evidence of a lack of due diligence.

4.2.3 Cargoworthiness

The obligation is not limited to the fitness of the vessel herself to sail. In order to be seaworthy, the ship must also be capable of carrying the cargo envisaged by the carriage contract. On the other hand, liability for stowage is quite often placed on the charterer or cargo-owner, and there is no common law presumption against shipowners excluding liability for bad stowage. The stowage obligation is not fundamental, and therefore the same principles of construction do not apply; in *Elder, Dempster & Co Ltd v Paterson, Zochonis & Co Ltd*,[32] the bill of lading exempted the shipowner from liability for bad stowage, but not unseaworthiness, and (once it had been held that the damage had been caused by bad stowage) protected the shipowners.[33] The line between bad stowage and providing a

---

27 [1984] 1 Lloyd's Rep 325, sentiments at 331.
28 *Northern Shipping Co v Deutsche Seereederei GmbH (The Kapitan Sakharov)* [2000] 2 Lloyd's Rep 255.
29 [2000] 2 Lloyd's Rep 255, headnote.
30 [2000] 2 Lloyd's Rep 255, 266 (Auld LJ).
31 [2000] 2 Lloyd's Rep 255, headnote.
32 [1924] AC 522.
33 Nor, of course, do the other consequences of seaworthiness being a fundamental obligation apply to bad stowage: see further sections [4.2.6]; [18.3.2].

vessel that is not fit to take the charterer's cargo (ie, is unseaworthy) can be important, and it can be quite a fine line to draw.[34]

In *Stanton v Richardson*,[35] the ship was fit to carry cargo apart from that provided by the charterer, because the pumps, although quite sufficient for all other purposes, were incapable of dealing with the extra moisture draining from the charterer's cargo (wet sugar). Her inability to carry cargo, which the charterer was contractually entitled to load, rendered the vessel unseaworthy, so that the shipowner was in breach of his implied obligation at common law. The case can be contrasted with *Elder, Dempster & Co Ltd v Paterson, Zochonis & Co Ltd*.[36] The shipper's cargo (casks of palm oil) were stowed at the bottom of the vessel, but these were overstowed with a very heavy cargo of palm kernels (which were loaded on top of the palm oil casks). The vessel was not fitted with 'tween decks, so that the weight of the kernels bore directly upon the casks, and split them open. A majority of the House of Lords held that this was bad stowage, but that the vessel was not unseaworthy. Thus the shipowner was protected by the clause in the bill of lading (which, as we have seen, covered bad stowage). One difference between these cases was that whereas the vessel in *Stanton v Richardson* was unfit to carry wet sugar at all, that in *Elder Dempster* could carry casks of palm oil, as long as the weight of cargo carried above them, unsupported by 'tween decks, was not too great.[37]

We discuss *Elder Dempster* further below, but there is also authority, in *The Apostolis*, that the seaworthiness obligation relates to something about the ship: where one cargo damages another that is bad stowage, not unseaworthiness.[38] *The Apostolis* concerned damage by fire spreading from another cargo, and there was held to be no breach of Art. III(1), the seaworthiness obligation in the Hague-Visby Rules. (There is no suggestion that the Hague or Hague-Visby Rules define unseaworthiness differently from the common law, though they modify the obligation in other respects.)[39]

4.2.4 When obligation attaches

The common law drew a distinction between the obligation to provide a seaworthy vessel, which attaches only at the start of the voyage,[40] for which liability is strict, and the obligation to care for the cargo otherwise, which continues throughout the period of the bailment of the cargo. The carrier's duties regarding the cargo, as we have seen, are strict but subject to exceptions.

As we will see in chapter 18, this division continues when the Hague-Visby Rules apply. The obligation to provide a seaworthy vessel is provided by Art. III(1), which applies only "before and at the beginning of the voyage". By contrast, duties otherwise regarding the cargo are dealt with in Art. III(2), which applies throughout the voyage, and requires that ". . . the carrier shall properly and carefully load, handle, stow, carry, keep, care for, and discharge the goods carried".[41] As we will see, Art. III(1) is paramount and III(2) is not, so the distinction continues to matter. (By paramount is

---

34 There is recent discussion of the distinction in *The Eems Solar* [2013] 2 Lloyd's Rep 487, noted [2014] LMCLQ 139. See also *Actis Co Ltd v Sanko Steamship Co. Ltd (The Aquacharm)* [1982] 1 WLR 119, discussed in another context in section [12.3.9], where the ship was perfectly capable of carrying the cargo, but had been overloaded.

35 (1874) LR CP 390, considered also below, section [4.2.11].

36 [1924] AC 522, a bill of lading contract, but the same principles apply to charterparties.

37 For another explanation of *Elder Dempster*, see section [4.2.5].

38 *A Meredith Jones & Co v Angemar Shipping Co Ltd (The Apostolis)* [1997] 2 Lloyd's Rep 241, 245 (Leggatt LJ); 257 (Phillips LJ). This can be reconciled with *The Kapitan Sakharov* [2000] 2 Lloyd's Rep 255, above, where the problems were exacerbated by the stowage of the second cargo under deck, rather than the second cargo itself. There was no proof that the shipowners had caused the fire to the other cargo in *The Apostolis*, whereas they had been responsible for stowage of the other cargo in *The Kapitan Sakharov*.

39 See section [18.3.1].

40 Eg, *McFadden v Blue Star Line* [1905] 1 KB 697. For a time charter the obligation attaches only at the commencement of the charter: eg, *The Madeleine* [1967] 2 Lloyd's Rep 224, 241 (Roskill J): "There was here an express warranty of seaworthiness and unless the ship was timeously delivered in a seaworthy condition, . . . the charterers had the right to cancel."

41 See further [4.3] below.

meant that a carrier in breach of Art. III(1) cannot rely on the excepted perils in the Rules, whereas a breach of Art. III(2) does not similarly preclude.)[42]

Should the UK ever adopt the Rotterdam Rules,[43] then the distinction between the start and the rest of the voyage will become largely blurred. The seaworthiness obligation in Art. 14 of Rotterdam would continue throughout the voyage. Art. 17(5) makes the obligation paramount again, so the main effect of this change would probably be to preclude carriers relying on excepted perils where Art. 14 was breached.

4.2.5 Stages

Though the authorities are rather inconclusive, the common law probably developed a doctrine of stages, further restricting the shipowner's obligation to the points of loading and sailing: that the ship must be fit to receive cargo on loading, and fit to sail on sailing, and that these are the only two occasions on which the obligation attaches. In *Maxine Footwear Co Ltd v Canadian Government Merchant Marine Ltd*, Lord Somervell, commenting on the common law position, said that "[when] the warranty was absolute it seems at any rate intelligible to restrict it to certain points of time",[44] and perhaps this was the justification for the doctrine.

In respect of fitness to receive cargo, in *McFadden v Blue Star Line*[45] cargo was damaged by defective packing of a valve-chest, a defect that existed prior to loading, and by an engineer failing sufficiently to screw down a sluice-door and a sea-cock, these omissions occurring after loading. Channel J held that there was a breach of the seaworthiness obligation only in respect of the valve-chest,

"that the defective fitting of the sea-cock and of the sluice-door, being defects which came into existence after the plaintiff's goods were loaded, were not breaches of the implied warranty of the fitness of the ship to receive the cargo; but that the defective packing of the valve-chest, being an existing defect at the time of the loading of the goods, was a breach of the warranty".[46]

This was despite the fact that all the omissions occurred before the vessel sailed.

In *The Thorsa*,[47] a cargo of chocolate was contaminated by its proximity to another cargo, of Gorgonzola cheese. The Court of Appeal held that there was no breach of the seaworthiness obligation, and the defendant shipowners were held entitled to rely on an exception in the bill of lading relieving them from liability for negligent stowage. Swinfen Eady LJ observed, however, that ". . . it would appear that the chocolate was put on board first and the cheese was stowed over it".[48] Phillimore LJ said:[49]

"Taking it as not proved that the cheese was there first, taking it as most probable that the cheese came there afterwards, I do not think that it made the ship unseaworthy *quoad* the chocolate."

---

42 See further generally section [18.3.2].
43 See further sections [18.3.1]; [21.4].
44 [1959] AC 589, 604, and see further section [18.3.1]. *Maxine* was a bill of lading case, where the Hague Rules applied, but of course the common law continues to apply to charterparties, unless the Hague Rules are incorporated into the charterparty.
45 [1905] 1 KB 697.
46 [1905] 1 KB 697, headnote.
47 [1916] P 257.
48 [1916] P 257, 260.
49 [1916] P 257, 263.

A possible implication is that had the cheese been loaded first, the vessel might not have been fit to receive the chocolate, and the decision might have been the other way.

The authorities are less than crystal-clear, however. In *Elder Dempster & Co Ltd v Paterson Zochonis & Co Ltd*,[50] where as we have seen cargo was damaged by other cargo later being loaded on top of it, the House of Lords could have decided the case simply on the basis that the ship was fit to receive the first cargo (palm oil) when that cargo was loaded. As Viscount Cave said:[51]

> "At the moment when the palm oil was loaded the [vessel] was unquestionably fit to receive and carry it. She was a well built and well found ship, and lacked no equipment necessary for the carriage of palm oil; and if damage arose, it was due to the fact that after the casks of oil had been stowed in the holds the master placed upon them a weight which no casks could be expected to bear."

Viscount Cave's speech as a whole was somewhat more equivocal, however, and it was in any case unnecessary to test the fitness of the vessel to carry palm oil on sailing, because the damage occurred between loading and sailing. *The Thorsa* and *Elder Dempster* were explained on a different basis in *The Apostolis*,[52] that a ship will be uncargoworthy only where the fault is as to the state of the ship. It is not enough for one part of the cargo to cause damage to another. This is certainly another possible explanation of both cases.

In summary, though there is authority that (at common law) the cargoworthiness obligation applies only at loading, and at no later stage, even during the loading process; the authorities are far from being unassailable.

As to whether the ship is required to be seaworthy prior to sailing, commonsense dictates otherwise to the extent that a ship, while being loaded, cannot be fit to sail. At the very least, bow doors, hatches, etc, need to be closed before the vessel departs. In *The Thorsa*, Phillimore LJ emphasised that (by contrast with fitness to receive the cargo of chocolate):[53]

> "When one is dealing with the structure of a ship, a ship may be and must be seaworthy according to stages."

By the time the ship goes to sea, on this view, the structure must be sufficiently seaworthy for a sea voyage. This would also extend to the cargo not being stowed in such a way as to endanger the safety of the ship.[54]

In conclusion, though the authorities are not absolutely clear, the best view seems to be that, at common law, the vessel must be fit to receive the cargo (cargoworthy) when the cargo is loaded, and fit to sail on sailing. The test for fitness to receive cargo is determined only when the cargo is loaded, but that for structural soundness of the vessel to go to sea is tested only when she goes to sea. The obligation attaches at these two points only and is not a continuing obligation.

Though as we saw above, the Hague and Hague-Visby Rules also limit the obligation to provide a seaworthy vessel to "before and at the beginning of the voyage", this application of the

---

50 [1924] AC 522. See section [4.2.3].

51 [1924] AC 522, 531–2.

52 [1997] 2 Lloyd's Rep 241, 245 (Leggatt LJ), 257 (Phillips LJ), Phillips LJ citing *The Thorsa* and *Elder Dempster*. Phillips LJ cited another part of *The Thorsa* [1916] P 257, and *Elder Dempster & Co Ltd v Paterson Zochonis & Co Ltd* [1924] AC 522, and it may be that this, rather than the application of the doctrine of stages, is the true rationale of these decisions. See further [4.2.3] above, and section [18.3.1] below.

53 [1916] P 257, 263, citing *Cohn v Davidson* (1877) 2 QBD 455.

54 Eg, *Smith Hogg Ltd v Black Sea and Baltic General Insurance Company* [1940] AC 997, where the stow of timber caused an eventually disastrous list.

doctrine of stages was rejected where the Hague or Hague-Visby Rules apply, the Privy Council taking the view in *Maxine Footwear* that Art. III(1) applied, as a continuing obligation, to the whole of the loading process, rather than applying only at specified points.[55] As we saw above, liability under the Rules is not strict, and there is less reason to be protective of the shipowner than at common law.[56]

Once the voyage is under way the seaworthiness obligation is at an end, but the shipowner remains under a duty (as bailee) to care for the cargo. This is an entirely different duty,[57] though the duty not to be negligent appears also, at common law at least, to be, like that to provide a seaworthy vessel, a fundamental obligation.[58]

A very different concept of stages can be seen in *The Vortigern*:[59] where a voyage is divided into stages, for example to allow rebunkering *en route*, the vessel will be unseaworthy unless she is adequately bunkered for each stage. It is not limited to an obligation on first sailing, just to have enough fuel for the first stage. The mischief addressed by *The Vortigern* (where on a long voyage, rebunkering was necessary) was to prevent shipowners benefiting from splitting the voyage into stages, and arguing that the obligation attached only to the first stage. After all, in the days of sail, they would have had to provision the vessel for the entire trip.

(In the early days of steamships range was a problem, because of their small size (relative to modern vessels), and high fuel consumption; this (and the fact that coal took up cargo space) was probably the main reason steamships were slow to catch on, for long ocean voyages. Consequently, vessels had to call in at intermediate ports *en route*, to rebunker.)

There is no suggestion that *The Vortigern* is affected by the Hague or Hague-Visby Rules. *Maxine Footwear* addresses a different aspect of the doctrine of stages, where (as we have seen) the responsibility of owners is reduced, whereas in *The Vortigern* it is of course increased.

We have said quite a lot about the fundamental nature of the seaworthiness obligation. It is time – in the next few sections – to fill out what we mean by that.

4.2.6 Fundamental obligation

The obligation to provide a vessel that is seaworthy at the start of the voyage is regarded as fundamental, and has its basis in the old law of bailment.[60] This has the following consequences:

1. It is difficult to contract out of it;
2. It is "paramount", in the sense that exceptions take subject to it;
3. Causation rules differ from other breaches;
4. The burden of proof is on the carrier.

However, it does NOT have the consequence that breach of the obligation voids the contract *ab initio*, as has been argued for deviation.[61]

We will now consider these consequences.

---

55 *Maxine Footwear Co Ltd v Canadian Government Merchant Marine Ltd* [1959] AC 589. See further generally section [18.3.1].
56 See further section [18.3.1].
57 See below [4.3]. Remember that even under Hague or Hague-Visby, it matters whether an obligation is classified as one of seaworthiness or (for example) stowage, or care of cargo, because Art. III(1) is paramount, whereas Art. III(2) is not. See section [18.3.2].
58 On seaworthiness as a fundamental obligation, see section [4.2.6].
59 [1899] P 140.
60 See section [3.2.1].
61 See section [4.4].

4.2.7 Contracting out of obligation

We have seen that in *Paterson Steamships Ltd v Canadian Co-Operative Wheat Producers Ltd*, Lord Wright observed that the duty to exercise due care, and the duty to provide a seaworthy vessel at the inception of the voyage, were fundamental obligations,[62] and that in *Smith, Hogg v Black Sea and Baltic General Insurance* he said that the clearest words are needed to contract out of liability for unseaworthiness.[63] We will see later in the chapter situations where a clause protects against liability for (for example) bad stowage, but not unseaworthiness. However, Gencon 1994, cl. 2 subjects the owners to liability only for:

> ". . . personal want of due diligence . . . to make the Vessel in all respects seaworthy and to secure that she is properly manned, equipped and supplied or by the personal act or default of the Owners . . .".

On its terms, this limits liability to one of "personal want of due diligence". It ought in principle to be enforceable, at least in the charterparty (though as we will see, the shipowner's liability to bill of lading holders may not be affected by cl. 2).[64]

4.2.8 Seaworthiness and causation

The position at common law is that the shipowner is not liable unless the loss is caused by unseaworthiness. In *The Europa*,[65] the vessel was unseaworthy at the start of the voyage, because scupper holes in the 'tween decks were imperfectly plugged, and when the vessel arrived at Liverpool, the port of discharge, she collided with the dock wall. There was no causal connection between the unseaworthiness and the collision. The charterparty exempted the shipowner from liability for "collision", and he was able to rely on this clause in spite of his prior breach in not providing a seaworthy vessel. The need for a causal connection may seem obvious, but there had been authority the previous year, in *Thorley (Joseph) Ltd v Orchis SS Co*, that a deviating carrier stepped outside the contract and became (in effect) a common carrier, whether or not the deviation was a cause of the loss.[66] In *The Europa*, the Court of Appeal held that the principles from *Thorley v Orchis* did not extend to unseaworthiness.

However, once it is shown that the loss has been caused by unseaworthiness, we have seen that the shipowner is not entitled to rely on excepted perils in the charterparty or bill of lading.[67] In *Smith Hogg & Co Ltd v Black Sea & Baltic General Insurance Co Ltd*,[68] the ship was loaded top-heavy (and hence unseaworthy at the start of the voyage) and toppled over. But the list had been exacerbated by a rebunkering operation, and therefore, at least in Lord Wright's view, the unseaworthiness was not the only cause of the loss. He thought it enough that unseaworthiness is *one* cause; it did not need even to be the predominant clause.[69] However, Lord Porter took the view simply that unseaworthiness had caused the loss; he noted that the bunkering operation on its own would not have done so, and also that there was nothing wrong with the bunkering operation. So the case is equivocal on the closeness of the causal relationship required. In *The Kamilla*,[70] without referring to *Smith Hogg*, Morison J adopted a test of "a proximate cause of the alleged damage", and this lower court case is the best resolution we have for the time being.

---

62 [1934] AC 538, 544: see section [3.2.1].
63 [1940] AC 997, 1004. See also *Nelson v Nelson* [1908] AC 16 (on negligence).
64 See section [15.1.4]. Gencon can be found at http://www.pfri.uniri.hr/~biserka/documents/gencon94.pdf.
65 [1908] P 84.
66 [1907] 1 KB 660, and see [4.4] below.
67 See section [3.2.1].
68 [1940] AC 997.
69 [1940] AC 997, 1005.
70 *Kamilla Hans-Peter Eckhoff KG v AC Oerssleff's EFTF A/B (The Kamilla)* [2006] 2 Lloyd's Rep 238.

As we have seen, *Smith, Hogg* is also authority that seaworthiness is an overriding obligation at common law, not qualified by excepted perils.[71]

4.2.9 Seaworthiness paramount

We have seen that, at common law, if the vessel is unseaworthy, the shipowner cannot rely on excepted perils.[72] This principle is continued in the Hague-Visby Rules,[73] at any rate to the extent that a carrier in breach of the obligation, under Art. III(1), to exercise due diligence to make the ship seaworthy "before and at the beginning of the voyage", cannot rely on the excepted perils in Art. IV(2). Nor can he rely on the Art. IV(6) dangerous cargo indemnity, considered later in this chapter.[74]

As we will see, however, when we look at Hague-Visby in detail, a different view has been taken of the relationship between Arts III(1) and IV(5), the package limitation. The package limitation (Art. IV(5)) applies even in respect of breaches of Art. III(1).[75] There is no very obvious principle at work here, other than detailed interpretation of the respective provisions themselves.

By contrast, Art. III(2) (which provides essentially for care of the cargo) is expressly subject to Art. IV, and so a breach of Art. III(2) does not preclude the carrier from relying on any of the excepted perils. It is not a fundamental or paramount obligation, in the same way as Art. III(1).[76]

4.2.10 Burden of proof

Also connected with the bailment origins of the seaworthiness obligation is the burden of proof.[77] Rules on burden of proof are important where there is no other evidence, or insufficient evidence to determine the truth.

We have seen that if the cargo-owner proves loss, the burden shifts to the carrier to show absence of fault, for example that the loss was caused by an excepted peril.[78] This will not avail him if he is in breach of a paramount obligation, such as that to provide a seaworthy vessel; in that case, only an exemption in relation to that paramount obligation, by express words, will protect him.[79] The burden of showing breach of a paramount obligation shifts back to the cargo-owner. In *The Glendarroch*, the explanation was that it operated as an exception within an exception, the burden being on the claimants (ie, the cargo-owners) to prove negligence or unseaworthiness.[80]

We will see that, in principle, the Hague and Hague-Visby Rules alter the position, only to the extent that want of due diligence must be shown, the burden of proof being on the carrier. In reality, however, the interplay between unseaworthiness and perils of the seas might place the burden of proof to a greater extent on the carrier.[81]

4.2.11 Effect of breach

When we look at deviation we will see an argument that a deviating shipowner has stepped outside, or abrogated the contract, and cannot rely on excepted perils, whether before or after the

---

71 Section [3.2.1].
72 Section [3.2.1].
73 In this respect the unamended Hague Rules are identical. See further section [18.3].
74 See section [4.6].
75 *The Happy Ranger* [2002] 2 Lloyd's Rep 357.
76 See further section [18.3.2].
77 See section [3.2.2].
78 *Albacora SRL v Westcott & Laurance Line Ltd* [1966] 2 Lloyd's Rep 53; *Gosse Millerd Ltd v Canadian Government Merchant Marine Ltd (The Canadian Highlander)* [1929] AC 223 (burden on carriers, in the latter case. to establish peril within Hague Rules Art. IV).
79 But if the Hague or Hague-Visby Rules apply, such an exemption would be rendered void by Art. III(8).
80 *The Glendarroch* [1894] P 226 (the fundamental obligation there being negligence).
81 See section [18.3.4].

deviation.[82] Whether this is a correct statement of the law for deviation is doubtful – though far from unarguable. It is an argument that has its origins in bailment, denying a carrier who has substituted a different adventure the benefit of excepted perils, whether relating to an event before or after the deviation has occurred.[83]

A similar argument has been advanced for a shipowner who fails to provide a vessel that is seaworthy at the start of the voyage, but this argument was rejected (as we saw) in *The Europa*,[84] and has been decisively rejected in the House of Lords in *Kish v Taylor* (Lord Atkinson expressly approving *The Europa*).[85] There, the (voyage) charterers (in breach) failed to provide a full cargo (of timber). In mitigation, the owners then overloaded the vessel so that she was unseaworthy. Because of the overloading she was forced, upon running into bad weather, to deviate in order to put into port for repairs, and this caused delay. The charterers could not rely on the deviation, it being justified as being in order to save life.[86] They tried to rely instead on the unseaworthiness as a defence to a deadfreight claim, but the House held that unseaworthiness did not affect the owners' claim against the charterers for deadfreight. The contract survived to allow the claim. The charterparty was not brought to an end by the unseaworthiness, and so the entire charterparty remained enforceable, including any exemption clauses, or common law exceptions, but in particular including the deadfreight clause.

We have seen that the obligation is not a condition but an innominate term.[87] If the vessel is unseaworthy the charterers can refuse to load, and if she cannot be made seaworthy within a frustrating time then (consistently with this categorisation) the charterers can repudiate. This was the result, fully 90 years before *Hongkong Fir* formalised the innominate term categorisation, in *Stanton v Richardson*.[88] The (voyage) charterer was entitled to ship wet sugar under the terms of the charterparty, but the vessel was unfit to carry this cargo (because she could not pump out the water), and hence not cargo-worthy, although she was seaworthy in every other respect.[89] The charterer unloaded the sugar, and refused to reload, and the issue was whether his refusal was justified. The jury found that the pumps could not have been replaced (so as to render the vessel reasonably fit to carry a reasonable cargo of wet sugar) within a frustrating time. In the Court of Common Pleas the charterer was held to be justified in his refusal, not because of the unseaworthiness in itself, but because it could not be remedied within a frustrating time.[90] On appeal to the Exchequer Chamber, the decision in the court below was upheld, and though this test was not specifically approved, Cockburn CJ did not demur, and made the point that it would be "months" before the ship could be made ready to take such a cargo.[91] This is also, of course, entirely consistent with the categorisation of the obligation as an innominate term.[92]

4.3 Duties in respect of the cargo

The starting point remains that the carrier, as bailee for reward, is under a duty to take reasonable care to keep the goods safe, to deliver them in the condition in which he took them, or to show that

---

82 The seaworthiness obligation operates only at the start, and so the deviation issues about retrospective abrogation of the contract (in section [4.4]) cannot really arise.

83 Especially Cashmore, *The legal nature of the doctrine of deviation* [1989] JBL 492. See generally below, [4.4].

84 Section [4.2.8].

85 *Kish (JE) v Charles Taylor & Sons* [1912] AC 604.

86 See further section [4.4].

87 Section [2.6.2].

88 (1874) LR 9 CP 390, on appeal from (1872) LR 7 CP 421. See further [2.6.1].

89 See section [4.2.3].

90 (1872) LR 7 CP 421, 437. The case is cited in *Universal Cargo Carriers Corp v Citati*, in [3.3.3] below, at 433.

91 (1874) LR 9 CP 390, 392.

92 For a similar type of reasoning, just a few months after *Stanton v Richardson*, see *Jackson v Union Marine Insurance Co* (1874–5) LR 10 CP 125, in section [6.6].

any damage was not caused by his neglect or default.[93] The bailment position is universally modified by contract, as we saw in chapter 3, and in reality there will be extensive excepted perils protecting the carrier. Since the obligations, other than the duty not to be negligent, and the seaworthiness obligation considered in the last section, are not fundamental or paramount, carriers experience no particular difficulty in taking advantage of these excepted perils.

Under Art. III(2) of both the Hague and Hague-Visby Rules, which are identical other than in respect of the package limitation, the standard of care is modified, in effect to one of due diligence. We saw in the previous section that unlike Art. III(1), Art. III(2) is not a fundamental obligation, and (unlike Art. III(1)) is subject to the excepted perils in Art. IV. This reflects the common law, that the seaworthiness obligation, but not (in the absence of negligence) that for care of the cargo otherwise, is paramount.

In the next chapter, we will see that shipowners frequently contract altogether out of responsibility for loading and discharging the cargo.[94] This can give rise to difficulty, in particular in terms of incorporating charterparty terms into bills of lading, and how this transfer of responsibility fits with the Hague-Visby Rules.[95]

4.4 Deviation

4.4.1 Duty of shipowner not to deviate

A deviation is a voluntary departure from an agreed or usual route. The duty on the carrier not to deviate had its origins in bailment, and a summary of the position is as follows:

1. At common law, deviation is only permitted if it is to save life at sea (eg, by avoiding dangerous weather). Deviation to save property is not permitted.[96]
2. Where the Hague or Hague-Visby Rules apply, Art. IV(4) allows any deviation in saving or attempting to save life *or property* at sea or *any reasonable deviation*.[97] Thus the shipowner has greater freedom to deviate.
3. Apart from deviations permitted under the common law, or the Hague or Hague-Visby Rules (if applicable), and any deviation that is allowed by an express clause in the carriage contract, the slightest deviation allows the cargo owner to repudiate the contract, possibly because the cargo owner can lose the benefit of his insurance cover if there is any deviation from the agreed route.

The more interesting question is whether the consequences are greater than those set out in (3).

4.4.2 Consequences of unjustified deviation

There is no doubt that an unjustified deviation is, at the very least, a breach of condition, and it follows that the slightest deviation allows the charterer or cargo-owner to repudiate the contract. If he does so, the principles in chapter 2 show us that from the moment of repudiation the carrier cannot rely on any carriage contract exemptions.[98]

---

93 See section [3.1].
94 See the FIO clauses in section [5.3].
95 See sections [15.2.4.1]; [18.4].
96 See section [4.4.3].
97 On Hague and Hague-Visby generally, see chapter 18, but the application of the Rules to deviation are dealt with here.
98 See section [2.10].

It used to be thought that the consequences were somewhat greater than that. By deviating, the carrier had voluntarily substituted a voyage different from the one he contracted to perform. He is no longer entitled to the benefit of exemptions, and indeed thereafter carries the goods as a common carrier. On one view, he is therefore disentitled from relying on contractual exemptions, whether covering the period before or after the deviation, unless the charterer or cargo-owner chooses to waive his rights. This view is not consistent with the normal law of contract and, if correct, puts deviation into a special position. In recent years, however, there has been an attempt to reconcile the law of deviation with the ordinary law of contract.

The issue is, which of these views is correct? This has not been conclusively resolved by the cases.

A starting point is the Court of Appeal decision in *Thorley (Joseph) Ltd v Orchis SS Co.*[99] The shipowner deviated from the agreed route, and the court took the view that he was no longer therefore performing the original contract of carriage, because he had substituted an altogether different voyage. Therefore he could not rely on any exemption clauses in the contract of carriage.

On a voyage from Cyprus to London the carrier deviated via ports in the eastern Mediterranean before continuing to London. At the end of the voyage the goods were damaged through the negligence of stevedores engaged by the carrier to unload the goods. The bill of lading contained a clause exempting the shipowners from liability for loss arising from the negligence of stevedores engaged by them in unloading the ship, but the Court of Appeal held that the carrier was not entitled to the benefit of any exemption clauses in the bill of lading.

One can take a narrow view of *Thorley v Orchis*. The damage did not occur until the end of the voyage, well after the deviation, and so, even on conventional contractual reasoning,[100] the Court of Appeal were justified in refusing to allow the carrier the benefit of the clause. This remains the case, even though the cause of any subsequent loss was not in any way related to the deviation. However, the tenor of the judgments is not so confined. Thus, Fletcher-Moulton LJ said:[101]

> "The cases shew that, for a long series of years, the Courts have held that a deviation is such a serious matter, and changes the character of the contemplated voyage so essentially, that a shipowner who has been guilty of a deviation cannot be considered as having performed his part of the . . . contract, but something fundamentally different, and therefore he cannot claim the benefit of stipulations in his favour contained in the bill of lading. In what position, then, does he stand? He has carried the goods to their place of destination, and is therefore entitled to some remuneration for that service, of which their owner has received the benefit. The most favourable position which he can claim to occupy is that he has carried the goods as a common carrier for the agreed freight."

In *Internationale Guano en Superphosphaat-Werken v Robert Macandrew & Co,*[102] *Thorley* was followed even to the extent of striking down exemptions taking effect prior to the deviation.

The idea that a shipowner who has deviated has performed an entirely different voyage has its origins in bailment, but though it might explain how the law has developed, it is not easy to see how it justifies it. A justification is sometimes found in marine insurance. Section 46(1) of the Marine Insurance Act 1946 provides:

> "Where a ship, without lawful excuse, deviates from the voyage contemplated by the policy, the insurer is discharged from liability as from the time of deviation, and it is immaterial that the ship may have regained her route before any loss occurs."

---

99 [1907] 1 KB 660.
100 Subject to the backdating of repudiation point below.
101 [1907] 1 KB 660, 669.
102 [1909] 2 KB 360.

The loss of cargo insurance might justify removing protection from the deviating carrier, though note that the insurer is discharged only as from the time of the deviation.

In *Hain SS Co v Tate and Lyle Ltd*,[103] Lord Atkin at least thought that the principles of the ordinary law of contract applied to deviation. What is clear in *Hain* is that the contract is not automatically displaced by deviation, and that the charterers were entitled to waive the deviation (thereby keeping the contract, including excepted perils, alive). However, though the original charterers, as prior holders of the bill, had waived the deviation, the House of Lords held that unless the indorsees also treated the original contract of carriage as subsisting, they were unaffected by the waiver. Though Lord Atkin analysed the case in ordinary contractual terms, Lord Wright said that the deviating shipowner could not "claim the benefit of the exceptions contained in the charter-party",[104] and his reasoning is not that far removed from that of the Court of Appeal in *Thorley*. Moreover, the cargo-owners had not actually repudiated by the time of the loss, yet, even so, the owners were not entitled to the benefit of the excepted perils. This suggests that the cargo-owner, on discovering the deviation, can backdate repudiation of the contract to the time of the deviation, and, if so, exemption clauses covering later events will not protect the shipowner. To this extent at least, *Hain* remains out of line with the conventional contract position. In the later Court of Appeal decision in *The Sara D*,[105] Lloyd LJ observed that it only Lord Maugham who refers expressly to the timing of repudiation, but the logic of the case requires it to be retrospective. It also makes sense, if the justification for the position is based on marine insurance.

The courts remain equivocal about deviation. In *Suisse Atlantique*, Lord Wilberforce thought that it should be assimilated into the general law of contract,[106] but by *Photo Production* he was less sure, and was more attracted by the view that it should be regarded as *sui generis*.[107] What is clear is that if deviation does indeed remain special, its principles are unlikely to be extended to other breaches of contract, however serious. Thus, for example, the Court of Appeal applied the normal law of contract in *The Antares (Nos 1 and 2)*,[108] and in *The Kapitan Petko Voivoda*,[109] in both of which a carrier who had loaded cargo on deck, thereby significantly increasing the risk to it, was held entitled to rely on the Hague Rules package limitation. In *The Sara D*,[110] the Court of Appeal refused to extend a backdated repudiation argument to a sale contract. We will return to this when we look at other serious breaches, such as misdelivery in chapter 20.

Even on a conventional view, a shipowner would lose the benefit of excepted perils, once a charterer or cargo-owner had validly repudiated. However, if the Rotterdam Rules are ever adopted in the UK, Art. 24 provides:[111]

> "When pursuant to applicable law a deviation constitutes a breach of the carrier's obligations, such deviation of itself shall not deprive the carrier or a maritime performing party of any defence or limitation of this Convention, except to the extent provided in article 61."

4.4.3 Justified deviations

All of the above applies only to unjustified deviations, not to deviations that are permitted by the contract, or to those that are otherwise justified.

---

103 (1936) 55 LL L Rep 159, the only case where the effect of deviation on contractual exemptions is extensively discussed in the House of Lords.

104 (1936) 55 LL L Rep 159, 177.

105 *State Trading Corporation of India Ltd v M Golodetz Ltd (The Sara D)* [1989] 2 Lloyd's Rep 277, 288.

106 *Suisse Atlantique Société d'Armement Maritime SA v NV Rotterdamsche Kolen Centrale* [1967] 1 AC 361, 434–5.

107 *Photo Production Ltd v Securicor Transport Ltd* [1980] AC 827, 845.

108 *Kenya Railways v Antares Co Pte Ltd (The Antares Nos. 1 and 2)* [1987] 1 Lloyd's Rep 424, 430 (Lloyd LJ).

109 *Daewoo Heavy Industries Ltd v Klipriver Shipping Ltd (The Kapitan Petko Voivoda)* [2003] 2 Lloyd's Rep 1.

110 [1989] 2 Lloyd's Rep 277.

111 Article 61 (Rotterdam) is on delay.

At common law a deviation is allowed to save life. In *The Teutonia*, Mellish LJ said:[112]

"Where a Master receives credible information that if he continues in the direct course of his voyage his Ship will be exposed to some imminent peril, as from Pirates, or Icebergs, or other dangers of navigation, he is justified in pausing and deviating from the direct course, and taking any step that a prudent man would take for the purpose of avoiding the danger."

In this particular case, the master had taken his German ship to Dover, rather than Dunkirk, fearing an outbreak of war between Prussia and France. This was held to be a justifiable deviation. There was also, as we have seen, a justifiable deviation in *Kish v Taylor*.[113] The common law justification is, however, narrow, and does not extend to the saving of property.[114]

Where the Hague or Hague-Visby Rules apply,[115] Art. IV(4) provides:

"Any deviation in saving or attempting to save life or property at sea or any reasonable deviation shall not be deemed to be an infringement or breach of this Convention or of the contract of carriage, and the carrier shall not be liable for any loss or damage resulting therefrom."

This provision obviously extends to saving property, and also to a reasonable deviation. What is reasonable was considered in *Stag Line Ltd v Foscolo, Mango & Co Ltd*[116] (though the value of the case as an authority is limited by the reluctance of the House of Lords to interfere with lower court findings of fact, and the judge's views as to reasonableness). Nonetheless, there is a test in Lord Atkin's speech:[117]

"The true test seems to be what departure from the contract voyage might a prudent person controlling the voyage at the time make and maintain, having in mind all the relevant circumstances existing at the time, including the terms of the contract and the interests of all parties concerned, but without obligation to consider the interests of any one as conclusive."

When the ship sailed from Swansea, superheater tests had not been completed because of the drunkenness of the stokers and the consequent delay in raising a full head of steam, so engineers were taken aboard, with the intention of landing them later. The ship later visited Lundy Island, which was not on the normal route to Constantinople, but the problem was still not fixed, and so the engineers were not landed until St Ives, further down the English coast. The ship then proceeded on a risky coastal course, where she was lost. In Lord Atkin's view, the route back at least was unreasonable. It was relevant but not conclusive that the deviation was entirely for the shipowners' benefit. However, Lord Atkin at least thought that the Hague Rules did more than merely codify *The Teutonia* (the view that had been taken by Scrutton LJ in the Court of Appeal),[118] but Lord Buckmaster expressed no opinion even as to this.

Stag Line does not clearly state the law, but it would probably be a mistake to conclude from it that Hague or Hague-Visby provide a wide exception.

---

112 *David Duncan v Daniel Augustus (The Teutonia)* (1871–73) LR 4 PC 171, 179.

113 Above, section [4.2.11].

114 *Scaramanga v Scamp* (1880) 5 CPD 295 (not justified to take ship in tow rather than just rescuing the crew).

115 See further chapter 18.

116 [1932] AC 328, on the Hague Rules – but Hague-Visby is identical in this respect.

117 [1932] AC 328, 350.

118 [1931] 2 KB 48, 61.

4.4.4   Deviation liberty clauses

A deviation, or liberty to deviate, clause specifically allows the carrier to deviate.

There is nothing inherently objectionable about deviation clauses. It is reasonable, for example, for a clause to allow the carrier to replenish bunker fuel, even if that requires deviating from the usual direct route. Indeed, voyage charterparties commonly include a P. & I. bunkering clause (the terms of which might also be incorporated into any bill of lading issued under the charter), allowing precisely that. Nor is it necessarily unreasonable, depending on the nature of the trade, for a carrier to insist upon a liberty to go via a number of ports, even if off the usual direct route, to pick up other cargo.

Some clauses allow the carrier a very wide liberty to deviate, however,[119] in which case the courts interpret them strictly against the carrier. The leading authority is *Glynn v Margetson & Co*,[120] where the House of Lords considered a clause in a bill of lading, allowing the carrier to deviate to a wide variety of ports, including any in Spain,

> "for the purpose of delivering coals, cargo or passengers, or for any other purpose what-soever".

The ship left Malaga in Spain on a voyage to Liverpool, but called first at Burriana, a port in east Spain and in the opposite direction from Liverpool. Because of the delay the shipper's cargo of oranges were delivered in a damaged condition, and the shipper sued the shipowner for breach of contract. The House of Lords held that the shipowner could not rely on the deviation clause. The printed clause must not be construed in such a way as to defeat the main object and intent of the contract, which was to carry the oranges from Malaga to Liverpool, and the liberty to deviate must therefore be restricted to ports that were in the course of the voyage. In the words of Lord Herschell:[121]

> "Where general words are used in a printed form which are obviously intended to apply, so far as they are applicable, to the circumstances of a particular contract, which particular contract is to be embodied in or introduced into that printed form, I think you are justified in looking at the main object and intent of the contract and in limiting the general words used, having in view that object and intent."

In chapter 15 we will look at *Leduc & Co v Ward*,[122] a Court of Appeal decision five years prior to *Glynn v Margetson*, which may be regarded as a precursor to it. The bill of lading incorporated a clause that allowed the carrier to call at any port in any order. The Court of Appeal held that the clause did not allow him to call at Glasgow in a voyage from Fiume to Dunkirk. It allowed only to proceed via ports that were substantially on the course of the voyage from Fiume to Dunkirk, and clearly going to Glasgow and back (an additional distance of some 1,200 miles) was not.

A similar principle of construction was adopted by the House of Lords in *Stag Line Ltd v Foscolo Mango & Co*. Here again, a clause that at first sight might have been thought wide enough to protect the shipowner was interpreted very restrictively, and did not do so. By a clause in the bill of lading the shipowners had

> "liberty . . . to call at any ports in any order, for bunkering or other purposes, . . . all as part of the contract voyage".

---

119 Eg, Gencon 1994, cl. 3.
120 [1893] AC 351.
121 [1893] AC 351, 360.
122 (1888) LR 20 QBD 475, and see section [15.1.4].

The shipowners failed in an argument that this clause justified them in the landing of the engineers. The deviation was not permitted by the clause in the bill of lading: "other purposes" should be construed only to allow a liberty to call at a port that had some purpose relating to the contract voyage. Lord Atkin said of the words in the deviation clause:[123]

> "They cannot be unlimited in scope, or they would authorise the shipowner to direct the ship to any part of the globe for any purpose he thought fit. Even if limited to port or ports on the geographical course of the voyage, as I think they clearly must be the purpose of the call must receive some limitation. The liberty could not reasonably be intended to give the right to call or take on board friends of the shipowner for the purposes of a pleasure trip . . . I think myself that the purposes intended are business purposes which would be contemplated by the parties as arising out of the contemplated voyage of the ship. This might include in a contract other than a contract to carry a full and complete cargo a right to call at port or ports on the geographical course to load and discharge cargo for other shippers. It would probably include a right to call for orders. But I cannot think that it would include a right such as was sought to be exercised in the present case . . . ."

So Lord Atkin's test was limited to "business purposes which would be contemplated by the parties as arising in carrying out the contemplated voyage of the ship". In the Court of Appeal Scrutton LJ had taken a much narrower view, that the clause simply justified bunkering.

On the other hand, in *G.H. Renton & Co Ltd v Palmyra Trading Corp of Panama*,[124] the House of Lords held that a clause allowing the carrier to discharge at any safe and convenient port in the event of strikes at the port of discharge (London) was effective to allow him to discharge the goods at Hamburg. A clause is not repugnant to the main objects of the contract where it modifies the carrier's obligations in the event of defined events that are outside the control of either party. The difference was that this clause applied only to specified events, rather than justifying deviations generally.

4.5 Obligation to proceed with reasonable despatch

Finally (on shipowners' obligations), whether or not expressly provided by the charterparty, it is an implied obligation that the shipowner will proceed with reasonable despatch, both on the approach voyage to the port of loading, and on the voyage from there to the port of discharge. Note that the obligation is always couched in terms of reasonable despatch, and not, for example, utmost speed. The obligation is not a condition, so breach of it will not give the charterer an automatic right to repudiate the charter. He will be able to do so, however, if the delay is sufficiently serious as to frustrate the adventure.[125]

The obligation to proceed with reasonable despatch is subject to the excepted perils on the voyage itself, so that if delay is caused by an excepted peril the shipowner will not be in breach of this obligation, and additionally the shipowner is entitled to the benefit of any exemption clauses expressly incorporated into the charterparty.

We consider reasonable despatch in the particular contexts of the approach voyage in chapter 6, and time charter routes in chapter 13.[126] In chapter 6 we will also look at the effect of excepted perils before the ship is delivered.

---

123 [1932] AC 338, 341.
124 [1957] AC 149, and see also section [18.4].
125 See *Jackson v Union Marine Insurance Co* (1874–5) LR 10 CP 125, in section [6.6].
126 Respectively sections [6.7]; [13.3].

4.6 Obligation not to ship dangerous cargo

This is an obligation on shippers not carriers. However, it is an obligation that can be transferred to subsequent holders of bills of lading, on the principles in chapter 16.[127]

The common law implied a term into carriage contracts not to ship dangerous cargo without the shipowner's consent. It is reasonable to suppose that there is also a right to refuse to load, and therefore to issue a bill of lading for the cargo. In that event there is unlikely to be a contract of carriage at all with the shipper,[128] and, in the event of dispute, the shipowner will need only to be concerned with his relationship with his head charterer (assuming there is a charterparty).

Where the Hague or Hague-Visby Rules apply, Art. IV(6) provides a liability that is concurrent with the common law. It allows that the goods "may be discharged destroyed or rendered innocuous by carrier without compensation", and provides that "the shipper of such goods shall be liable for all damages and expenses directly or indirectly arising out of or resulting from such shipment".

4.6.1 What is dangerous cargo?

Of course there are cargoes which are dangerous in a classic, traditional sense. Ship and cargo exploded in *The Ythan*, *The Fiona* and *The Aegean Sea*.[129] There is no doubt that the term "dangerous cargo" encompasses such cargoes. This does not mean that they cannot be carried at sea, rather that the carrier must be aware of, and consent to, the risks. No doubt they can be carried safely, with the appropriate care.

But the concept extends beyond cargoes of this type. In *Chandris v Isbrandsen-Moller Co Inc*,[130] turpentine was held to be dangerous. There was no real doubt about this, the issue being whether an *ejusdem generis* interpretation to a clause prohibiting the shipment of "acids, explosives, arms, ammunition or other dangerous cargo". The shippers attempted (unsuccessfully) to argue that "other dangerous cargo" should be given a restricted meaning. The only damage in *Chandris* was delay (which was compensated by a demurrage payment).[131] The authorities at Liverpool refused to allow discharge directly, but only into the river into craft, with the result that the discharge took 16 days longer than it would otherwise have done. (Their nervousness was perhaps explained by the date, the vessel arriving on 25 May 1941, shortly after very heavy bombing of the city by the German air force.)

Even turpentine is highly inflammable, but a cargo that was merely corrosive was accepted as dangerous in *The Berge Sisar*.[132] In *The Giannis NK*,[133] the cargo was physically dangerous to other cargo, but only indirectly. It was contaminated by Khapra beetle, and though the beetle would not have affected the neighbouring cargo (so that there was no direct physical danger to the other cargo), the contamination led to all the cargo on ship being dumped at sea. Lord Lloyd said that he could:[134]

---

127 Carriage of Goods by Sea Act 1992, as argued in, eg, *Borealis AB v Stargas Ltd (The Berge Sisar)* [2002] 2 AC 205; *Aegean Sea Traders Corp v Repsol Petroleo SA (The Aegean Sea)* [1998] 2 Lloyd's Rep 39; *Primetrade AG v Ythan Ltd (The Ythan)* [2006] 1 Lloyd's Rep 457. Binding a subsequent holder by implied contract was argued in *The Athanasia Comninos and The Georges Chr Lemos* [1990] 1 Lloyd's Rep 277, and see sections [4.6.3]; [16.8]. In none of these cases was the argument successful, but it could have worked in principle. See generally section [16.7] on liabilities.

128 See further section [15.1.3].

129 Respectively *The Ythan* [2006] 1 Lloyd's Rep 457; *Mediterranean Freight Services Ltd v BP Oil International Ltd (The Fiona)* [1994] 2 Lloyd's Rep 506; *The Aegean Sea* [1998] 2 Lloyd's Rep 39.

130 [1951] 1 KB 240, rvsd other grounds (1950) 84 Ll. L Rep 347.

131 See section [9.5].

132 [2002] 2 AC 205; see section [16.7].

133 *Effort Shipping Co Ltd v Linden Management SA (The Giannis NK)* [1998] 1 AC 605.

134 [1998] AC 605, 613.

". . . see no reason to confine the word 'dangerous' to goods which are liable to cause direct physical damage to other goods."

At the same place, Lord Lloyd left open the question whether the concept extended to cargo that is simply legally dangerous. (In the case itself, the action was actually brought by shipowner, against the shippers under the bill of lading, for delay.)

In *The Giannis NK*, the bill of lading was subject to the Hague Rules, and was brought under the Art. IV(6) indemnity. This was held to be a standalone provision, providing for no-fault liability, and not qualified by Art. IV(3):

"The shipper shall not be responsible for loss or damage sustained by the carrier or the ship arising or resulting from any cause without the act, fault or neglect of the shipper, his agents or his servants."

Art. IV(3) is consistent with the fault-based regime that pervades the Hague and Hague-Visby Rules. But the majority view was that Art. IV(6) was free-standing, in spite of general tenor of the Rules towards a due diligence regime, and that in any case the dumping allowed in Art. IV(6) cannot depend on shipper fault. Though it did not arise in *The Giannis NK*, there are also remarks, *obiter*, that liability at common law is also strict.[135]

4.6.2 Arts. III(1) and IV(6)

We will see in chapter 18 that the Art. III(1) obligation, to provide a seaworthy vessel, is overriding under the Hague and Hague-Visby Rules (where they apply).[136] In this context, a shipowner who is in breach of Art. III(1) cannot make use of Art. IV(6). In *The Kapitan Sakharov*,[137] there was a fire and explosion caused by the shipment of a dangerous cargo in a container, but it was made worse by the shipment of second dangerous cargo, the carriage of which (though he was unaware of it) put the carrier in breach of Art. III(1) of the Hague Rules. The Court of Appeal held the carrier not entitled to claim an indemnity under Art. IV(6). *The Kapitan Sakharov* follows the earlier decision, also in the Court of Appeal, in *The Fiona*,[138] where a dangerous cargo of oil had exploded, but a contributory cause of the explosion was its contamination by a previous cargo, which rendered the vessel unseaworthy and put the shipowner in breach of Art. III(1). *The Kapitan Sakharov* goes further than *The Fiona*, since in the latter case the unseaworthiness of the vessel was not the dominant cause of the subsequent loss of vessel and cargo.

4.6.3 Who bears the risk?

The gravamen of the breach lies not in shipping dangerous cargo as such, but in shipping dangerous cargo of whose nature the shipowner is unaware. There are many cargoes that are normally safe to ship, but where the particular cargo is dangerous, or needs special precautions. *The Athanasia Comninos* concerned coal that was claimed to be unusually gassy, and hence more likely to explode than coal generally.[139] Another type of cargo that has become topical recently, mostly because of increases in tonnages shipped, is nickel ore fines, nickel having uses in batteries and electronics. Some nickel

---

135 [1998] AC 605, 619 (Lord Lloyd).
136 See section [18.3].
137 *Northern Shipping Co v Deutsche Seereederei GmbH (The Kapitan Sakharov)* [2000] 2 Lloyd's Rep 255.
138 [1994] 2 Lloyd's Rep 506.
139 [1990] 1 Lloyd's Rep 277 (Mustill J), a case reported 11 years after it was decided.

ore cargoes are prone to liquefaction, where it behaves like a liquid and hence renders ships very unstable. On the other hand, most nickel ore is perfectly safe. But merely because a shipowner has consented to carry nickel ore does not imply that he has consented to carry cargo that is prone to liquefaction.

In *The Athanasia Comninos*, the carrier had agreed to carry cargo with known dangers, but where the dangers were unusually high. The cargo was coal, which it was claimed had an unusually high methane content, and that exploded. Mustill J pioneered the risk analysis later adopted, in different contexts, in *The Island Archon* and *The Achilleas*:[140]

> "In my view, it is essential when looking for such a test to remember that we are here con-
> cerned, not with the labelling in the abstract of goods as 'dangerous' or 'safe', but with the
> distribution of risk for the consequences of a dangerous situation arising during the voyage.
> The character of the goods does, of course, play an important part in creating such a situa-
> tion. But it is not the only factor. Equally important are the knowledge of the shipowner as
> to the characteristics of the goods, and the care with which he carries them, in the light of
> that knowledge."

The shipowner had agreed to the carriage of coal, with its associated dangers, but this was particularly gassy (high methane content), and hence more likely to explode. Mustill J rejected the idea that the owners must be taken to have consented to the carriage of coal, however gassy. (There were two cargoes considered, and the shipowner succeeded in respect of one but not the other.) In identifying the risks, Mustill J used as a test the adoption of proper methods of carriage. If the carrier adopts proper methods, appropriate to goods of that description, he will normally be protected. It was accepted, however, that there will always be some risk, even if proper methods are used, and that in respect of that bad luck category the carrier takes the risk. Mustill J also said that "the risks must be of a totally different kind (whether in nature or degree) from those attached to the carriage of the described cargo, before shipment of the particular cargo can be regarded as a breach of duty".[141]

The case was decided on the common law, and Hague Rules points are left open, but there is no reason to suppose the risk analysis would be inapplicable under the Rules.

4.7 Questions

These questions are on the obligation to furnish a seaworthy vessel, discussed in section [4.2]. Let us begin with a quick question, just for you to think about, to see if you have formed a view on when cargo can render a ship unseaworthy.

Question 4.1

Why was there a breach of the seaworthiness obligation in *Smith, Hogg v Black Sea and Baltic General Insurance* and *The Kapitan Sakharov*,[142] but not in *The Thorsa, Elder Dempster & Co Ltd v Paterson Zochonis & Co Ltd* [1924] AC 522 or *The Apostolis*.[143]

---

140 [1990] 1 Lloyd's Rep 277, 282. A risk analysis was later used in *The Island Archon* [1994] 2 Lloyd's Rep 227 and *The Achilleas* [2009]
    1 AC 61: see sections [3.6]; [13.4].
141 [1990] 1 Lloyd's Rep 277, 284.
142 Respectively [1940] AC 997; [2000] 2 Lloyd's Rep 255.
143 Respectively [1959] AC 589; [1916] P 257; [1997] 2 Lloyd's Rep 241.

Next few questions

Let us make sure we understand when the obligation attaches. (It is not entirely clear. There is authority for the doctrine of stages at common law, but it is rather shaky.)

Question 4.2

Cargo A is loaded without problems. Cargo B is loaded next and contaminates Cargo A, before the ship sails. Is the ship unseaworthy?

Cargo B is loaded without problems. Cargo A is loaded next and is contaminated by Cargo B, before the ship sails. Is the ship unseaworthy?

Question 4.3

This question is based on a passage in Baughen, *Shipping Law*, 6th ed (2015), Taylor & Francis, 90, discussing *Elder Dempster & Co Ltd v Paterson Zochonis & Co Ltd*:[144]

> "If, however, contractual commitments had already been entered into in respect of carriage of the palm kernel cargo from the second port at the time that the palm oil was loaded at the first port, it is likely that the vessel would have been unseaworthy as regards the palm oil."

Do you think this is correct? Is a ship unfit to carry cargo when loaded, if contractual commitments have already been made to carry a heavy cargo on top, when that heavy cargo will crush the lighter cargo underneath?

Question 4.4

Puffer loads a cargo of Gorgonzola, followed by a cargo of chocolate. When the chocolate is loaded, the only place remaining for it is on top of the Gorgonzola, in a hot and poorly-ventilated hold. By the end of the voyage the chocolate smells so bad as to have become unmerchantable.

Puffer is chartered under a voyage charter, under which liability for bad stowage is excluded. The charterer claims that the damage has been caused by unseaworthiness, not bad stowage.

Advise the charterer. Would your advice have been different had the chocolate been loaded first?

Comments

These three questions are all on when the obligation attaches, and the last is of course inspired by *The Thorsa*.[145] You may think the main part of Question 4.4 is on all fours with that case, but it gets more interesting if the chocolate is loaded first. The issue is when the seaworthiness obligation ends, at any rate where the issue is fitness to receive cargo, since the ship may well be seaworthy on loading, if not on sailing. Have a look at *McFadden v Blue Star Line*,[146] particularly regarding the sea-cock and sluice-door. You might also look at comments made on *The Thorsa* in *Elder Dempster & Co Ltd v Paterson Zochonis & Co Ltd*.[147] Don't necessarily expect a clear answer. That is not how case law always works.

The charterparty is of course governed by the common law, but you might consider whether the position would be the same for a bill of lading to which Hague-Visby applied, or for that matter

---

144 [1924] AC 522.
145 [1916] P 257.
146 [1905] 1 KB 697.
147 [1924] AC 522.

Rotterdam, in the unlikely event that Rotterdam becomes part of English law. You might also have a look at the question at the end of chapter 21.

Finally on seaworthiness

A topical question:

Question 4.5

What obligations, if any, in your view, are imposed on a shipowner who intends to sail through an area where there is a known piracy risk?

Comment

The vessel must be fit for the particular voyage, and presumably could be unseaworthy if she set off for such an area without being reasonably well-equipped to repel pirates. On the voyage itself, though shipowners will not be liable in respect of a piratical attack in itself,[148] they will be if that loss is occasioned by a lack of care, for example if the crew could have repelled the pirates, but did not.[149]

---

148 Comments in *Trafigura Beheer BV v Navigazione Montanari SpA (The Valle di Cordoba)* [2015] EWCA Civ 91. See further section [22.4] and generally Todd, *Charterparties and piracy today* (2014), CreateSpace.

149 *Petroships Pte Ltd v Petec Trading and Investment Corp (The Petro Ranger)* [2001] 2 Lloyd's Rep 348 (where there was a lack of care at the stage of recovering the cargo).

Part 2

Voyage charterparties

Chapter 5

Nature of voyage charterparties

Chapter Contents

5.1 Introduction

This relatively short chapter introduces the fundamentals of the voyage charter, and looks at two related types: the consecutive voyage charter and the contract of affreightment. Recall that under all types of a voyage charterparty, freight is paid for the voyage (or voyages), which though it might depend upon tonnage carried, does not depend on the length of time the voyage (or voyages) take. Risk of delay is therefore on the shipowners, at least to the extent that other terms in the charterparty do not alter the delay risk allocation.

The requirements on owners to provide a seaworthy vessel, to stow and care for the cargo, and to make reasonable despatch, apply to voyage charters as they do to other contracts for the carriage of goods by sea, as do the requirements on shippers not to ship dangerous cargo. These have already been addressed in chapter 4.

5.2 Terms of voyage charterparties

All charterparties, whether in voyage time or demise form, will include the place where the contract is made, the date of the charterparty, names and domicile of the contracting parties, the name, present position and description of the vessel.

Statements in a voyage charterparty describing the vessel are generally less extensive in (at any rate dry-cargo) voyage than in time charterparties. Typically, in a voyage charterparty her name will be identified, and her present position. The carrying capacity of the vessel is an important consideration for voyage charterers, and will invariably be stipulated in the charterparty. Sometimes the class of the ship will also be stated. Voyage charterparties may contain warranties as to the performance of the vessel (eg, power and speed) and her condition, but these are not included, for example, in Gencon. Time charterers are more likely to be interested in the performance of the vessel than voyage charterers, and demise charterers are more likely to be concerned with her condition, although voyage charters also sometimes include a warranty as to the condition of the vessel.

Where the form is divided into parts the description of the vessel will normally be filled in, in Part I. As we have seen, where there is a conflict between Parts I and II, Part I will normally prevail,[1] and indeed the some forms, such as BPVOY4, provide this.

The shipowner will undertake to provide a seaworthy vessel, and, as we have already seen, this would be implied into the charterparty, whether expressed or not.[2]

Voyage charters contain clauses determining loading and discharging places, which are often agreed within ranges at charterer's option. The cargo will be stipulated (whereas in time charters it is more common to detail cargoes that cannot be carried), and voyage charterparties contain clauses relating to freight, laytime and demurrage, which would of course be inappropriate in time and demise charters.[3] Voyage charters also usually contain a deviation clause (ie, liberty to deviate), and a cesser clause.

Voyage and time charters will also contain war and strike clauses, although the requirements for these clauses differ slightly in time charterparties.[4]

Arbitration clauses, and commission and brokerage clauses, would be appropriate for inclusion in any type of charterparty.

---

1 See further section [22.2].
2 Section [4.2].
3 See sections [1.3]–[1.5].
4 See sections [12.10] and [22.4] for time charter war clauses.

Speed is relatively unimportant in a voyage charter, where the risk of delay is on the owners, but some tanker voyage charterparties nonetheless concern themselves with speed. Speed clauses in voyage forms are quite unlike their time counterparts, however, their purpose being merely to ensure arrival at a convenient time. Typically, the owners undertake to proceed (or use best endeavours to proceed) at a base speed, the charterers having the option to order the vessel to increase speed, in which case the freight rate is adjusted to compensate the shipowner for increased fuel consumption. While the owners will be liable in damages for failure to comply, delay will not inevitably cause the charterers loss, as it will in a time charterparty, where they are paying hire calculated on a time basis. Any loss is likely to be consequential on failure to arrive at the desired time. In other respects, risk of delay remains on the shipowner, and is unaffected by the speed clause.

It is also normal for charterers to be able to require the master to issue bills of lading. This is also true of time charterparties, but it is also common for both time and voyage charters to contain some stipulation as to bills of lading that may be issued. This is for the protection of the shipowner. The main issues here are if the bill of lading imposes greater duties on the shipowner than the charterparty – is the shipowner entitled to an indemnity?[5]

There may be a paramount clause incorporating the Hague or Hague-Visby Rules, a New Jason clause and a both-to-blame collision clause,[6] but these are not universally included. None is included in Baltime or Gencon, for example.

5.3 FIO and gross terms

Voyage charterparties need to determine who is responsible for the handling of the cargo at loading and discharge ports. The commonest variations are *gross terms* and *free in and out* (or FIO). The shipowner pays all the costs in a gross terms charter, whereas the charterer pays loading and discharge expenses of the cargo in an FIO charter (sometimes referred to as "*nett terms*"). There are other variations, such as *net form*, where the charterer pays everything, including the port charges between loading and discharge (whereas under an FIO charter these are paid by the shipowner).

Where "FIO and free stowed trimmed" (FIOST) is chosen by the parties, all loading, stowage, trimming and discharge costs are borne by the charterer (for example), "free of any risk, liability and expense whatsoever to the Owners".

These division of responsibility clauses occasion no particular legal difficulty as charterparty terms, but there are issues about their incorporation into bills of lading, and also issues revolving around the Hague-Visby Rules, which we consider in detail later in the book.[7]

5.4 Classification of terms

Some forms make representations concerning the vessel conditions of the charter, or allow the charterers to cancel in the event of misrepresentations. For example, BPVOY4 makes it "a condition of this Charter that the responses in the BP Shipping Questionnaire are correct as at the date hereof".[8] Although in *L. Schuler AG v Wickman Machine Tool Sales Ltd*,[9] the House of Lords did not treat as conclusive the description of a term of a contract as a condition, this was only because that particular

---

5 See generally section [13.7].

6 These are deal with US case law developments, and are not covered in this book.

7 Chapter 18.

8 The questionnaire is an appendix to the form and comprises essentially questions relating to the vessel. An example can be found at http://www.marinetanker.com/ankets/bp.pdf.

9 [1974] AC 235 (Lord Wilberforce dissenting). See also section [2.6.2].

construction, in that particular contract, led to a very unreasonable result. The breach was trivial, and it would have been quite unreasonable to construe it as bringing the long-term commercial contract to an end, even if it were described as a condition. Such reasoning would not appear to be applicable to most representations about the vessel. So if the form makes the representation a condition, it probably will be.

In chapter 6 we will see that the present position of vessel, and expected readiness statement, are both conditions.[10] In chapter 2 we saw that in *The Seaflower*,[11] a "majors approval clause" was held to be a condition, though it was not stated to be a condition. It is true that this was a time charterparty, but there is no reason to suppose that it would be treated differently in a voyage form. A point about this clause was that it was very certain, in the sense that it was obvious that there was either a breach or there was not. Vague terms, such as the speed clause in *The Apollonius*, are unlikely to be conditions.[12]

It seems unlikely, however, that terms generally in voyage charterparties will be regarded as conditions. We have seen that the seaworthiness obligation is not a condition but an innominate term, partly because the consequences of a breach can range from the very trivial to the very serious.[13] However, if the seaworthiness obligation is not a condition then that must surely also be true of many lesser descriptive terms. Indeed, in many charterparties (especially in time charters) they are described as warranties (though it is hard to see why a really serious breach should not allow the charterer to repudiate, which would of course make them innominate terms).

We will see in chapter 6 that cancelling clauses do not give rise to contractual undertakings at all.[14]

5.5 Consecutive voyage charters

The consecutive voyage charterparty, even if expressed to be for a period of time, may be regarded as a species of voyage charter, and shares its fundamental features. There will be freight, laytime and demurrage provisions, and the risk of delay will be on the owners.

The difference is simply that a consecutive voyage charterparty covers a number of voyages. Its duration can be defined either as a fixed number of voyages, or the maximum number of voyages that can be fitted into a period of time. The same voyage may be repeated, or the charterer may be able to choose between different voyages.

There is, at any rate in theory, no reason why ordinary voyage terms cannot be used, without amendment, in a consecutive voyage charterparty. Indeed, the earliest voyage charterparties simply contained a provision that the voyage be repeated times. This is by no means ideal, however, especially for longer duration charters. It also does no more than provide for a shuttle service, with the same voyage being repeated the stipulated number of times. Today there are better suited, and more flexible, forms of agreement.

Sometimes the number of voyages is fixed by reference to a period of time, as for example in *Suisse Atlantique Societe d'Armament Maritime SA v NV Rotterdamshe Kolen Centrale*.[15] This would almost invariably be the form where the charterer could choose from a wide range of voyages. Were the duration to be

---

10 See sections [6.4]–[6.6].

11 BS & N Ltd (BVI) v Micado Shipping Ltd (Malta) (The Seaflower) [2001] 1 Lloyd's Rep 341, in section [2.6.2].

12 Cosmos Bulk Transport Inc v China National Foreign Trade Transportation Corp (The Apollonius) [1978] 1 Lloyd's Rep 53, also a time term but voyage charters also contain vague undertakings. Actually the classification of the term was not an issue in the case, since only damages were claimed.

13 See section [2.6.1].

14 See section [6.2].

15 [1967] 1 AC 361, and see section [5.6].

defined simply in terms of a number of voyages, then if the market fell the charterer could get out of the charter early by opting only for very short voyages.

Despite reference to a period of time, the consecutive voyage charter is fundamentally different from a time charterparty proper. The freight payable will depend on the number of loaded voyages actually made. In a time charterparty the hire depends only on the period for which the vessel is hired, and is quite independent of the number of voyages. Hence, as in a single voyage charterparty, it is the shipowner in a consecutive voyage charter, not the charterer, who bears the risk of delay, whereas it is the charterer with a time charterparty.

Thus, laytime and demurrage provisions are as important in this type of charter as in a charterparty for a single voyage. Indeed, *Suisse Atlantique* is an important authority on demurrage, and is discussed fully in the demurrage chapter.[16]

5.6 Terms common to the consecutive voyage charterparty

With the simplest consecutive voyage charterparties, which simply contains a provision that the voyage be repeated . . . times, the charterer does not get a choice of voyages, but is only entitled to repeat the same voyage the agreed number of times. Even with a shuttle service, which this provides, and even if the number of voyages agreed is small, other terms are desirable, in addition to the simple stipulation that the voyage be repeated . . . times. In particular, the cancelling clause should apply only to the first voyage, as the shipowner obviously cannot guarantee when the vessel will be ready to load on subsequent voyages (because delays may be caused by the charterer).

Nevertheless, for shuttle services it is quite common for the parties simply to adapt a standard form single voyage charterparty. This could be a one-off addition, as in *The Nema*.[17] A standard form of charterparty, C (Ore) 7, was adapted to provide a shuttle service during 1979 between Sorel (on the St Lawrence River) and Calais or Hartlepool at charterers' option, the charter to remain in force for six voyages, or at charterers' option, 7. The cancelling clause was adapted to apply to the first charterparty only, except that the charterers also had an option to cancel any voyages where the vessel had not been presented at loading port by 5 December 1979 (because of likely ice difficulties at Sorel). Maximum and minimum intervals between voyages were stipulated (at 30 and 50 days), but otherwise the standard voyage charterparty was not significantly adapted.[18]

In neither *The Nema* nor in *Suisse Atlantique* did the charterer have any significant choice as to where the vessel was to go. The same voyage was simply repeated, although the charterer in *The Nema* had a choice of two ports at the European end of each voyage. If it is envisaged that the charterer should be able to choose from a wide range of voyages, then somewhat more complex forms are required, preferably a form drafted for this specific purpose.

Standard form consecutive voyage charterparties are occasionally encountered in the tanker trade, and there are essentially two types. The major oil company standard forms (eg, Shellconsec) are intended to be used on their own, but Intertanko's Interconsec 76 adopts a different approach.[19]

---

16 Section [9.8].

17 *Pioneer Shipping Ltd v B.T.P.Tioxide Ltd (The Nema (No. 2))* [1982] AC 724.

18 The charterparty in *The Nema* was later varied, but the variation is irrelevant to the present discussion.

19 Linked from https://www.bimco.org/Chartering/Clauses_and_Documents/Documents/Voyage_Charter_Parties/ INTERCONSEC_76.aspx.

Interconsec 76 is not intended to be used on its own. Each individual voyage is governed by its own standard form voyage charterparty, and Interconsec merely provides the additional terms appropriate to a series of voyages. It has been drafted for use with Intertankvoy 76, but could easily be adapted for use with any other standard tanker voyage charter, and possibly even for dry cargoes. It therefore contains all the terms that are desirable in a consecutive voyage charter, but that are not required in charterparties for a single voyage.

The parties can agree either on a number of consecutive voyages, or for the maximum number that the vessel can load within a stipulated period. The latter is more suitable if the charterer can choose between a number of voyages of differing lengths. Also, the cancelling date is stated to refer to the first voyage only, because from then on delays are more likely to be caused by the charterer (on loading and discharge) than by the shipowner.

Freight is paid only on loaded voyages, of course, and so if the charterers have a choice of voyages, it is important to the shipowner that a reasonable proportion are loaded. Under Interconsec the charterers undertake that at least half the total distance will be loaded, excluding the initial approach voyage (over which they have no control), but including the voyage from final port of discharge back to first port of loading.

If it is not envisaged that the consecutive voyage charter will remain in force for long, no further terms may be necessary. Where a long charter is envisaged, however, some clauses more commonly to be found in time charterparties may become appropriate. For example, although each voyage in Interconsec is governed by the war clause in the individual voyage charterparty, there is an additional war clause, which is effectively the same as those found in time charters.[20]

Also, just as it is important for owners to be able to get out of time charterparties if the charterer cannot or will not pay, it is more important to guard against late (or non-) payment of freight with a consecutive voyage charter than with a charterparty for a single voyage. So again to use Interconsec as an example, for non-payment of freight there is a provision similar to a withdrawal clause in a time charterparty.[21] This gives the owners the right to cancel remaining voyages under the charter, if freight due has not been paid and 96 hours have elapsed after notice has been given to the charterers. This is just like a time charter withdrawal and anti-technicality clause.[22]

To protect them against the possible bankruptcy of the charterers, the owners are also entitled under Interconsec to refuse to load for a new voyage if freight is still due, and to count any time lost thereby as part of the laytime. Interconsec also provides for the payment of interest on late payments of freight at an agreed rate. These clauses are also akin to those found in some standard time forms, but are not to be found in single voyage forms.

5.7 Contracts of affreightment

A contract of affreightment (COA) is also related to a voyage charter, but is a contract to lift a specified tonnage of cargo over a period, and is often referred to as a tonnage contract. It envisages a number of voyages, and allows substitution of vessels. This contrasts with normal charterparties, whether in time or voyage form, where though charterers can usually sublet the vessel, the owner's performance is personal, and he cannot substitute another vessel.

---

20 On which see further section [13.10].
21 On time charter withdrawal clauses see section [12.1.2].
22 On which see further sections [11.2.1] and [11.2.4].

5.8 Question

Suppose a FIOST charter, under which charterers undertake stowage, and shipowners do not.[23] A bill of lading is issued, incorporating the terms of the charterparty, and under which the shipowners are the contracting carriers. The goods are damaged during stowage. The holders of the bill of lading (who are not the charterers) wish to sue in contract. Who do they sue?

Comment

Quite possibly they have no contract action against anybody. They cannot sue the charterers because they have no contract with them. They cannot sue the shipowners because the shipowners are not responsible for stowage.

You really need also to look at other chapters, chapter 15 on incorporation of charterparty terms into bills of lading,[24] and chapter 17 on the identity of the contracting carrier.[25] If, as is almost certain to be the case, the Hague or Hague-Visby Rules apply to the bill of lading, you also need to look at chapter 18.[26] However, the problem originates from the FIOST provision considered in this chapter.

There is a slightly more detailed question on a similar clause at the end of chapter 18.

---

23 See section [5.3].
24 Section [15.2].
25 Section [17.1].
26 Esp section [18.4].

Chapter 6

The approach voyage and the voyage

Chapter Contents

6.1 Approach voyage: introduction

The approach voyage covers the period from the time the charterparty is made until the vessel arrives at the port of loading. It would obviously be very unusual for the vessel already to be at the port of loading when the charterparty is made.

The time of arrival of the vessel for loading is obviously of great importance to the charterer, but it is not something that the shipowners can necessarily guarantee with any precision. As Devlin J observed at the start of his judgment in The North Anglia:[1]

> "A charterer manifestly wants, if he can get it, a fixed date for the arrival of the ship at the port of loading. He has to make arrangements to bring down the cargo and to have it ready to load when the ship arrives, and he wants to know, as near as he can, what that date is going to be. On the other hand, it is to the interest of the shipowner, if he can have it, to have the date as flexible as possible. Because of the inevitable delays due to bad weather or other circumstances that there might be in the course of a voyage, he can never be sure that he can arrive at a port on a fixed and certain day."

Where (as must be common, and as in The North Anglia itself) the vessel is engaged on a previous fixture, Devlin J might have added that quite apart from potential delays on the voyage itself, there are the (probably far greater) uncertainties as to the time taken to discharge (and in The North Anglia load) the cargo under the previous fixture. In reality, the best the shipowner can do is to give an estimate, and to proceed with reasonable despatch. He will not normally undertake to arrive by a certain date.

As a consequence, there are a number of intertwined obligations dealing with the approach voyage. It is universal to include in a voyage charterparty an expected readiness to load date,[2] and (in any type of charterparty) a cancelling date. Under the cancelling clause, the owner does not promise to arrive by the cancelling date, but the clause gives the charterers the right to cancel (and nothing else), should the vessel not have arrived by then. The owners also typically make statements about the present position of the vessel, and/or estimated time of arrival (ETA), and/or when she is expected ready to load. None of these are to be construed as contractual promises to arrive at any particular time, but at least the owner promises that the statement or statements are true when made, in the sense that the estimated times are genuinely and reasonably held. These statements and terms must be express; they will not be implied by the courts.

Because the shipowners cannot guarantee the arrival time, the cancelling date will be later than the expected readiness date. It is really a long-stop provision only, triggered some time after the vessel would normally be expected to arrive.

Additionally to any of this, and whether it is in the charterparty or not, the owner undertakes to proceed to the loading port with reasonable despatch.[3] This obligation is implied into the charterparty.

As we have seen, the obligation to proceed with reasonable dispatch is common to all carriage contracts,[4] and so we will deal here only with that aspect of it that relates to the approach voyage. Cancelling clauses can also be found in time and demise charterparties, and the principles here also apply there.[5]

---

1 *Evera SA Comercial v North Shipping Co Ltd* (*The North Anglia*) [1956] 2 Lloyd's Rep 367. See further section [6.6].
2 Or something similar, such as ETA (estimated time of arrival).
3 Or "reasonable dispatch". Both spellings are used – indiscriminately as far as I can tell.
4 See section [5.4].
5 See section [11.2].

6.2 Cancelling clause

The cancelling clause is pretty well universal to be included in any charterparty. This gives the charterer the option of terminating the charterparty if the vessel is not actually ready to load before the cancelling date. That is all it does. The shipowner is not in breach of charter, still less a breach of condition, merely by missing the cancelling date. In *Smith v Dart & Son* A.L. Smith J observed that:[6]

> "The shipowner does not contract to get there by a certain day, but says: 'If I do not get there you may cancel'."

Because there is no breach there are of course no damages:[7]

> "The mere fact that [the voyage charterers] lawfully exercised their option to cancel the charter-party did not entitle them to claim damages."

The right to cancel under the voyage clauses depends on the vessel not being ready to load by the cancelling date. This is the same test as for notice of readiness considered in the laytime chapter.[8] In *Smith v Dart* itself, that meant that the vessel had to have been granted *free pratique*, and to be in all respects ready to load, prior to the cancelling date.

Just as with time charter cancelling clauses considered in chapter 11,[9] and again because not to arrive by the cancelling date is not a breach of charter, there is no anticipatory right to cancel. The cancelling date must pass, before the charterers can invoke the clause – otherwise they are them-selves in repudiatory breach of charter.

Because the cancelling clause is triggered simply by the non-arrival of the vessel, and does not depend on the owner's conduct, it follows that it overrides other stipulations in the charterparty, so that, for example, it applies even if the delay on the approach voyage was caused by an excepted peril, or for some other reason for which the owner is not responsible under the terms of the charterparty. If the owner is to have the benefit of exceptions they must therefore be expressly included in the cancelling clause itself. This is sometimes done. For example, delays due to ice and war risks extend the cancelling time under cl. 6 of Tankervoy 87.

Because failure to arrive by the cancelling date is not a breach of contract by the shipowner, still less a breach enabling the charterer to repudiate, it follows that there is no anticipatory breach doctrine, so the charterer cannot cancel early, even if it is clear that the shipowner will not arrive in time (unless the shipowner has committed an independent breach, as in *The Mihalis Angelos*).[10] It further follows that if the charterer does purport to cancel early, that itself amounts to a repudiatory breach of the charterparty. On the principles discussed in chapter 2, however, if the owner elects to keep the contract alive, as in *The Simona*, all its terms continue to operate, including the cancelling clause.[11] Once the cancelling date arrives the charterer will therefore have a fresh entitlement to cancel, unless of course the ship has arrived by then. In *The Simona*, the charterers purported to cancel

---

6 *Smith v Dart & Son* (1884) 14 QBD 105, 110, cited in *Marbienes Compania Naviera SA v Ferrostaal AG (The Democritos)* [1976] 2 Lloyd's Rep 149 (on which see further section [11.2]).

7 *Geogas SA v Trammo Gas Ltd (The Baleares)* [1993] 1 Lloyd's Rep 215, 229 (Steyn LJ).

8 See section [8.6].

9 Section [11.2].

10 See section [6.3]. (Lord Denning MR alone took a different view of the cancelling clause in *The Mihalis Angelos*.)

11 See section [2.6.3]; also [11.2] (on *The Simona*).

before the cancelling date but the owners elected not to treat this breach as bringing the contract to an end. Lord Ackner said:[12]

> "It is common ground that the action of the charterers in giving the notice purporting to cancel the contract was premature. It constituted an anticipatory breach and repudiation of the charterparty, because the right of cancellation could not be validly exercised until the arrival of the cancellation date, some seven days hence. It is equally common ground that this repudiation was not accepted by the owners."

The consequence (of the non-acceptance) was that the contract terms, including the cancelling date, survived, and the charterers could cancel perfectly validly, when the vessel was still not ready to load by that date.[13] Of course, the position would have been quite different had the owners elected, as they were entitled, to treat the original (early) purported cancellation as bringing the contract to an end.[14]

The cancelling date will be stipulated (as with the expected readiness date below, usually in Part I where the standard form is divided into two parts), and will be some time after the expected readiness date. Thus the cancelling clause only operates where the shipowner is late by a margin.

The operation of the cancelling clause is usually hedged about with restrictions, charterers not being given an unfettered freedom to cancel on the stipulated date, unless the vessel is ready to load by then. Shipowners need protection against a wasted voyage. If the charterer does not exercise his option to cancel until the approach voyage (which is usually in ballast) is almost complete, the shipowner's bargaining power will be very weak should the charterer attempt to renegotiate freight rates. If the shipowner refuses, the charterer simply cancels the charter, and the approach voyage will probably be wasted so far as the shipowner is concerned. To guard against this, the standard forms typically require the charterer to declare some time in advance whether or not he intends to exercise his option to cancel, a new cancelling date being substituted if the option to cancel is not exercised. The position is similar with the time charter forms, and there is quite a bit of difference between tanker and dry-cargo forms, the tanker forms (as usual) having a significantly greater pro-charterer bias.

6.3 Expected readiness to load

Even if the charterer cannot use the cancelling clause, another right to throw up the charter may arise from the expected readiness clause. Often the general readiness clause will be included as part of the general description of the vessel. Anyway, voyage charterparties invariably state when the vessel is "expected ready to load".

By contrast with the cancelling clause, the right to repudiate is untrammelled, but the expected readiness clause operates in a very different way from the cancelling clause. We saw how, in *The North Anglia*, Devlin J explained why shipowners were reluctant to guarantee arrival dates, and there are similar comments by Greer LJ in *Monroe Bros Ltd v Ryan*.[15] These comments were used to explain why the expected readiness to load clause came into being instead.

Thus, whether the charterer can use the cancelling clause depends on whether the vessel is actually ready to load by the cancelling date. By contrast, Lord Sterndale MR held in *Samuel Sanday & Co v Keighley, Maxted & Co* that whether there is a breach of the expected readiness condition:[16]

---

12 *Fercometal SARL v Mediterranean Shipping Co SA (The Simona)* [1989] AC 788, 796: see also section [2.6.3].
13 Readiness to load appears to have the same meaning here as for voyage charterparties: see section [8.6].
14 The report does not state why the owners elected to keep the charterparty alive.
15 [1935] 2 KB 28, 36.
16 (1922) 10 Ll L Rep 738, 740.

" . . . is to be interpreted as meaning that in view of the facts, as known to the seller at the time of his making the contract and making the statement 'expected ready to load,' the expectation was one which was made . . . honestly and upon reasonable grounds".

In other words, the test is the shipowner's state of mind at the time he made the statement, and is unaffected by what happens later. It is immaterial when the vessel actually becomes ready to load. Thus, even if the vessel is able to load by the expected readiness date, the shipowner will still be in breach if he could not reasonably have expected to be ready by that date when the charterparty was made. Conversely, however late the vessel actually arrives, there will be no breach of this condition so long as the shipowner reasonably expected to be able to meet the date when he entered into the contract. This is all subject to the qualification, however, that there is an inter-relationship between the expected readiness date and the obligation to make reasonable despatch.[17]

We saw in chapter 2 that the expected readiness to load date is a condition of the charterparty, so that the slightest breach allows the charterer to repudiate the charterparty, for any reason.[18] (Of course, it is also a breach of contract, giving rise to a claim for damages as well, should there be any loss.) The Mihalis Angelos concerned a voyage charterparty to carry a cargo of apatite (mineral ore), from Haiphong in North Vietnam to a North European port.[19] It was dated 25 May 1965, and the vessel was described as "expected ready to load . . . about July 1, 1965", although on 25 May the vessel was on a laden voyage under a previous fixture, and the shipowner could not have reasonably expected to be ready to load at Haiphong by about 1 July. The cancelling date (from a Gencon form) was 20 July 1965.

By 17 July the vessel had still not arrived, but the charterers were in any case having difficulty obtaining a cargo of apatite due, they thought, to American bombing of the railway line to the port. They therefore cancelled the charter on the (incorrect) ground of force majeure. (Note that they did not purport to cancel under the cancelling clause, and in any event the cancelling date had not yet passed.)

One of the questions for decision by the Court of Appeal was whether the charterers were justified in throwing up the charter on the 17th. The court unanimously held that they were, on the ground that the shipowner had breached the expected readiness clause. The charterers could rely on this breach of condition even though earlier they had advanced a different reason (force majeure). Whether an innocent party is entitled to repudiate a contract depends solely on whether the guilty party had committed a breach that entitles him to repudiate.[20] What the innocent party gave as his reason at the time of the repudiation is entirely irrelevant.

The Mihalis Angelos is a demonstration of the charterer's right to repudiate the charter independently of the cancelling clause. There may be other possibilities as well. For example, the shipowner must proceed with reasonable despatch on the approach voyage, and if in breach of this obligation he proceeds so slowly as to frustrate the commercial nature of the adventure, that also should allow the charterer to repudiate.[21]

There was another issue in The Mihalis Angelos. The decision was only a few years after Hongkong Fir, and it may be that the Court of Appeal were not fully confident that their condition reasoning would survive an appeal. So they also considered the position, were they wrong on the condition issue, in other words on the assumption that the charterers had wrongfully repudiated. Even on

---

17 Considered below in section [6.6].

18 Section [2.6.2]. Often the motivation will be a falling market, but in The Mihalis Angelos itself the charterers had no cargo, the railway lines to the loading port having been bombed during the Vietnam war.

19 Maredelanto Compania Naviera SA v Bergbau-Handel GmbH (The Mihalis Angelos) [1971] 1 QB 164.

20 The principles are discussed at section [2.6].

21 See section [6.6]. Note that the obligation to proceed with reasonable despatch is not a condition.

this assumption the shipowners were entitled to no damages; the charterers would certainly have cancelled, once the cancelling date arrived, and the owners had therefore suffered no loss. There are some difficulties with this reasoning, because had the owners validly repudiated, it is surely at least arguable that the cancelling clause would no longer be effective.[22] However, this aspect of *The Mihalis Angelos* has been extended, applying what was described as "the compensatory principle", in *The Golden Victory*, which we examine in chapter 11.[23] We can assume, therefore, that this alternative reasoning in *The Mihalis Angelos* is good law.

6.4 ETA

ETA (expected time of arrival) clauses are not universal. They are more commonly found in the tanker than dry-cargo standard forms (an example being BPVOY4, cl. 4), and are sometimes added by the parties.

In *The Myrtos*, Leggatt J took the view that an ETA clause was analogous to an expected readiness to load clause, except in so far that the time at which a vessel arrives is usually before the time at which she is ready to load.[24] He treated the two clauses as being otherwise essentially the same. The shipowners were required to nominate the vessel 20 days prior to the ETA, and as far as can be ascertained from the report, when *Myrtos* was nominated she was still engaged under another charterparty. Consequently she sailed late and arrived well over 20 days after nomination. The charterers successfully claimed damages (although the report does not make clear what loss they had suffered).

Like the expected readiness clause, an ETA clause looks to the reasonableness of the owner's estimate at the time when it was given, rather than at subsequent events. If the vessel arrives late, for unexpected reasons, the shipowner is not in breach of an ETA clause. Though the issue did not arise in *The Myrtos* (because the charterers claimed only damages), the logic of treating ETA as analogous to expected readiness to load is that if the shipowner gives the charterer an ETA that he does not believe honestly and on reasonable grounds, he commits a breach of condition entitling the charterer to repudiate, even if the vessel arrives before the cancelling date.

The actual issue in *The Myrtos* was whether the shipowners had also failed to proceed to the loading port with reasonable despatch. This was tied into the ETA, just as in *The North Anglia* it was tied into the expected readiness date. We therefore return to the case in the discussion of reasonable despatch.[25]

6.5 Present position and other clauses

Some charterparties also give the present position of the vessel. In the old case of *Behn v Burness*,[26] the charterer was held entitled to repudiate because the vessel was stated to be "now in the port of Amsterdam", when in fact she was 62 miles away from there, and it is usually assumed therefore that the position of the vessel at the date of the charterparty is a condition. In *Bentsen v Taylor, Sons & Co*, the Court of Appeal held though that an incorrect statement that the vessel was about to sail from a particular port could give the charterer the right to repudiate.[27]

---

22 Reasoning similar to that in *Gill & Duffus SA v Berger & Co Inc* [1984] AC 382, in an international sale context.

23 See section [11.3.2].

24 *Mitsui OSK Lines Ltd v Garnac Grain Co Inc (The Myrtos)* [1984] 2 Lloyd's Rep 449. (We will see more on the definition of arrival in section [8.5].)

25 See section [6.6].

26 *Behn v Burness* (1863) 3 B & S 751.

27 [1893] 2 QB 274. In the event, the charterers were held to have waived their right to repudiate.

The reasoning in *Bentsen v Taylor* has superficial similarities with innominate terms in chapter 2.[28] But the test stated by Bowen LJ was what:[29]

> "the effect of a breach of such a condition would be on the substance and foundation of the adventure; not the effect of the breach which has in fact taken place, but the effect likely to be produced on the foundation of the adventure by any such breach of that portion of the contract".

This is not looking at the effect of the particular breach, as one would to decide whether a breach of an innominate term was a frustrating breach, but the likely effect of the breach of such a term in general. This is consistent with the test for a condition,[30] and with what Diplock LJ said in *Hongkong Fir*, where of a condition:[31]

> " . . . it can be predicated that every breach of such an undertaking must give rise to an event which will deprive the party not in default of substantially the whole benefit which it was intended that he should obtain from the contract . . .".

A statement that the vessel is in a particular place, or is about to sail from a particular port, is of this nature. However, it might depend on the circumstances, as Bowen LJ also said:[32]

> "Having regard to the time of the year at which it is intended to prosecute the voyage, delay in its commencement, if it is protracted beyond a certain point, may in many cases be so vital a matter as to render the voyage impossible, or the risk may be so much increased as to make it no longer possible to have a voyage of the same kind."

There is at least the possibility, therefore, that for a charterparty entered into at a different time of year the categorisation of the term might be different. But for any given charterparty, if the term is a condition, its breach will always give the option of repudiation, whatever the effect of the actual breach.

6.6 Reasonable despatch

There would be little point in requiring the shipowner to state an expected readiness date if he was not also under an obligation to proceed to the port of loading. However, whether or not expressly provided by the charterparty, there is an implied obligation that the shipowner will proceed with reasonable despatch.[33] This obligation applies both on the voyage itself, and on the approach voyage to the port of loading.

The obligation, as it applies to the approach voyage, was comprehensively discussed by Devlin J in *The North Anglia*.[34] It is to be interpreted in the light of the expected readiness date. Adopting earlier authority, and in particular *Monroe Bros Ltd v Ryan*,[35] a Court of Appeal decision by which he was of course bound, Devlin J thought that the obligation was that the vessel should start from wherever

---

28 See section [2.6].
29 [1893] 2 QB 274, 281.
30 Section [2.6.2].
31 [1962] 2 QB 26, 69 (Diplock LJ).
32 [1893] 2 QB 274, 282.
33 See section [4.4].
34 *Evera SA Comercial v North Shipping Co Ltd (The North Anglia)* [1956] 2 Lloyd's Rep 367.
35 [1935] 2 KB 28. Also *Louis Dreyfus & Co v Lauro* (1938) 60 Ll L Rep. 94 (Brandon J).

she may happen to be, at a date when, by proceeding with reasonable despatch, she will arrive at the port of loading by the expected date.[36] It is of course common (as indeed was the case in The North Anglia itself) for the vessel still to be engaged on a prior fixture when the charterparty is made, in which case she has obviously committed herself to complete that fixture before proceeding to the approach port. The formulation in The North Anglia allows the vessel to complete a prior fixture, or even to make a prior fixture, as long as she is able to set out for the loading port with sufficient time to arrive by the expected readiness date. If she does so, but is delayed by an unexpected occurrence on the approach voyage, the owner is protected. If, however, the vessel does not set out in time, the owners will be liable, whatever the reason for the delay in setting out. As Greer LJ observed in Monroe, charterparty exceptions apply to the charter voyage, and "[include] the period of time when she is steaming with all convenient speed to arrive at the loading port", but "do not apply to matters which may happen before the ship has entered upon the voyage [including the approach voyage] dealt with by the charterparty",[37] unless, of course, the charterparty explicitly makes provision for such a delay. As Devlin J said in North Anglia, "if a shipowner wants to make the beginning of one voyage contingent upon the conclusion of the one before, he must say so in clear terms".[38]

In The Myrtos, Leggatt J adopted the principles from The North Anglia to an ETA clause, the only difference between the clauses being the difference between arrival and readiness to load.

In North Anglia itself the obligation was to set out in sufficient time from the port of discharge under the previous fixture, but it has been observed that the test is not stated in such restrictive terms. In The Baleares, it was held that the obligation is to set out from wherever she may be, in time to reach the loading port at or around the expected readiness date.[39]

The obligation is not a condition. In Jackson v Union Marine Insurance Co Ltd,[40] the vessel was stranded on what amounted to the approach voyage, to commence another (transatlantic) voyage under a voyage charter. The vessel was required to proceed "with all possible dispatch", for breach of which obligation the sole remedy was accepted (in the Exchequer Chamber) to be damages.[41] However, the vessel would have taken so long to repair as to render the second voyage useless, and the issue was whether the charterers were entitled to repudiate, and charter in another vessel.[42] Bramwell B, in the majority, thought that there was a second implied condition, to arrive before the contemplated voyage was frustrated,[43] and that the charterers were entitled to repudiate for breach of this obligation. In Hongkong Fir, considered in detail in chapter 2, Diplock LJ thought that today, the Jackson obligation would be reanalysed as an innominate term:[44]

" . . . to take Bramwell B.'s example in *Jackson v Union Marine Insurance Co Ltd* itself, breach of an undertaking by a shipowner to sail with all possible dispatch to a named port does not necessarily relieve the charterer of further performance of his obligation under the charter-party, but if the breach is so prolonged that the contemplated voyage is frustrated it does have this effect."

---

36 [1956] 2 Lloyd's Rep 367, 372.

37 [1935] 2 KB 28, 38, citing the then current edition Carver, *Carriage of Goods by Sea*.

38 [1956] 2 Lloyd's Rep 367, 376. For an example of such a clause, see (eg) Tankervoy 87, cl. 3 (lines 125–6).

39 *Geogas SA v Trammo Gas Ltd (The Baleares)* [1993] 1 Lloyd's Rep 215, eg 226 (Niell LJ). It was important to determine when the obligation commenced in order to assess damages, since the market (for LPG) was rising continually over the relevant period.

40 (1874–5) LR 10 CP 125.

41 (1874–5) LR 10 CP 125, 143 (Bramwell B).

42 The issue arose in a marine insurance context, but that was nonetheless the issue.

43 (1874–5) LR 10 CP 125, 147. This part of the case was cited in support of his judgment by Diplock LJ in *Hongkong Fir* below, though Diplock LJ would have preferred to avoid having to resort to the second implied condition reasoning. It is not obvious how it can be avoided, however, given that there is no other breach.

44 [1962] 2 QB 26, 70. *Hongkong Fir* is discussed in depth in section [2.6.1].

Jackson itself went further, since, because it was subject to a perils of the seas exception, there was no breach at all of the obligation to proceed "with all possible dispatch". The implied condition was the only term broken, which allows the possibility of there being a self-standing implied condition that the vessel will arrive before the contemplated voyage is frustrated.

6.7 Question

Adam owns a coal carrier, *Smoker*, and charters it to Caroline for a voyage from Port C (Charterparty B). Adam gives an expected readiness date of 15 June, and the cancelling date is 1 July. The vessel is stated to be "about to sail from Port A".

When Adam and Caroline enter into Charterparty B, *Smoker* is in Port A, and is loading under an existing charterparty (Charterparty A) to Belinda, for a voyage to Port B. Five days after entering into Charterparty B, *Smoker* leaves Port A. She is delayed in Port B, so that by the time *Smoker* leaves Port B for her ballast voyage to Port C, there is no possibility of her reaching Port C by 15 June. Sometime after 15 June, but before 1 July, she has still not arrived. Caroline is anxious to get out of Charterparty B quickly, since she can secure an alternative vessel cheaply, but only if she is ready to load her cargo of coal almost immediately.

Advise the parties.

Comment

Caroline can safely cancel if Adam has committed a breach of condition; but has he? He may well have believed the expected readiness date when given, and nor is it entirely clear that he has broken a condition in respect of the "about to sail" statement. There may have been unexpected delays in leaving Port A, so that, again, the statement could be truthful when made.

If Caroline wrongfully repudiates, Adam should consider carefully whether to accept the repudiation as bringing the contract to an end. If he does not, and does not arrive by the 1st, he risks Caroline cancelling anyway, as in *The Simona*.[45]

There may also be a breach of the obligation to proceed with reasonable despatch, in leaving Port B too late, but while that may entitle Caroline to damages, it is not a breach of condition, and will not necessarily allow her to repudiate the charterparty.[46]

---

45 [1989] AC 788, in section [6.2].
46 Have another look generally at section [6.6].

Chapter 7

Freight

7.1 Introduction

For reasons that seem mostly to be historical, special principles apply to freight payments, in particular the rules as to set-off where there is damage to, or short delivery of, the goods.[1] It is difficult to justify the special treatment given to freight, in anything other than historical terms.[2]

The carrier has a common law lien on the goods for freight. Consequently if, for example, a voyage charterer ships his own goods and sells them on, the purchaser (or if there are further sales the eventual receiver) will be unable to obtain the goods until freight is paid. In principle, the voyage charterer remains contractually liable for the freight, a liability that would be more than academic, were the goods to be worth less than the freight, leading to their abandonment by the receiver.[3] In the nineteenth century (though much less commonly today) it was common for charterparties to include cesser clauses, requiring the shipowner to proceed against the receiver rather than the charterer (or to be more accurate, preventing him from proceeding against the charterer). This made sense, particularly if under the sale contract, the purchasers were required to pay the freight.[4]

7.2 Delivered freight

Were a charterparty (or bill of lading) to contain no provision to the contrary, at common law freight would be earned and payable on delivery, and would be calculated on the basis of the amount of cargo actually delivered. In practice the charterparty always stipulates for freight, and both the time at which it becomes payable and the basis of calculation may be varied. Freight earned and payable on delivery remains common, especially in the tanker trade, though advance freight is more common for dry-cargo, and even for tankers, it is more often calculated on the intaken (ie, loaded), rather than delivered, quantity of cargo.[5]

If freight is earned on delivery, then as long as the goods arrive, it is payable whether or not they arrive damaged. In *Dakin v Oxley*,[6] freight was earned and payable on delivery. Because of the negligence of the master, a cargo of coal deteriorated so much that when it arrived it was worth less than the freight, and the charterer therefore abandoned it to the shipowner. In the Court of Common Pleas Willes CJ held that the charterer was liable for the freight in spite of the damage:[7]

> "The true test of the right to freight is the question whether the service in respect of which the freight was contracted to be paid has been substantially performed; and, according to the law of England, as a rule, freight is earned by the carriage and arrival of the goods ready to be delivered to the merchant, though they be in a damaged condition when they arrive."

To obtain compensation for the loss he should have sued for damages in a cross-action. This need not be a problem, unless the shipowner's financial position is doubtful, or where (as in *Dakin*) the cargo's worth (and hence the damages) would be less than the freight, or where the limitation period is longer for the freight claim than for the cross-action.[8]

---

1 See section [7.6].

2 See section [7.6], and in particular comments made in *Aries Tanker Corp v Total Transport Ltd (The Aries)* [1977] 1 WLR 185.

3 As in (eg) *Sewell v Burdick* (1884) 10 App Cas 74, a case discussed in sections [16.3] and [16.7].

4 See further section [7.9].

5 See section [7.5].

6 (1864) 15 CB (NS) 646.

7 (1864) 15 CB (NS) 646, 665, cited in *Kish (JE) v Charles Taylor & Sons* [1912] AC 604, 616.

8 See section [7.6].

Dakin v Oxley was upheld by the Court of Appeal in *The Brede*,[9] where the issues were whether the charterers could set-off damages against freight, and the nature of the time bar in the Hague Rules. *The Brede* was upheld by the House of Lords in *The Aries*,[10] where the issues were essentially the same.[11]

If freight is earned on delivery, this of course depends on the goods arriving, at the contractual destination port. In *Hopper v Burness*,[12] the ship, which was bound for Point de Galle (Sri Lanka) from Cardiff, was damaged by heavy weather and forced to put into the Cape of Good Hope, a port *en route*. In order to obtain funds to repair the ship the master justifiably sold part of the cargo (which actually fetched more than it would have, had the ship proceeded to Point de Galle). The Court of Common Pleas held that freight could not be claimed. A similar conclusion was reached in *St Enoch Shipping Co Ltd v Phosphate Mining Co*,[13] where a British ship, bound for Hamburg from Florida in the United States, was unable to discharge there because of the outbreak of the World War I. She diverted to Runcorn on the River Mersey. Rowlatt J held that the shipowners were not entitled to freight.

In both *Hopper v Burness* and *St Enoch Shipping* there was only one discharge port provided for in the charterparty. In *The Teutonia*,[14] which was distinguished in *St Enoch*, the consignees had a choice of discharge ports, and nominated Dunkirk (in France). Again because of the outbreak of war (this time the war between France and Germany which began in July 1870), the (German) ship could not proceed there, and the master went instead to the nearest alternative port named in the charterparty, which was Dover (in England). The charterparty provided for a freight rate, had the consignees nominated Dover as the discharge port, and the shipowners were held entitled to this freight. The charterparty having become impossible to perform, on its true construction the consignees were entitled to take delivery, and the shipowner to deliver, at the nearest neighbouring port.[15] In effect, in the circumstances that had arisen, Dover had become the contractual discharge port. The case differs from *St Enoch*, in that in the later case there was no alternative port.

In *Cargo ex Argos*,[16] petroleum was shipped from London to the discharge port of Le Havre, also in France, where during the same Anglo-Prussian war the port was full of munitions, making it impossible to discharge the cargo of petroleum. The master arrived at Le Havre, entered the port and did all he could to discharge the cargo, but was ultimately thwarted by the authorities. Eventually he returned to London, the port of loading where the cargo was discharged. The shipowners successfully claimed freight, Sir Montague Smith in the Privy Council observing that "what is a compliance with [the discharge] obligation must depend on and vary with the existing state of things in the port".[17] In both this case, and *The Teutonia*, the contract on its true construction, in the events that occurred, did not require the physical delivery of the goods to the nominated or provided discharge port, and in each case the shipowner had performed his contractual obligations.

---

9 *Henriksens Rederi A/S v THZ Rolimpex (The Brede)* [1974] QB 233.
10 *Aries Tanker Corp v Total Transport Ltd (The Aries)* [1977] 1 WLR 185.
11 See further section [7.6].
12 (1876) 1 CPD 137. See also *Hunter v Prinsep* (1808) 103 ER 818.
13 [1916] 2 KB 624.
14 *David Duncan v Daniel Augustus (The Teutonia)* (1871–3) LR 4 PC 171.
15 (1871–3) LR 4 PC 171, 182–183 (Mellish LJ).
16 *Gaudet v Brown (The Argos)* (1872) LR 5 PC 134.
17 (1872) LR 5 PC 134, 160.

In tanker charterparties, it is common for freight to be earned on delivery, but calculated on intaken quantity of cargo.[18] In such cases, if any of the cargo arrives, freight is payable on the entire cargo. This was the situation in *The Aries*, discussed more fully below.[19]

The condition precedent for payment of freight on *Dakin v Oxley* principles is that the goods arrive. What arrives must therefore remain in such a state as to be identifiable as the goods. If the cargo is so badly damaged that it cannot be regarded as the original goods at all, the charterer may have a defence to a claim for freight. In *Asfar & Co v Blundell*,[20] no freight was held payable where the goods that had arrived were so badly damaged that "the nature of the thing has been altered". Dates had sunk in the Thames, but were raised and delivered. Though they still retained the appearance of dates, and although they were of considerable value for the purpose of distillation into spirit, they were so impregnated with sewage and in such a condition of fermentation as to be no longer merchantable as dates. They were "simply a mass of pulpy matter impregnated with sewage and in a state of fermentation",[21] and were no longer fit for human consumption. The Court of Appeal held that no freight was payable.

Asfar was considered in *The Caspian Sea*,[22] where the charterers alleged that the cargo was "Bachaquero Crude" oil, whose "special value lies in the fact that it is free of paraffin and is therefore suitable for the production of lubricating oils of high quality and value",[23] had been contaminated by the residues of a previous cargo, which contained paraffin. Donaldson J, in the Commercial Court, proceeded on the assumption that the charterers' allegations were correct. Of course he was bound by *Asfar & Co v Blundell*, and did not share the doubts about the decision that had been expressed in the textbooks,[24] but he took the view that the test was *not* whether what was delivered was identical commercially with the cargo loaded, but whether it could still be described in the same terms. The issue was whether the cargo:[25]

> "could in commercial terms, bear a description which sensibly and accurately included the words 'Bachaquero Crude', eg 'Bachaquero Crude contaminated with paraffin or low sulphur oil residues'. The question is whether an honest merchant would be forced to qualify the description applicable to the goods on shipment to such an extent as to destroy it."

It was irrelevant that the cargo may not have been of merchantable quality (as the term is used in the sale of goods legislation).

The case was remitted to the arbitrators, and so the result was not reported. What is clear, however, is that *Asfar v Blundell* was narrowly construed, by a test that is more one of form rather than substance. There must also be some doubt about the correctness of *The Caspian Sea*, since the test in *Asfar v Blundell* fairly clearly was one of merchantable quality.[26] Moreover, Lord Esher MR (in the earlier case) had observed that "there had been no change in [the nature of the goods], and they still were dates", while Kay LJ agreed "that the substance of the dates still remained, and that they had not been changed into anything but dates in a peculiar condition".[27] This does not seem to be consistent with the test adopted in *The Caspian Sea*.

---

18 See section [7.5].

19 See section [7.6].

20 [1896] 1 QB 123. Freight was payable as a lumpsum on delivery. See section [7.3] for lumpsum freight.

21 [1896] 1 QB 123, 127 (Lord Esher MR). The case arose on an insurance policy, taken out by the charterers, on profits; this depended upon whether they received more for the bills of lading freight than they paid as chartered freight, the difference between the two being their profit. There was held to be a total loss of the subject matter of the insurance.

22 *Montedison SPA v Icroma SPA (The Caspian Sea)* [1980] 1 Lloyd's Rep 91.

23 [1980] 1 Lloyd's Rep 91, 93 (Donaldson J).

24 [1980] 1 Lloyd's Rep 91, 95, referring to the then edition of *Scrutton on Charterparties*, 18th ed (1974).

25 [1980] 1 Lloyd's Rep 91, 96.

26 [1896] 1 QB 123, 128 (Lord Esher MR); 129 (Lopes LJ).

27 [1896] 1 QB 123, respectively 127 (Lord Esher MR); 132 (Kay LJ).

7.3 Lumpsum freight, freight *pro rata itineris* and back freight

Lumpsum freight is occasionally (but rarely nowadays) chosen by the parties, in which case the freight payable does not depend on tonnage carried at all. The sum is fixed in advance, whatever weight of cargo the charterer loads, the shipowner usually guaranteeing a number of cubic metres for the use of the charterer. This is especially useful for mixed cargo charters, where the cargoes are of varying density.

The same principle applies to lumpsum freight as to freight calculated on intaken cargo: the whole lumpsum freight is payable, as long as any of the cargo is delivered. The House of Lords so held in *William Thomas & Sons v Harrowing Steamship Co*,[28] where the vessel was driven ashore near the discharge port (Port Talbot) and some, but not all, the cargo was recovered and deposited on dock premises. The shipowners were entitled to recover the entire lumpsum freight.

We know that where freight is payable on delivery, no freight is earned unless the goods are delivered at the agreed port of discharge.[29] If the charterer voluntarily accepts the goods at an intermediate port, however, a new contract between shipowner and charterer may be implied; the charterer will be required to pay not the full freight, but freight *pro rata itineris*, a proportion of the freight to compensate the shipowner for carrying the goods part way to the destination. This liability arises not under the original charterparty, but is a *quantum meruit* claim under the newly implied contract. Whether such a contract can be implied will depend on the particular facts, and requires *voluntary* acceptance of the goods by the charterers. It is not lightly inferred, and was not in either *Hopper v Burness* or *St Enoch*, where the charterers had no choice but to accept discharge of cargo in the intermediate port. This explanation by Brett J in *Hopper v Burness* was adopted by Rowlatt J in *St Enoch*:[30]

> ". . . such freight . . . is only payable when there is a mutual agreement between the charterer or shipper and the captain or shipowner, whereby the latter being able and willing to carry on the cargo to the port of destination, but the former desiring to have the goods delivered to him at some intermediate port, it is agreed that they shall be so delivered, and the law then implies a contract to pay freight *pro rata itineris*."

Perhaps unsurprisingly, successful claims for freight *pro rata itineris* seem to be very rare.[31]

A slightly different type of case, arising this time from implied authority in the charterparty, rather than a new implied contract, is the Privy Council in *Cargo ex Argos*.[32] As we know from the previous section, the vessel sailed from London and reached the port of discharge (Havre), but was prevented from discharging by the port authorities. Nor was it possible to discharge in neighbouring ports, so the master brought the goods back to England. The shipowner successfully claimed not only freight, but also compensation for bringing the cargo back to England. The court held that the master had an implied authority to deal with the cargo for the benefit of the shipper, and hence to save the goods if possible, rather than throw them overboard, as long as the expense involved in saving them was not greater than the value of the cargo. Bringing the cargo back to London was probably the cheapest method of saving it, so the shipper was liable to compensate the shipowner on the basis of this implied authority given to the master.

---

28 [1915] AC 58.
29 See section [7.2].
30 Respectively (1876) 1 CPD 137, 140 (Brett J); [1916] 2 KB 624, 627 (Rowlatt J).
31 In *Hopper v Burness*, *Baillie v Mogdigliani* 6 TR 421, n is cited; in *St Enoch Shipping Co Ltd v Phosphate Mining Co*, *O'Neill v Armstrong* [1895] 2 QB 70, affd 418 (CA).
32 (1872) LR 5 PC 134.

These cases demonstrate that the need to take account, not only of the formal freight position under the charterparty, but also of any implied authority the master may have, and any inference of voluntary acceptance by the charterer for the goods to be discharged elsewhere.

7.4 Advance freight

It was established as long ago as *De Silvale v Kendall* that if the contract of carriage stipulates that freight is to be paid in advance, once it is paid it cannot be recovered, even if ship and cargo are totally lost on the voyage, and no cargo at all delivered.[33] Advance freight is commonly stipulated in dry-cargo, but less commonly in tanker charterparties.[34]

The important point is when freight is earned. This may or may not be before it becomes payable. If freight has been earned, then it will be payable whatever happens afterwards; the freight payment is protected even if the vessel and/or cargo is lost on the voyage – the "freight risk" is on the charterer. It cannot, however, be recovered, if ship and cargo are later lost, whether or not it has been earned.

A clause providing for advance freight has to be clear and, in particular, the courts are reluctant to hold that freight is due in advance of payment, unless the charterparty clearly so states. For example, in *The Lorna I*,[35] the clause provided:

"Freight non returnable cargo and/or vessel lost or not lost"

but also

"to be paid . . . 75% . . . within 5 . . . days after Master signed Bills of Lading . . .".

The vessel sank, and all the cargo was lost, after bills of lading were signed but before five days had elapsed.

Had the clause provided that freight was earned on shipment, the shipowners would have been entitled to it, and had the charterers actually paid the freight before the vessel had sunk, they would have been unable to recover it.[36] Only if there had been a total failure of consideration would freight that had been paid be recoverable, on analogy with the total failure of consideration doctrine applicable in frustration cases considered in chapter 2.[37] This however was not the position in *The Lorna I*. No freight had been paid, and though the clause made clear when freight became *payable* (75 per cent within five days of signing bills of lading), it did not stipulate that it was *earned* at an earlier time (for example, on shipment). The Court of Appeal held that the shipowners were not entitled to claim any freight, and refused to imply a term "Freight to be earned on shipment". If the shipowners intend freight to be earned before it becomes payable, they must expressly stipulate to that effect.

---

33 (1815) 4 Maule and Selwyn 37.

34 See further section [7.5].

35 *Compania Naviera General SA v Kerametal Ltd (The Lorna I)* [1983] 1 Lloyd's Rep 373. Similarly *The Samos Glory* [1986] 2 Lloyd's Rep 603, where again there was no provision for freight to be earned on shipment.

36 [1983] 1 Lloyd's Rep 373, 376 (col 1) (O'Connor LJ). This was the effect of "freight non-returnable, cargo and/or vessel lost or not lost". The authority (cited by Dillon LJ at the same place) was the then-current edition of *Scrutton on Charterparties*, 18th ed (1974), 332.

37 Eg, Dillon LJ, ibid, citing *Fibrosa Spolka Akcyjna v Fairbairn Lawson Combe Barbour Ltd* [1943] AC 32. For frustration generally see section [2.12].

Conversely, the clause unambiguously stated that freight was deemed earned on shipment in the Court of Appeal decision in *The Karin Vatis*.[38] Although freight became payable only some time after loading, the Court of Appeal held, distinguishing *The Lorna I*, that the phrase "freight deemed earned as cargo loaded" put the charterers under an obligation for the entire freight payment as soon as the cargo was loaded. The owners were entitled to retain the freight that had already been paid, and to claim such as remained outstanding. Lloyd LJ also thought that "earned", "deemed earned" and "considered as earned" all meant the same, namely that the shipowners have done all that is required of them to earn their freight once the cargo has been loaded.

The same view was taken a year later by the House of Lords in *The Dominique*, where the charterparty provided that freight "shall be prepaid within five days of signing and surrender of final bills of lading, full freight deemed to be earned on signing bills of lading . . .". After the bills of lading had been signed, but before the lapse of five days, the vessel was arrested due to a repudiatory breach of charterparty by the shipowners, accepted by the charterers as bringing the charterparty to an end. Freight had, however, been earned before the repudiation, and remained payable, though the charterers had to tranship the cargo on to another vessel. *The Dominique* is discussed in detail below.[39]

7.5 The standard forms

Freight is normally payable in advance in dry cargo charters and on delivery in tanker charters. It may be payable on intaken quantity, bill of lading quantity or delivered quantity. There are no clear conventions. Exceptionally, lumpsum freight is payable.

Prepaid or advance freight is common with dry-cargo (but not tanker) charters, probably because the clause is clearly to the shipowner's advantage, and the shipowner's bargaining position tends generally to be stronger in dry-cargo (but not tanker) charters. Also, a lien can be enforced for unpaid freight, as long as freight has become earned prior to delivery – but a lien on a tanker cargo is in practice useless, because the shipowner has nowhere to store the cargo, and has to make delivery, freight paid or not.[40] Possible variations where freight is earned on delivery are payment concurrently with discharge (often in practice day by day on the out-turn), or after delivery (again day by day, but adjusted on final delivery). The latter is rarely agreed for dry cargoes, perhaps because the shipowner's lien is of no value once the goods have been delivered,[41] but it is commonly agreed for tankers, where the lien is of less value in any event.[42]

Freight is also frequently made payable in advance in bill of lading contracts. Here the shipowner is often in an even stronger bargaining position, and in addition purchasers of goods covered by the bill of lading may require a "freight prepaid" bill of lading, especially if the sale contract is on CIF terms.

By contrast, but under all the standard tanker forms, freight is payable at, or even after, delivery. The charterers are generally in a stronger bargaining position than their dry-cargo counterparts, and the shipowner's lien on cargo to secure payment of freight is of less value than with dry cargo. This is because whereas it is relatively easy for the shipowner to store (eg) grain in a warehouse, there are considerable difficulties in finding storage for tanker cargo once it has been discharged. None of the tanker standard forms stipulate prepayable freight, and a common stipulation is for payment after discharge. This would, of course, be inappropriate unless the shipowner were certain of the charterer's ability to pay, since he is, in effect, extending unsecured credit to the charterer. If the

---

38 *Vagres Compania Maritima SA v Nissho-Iwai American Corporation (The Karin Vatis)* [1988] 2 Lloyd's Rep 330.

39 Section [7.6].

40 See section [7.9] on liens.

41 See sections [7.5]; [7.9].

42 Eg. BPVOY 4, cl. 31.4 (immediately after completion of discharge).

charterer cannot pay, and the cargo has been sold on the voyage, the shipowner may be able theoretically to claim against the receiver of the cargo on the bill of lading contract (though the lien on the cargo cannot be enforced after delivery). Since the charterer is often a major oil company who can, of course, pay, this may not usually matter.

Indeed, from the point of view of an oil company charterer, an advantage of stipulating payment after discharge is precisely that it prevents the owner from exercising a lien against the cargo. A precursor to the modern Shellvoy forms, Shellvoy 3, went further, and cl. 30 (ii) actively prevented the owners from taking any proceedings on the bill of lading for the recovery of freight. Thus, the owners could not claim against any purchaser or receiver of the cargo. They were limited to claiming against the charterer, and the lien against cargo could not be used. A clause such as this enabled the charterer to sell CIF, without giving the purchaser any credit for freight, even if he was unwilling to pay freight in advance.[43] This would been acceptable to the purchaser, because he knew that the shipowner could not proceed against him, or any later purchasers, for the freight. The clause may also have been acceptable to the shipowner so long as Shell were the charterer: the charterer remains liable for freight (and demurrage) even if the cargo is sold on the voyage, and Shell are obviously solvent. However, the Shellvoy 3 clause was an unusual feature of that particular standard form, and has not been repeated in later revisions of Shellvoy.[44]

There are various ways in which the quantity of cargo (on which freight is payable) can be calculated. The common law basis is delivered cargo, but this is obviously impossible if the freight is made payable before delivery, and other possibilities are intaken cargo or the quantity stated in the bill of lading. Even if no cargo is lost on the voyage, the intaken quantity may exceed the out-turned quantity, especially if, for example, it is difficult to discharge the whole of a bulk cargo that is carried loosely in the holds. Another possibility is (eg) ice on timber at the loading port, which melts on the voyage. Arguably it is reasonable for freight to be paid on intaken quantity in this case, because the ice affects the tonnage the shipowner can load. With tankers some cargo loss is inevitable through evaporation, contamination, clingage or sedimentation, so that intaken quantity will always differ from out-turned quantity.[45] In tanker charters intaken rather than out-turned quantity is usually the basis of the freight calculation, even though freight is not normally made payable until delivery.

There ought (in theory) to be no difference between bill of lading weight and intaken quantity, but Gencon 94 and Tankervoy 87 use intaken quantity, rather than bill of lading quantity, as the basis of calculation. Shipowners might be wary of allowing bill of lading quantities to be taken as conclusive against them, especially as quantity stated in the bill of lading is usually measured by the shipper, rather than the carrier.[46] If freight were accepted on bill of lading quantities, it is at least arguable that the shipowner would be estopped from later denying the accuracy of the bill of lading quantity, in an action by a cargo-owner for short delivery. It will make a difference only if the claimant pays the freight in reliance on the bill of lading quantity (only likely if the receiver of the cargo pays freight on delivery), and there is no other basis for an estoppel.[47] Tankervoy favours shipowners too much for general acceptance in the oil market, however, and Shellvoy uses bill of lading quantity (unless there is a minimum quantity guaranteed by the charterers). BPVOY 4 also uses bill of lading quantity. The difference is probably explained by the relative bargaining strengths of the parties.

---

43 This is not really necessary. It was established as long ago as *Ireland v Livingston* (1872) LR 5 HL 395, that CIF contracts are possible, even where the receiver pays the freight, as long as credit is given for it.

44 See, eg, Per Gram, *Chartering Documents* (1981), LLP, 35. Many oil sales are on FOB terms in any case.

45 See further section [22.5].

46 See, eg, Per Gram, *Chartering Documents* (1981), LLP, 27.

47 On estoppels generally, see sections [19.4]; [19.5]; [19.8].

7.6 Setting off damages against freight

While the shipowner may, if vessel and/or cargo is lost, potentially be liable to the charterer in damages, it has been clear since at least *Dakin v Oxley* that the proper recourse is a cross-action. Charterers are not entitled to deduct damages from freight, and to do so can be very unwise, since it is likely that the one-year time bar in the Hague or Hague-Visby Rules will apply to the damages, but not to the freight claim.

In *The Brede*,[48] a cargo of rice was damaged by water entering the hold because of unseaworthiness. The charterers withheld about £2,500 from the balance of freight due after delivery, and after about two years the owners (in arbitration proceedings) claimed the full amount calculated on the delivered cargo, to which they were eventually held entitled by the Court of Appeal. The court followed *Dakin v Oxley*,[49] among other authorities: the charterers were not entitled to set up the damage as a defence, but should cross-claim in damages. However, by the time the shipowners pursued their claim for the balance of the freight, the charterers' cross-action was time-barred by the Hague Rules. The case thus highlights the dangers for charterers of withholding freight instead of pursuing a separate claim for damages. The common law limitation period of six years applied to the freight claim, but the Hague Rules time bar, which applied to the cross-claim, enforced a one-year limit. Had the charterers in *The Brede*, instead of withholding freight, sued for damages in a separate action, they may have succeeded, but instead they took a gamble on the shipowners not pursuing their claim for the disputed freight. As it was, by the time the arbitration proceedings were commenced two years had elapsed, and the charterers were by then time-barred under the Hague Rules.

The correctness of *The Brede* was unsuccessfully challenged three years later in *The Aries*,[50] where the earlier case was expressly upheld by the House of Lords. In *The Aries* a cargo of petroleum was short-delivered, and the charterers deducted the value of the shortfall from the freight (which, as is often the case with tanker charterparties, was payable on delivery, but on intaken quantity). The House of Lords held that the charterers were not entitled to withhold freight in respect of the cargo. As in *The Brede*, by the time the owners brought proceedings to recover it they were out of time to claim damages, because of the Hague Rules. The owners were therefore able to recover the balance of freight due but the charterers were too late to cross-claim in damages. Although Lord Salmon accepted that no justification for the rule had ever been defined (and indeed, other jurisdictions, and in particular the United States, adopt different principles, bringing freight into line with any other claim under the contract), he was reluctant to overturn "a rule of commercial law which has stood so long and upon the faith of which thousands of contracts have been made and are daily being made".[51] He thought that so well-known and long-standing a rule could now only be altered by Parliament, and not by the courts.

Even had the rule against deduction not been adopted, the charterers would still not have succeeded in *The Aries*, because of the view that was taken on the nature of the Hague Rules time bar. He observed that while most English statutes of limitation bar the remedy while leaving the claim itself in existence, this was not invariably true, and the effect of Art. III(6) of the Hague Rules was that the

---

48 *Henriksens Rederi A/S v THZ Rolimpex (The Brede)* [1974] 1 QB 233.
49 See section [7.2].
50 [1977] 1 WLR 185.
51 [1977] 1 WLR 185, 195. For other instances of where certainty is regarded as a matter of importance in contracts for the carriage of goods by sea, see (eg) section [8.5.1].

charterers' claim in that case (for short delivery) "had not merely become unenforceable by action, it had simply ceased to exist".[52] It would therefore have applied, even to a set-off.[53]

In neither The Brede not The Aries was it suggested that the shipowner's breach went to the root of the contract, but in The Dominique[54] the House of Lords reaffirmed the special protection given by English law to a shipowner's claim to freight under a voyage charterparty, and indeed extended it to a repudiatory breach of the charterparty, accepted by the charterers as bringing the contract to an end. The charterparty provided that freight was earned on signing of bills of lading, although it did not become payable until five days later. Bills of lading were signed and the vessel sailed, and so freight had therefore been earned, but before it was paid (or had become payable), The Dominique was arrested. The charterers treated the owners' conduct as a repudiation of the charterparty, and justifiably elected to terminate it, the cargo being transhipped on to another vessel. The House held that the shipowners were nonetheless entitled to their advance freight.

The case is little more than a reaffirmation of well-established principles applicable to advance freight. The charterers' main argument was that these principles did not apply to a *repudiatory* breach by the owners, accepted as such by the charterers, as bringing the charterparty to an end. It is true that the earlier cases were not concerned with repudiatory breaches by the owners, but Lord Brandon (who delivered the only substantive speech) saw no reason to distinguish between repudiatory and non-repudiatory breaches, and gave three reasons why they should not be treated differently:[55]

First, a repudiatory breach (for example, a deviation late on the voyage) need not cause as much loss as some non-repudiatory breaches (for example, a loss of part of the cargo).

Secondly, he observed that the charterers will not suffer significantly from the rule against deduction, as long as the owners' financial position is such that a counterclaim for damages can be enforced against them (but this is not necessarily so, as we have seen, since different time limits may apply to the counterclaim than to the freight claim).

Thirdly, the decision in The Dominique brought the effect of a repudiatory breach into line with that of frustration of the charterparty. It will be recalled from chapter 2 that if a contract is frustrated payments that have already become due remain payable, and payments that have been made can be recovered only on a total failure of consideration (which there will not be, at any rate once the voyage has started).[56] Lord Brandon observed,[57] that the Law Reform (Frustrated Contracts) Act 1943 was expressly stated not to apply to voyage charterparties,[58] and that:

> "The legislature must have had a reason for this exclusion and the only reason which it seems to me that it could have had is an unwillingness to create a situation in which, following the frustration of contracts of this kind, advance freight already due could, if paid, be recovered back in whole or in part, or, if not paid, cease to be payable in whole or in part. In other words the legislature was preserving, in the context of the premature termination of such contracts by frustration, the indefeasibility of an accrued right to advance freight. The attitude of the legislature in this respect seems to me to make it difficult to say that, when a voyage charterparty or other contract for the carriage of goods by sea is prematurely terminated by the owner's

---

52 [1977] 1 WLR 185, 188. In *Feest v South West Strategic Health Authority*, a case on the Athens Convention on the carriage of passengers, Lord Wilberforce's speech is described by His Honour Judge Havelock-Allan QC as the "zenith of expression of the English rule": [2014] 1 Lloyd's Rep Plus 25, [21], though in The Aries, Lord Salmon expressed some doubts (at 196). There is further discussion of the distinction in *Yew Bon Tew v Kenderaan Bas Mara* [1983] 1 AC 553.
53 See further chapter 18 on the Hague Rules.
54 *Bank of Boston Connecticut v European Grain and Shipping Ltd (The Dominique)* [1989] AC 1056.
55 [1989] AC 1056, the discussion beginning at 1107.
56 Section [2.12].
57 [1989] AC 1056, 1108–9, the quote being at 1109.
58 See section [2.12.2].

repudiation of it, the indefeasibility of an accrued right to advance freight should not be similarly preserved by applying the rule against deduction to the situation so created."

Lord Brandon's speech simply brings repudiation into line with frustration. The position is of course
different if a repudiatory breach occurs *before* freight is earned, and the charterers elect to bring the
charterparty to an end. The effect of such an election is to relieve each party of further performance
under the charterparty, and since freight has not yet been earned, the charterers are relieved of
their obligation to pay it. *The Dominique* is therefore limited to advance freight, where the repudiatory
breach occurs only after freight in earned.[59]

7.7 Cargo retention and similar clauses

When oil prices rapidly rose in the 1970s, first following the OPEC embargo in 1973 and later the
Iran–Iraq war five or so years later, cargo-owners and charterers were concerned to protect themselves against shortfalls of cargo. Having the stronger market power in this market, they began to
insist on the inclusion in tanker charterparties of out-turn loss or cargo-retention clauses. These
allow for the deduction of shortfall from freight, and to that extent reverse the effect of *The Aries*.[60]
They are intended really to guard against inefficient discharge of the cargo.

We know that the usual position in tanker charters is that freight is calculated on intaken
cargo,[61] and as a result of *The Aries* if there is a shortfall charterers cannot make any deduction from
freight to compensate them for this shortfall. Not only do the charterers have to pay the full freight,
but they cannot withhold the value of any cargo short delivered, being left to a separate damages
action against the shipowner.

The effect of out-turn loss and cargo retention clauses is to allow charterers to deduct from the
freight the *value* of the cargo short delivered (and not merely to deduct the *freight* that would have been
payable on it).[62] Yet although they are intended to achieve a similar result, the method by which they
do so is quite different.[63] Though it seems to be the cargo-retention clause that has found favour in
the standard forms,[64] of the two the out-turn loss clause is the easier to operate. It assumes an inevitable transportation loss, perhaps of 0.3 per cent or 0.5 per cent. Any loss of less than this amount
is assumed to be a transportation loss, which the charterer bears, but under the clause the charterer
is entitled to deduct from freight the *value* of any shortfall over and above the stipulated percentage,
because it is assumed not to be an inevitable transportation loss.[65]

The cargo retention clause is much more difficult to operate. It penalises the shipowner for
inefficient discharge, rather than making assumptions about how much of the shortfall is due to an
inevitable transportation loss, and is directed towards the amount of cargo retained on board, rather
than the amount discharged. It allows the charterer to deduct from intaken quantity freight the value
of any oil retained aboard the vessel that could have been discharged (the usual term is "pumpable",
but BPVOY 4, cl. 33, uses the term "liquid"). Operation of the cargo retention clauses requires accurate measurement of oil remaining on board (ROB quantity). This is likely to be more difficult than

---

59 There is quite a nice problem question (for which I do not take all the credit) in chapter 23.
60 See section [7.6].
61 See section [7.5].
62 Assuming it is properly triggered; it had not been in *The Protank Orinoco* [1997] 2 Lloyd's Rep 42, because no determination had
been properly made by an independent surveyor, as required to trigger the clause, and the charterers were not allowed to deduct
from freight the value of any cargo remaining on board after discharge.
63 Among the difficulties inherent in the use of such clauses is that there are practical difficulties in measuring with accuracy the
amount of cargo intaken or delivered, and hence the amount of any shortfall. See further section [22.5].
64 Eg, BPVOY4, cl. 33; Shellvoy 6, cl. 48.
65 On the interpretation of these clauses by the courts, see section [22.5].

measurement of oil discharged, since the quantities are likely to be small, lying at the bottom of large tanks. Even inspection of the cargo remaining on board can be difficult if an inert gas system is in operation. Unlike the out-turn loss clause, it can apply even where the delivered quantity exceeds that intaken, for example if the cargo becomes mixed with the residue of a previous cargo carried. Sometimes the use of out-turn and cargo retention clauses is combined in the same charterparty.

7.8 Deadfreight

Deadfreight is not in reality a freight payment at all, but is compensation to the shipowner for the charterer failing to load a full and complete cargo. Recall that freight almost always depends upon tonnage or volume of goods shipped or delivered. Consequently, in order to protect the shipowner's right to freight, it is usual for voyage charterers to undertake to load a "full and complete cargo". If the charterer breaches this undertaking, deadfreight becomes payable. This is not freight, but is in effect damages for breach of the undertaking. In the words of Lord Atkinson in *Kish v Taylor Sons & Co*:[66]

> ". . . dead freight is defined to be the compensation payable to be the compensation payable to the shipowner when the charterer has failed to ship a full cargo. [By contrast, freight] is the recompense which the shipowner is to receive for carrying the cargo to its port of discharge. The two things are wholly dissimilar in their nature, though, of course, the freight the shipowner would have earned if the charterers had fulfilled their contract will in most cases be a fair measure of the damages which he is entitled to recover."

This is only a starting point for the calculation of damages, since the ordinary principles of contractual damages apply to deadfreight. For example, the shipowner may be required to mitigate his loss by obtaining other cargo (as in *Kish v Taylor* itself). If he does so, his damages will be reduced by the amount of the extra freight so earned. If he does not, they will be reduced by the amount he ought reasonably to have earned.[67]

7.9 Lien and cesser

Shipowners have a common law lien on cargoes, to secure common law freight. Since the common law lien is enforceable against the cargo, it is not necessary to incorporate a lien clause, either into the charterparty or bill of lading.

At common law, freight is payable on delivery, on delivered quantity.[68] Where the common law position is departed from, for example where freight is payable in advance, or on intaken quantity, it is not so clear that the common law lien applies. Nor does the common law lien apply to other charges, such as deadfreight or demurrage. If shipowners wish to protect these payments by lien, then they must do so by a clause in the charterparty, also incorporated into any bills of lading issued.[69] Moreover, the Carriage of Goods by Sea Act 1992 must apply, for the bill of lading to bind receivers of cargo.[70]

Lien clauses are not universal in voyage charterparties, and are not seen in tanker charters. In practice a lien on an oil cargo would be useless, since there would be nowhere to store it; in any case,

---

66 [1912] AC 604, 613–4.
67 This is an application of the principles in section [2.9.2].
68 See section [7.2].
69 On incorporation, see section [15.2].
70 See generally section [15.7].

many tanker forms provide for freight to be paid after delivery, in which case the liability to pay does not arise until after the shipowner loses possession of the cargo.[71]

While cesser clauses were common in the nineteenth century, they are not found in any of the main standard forms today, and have been described as "that most esoteric of subjects".[72] They are rare, and infrequently give rise to litigation, perhaps because tanker charterers do not want them, and dry-cargo shipowners will not agree to them. Their effect is to relieve the charterer of liability once the cargo is shipped. For claims arising after shipment the shipowner must look to the receivers of the cargo, and not to the charterer. (Of course this is not something the shipowner wants, because whereas he chooses the charterer, he knows nothing of the solvency and reputation of the receiver.)

Here is a diagrammatic representation of a cesser clause. The shipowner is required to proceed against the receiver, this contractual relationship being on the basis of the principles in chapter 16.

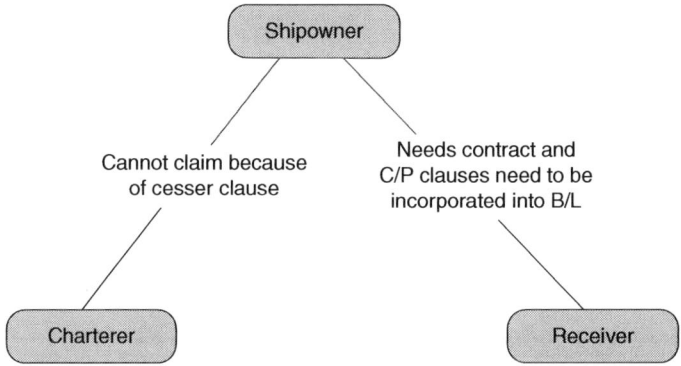

Though cesser clauses are rare today, their historic use probably influenced, and certainly explains, the development of some aspects of the law.[73]

The assumption is that the lien will operate to give the shipowner an effective remedy against the cargo owner. Indeed, the courts have interpreted cesser clauses as relieving charterers from liability only to the extent that the shipowner is protected, not only in theory but also in practice, by a lien against the receiver, unless the cesser clause is clearly expressed to the contrary. That lien and cesser clauses should be interpreted together in this way has been assumed since *Clink v Radford & Co*,[74] and in *The Aegis Britannic*[75] the Court of Appeal extended the principle to interpreting a cesser clause as inapplicable, where the receivers would not be liable in practice in Iraq, owing to local conditions. (This is perhaps why cesser clauses are not to be found in the standard tanker forms, since, as already observed, the lien is of little use for tanker cargoes.)

---

71 See further section [7.5].

72 *Marvigor Compania Naviera v Romanoexport State Co for Foreign Trade (The Corinthian Glory)* [1977] 2 Lloyd's Rep 280, 285 (Donaldson J), a case where the charterers were held to have waived their right to cesser.

73 See, eg, sections [15.2.1] and [16.2].

74 [1891] 1 QB 625.

75 *Action SA v Britannic Shipping Corporation Ltd (The Aegis Britannic)* [1987] 1 Lloyd's Rep 119, applying *The Sinoe* [1972] 1 Lloyd's Rep 201.

We saw earlier that Shellvoy 3 had an anti-cesser clause, requiring the shipowner to sue the charterer only for freight, and not the receiver. This was to facilitate charterers selling cargo on CIF terms, but it has no counterpart in any of the modern tanker forms.[76]

Liens on sub-freights raise entirely different issues, and are considered further in chapter 12.[77]

7.10 Questions

Question 7.1

Elizabeth has chartered an oil tanker for a voyage. Under the charterparty, which incorporates a one-year time bar for claims in respect of the goods, freight is payable on delivery, calculated on the intaken quantity of cargo. Elizabeth loads 40,000 tons of a cargo described as "Top quality lubricating oil, suitable for two-stroke motorcycles".

Advise Elizabeth as to whether she would be well advised to withhold payment of freight in the following ALTERNATIVE circumstances:

(i) The oil is contaminated by a previous cargo, so that although it is still suitable for tractors, it can no longer be described as "top quality", and would damage the engine of a two-stroke motorcycle;

(ii) Only 30,000 tons of oil arrives, the remainder having been lost due to the unseaworthiness of the vessel.

Comment

This question is of course about deductions from freight, and the second part is almost on all fours with *The Aries*.[78] For the first part, the cargo arrives (and so freight is payable) – or does it? What arrives is not "Top quality lubricating oil, suitable for two-stroke motorcycles". The facts are quite a long way removed from *Asfar & Co v Blundell*,[79] but you might think that the issue is how far the principles in that case extend. There is discussion in *The Caspian Sea*,[80] and you need to consider whether the test in that case is correct, and, if so, how it applies here. (Note that there is no decision as such in *The Caspian Sea* – the importance of the case lies in the test stated by Donaldson J.)

The next question is based, very loosely, on the IMLAM[81] moot in 2014. It raises quite a nice issue about what is meant by total failure of consideration, and also about provision for advance freight.

Question 7.2

The charterparty provides:

"Freight deemed earned in full, discountless and non-returnable, and 50% of minimum freight payable upon signing contract."

---

76 See section [7.5].
77 See section [12.1.8].
78 [1977] 1 WLR 185.
79 [1896] 1 QB 123.
80 [1980] 1 Lloyd's Rep 91.
81 International Maritime Law Arbitration.

Charterers pay 50 per cent of the freight, on signing the contract. The vessel needs to bunker for the voyage, proceeds to the bunkering port *en route* to the port of loading, and is destroyed by an explosion during the bunkering operation.

Charterers claim return of the 50 per cent freight paid, and owners claim the remaining 50 per cent freight.

Advise the parties.

Note:

Of course you will need to consider whether this is covered by *The Dominique*,[82] but you might also want to look at authorities on total failure of consideration, such as *Fibrosa Spolka Akcyjna v Fairbairn Lawson Combe Barbour Ltd* and *The Julia*.[83]

You might also consider whether the words of the clause really provide for advance freight, and will need to look at *The Lorna I* and *The Karin Vatis*.[84]

---

82 [1989] AC 1056.

83 Respectively [1943] AC 32; *Comptoir d'Achat et de Vente du Boerenbond Belge SA v Luis de Ridder Ltda (The Julia)* [1949] AC 593, both in section
    [2.12].

84 Respectively [1983] 1 Lloyd's Rep 373; [1988] 2 Lloyd's Rep 330, in section [7.4].

Chapter 8

Loading and discharge (1): introduction and laytime

Chapter Contents

8.1 Time for loading and discharge: an overview

You know that in a voyage charter the freight paid does not depend on the length of time the voyage takes, and so, in the absence of contrary terms, the risk of delay is on the shipowner.[1] But time taken for loading and discharge are to a large extent within the control of the charterer, directly perhaps if he is responsible for loading or discharge, but also indirectly, because he will have a say in the ports of loading and discharge. Congestion in particular can significantly affect loading and discharge times, and there is a good case for congestion risks being on charterers, rather than owners.

The laytime and demurrage regime is intended to discourage charterers from delaying loading and discharge, or, to be more accurate, to compensate the owners for increased time taken. The essence of the regime is that charterers are allowed the laytime in which to pursue their cargo-handling operations. If they exceed the laytime they are in breach of contract, in which case demurrage is universally agreed as liquidated damages. In some (but not all) charterparties, they are rewarded by despatch money, should they load and discharge within the laytime.

Thus, you already know that charterers pay for laytime within the freight:[2]

> "the sum agreed for freight in a charter covers the use of the ship for an agreed time for loading or discharging".

You also know that a reasonable laytime would be implied if not (as it universally is) expressed.[3] You know that if the laytime is exceeded, the charterers are in breach of an innominate term of the contract.[4] Thus they are liable for damages for breach, but in reality, these are always fixed as demurrage. Demurrage is therefore liquidated damages for exceeding the laytime:[5]

> ". . . if [the laytime] is exceeded the charterers are in breach; demurrage is the agreed damages to be paid for delay if the ship is delayed in loading or discharging beyond the agreed period".

This analysis probably dates from (or at least was settled in) *Aktieselskabet Reidar v Arcos*.[6] Because demurrage is liquidated damages, it must be a genuine pre-estimate – a demurrage rate that is set too high will risk being struck down as a penalty clause.[7]

This subject is very large, and entire books have been written, just on the commencement of laytime, for example.[8] In this principles book, we will concentrate on the following main areas:

(a) the beginning of the process – commencement of laytime;
(b) avoiding the laytime regime;
(c) "traditional" allocation of risk – how to achieve it;

---

1 Section [1.3].
2 *Inverkip SS Co v Bunge & Co* [1917] 2 KB 193, 200 (Scrutton LJ). See also section [1.4].
3 Section [1.4].
4 See the discussion of *Universal Cargo Carriers Corp v Citati* [1957] 2 QB 401, in section [2.6.1].
5 *Compania Naviera Aeolus SA v Union of India* [1964] AC 868 at 899 (Lord Guest), cited by Lord Diplock in *Dias Compania Naviera SA v Louis Dreyfus Corporation* [1978] 1 WLR 261 at 263.
6 *Aktieselskabet Reidar v Arcos Ltd* [1927] 1 KB 352.
7 See section [2.9.4].
8 Eg, Davies, *Commencement of Laytime*, 4th ed (2006), Taylor & Francis. The leading reference work on laytime is Baughen, *Summerskill on Laytime*, 5th ed (2013), Sweet & Maxwell/Thomson Reuters.

and in the next chapter:

(d)   avoiding the demurrage regime;
(e)   exceptions to laytime and demurrage.

8.2 Stages of a voyage

The laytime and demurrage regime applies only to loading and discharge processes, and we need to identify when these begin and end. Delays outside this period are not compensatable at all unless caused by a breach of the charterparty by the charterer; in that case the owners can claim damages for detention (which are based on market rates at the time of the breach). By contrast, demurrage rates will generally be based on the freight rates agreed in the contract.

In *The Johanna Oldendorff*,[9] Lord Diplock identified four stages to a voyage charterparty as follows:

"The adventure contemplated by a voyage charter involves four successive stages. They are:

(1)   The loading voyage, viz. the voyage of the chartered vessel from wherever she is at the date of the charter party to the place specified in it as the place of loading.
(2)   The loading operation, viz. the delivery of the cargo to the vessel at the place of loading and its stowage on board.
(3)   The carrying voyage, viz. the voyage of the vessel to the place specified in the charter party as the place of delivery.
(4)   The discharging operation, viz. the delivery of the cargo from the vessel at the place specified in the charter party as the place of discharge and its receipt there by the charterer or other consignee."

The laytime and demurrage regimes apply to stages (2) and (4). If delay is caused by a charterer breach *outside* one of those two periods, the shipowner's remedy is to sue for damages for detention. (This is a trick shipowners can use when they wish to avoid a low demurrage rate.)[10] It is therefore important to be able to distinguish between the stages, to determine when each begins and ends.

8.3 Commencement of laytime

We need to know when laytime starts to trigger the laytime/demurrage regime, and also because delays outside periods (2) and (4) are not subject to the regime.

Remember that any aspect of a charterparty can be altered by the contracting parties, and that in this area significant provision is usually made. But all alterations need to be seen against the basic backdrop – what would happen if the parties made no provision? So we have the following basic timeline (unless altered by the parties):

Time line

Ship "arrives";
Notice of readiness (NOR);[11]

---

9   [1974] AC 479, 557; also *Dias Compania Naviera SA v Louis Dreyfus Corporation* [1978] 1 WLR 261, 263; *Aldebaran Compania Maritima SA Panama v Aussenhandel AG Zurich (The Darrah)* [1977] AC 157, 164.

10   See sections [8.8]; [22.3].

11   Technically, at common law NOR is not required at discharge (though it is invariably provided for): *Transgrain Shipping BV v Global Transporte Oceanico SA (The Mexico I)* [1990] 1 Lloyd's Rep 507, 513 (Mustill LJ).

Laytime commences (triggered by NOR);

Demurrage after laytime expires;

Damages for detention if demurrage expires.[12]

The general principle is that, once the vessel has arrived, the master can give notice of readiness to load or discharge (as long as the vessel is in all respects ready), after which the laytime provisions of the charterparty take over (note that laytime does not necessarily start immediately – this depends on the charterparty).

Commencement of laytime timeline

• Arrival—— NOR- – commencement of laytime

It is however open to the parties to agree for laytime to start earlier, for example by expressly advancing the time when notice of readiness can be given, or the time from which time starts to count. The parties sometimes choose any of these:

• NOR- – start of laytime- – arrival
• Start of laytime—— NOR- – arrival

8.4 Traditional allocation of delay risks

A traditional allocation of delay risks is to make charterers responsible for congestion, since they choose the loading and discharging ports, but not for (for example) weather, over which the charterers have no control.[13] Thus, charterers should bear the risks of congestion, and other risks that relate specifically to the port or berth they have chosen. Shipowners should bear navigation risks. This is a fairly standard distinction, and for example the majority arbitrators in *The Fjordaas* observed that:[14]

> "It is a fundamental and basic fact that [in] voyage charterparties responsibility for navigational matters rests squarely on the shoulders of Owners and not Charterers."

Later in the chapter we look at ways of achieving this result (which is not straightforward).[15]

First, however, we will look at arrival, and at NOR, in other words at the commencement of laytime.

8.5 Definition of arrived ship

As we know (unless the charter otherwise provides – and it often does), the arrival of the ship triggers the entitlement for the owners to give NOR, which (again unless otherwise provided) triggers the commencement of laytime. So the definition of an arrived ship is vital to know when laytime starts.

---

12 Demurrage is the subject of chapter 9.

13 See, eg, *Bulk Transport Group Shipping Co Ltd v Seacrystal Shipping Ltd (The Kyzikos)* [1989] AC 1264.

14 *Arnt J Moerland (K/S) v Kuwait Petroleum Corp (The Fjordaas)* [1988] 1 Lloyd's Rep 336, 340.

15 Section [8.8].

Traditionally, a distinction is made between port and berth charterparties. In the Court of Appeal in *Stag Line Ltd v Board of Trade*,[16] the charterers had an express right under the charter to order the vessel, on reaching the nominated port, to load at a particular place within the port. This was therefore a berth charterparty, and the vessel did not arrive until she had reached the berth. The test accepted in *Stag Line* was:[17]

> "... if the berth at which the vessel ultimately had to load or discharge is named in the charter-party ... she is not an arrived ship until she arrives at the berth. If, on the other hand, no berth is named in the charterparty and no power of nomination is expressly given, and she proceeds to the berth ordered by the charterers merely by virtue of the implied right which the charter-ers have to select the loading berth, then she becomes an arrived ship when she arrives at the port or place named in the charterparty."

With a port charterparty, by contrast, the vessel needs only to arrive at the port. Tanker voyage char-ters are commonly (but not invariably) port charters (or variations thereon).

It is obvious that under a berth charterparty, the arrival of the ship is late, whereas under a port charterparty, the ship arrives much earlier. In general, an early arrival places risk of delays thereafter on the charterers, whereas of course the converse is true if the vessel arrives late. This is in reality a great oversimplification, because very few charterparties are pure berth or port charterparties. (The fine tuning we will consider in greater detail later in the chapter.)[18] A common variation, however, is the berth charterparty with a WIBON clause, allowing NOR to be tendered "whether in berth or not". "Berth or no berth" has the same meaning. The effect of a WIBON clause was the issue in *The Kyzikos*.[19] *The Kyzikos* achieves the "traditional" allocation of delay risks, whereas neither the port nor berth charter do this on their own. It places the delay risks on to the charterers in respect of congestion, but not weather (in the case itself, fog). There are problems with *The Kyzikos* method, though, as we will see.

For a port charterparty, the test for whether the vessel has become an arrived ship was stated by the House of Lords in *The Johanna Oldendorff*:[20] the ship becomes an arrived ship when she is under the immediate and effective disposition of the charterer. This can be before she has arrived within the commercial area of the port, as indeed in the case itself. Prior to this case there was House of Lords authority in *The Aello*,[21] that the vessel arrived only once she was within the commercial area of the port. This is much later than the test in *The Johanna Oldendorff*, and is effectively a geographical test. The problem in *The Aello* was that, because of temporary congestion, the port authority at Buenos Aires ordered waiting vessels to a point some 22 miles from the loading area. The House of Lords held that the *Aello* was not an arrived ship, although the shipowners had done all that they could have done to reach the port of Buenos Aires.

In *The Aello* itself, the charterers were held to be in breach in failing to provide a cargo in time to enable the ship to perform its obligation, of becoming an "arrived ship" under the contract. They were therefore liable for damages for detention – effectively shifting the delay risk back to them. Here, damages were simply loss of demurrage, and repayment of despatch, but, as we will see when we look at reachable on arrival clauses, a late arrival time, coupled with a damages for detention claim, have caused problems that might not have been appreciated at the time of *The Aello*.[22]

---

16 [1950] 2 KB 194.
17 [1950] 2 KB 194, 195.
18 Section [8.8].
19 [1989] 1 AC 1264, reversing [1987] 1 WLR 1565.
20 [1974] AC 479.
21 *Sociedad Financiera de Bienes Raices SA v Agrimpex Hungarian Trading Company for Agricultural Products, et è Contra (The Aello)* [1961] AC 135.
22 See section [22.3].

The main reason for moving to an earlier arrival time in The Johanna Oldendorff was changes in shipping practice, in particular use of larger ships and better communications – leading to ships waiting further from the berth. The test in The Johanna Oldendorff is not a test based on distance as such.

8.5.1   *The Johanna Oldendorff* and precedent

In The Johanna Oldendorff, the House of Lords took the unusual step of overruling its own previous decision, something that the House accepted that it could do only since 1966,[23] and even then only with great caution in commercial and property disputes. On The Aello as an authority, Lord Reid in The Johanna Oldendorff observed that:[24]

> "A main objective of the law should be that it should appear sensible and easy of application by those whose affairs it governs. I would not think it sufficient to justify our intervention that the criterion approved in *The Aello* is illogical but if in addition we find that it causes uncertainty in practice then I think that we ought to intervene.
>   . . .

In the Court of Appeal [in this case] . . . Roskill LJ said that he reached his decision 'with consider-able reluctance' and added:[25]

> 'It is now over 12 years since *The Aello* was finally decided. It is widely known that it was not a popular decision either in St. Mary Axe or in the Temple. It is also widely known that its appli-cation has from time to time caused difficulty not only to brokers but also to arbitrators and umpires and indeed to judges.'
>   . . .
>   . . . As things stand at present there must be numerous cases where parties' advisers can only guess what line the court will take.
> So in my judgment this is certainly a case in which this House ought to exercise its power to alter its previous decision."

The point of this exposition is to demonstrate that The Aello test was unpopular with practition-ers and traders and created uncertainty. Note in particular the emphasis on certainty.[26] The earlier arrival time in The Johanna Oldendorff seems to have been greatly preferred.

8.5.2   *The Johanna Oldendorff* itself

In The Johanna Oldendorff, although the parties contracted on the basis of a standard form,[27] there was a specially added clause 19. The destination was to be London, Avonmouth, Glasgow, Belfast, Hull or Liverpool/Birkenhead as directed by charterers or their agents, but whereas the added clause 19 stated clearly when laytime was to start in the event of arrival at Avonmouth, Glasgow or Hull it was silent where Liverpool/Birkenhead was chosen. (Elsewhere in the charterparty was a WIBON clause – which we will look at later.) This is a case where the problems were caused by a poorly considered amendment.[28]

The master was directed to Liverpool/Birkenhead and was ordered by the port authority to anchor at the bar light vessel, some 17 miles from the berth. The question was whether laytime

---

23 Practice Statement (Judicial Precedent) [1966] 1 WLR 1234.
24 [1974] AC 479, 533–5.
25 [1972] 3 WLR 623, 647–8.
26 We have seen this elsewhere, eg, section [7.6].
27 Baltimore Berth Grain Charterparty Form C.
28 See section [1.10]. As a matter of construction, amendments prevail: section [22.2.3].

started to run then or not until she had berthed. Although the bar was within the legal limits of the port, that was held by the House of Lords not to be conclusive. However, since the anchorage was at a place where waiting ships usually lay, she was presumed to be within the immediate and effective disposition of the charterer, and therefore an "arrived ship". Only in extraordinary circumstances would a ship at such a place not be within the immediate and effective disposition of the charterer.

Nonetheless, The Johanna Oldendorff creates only a presumption, and so some forms and clauses continue specifically to provide for the result in the case. Thus, for example, cl. 1 of BIMCO's Charterparty Laytime Definitions 2013 provides:[29]

> "PORT shall mean any area where vessels load or discharge cargo and shall include, but not be limited to, berths, wharves, anchorages, buoys and offshore facilities as well as places outside the legal, fiscal or administrative area where vessels are ordered to wait for their turn no matter the distance from that area."

The then-new Johanna Oldendorff test was applied, also by the House of Lords, in The Maratha Envoy – but with the elaboration that "the place where the vessel is waiting must be within the port".[30] Lord Diplock made the observation that:[31]

> "it is an important function of a court, and particularly of your Lordships' House, to provide [charterers and shipowners] with legal certainty at the negotiation stage as to what it is that they are agreeing to".

This is an important general point. The parties can change what they do not like, but it is important that the default position be certain.[32]

The vessel was waiting at the Weser Lightship, but there were four ports on the Weser, and she had not reached Brake (one of the four ports).[33] Consequently she was not an arrived ship. It was conceded that ". . . the Weser Lightship anchorage is outside the legal, fiscal and administrative limits of the port of Brake". It lies 25 miles from the mouth of the river in an area in which none of the port authorities of Weser ports does any administrative acts or exercises any control over vessels waiting there". This particular problem is often resolved by the inclusion of a Weser Lightship clause:[34]

> "If vessel is ordered to anchor at Weser Lightship by port authorities, since a vacant berth is not available, she may tender notice of readiness upon arriving at anchorage near Weser Lightship, as if she would have arrived at her final loading/discharging port. Steaming time for shifting from Weser Lightship to final discharging port, however, not to count."

Another possibility is cl. 18(b) of Norgrain 89:[35]

> "If . . . the Master warrants that the vessel is physically ready in all respects to load or discharge, the Master may tender notice of readiness, by radio if desired, from the usual

---

29 Which can be found at https://www.bimco.org/Chartering/Clauses_and_Documents/Clauses/Laytime_Definitions_for_Charter_Parties_2013.aspx.

30 Federal Commerce and Navigation Co Ltd v Tradax Export SA (The Maratha Envoy) [1978] AC 1.

31 [1978] AC 1, 8.

32 Se, eg, section [7.6].

33 Though she had "shown her chimney", making a "voyage of convenience" whereby she had proceeded up the river until she was opposite the port of Brake, turned round in midstream and immediately returned to her original anchorage: [1978] AC 1, 12. This did not, of course, make her an arrived ship.

34 This clause is set out at [1978] AC 1, 6.

35 North American Grain Charterparty 1973, as amended May 1989, which can be found at https://www.bimco.org/~/media/Chartering/Document_Samples/Voyage_Charter_Parties/Sample_Copy_NORGRAIN_89.ashx.

anchorage outside the limits of the port, whether in free pratique or not, whether customs cleared or not . . .".

We consider later the problems surrounding free pratique and customs clearance.

We see something similar in Tankervoy 87, cl. 8 of which allows NOR to be given "when the vessel has arrived at a customary anchorage or waiting place . . . and is ready to load or discharge".

8.6 Validity of notice of readiness (NOR)

A WIBON clause, as we have seen, allows a "traditional" allocation of delay risks. This allows for NOR to be tendered before the vessel arrives (at the berth), but there is a problem with this approach. In order for a valid NOR to be given, the vessel has to be in all respects ready to load or discharge, and sometimes this will simply not be the case, where the vessel is not in berth. For example, the charterers' cargo may be overstowed, or free pratique may not have been granted.

Free pratique and customs clearance can cause special difficulty, since it may not be known whether they will be granted until the vessel is actually in berth. The gives rise to the problem of so-called inchoate NOR.

8.6.1 The problem

Suppose the ship has arrived, or NOR can otherwise be given in principle, but the ship has not yet berthed. With a port charterparty this is obviously a possibility, as it is with a berth charter, coupled with a WIBON clause. Suppose, however, the ship is not in fact in all respects ready to load. It may be that NOR cannot be given in reality, whatever the position in principle.

If the master knows that free pratique will not be granted, as in The Tres Flores,[36] then he cannot give valid notice of readiness. However, the position is different if he believes that it is a mere formality. In The Delian Spirit,[37] notice was given before free pratique had been obtained, although she was in all other respects ready to load. It may not be possible for free pratique to be given until the vessel is actually at berth, and the Court of Appeal held the notice valid. The headnote to the Court of Appeal decision reads:

> "That where a vessel had an apparently clean bill of health the fact that free pratique was not obtained until she was at her berth did not invalidate the notice of readiness or her status as an arrived ship."

Lord Denning MR commented that:[38]

> "I can understand that, if a ship is known to be infected by a disease such as to prevent her getting her pratique, she would not be ready to load or discharge. But if she has apparently a clean bill of health, such that there is no reason to fear delay, then even though she has not been given her pratique, she is entitled to give notice of readiness, and laytime will begin to run . . . I therefore hold that the notice of readiness is good."

---

36 *Compania de Naviera Nedelka SA v Tradax International SA (The Tres Flores)* [1974] QB 264.
37 *Shipping Developments Corporation SA v V/O Sojuzneftexport (The Delian Spirit)* [1972] 1 QB 103.
38 [1972] 1 QB 103, 124.

The Delian Spirit was applied in *The Antclizo* (No. 2),[39] a case whose interest for present purposes might be simply that it reached the Court of Appeal (on appeal from arbitration) an incredible 18 years after discharge had been completed.

The Delian Spirit was distinguished in *The Tres Flores*,[40] where the cargo of maize was infested with pests, and free pratique would not have been granted as a formality. Here again is a quote from the headnote:

"(1)   in order for a notice of readiness to be good the vessel must be ready at the time that the notice is given and not at a time in the future; in this case, it could not be said that at the time when notice of readiness was given the ship was in a business and mercantile sense ready to load;

(2)   the vessel must be completely ready in all her holds to receive the cargo at any moment when she is required to receive it . . ."

This makes shifting of delay risks on to charterers, even for congestion risks, a lot more difficult. The common law position is often, however, departed from in reality; it can, of course, be altered by express provision in the charterparty.[41]

8.6.2   Inchoate NOR

Another question then arises: suppose an NOR is given early, before the vessel is in all respects ready to load or discharge; can this invalid NOR take effect once the situation changes, so that the vessel is in all respects ready to load or discharge.

In *Christensen v Hindustan Steel Ltd*,[42] Donaldson J held, in a case arising under a heavily amended Gencon charter, which made no express provision apart from requiring notice to be served during normal office hours, that a notice indicating only that the vessel is about to become ready to load or discharge will not be valid. The vessel must be ready to load or discharge at the time at which the notice is given. Furthermore, although there was a suggestion (in *The Massalia* (No. 2))[43] that such an invalid notice will become valid when the vessel becomes ready, this was doubted in *Christensen* itself, and the "inchoate NOR" idea has since been disapproved by the Court of Appeal in *The Mexico 1*.[44]

In *The Mexico 1*, NOR at discharge was given when the vessel was overstowed. This was clearly invalid when given, and Mustill LJ rejected the idea of an inchoate notice, which could come into effect later, once the fact situation had changed. The entire certainty of the NOR regime would be negated, were that to be the law. The inchoate NOR doctrine was disapproved – both:

(a)   in its purest form (namely as an invalid notice automatically taking effect as at the moment when the ship became ready); and

(b)   in a modified version whereby the notice might become effective not simply when the ship became ready for discharge, but when the charterers first knew or had the means of knowledge that it was ready.

39 *Antclizo Shipping Corporation v Food Corporation of India (The Antclizo (No. 2))* [1992] 1 Lloyd's Rep 558.

40 [1974] QB 264.

41 Note, for example, the detailed provision made in Norgrain 89. On the effect of clauses altering the common law position see (eg) *Cobelfret NV v Cyclades Shipping Co Ltd (The Linardos)* [1994] 1 Lloyd's Rep 28 [1994] 1 Lloyd's Rep 28; *United Nations/ Food and Agriculture Organisation –World Food Programme v Caspian Navigation Inc (The Jay Ganesh)* [1994] 2 Lloyd's Rep 358.

42 [1971] 1 Lloyd's Rep 395.

43 *Government of Ceylon v Societe Franco-Tunisienne d'Armement-Tunis (The Massalia) (No. 2)* [1962] 2 QB 416.

44 [1990] 1 Lloyd's Rep 507.

The main argument in *The Mexico 1* was purposive; to decide otherwise would be to deprive the charterers of the benefit of the NOR, for which (on discharge) the contract had expressly provided as the only way of starting commencement of laytime.

The Mexico 1 was followed by Thomas J in *The Agamemnon*;[45] NOR that was given before the vessel had arrived did not become valid automatically on her arrival (as defined in the charterparty).

This led charterers in *The Happy Day* to argue that the NOR never came into effect, even once discharge had actually begun – an argument that found favour at first instance.[46] There the vessel took over three months to discharge, but Langley J held that laytime had never even started to run, because the initial NOR was invalid. In *The Mexico 1*, the charterers conceded that laytime would run once discharge actually began, but Mustill LJ confessed himself unsure as to the mechanism by which this would occur. However, the purposive argument from *The Mexico 1* does not obviously apply, once discharge has actually begun.

Langley J was reversed when *The Happy Day* went to the Court of Appeal,[47] where a mechanism was found: discharging without objection was taken to amount to a waiver by the charterers of their right to object to the invalidity of the NOR. So the commencement of laytime was triggered in the end by the commencement of discharge. Alternatively the charterers, or people authorised to act on their behalf, may be taken by their conduct to have accepted an invalid NOR. This was held to have occurred in *The Northgate*.[48]

Nevertheless, the general principle remains that an invalid NOR is just that, unless the charterers (or those acting on their behalf) can be said to have acted in such a way as to have waived their right to object, or to be estopped from objecting. Waiver and estoppel were discussed at length in the Court of Appeal in *The Happy Day*. Both depend on a representation, express or implied, made by the charterers. Potter LJ said:[49]

"Laytime can commence under a voyage charter-party requiring service of a notice of readiness when no valid notice of readiness has been served in circumstances where:

(a)   a notice of readiness valid in form is served upon the charterers or receivers as required under the charter-party prior to the arrival of the vessel;

(b)   the vessel thereafter arrives and is, or is accepted to be, ready to discharge to the knowledge of the charterers;

(c)   discharge thereafter commences to the order of the charterers or receivers without either having given any intimation of rejection or reservation in respect of the notice of readiness previously served or any indication that further notice of readiness is required before laytime commences."

This will usually be the case where the charterers discharge without exception.

This discussion assumes that the notice is tendered too early. In *The Petr Schmidt*,[50] the notice was required to be tendered within office hours, and was in fact telexed when the office was closed. In all other respects the notice was valid; the vessel had arrived and was ready to discharge, as soon as the notice was issued. The Court of Appeal held that the notice became effective once the offices had opened, but only because it was effectively given then, since the telex had simply remained in the charterers' telex machine. Evans LJ also accepted that ". . . if the statements made in the notice are in

45 *TA Shipping Ltd v Comet Shipping Ltd (The Agamemnon)* [1998] 1 Lloyd's Rep 675.

46 *Glencore Grain Ltd v Flacker Shipping Ltd (The Happy Day)* [2001] 1 Lloyd's Rep 754.

47 [2002] 2 Lloyd's Rep 487.

48 *Ocean Pride Maritime Limited Partnership v Qingdao Ocean Shipping Co (The Northgate)* [2008] 1 Lloyd's Rep 511.

49 [2002] 2 Lloyd's Rep 487, [85].

50 *Galaxy Energy International Ltd v Novorossiysk Shipping Co (The Petr Shmidt)* [1998] 2 Lloyd's Rep 1.

fact incorrect when the notice is tendered, received or given . . .",[51] and that the statement that the ship was ready implied that it was ready when the statement was made, and also when the message was received (ie, when the notice was tendered, on the opening of the office). It follows that the decision also depended on the vessel being physically ready to discharge when the telex was sent, and consequently that if the vessel had not arrived by then, it would not be possible to cure an invalid NOR simply by arguing that the notice was still in the charterers' telex machine when the vessel did arrive.

8.7 Breach before NOR

If the ship arrives, and NOR is tendered, laytime begins, after the expiry of which demurrage is payable in an orderly fashion, as liquidated damages for delay, As you know, the laytime and demurrage regime is all about apportioning risks for delay. It would also seem that both owners and charterers usually prefer a demurrage regime, rather than the alternative, which is that charterers become liable for damages for detention. The convenience of prompt and regular payment, and of fixed damages, usually outweigh any disadvantages.

However, it might be in the interests of one of the parties to argue for damages for detention, when the case is actually litigated. For example, if the demurrage rate is too low the owners will want to avoid it. We will leave some ways of avoiding the demurrage regime until the next lecture, but for the moment we should remember that demurrage is payable only in respect of delays that follow the end of the laytime. If, on the other hand, delay (because of a charterer breach) occurs before the laytime has been triggered, then damages for detention will be payable. This is not normally what the parties want, but because of market fluctuations or other reasons, shipowners in particular sometimes argue it.

The stages in *The Johanna Oldendorff* are important in that it is only for delays in stages 2 and 4 that the laytime/demurrage regime applies.[52] If delay is caused by a breach at stage 1 or 3, the regime is not triggered, and damages are for detention. This is a device that shipowners can use to avoid the demurrage regime.

In this regard, in the absence of express provision to the contrary, laytime and demurrage provisions can only operate once a valid notice of readiness has been given. Where delay occurs before that time, damages are in principle at large, for detention. We saw this in *The Aello*,[53] but it was one of the problems (as perceived by the charterers) with the early reachable on arrival cases, in chapter 22.[54]

Where the charterers have the option of nominating a range of loading or discharge ports, the possibility arises that they can, by failing to nominate, prevent the vessel from becoming an "arrived ship". In *The Timna*,[55] Donaldson J held that the master could not in that case himself nominate the port and thereby cause the vessel to become an "arrived ship". However, the charterers were liable in damages (for detention) for their failure to nominate, because they were thereby in breach of contract. The Court of Appeal upheld Donaldson J's decision on the damages for detention claim.[56] In the event, it seems that the shipowners were content to claim at the demurrage rate, but had damages at large been higher, there is no reason in principle why they should not have claimed at the higher rate.

---

51 [1998] 2 Lloyd's Rep 1, 5.
52 See section [8.2].
53 See section [8.5].
54 See section [22.3].
55 *Zim Israel Navigation Co Ltd v Tradax Export SA (The Timna)* [1970] 2 Lloyd's Rep 409.
56 [1971] 2 Lloyd's Rep 91.

As a general proposition, if it is through a breach of the charterers, by failing to nominate, that the vessel does not become an "arrived ship", they will be liable for breach of contract. Because notice of readiness cannot be given, damages will be at large and unaffected by the demurrage provisions. In *The Boral Gas*, Evans J said:[57]

"At the relevant time the laytime had neither begun nor expired, and so no claim for demurrage can arise. The agreed demurrage figure nevertheless may be regarded as the appropriate amount to award as unliquidated damages – this is a question of fact for the arbitrators to consider and decide."

In *The Boral Gas* the breach was a failure by charterers to supply pre-coolant; this occurred before the laytime regime had begun, and hence damages were for detention. In none of the cases has an amount been claimed that differs from the demurrage rate – but obviously it could, if the market had moved. On a rising market damages for detention are likely to exceed the demurrage rate, whereas on a falling market the shipowners would generally be better off claiming demurrage. But even on a falling market, it cannot be assumed that damages will necessarily be limited to the lower prevailing market rate. In *The Mass Glory*,[58] the vessel was unable to berth, and hence tender a valid notice of readiness, because of a breach by the charterers relating to documents. The charterparty was a sub-charter, the disponent owners having themselves chartered the vessel on a time basis, and the effect of the delay was to cause a late redelivery under the time charterparty. Since, on a falling market, the disponent owners would (barring the delay) have made timely redelivery, the effect of the delay was to render them liable for additional hire payments. These were, in principle, recoverable on the damages for detention claim, under the sub-charter; since the market had fallen significantly, these hire payments were higher than current market rates. However:[59]

". . . in general damages for the detention of a vessel are to be calculated by reference to the prevailing market rate. A ship is a profit-earning chattel and the market rate therefore normally provides the best guide to her earning capacity at any given time. Unusually profitable employment that might for one reason or another have been available to her will not normally be taken into account because it will not have been within the defendant's reasonable contemplation. It will therefore be regarded as too remote in law to be recoverable."

It follows that recovery at above the prevailing market rate is unusual.

As with anything to do with charterparties, the principles in this section are subject to express provision to the contrary; sometimes (as with the WIBON clause) NOR can be given whether the vessel has become an arrived ship or not.

In chapter 22, we look at a specific instance where a breach prevented the vessel from arriving. It is chosen because there is a reasonably substantial body of case law on the area, and because the leading case, in the House of Lords, has an interest beyond the immediate situation. It concerns the "reachable on arrival" clause in the Exxonvoy tanker form, and the subsequent history of that clause.[60]

---

57 Rashtriya Chemicals and Fertilizers Ltd v Huddart Parker Industries Ltd (The Boral Gas) [1988] 1 Lloyd's Rep 342.
58 Glencore Grain Ltd v Goldbeam Shipping Inc (The Mass Glory) [2002] 2 Lloyd's Rep 244. It is an interesting question whether the decision would have been the same, had the vessel been an "arrived ship": see the discussion of *Akt Reidar v Arcos* in section [9.6].
59 [2002] 2 Lloyd's Rep 244, [52].
60 See section [22.3].

8.8 Achieving traditional allocation of risk

We now turn to devices that might be used to achieve the traditional allocation of risk, neither of which are achieved by the port or berth charter *simpliciter*. A port or berth charter, on its own, is too blunt an instrument. Essentially, there are two types:

* late arrival, but earlier tendering of NOR in some circumstances;
* early arrival with exceptions in some circumstances.

There are, however, problems with each type.

8.8.1 Late arrival, and earlier tendering of NOR

This is how WIBON works. The WIBON clause is used in a berth charterparty, under which arrival is late, but it allows notice of readiness to be tendered "whether in berth or not". The clause has been held by the House of Lords not to allow owners to tender NOR where delay is caused getting into berth by bad weather, though not by congestion, thereby achieving a traditional allocation of delay risks.[61] "WIBON" applied only where a berth was not available, not where a berth was available for the vessel on her arrival, but was unreachable by reason of bad weather.

Other clauses can also work. In *The Radnor*,[62] a berth charterparty contained the clause, "Time lost in waiting for berth to count as loading time", and the Court of Appeal held that this put the risk of delay through congestion on to the charterer. Time lost in waiting for berth was to be treated as laytime, the argument of the charterer being rejected, that it could not do so because no valid notice of readiness could have been given at that time. Had the charterer's argument succeeded, of course, the clause would have had no effect at all.[63] This aspect of *The Radnor* was approved by the House of Lords in *The Darrah*.[64]

There are, however, two pitfalls that should be avoided. First, there is the danger, with arrival being defined late, that the laytime and demurrage regime will not be triggered at all, but that instead damages will be for detention.[65] Secondly, it is sensible not to make valid tender of notice of readiness the only trigger for the commencement of laytime, as for example in a WIBON clause, because of the courts' refusal always to recognise the concept of an inchoate NOR.[66] There is also the problem around cases such as *The Tres Flores*, but these can be dealt with by appropriate provision in the charterparty.

8.8.2 Early arrival, but with exceptions

This obviates the problems in the previous section, and is common with tanker charters, which are usually port charters, but allowing for interruptions to laytime and demurrage.

---

61 See, eg, Bulk Transport Group Shipping Co Ltd v Seacrystal Shipping Ltd (The Kyzikos) [1989] AC 1264.

62 North River Freighters Ltd v HE President of India (The Radnor) [1956] 1 QB 333.

63 However, in Inca Compania Naviera SA v Mofinol Inc (The President Brand) [1967] 2 Lloyd's Rep 338, 347, Roskill LJ took the view (citing The Radnor) that "that it is only by very clear language that a shipowner can cast on to a charterer a liability to pay for any loss of time before the point of time at which laytime starts in accordance with the laytime and demurrage provisions of the particular charter-party". The President Brand is discussed fully in section [22.3].

64 Aldebaran Compania Maritima SA Panama v Aussenhandel AG Zurich (The Darrah) [1977] AC 157. ("Time lost in waiting for berth to count as laytime"). The actual calculation in The Radnor should, however, be regarded as suspect, because a Sunday should have been excluded: [1977] AC 157, 166–8 (Lord Diplock).

65 See further the reachable on arrival clauses in section [22.3].

66 See section [8.6.2], above.

Among the problems are that exceptions are interpreted *contra proferentem*, and the issues arising from the maxim, "once on demurrage always on demurrage", considered in the next chapter.[67]

8.9 Laytime and standard forms

There are many variations among the standard forms, as to the definition of the arrived ship, as to when notice of readiness can be tendered, and as to when laytime starts, usually (as we have seen) after NOR has been tendered. Laytime itself may run SHEX (Sundays and holidays excepted) or SHINC (included). Particularly for dry cargo, laytime may run only during a "weather working day", or "weather permitting". There may be a number of hours or days, which may or may not be for both loading and discharge, or a rate may be specified. Rates may be qualified, eg "per working hatch".[68]

These variations are of immense interest, and are vital for practitioners working in the area. Unfortunately they are beyond the scope of this Principles book. BIMCO have, however, drafted *Charterparty laytime definitions*, the latest version of which were revised in 2013. There is also a useful downloadable commentary.[69]

It is important to be aware of the standard forms though. Charterparties are not governed by legislation and pretty well everything can be altered by the parties. A lot of the law on laytime and demurrage is really no more than the default position. The standard forms remind us of that.

8.10 Question

The ship arrives and the shipowners declare NOR. Before she can berth, she grounds in the fairway, and is delayed. She eventually gets into berth, and the charterers discharge before the expiry of the laytime. The grounding (which causes no physical damage to the ship) is nonetheless the result of the charterers ordering the vessel to an unsafe berth, in breach of the safe berth clause in the charterparty. The shipowners sue for damages for detention, from the breach of the safe port obligation. Advise the parties.

Comment

If the ship were already on demurrage, and a breach of an independent obligation (such as a safe berth clause) occasioned additional delay, there is authority (in the next chapter) that the ship-owners would be limited to a demurrage claim, and could not claim damages for detention in respect of the delay.[70] Here, they are attempting to use breach of an independent obligation to deprive the charterers of some of their laytime. If the demurrage authorities apply to laytime, they should not be able to do this. But do they? Have a look at *TheVine* in section 9.5, and in particular the following passage from Teare J's judgment:[71]

67 See section [9.9].

68 Or "available working hatches", as interpreted in *President of India v Jebsens (UK) Ltd (The General Capinpin, Proteus and Free Wave)* [1991] 1 Lloyd's Rep 1.

69 The definitions can be found at https://www.bimco.org/Chartering/Clauses_and_Documents/Clauses/Laytime_Definitions_ for_Charter_Parties_2013.aspx, the PDF commentary also being linked from this site.

70 See section [9.5].

71 *Emeraldian Limited Partnership v Wellmix Shipping Ltd (The Vine)* [2011] 1 Lloyd's Rep 301, [81], and look especially at the part I have marked out in bold. The case is discussed further in section [9.5]. Citations are to Independent Petroleum Group Ltd v Seacarriers Count Pte Ltd (The Count) [2008] 1 Lloyd's Rep 72 and Inverkip SS Co Ltd v Bunge & Co [1917] 2 KB 198.

"... The Charterers have a number of obligations under the charterparty. One is to load within the laydays. If that is breached demurrage is payable. Another is to nominate a safe berth. If that is breached it may cause damage to the vessel or it may cause delay: see *The Count* ... If delay is caused damages for such delay are to be measured by the demurrage rate which is the agreed rate of damages for delay: see *Inverkip SS v Bunge* ... **The fact that there may have been no breach of the obligation to load within the laydays does not disable the Owners from claiming the agreed rate of damages for delay caused by breach of another obligation.**"

However, there is also authority that the charterers are entitled to the laytime as paid for within the freight,[72] and these comments appear to run contrary to remarks in *The President Brand* and *The Delian Spirit* in chapter 22.[73] In fact, in *The Vine*, the issue was whether the charterers were entitled to claim laytime exceptions. Teare J held that the exceptions did not cover the situation in any event, but that, if they had, the charterers would have been unable to rely on them anyway, for the reason in the above passage. There is also a footnote to the paragraph, however, which may provide a better explanation:

"If the correct analysis is, as submitted by [counsel], that where an event was caused by a breach of the safe port warranty such an event cannot, as matter of construction, fall within an exception to laytime then the same result follows. There is no difference in substance."

This reasoning would not, of course (unlike that in the main passage), permit the owners to avoid the laytime, as they are attempting in the problem question.

Alternatively, perhaps these statements in *The Vine*, which are no more than first instance *dicta*, are wrong.

---

72 Section [9.1].
73 *Inca Compania Naviera SA v Mofinol Inc (The President Brand)* [1967] 2 Lloyd's Rep 338; *Shipping Developments Corp v V/O Sojuzneftexport (The Delian Spirit)* [1972] 1 QB 103, in section [22.3.5].

Chapter 9

Loading and discharge (2): demurrage

Chapter Contents

9.1 Nature of demurrage

Demurrage provisions are universal in voyage charterparties (although a charterparty would be workable without them, and there is no need to imply them, if they are not there). Demurrage is payable by the charterer once the laytime agreed for loading or discharging the cargo has expired, its purpose being to compensate the shipowner for any additional delay caused by the charterer's breach of contract in exceeding the agreed laytime. In *The General Capinpin*, Lord Templeman observed:[1]

> ". . . when a shipowner agrees to carry in his ship a cargo of a charterer, the responsibility for loading and unloading the cargo may be imposed on the charterer . . . On a single voyage charter the shipowner wishes the adventure to be completed as soon as possible so as to free his ship for another voyage. The speedy unloading of the vessel by the charterer is encouraged by a stipulation in the charterparty that if the charterer does not discharge the cargo within a certain time, known as 'laytime' after the vessel is ready to be unloaded the charterer will pay a daily fine, known as 'demurrage' . . ."

Lord Templeman went on to say that ". . . if on the other hand the charterer discharges the cargo before the expiry of the laytime, the owner will pay the charterer a reward known as 'despatch money' for every day saved". Some (but by no means all) voyage charterparties also include a despatch clause, which (as Lord Templeman observes) compensates the charterer for completing loading, even before the laytime has expired. You might also occasionally see a Jupiter clause, which gives the owners the option to cancel, once the ship has been on demurrage for a stipulated period.[2]

Demurrage is conceptually very different from laytime. The charterer has a contractual right to use the laytime period provided in the charterparty, because it is included in the freight payment. Scrutton LJ said in *Inverkip SS Co Ltd v Bunge & Co*, in a passage approved in many subsequent cases:[3]

> "The sum agreed for freight in a charter covers the use of the ship for an agreed time for loading and discharging, known as 'the lay days,' and for the voyage . . . ".

The charterer is in breach of contract, however, if he delays the vessel beyond the laytime (or lay days). He has no contractual right to delay the vessel further and pay demurrage. Rather, demurrage is liquidated (ie, agreed) damages for the charterer's breach in failing to load or discharge within the laytime. That this was the correct analysis became clear about 90 years ago, in *Aktieselskabet Reidar v Arcos Ltd*.[4] In *Dias Compania Naviera SA v Louis Dreyfus Corp*, Lord Diplock quoted with approval Lord Guest in *The Spalmatori*:[5]

> "[if the laytime is] exceeded the charterers are in breach; demurrage is the agreed damages to be paid for delay if the ship is delayed in loading or discharging beyond the agreed period".

Were there no demurrage provisions, the shipowner would be entitled to damages at large for detention of the vessel beyond the laytime. Such damages would be calculated on the principles applicable to any other breach of contract. In practice, the basis of the calculation would be the

---

1 *President of India v Jebsens (UK) Ltd (The General Capinpin)* [1991] 1 Lloyd's Rep 1, 3. Lord Templeman's was a dissenting speech (although nothing turns on this for present purposes). This passage is about discharge, but identical principles apply to loading.

2 See section [9.3].

3 [1917] 2 KB 198, 200.

4 [1927] 1 KB 352.

5 [1978] 1 WLR 261, 263 (Lord Diplock), quoting *Compania Naviera Aeolus SA v Union of India (The Spalmatori)* [1964] AC 868, 899 (Lord Guest).

freight the shipowner could earn over the period. However, the shipowner would have to prove loss, and the normal contractual rules as to remoteness of damage would apply.[6] The shipowner would also be required to mitigate his loss.[7] The effect of demurrage provisions is that, instead of paying contractual damages for detention, the charterer pays demurrage at an agreed rate, if he fails to complete the cargo handling within the lay days. The advantage to the shipowner of a demurrage provision is therefore that he can claim the requisite sum without having to prove (or mitigate) loss. Another advantage is that they are usually paid at the time, whereas a damages claim will generally lead to delayed payment.

On the other hand, were demurrage rates set higher than damages at large for detention of the vessel, they would risk being struck down as contractual penalty clauses.[8] In practice, therefore, demurrage rates are often lower than damages at large for detention would be. This is especially likely if the market has risen since the conclusion of the charterparty, since damages for detention will be calculated on the basis of current freight rates, whereas the demurrage rate will have been agreed on the basis of the earlier (lower) market rate. The only situation where demurrage rates are likely to be higher than damages for detention is on a rapidly falling market, where freight rates have fallen considerably since the charterparty was concluded. No doubt, for example, the shipowners would have been content to claim demurrage in the well-known case, *Suisse Atlantique Société D'Armement Maritime SA v NV Rotterdamsche Kolen Centrale*,[9] where the market had fallen substantially on the reopening of the Suez Canal in 1957, except that, presumably due to an oversight, the agreed demurrage rates had in any case been set unrealistically low.[10]

Because demurrage rates are typically lower than damages for detention, shipowners often try to avoid the demurrage provisions in the charterparty and sue for general contractual damages instead (as in *Suisse Atlantique* itself). We examine possible ways of doing this later in the chapter.[11]

Demurrage covers only delays after the expiry of the laytime, and is not applicable (unless expressly provided for) if the delay prevents laytime from starting at all. It was for this reason that damages for detention were successfully claimed in the early reachable on arrival cases, and in *The Timna*, considered in the last chapter.[12] The reasoning in those cases would also have limited the shipowner to damages for detention in all circumstances, however, whereas often it will be more convenient for the parties to extend demurrage to cover charterers' failure to nominate as well. This is sometimes done in tanker charterparties.[13]

The demurrage regime ends once loading and/or discharge is complete. Delays after this time (for example where a ship is delayed in getting out of a port because of breach of a safe port clause),[14] will be compensated by general contractual damages.

9.2 Length of time on demurrage

Occasionally charterparties provide for a limited time on demurrage. Thus, for example, the pre-1994 version of Gencon provided:

---

6 Described briefly in section [2.9.1].
7 Described briefly in section [2.9.2].
8 On which see further section [2.9.4].
9 [1967] AC 361, discussed further in sections [9.8] and [9.9].
10 See further section [9.9].
11 See sections [9.4]–[9.7].
12 See section [8.7].
13 Eg, Tankervoy, cl. 2 (Nomination/Renomination clause).
14 See sections [13.9] and (esp) [13.10].

"Ten running days on demurrage at the rate stated . . . to be allowed Merchants altogether at ports of loading and discharging."

After 10 days damages would be for detention, but the parties did not care for this, and it is not replicated in the latest version of the form. It would seem to be rare today. In *The Saturnia*, Sir John Donaldson MR observed that:[15]

"Formerly it was much more common than it is today to have a limited number of days during which the vessel could be on demurrage paying the demurrage rate. The charter stipulated a laytime. Then, having failed to fulfil the obligation to load and discharge the vessel within the laytime, the charterer was in breach, but, during the allowed time on demurrage, he was entitled to limit his damages to a liquidated amount per day. Thereafter damages were at large, and it was merely a matter of proving what damage had been suffered."

There is no equivalent in other modern forms, and even when pre-1994 Gencon itself was used, the 10-day provision was often struck out. Some standard forms have a cancelling clause allowing the shipowner to repudiate the charterparty and withdraw the vessel after a stipulated time on demurrage, but even these clauses are relatively unusual.[16] The usual position is for demurrage to continue into the indefinite future, since it is usually in the interests of both parties to agree liquidated damages. Indeed, as has already been observed, tanker charterparties often apply the demurrage rate to charterers' failure to nominate also.

9.3 Jupiter clauses

From the point of view of the owners, with indefinite demurrage there is always the danger, with very long delays, of the vessel being tied up indefinitely on demurrage, which may well be much lower than the freight that could otherwise be obtained. This could occur in the ordinary course of events, for example where congestion delays are very long. On the other hand, it could be a deliberate policy of the charterers, as in *Suisse Atlantique*, for example.[17] There, under a consecutive voyage charterparty, due to a combination of a sharply falling freight market and a fall in charterers' tonnage requirements, it became cheaper for the charterers to keep the vessel on demurrage indefinitely, chartering in alternative tonnage at the new market rates, to the limited extent that it was required. Mention should also be made of the *Jupiter* saga.[18] Jupiter (a company) entered into a number of voyage charterparties, apparently on Beepeevoy forms, for tankers in the Gulf. The charterparties were presumably entered into on a speculative basis since Jupiter had secured no cargo. They refused to admit their failure to obtain cargoes, and many vessels were consequently kept waiting for long periods on demurrage. Another problem was that (as with many voyage forms today also) there was no stipulation for time of payment of demurrage, and it was assumed (but never held) to be payable under these charterparties along with freight, at destination. In the event, it seems, demurrage was never paid.

Obviously, shipowners prefer to be protected from these possibilities, but if there is no limit to the time on demurrage, the general rule is that because demurrage is liquidated damages for detention of the vessel, if the shipowner's loss is in reality due to detention of the vessel, or delay in loading or discharge, he is limited to a claim for demurrage, and cannot sue for damages at large, and

---

15 *Superfos Chartering A/S v NBR (London) Ltd (The Saturnia)* [1987] 2 Lloyd's Rep 43, 45.

16 Eg, (as in Tankervoy, cl. 7, and the 1994 Gencon provision, set out here).

17 See further section [9.8] below, and also section [5.5].

18 Which is related by Per Gram, *Chartering Documents*, Lloyd's of London Press (1981), 18.

devices to avoid the demurrage provisions generally do not work.[19] In that case, the only way around the demurrage clause is where the charterer's breach is sufficiently serious to allow the shipowner to repudiate the contract, and the shipowner does so repudiate. In that event the demurrage provisions would not apply to any delay *after* repudiation occurred. This requires that the delay amounts to a frustrating breach, and that the owners elect to repudiate (not always an easy call if demurrage is being paid regularly and on time).[20]

It is for this reason that some charterparties include a Jupiter clause, which gives them an option. Thus, for example, Tankervoy 87 gives the owners the option of cancelling after 20 days' demurrage has accrued before loading has begun, but allows them alternatively to keep the charter alive and claim demurrage. Gencon 94 (cl. 7) protects in a different way, allowing termination of the charterparty in the event of non-payment. This does not, of course, protect owners against a low demurrage rate.

9.4 Avoidance of demurrage regime by repudiating

Even if the charterer's breach is sufficiently serious to allow the shipowner to repudiate the contract, the shipowner must do so: if he elects to keep the contract alive, he will be bound by all its terms, including the demurrage provisions. As Lord Diplock commented in *Dias Compania Naviera SA v Louis Dreyfus Corp*:[21]

> "If laytime ends before the charterer has completed the [loading or] discharging operation he breaks his contract. The breach is a continuing one; it goes on until discharge is completed and the ship is once more available to the shipowner to use for other voyages. But unless the delay in what is often, though incorrectly, called re-delivery of the ship to the shipowner, is so prolonged as to amount to a frustration of the adventure, the breach by the charterer sounds in damages only. The charterer remains entitled to continue the discharge of the cargo, while remaining liable in damages for the loss sustained by the shipowner during the period for which he is being wrongfully deprived of the opportunity of making profitable use of his ship. It is the almost invariable practice nowadays for these damages to be fixed by the charterparty at a liquidated sum per day or *pro rata* for part of a day (demurrage) which accrues throughout the period of time for which the breach continues."

The shipowner's only option, therefore, is to get out of the charterparty altogether, unless he can argue an independent breach, based on the principles in the next section.

9.5 Independent breach?

Once the laytime regime has started, so that we are in stage (2) or (4) (on the *Johanna Oldendorff* classification in the last chapter),[22] the laytime and demurrage regime will usually apply to any delay, even if caused by a separate breach by the charterer. This is different from the cases we have already considered, where a separate breach prevents the ship from arriving in the first place.

---

19 See further below, sections [9.4]–[9.8].

20 See further section [9.8]. A case in a slightly different context, where laytime and demurrage terms had been incorporated into an international sale contract, and where FOB buyers could not repudiate until a frustrating time had elapsed, is *ERG Raffinerie Mediterranee SpA v Chevron USA Inc (The Luxmar)* [2007] 2 Lloyd's Rep 542.

21 [1978] 1 WLR 261, 263–4.

22 See section [8.2].

In *Inverkip SS Co Ltd v Bunge & Co*,[23] the shipowner failed in an attempt to avoid the demurrage provisions, on the grounds of an independent breach by the charterer. The shipowner had elected to keep the contract alive, but it was by no means clear either that he would have been entitled to repudiate, or even that the charterer had in act committed any independent breach of contract. Under the charterparty, the port of loading was originally agreed as Galveston, but Galveston was seriously damaged by a tidal wave, and the agreement was varied, substituting Newport News as loading port, and reducing the freight. All other terms of the charterparty remained as before, five days being agreed as laytime. Naturally in the circumstances, other vessels also diverted from Galveston. Newport News became very congested but, more importantly, so did the nearby railway network, and the charterers had difficulty getting the cargo to Newport News. The result was that considerably after the laytime had expired the charterers had not even begun to load. The shipowners threatened to withdraw the vessel, but in the end did not do so (ie, kept the contract alive), and she was eventually loaded nearly a month after the expiry of the lay days.

The shipowners accepted that they were limited to demurrage until a reasonable time after the lay days had expired, but claimed damages for detention for the delay beyond that time. The Court of Appeal held that they were entitled only to the (much lower) demurrage payment for the whole period of delay. The findings of fact, as described by Scrutton LJ, were that the vessel was "kept an unreasonable time", but:[24]

"I cannot make any finding of commercial frustration of the adventure, the delay being provided for by demurrage."

One of the shipowners' arguments was that the charterer had broken an independent term of the contract by failing to have a cargo ready for loading when the vessel arrived, and that the demurrage provisions did not apply to that breach of contract. Scrutton LJ doubted whether the inability of the charterers to have the cargo ready when the vessel arrived *was* a breach of contract, but even if it was Warrington LJ thought that the demurrage payment covered delay for any reason, and not just for delay in loading or discharging the cargo. Scrutton LJ observed that:[25]

"If there was a breach in not having cargo ready . . . the only consequence is detention of the ship, and the damages for that, which is the same detention, however it arises, are agreed in the charter and have been paid."

Whether or not the charterers had committed an independent breach of the charterparty was irrelevant.

A case in a similar vein is *Chandris v Isbrandsen-Moller Co Inc.*[26] The charterer had shipped dangerous cargo (turpentine), undoubtedly thereby committing a breach of contract, but the shipowner did not repudiate as he was entitled, and accepted the cargo. In other words, he elected to keep the charterparty alive. Because of the dangerous nature of the cargo, it took 16 days longer to discharge than it would otherwise have taken, but Devlin J held that the shipowner could only claim demurrage for these additional 16 days. Devlin J commented that:[27]

---

23 [1917] 2 KB 198. (Scrutton LJ observed that "the rate of demurrage (about £47 a day) was low for that time": [1917] 2 KB 198, 199.) The owners' claim for damages for detention was £200 a day.

24 [1917] 2 KB 198, 201.

25 [1917] 2 KB 198, 203.

26 [1951] 1 KB 240, rvsd CA on other grounds, also reported [1951] 1 KB 240. See also section [4.6.1].

27 [1951] 1 KB 240, 249.

"The demurrage rate in this case appears to have been a good deal lower than the freight market rate, and I suppose I need not shut my eyes to the fact that a sum produced by demurrage is generally less than damages for detention, which are, presumably, assessed by reference to the market rate of freight at the time of the breach."

He also observed that though demurrage was generally lower than damages for detention:[28]

". . . even though the former may be designed to be lower, there is always the possibility of a slump in freight rates . . .".

(In such a case, of course, it would be the charterers who would wish to avoid the demurrage rate.)

In the particular case it was the shipowner who wished to avoid the demurrage rate. He could not do so, by arguing that the delay was caused by a breach of a different term of the contract. (The case subsequently went to the Court of Appeal, but on another issue.)[29]

The logic of these cases is that all delay will be at the demurrage rate, even if caused by an independent breach. Though the cases concern demurrage, the statements in Inverkip, that laytime is included in the freight, would surely suggest that laytime also cannot be avoided, simply by claiming that the delay is caused by an independent breach, at any rate if the delay occurs during stages (2) or (4) of the voyage.[30] Much of the point of Inverkip would be lost if laytime could be avoided by claiming an independent breach. In The Vine, however,[31] the ship was prevented from getting into berth, in circumstances that Teare J held rendered the port unsafe. In other words, there was a breach of the independent safe berth warranty.[32] As a consequence the vessel was delayed for a considerable time, but this was after the laytime had started. The charterers failed in an argument that they were protected by a clause which (they argued) provided that in these circumstances, time lost should not be computed as laytime. (Had the charterers been successful, they would have loaded within the laytime.) Teare J also held that even if they had been successful, the owners were entitled to damages for delay, caused by breach of an independent obligation (ie, breach of the safe port clause).[33] (He awarded the agreed rate for damages for delay, ie, demurrage, but presumably, since this was a damages for detention claim, the demurrage limit could have been avoided, had the market risen.) Moreover, Teare J's reasoning, if correct, deprived the charterers of their laytime, even though the ship was an arrived ship and laytime had started. It is not at all clear how this reasoning can be reconciled with the views expressed in this section, nor with The President Brand and the views in the Court of Appeal in The Delian Spirit, both discussed in chapter 22.[34]

9.6 Different type of loss and/or breach of different obligation

In Inverkip and Chandris, the only loss to the shipowner was loss of ability to earn freight elsewhere because of the detention of the vessel. This is covered by the demurrage clause, even if the cause of

28 [1951] 1 KB 240, 250.

29 Also reported [1951] 1 KB 240 (interest on arbitration award).

30 See section [8.2] for the description of the stages. Cf. sections [8.7] and [22.3], where breach occurs before NOR, but even in the cases considered in [22.3], once the ship had arrived, the charterers were held entitled to their laytime.

31 Emeraldian Limited Partnership v Wellmix Shipping Ltd (The Vine) [2011] 1 Lloyd's Rep 301.

32 On which see generally section [13.9].

33 [2011] 1 Lloyd's Rep 301, [81].

34 Respectively Inca Compania Naviera SA v Mofinol Inc (The President Brand) [1967] 2 Lloyd's Rep 338; Shipping Developments Corp v V/O Sojuzneftexport (The Delian Spirit) [1972] 1 QB 103, in section [22.3.5].

that detention was a breach of a different term by the charterer. The position is different, however, if the delay causes damage of a nature that is entirely different to detention. In that case the shipowner might be able to sue for damages at large for the subsequent breach, as in the Court of Appeal decision in *Aktieselskabet Reidar v Arcos Ltd*,[35] where the delay affected the amount of cargo the vessel was able to carry, as a result of differences between summer and winter loading marks (the delay being of sufficient length that the winter marks applied, allowing less cargo to be loaded). Atkin LJ said:[36]

> "If the lay-days expire without a full cargo having been loaded the charterer has broken his contract. The provisions as to demurrage quantify the damages, not for the complete breach, but only such damages as arise from the detention of the vessel."

This is also the explanation of the case, adopted later by Devlin J in *Chandris*.

What is not clear is whether *Reidar* requires in addition a breach of another term of the charterparty. Sargant and (probably) Atkin LJJ (but not Bankes LJ) considered that there had also been two breaches of two separate obligations, the second being a failure to load a full and complete cargo. Bankes LJ said that:[37]

> "I see a difficulty upon the facts in saying that the vessel did not load a full and complete cargo, as it appears to me that the time for ascertaining whether she had or had not a full cargo is the time when she sailed. At that time, assuming her destination to be a port in the United Kingdom, she had a full and complete cargo."

It may be that recovery above the demurrage rate requires not only that the additional loss be different in character from the loss of use, but also that it stemmed from a breach of an additional obligation.[38] However, in *Suisse Atlantique*, whereas Sellers LJ stressed both aspects of *Reidar*, Diplock LJ would have distinguished it on either basis.[39]

Cases such as *Arcos* are likely to be rare: in most situations, unless the shipowner validly repudiates the charterparty, he is bound by the demurrage provisions in respect of any delay after the laytime period has expired.

Where, as in *Arcos*, the loss was not detention at all, the laytime provisions would not have affected it. Presumably, however, had the change from summer to winter marks occurred while laytime was still running, the charterers would not have been in breach at all, and there would have been no damages, despite the loss not being detention.

9.7 Repudiating the charterparty

If for a voyage chaterer to exceed the laytime were a breach of condition, any shipowner dissatisfied (perhaps because of the state of the market) with the demurrage rate, could avoid it simply by repudiating the charter, and suing for damages at large, for detention. Clearly this would be an undesirable result, but on the other hand the shipowner should not be required to keep his ship available for ever, while the charterer (for example) struggles to find a cargo.

It is clear that exceeding the laytime does not amount to a breach of condition. In the absence of any contrary clause in the charterparty, on the principles in chapter 2, the shipowner can therefore

---

35 [1927] 1 KB 352.
36 [1927] 1 KB 352, 363. Lay days are just another term for laytime.
37 [1927] 1 KB 352, 358.
38 See (eg) the very full review in *Richco International Ltd v Alfred C Toepfer International GmbH (The Bonde)* [1991] 1 Lloyd's Rep 136 (Potter J).
39 [1965] 1 Lloyd's Rep 533 (CA), affd [1967] AC 361 (HL). See also section [9.8].

repudiate, and hence avoid the demurrage provisions for any subsequent delay, only if the delay itself is so long as to frustrate the commercial object of the adventure, in which case the charterer's breach is a repudiatory breach.[40] This would have to be quite a substantial delay. In *Inverkip v Bunge*, many weeks had passed before the charterer even began to load. As we have seen, the shipowner chose not to repudiate, but in any case Scrutton LJ thought that the delay had not been long enough to allow him to do so. The test (whether or not the charterer's breach is repudiatory) is not the expiry of a reasonable time (which had passed), but either a refusal by the charterer to perform at all, or the expiry of so long a time as to frustrate the commercial adventure. Scrutton LJ thought that the shipowners could not validly have withdrawn the vessel on this test, even had they chosen to do so (although Warrington LJ expressed no opinion on whether they were entitled to do so).

This was one of the issues considered by Devlin J in *Universal Cargo Carriers Corp v Citati*.[41] At what point is the shipowner entitled to sail the ship away, when the charterer has not provided a cargo at the loading port?[42] Devlin J thought it well-settled that "the obligation to load within the lay days is a warranty only and not a condition",[43] but said this, right at the start of his judgment:[44]

> "Where time is not of the essence of the contract – in other words, when delay is only a breach of warranty – how long must the delay last before the aggrieved party is entitled to throw up the contract? The theoretical answer is not in doubt. The aggrieved party is relieved from his obligations when the delay becomes so long as to go to the root of the contract and amount to a repudiation of it."

Later in his judgment he took the view, adopting (among others) Brett J's views in *Stanton v Richardson*,[45] that this is the same test as that used to determine whether a contract is frustrated.[46] If the shipowner repudiates, all contract clauses subsequently go, including the demurrage clause – so any damages claim will be for detention.

In *Citati* itself, the shipowners withdrew even before the laytime had expired.[47] Whether he was entitled to do so depended on whether there was an anticipatory breach. According to Devlin J, and in accordance with the principles in chapter 2,[48] the charterers would have committed an anticipatory breach allowing the shipowners to withdraw if either they had renounced their obligations under the charterparty (in effect refusing to perform), or it had become impossible to perform them. The shipowners need not wait for an anticipatory breach to occur, but may repudiate as of that moment. A refusal to perform may be inferred not only from express words, but also from conduct, as interpreted at the time of the repudiation. In *Citati* itself, the owners' claim on renunciation failed.[49]

The owners may also repudiate if the charterers cannot perform the contract within a frustrating time. From chapter 2,[50] this is an objective test, and does not depend on what the owners

---

40 See section [2.6.1].

41 [1957] 2 QB 401.

42 Where there are delays at discharge cargo will often remain on board, in which case the remedy is of course a damages claim, but for detention, not limited by the demurrage clause.

43 [1957] 2 QB 401, 429–30.

44 [1957] 2 QB 401, 426.

45 [1957] 2 QB 401, 433, citing *Stanton v Richardson* (1872) LR 7 CP 421. See generally sections [2.6.1]; [2.7]; [4.2.3].

46 Section [9.5]. Also *ERG Raffinerie Mediterranee SpA v Chevron USA Inc (The Luxmar)* [2007] 2 Lloyd's Rep 542, [23].

47 The case arose on an appeal from arbitration, and the court determined only what tests were to be applied. The question whether the shipowners were in fact entitled to repudiate was referred back to the arbitrator.

48 See section [2.7].

49 When we look at punctual payment of hire in time charterparties, we see a case where renunciation succeeded: see section [12.1.6].

50 Section [2.7].

thought. So in *Citati*, the owners' withdrawal would have been justified, in the opinion of Devlin J, even though it took place even while laytime was still running, if at the time of the withdrawal the charterers had become wholly and finally disabled from finding and loading a cargo before the delay had become so long as to frustrate the adventure. They would then have succeeded on the grounds of impossibility of performance, although they had failed on renunciation. Conversely, if the charterers could have loaded before the delay had become such as to frustrate the adventure, the withdrawal by the shipowners would have been wrongful, even if the owners were certain of the charterers' inability to do so when they withdrew the vessel. The court was unable to decide this question on the facts as found by the arbitrator, so it had to be referred back to him.

Citati principles can apply to other breaches (eg, *Stanton v Richardson*, on seaworthiness).[51]

9.8 Must elect to repudiate

Even once a frustrating time has passed, so as to render the charterer's breach a repudiatory breach, the shipowner must *actually* repudiate in order to avoid the demurrage provision. We can see this in the discussion of *Suisse Atlantique Société D'Armement Maritime SA v NV Rotterdamsche Kolen Centrale*, in the next section. If the contract is not repudiated, all its terms continue to apply, including the demurrage clause.

The essential problem is that to throw up the charterparty can be risky for the shipowner, especially if the charterer is happy to pay demurrage, and continues to reassure the owner that completion of loading or discharge is imminent. By repudiating he may be throwing away the certainty of a continuing demurrage payment (albeit perhaps inadequate to compensate for his losses), for the uncertain prospect of claiming damages for detention. The owner considered repudiating in both *Inverkip v Bunge* and *Suisse Atlantique*, but did not do so. In *Suisse Atlantique* the freight market was depressed, market freight being much lower than charter freight. It would be a difficult decision for an owner to sail away in these circumstances, relinquishing irrevocably his claim to freight under the charterparty, especially if he was unlikely to be able to obtain alternative cargo.[52]

The other problem is that if the shipowner repudiates, not only does he lose his existing rights under the charterparty, but he also risks an action by the charterer for wrongful repudiation, since it is difficult to know in advance of actual litigation what will be held to be a frustrating time. One of the reasons why Jupiter was able to tie up so many vessels on demurrage for so long was that they threatened wrongful repudiation actions whenever the shipowners were tempted to sail away, and shipowners were unprepared to take this risk.[53]

9.9 Application to consecutive voyages

Suisse Atlantique Société D'Armement Maritime SA v NV Rotterdamsche Kolen Centrale (The General Guisan) is an application of the principles discussed in the previous sections. In the Court of Appeal it is also a leading authority on demurrage, and in the House of Lords on the law applicable to fundamental breaches of contract.[54]

In the Court of Appeal, Diplock LJ began his judgment with the words "I am afraid I think this is a very simple case", and indeed the arguments advanced in that court consisted largely of

---

51 See section [4.2.3].

52 This was a consecutive voyage charter, so earning future freight would have been at least a possibility, as it would under a single voyage charter, if the delay was at loading and freight was earned (eg) on delivery.

53 See section [9.3] above. Also Per Gram, *Chartering Documents* (1981), LLP, 18.

54 [1965] 1 Lloyd's Rep 533 (CA), affd [1967] AC 361 (HL).

well-charted ground. Entirely new arguments were advanced in the House of Lords, however, considerably complicating an otherwise essentially simple case.

The General Guisan was chartered under a charterparty (in the Americanised Welsh Coal Charter form) that was to remain in force "for a total of two years consecutive voyages", but *Suisse Atlantique* provides a good illustration of how, in spite of the reference to a period of time, consecutive voyage charterparties differ from time charterparties. The fundamental difficulty facing the shipowners in the case was that the freight payable depended on the number of loaded voyages actually made. In a time charterparty the hire would have been independent of the number of voyages. A secondary point of interest is that the in *Suisse Atlantique* the particular route was defined, whereas usually (but not always) a time charterparty gives the charterer a discretion as to routes.[55]

In *Suisse Atlantique*, owing to delay by the charterers, only eight voyages were completed, rather than the 14 that would have been possible had all loading been completed within the laytime. In the Court of Appeal, Sellers LJ observed that:[56]

> "The freight rate was high, probably under the influence of the closing at that time of the Suez Canal; but the demurrage rate possibly had not been relatively increased and remained relatively low. When freight rates fell, as they did soon after the charter-party, it no doubt proved an expensive way of carrying coal across the Atlantic."

Obviously, when the Suez Canal reopened freight rates dropped again, it became cheaper for the charterers to use other vessels to carry their coal, and keep the *General Guisan* on demurrage. Also, a number of similar disputes arose from coal charters at around this time because the coal market collapsed, and charterers cut their losses by reducing the number of voyages made.[57]

The charterers claimed that they were required only to pay the low demurrage rate fixed in the charterparty. The shipowners claimed damages at large for detention, a much higher sum.[58] The Court of Appeal held, on the normal principles earlier in this chapter, that the owners could claim only demurrage (which had been fixed at an unrealistically low rate) and not damages at large for detention. There is little in the Court of Appeal that adds to the principles discussed above.[59]

The case went to the House of Lords on a completely different point. The shipowners argued for a doctrine of fundamental breach of contract, for which there was limited authority at that time. Essentially the argument ran that as a matter of law exemption clauses, and other clauses limiting liability (such as the demurrage clause in the case), cannot be relied on by a party who is in fundamental breach of contract; this doctrine precluded the charterers from relying on the demurrage clause. The House of Lords held that there was no such doctrine. Whether an exemption clause (or a clause limiting liability, as here) covers the breach depends simply upon its construction, and not on any rule of law as argued by the shipowners. No doubt, as a matter of construction, the courts would be loath to construe an exemption clause so as to cover a really serious breach,[60] but if it is clearly enough expressed then there is no rule of law to prevent it from applying. Here, the demurrage clause clearly protected the charterers, and they did not lose its protection merely because their breach was serious.

---

55 See further sections [5.5] and [5.6].
56 [1965] 1 Lloyd's Rep 533, 537. The contract was entered into when the Suez Canal was closed, in 1956. The canal reopened in 1957, resulting in plummeting freight rates.
57 See Per Gram, *Chartering Documents*, 50.
58 Damages based on the prevailing freight rate would not have been high, the market having collapsed, but the damages claimed would have included lost freight while the canal was still closed, and rates therefore much higher.
59 Sections [9.4]–[9.8].
60 See the discussion of *Glynn v Margetson* at [4.4.4], [22.2].

It was common ground in *Suisse Atlantique* that if the charterers had committed a fundamental breach by keeping the vessel on demurrage (a question of fact for the arbitrators, which was not decided), the shipowners could have sailed away, and entered a fresh charterparty with other charterers. Had they done so, then they would have been able to sue at large *from that time*, unencumbered by the demurrage clause: the charterparty, justifiably repudiated, would have been at an end. However, the owners had chosen not to do this, and expressly kept the contract alive. (The market having fallen substantially on the reopening of the Suez Canal, any new fixture might not have been favourable.) They accordingly remained bound by its terms, including the demurrage clause.

Suisse Atlantique was a consecutive voyage charter where, of course, the risk of delay was on the owners. Such a dispute would have been inconceivable had a time charter been used, throwing the risk of delay on the charterers.

9.10 Once on demurrage always on demurrage

There is a maxim: once on demurrage always on demurrage. Exceptions that apply to laytime do not extend to demurrage. One justification is that, if the peril triggering the clause begins before the end of the laytime, neither party can be blamed. If it begins after the laytime has ended, on the other hand, the shipowners can argue that had the charterers fulfilled their contractual obligations, and completed cargo-handling within the time allowed, the peril would have had no effect on cargo-handling, since it would already have been completed. We can find statements for this justification in *The Saturnia*,[61] *Compania Naviera Aeolus SA v Union of India*,[62] and *The Kalliopi A*.[63]

Another justification is, quite simply, that laytime and demurrage are different things. We can see this view in both *Union of India* and *Dias Compania Naviera SA v Louis Dreyfus Corporation*,[64] and in *Aktieselskabet Reidar v Arcos Ltd*, where (after defining laytime) Atkin LJ he says:[65]

> ". . . demurrage days are days in which the charterer is in breach, and this view alone explains what I conceive to be the well established principle that, unless by express stipulation, exceptions that would protect the charterer during lay days no longer protect him during demurrage days".

Demurrage, in other words, is very different from laytime (this was the case, remember, which really established the definitions of these two terms). An ambiguous clause is no protection: if it is intended to cover demurrage it needs to be clearly so expressed.

What if the exception starts during the laytime? Do you get to demurrage at all? In *The Kalliopi A*, the circumstances relied on by the charterers (congestion) continued throughout the laytime and demurrage period. The parties conceded that the charterparty was not to be drafted in such a way that the exceptions *interrupted* laytime. Had it done so, it would have prevented expiry of the laytime and hence any liability for demurrage. As it was, demurrage started at the usual time and the exceptions no longer operated.

---

61 *Superfos Chartering A/S v NBR (London) Ltd (The Saturnia)* [1987] 2 Lloyd's Rep 43.

62 [1964] AC 868.

63 *Marc Rich & Co Ltd v Tourloti Compania Naviera SA (The Kalliopi A)* [1988] 2 Lloyd's Rep 101.

64 [1978] 1 WLR 261.

65 [1927] 1 KB 352, 363.

Here is a diagrammatic representation of what was argued (these are time lines running from left to right):

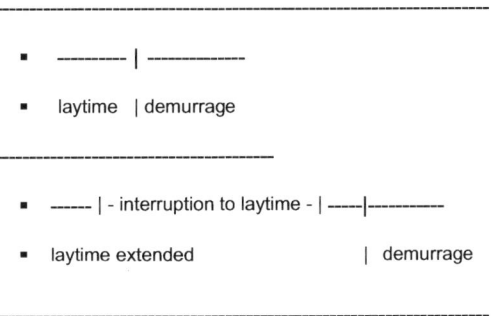

The top part of this time line shows what would have happened, had there been no congestion; the laytime would have expired, and demurrage run as normal. But from the bottom part you can see what can happen if the exception interrupts laytime; because the laytime period is extended, demurrage does not begin at all (the starting point is simply postponed). If it were otherwise, then the interruption would have no meaning. As we have seen, in *The Kalliopi A* itself, the parties conceded that the exceptions did not interrupt laytime, and so the second part of the diagram did not there represent the actual case.

Unfortunately, *The Kalliopi A* has been extended to charterparties where the exceptions arguably *should* have interrupted laytime (and hence prevented demurrage running at all). In *The Lefthero*,[66] this issue does not appear to have been appreciated, and the Court of Appeal purported simply to follow *The Kalliopi A*, though there was no similar concession in the later case. However, the court looked at charter as a whole and took the view that the "underlying objective . . . was to compensate the owners for any delay due to the operation of the convoy system".[67] The result was that, as in *The Kalliopi A*, the clause was not treated as interrupting (and hence extending) laytime. *The Lefthero* was applied in *The Solon*.[68] The problem was at least now clearly appreciated:[69]

> "When the event started to operate, if it were to have the effect of extending the laydays, it would necessarily also have an effect on the obligation to pay demurrage, as the laydays would be extended for the appropriate period; the consequence would be that the obligation to pay demurrage would either never arise or be reduced by an amount equivalent to the extension of the laydays."

But Thomas J decided that this was not the consequence, and followed *The Lefthero*. Ultimately, this was treated as a construction issue, looking at the charterparty as a whole. The case concerned the construction of cl. 28, which stated that strikes were "always excepted", and in Thomas J's view:[70]

> ". . . the clause has to demonstrate a clear intention that the exception should apply even when the vessel is on demurrage whether or not the operation of the peril arises from the earlier

66 *Ellis Shipping Corporation v Voest Alpine Intertrading (The Lefthero)* [1992] 2 Lloyd's Rep 109. *The Lefthero* was considered in a slightly different context in *Stolt Tankers Inc v Landmark Chemicals SA* [2002] 1 Lloyd's Rep 78.

67 [1992] 2 Lloyd's Rep 109, 113.

68 *Cero Navigation Corp v Jean Lion & Cie (The Solon)* [2000] 1 Lloyd's Rep 292.

69 [2000] 1 Lloyd's Rep 292, 298.

70 [2000] 1 Lloyd's Rep 292, 296.

breach by the charterer of his obligation to discharge within the laydays. For a clause to have such a clear intention requires language that leaves one in no doubt that that is what the parties intended. Clause 28 falls short of demonstrating such an intention."

It was possible to give content to the clause without it including an exception to the obligation to load within the laydays. For example, the clause:[71]

". . . covers cases of prevention as well as delay; it covers liabilities in unliquidated damages, as for example damages for failure to load or damages for detention; . . .".

So, *The Kalliopi A* and *The Lefthero* were applied.

No doubt this is a possible interpretation of this clause, and there have been later cases where a very narrow construction has been applied to similar clauses, on the grounds that they are ambiguous.[72] Nonetheless what seems to have happened, in reality, is that a principle that had some merit in according demurrage special treatment has been extended without great thought to apply to laytime as well.

9.11 Question

Mabel charters *Gencarrier* to Paul for a voyage. The loading port is Archangel, which is known to ice up in winter. The vessel arrives in September, at a time when, if the vessel loads within the laytime, she is likely to be able to leave port before being iced in. No cargo is ready, however, until well after the laytime has been exceeded. Because of the delay *Gencarrier* is iced in for the winter.

On the assumption that they would be higher than the demurrage rate, advise Mabel whether she can claim damages for detention, and, if so, from when.

Comment

We know from section [9.6] that if the loss is of a different type from delay (as it is here) it might be possible to avoid the demurrage limit, but the authorities do not speak with one voice on whether an additional breach is also required (which is not the case here).[73] It would be a different matter if Paul had a choice of loading ports in Russia, and the icing-up propensities of Archangel made it an unsafe port in the autumn. Then there may also be a breach of the safe port obligation in chapter 13,[74] in which case the additional breach requirement would also be satisfied.

There is also, in any case, the possibility, for a very long (actual or anticipated) delay, of the owners repudiating the charterparty, on the principles in *Universal Cargo Carriers Corp v Citati*.[75] If they do so, they can of course avoid the demurrage limit.

---

71 Ibid.
72 Eg, *Frontier International Shipping Corp v Swissmarine Corp Inc* (*The Cape Equinox*) [2005] 1 Lloyd's Rep 390.
73 Compare the judgments in *Aktieselskabet Reidar v Arcos Ltd* [1927] 1 KB 352; see also *The Bonde* [1991] 1 Lloyd's Rep 136.
74 Section [13.9].
75 [1957] 2 QB 401, in section [9.7].

Part 3

Time charterparties

Chapter 10

Nature of time charterparties

Chapter Contents

10.1 Main features of time charters

Part 3 of the book examines time charterparties. This part of the book is shorter than that on voyage charterparties, because many time charterparty clauses are similar to clauses in voyage forms.

Some of the main features of time charters, and the fundamental distinction between time and voyage charters, have already been set out.[1] This chapter looks at the time charter in greater depth, and in particular the difference between time and demise charters. It will be seen that though the time charter shares some of its terms with the demise charter, it is not only a very much more sophisticated instrument, but also one that is different in nature. This has significant consequences for the law, as set out in this part of the book.

A point that was made in chapter 1 was that all charterparties are contracts whose terms are largely unregulated by the law, and that can therefore be altered by the parties.[2] However, the distinction between time and demise charters has legal consequences which cannot be altered by the parties, partly because of restrictions on the remedies provided by the law. The property consequences later in this chapter, for example, follow from very nature of a time charter.[3] They could not be altered without converting the charterparty back into a demise charter. Similarly, the law on withdrawal in chapter 12 has been affected by the very nature of the time charterparty, and in particularly by the service element in the charterparty. The shipowner is doing far more than merely providing the ship.[4]

Time and demise charterparties are both period charters, under which (as we saw in chapter 1) the charterers pay hire. Unlike voyage charter freight, hire is payable on a time basis. Under a time (or demise) charter, therefore, the risks of unforeseen events causing delay fall (subject, as ever, to contrary agreement) on the charterers. Unlike their voyage counterparts, time charterers will pay more for a voyage that takes longer. Conversely, the shipowners can more accurately calculate their costs.

The time charter developed from the earlier demise form, as a more complicated instrument. Though, because of this development, time and demise charters share many common terms, they are in fact very different types of contract. A demise charterparty is essentially a chattel lease. It is the demise of the ship. It is also described as a bareboat charter. The shipowners provide just the ship, and transfer possession of her to the charterers. The charterers provide their own crew, and there is no service element to a demise charter. Under a time charterparty, by contrast, the shipowners allow the charterers the use of the ship, and the services of the master and crew. It is a contract for services, not merely hire. Indeed, they do not transfer possession of the ship to the charterers. The nature of a time charterparty has been often described, as for example in the following passage from Lord Wilberforce's speech in The Laconia:[5]

> "As has often been pointed out, the description of a time charter as a hire or demise of a ship is very misleading: all that the owner does, in fact, is to agree to provide services, those of the master and the crew . . . in sailing the ship for the charterers' purposes . . . It must be obvious that this is a very different type of creature from a lease of land."

---

1 Section [1.3].

2 Sections [1.3]; [1.7].

3 Section [1.6].

4 Eg, *Scandanavian Trading Tanker Co AB v Flota Petrolera Ecuatoriana (The Scaptrade)* [1983] 2 AC 694, the passage from Lord Diplock's speech set out below: section [10.6], and see generally section [12.1.2].

5 Lord Wilberforce in *Mardorf Peach & Co Ltd v Attica Sea Carriers Corporation of Liberia (The Laconia)* [1977] AC 850 at 870A to C – cited in *The Astra* [2013] 2 Lloyd's Rep 69, [40]. On *The Astra* see further [12.1.6].

Because it is essentially a contract to provide services it is therefore legitimate, in my view, to describe a time, but not a demise charterparty as a contract for the carriage of goods by sea, since that is the function of the crew, whose services are being provided.

The difference between the two types was also described, by MacKinnon LJ in *Sea and Land Securities v Dickinson*, as follows:[6]

> "A time charterparty is, in fact, a misleading document, because the real nature of what is undertaken by the shipowner is disguised by the use of language dating from a century or more ago, which was appropriate to a contract of a different character then in use. At that time a time charterparty (now known as a demise charterparty) was an agreement under which possession of the ship was handed by the shipowner to the charterer for the latter to put his servants and crew in her and sail her for his own benefit. . . . The modern form of time charterparty is, in essence, one by which the shipowner agrees with the time charterer that during a certain named period he will render services by his servants and crew to carry the goods which are put on board his ship by the time charterer. . . . [Between] the old and the modern form of contract there is all the difference between the contract which a man makes when he hires a boat in which to row himself about and the contract he makes with a boatman that he shall take him for a row."

In addition to paying hire, time charterers are typically responsible for providing the bunker fuel. It follows that, for this reason, as well as because they bear the delay risk, they are interested in making the voyage as short as possible. The interest of the owners may be different, and we see the consequences of this when we consider routeing, war clauses, and piracy.

Under a time charterparty, the charterers are (within any trading or other limits in the charterparty) entitled to direct the master as to the employment of the ship. The operational control of the vessel remains with the master, however, and time charterers are not entitled to give orders as to navigation, or the safety of the ship.

It must be clear from this that the time form is quite a complex provision, certainly far more so than the earlier demise counterpart. The distinction between navigation, which is within the owners' discretion, and employment, which is for the charterers to determine, is not always straightforward, having been recently litigated as far as the House of Lords, for example, in *The Hill Harmony*.[7] Conversely, orders as to employment can cause loss to the owners, so that indemnities have to be provided to cater for that possibility.[8]

The issue of bills of lading is also more complex for time charters. Under the demise form the master acts for the charterers, who can potentially incur liability in respect of bills signed on their behalf.[9] Under a time charter, by contrast, bills of lading will typically be issued as directed by the charterers, but the master will typically sign for the shipowner, who will therefore incur any potential liability. Time charters may therefore place restrictions on the issue of bills, and provide for indemnities should the shipowner suffer loss.[10]

10.2 Use of time and demise charters

Whether or not agreements resembling time charters existed earlier, they were little used until the latter part of the nineteenth century, when steamships had finally developed sufficiently to be able to

---

6 [1942] 2 KB 65, 69.

7 *Whistler International Ltd v Kawasaki Kisen Kaisha Ltd (The Hill Harmony)* [2001] 1 AC 638 (see further section [13.3]).

8 See section [13.2].

9 *Baumwoll* below [10.8], and see more generally chapter 19.

10 See further section [13.7].

be used reliably and economically on long haul routes, and there developed a demand for charters for a longer term than a single voyage:[11]

"... the time charter was, it seems, unknown until the second half of the last century when the development of the steamship made the duration of voyages accurately predictable and accordingly merchants and others were prepared to charter ships upon a time and not only upon a voyage basis."

Similar comments can be found in Evans LJ's judgment in *The Island Archon*, when talking of:[12]

"... authorities dating back to the beginning of the present century when time charter-parties became more common or at least more frequently the subject of dispute in the Courts. The reason for this may have been the fact that shipping movements could be predicted more reliably with steamships than with sail, and this led to charterers being more willing to pay hire for the use of the ship's services throughout an agreed period."

When ocean voyages were predominantly made by sail, the master and crew (who under a time charterparty are engaged by the owners) could significantly affect sailing time, but to travel faster in bad weather was both harder work and more dangerous. Presumably charterers were unattracted by a charter where the owners (and hence master and crew) had no interest in hurrying the voyage. With the advent of steam, the speed of the vessel could be more readily guaranteed.

Both voyage and demise types are older, and time forms typically borrow clauses, not always appropriately, from the older demise variety.

Today, the time charterparty performs a number of functions, for example:

A prospective purchaser of a vessel, who is unsure of the market, may take an option to purchase, but delay taking up the option until a long time charter has been fixed (a "bankable charter").[13] Moreover, the financing of the vessel may depend on a bankable charter being fixed in advance of the purchase being made. It is not uncommon for purchasers to time charter back to the seller, nor indeed for demise charterers to time charter back to the owners.[14]

A tramp trader may decide to speculate on a freight rate rise, taking a time charterparty and trading on his own account as disponent owner, either on a bill of lading basis or by sub-charter. It seems to be common for first shipping ventures to be on speculative short-term time charters.[15]

A liner or other operator (especially common with oil companies) may need to add temporary tonnage to his fleet.[16]

The demise form, from which the time charterparty developed, was less convenient unless the charterer wanted to take over responsibility for the management and operation of the vessel. In reality, a time charterer will not normally want to do this, preferring to rely on the expertise of the shipowner, but he will want to direct where the vessel is to trade, or, in other words, her

---

11 *The Albazero* [1977] AC 774, 808 (Roskill LJ). Whereas steam liners existed as early as the 1830s, sail continued to predominate for cargo, for another 40 years or so. This was especially true for longer routes, and for cargoes where speed was relatively unimportant, principally because the need to carry coal reduced the cargo-carrying capacity of the vessel. As late as the end of the century we see the need for coaling stations in *The Vortigern* [1899] P 140, which we considered in section [4.2.5].

12 *Triad Shipping Co v Stellar Chartering & Brokerage Inc (The Island Archon)* [1994] 2 Lloyd's Rep 227, 232.

13 The term used in Per Gram, *Chartering Documents* (1981), LLP, 51. A similar type of transaction can be seen in *The Ocean Frost* [1986] 1 AC 717.

14 Eg, *Candlewood Navigation Corp Ltd v Mitsui OSK Lines Ltd (The Mineral Transporter)* [1986] AC 1, in section [10.7].

15 See, eg, the description in Williams, *Chartering Documents*, 4th ed (1999), LLP, at 61.

16 Eg, *Elder Dempster & Co v Paterson, Zochonis & Co* [1924] AC 522, in section [17.1.6] on this issue.

employment. Conversely, the shipowner may be reluctant to part with control over the vessel to the extent envisaged under a demise charter, preferring to keep his own master and crew aboard.

Whether for these or other reasons, charterparties by demise are rarely (if ever) used today for the general carriage of goods. Even compulsory requisition is usually by time charter,[17] whereas demise charterparties have been used in the past, the charterers being the requisitioning government. Charters by demise are sometimes used for (eg) holiday yachts, which might be chartered for the summer, the charterers providing their own crew.[18] This is pretty insignificant by comparison with time charter usage, however, and about 70 years ago MacKinnon LJ remarked that demise charterparties were virtually obsolete.[19] But whereas that might still be true for carriage of goods as such, demise charterparties are still used today, to finance the acquisition of ships. The owners might be a finance house or bank, but their ownership will be only nominal, in the sense that they will not wish to be involved in the management of the ship. They retain ownership purely for security, rather as a finance company retains ownership of a car under a hire purchase agreement. Indeed, BIMCO's standard form demise charterparty, Barecon 2001, allows for a genuine hire purchase agreement to be entered into as an option.[20] The charterers will wish to be in full possession of the ship, and will act to all intents and purposes as if owners. Clearly a demise charter is best suited to this type of arrangement, because the charterers will wish to engage their own master and crew, and operate the vessel as if she were their own. Often this type of charterparty is very long term, possibly up to the expected life of the vessel. For example, in a sale and lease-back arrangement, the operator will purchase a newbuilding, sell it to a finance house, and then lease it back from the finance house on a long-term demise basis.[21]

10.3 Some time charterparty clauses

As we saw in chapter 1, time charters, like their demise cousins, are period charters, and risk of delay is on the charterers.

A time charterparty typically begins with the date of the charterparty, the names and domicile of the contracting parties, the name, present position, description and condition of the vessel. There will be hire clauses, and, associated with these, withdrawal provisions for non-, late or under-payment, and an off-hire clause. The charterers will have the use of the vessel for an agreed period, which is typically fixed as a number of calendar months (except for trip-time charterparties).[22] It is obviously difficult for the charterers to be able to predict exactly when the last voyage will be completed, so a margin is usually agreed at charterers' option to allow for the final voyage to be completed. There may also be a final voyage clause giving the charterers further discretion as to the period of the charter. Provision will be made for times and places of delivery of the vessel to the charterers, and redelivery at the end of the period to the shipowners.[23]

---

17 Eg, *Larrinaga Steamship Co Ltd v The King (The Ramon de Larrinaga)* [1945] AC 246; (1944/45) 78 Ll L Rep 167, in section [13.3].

18 Time charters are also used, if the owners are providing skipper and crew: Coles and Lorenzon (eds), *The Law of Yachts and Yachting*, (2011), Informa, ch. 8.

19 *Sea and Land Securities Ltd v William Dickinson & Co Ltd* [1942] 2 KB 65, 69.

20 Barecon 2001, Part IV. The form is available at http://www.pfri.uniri.hr/~biserka/documents/Sample_Copy_BARECON_2001. pdf. It also has a flagging-out option.

21 Eg, in *More OG Romsdal Fylkesbatar AS v Demise Charterers of the ship Jotunheim (The Jotunheim)* [2005] 1 Lloyd's Rep 181, in section [12.1.2], a demise charter was used to effect hire-purchase, albeit on a term of just 48 months.

22 Section [10.4].

23 See chapter 11.

Although the master and crew are engaged by the owners in a time charter, the master is under the orders of the charterers as to the employment of the vessel, ie, must go where the charterers direct. The charterparty usually provides, however, for some geographical limits on where the vessel may operate, for example to prevent potential danger to the ship.[24] Many, but not all, time charters provide indemnity provisions, since compliance with charterers' order may occasion loss to the shipowners.

Although many time clauses are similar to those found in voyage forms, because in a time charterparty the charterers rather than the owners bear the risk of delay, there are substantial differences between the two types of charter. For example, time charterparties always contain stipulations as to the speed of the vessel, whereas voyage charterparties need not, and rarely do.[25] The speed of the vessel is of obvious importance to time charterers, because on it directly depends the number of voyages they can complete within the period. It is of far less importance to voyage charterers, who pay the same freight for the voyage however long it takes.

Time charterparties also share a number of terms with the older demise form. Both types are period charter, and time clauses developed from the demise form. Hire clauses appear in both, and both contain delivery and redelivery clauses. Other similarities include the cancelling clause, delivery laydays (if agreed),[26] remedies for non-payment of hire, for example the owners' lien on cargoes and sub-freights, and the shipowner's right to withdraw for non-payment of hire.[27] Both time and demise charterers are responsible for the provision of bunker fuel, so they have an obvious interest in the vessel's consumption. Also, since hire is on a period basis, the charterers need to know the vessel's speed in order to calculate the number of voyages they can make. Other clauses shared between the two types are the war clause, commission clause, and law and arbitration clause.

10.4 Trip-time charters

Although under a time charter the period is usually based upon an agreed number of calendar days or months, it can alternatively be for a single voyage, or series of voyages. A charterparty in time form used for a single voyage is known as a trip-time charterparty, and such charters are not uncommon; whereas on rising markets owners can be reluctant to fix their vessels for long periods, no such reluctance affects the trip time charterparty.

A trip time charterparty resembles a voyage charter in that the charterers are unlikely to have the same choices as to ports visited, routes, etc, and so much of the general law that applies to time charterparties will not apply. However, the fundamental characteristic of a time charterparty remains that risk of delay is on the charterers. In this fundamental sense, a trip time charterparty is very different from its voyage cousin.[28]

As discussed in chapter 1,[29] where the charter is on a voyage basis, freight is payable to the shipowner. Freight is usually calculated on the tonnage of cargo carried, and not on the time that the voyage takes. If the charter is in consecutive voyage form, freight is calculated on the tonnage of cargo carried and the number of voyages completed, but is again independent of the time that the series of voyages take. Under a trip time charterparty, on the other hand, the hire payable depends on the time that the vessel is used by the charterer, and does not depend on the tonnage of cargo carried.

---

24 See chapter 13.
25 But see section [5.2], where the speed clauses in some voyage charters are described.
26 These essentially fix first and last days for delivery.
27 See respectively sections [12.1.8]; [12.1.2].
28 See section [1.4].
29 Sections [1.3]; [1.4].

A consequence of using the time form, even for a single voyage, is to place the risk of delay on the charterers, rather than the owners. The Doric Pride involved a trip time charter, where Rix LJ observed that:[30]

". . . under a time charter the risk of delay is fundamentally on the charterer, who remains liable to pay hire in all circumstances unless the charterer can bring himself within the plain words of an off-hire provision".

In The Eugenia,[31] the Baltime form was used for a single voyage "to India via the Black Sea". Because this was a time charter the charterers had to bear the cost of delay through being caught in the Suez Canal.[32] It follows that whereas if a charter in voyage form is used it is easier for the charterers to calculate their costs, because they are independent of the time the voyage takes, it is easier for the shipowners if the charterparty is in trip-time form, since now it is the charterers who bear the risk of delay.

In The Democritos,[33] the charterparty was "for about a trip via port or ports via the Pacific, duration about 4 to 6 months". Though it must have been intended for a single voyage, this was held to be a time and not a voyage charter. Lord Denning MR thought that the reference to the trip simply stated "the trading limits within which the vessel is to trade during the time charter".[34] Although the contract there was not absolutely locked down into a single trip, the case provides another example of a time charter intended for a single voyage.

10.5 Distinction between time and demise charters

Despite their sharing many common terms, time and demise charters are very different creatures. The main distinctions have already been mentioned,[35] that under a time (but not demise) charter, the shipowners provide not only the vessel herself, but also the services of the master and crew, and that under a demise (but not time) charter, charterers take over full possession of the vessel. Under a time charter, although the master is under the directions of the charterer, the owners retain possession of the vessel. It follows that the demise terms "delivery" and "redelivery" are, strictly speaking, inappropriate in time charterparties, where possession of the vessel remains with the owner. Yet these terms, which make perfect sense in a demise charter, are universally used, albeit inaccurately, in time charters; the time charterparty developed from its demise forebear, rather than from first principles in its own right, and some of the terms of time charterparties are throwbacks. In The Berge Tasta, Donaldson J contrasted the two types as follows:[36]

"Under a time charterparty, not being a charter by way of demise, the shipowner undertakes to make the vessel available to the charterer for the purposes of undertaking ballast and loaded voyages as required by the charterer within a specified area over a stated period. The shipowner's remuneration known as 'time chartered freight' or 'hire' is at a fixed rate for a unit of time

30 Hyundai Merchant Marine Co Ltd v Furnace Withy (Australia) Pty (The Doric Pride) [2006] 2 Lloyd's Rep 175, [28]. (The charterers successfully brought themselves within the off-hire provision: section [12.3.6].)

31 Ocean Tramp Tankers Corporation v V/O Sovfracht (The Eugenia) [1964] 2 QB 226.

32 The charterers argued that the charterparty had been frustrated by the closure, and that they were relieved of any obligations under it, but the Court of Appeal did not accept this argument: see further section [2.12.3]. Another consequence of this being a time charter was that the charterers were in breach of the (Baltime) war clause, even though they had done no more than order the vessel to take the normal route for the voyage: [1964] 2 QB 226, 237 (Lord Denning MR). On time charter war clauses generally, see sections [13.10]; [22.4].

33 Marbienes Compania Naviera SA v Ferrostaal AG (The Democritos) [1976] 2 Lloyd's Rep 149, in section [11.2].

34 [1976] 2 Lloyd's Rep 149, 153.

35 See section [10.1].

36 Skibsaktieselskapet Snefonn v Kawasaki Kisen Kaisha Ltd (The Berge Tasta) [1975] 1 Lloyd's Rep 422, 424.

> regardless of how the vessel is used by the charterer. Risk of delay thus falls on the charterer. The shipowner meets the cost of maintaining the vessel and paying the crew's wages, but the cost of fuel and port charges fall on the charterer. At the end of the period covered by the time charter the vessel is said to be 'redelivered' to the shipowner. This is a misleading term for the vessel never leaves the possession of the shipowner. All that is meant is that the time charter then ends in exactly the same way as a voyage charterparty ends when the last cargo is discharged."

Note the point that he makes about risk of delay, Donaldson J contrasting the time charter with the voyage form, in this respect.[37]

In a time charterparty the owners remain responsible for the maintenance of the vessel, and there is also typically an off-hire clause that allows the charterers to withhold hire for periods when the vessel is unserviceable.[38] In a demise charterparty, however, the charterers are responsible for her maintenance, and there is no off-hire clause. Thus, the obligation to maintain the vessel (typically in a state of good repair and efficient operating condition with unexpired classification at all times throughout the period) falls upon the charterers, and the owners are typically entitled to redelivery at the end of the period "in the same or as good structure, state and condition and class, fair wear and tear excepted" as on delivery.[39] There will also be inspection and withdrawal clauses to assist owners in the enforcement of the maintenance obligation. However, because demise charterparties are often for a very long term, there may be some provision protecting the charterers if there are hidden defects that appear early in the period, or if expensive alterations are necessary during the term in order for the vessel to continue to operate legally (because of changes in legislation, for example, relating to safety).[40]

Demise (but not time) charterers are often required to take out hull insurance on the vessel, especially if the fixture is long term.[41] Usually the charterers insure the hull and machinery up to the agreed value (although sometimes the owner takes out insurance to charterers' account). Typically the charterers make insurance claims and carry out repairs, but in the event of total loss the insurance payments are made to the owners, who then redistribute the moneys according to the respective interests of themselves and the charterers. Salvage and towage, on the other hand, is usually for charterers' sole benefit.[42]

10.6   Time charterparties and third parties

Another difference between the time and demise charterparty is that a demise charterparty probably gives the charterer a property interest in the ship. However, because of its nature this is almost certainly not true of a time charter. Generally speaking, a time charter creates obligations that are enforceable only against the other party to it. Consequently, if the shipowner sells the ship, the new owner is not bound by the charterparty. If he refuses to perform it, the charterer's recourse is against the original owner.

It is different with a demise charter. Certainly, at the very least, the charterer obtains possession and becomes a bailee of the vessel, but a demise charterer is probably also regarded as an equitable lessee of the vessel, which gives him a property interest, enforceable against third parties. Very briefly, contracts that are enforceable in equity are capable of creating equitable property interests.[43] While

---

37 See further section [1.3]. Note also that "hire" used to be called "time chartered freight": see further sections [12.1.8]; [12.2].

38 See section [12.3].

39 Eg, Barecon 2001, cl. 15. See also *Attica Sea Carriers Corp v Ferrostaal Poseidon Bulk Reederei GmbH (The Puerto Buitrago)* [1976] 1 Lloyd's Rep 250, in section [11.3.1].

40 See generally Barecon 2001, cl. 10 on the maintenance obligation, and cl. 8 for inspections.

41 Eg, Barecon 2001, cl. 13 (but cf. the optional cl. 14, under which owners insure). This was an issue in *Gard Marine & Energy Ltd v China National Chartering Co Ltd (The Ocean Victory)* [2015] 1 Lloyd's Rep 381.

42 See generally, Per Gram, *Chartering Documents*, ch. 4.

43 See generally section [3.4].

such contracts do not always create property interests,[44] equitable property interests certainly cannot be created unless the equitable remedy of specific performance is available, to enforce the contract. The effect of this remedy is to render non-performance of the contract a contempt of court, and, not surprisingly, it is a remedy that is rarely granted. All equitable remedies are discretionary, and, for example, can be lost if the claimant has behaved in an inequitable fashion,[45] and (because enforcement would be difficult in practice) specific performance is not available for contracts that require constant supervision, in other words contracts with a service element.[46] Specific performance is not therefore (because of the service element) available to enforce a time charterparty. In *The Scaptrade*, Lord Diplock observed that:[47]

> "A time charter, unless it is a charter by demise, with which your Lordships are not here concerned, transfers to the charterer no interest in or right to possession of the vessel; it is a contract for services to be rendered to the charterer by the shipowner through the use of the vessel by the shipowner's own servants, the master and the crew, acting in accordance with such directions as to the cargoes to be loaded and the voyages to be undertaken as by the terms of the charterparty the charterer is entitled to give to them. Being a contract for services it is thus the very prototype of a contract of which before the fusion of law and equity a court would never grant specific performance . . . ."

By contrast, because there is no service element to a demise charter, and hence no continuing obligations requiring supervision, specific performance can (in principle at least) be awarded to enforce it.

In *The Stena Nautica* (No. 2), the Court of Appeal granted specific performance of a demise charterparty.[48] A probable consequence is that demise charterers have an equitable title that binds third parties, such as a new owner, or indeed subsequent demise charterer. In other words, the new owner, or subsequent demise charterer, can be required to enforce the original demise charterparty, the only person who takes free being a *bona fide* purchaser with neither actual nor constructive notice of it.[49] The position is as in the following diagram, where "BFPWN" stands for "*bona fide* purchaser without notice":

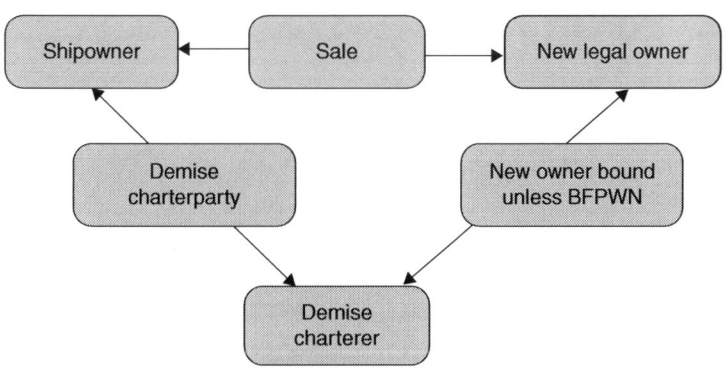

---

44 Eg, *National Provincial Bank Ltd v Ainsworth* [1965] AC 1175.
45 See section [3.4].
46 Ibid.
47 [1983] 2 AC 694, 700–1.
48 *CN Marine Inc v Stena Line A/B* (*The Stena Nautica*) (*No. 2*) [1982] 2 Lloyd's Rep 336.
49 See section [3.4], this diagram being the same shape, showing the party to be bound at the top right.

The Stena Nautica does not go this far, because, though there is at least an allusion to property issues in Lord Denning MR's judgment,[50] the decision in the end was simply that the demise charterer was entitled to specific performance against the original shipowner. But though the property consequences do not always follow from the remedy, there is nothing in *The Stena Nautica* to suggest that the demise charterers were limited to suing the original shipowner.

Whatever the position for demise charters, a time charterparty is a service contract, and specific performance is not available for a contract which envisages continuing obligations requiring supervision.[51] The starting point must be that time charterparties take effect only as contracts between the parties to the charterparty, and do not give the charterer the equivalent of a proprietary interest in the vessel. Certainly, there should be no possibility of a property interest under a contract that is essentially to perform services, for which specific performance is not available. In the absence of a property interest, the starting point is that the English privity of contract doctrine therefore applies, which states that a contract between two parties (ie, shipowners and charterers) does not bind any other person.[52] On this view, if the shipowners sell the vessel, the new owners are not directly bound by the terms of any time charterparty to which the sellers were subject. If the new owners refuse to honour it, the charterers can undoubtedly claim damages against the original shipowners, but cannot directly enforce the charterparty against the new owners. The position now therefore becomes as follows:

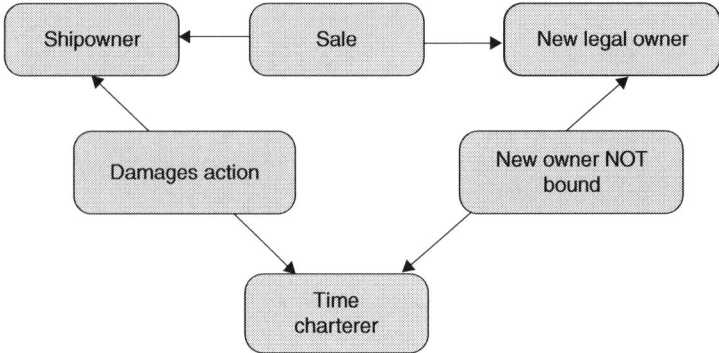

Although a time charterparty creates no proprietary interest, and although specific performance is not available, time charters can be enforced by injunction, also an equitable remedy. There are circumstances in which subsequent owners can therefore be bound, at least to the extent of being restrained from acting contrary to the terms of the charterparty. The issue is the extent of the principle, and consequent upon that, the circumstances in which they can be bound.

In the early case of *De Mattos v Gibson*,[53] a mortgagee of a vessel, who had notice of a prior voyage charterparty, could in principle be restrained from acting inconsistently with the charterparty. In an oft-quoted passage, Knight Bruce LJ said:[54]

---

50 [1982] 2 Lloyd's Rep 336, 344.
51 Eg, *The Scaptrade* [1983] 2 AC 694, a decision of the House of Lords considered in depth, in section [12.1.2].
52 See further chapter 17, and esp. on binding non-parties (though in a different context), sections [17.4]; [17.5].
53 (1858) 4 De G & J 276.
54 (1858) 4 De G & J 276, 282.

"Reason and justice seem to prescribe that, at least as a general rule, where a man, by gift or purchase, acquires property from another, with knowledge of a previous contract, lawfully and for valuable consideration made by him with a third person, to use and employ the property for a particular purpose in a specified manner, the acquirer shall not, to the material damage of the third person, in opposition to the contract and inconsistently with it, use and employ the property in a manner not allowable to the giver or seller."

In *Lord Strathcona Steamship Co Ltd v Dominion Coal Co Ltd*,[55] the Privy Council appeared to accept that *De Mattos* was based on the principle of *Tulk v Moxhay*.[56] This was a case involving an equitable property interest in land, enforcement of which depends on the purchaser having actual or constructive notice of the prior contract.[57] In *Strathcona* itself, however, the purchaser had actual (not merely constructive) notice of the prior time charter, and have expressly covenanted with his seller to perform it. In *Port Line Ltd v Ben Line Steamers Ltd*, Diplock J observed that *Tulk v Moxhay* had been restricted to particular types of negative covenants in relation to land,[58] and thought that even if *Stratchcona* were correct (which he doubted), it was based not on *Tulk v Moxhay*, but on *Lumley v Gye*,[59] the foundation of the modern law of interference with contract. (Interference with contract is a common law tort action where an injunction can be granted to prevent third parties to contracts from deliberately interfering with them.) The principles in *De Mattos* were properly limited to cases where the purchaser had express notice, and the remedy was limited to the negative one, of restraining the purchaser from acting inconsistently with the prior charterparty.

In *Port Line Ltd v Ben Line Steamers Ltd*, the claimants had time chartered a vessel from Silver Line Ltd. Silver Line sold the vessel to the defendants, who then chartered it by demise back to Silver Line for the unexpired period of the plaintiffs' time charter. The demise charterparty contained a clause:

"If the ship be requisitioned this charter shall thereupon cease".

There was no similar clause in the plaintiffs' time charterparty (but the defendants were unaware of this). It seems likely that the defendants demised the vessel back to the original owners, to enable them to perform the plaintiffs' time charter.

The sale of the vessel to the defendants occurred in February 1956, and in August of that year the vessel was requisitioned for use during the Suez crisis. The defendants received compensation for the requisition from the Crown, and the plaintiffs claimed, not to enforce the time charterparty as such, but a share of the requisition compensation, in their capacity as time charterers. Diplock J rejected their claim.

The defendants (the new owners of the vessel) had been wrong in their belief that the time charter had ceased on requisition, but advanced two main arguments. First, they claimed that the plaintiffs' time charterparty had been frustrated by the requisition. Secondly, even if it had not been frustrated, it was binding only on Silver Line, the original shipowners, not themselves, the new owners. They failed on the first argument,[60] but succeeded on the second. As it was necessary only for the defendants to succeed on one argument or the other, the claimants' claim failed. On the second ground, Diplock J held that time charterparties do not bind third parties. Diplock J concluded that *Strathcona* was wrong, or alternatively, that it should be limited to its facts. In *Port Line*, by contrast with *Strathcona*, the purchasers knew only of the existence of the

---

55 [1926] AC 108.
56 (1848) 2 Ph 774.
57 See section [3.4.2].
58 [1958] 2 QB 146, 154.
59 (1853) 2 E & B 216: [1958] 2 QB 146, 165.
60 See further section [2.12.2].

charterparty, not of its terms (indeed, they thought, wrongly, that it would cease upon requisition). In *Strathcona* the charterers were claiming only a negative remedy (an injunction restraining inconsistent use) the claimants in *Port Line* were claiming a share of the compensation paid by the Crown, under s. 4(3) of the Compensation (Defence) Act 1939. This required that they had to "be entitled to possession of, or to use, the vessel, . . . but for the requisition". It was a positive remedy that depended on establishing a property interest. Diplock J was not prepared to extend the principles of *Strathcona* this far.

As we have seen, Diplock J's view was that *Strathcona*, if correct at all, was based on the principles of *Lumley v Gye*. There was, however, the additional feature in *Strathcona* that the vessel was acquired expressly subject to the charterparty, leading to an argument that the purchaser became a constructive trustee, and hence bound directly to the contractual terms.[61] Reasoning similar to this can be found in other cases, of which the best known is probably the judgment of Lord Denning MR in *Binions v Evans*,[62] where purchasers of land were held bound by a "tenancy agreement" to which they took expressly subject. *Binions v Evans* has since been applied elsewhere (albeit only in cases involving land). The problem with this reasoning in a time charter context, as Diplock J pointed out in *Port Line*, is that it is, in any case, difficult to see how the positive obligations under the charterparty can be enforced in equity, given the service element. On this view, the constructive trust reasoning adds nothing to the previous discussion.

> We can perhaps conclude that the new owner will be bound:
> −if he has actual knowledge of the charterparty (including its terms); and
> −only by injunction (restraining him from acting inconsistently).

The injunction will in any case not be available as of right, but is discretionary, as are all equitable remedies.

10.7 Property and tort actions

If the vessel is damaged, the lack of a proprietary interest in the vessel will prevent time charterers from having title to sue in negligence. In *The Mineral Transporter*,[63] the plaintiffs were time charterers of *The Ibaraki Maru*, which was damaged in a collision with *The Mineral Transporter*, a vessel owned by the defendants. The collision was caused by the defendant shipowners' negligence, and the plaintiffs suffered a loss of profits during the time the vessel was undergoing repairs. Also, the hire they paid over that period was wasted. The Privy Council held that the plaintiffs could not recover in negligence from the owners of the other vessel, because they had suffered economic loss only.

The position of a demise charterer is different. This was recognised in *The Mineral Transporter* itself: the plaintiffs were sub-charterers, the head charterparty being by demise, and it was accepted that the head charterers would have been entitled to sue.[64] Here is a diagrammatic representation of the parties in *The Mineral Transporter*:

---

61 [1926] AC 108, esp. 124–5.
62 [1972] Ch 359, 368.
63 [1986] AC 1.
64 Their possessory rights as bailees would be sufficient to found an action in negligence: see further generally on title to sue in negligence section [16.9].

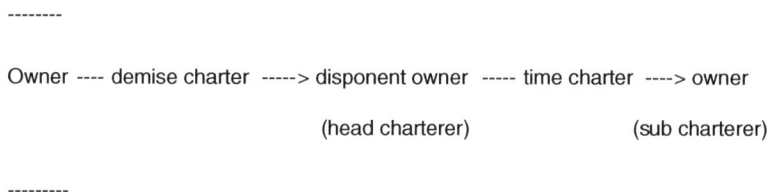

In *Elliott Steam Tug Co Ltd v Shipping Controller*,[65] an earlier Court of Appeal decision, which figured significantly in *The Mineral Transporter*, Scrutton LJ observed that "charterers under a charter not amounting to a demise do not and cannot sue . . . a wrongdoer who has sunk by collision their chartered ship",[66] a possible implication perhaps being that a demise charterer could sue.

10.8 Test for demise charterparty

Given the significant differences between the two types, it is necessary to be able to distinguish between them. In *Baumwoll Manufactur von Carl Scheibler v Christopher Furness*,[67] the master and crew were chosen and paid for by the charterer, except that the owner chose the chief engineer. The House of Lords treated this as a demise charter, though the word "demise" did not appear in the document. Consequently, the master signed bills of lading as agent of the charterer, not the owner, whereas in general the opposite is the case in time charters.[68] Unlike a time charterer, a demise charterer takes over the management and control of the ship, and possession of the ship. The test in *Baumwoll* was whether the agreement "put the vessel altogether out of the power and control of the then owner, and vested that power and control in the charterers, so that during the time that this hiring lasted she must be regarded as the vessel of the charterers, and not as the vessel of the owner".[69] In *Baumwoll* this depended on which party engaged the master and crew. In charterparties by demise, the master and crew are engaged as agents of the charterers, rather than the shipowners (even though the owners may retain a voice in the nomination of the master and some other crew members). Thus, for example, in *Baumwoll Manufactur von Carl Scheibler v Furness* the charterparty provided that:

> ". . . the charterers shall provide and pay for all the provisions and wages of the captain, officers, engineers, firemen, and crew".

The owners retained a voice in the nomination of the chief engineer, but even he was to be paid by the charterers. This was held by the House of Lords to be a charterparty by demise.

10.9 Question

Croaker is demised to Meathook for five years, and sub-chartered to Porkgrind for the same period. Under the sub-charter, Meathook appoint, and pay the wages of, master, engineer and crew. Croaker is then sold to Bullybeef.

---

65 [1922] 1 KB 127.
66 [1922] 1 KB 127, 139.
67 [1893] AC 8.
68 See further section [17.2].
69 [1893] AC 8, 14 (Lord Herschell).

Answer both parts

(i) Advise Bullybeef as to the extent to which, if at all, he needs to concern himself with the terms of either charterparty, and the manner in which either or both charterparties might affect him. Do we need any more information, before we can give this advice?

(ii) Would your advice have been different had Porkgrind paid the wages of master, engineer and crew, even though the master and engineer had been appointed by Meathook?

Comment

This is a relatively straightforward question, based on the material in sections [10.6] and [10.8]. Is it a demise or time charter and, if the latter, to what extent does it affect the purchaser?

Chapter 11

Period of charter: delivery and redelivery

This chapter is about the period of the charter, and in particular issues concerning delivery and redelivery. Redelivery disputes especially are often motivated by market fluctuations. Many of the principles in this chapter are specific applications of the general principles in chapter 2.[1]

11.1 Margins for the term

Unless the charterparty is for a trip, it is likely that the term will be agreed as a number of calendar months. In practice, it is impracticable to expect the charterers to be able to estimate the duration of the final voyage exactly. For this reason it is common (but by no means universal) to agree margins. INTERTANKTIME, for example, provides for the period to be agreed "14 days more or less at Charterers' option".[2] NYPE 1946 qualifies the period with the word "about".[3] In the absence of such express provision, the courts will imply a reasonable margin, but where there is an express MOLCOPT clause, any implication for an additional margin is negated. The charterers have the expressly agreed option, and nothing more. The position was summarised by Bingham LJ in *The Peonia*:[4]

> "Where a time charter-party stipulates a definite date for the termination of the charter period without any express margin or tolerance the Courts imply a reasonable margin or tolerance to allow for the exigencies of maritime business.[5] Where the parties have expressly agreed a margin or tolerance (as by agreeing a minimum and maximum period for the charter or a 'more or less' provision) such implication will not be made."[6]

In the particular case the period was "about minimum 10 months maximum 12 months", and Bingham LJ continued:

> "In the present case the words 'minimum 10 months maximum 12 months' which, standing alone, would ordinarily be effective to exclude the implication of any additional margin or tolerance are prefaced by the word 'about', which is effective to provide for such an additional margin or tolerance."

It was not enough, however, to justify the five-week overrun in the case. In the earlier case of *The Democritos*,[7] the Court of Appeal refused to interfere with the five-day latitude thought appropriate by the arbitrators, where the period was " . . . for about a trip via port or ports via the Pacific, duration about 4 to 6 months . . . ".

By the time of the House of Lords decision *The Gregos* a few years later, the principles were regarded as established.[8] The period was "about 50 to maximum 70 days", and Lord Mustill commented that:

---

1 In particular sections [2.6]–[2.7].

2 The acronym "MOLCOPT" is used for "more or less in charterers' option".

3 There is, however, no such qualification in the later (but little used) NYPE 1993, nor in the proposed NYPE 2014, a draft for comments for which can be found at https://www.bimco.org/~/media/News/2014/NYPE_93_v_NYPE_2014_comparison.ashx.

4 *Hyundai Merchant Marine Co Ltd v Gesuri Chartering Co Ltd (The Peonia)* [1991] 1 Lloyd's Rep 100, 107.

5 Bingham LJ cites *Gray & Co v Christie & Co* (1889) 5 TLR 577; *Watson Steamship Co v Merryweather & Co* (1913) 18 Com Cas 294; *The London Explorer* [1972] AC 1; *Alma Shipping Corp of Monrovia v Mantovani (The Dione)* [1975] 1 Lloyd's Rep 115 (where however Orr LJ dissented on the tolerance issue).

6 Bingham LJ cites (again) *Watson v Merryweather* and *The Dione*.

7 *Marbienes Compania Naviera SA v Ferrostaal AG (The Democritos)* [1976] 2 Lloyd's Rep 149. This was held properly to be a time charterparty, though envisaged for a trip. See further sections [1.3]; [10.4].

8 *Torvald Klaveness A/S v Arni Maritime Corp (The Gregos)* [1994] 1 WLR 1465 (discussed at [11.5] below).

"In the early stages of these proceedings there was an issue about the meaning of 'maximum 70 days.' Did this allow a margin for later redelivery in unforeseen circumstances? The arbitrator held that there was no room for such a margin. This is now accepted as correct."

Only the minimum there was qualified by "about". There can be little doubt that the inclusion of a MOLCOPT provision negates implication of a further margin, unless it is itself qualified with the word "about", as was the charterparty in *The Peonia*.

11.2 Delivery

Though time charterparties have no equivalent to the voyage charter expected readiness date, they universally have a cancelling date. As with voyage charters in chapter 6,[9] this gives just a right to cancel and nothing else. It is not a breach of contract for owners to arrive only after the cancelling date.

In *The Democritos*, neither Lord Denning MR nor Bridge LJ thought that this placed an absolute obligation on the owners to arrive before the date, merely an obligation to use reasonable diligence. Lord Denning said that:[10]

"There is, of course, an implied term that the owners will use reasonable diligence to deliver the ship in a fit condition by [the cancelling date]. But that is not an absolute obligation. So long as they have used reasonable diligence, they are not in breach. In this case it is found that reasonable diligence was used, so there is no breach by them of that implied obligation."

Though it is not clear, it may be that this is no more than a restatement of the obligation to proceed with reasonable despatch.

In other respects the time charter cancelling date is treated identically to a voyage cancelling date, Lord Denning MR observing that:[11]

"[its] effect is that, although there may have been no breach by the owners nevertheless the charterers are, for their own protection, entitled to cancel if the vessel is not delivered in a proper condition by the cancelling date. That is the sole effect."

Note, then, that there is no contractual obligation to deliver by the cancelling date. If the ship has not arrived the charterers can cancel, but in *The Madeleine*, Roskill J said that there was no doctrine of "anticipatory right to cancel under the clause".[12] They cannot therefore cancel in advance of the date, and if they do then they will themselves be in repudiatory breach of contract. On the principles in chapter 2,[13] the owners can elect to treat the contract as at an end or to keep it alive, but if they do the latter then all its terms survive, including the cancelling clause. *The Simona* applies here, in exactly the same way as to voyage charters, considered in chapter 6.[14]

As with voyage charterparties, there is some variation among the standard forms, some cancelling clauses being varied to protect the shipowner from a wasted voyage.[15]

---

9 Section [6.2].

10 [1976] 2 Lloyd's Rep 149, 152. (Lawton LJ did not deal with this issue.)

11 Ibid.

12 *Cheikh Boutros Selim El-Khoury v Ceylon Shipping Lines Ltd (The Madeleine)* [1967] 2 Lloyd's Rep 224, 245. There was also a seaworthiness issue, discussed in section [4.2].

13 Sections [2.6.3]; [2.10].

14 Section [6.2].

15 Eg, Baltime 1939 (2001 revision), cl. 21 (declaration within 48 hours of receiving notice); Intertanktime 80, cl. 2 (owners option to call on charterers to declare as early as seven days before expected sailing date). Cf. discussion of the voyage clauses in section [6.2].

11.3 Early redelivery

11.3.1 Hire for remainder of term

If redelivery is made early then in principle the shipowner is entitled to claim hire until the end of the term. Alternatively, since it would make little sense to redeliver early other than on a falling market, damages would be assessed on the basis of the charter hire rate, since that is the owners' entitlement. A hire claim is still preferable to damages, because it avoids mitigation principles,[16] and because of the requirement that it be paid punctually in advance.[17]

There have been cases, however, where the charterers have attempted to hold the owners to a damages claim, arguing that the principles in *White and Carter (Councils) Ltd v McGregor* in chapter 2 do not apply to time charterparties, or that, if they do, their case falls within one of the exceptions.[18] It will be remembered that *White and Carter* established that a wronged party is not compelled to accept a breach by a contract-breaker as bringing the contract to an end. To the extent that the case applies in a time charter context, it would allow shipowners to insist on keeping the contract alive and claiming hire, at least until the earliest redelivery date in the charterparty. However, Lord Reid's speech envisaged exceptions that, though not explicitly adopted by his brethren, have been accepted as authoritative in later cases.

The first exception is that *White and Carter* does not apply where the co-operation of the other party is required. However, whereas a time charterer requires the co-operation of the shipowner in order to perform, the converse is not true. So the co-operation exception does not rule out hire payments under time charters, as is in any case clear from *The Odenfield* and *The Aquafaith*.[19]

The second exception precludes the shipowners from claiming hire where they have no legitimate interest in so doing. However, it seems from the authorities that, at least for the period prior to the first allowable redelivery date, the owners will usually have a legitimate interest in continuing to claim hire, and will therefore be able to rely on *White and Carter*.

Lord Reid also said that the court will not prevent an attempt to enforce the contract, where to do so is merely unreasonable.[20] In Lloyd J's opinion in *The Alaskan Trader* (No. 2),[21] the conduct of the innocent party must not be merely unreasonable, but *wholly* unreasonable, before Lord Reid's second exception can apply. If so, then on general equitable principles, the court will prevent him from enforcing the contract according to his strict legal rights. In the next chapter we will come across the hostility of the House of Lords towards the application of equitable principles to charterparties,[22] and this is also instanced in the severe limits placed on the second exception to *White and Carter*. Equity intervenes here not to rewrite the contract, nor to even prevent the election by the innocent party to keep the contract alive, but merely to restrict his range of remedies should his conduct be wholly unreasonable. Moreover, the injured party is himself claiming virtually the equivalent of the equitable remedy of specific performance of his contract, and so we are not seeing equity making large inroads into the law of charterparties here.

To the extent that an owner's interest in the charter is merely to protect him against a downturn in the market, damages can do this.[23] However, shipowners also rely on punctual payment of hire, to pay the master or crew, to service a mortgage on the ship, or perhaps as other security for a

---

16 Discussed in section [2.9.2], where the exceptions are more fully set out.

17 See, eg, *Isabella Shipowner SA v Shagang Shipping Co Ltd (The Aquafaith)* [2012] 2 Lloyd's Rep 61, [47] (comments by Cooke J).

18 [1962] AC 413, discussed in section [2.8].

19 Respectively [1978] 2 Lloyd's Rep 357; [2012] 2 Lloyd's Rep 61. Both cases are discussed further below.

20 See section [2.8].

21 *Clea Shipping Corp v Bulk Oil International Ltd (The Alaskan Trader) (No. 2)* [1983] 1 Lloyd's Rep 645.

22 Section [12.1.2], especially the comments of Lord Diplock in *Scandinavian Trading Tanker Co AB v Flota Petrolera Ecuatoriana (The Scaptrade)* [1983] 2 AC 694, esp. 701 (at any rate for time charterparties).

23 See section [2.9].

loan.[24] To force owners to claim damages, and to mitigate their loss, deprives them of the advantage of punctual payment. Owners should therefore have a legitimate interest in continuing to claim hire, so there is a good argument that they ought to be able simply to claim the hire due on *White and Carter* principles, at any rate for a considerable time after the charterers' breach. By and large the cases support the principle. In cases where the owners have been unable to claim the hire, there have been additional factors, and it has not been simply a case of owners legitimately enforcing their good bargain.

The Odenfeld lends support to this conclusion.[25] Two years into a ten-year time charterparty the market collapsed, and the charterers refused to pay further hire. The owners sued for the hire due for the following nine months, and succeeded. The charterers' argument, that the owners should regard their breach as bringing the charterparty to an end, was rejected by Kerr J. Only if the owners' election to keep the contract alive was wholly unreasonable would equity intervene to prevent them from doing so. Kerr J did not go so far as to say that the owners could continue to claim hire for the whole of the rest of the ten-year period, but if there is a cut-off time (after which the owners would no longer be regarded as having a legitimate interest), it is certainly more than nine months after the charterers' breach in refusing to pay further hire.

A similar position was adopted in *The Aquafaith*.[26] The charterers redelivered about three months early on a charter of about five years, and Cooke J held that the owners were entitled to claim hire. A time charter was, he thought, a contract that could be performed without the charterers' co-operation. The shipowner would only be deprived of his right where it would be wholly unreasonable to keep the contract alive, and this was for the charterers to show. It would have been difficult for the owners to find a substitute charter given the state of the market, and, in any case,[27] it was equally open to the owners or the charterers to employ the vessel on the market, in what had become very difficult market conditions following the large drop in rates. Damages would not have been an adequate remedy given the charterers' poor financial situation, the point being made that charterparty hire is payable in advance.[28]

There are cases where *White and Carter* has not been applied, but they are quite exceptional, and far removed from the norm. *The Puerto Buitrago* involved a demise charterparty.[29] A demise charter differs from a time charterparty, of course, in that the obligation to maintain the vessel is on the charterers, rather than the shipowners.[30] (*White and Carter* principles apply, of course, to all contracts.)

When the time came to redeliver the vessel, extensive repairs were necessary. It was estimated that these would cost the charterers about $2 million, but that the vessel, even when repaired, would be worth only $1 million. The charterers refused to carry out the repairs, and purported to redeliver the vessel.

The owners refused to accept redelivery, claiming that the charterers were obliged to repair the vessel before they could redeliver the vessel. Accordingly, they argued that hire continued to be payable under the charterparty until the repairs were made and redelivery of the vessel in a repaired state effected. The Court of Appeal rejected this argument, on the basis that the obligation to repair was not a condition precedent to redelivery, or in other words that the charterers were entitled to redeliver the vessel even if still unrepaired. No doubt, the charterers would have been liable in damages for breach of the maintenance obligation, but these could not have exceeded $1 million, the

---

24 Eg, observations of Lord Diplock in *The Scaptrade* [1983] 2 AC 694, 702.

25 *Gator Shipping Corp v Trans-Asiatic Oil Ltd SA (The Odenfeld)* [1978] 2 Lloyd's Rep 357.

26 [2012] 2 Lloyd's Rep 61, noted Winterton [2013] LMCLQ 6.

27 [2012] 2 Lloyd's Rep 61, [48].

28 [2012] 2 Lloyd's Rep 61, [47].

29 *Attica Sea Carriers Corp v Ferrostaal Poseidon Bulk Reederei GmbH (The Puerto Buitrago)* [1976] 1 Lloyd's Rep 250.

30 See section [10.5].

value of the vessel when repaired, because that sum was clearly the maximum extent of the owners' loss. That was enough to dispose of the case.[31]

The court went on, however, to consider the position on the assumption that the main basis for the decision was wrong. They held that even if repairing the ship was a condition precedent to redelivery, the owners had to treat the charterers' breach as a repudiation of the charterparty. They had no legitimate interest for electing to keep the charterparty alive, and to claim hire into the indefinite future. This is an application of the second of Lord Reid's exceptions in *White and Carter*. Orr LJ thought that *White and Carter* was also distinguishable because here the owners could not continue to perform without the co-operation of the demise charterers, presumably because they were obliged to maintain the vessel, but the court also took the unanimous view that the owners had no legitimate interest in claiming the charter hire rather than damages. As Lord Denning MR observed:[32]

> "What is the alternative which the shipowners present to the charterers? Either the charterers must continue to pay the charter hire for years to come, whilst the vessel lies idle and useless for want of repair. Or the charterers must do repairs which would cost twice as much as the ship would be worth when repaired – after which the shipowners might sell it as scrap, making the repairs a useless waste of money . . . I do not think the law allows them to do this."

The situation in *The Puerto Buitrago* is quite different from that in *The Odenfeld* and *The Aquafaith*, where the owners continued to claim hire during the time charter period, possibly to protect their overheads and commitments to third parties. In *The Puerto Buitrago*, the owners were attempting to claim hire beyond the charter period, indeed into the indefinite future, and using what was clearly a device in order to do so. They had had the benefit of their bargain, because the charter period was at an end, and the charterers were not trying to pull out early. It is difficult to see that the shipowners had a legitimate interest in claiming more than damages for the reduction in value to their vessel. *The Puerto Buitrago* is therefore a case well outside the norm, from which it is difficult to generalise.

Kerr J in *The Odenfeld* felt that *The Puerto Buitrago* was an extreme case,[33] but Lloyd J followed it in *The Alaskan Trader* (No. 2).[34] The case is, like *The Puerto Buitrago*, rather extreme, and the owners were arguably using a device to claim more than their legitimate due. This case concerned a two-year time charterparty, and, after a year, the vessel broke down. It was clear that she would not be repaired for several months, and the charterers therefore indicated that they had no further use for her (perhaps motivated by hire rates having dropped by about 40 per cent). Lloyd J held that "[the] owners could have treated the charterers' conduct as a repudiation of the charter-party", from which it followed, in his view, that the charterers could not treat the breakdown as a ground *themselves* for repudiating the charter.[35] The charterers were therefore in breach in telling the owners that they had no further use for the vessel.

Far from treating the contract as repudiated, the owners spent a considerable sum repairing the vessel, and then told the charterers that she was again at their disposal. They kept a full crew aboard until the end of the charterparty period, but the charterers declined to give the master any orders, though they continued to pay hire "without prejudice". At the end of the charterparty period, the owners sold the vessel for scrap, suggesting surely that she had not been worth repairing. The

---

31 Consequently, Cooke J observed in *The Aquafaith* [2012] 2 Lloyd's Rep 61, [11], that "[in] *The Puerto Buitrago*, the Court of Appeal considered the *White and Carter* decision on an *obiter* basis". This aspect of *Puerto Buitrago* was distinguished in *The Rijn* (not, I suggest, very convincingly), which is discussed in section [11.4].

32 [1976] 1 Lloyd's Rep 250, 255.

33 [1978] 2 Lloyd's Rep 357, 373.

34 [1983] 1 Lloyd's Rep 645.

35 [1983] 1 Lloyd's Rep 645, 646. The reasons why the breakdown did not put the owners in repudiatory breach are not made clear, but presumably it was insufficiently serious on the principles in section [2.7].

charterers claimed return of the hire paid, and the owners claimed to retain the hire from the time the vessel was repaired until the end of the charterparty period. Lloyd J held that they were not entitled to do so, and that the charterers were entitled to its return.

This is again, like *The Puerto Buitrago*, a somewhat extreme case. Not only were there expensive repairs to a vessel that was, immediately after the expiry of the charterparty period, sold for scrap, but it was also considerably more expensive to maintain a full crew aboard the vessel than to lay her up. It is no surprise that Lloyd J held that the owners had no legitimate interest in continuing to claim hire for the remainder of the period.

The normal position remains, however, that the injured party (the shipowner in these cases) does not have to accept a breach by the other party as putting an end to the agreement. *White and Carter* is applicable to claims for time charterparty hire, unless the situation is wholly exceptional, as in *The Alaskan Trader* (No. 2). The shipowner will probably have a legitimate interest, at least until the end of the charter period. The situation might be different if the shipowner attempts to claim hire into the indefinite future, for example where the vessel cannot be redelivered.[36]

11.3.2 Damages

If the owners elect to treat the contract as repudiated, they will be unable to claim hire, but will be limited to a damages claim. (The owners might so elect, in order to fix the vessel elsewhere, even on a falling market, thereby mitigate their losses to some extent.) The starting point for the calculation will be the hire they would have earned for the remainder of the term, until the earliest lawful redelivery date, less hire actually earned, or that could reasonably have been earned. A damages claim will be subject to the compensatory principle, and also to mitigation.[37]

There is also the so-called "compensatory principle", which reminds us that damages only compensate for losses that have been sustained. We have already seen an embryonic form of this principle in *The Mihalis Angelos* in chapter 6.[38] In assessing damages, the courts will have regard to what would have occurred, in the absence of a breach. The compensatory principle was examined and applied in the House of Lords in *The Golden Victory*,[39] *The Mihalis Angelos* being applied (and extended). Time charterers wrongfully redelivered early (on a falling market), in 2001, the earliest allowable date being not until 2005. The owners accepted that breach as terminating the charter, and claimed damages based on the difference between contract and market hire, for the remainder of the period. There was, however, a clause that would have enabled the charterers to cancel in any event, on the outbreak of war in Iraq, which occurred in 2003. Since they clearly would have done so, the owners were held entitled to damages only up to this point, and not for the remainder of the term of the charter.[40] The case is an extension of *The Mihalis Angelos*, but in the former case it was clear at the time of the cancellation that the shipowner's rights would have been valueless, even had the charterparty continued, whereas in *The Golden Victory* it became clear only months after the charterers' repudiation, when war in Iraq became inevitable.

The Golden Victory was a 3–2 majority decision only, and it has been quite heavily criticised.[41] Lord Bingham in particular delivered a strong dissenting speech, emphasising the need for certainty, requiring damages to be quantified at the time of the breach, and not to depend on the vagaries of

---

36 See (in another context) section [13.9.6].

37 See generally the principles in section [2.9].

38 Section [6.3].

39 *Golden Strait Corp v Nippon Yusen Kubisha Kaisha (The Golden Victory)* [2007] 2 AC 353.

40 The case was unusual in that, by the time of the arbitration proceedings, these subsequent events were known. Had damages been assessed earlier, as would of course be usual, then of course the 2003 events could not have been taken into account.

41 Eg, the citations in *Flame SA v Glory Wealth Shipping Pte Ltd (The Glory Wealth)* [2013] 2 Lloyd's Rep 653, [11]–[16] (Teare J).

what happened later.[42] The majority view was that certainty should give way to the "compensatory principle", on which the decision was said to be based.

There are authorities which are difficult to reconcile with The Golden Victory, and prior to The Glory Wealth,[43] it could be argued that The Golden Victory applied only to a cancelling clause, which would operate regardless of any performance by the shipowners. (Had the situation instead been that the charterers would have repudiated in 2003, because the owners would have been unable to perform, the owners would have argued that their election to terminate relieved them of any obligation to perform in any event.)[44] However, in The Glory Wealth, Teare J held that the principles in The Golden Victory and The Mihalis Angelos extended to the situation where further performance would have been required before a later termination could occur. The Glory Wealth concerned a contract of affreightment,[45] and the allegation was that, had the charterers not wrongfully terminated it, the owners would later have been unable, because of financial problems, to perform if the charterers had called upon them to do so. Teare J, after fully reviewing the authorities, thought that had the allegation been made out (in the event it was not), it would have accordingly reduced the damages payable to the shipowners. This is said to be an application of the "compensatory principle", but takes no account of the shipowners being relieved of their obligation to perform in the future, because of the repudiation.[46]

Since drafts for this book were written, the Supreme Court (in a different context) has strongly supported the sentiments expressed by the majority in The Golden Victory.[47] Though the particular issue in The Glory Wealth was not there at issue, it looks more likely than it did before that Teare J's decision in that case is correct, and that the "compensatory principle" applies to future inability to perform, as well as to the cancelling clause situation in The Golden Victory itself.

There is another principle, in the next section, that it should be assumed that the guilty party would (had he not been in breach) have performed the contract in the manner least favourable to the other party. This makes an assumption as to future (hypothetical) performance, rather than attempting to predict what might actually have happened. This principle also has the effect of restricting damages.

Another principle is mitigation. The owners must reasonably mitigate their loss. If they do so, damages will be reduced to the extent that they successfully mitigate, which is one reason why any hire received under a substitute fixture is deducted from the damages award.[48] If they fail to mitigate, hire which could reasonably have been earned would also be deducted, and it is in this respect that they may be seen to be under a duty to mitigate. In chapter 2 we also saw that a sale of the vessel is not taken into account to reduce the damages. It is not sufficiently closely related, causally, to the breach, to be taken into account.[49]

11.4 Redelivery to wrong port

If redelivery is made to the wrong port, the shipowners can continue to claim charter hire until proper redelivery is made, but it is assumed that the charterers will redeliver to the nearest port

---

42 In the usual case, they would, of course, have been quantified much earlier, and later events could not have been taken into account.

43 [2013] 2 Lloyd's Rep 653.

44 See in particular (albeit in a sale context) Gill & Duffus SA v Berger & Co Inc [1984] AC 382, 390, 392 (Lord Diplock).

45 See further section [5.7].

46 As in Gill & Duffus SA v Berger & Co Inc [1984] AC 382.

47 Bunge SA v Nidera BV [2015] UKSC 43 (SC).

48 Another is that they should not be compensated for losses they have not suffered.

49 Section [2.9.2], discussing Fulton Shipping Inc of Panama v Globalia Business Travel SAU (The New Flamenco) [2014] EWHC 1547 (Comm); [2014] 2 Lloyd's Rep 230.

in the redelivery range. In *The Bunga Kenanga*,[50] therefore, it was said that damages should only put the owners in the position they would have been in had the charterers performed in the manner least favourable to the owners. This is consistent with normal contractual principles, where the contract-breaker has a choice as to how to perform.[51] A similar principle was applied in *The Rijn*,[52] where damages were assessed on the basis that the voyage to the nearest permissible redelivery port would be in ballast, since that would have been quicker, even though the likelihood in practice would have been for the charterers to make the voyage with a loaded vessel.

In *The Rijn*, the vessel was required to be redelivered to "a safe port SOUTH JAPAN", but when she arrived at Galveston (USA), the charterers notified the owners that the time charter was terminated "as is, where is". The owners fixed the vessel for an alternative voyage, and therefore presumably accepted that the charterparty was at an end. Mustill J held that they were entitled to damages based on "the difference between the net profit which they would have earned if the voyage had continued, and their net receipts under the substitute fixture".[53] (Assuming the market was falling, earnings under the substitute fixture would have been at the current market rate, and hence lower than contract hire.) The charterers argued that they should be limited to compensation for redelivering the vessel at the wrong port, at the current market rate. The argument appears to have been that, since even though they were at the wrong port, they had nonetheless effectively redelivered, thereby bringing the charterparty to an end, the charter hire rate was not relevant to the assessment of that compensation. In *The Puerto Buitrago*, as we have seen,[54] the obligation to repair the vessel (under a demise charter) was held not to be a precondition to redelivery. By analogy, argued the charterers, nor was delivering in the right place. Mustill J was unimpressed, commenting that there is no true analogy between the two situations. In *The Puerto Buitrago* situation, "[both] legal and commercial considerations demand that the charter shall come to an end, even if the condition of the vessel on redelivery is unsatisfactory". In the situation in *The Rijn*, however, "the contractual service is defined in terms of the place or time, or both, at which the vessel is redelivered. The stipulation concerning the vessel's condition on redelivery is not part of this definition".[55] So whereas a demise chartered vessel can be validly redelivered in any condition, whether or not the charterers are thereby in breach of contract, a vessel (presumably under either a time or a demise charter) cannot be validly redelivered at any place; charter service continues until the ship reaches the contractual redelivery range, the voyage to the redelivery range forming part of the chartered service. The owners were therefore entitled to continued hire, on the basis of the charterparty hire clause:[56]

"4. That the Charterers shall pay for the use and hire of the said vessel . . . commencing on and from the day of her delivery . . . hire to continue until the hour of her redelivery in like good order and condition ordinary wear and tear excepted, to the Owners . . . at a safe port South Japan (not north of Tokyo Bay)/Singapore Range . . . ".

Mustill J's distinction between the situations in *The Puerto Buitrago* and *The Rijn* is not, I suggest, very convincing. He does not explain why the condition of the ship should be treated differently, in this context, from her geographical location, and it is hard to find a principled distinction between the two situations.

---

50 *Malaysian International Shipping Corp v Empresa Cubana de Fletes (The Bunga Kenanga)* [1981] 1 Lloyd's Rep 518.
51 See section [2.9.3], but cf. the discussion of *The Delian Spirit* [1972] 1 QB 103, in section [22.3].
52 *Santa Martha Baay Scheepvaart and Handelsmaatschappij NV v Scanbulk A/S (The Rijn)* [1981] 2 Lloyd's Rep 267.
53 [1981] 2 Lloyd's Rep 267, 269.
54 Section [11.3.1].
55 [1981] 2 Lloyd's Rep 267, 270.
56 Set out at the beginning of the judgment: [1981] 2 Lloyd's Rep 267, 268.

Another argument (this time advanced by the owners) dealt with in The Rijn, concerned The Mihalis Angelos, an argument that we considered in chapter 6.[57] The argument was that, in assessing damages, regard should be had to what the contract-breaker would actually have done by way of performing his side of the bargain, if the contract had continued in existence. The charterers would have made a laden voyage to Japan. Mustill J's view was that:[58]

> " . . . the reasoning of The Mihalis Angelos could be applied, if at all – and I express no view as to whether it could be applied even then – if the arbitrators had found that the charterers would definitely have ordered the ship on a laden voyage for the carriage of grain from Galveston to Japan, if they had not repudiated the contract. They have found no such thing, and there is no reason to suppose that this was in fact the case."

He also said that in The Mihalis Angelos, "[the shipowner] could not have performed the contract himself in any way which would have avoided cancellation". But surely there is no conflict anyway, between The Mihalis Angelos and the test adopted in The Bunga Kenanga and The Rijn; in The Mihalis Angelos, the charterers would no doubt in fact have cancelled, but given that the ship would certainly not have arrived in any case, prior to the cancelling date, the charterers would also have cancelled, on the test that "for the purpose of calculating damages [the charterers] would have chosen the way which would have brought least benefit to the [owners]".[59] It is not necessary, in other words, to look at what the charterers would actually have done, to justify the reasoning in The Mihalis Angelos. It follows that, even had it been possible to show that the charterers would definitely have ordered the ship on a laden voyage, The Mihalis Angelos should not have precluded the award of damages that was made in The Rijn.

Note that in The Rijn, we are looking at what the guilty party would be assumed to have done, had he performed the contract. Recall also that, for this part of The Mihalis Angelos, the court is assuming (contrary to the actual decision) that the charterers are the guilty party.[60] The is quite different from The Glory Wealth in the last section, where Teare J looked at what the innocent party would have done, had there been no breach.

11.5 Late redelivery

It would not generally be in the charterers' interests to redeliver late on a falling market, since they should be able to obtain cheaper tonnage elsewhere, but in The London Explorer[61] they were delayed (with no breach on their part) by strikes. The House of Lords held that charter hire remained payable until redelivery was made, and that the charterers were not entitled to tender the lower market freight rate for the overrun. Many charterparties expressly so provide anyway.[62]

11.5.1 Late redelivery as a breach?

It is far more common, of course, for the charterers to attempt to extend the charter on a rising market, since alternative tonnage will now be more expensive. There were dicta in The London Explorer,

---

57 Section [6.3].

58 [1981] 2 Lloyd's Rep 267, 270.

59 [1981] 2 Lloyd's Rep 267, 269.

60 On the main part of the decision, see section [2.6.2].

61 Timber Shipping Co SA v London & Overseas Freighters Ltd (The London Explorer) [1972] AC 1.

62 Eg, Shelltime 4, cl. 8 (line 177). Shelltime 4, as revised in 2003, can be found at http://shippingforum.files.wordpress.com/2012/08/shelltime-4-as-revised-20031.pdf.

especially in Lord Reid's speech, that failure to make timely redelivery is not of itself a breach of contract,[63] and this view was taken to be the law by Lord Denning MR in *The Democritos* and *The Dione*. In the latter case he said (citing *The London Explorer*):[64]

" . . . the charter is presumed to continue in operation until the end of the final voyage, even though that extends beyond the charter period. The hire is payable at the charter rate until redelivery, even though the market rate may have gone up or down."

The consequence of late redelivery, on this view, if there is no other breach, was simply to extend the time for which charterparty hire is payable. It was probably because this view was taken that the emphasis was on the final voyage order (on which see further, later in this section).

It is now clear from *The Peonia* and *The Gregos* that the Denning view is incorrect, and that late redelivery it is of itself a breach, even if redelivery is delayed, through unexpected circumstance and no fault of the charterers.[65] It follows from this that, though on a falling market the shipowner can continue to claim hire for the overrun, on a rising market he can claim damages, which of course will be based on the now higher market rate.[66] This will not depend on establishing that the final voyage order is itself a breach of contract.

On a falling market, on the other hand, even on this view, the principles in *White and Carter* should normally entitle the owners to claim hire until redelivery is actually made, and not be limited to (lower) contractual damages.[67] *White and Carter* ought to allow the owners the option to claim hire, at any rate for short extensions. The position might be different where (for example) the vessel has become entrapped, indefinitely delaying redelivery.[68] The question would then arise as to the extent of the owners' legitimate interest, which, at the very most, would surely be limited to the value of the vessel.

There remains a separate question, whether the owners are required to comply with the last voyage order. In *The Gregos*, Lord Templeman thought that to redeliver late was a breach of condition, but Lord Mustill (with whom the others agreed) thought that it was only a breach of innominate term.[69] Whereas on Lord Templeman's view the owners would therefore never be required to obey an illegitimate last voyage order, Lord Mustill's position would be slightly more complicated.[70]

It is worth observing, however, that this is a time term, and that, as we will see in the next chapter, time terms in commercial contracts are usually conditions.[71] Lord Mustill did not think that the justifications for this extended to a short delay in redelivery; certainly, the arguments in the next chapter, from *The Laconia* and *The Scaptrade*, on the importance of punctual payment of hire,[72] do not apply to the obligation to make timely redelivery. In *The London Explorer*, Lord Reid said that there was "good authority, for the proposition that there is a presumption that a definite date for

---

63 [1972] AC 1, esp. at 15, *dicta* because redelivery not having been made, the owners were suing not for damages, but for hire under the charterparty.

64 [1975] 1 Lloyd's Rep 115, 117.

65 Respectively *The Peonia* [1991] 1 Lloyd's Rep 100; *The Gregos* [1994] 1 WLR 1465.

66 Consistently with the principles in *The Bunga Kenanga* and *The Rijn*, that damages should only put the owners in the position they would have been in, had the charterers performed in the manner least favourable to the owners, it is assumed that the charterers would have extended the charter until the last possible contractual redelivery date. Damages above the hire rate are only available thereafter, therefore.

67 Discussed in section [11.3].

68 See further section [13.9.6].

69 [1994] 1 WLR 1465, 1476.

70 See section [11.5.3].

71 See section [12.1.6].

72 See section [12.1.2].

the termination of a time charter should be regarded as an approximate date only".[73] We saw at the start of the chapter that some leeway is allowed, and there is in any case often an express MOLCOPT clause. Where the latitude is given by an implied term, it is likely to be imprecise, and not therefore well-suited to condition reasoning. Anyway, Lord Mustill found "it hard to accept that timely re-delivery is a condition of the contract".[74]

11.5.2 Damages for late redelivery

Obviously, late redelivery on a rising market will cause loss to the owners, but normally this will be compensated by damages calculated on the difference between current market and contract hire rates, the market rate being the higher, of course, on a rising market.

The Achilleas was unusual in that this measure did not fully compensate.[75] Relying on timely re-delivery, the owners had agreed a very profitable follow-on charter when charter rates were high. By the time it became clear that redelivery would be made late, charter rates had fallen sharply, and the owners had had to agree a much reduced rate for a follow-on charter. This was held to be reasonably foreseeable, given the state of the market, or at any rate the charterers, at the time when the contract had been made, ought to have realised that it was not unlikely to result, from the breach of contract caused by returning the vessel late. Under normal remoteness of damage principles, this loss would have been recoverable (even though the charterers had not been put on notice of the existence of the follow-on charter),[76] but the House restricted damages for late redelivery to the difference between market and contract rates. (Because the market had by now fallen again, this gave a much lower figure than the loss occasioned by the renegotiation of the follow-on charter.) The issue was said to be whether the compensation was of a "kind" or "type" for which the contract-breaker ought fairly to be taken to have accepted responsibility, bearing in mind that there has been a uniform series of *dicta* over many years in which judges have said or assumed that the damages for late delivery are the difference between the charter rate and the market rate. The charterers had not taken the risk of such loss.[77]

The Achilleas is an exceptional case that will probably rarely be applied. An argument based on it failed in *The Sylvia*;[78] the charterers lost a lucrative sub-charter (during the period of the charter) because the vessel was detained due to violation of s. 19 of SOLAS,[79] and Hamblen J held that they were entitled to recover in respect of those losses, and were not limited to the difference between contract and market hire over that period. Hamblen J applied the normal rules of remoteness, observing that only in relatively unusual cases might a consideration of assumption of responsibility be required. *The Achilleas* concerned a well-known rule for calculation in a specific circumstance. That is central to the reasoning, and the decision is probably limited to that situation.

A slightly different issue was considered in *The Paragon*.[80] A clause of the charterparty provided:

"The Charterers hereby undertake the obligation/responsibility to make thorough investiga-tions and every arrangement in order to ensure that the last voyage of this Charter will in no

---

73 [1972] AC 1, 14.

74 [1994] 1 WLR 1465, 1476.

75 *Transfield Shipping Inc v Mercator Shipping Inc (The Achilleas)* [2009] 1 AC 61. See also section [2.9.3].

76 As set out in *Hadley v Baxendale* (1854) 9 Exch 341 and *C Czarnikow Ltd v Koufos (The Heron II)* [1969] 1 AC 350, both cited in *The Achilleas*.

77 On analysis in terms of the risks the parties have undertaken to bear, see further section [3.6].

78 *Sylvia Shipping Co Ltd v Progress Bulk Carriers Ltd (The Sylvia)* [2010] 2 Lloyd's Rep 81, appd *Maestro Bulk Ltd v Cosco Bulk Carrier Co Ltd (The Great Creation)* [2015] 1 Lloyd's Rep 315. The Achilleas was also distinguished in *Saipol SA v Inerco Trade SA* [2015] 1 Lloyd's Rep 26.

79 International Convention for the Safety of Life at Sea: see http://www.imo.org/About/Conventions/ListOfConventions/Pages/ International-Convention-for-the-Safety-of-Life-at-Sea-%28SOLAS%29,-1974.aspx for a general description.

80 *Lansat Shipping Co Ltd v Glencore Grain BV (The Paragon)* [2009] 2 Lloyd's Rep 688.

way exceed the maximum period under this Charter Party. If, however, Charterers fail to comply with this obligation and the last voyage will exceed the maximum period, should the market
rise above the Charter Party rate in the meantime, it is hereby agreed that the charter hire
will be adjusted to reflect the prevailing market level from the 30th day prior to the maximum
period [d]ate until actual redelivery of the vessel to the Owners."

It can be seen that the last part of the clause purports to allow owners to claim damages based on the
market rate for 30 days prior to redelivery. Obviously, if the market rate has risen above that provided
by the charter, this gives the owners more than the normal compensation for late redelivery. The
Court of Appeal held that this was not a genuine pre-estimate of damage, and was a penalty clause.
As we saw in chapter 2,[81] penalty clauses are unenforceable, and that was therefore the fate of this
part of this clause.

11.5.3 Last voyage orders

As we have seen, however, possibly because of the now-discredited dicta from The London Explorer (that
late redelivery is not itself a breach) the courts, in cases prior to The Gregos, concentrated on the order
for the last voyage. Whether or not it was a breach to redeliver late, to order the vessel on a final voyage that was likely to lead to late redelivery was another matter altogether. A distinction was drawn
between legitimate and illegitimate last voyage orders. This definition (which is uncontroversial) is
taken from the recent case of The Paragon:[82]

"An order given by charterers for a 'legitimate last voyage' is an order for the employment
of the vessel on a voyage which can reasonably be expected to be performed by the time for
redelivery under the charterparty. By contrast, an order for an illegitimate last voyage is an
order for the employment of the vessel on a voyage which cannot reasonably be expected to be
performed by the time for redelivery."

In The Dione, and again in The Democritos, to give an illegitimate last voyage order was effectively
regarded as a repudiatory breach of contract. If the owners did not accept it, this allowed them to
claim the market rate as from that moment. If they accepted the order then they would be entitled to
claim only hire, at any rate up until the redelivery date. As Lord Denning MR observed in The Dione:[83]

"If the charterer sends the vessel on an illegitimate last voyage – that is, a voyage which it cannot be expected to complete within the charter period, then the shipowner is entitled to refuse
that direction and call for another direction for a legitimate last voyage. If the charterer refuses
to give it, the shipowner can accept his conduct as a breach going to the root of the contract,
fix a fresh charter for the vessel, and sue for damages. If the shipowner accepts the direction
and goes on the illegitimate last voyage, he is entitled to be paid – for the excess period – at
the current market rate, and not at the charter rate . . . The hire will be payable at the charter
rate up to the end of the charter period, and at the current market rate for the excess period
thereafter."

This is consistent with the giving of the order, or at least the refusal to give a valid order, amounting to a repudiatory breach, which the owners may or may not accept as bringing the contract
to an end. Even if they accept the order, and go on the voyage, there is still a breach, entitling

---

81 Section [2.9.4].
82 [2009] 2 Lloyd's Rep 688, [8], citing The Peonia [1991] 1 Lloyd's Rep 100.
83 [1975] 1 Lloyd's Rep 115, 118, cited in The Democritos [1976] 2 Lloyd's Rep 149, 153.

the owners to damages, based on the market rate, for the overrun. But if they go on the voyage, they elect to keep the charter alive, and therefore to continue the charter hire rate until redelivery. There is an elaboration by Steyn J in *The Black Falcon*:[84]

> "in circumstances where the owner undertook the illegitimate last voyage without waiving their rights to claim damages the charterer's obligation was to pay the charter rate until the last permissible date for redelivery and thereafter to pay the market rate until actual redelivery . . . ".

For the charterers to be entitled to pay hire (on a rising market) rather than damages until the *last permissible date for redelivery* is consistent with the principles in *The Bunga Kenanga*, and *The Rijn*;[85] the charterer is entitled to the assumption that he would have performed in the manner least beneficial to the owner (and of course on a rising market he would keep the charter going as long as possible).

In *The Paragon*, the owners argued that they went on the last voyage, only outside the charterparty, so that the last voyage would be at market rate. Though this conclusion is no doubt possible in principle, the argument did not impress Lord Clarke, who said:[86]

> " . . . in the ordinary case in which charterers give orders for an illegitimate last voyage there is no basis for implying a request by the charterers that the owners should perform such a voyage outside the charterparty and on terms that they will pay for the voyage at the market rate".

In other words, such a voyage is usually undertaken within the charterparty, and hence at the charter hire rate.

That is the illegitimate last voyage. By contrast, because it was thought that late redelivery was not itself a breach, a *legitimate* last voyage order was assumed to lock the owners into the charter hire rate, even if the vessel was in fact redelivered late. The no-breach assumption must now however be regarded as wrong, in the light of *The Peonia* and *The Gregos*. In *The Peonia*, Bingham LJ said:[87]

> "It would seem to me (although challenged by the charterers) that every time charter must have a final terminal date, that is a date by which (in the absence of an exonerating cause) the charterer is contractually obliged to redeliver the vessel . . . the nature of a time charter is that the charter is for a finite period of time and when the final terminal date arrives the charterer is contractually bound (in the absence of an exonerating cause) to redeliver the vessel to the owner. . . . "

In *The Gregos*,[88] all their Lordships agreed that to redeliver late was, in fact, a breach of charter. On a rising market, therefore, the owners can *always* claim damages based on market rates, after the last date for redelivery has passed, whether or not the last voyage order was legitimate.

11.5.4 *The Gregos*

A number of issues that were previously unclear were resolved in the House of Lords in *The Gregos*. Final voyage instructions were given that, at that time, were reasonable (that is to say, that timely

---

84 *Shipping Corp of India Ltd v NSB Neiderelbe Schiffahrtgesellschaft mbH & Co (The Black Falcon)* [1991] 1 Lloyd's Rep 77, this passage being taken from the headnote. See also *The Paragon* [2009] 2 Lloyd's Rep 688, [12].

85 See section [11.4].

86 *Lansat Shipping Co Ltd v Glencore Grain BV (The Paragon)* [2009] 2 Lloyd's Rep 688, [25].

87 [1991] 1 Lloyd's Rep 100, 106.

88 [1994] 1 WLR 1465.

redelivery in accordance with the charterparty could reasonably have been expected), and the vessel proceeded towards the loading port, but by the time notice of readiness to load was given, the navigable channel between the loading port and the river mouth had become obstructed by the grounding of another vessel, rendering it unreasonable to expect the voyage to be completed in time. The charterers nonetheless persisted in their order, and the owners complied, but subject to a without prejudice agreement.

The charterers were held to be in repudiatory breach. In Lord Templeman's view the analysis was straightforward. Because in his view late redelivery was a breach of condition, to give an order that prevented timely redelivery was itself a repudiatory breach.[89] Lord Mustill took a different view on the categorisation of the term, and concentrated instead, not on the order that was given, but on the failure to give a legitimate last voyage order. In his view this evinced an intention no longer to be bound:[90]

> "the charterers' persistence in it after it had become invalid showed that they did not intend to perform their obligations under the charter. That is to say, they 'evinced an intention no longer to be bound' by the charter. This was an anticipatory breach, which entitled the owners to treat the contract as ended."

This was renunciation, in other words.[91]

Either view would have entitled the owners to damages, based on the market rate, for the over-run (remember that the market rate had risen above the hire rate, but that the owners had complied with the order, thereby keeping the charterparty alive). The damages actually awarded were much higher than this, however. The owners, in reliance on timely redelivery, had fixed a profitable charter, with a concern called Navios, and were compensated for the loss of this:[92]

> "The arbitrator then proceeded to damages, and arrived at an award of [nearly £300k], comprising the difference between the charter hire and the hire obtainable on the alternative fixture with Navios, plus the bonus which Navios would have paid to recognise the immediate availability of the ship."

This was far more than the difference in rates for a few days' delay, and looks at first sight difficult to square with *The Achilleas*, above.[93] The reason for the unusually large award was that owners only went on the last voyage "without prejudice". It was for breach of the without prejudice agreement that the arbitrators' award (which was upheld) could be justified:[94]

> "The reason was, I believe, that what the arbitrator did was not to award damages [for breach of the charterparty] but to enforce the terms of the without prejudice agreement, and to remunerate the owners for performing a voyage from which, in consequence of the charterers' wrongful act, they would otherwise have been free."

Note then, that this is not damages for breach of the charterparty, but for the without prejudice agreement, which was considered to be a separate agreement.

---

89 [1994] 1 WLR 1465, 1467.
90 [1994] 1 WLR 1465, 1476.
91 As discussed in sections [2.7] and [12.1.5].
92 [1994] 1 WLR 1465, 1471 (Lord Mustill).
93 Section [11.5.2].
94 [1994] 1 WLR 1465, 1477 (Lord Mustill).

11.5.5 Last voyage orders after *The Gregos*

Because in *The Gregos* it was accepted that redelivery was of itself a breach of contract, it follows that if the owner accepts the order and performs the last voyage, it makes no difference whether the order is legitimate or not. As Lord Clarke MR in *The Paragon* observed:[95]

> "It can thus be seen that, when the illegitimate last voyage is performed, the measure of damages is the same as in the case of a legitimate last voyage."

A similar view was also taken by Bingham LJ in *The Peonia*.[96] In either event hire is payable until (assuming market hire now exceeding the charter hire rate) the last possible redelivery date, and damages (based on market hire) thereafter.

Suppose, however, the owners are minded to reject the voyage instructions. Prior to *The Gregos*, they would be entitled to do this if the last voyage order were illegitimate. The same would be true, on Lord Templeman's view in *The Gregos*; if late redelivery is a breach of condition, the same would be true of giving an illegitimate voyage order. On Lord Mustill's view, the entitlement to refuse would arise only if the delay in redelivery would be a frustrating delay, or if the charterers persisted in their illegitimate last voyage order (hence renouncing the charterparty). Probably this makes little difference in practice, except that owners would be wise to insist on a legitimate order, to force the charterers to persist in a refusal. This is also the position taken by Lord Clarke MR in *The Paragon*: it is the persisting in the illegitimate last voyage order that is a repudiatory breach, not just the giving of it, unless it amounts to evincing an intent not to be bound by charterparty.

Conversely, if the charterparty is validly repudiated and the owners refuse to perform the final voyage, damages based on current market rates would be awarded as from the date of the repudiation.

In the light of this, we need to consider how final voyage clauses alter the situation.

11.6 Final voyage clauses

As with anything else concerning charterparties, the parties are free to make whatever changes to the regime they choose.[97] A common alteration, particularly in the pro-charterer tanker market, is the final (or last) voyage clause. These clauses give charterers additional rights in relation to the last voyage. They are, however, interpreted against the charterer, giving the minimum necessary to give some effect to the clause. Thus, for example, once it had been held that late redelivery itself is a breach, effect could be given to the clause in *The Peonia*, which stated only that: "Charterers have further option to complete last voyage within . . . trading limits", by construing it simply to protect against lateness arising from an unforeseen circumstance, a legitimate order having been given. The charterers failed in their argument that it allowed them to give an illegitimate order, an argument that, as we saw in chapter 1, Bingham LJ rejected on the grounds that this very wide interpretation would "disturb in . . . a radical manner the ordinary rule whereby risk of delay under a time charter-party (in the absence of breach by the owner) falls on the charterer".[98] A similar view was taken by Steyn J in *The Black Falcon*, where the clause was as follows:[99]

---

95 [2009] 2 Lloyd's Rep 688, [11], after citing Lord Denning MR in *The Dione* [1975] 1 Lloyd's Rep 115. Lord Clarke also observes that the damages award in *The Gregos* depended on the without prejudice agreement: at [21].

96 [1991] 1 Lloyd's Rep 100, 114.

97 See section [1.8].

98 [1991] 1 Lloyd's Rep 100, 117. See section [1.8].

99 *Shipping Corp of India Ltd v NSB Neiderelbe Schiffahrtgesellschaft mbH & Co (The Black Falcon)* [1991] 1 Lloyd's Rep 77.

"Charterers having option to complete last round voyage under performance prior to redelivery at charterparty rate . . . ."

In each case, the clause was construed as narrowly as possible to give it effect, and certainly not so as radically to alter delay risk allocation under a time charterparty.

Nothing about charterparties, even the delay risk allocation, is set in stone, of course, and therefore if the clause is sufficiently clear, it can give the charterers the right to give even an illegitimate last voyage order. This was the position taken in *The World Renown*,[100] but the clause has to be very clear, since otherwise the alternative construction remains possible. That in *The World Renown*, which was a standard Shelltime clause (18), differed from those in *The Peonia* and *The Black Falcon*:

"Notwithstanding the provisions of clause 3 hereof [period clause], should the vessel be upon a voyage at the expiry of the period of this charter. Charterers shall have the use of the vessel at the same rate and conditions for such extended time as may be necessary for the completion of the round voyage on which she is engaged and her return to a port of redelivery as provided by this charter."

The important part was the first phrase. It made clear, in the view of the Court of Appeal, that the final voyage clause (18) overrode even the period clause (3), and that this allowed the charterers to make even a final illegitimate last voyage. Had it not been for the first phrase, the clause would have been interpreted in the same way as those in *The Peonia* and *The Black Falcon*, allowing only a last legitimate voyage.

While no doubt a clear clause should allow for even an illegitimate last voyage to be ordered, I suggest that the distinction drawn in *The World Renown* is unconvincing. It reads too much into the first phrase of the clause.

11.7 Question

Bridget's has a vessel on time charter from Charles. The period was agreed as two years from 31 January 2013, and there is no MOLCOPT provision. Hire rate is £20,000 per day. On 1 December 2014 Bridget orders the vessel on a final voyage, which both parties expect will allow redelivery on 28 January 2015. Charles is delighted because the market has risen and he is able, relying on timely redelivery, to fix the vessel with Eleanor for £50,000 a day. As it turns out, unexpected delays, caused by a vessel sinking and blocking the fairway into the redelivery port, mean that redelivery is not made until 28 March 2015. This causes Charles to lose his profitable charter with Eleanor. During February and March the market rate is £30,000 per day.

(i)   Advise Charles as to whether he has an action against Bridget, and, if so, the basis upon which damages will be assessed.

(ii)   Would your answer be different if neither party had expected redelivery by 31 January and Charles had refused to go on the final voyage except on the basis of a without prejudice agreement (similar to that in *The Gregos*),[101] which the parties had made.

---

100 *Chiswell Shipping Ltd v National Iranian Tanker Co (The World Symphony and The World Renown)* [1992] 2 Lloyd's Rep 115 (CA), appd *Petroleo Brasilero SA v Kriti Acti Shipping Co SA (The Kriti Acti)* [2004] 1 Lloyd's Rep 712 (CA) (where the later court was of course bound by the earlier). There is, however, the suggestion (no more) in *The Kriti Acti* that " . . . a last voyage of an extreme length would be precluded . . . by reference to the principle in *Glynn v Margetson & Co* [1893] AC 351": [2004] 1 Lloyd's Rep 712, [23] (Mance LJ), and see section [22.2] on *Glynn v Margetson*.

101 [1994] 1 WLR 1465.

Comment

It would seem that Bridget is in breach by redelivering late, but what are the damages? This is a rising market, so Charles should have no difficulty claiming £10,000 a day for the overrun. But what about the lucrative fixture? Damages in respect of this would appear to be ruled out by *The Achilleas*.[102] Fact situation (ii), however, is very similar to the situation in *The Gregos* itself.[103] Charles enforces not the charterparty, but the without prejudice agreement, and can probably claim in respect of the Eleanor fixture as well.

---

102 [2009] 1 AC 61, in section [11.5.2].
103 See section [11.5.4].

Chapter 12

Time charterparty hire

12.1 Punctual payment of hire

12.1.1 The obligation

Hire is the main consideration moving from time charterers.[1] Punctual payment is relied on by shipowners, who will themselves have other commitments, to pay crew, perhaps under a chattel mortgage, perhaps themselves to pay hire under a head charter. Punctual payment is therefore provided universally in time charters, and we can start with cl. 5 of the widely-used NYPE 1946 form, which provides:[2]

> "Payment of said hire to be made in New York in *cash* in United States Currency, monthly in advance,[3] and for the last month or part of same the approximate amount of hire, and should same not cover the actual time, hire is to be paid for the balance day by day, as it becomes due, if so required by Owners, unless bank guarantee or deposit is made by the Charterers, other-wise *failing the punctual and regular payment of the hire*, or bank guarantee, or on any breach of this Charter Party, the *Owners shall be at liberty to withdraw the vessel from the service of the Charterers*, without prejudice to any claim they (the Owners) may otherwise have on the Charterers."

Note the requirement for cash, and also for shipowners to have the liberty to withdraw, failing the punctual and regular payment of the hire.

Commercially recognised methods of transferring money that give the shipowners uncondi-tional use of the funds transferred, are also encompassed within the term "cash". Examples are inter-bank transfers, bankers' drafts and bankers' payment slips. The House of Lords held in *The Chikuma*,[4] however, that where the charterparty provided for payment in cash, the shipowners were entitled to receive cash or the equivalent of cash, but that this required immediate and *unconditional* use of the funds. *The Chikuma* was chartered on the NYPE 46 form.[5] Over more than six years (80 payments), the charterers had paid the monthly hire directly into the owners' bank (in Genoa in Italy) on the day that hire fell due. On the 81st instalment, the charterers made the payment as usual. Under Italian banking practice at that time, although the payment had been made into the bank on the due date, the money could not be withdrawn without interest until some four days later. The owners withdrew the vessel on the basis of cl. 5.

Had the owners withdrawn the money immediately, the interest would have amounted to about $70–100, an amount described by Lord Denning MR in the Court of Appeal as "trifling".[6] Lord Denning also observed that, following a slump:[7]

> ". . . [freights] are rising again. Here we are – owners are seeking to find some technicality, or some slight lapse on the part of the charterers or their bankers, on which they can with-draw the vessel."

As with many cases on withdrawal, the issue appears to have been purely financial. On a rising market, owners will of course wish to withdraw, to refix the vessel at the new (higher) market rate.

---

1 Demise charters also.
2 My emphasis.
3 Sometimes semi-monthly.
4 *Awilco A/S v Fulvia SpA di Navigazione (The Chikuma)* [1981] 1 WLR 314.
5 As indeed are many of the cases in this chapter. It remains probably the most widely used form in dry-cargo use. Conversely, none of the cases in this chapter deals with the later NYPE 93 form.
6 [1980] 2 Lloyd's Rep 409, 412.
7 [1980] 2 Lloyd's Rep 409, 411.

The House of Lords (reversing the Court of Appeal) held the owners' withdrawal justified. The owners had not received the equivalent of cash on the due date, because the funds transferred could not be used to earn interest. Therefore they did not have unconditional use of the money.

It is of course also necessary for the money to reach the owners. It is the time of receipt that matters for withdrawal purposes. This was the main issue in *The Brimnes*,[8] a decision of the Court of Appeal approved in *The Chikuma*. Risk of banking delays is therefore on the charterers.

Other forms are generally similar. Shelltime 4, cl. 9 requires payment in "immediately available funds". This seems to be the same as the meaning given to "cash" in *The Chikuma*. BPTIME 3, cl. 8 requires "funds available to Owners on the due date". However, in mitigation, it goes on to provide:

> "If, however, in a given month the due date is a non-banking day in the United States (if hire is to be paid in US Dollars) or in the country stated in PART 1, Section I, then the subject month's hire shall be paid on the next banking day."

12.1.2 Withdrawal for late payment

Withdrawal is one of the remedies for failure punctually to make payment of hire. It will only be used, of course, when the shipowners wish to end the charterparty. As we saw in the last section, the usual reason is that the market is rising. Often, indeed, the ship continues in service (and it is not easy physically to withdraw anyway, in middle of voyage), but if the withdrawal is valid, the continuation will be at the market rate, rather than the charter hire rate. In *The Astra* and in *Spar Shipping*, both discussed later in this chapter, the owners withdrew on a falling market.[9] Reasons for this might include fear over the charterer's liquidity, or ability or willingness to stay in the charterparty. Withdrawal on a falling market seems to be rare, however.

It may be that a withdrawal clause is like a cancelling clause in providing just the right and nothing more. But a cancelling clause is not associated with any particular breach of contract, whereas the withdrawal clause here provides a remedy for failure to make punctual payment, which is a breach of contract. The withdrawal clause does not therefore stand on its own, as a cancelling clause does. In *The Afovos*, Lord Diplock said the inclusion of a withdrawal clause made the breach of contract a breach of condition.[10] This point, however, cannot be said to have been determined by the authorities, which we consider further below.[11]

Particularly the older dry-cargo standard forms often allow withdrawal for the slightest breach of the hire clause by the charterers, for example payment one day late. This could be due to an oversight by the charterers, or arise from a difficulty in the banks' making payment. The argument has been advanced that it is unfair on charterers for shipowners to be allowed to rely strictly on such a clause, and respond to a technical breach with the extreme remedy of withdrawal.[12] This argument seems especially persuasive on a rising market, if the only reason for the owners' withdrawing is to recharter the vessel at higher rates.

On the other hand, hire is payable in advance to enable the owners to pay the necessary wages for the service that he has agreed to provide under the charter, and to service any mortgage commitments on the vessel. Moreover, if the charterers can resist withdrawal they in their turn can profit from the higher rate, by sub-chartering the vessel. As Lord Diplock noted in *The Scaptrade*:[13]

---

8 *Tenax Steamship Co Ltd v The Brimnes (Owners)* [1975] QB 929.

9 Section [12.1.6].

10 *Afovos Shipping Co SA v R. Pagnam & F. Lli (The Afovos)* [1983] 1 WLR 195, 203. See section [12.1.4] for detailed coverage of *The Afovos*.

11 See section [12.1.6].

12 Eg, Lord Denning MR in *The Laconia* [1976] QB 835, 847 (CA), rvsd HL [1977] AC 850 (see immediately below).

13 *Scandinavian Trading Tanker Co AB v Flota Petrolera Ecuatoriana (The Scaptrade)* [1983] 2 AC 694, 703.

"The freight market is notoriously volatile. If it rises during the period of a time charter, the charterer is the beneficiary of the windfall which he can realise if he wants to by sub-chartering at the then market rate. What withdrawal of the vessel does is to transfer the benefit of the windfall from charterer to shipowner."

In any case, the position is now fairly clear; the courts interpret withdrawal clauses literally. There is no period of grace, unless stipulated in the charterparty.

In *The Laconia*,[14] the market monthly hire rate had risen from the contract rate of $3.10 per ton to $5.59 per ton, so that the owners were keen to (and did) withdraw the vessel to take advantage of the higher rate.

You might note in passing that this is one of the cases where there was cargo on board, and so the ship remained in service. The actual effect of the withdrawal was that:[15]

"The charterers, in order to complete a voyage, agreed to pay $8 per ton pending a reference to arbitration of the question whether the owners were entitled to withdraw the vessel."

The hire clause in *The Laconia* also came from the 1946 revision of the New York Produce Exchange form, set out above,[16] from which (as you can see) there is a withdrawal provision, but no grace period.

The seventh and last (semi-monthly) instalment of hire fell due on a Sunday, when the banks in London were closed, and consequently the owners did not receive the money due until the Monday. The House (reversing the Court of Appeal) interpreted the clause literally, so that the payment by the charterers one day late allowed the shipowners to exercise their right of withdrawal.

A number of different withdrawal clauses were considered by the House of Lords. Lord Wilberforce noted that:[17]

"there is a range of forms available varying from the very strict to those with substantial periods of grace. The parties choose as they will, or as their market strength allows".

Shipowners and charterers are regarded as being capable of looking after themselves, and, if the charterers enter into an unwise bargain, the courts will not protect them from the consequences of their so doing. If charterers want a period of grace, it is up to them so to stipulate during charterparty negotiations.

The House also held that the charterers could not avoid the consequences by later tendering an unpunctual payment.[18] Had the owners accepted the later payment they would have waived (and hence lost) their right to withdraw, but in *The Laconia* they had instructed the bank to refuse payment. The owners will also be taken to have waived their rights if they do not give notice of withdrawal within a reasonable (short) time.[19]

In the House of Lords, the charterers in *The Laconia* attempted to advance the argument that a withdrawal clause in a time charterparty should be regarded as analogous to a forfeiture clause for a lease of land. The point of this argument is that, in appropriate circumstances, equity grants relief

14 *Mardorf Peach & Co Ltd v Attic Sea Carriers Corp of Liberia* (The Laconia) [1977] AC 850.
15 This is taken from the headnote. Note that $8 was significantly higher than either market or charter rates (the market rate being above the charter rate).
16 Section [12.1.1].
17 [1977] AC 850, 869.
18 Overruling CA contrary authority in *Empresa Cubana de Fletes v Lagonisi Shipping Co Ltd* (The Georgios C) [1971] 1 QB 488.
19 On waiver see generally [1977] AC 850, 872 (Lord Wilberforce).

against forfeiture by landlords of leases of land, effectively allowing time for tenants to pay, and the charterers argued that the same should apply to a withdrawal clause in a time charterparty.[20]

The argument had not been advanced in the lower courts in *The Laconia*,[21] and was therefore not considered by the House of Lords, but it *was* considered and rejected in *The Scaptrade*.[22] This case concerned the Shelltime 3 charter, whose withdrawal clause was similar to the NYPE, providing that:

". . . in default of such payment owners may withdraw the vessel from the service of the charterers, without prejudice to any claim owners may have on charterers under this charter".

Payment was made four days late, and the shipowners gave notice of withdrawal, but rechartering the vessel back to the charterers without prejudice. The rate of hire under the new charterparty was to await the litigation that followed (to determine whether the withdrawal was valid).

In the event, the withdrawal was held valid, so that the rate for the new charter was the current market rate, higher (on a rising market) than that agreed under the original charter.

Lord Diplock (who delivered the only substantive speech), rejected any analogy between time charterparty withdrawal and forfeiture clauses: time charterparties were not analogous to leases of land, primarily because the shipowner has to provide the services of the master and crew, as well as the vessel herself.[23] To grant an injunction restraining the owners from exercising their right of withdrawal was therefore tantamount to granting a decree of specific performance to enforce a contract for services, something that equity (as we have seen) will not do:[24]

". . . in respect of that category of contracts, even in the event of breach, this is a remedy that the English courts have always disclaimed any jurisdiction to grant. This is, in my view, sufficient reason in itself to compel rejection of the suggestion that the equitable principle of relief from forfeiture is juristically capable of extension so as to grant to the court a discretion to prevent a shipowner from exercising his strict contractual rights under a withdrawal clause in a time charter which is not a charter by demise."

In *The Scaptrade* the charterers also sought to advance:[25]

". . . a more general proposition that wherever a party to a contract was by its terms given a right to terminate it for a breach which consisted only of non-payment of a sum of money and the purpose of incorporating the right of termination in the contract was to secure the payment of that sum, there was an equitable jurisdiction to grant relief against the exercise of the right of termination".

The right to terminate the contract here is the withdrawal clause, and the charterers argued that the purpose of such a clause is essentially to secure the payment of money. Therefore, argued the charterers, equity can grant relief against its exercise.

Lord Diplock rejected this more general argument also,[26] on the grounds that it is not the purpose of a withdrawal clause in a time charterparty merely to secure the payment of a sum of money. It secures to the owners a fund from which they can meet the expense of providing the services they

---

20 On equitable principles generally, and the reluctance of the courts to apply them to arm's length relationships, see also section [3.4.4].

21 [1977] AC 850, 873 (Lords Wilberforce, Simon); 878 (Lord Salmon).

22 [1983] 2 AC 694.

23 See section [10.5].

24 [1983] 2 AC 694, 701.

25 Ibid.

26 [1983] 2 AC 694, 702.

have promised under the charter itself. Lord Diplock mentioned in particular the payment of wages of the master and crew, and the insurance and maintenance of the vessel.

It is clear from *The Scaptrade*, therefore, that equity will not intervene to grant relief against the exercise of a withdrawal clause in a time charterparty.

Lord Diplock states at the end of his speech,[27] that it "has been directed exclusively to time charters that are not by demise", and that "[identical] considerations would not be applicable to bareboat charters" (where, of course, there is no service element). In *The Jotunheim*,[28] Cooke J would have been prepared in principle to apply equitable relief in a demise charter that was being used as part of a hire-purchase arrangement, but on the facts refused relief; the charterers' conduct was not meritorious (since they had been persistently late in making payments). In *The Jotunheim*, the charterparty was used as a hire-purchase agreement, and of course there was no service element, and it was reasonable to view the purpose of the termination clause as essentially to secure payment.[29] If it were otherwise, then the court will not have jurisdiction, even where there is no service element. This was the view taken by Hamblen J in *Celestial Aviation Trading v Paramount Airways*,[30] where the charterparty (of an aircraft) was short term, compared with the economic life of the aircraft, and there was no hire-purchase element. Hamblen J, distinguishing *The Jotunheim*, thought that the owners had a very real continuing interest in the aircraft themselves, not just in the payment of rent. Therefore the termination provision was not inserted essentially to secure the payment of money, and equitable relief was not available, even in principle.[31]

It seems probable, then, that even where the charter is by demise, equitable relief will be available only where the owners have no reversionary interest in the vessel, as with a long-term charter culminating in a hire purchase option.

In *The Laconia*, the withdrawal was not "real", in the sense that the vessel was actually withdrawn from the service of the charterers. It was more convenient to continue the voyage, the effect of the valid withdrawal being that continuation was at market, not contract, hire rate. This was a dispute just about money, on a rising market, as is the case at the beginning of the next section, and as indeed are many of the withdrawal cases. In *The Kos*,[32] the charterers' cargo had already been loaded by the time of the withdrawal, but the charterers refused the owners' offer to continue the voyage at the higher market rate. The cargo was unloaded, and the owners successfully claimed hire for the period of the unloading, plus bunker fuel for the same period. One basis for the claim was the employment and indemnity clause in the Shelltime charterparty, the Supreme Court (with Lord Mance dissenting on this issue) holding that the charterers' order to load the cargo was a proximate cause of the owners' loss. The causation aspects of this case are discussed further in the next chapter.[33]

12.1.3 Withdrawal for deduction from hire

There are also withdrawal consequences attendant on deduction from hire, unless expressly provided for by the charterparty, as is shown by *The Mihalios Xilas*.[34] *The Mihalios Xilas* was chartered on an amended version of the Baltime form, which did not allow deductions from hire, except in the case of the last month's hire. For the last month, the charterers were allowed to deduct estimated

---

27 [1983] 2 AC 694, 704.
28 *More OG Romsdal Fylkesbatar AS v Demise Charterers of the ship Jotunheim (The Jotunheim)* [2005] 1 Lloyd's Rep 181.
29 [2005] 1 Lloyd's Rep 181, [46]–[53] on jurisdiction; [54]–[68] on discretion. Had the charterparty been performed, the owners would have retained no interest in the vessel, and the charterparty really was operating just as a payment mechanism.
30 [2011] 1 Lloyd's Rep 9.
31 [2011] 1 Lloyd's Rep 9, discussion of jurisdiction starting at [41].
32 *ENE Kos 1 Ltd v Petroleo Brasileiro SA (The Kos) (No. 2)* [2012] 2 AC 164.
33 See section [13.6].
34 *China National Foreign Trade Transportation Corporation v Evlogia Shipping Co SA of Panama (The Mihalios Xilas)* [1979] 1 WLR 1018.

bunker costs, owners' disbursements and other items of owners' liability. The charterers purported to make such deductions to the last month's hire, but the umpire found that in fact they would have been unable to redeliver the vessel until the next month. It therefore followed that this was not the last month's hire, and that therefore they were not entitled to make any deductions at all. Thus, too little hire was paid for the month, because unauthorised deductions had been made, but it was not paid late (in fact it was paid a day early). On *Laconia* principles, the shipowners were able validly to withdraw.

As with other cases we have seen, the effect of withdrawal, where the vessel was about to embark upon her final voyage to the port of redelivery, was that the owners could claim the market rate from the charterers after notice of withdrawal had been given, but on the settling of accounts they would have had to return any hire paid that was not earned by that date. The withdrawal was to the owners' benefit, assuming a rising market.

Similar principles were applied by Bingham J in *The Lutetian*,[35] where, in principle at least, the owners were held entitled to withdrawal following an unlawful deduction of estimated future off-hire.[36]

Clearly then, if the charterers are to be entitled to make deductions from hire, as they are in tanker time charters, it must be possible for the charterers either to be able to calculate such deductions with certainty, or to be given an express right to estimate the correct deductions. The certainty point has especial relevance for the drafting of off-hire clauses,[37] but in any case tanker charterers are often entitled to make deductions on the basis of reasonable estimates. Beepeetime 2, cl. 13 allowed deductions in respect of:[38]

"... (1) any advances for disbursements made on Owners' behalf; (2) any amount or expenses in respect of actual or estimated off hire periods; (3) any expenses incurred by Charterers which may reasonably be estimated by them to relate to such off hire periods . . .".

12.1.4 Anti-technicality clauses

Many charterparties (including the current revision of NYPE, and nearly all tanker charters) mitigate the effect of the above cases by making anti-technicality provision. These allow for a grace period before withdrawal, the duration of which varies between the forms. In cl. 11 of NYPE 93, for example, it is filled in by the parties; seven days' grace after notice is the period stipulated in Shelltime 4, cl. 9, and Intertanktime 80 (cl. 4) allows 144 hours' (ie, six days') grace after notification by the owner.[39] The intention of such a clause is to mitigate against the effects of *The Laconia*.

A similar anti-technicality clause, which was added to a NYPE 46 form,[40] operated successfully to protect the charterers in *The Afovos*.[41] The added clause required the owners to give 48 hours' notice before withdrawal, and not to withdraw the vessel if hire was paid within the 48 hours. The House of Lords held that the notice of withdrawal could not be given until after the time at which, apart from the anti-technicality clause, the right of withdrawal would accrue (in other words, only once payment was late). Payment was due on 14 June, so that the charterers were entitled to make

---

35 *Tradax Export SA v Dorada Compania Naviera SA (The Lutetian)* [1982] 2 Lloyd's Rep 140.

36 However the shipowners ultimately failed on *Afovos* principles: [1982] 2 Lloyd's Rep 140, 154–5. Note that this is the CA decision in *The Afovos* [1982] 1 Lloyd's Rep 562, which was affirmed in the HL (see generally section [12.1.4]).

37 See [12.3].

38 See also, eg, BPTIME 3, cll. 8.5 and 8.6.

39 Possibly, in reality, the parties prefer shorter grace periods. 48 hours was agreed in *The Afovos* [1983] 1 WLR 195, and in *Kuwait Rocks Co v Amn Bulkcarriers Inc (The Astra)* [2013] 2 Lloyd's Rep 69 (section [12.1.6]), it was two banking days.

40 There is, of course, no anti-technicality provision in NYPE 46, unamended.

41 [1983] 1 WLR 195. The anti-technicality clause was added: cl. 31.

payment at any time up to midnight on 14/15 June. Because of a banking error (through no fault of the charterers), it was not actually made until 19 June.

Meanwhile, the shipowners gave notice of withdrawal.[42] Their notice of withdrawal was given at 4.40 p.m. on 14 June, and of course payment was not made within 48 hours of that time. The House of Lords held, however, that the right to withdraw, apart from the clause, did not accrue until 15 June. The shipowners' notice was not a valid notice of withdrawal, therefore, however unlikely it appeared at the time it was given, that payment would be made on time. Hence, the purported withdrawal was invalid.

It follows that there is no anticipatory right to withdraw, and that the time for punctual payment must have passed, before the owners are entitled to give notice and invoke the grace period.

In Lord Diplock's view, the withdrawal remedy made failure to make punctual payment a breach of condition,[43] and, on this basis, one might have expected the shipowners to be entitled to repudiate for anticipatory breach. But Lord Diplock thought the anticipatory breach doctrine limited to "fundamental", or root of contract breaches, and that it did not apply to mere breaches of condition.[44] Though a breach of condition, the owners had to wait until the breach had occurred.

Apart from the timing issue, the notice must be clear and unambiguous. It must be a notice that the owners *will* withdraw.[45] This does not, however, commit them when the time for payment has passed; they always have the option to keep the charterparty alive and accept late payments.

12.1.5 Other remedies for late payment

Withdrawal is an extreme remedy, and will normally be attractive to shipowners only on a rising market. On a falling market the shipowner would prefer to keep the charterparty alive and sue for hire as it falls due. If (perhaps fearful of the charterer's ability to continue with the charterparty) he withdraws, he can still sue for hire due until the date of the withdrawal, but a claim for loss of future earnings (based on hire until the end of the charterparty) will be problematic, either because the decision to withdraw will include withdrawal of the services of master and crew, or because the withdrawal, rather than the charterer's breach, will be seen as the cause of the future losses. It is a different matter if the charterers are seen as being in repudiatory breach, the withdrawal being seen as an election by the owners to terminate.[46] There have been two recent first instance cases, where the charterers were treated (because of repeated late payments) as *refusing* to make punctual payment of hire, and hence (because of the importance to owners of payment in advance) to have *renounced* the charterparties.

Like *The Afovos*, *The Astra* concerned a NYPE form – but with an added cl. 31 (anti-technicality provision).[47] During the recent (2008) recession, the charterers continually demanded a hire reduction, eventually threatening bankruptcy unless they achieved this objective. They made a number of very late payments, and eventually (despite the market being very low) the owners invoked the anti-technicality clause and withdrew. They claimed damages for breach up to earliest redelivery

---

42 In reality, as is often the case, the charterers continued to use the vessel for the rest of the charter period, but without prejudice to the rights of the shipowners. Thus, if the shipowners' purported withdrawal was effective, they were entitled to the market hire rate at the time of the purported withdrawal. This was much higher than the contract rate: indeed, the difference amounted to some $2.5 million. Conversely, if the purported withdrawal was invalid, the owners were entitled only to hire at the original rate.

43 Section [12.1.2], but this statement, which is not part of the *ratio* of the case, may not be correct: see further section [12.1.6].

44 [1983] 1 WLR 195, 203. For a definition of "fundamental breach" he referred to his own speech in *Photo Production Ltd v Securicor Transport Ltd* [1980] AC 827, 849: [1983] 1 WLR 195, 202. Cf. *Spar Shipping v Grand China Logistics Holding (Group) Co Ltd* [2015] EWHC 718 (Comm), [144] (Popplewell J). On *Spar Shipping*, see further section [12.1.6]. On anticipatory breach generally, see section [2.7].

45 [1982] 2 Lloyd's Rep 140, also at section [12.3.1].

46 See generally section [2.6].

47 [2013] 2 Lloyd's Rep 69.

date, being effectively the hire lost, less earnings they could have made over the same period. For them to be able to do this, it was assumed they needed to show the charterers to be in repudiatory breach, the owners accepting the breach as bringing the charterparty to an end; otherwise there would have been no damages for the loss of charter as such, just a claim to the hire late paid.[48] Flaux J held that the charterers had (by their persistent demands, late payments and threats of bankruptcy) renounced the charterparty.[49] Consequently, the claim for future hire could be made. A similar case is *Spar Shipping v Grand China Logistics Holding (Group) Co Ltd*,[50] a decision of Popplewell J, decided just before this book went to press.

In each case, that was enough to decide the case. The overwhelming majority of the judgment in *The Astra*, however, is devoted to an argument (not in the event necessary for the decision) that failure punctually to pay hire amounts to a breach of condition. Flaux J said that "both parties' counsel urged me to decide this issue and therefore I propose to do so".[51] A large part of *Spar Shipping* is devoted to the same issue, with Popplewell J taking the opposite view to Flaux J. So we now turn to consider that question.

12.1.6 Punctual payment term condition?

Prior to *The Astra* it had been widely thought, partly on the basis of Coughlin, *Time Charters*, that the punctual payment obligation was only an "intermediate term".[52] There were a number of authorities, both for and against this proposition,[53] but nothing in any sense conclusive. In *The Astra*, Flaux J was not surprised at the lack of authority because withdrawal usually took place on a rising market – in which case there would be no loss of charter losses.[54] It is probably correct to say that he was not constrained one way or the other, by previous authority. He took the view that the obligation to make punctual payment was a condition. In *Spar Shipping*, Popplewell J took the opposite view (assuming it was not expressly made a condition in the charterparty).[55] Consequently, to add to the previous inconclusive authority, we now have two contradictory views, each of which is just *obiter dicta* at first instance. It is going to take a higher court to resolve this. All I will do here is to state briefly the arguments.

Flaux J drew support from *The Laconia*, emphasising as it did both the importance of punctual payment, and the need for certainty.[56] He also made general observations on time clauses being conditions in commercial contracts.

---

48 It is not entirely clear why this assumption was made, since as Flaux J himself observed, the damages claimed were "the very loss which the owners would suffer on a falling market . . . by virtue of early withdrawal of the vessel for breach of the obligation to make punctual payment of hire . . .": [2013] 2 Lloyd's Rep 69, [32]. So why could they not be claimed on normal contractual principles? Maybe causation was perceived to be the problem, that in the absence of repudiation, the owners would be seen to have brought the loss on themselves, by withdrawing the vessel.

49 This part of the case involved an interpretation of *The Nanfri*, section [2.7]. Flaux J held that the arbitrators had applied the right test, and "that the charterers were determined to perform the charterparty in a manner which deprived the owners of the substantial benefit they should have obtained from further performance": [2013] 2 Lloyd's Rep 69, [27].

50 [2015] EWHC 718 (Comm).

51 [2013] 2 Lloyd's Rep 69, [33]. The discussion occupies nearly 90 paragraphs, up to [121].

52 [2013] 2 Lloyd's Rep 69, [34] (Flaux J citing *Time Charters*, 6th ed (2008), Informa, [16.132]). See now 7th ed (2014).

53 Eg, *dicta* in Brandon J's judgment in *The Brimnes* [1973] 1 WLR 386 affd CA [1975] 1 QB 929. But Brandon J had founded heavily on *The Georgios C* [1971] 1 QB 488, which was overruled in *The Laconia*: [2013] 2 Lloyd's Rep 69, [63]. There are authorities the other way, principally *The Afovos*, in sections [12.1.2]; [12.1.4]: see [2013] 2 Lloyd's Rep 69, [90]. There are *dicta* in *The Kos*, both at first instance ([2010] 1 Lloyd's Rep 87) and in Lord Mance's speech in the Supreme Court ([2012] 2 AC 164), supporting the innominate term view, and there are of course time terms which are not conditions – eg, *Torvald Klaveness A/S v Arni Maritime Corp (The Gregos)* [1994] 1 WLR 1465 (see section [11.5]).

54 Flaux J made observations to this effect at [54] and [75].

55 [2015] EWHC 718 (Comm), issue 2, starting at [92].

56 [2013] 2 Lloyd's Rep 69, [77].

In summary, Flaux J's main reasons were:[57]
- the wording of the clause, which was sufficiently serious to be a condition;
- time terms being usually conditions;[58]
- the anti-technicality clause making time of the essence;[59]
- certainty;[60]
- authority (though as we have seen this was equivocal).

His conclusion was that, therefore, the owners could claim on termination for loss of bargain.[61]

It might be thought that *The Astra* renders valueless anti-technicality clauses, but one of the authorities relied upon by Flaux J was *The Afovos*.[62] In *The Afovos*, Lord Diplock thought it was the withdrawal provision that created the condition, and, of course, that does not operate until after anti-technicality grace periods have expired.[63] However, whatever the consequences of the breach of condition, the renunciation, or any other root of contract breach, would have entitled the owners to repudiate without regard to the anti-technicality clause.[64] As to the continued need for the withdrawal clause, given that (if *The Astra* is correct) the owners can repudiate anyway, according to Lord Diplock, the withdrawal clause is what makes the punctual payment obligation a condition in the first place.

In the later case, Popplewell J regarded the withdrawal authorities as of no value, since they were deciding a different issue. He was impressed by first instance *dicta* in *The Brimnes*,[65] and at first instance and in the Court of Appeal in *The Georgios C*,[66] taking the view (contrary to Flaux J) that these *dicta* were unaffected by the overruling of the later case in *The Laconia*.[67] These were among the authorities that had impressed the editors of *Time Charters*, prior to *The Astra*. Popplewell J thought that Lord Diplock had been wrong to treat the withdrawal clause as making punctual payment a condition in *The Afovos*, and observed that this view was not necessary to the decision in *The Afovos*. Conversely, he drew support from *dicta* in *The Kos*, also a decision of the highest court.[68] He considered the tests for treating terms as conditions, in the absence of express provision.[69] Fundamentally, he regarded a withdrawal clause as essentially similar to a cancelling clause, providing a termination remedy, and nothing else. But in view, the obligation to make punctual payment was an innominate term, not a condition, and therefore permitted repudiation only where sufficiently serious as to go to the root of the contract.

It is clear that the views of both Flaux and Popplewell JJ are arguable, and both draw some support (though nothing directly) from decisions of the highest courts in the land. The state of the authorities does not permit the drawing of any kind of conclusion as to what the law is; that will have to await a decision of a higher court.

---

57 [2013] 2 Lloyd's Rep 69, [109] ff.
58 Flaux J cited *Bunge Corp, New York v Tradax Export SA, Panama* [1981] 1 WLR 711: [2013] 2 Lloyd's Rep 69, [82]–[87]. Different considerations arguably apply to international sale contracts, however: section [2.6.2].
59 This was not crucial to his reasoning, and indeed it would have been surprising if a clause intended to protect charterers had the effect of strengthening the owners' position.
60 Flaux J cited *The Laconia* (section (12.1.2]) and *Bunge v Tradax*: [2013] 2 Lloyd's Rep 69, [114]–[116].
61 [2013] 2 Lloyd's Rep 69, [118].
62 See section [12.1.4].
63 Ibid.
64 A point made by Lord Hailsham: [1983] 1 WLR 195, 201.
65 [1973] 1 WLR 386.
66 *Empresa Cubana de Fletes v Lagonisi Shipping Co Ltd (The Georgios C)* [1971] 1 QB 488.
67 [2015] EWHC 718 (Comm), [120]–[137].
68 [2012] 2 AC 164: see [2015] EWHC 718 (Comm), [151]–[153].
69 The authorities discussed in section [2.6.2].

12.1.7 *The Astra* and the penalty clause argument

In *The Astra*, the owners also advanced an argument based on the following clause:

> "In the event of the termination or cancellation of the Charter by reason of any breach by or failure of the Charterers to perform their obligations, Charterers shall, in addition to any amounts due to Owners at the date of termination or cancellation, pay to the Owners compensation for future loss of earnings in respect of the unexpired period of the Charter on the basis of the difference between the market rate and [the charter hire rate]."

The charterers argued that this was a penalty clause, and hence unenforceable, on the principles in chapter 2.[70]

Because the owners succeeded on the basis of repudiation, there was no need to consider this clause, but Flaux J thought that it was not a penalty clause, interpreting "any breach" in cl. 5, to cover only to a repudiatory breach or a breach of condition. This may not be a very obvious interpretation, but he felt that it was justified by House of Lords authority.[71] But even if this was wrong, the existence of this clause could be used to support the conclusion that the parties intended non-punctual payment to be a breach of condition, justifying the damages calculation in the clause.[72]

12.1.8 Lien

Liens to secure payment of hire can provide the shipowner with some protection against the financially embarrassed charterer. Where the charterer is trading on his own account, it is the shipowner who may be left with liabilities to cargo-owners, but at least if the hire is secured, he should not thereby be placed in financial difficulty.

Liens may be on cargoes (though probably difficult to enforce in practice), or on moneys due under any sub-charterparty, whether freight or hire, or other money such as sub-charter demurrage, or general average contributions.[73]

Liens on cargoes are in principle covered by the discussion on voyage charters,[74] except that no lien is available at common law, to secure hire. A contractual lien on the cargo is of course possible, but it only operates against the charterer's cargo, unless the lien clause is also incorporated into any bills of lading issued under the charterparty.[75] Then the lien for unpaid hire can be enforced against the receiver as well, as long as the receiver is bound by s. 3 of the Carriage of Goods by Sea Act 1992.[76]

Liens on sub-freights are conceptually different from liens on cargo. They were considered in *The Spiros C*.[77] Such liens are not generally needed to secure freights on bill of lading contracts, since usually the shipowner will have a direct contractual nexus with the cargo-owner,[78] and will be able simply to direct payment of freight to himself. It is a different matter with sub-charter freights,

---

70 See section [2.9.3].

71 *Antaios Compania Naviera SA v Salen Rederierna AB (The Antaios) (No. 2)* [1985] AC 191, 200–1 (Lord Diplock): [2013] 2 Lloyd's Rep 69, [29]–[30].

72 [2013] 2 Lloyd's Rep 69, [31].

73 Shelltime includes demurrage and NYPE general average contributions.

74 In section [7.9].

75 As in *Federal Commerce and Navigation Inc v Molena Alpha Inc (The Nanfri)* [1979] AC 957.

76 See section [16.8] on liabilities.

77 *Tradigrain SA v King Diamond Shipping SA (The Spiros C)* [2000] 2 Lloyd's Rep 319, the CA adopting Lloyd J's analysis in *Care Shipping Corp v Latin American Shipping Corp (The Cebu) (No. 1)* [1983] QB 1005.

78 On the basis of the discussion in section [16.8].

where there is no direct contractual nexus; in that case, the lien operates as an equitable assignment of the debt from charterer to shipowner.[79] Then, according to Rix LJ in *The Spiros C*:[80]

"The shipowner perfects his right of lien by giving notice to the debtor: if the notice is in time to pre-empt payment of the relevant sub-freight, then the shipowner is entitled to payment from the debtor, even though he otherwise has no direct contractual relationship with him. But if the shipowner's notice to pay comes too late, and the sub-freight has already been paid, then the lien fails to bite on anything."

They are the assignment of a debt (owed by sub to head-charterer), and, once the debt has been paid, there is nothing on which the lien can bite. It might be different if sub-freight or sub-hire had been paid to a third party, unless with the authority of the head-charterer, since that would not amount to payment of the debt at all. Also, because this is an equitable property right, on the principles in chapter 3,[81] it should be possible to follow the debt into the hands of the third party, if he has notice of it.[82]

Priorities of equitable assignments depend on the rule in *Dearle v Hall*,[83] ie, the order in which notice is given to the debtor. This can significantly weaken the shipowner's protection, as in *The Attika Hope*,[84] where the charterers had, unbeknown to the shipowners, assigned the sub-freights to a third party; the third party gave notice to the sub-charterers, before the shipowners informed the sub-charterers that they were exercising their lien on sub-freights. Steyn J held that the sub-charterers were required to pay the freight to the third party, thereby depriving the shipowners of the efficacy of their lien.

The NYPE 46 lien encompasses only sub-freights, but sub-hire was added in the 1993 revision to NYPE.[85] In *The Cebu (No. 1)*,[86] Lloyd J held that the earlier wording alone sufficed to give the owners a contractual lien on any remuneration earned by the charterers from the employment of the vessel, including sub-charterparty hire. (Although the actual decision was limited to trip time charterparty hire, the reasoning extended to all hire.) His reasoning in essence was that the term "freight" was often used in a wider sense to include what was historically called "time freight" or "time-chartered freight", and that there had been a progressive tendency for the law to assimilate the rules relating to voyage and time charters.

Steyn J refused to follow Lloyd J, however, when the matter arose for reconsideration in *The Cebu (No. 2)*.[87] He felt that Lloyd J's observations as to the meaning of "freight" were based on nineteenth century usage, and were now out of date. Certainly by the time of the conclusion of the head charterparty in 1979, the vocabulary of the shipping trade had for many years used the word "hire" for sums payable under time charters, and restricted the word "freight" to voyage charterparties and bills of lading. The ordinary meaning of the term "freight" clearly therefore excluded "hire". Steyn J also observed that the exercise of rights of lien in respect of hire under a sub-time charterparty was more complicated than in respect of freights under a voyage charterparty, since the accounting

---

79 Differing views have been expressed on this. The authorities are all reviewed in *Western Bulk Shipowning III A/S v Carbofer Maritime Trading ApS (The Western Moscow)* [2012] 2 Lloyd's Rep 163, where Christopher Clarke J adopts the conventional view. A different view (essentially that the liens give only a non-proprietary interception right) was adopted by Lord Millet in *Agnew v Commissioners of Inland Revenue* [2001] 2 AC 710. If that view is correct, it gives no right against the sub-charterer himself.

80 [2000] 2 Lloyd's Rep 319, [11].

81 Section [3.4.2].

82 [2012] 2 Lloyd's Rep 163, [48].

83 (1828) 3 Russ 1.

84 *G & N Angelakis Shipping Co SA v Compagnie National Algerienne de Navigation (The Attika Hope)* [1988] 1 Lloyd's Rep 439.

85 Clause 18 in both cases.

86 *Care Shipping Corp v Latin American Shipping Corp (The Cebu) (No. 1)* [1983] QB 1005.

87 *Care Shipping Corp v Itex Itagrani Export SA (The Cebu) (No. 2)* [1993] QB 1.

position under a time charterparty was more complex. He cited *The Nanfri*,[88] where (as will become apparent in the next section) the majority of the Court of Appeal drew a clear distinction between freight and hire; Lloyd J had distinguished *The Nanfri* on the grounds that it went against the general trend, and that the Court of Appeal needed to consider only a rule relating to voyage charterparties that it clearly regarded as anomalous.[89]

The trend of modern cases probably lends support to Steyn J's reasoning, in which case sub-charter hire will need to be expressly included, as in NYPE 93.

Whether the lien is exercised on sub-freight or sub-hire, the shipowner must give notice in time to intercept the payment. In *The Spiros C*, the sub-freight had already been paid, but (at the request of the charterers) as an advance, and to a third party. The shipowners attempted to argue that what had been paid was not the sub-freight under the sub-charterparty, but this argument was rejected in the Court of Appeal. The shipowner was held to have delegated the whole manner and mode of the collection of the freight to the time charterer. If the time charterer was prepared to accept freight paid in advance to a third party, there was no reason why the shipowner should consider that such arrangements, even if they were different from that contemplated by the original charter, were outside the scope of the delegated authority to his time charterer. In the absence of clear provision to the contrary, therefore, the charterer is given a very wide discretion as to how sub-charter freights (and presumably hire) are to be collected.

12.2 Equitable set-off

With voyage charterparties (as we saw in chapter 7), there is a general principle that freight must be paid to the shipowners in full, even if there is short delivery of the cargo, or it is delivered in a damaged condition.[90] The charterers must pay the full freight (in the absence of an out-turn loss clause), and cannot set off any damages to which they may be entitled against the freight. They must sue for damages in a separate action. This is generally recognised to be an anomalous rule, but was nevertheless restated by the House of Lords in *The Aries*.[91] The question is, do the rules that apply to freight also apply to hire?

As we saw in the discussion of *The Cebu* (No. 1) in the last section, hire used to be called time-chartered freight, and today's clear distinction between freight and hire is a fairly modern concept. Nevertheless, in *The Nanfri*, Lord Denning MR observed that:[92]

> "'Freight' is payable for carrying a quantity of cargo from one place to another. 'Hire' is payable for the right to use a vessel for a specified period of time, irrespective of whether the charterer chooses to use it for carrying cargo or lays it up, out of use. Every time charter contains clauses which are quite inappropriate to a voyage charter, such as the off-hire clause and the withdrawal clause. So different are the two concepts that I do not think the law as to 'freight' can be applied indiscriminately to 'hire'."

Treating time charter hire as different from freight, the case may provide a limited exception, for hire, from the *Aries* rule, under the doctrine of equitable set-off.

---

88 [1978] 1 QB 927, discussed in section [12.2].

89 This will become clearer in section [12.2].

90 Section [7.2].

91 *Aries Tanker Corp v Total Transport Ltd (The Aries)* [1977] 1 WLR 185, in section [7.2].

92 *Federal Commerce and Navigation Inc v Molena Alpha Inc (The Nanfri)* [1978] 1 QB 927 (affd HL on other grounds [1979] AC 957: see section [13.7]). This passage is at [1978] 1 QB 927, 973.

In *The Nanfri*, time was lost due to breakdowns of machinery, and reduction in speed due to defects in the hull machinery and equipment. The charterers deducted hire, and the owners responded by withdrawing all authority from the master to sign bills of lading on behalf of the charterers. The master could still sign bills of lading on the shipowners' behalf, but he was not to sign any "freight pre-paid" bills, and to indorse any bills:

> "All terms, conditions and exceptions of the charterparty . . . including the lien clause . . . on bill of lading freight as well as sub-freight belonging to the time charter, are herein incorporated."

The owners' conduct amounted to a breach of the employment and indemnity clause in the charterparty,[93] unless the charterers' prior deduction itself amounted to a repudiatory breach, which was (by this conduct) accepted by the owners as bringing the charterparty to an end.

The charterers treated the *owners'* conduct as a repudiatory breach of the charterparty, and purported to repudiate it (very low market rates then prevailing, as compared to the contract hire rate). This argument depended on them being entitled to deduct hire. By a 2–1 majority,[94] the Court of Appeal held that the charterers were so justified, under the doctrine of equitable set-off. Lord Denning MR limited the doctrine to breaches by the shipowner that:[95]

> "wrongly deprived the charterer of the use of the vessel or . . . prejudiced him in the use of it".

Goff LJ broadly agreed with this, but also thought that the charterers were also entitled to make deductions on the basis of the express wording of the (amended Baltime) off-hire clause in the charterparty. Cumming-Bruce LJ dissented on equitable set-off, on the basis that time charterparty hire was to be treated similarly to voyage charterparty freight, but he agreed that a clause in the Baltime charter expressly provided for the deductions that had been made.

We therefore have a 2–1 majority view expressed by the Court of Appeal, where Goff LJ would have reached the same result on the express wording of the charterparty (as indeed would Cumming-Bruce LJ). On appeal, the House of Lords expressly left open the issue of the basis of any deduction, concentrating entirely on the repudiation issue.[96] The authority for application of the equitable set-off doctrine to hire is therefore not particularly strong. There have, however, been a number of first instance decisions accepting Lord Denning's view (though not applying it). Recall that it requires the breaches by the shipowner to have "wrongly deprived the charterer of the use of the vessel or . . . prejudiced him in the use of it". Hence, *The Nanfri* was distinguished in *The Leon*,[97] where the charterers suspected that the master and chief engineer had been fraudulently persuading the bunker supplier to deliver less bunker fuel than the charterers had ordered, but had been invoicing the charterers for the full quantity. The difference, it was alleged, they pocketed themselves, as cash. The charterers claimed that the total amount of the fraud amounted to nearly $300,000, and refused to pay a month's hire, of just under $200,000, claiming that they were entitled to set off their damages against hire payments as they fell due. In an appeal from arbitration, Hobhouse J held that they were not entitled to do so, observing that:[98]

---

93 See section [13.7].

94 Cumming-Bruce LJ dissented on the equitable set-off issue.

95 [1978] 1 QB 927, 976.

96 On which see further section [13.7]. The owners' breach was serious, making it difficult for the charterers to carry any cargo sold on CIF terms, where a freight prepaid bill would normally be expected.

97 *Leon Corporation v Atlantic Lines and Navigation Co Ltd (The Leon)* [1985] 2 Lloyd's Rep 470.

98 This is taken from the headnote. Lawton LJ tentatively agreed (CA, 18 October 1985), but the CA was concerned with a different issue.

"none of the breaches [alleged] . . . affected the use of the vessel and none were capable in law of justifying a conclusion that they prejudiced the charterers or their use of the vessel".

Of course this is true – they had nothing to do with the use of the vessel as such.

Other (first instance) cases where charterers were held not entitled to set off include *The Aditya Vaibhav*,[99] and *The Li Hai*.[100] These cases proceed on the assumption that Lord Denning's position is correct, but I would suggest that the law is not yet clearly determined.

Remember also that if the deductions are not permitted then, in principle, the shipowner can withdraw.[101]

12.3 Off-hire

12.3.1 General principles

Off-hire clauses can effectively stop the clock running for the time that the vessel cannot be said to be at the disposal of the charterers.

The general principle is that hire continues to run even if the shipowners are in breach of the charterparty, unless the charterparty expressly provides to the contrary. So, for example, if the owners are in breach by failing to maintain the vessel, and, for that reason, the charterers are unable to make full use of her, hire remains payable at the full rate unless the charterers can bring themselves within the terms of an off-hire clause.

The onus is on the charterers to bring themselves within the clause, and the list of events within it, putting the vessel off-hire, is exhaustive.

There are many authorities for this proposition, but the law is summed up in *The Saldanha*, where Gross J reminds us:[102]

". . . that the applicable principles are beyond argument. As is hornbook law and was clearly expressed in the award, under a time charterparty, hire is payable continuously unless charterers can bring themselves within any exceptions, the onus being on charterers to do so. Doubt as to the meaning of exceptions is to be resolved in favour of owners. Unless within the ambit of the exceptions, the risk of delay is borne by charterers. The justice of the matter is to be found in the bargain struck by the parties. Mr Baker QC, for owners, put it well in his skeleton argument:

'There is no relevant concept of fairness other than the contractual balance struck by the off-hire clause, construed in accordance with well-known orthodoxy.'"

It follows that the definition of off-hire exceptions in the off-hire clause is fundamental.

---

99 *Century Textiles and Industry Ltd v Tomoe Shipping Co (Singapore) Pte Ltd (The Aditya Vaibhav)* [1991] 1 Lloyd's Rep 573 (vessel delayed but charterers not entitled to set-off for any period longer than the delay – charterers had also wrongly deducted consequential losses).

100 *Western Bulk Carriers K/S v Li Hai Maritime Inc (The Li Hai)* [2005] 2 Lloyd's Rep 389 (deduction for bunker cancellation fee not permitted; this could in principle have led to withdrawal of vessel for under-payment, except that the owners did not give effective notice under anti-technicality clause (they had failed to give a clear and unambiguous ultimatum to the charterers: see [70] *et seq*). See generally section [12.1.2].

101 As in *The Li Hai*; see also *The Lutetian* [1982] 2 Lloyd's Rep 140, in section [12.1.4].

102 *Cosco Bulk Carrier Co Ltd v Team-Up Owning Co Ltd (The Saldanha)* [2011] 1 Lloyd's Rep 187, [7]. This case is fully discussed in section [12.3.6].

It is also a matter of construction of the charterparty whether deduction from hire, in respect of off-hire is also permitted. In *The Lutetian*,[103] the NYPE clause allowed deduction for past off-hire, and in respect of owners' estimates of future off-hire, but not deduction from advance payment in respect of charterers' estimates of future off-hire. For the charterers to make such a deduction would have allowed the owners to withdraw the vessel, had they properly complied with the withdrawal provisions. Charterparties can of course permit such deduction, as did Beepeetime 2, cl. 13 (but, curiously, there is no equivalent provision in BPTIME 3).

12.3.2 Different off-hire clauses in the standard forms

There is a wide difference between off-hire clauses, reflecting the relative bargaining strengths of the parties. In general, as one would expect, tanker off-hire clauses are more beneficial to the charterers.

Baltime is a pro-shipowner charter, even by dry-cargo standards, and cl. 11 provides what is probably the minimum off-hire concession commonly seen today:

> "(A) In the event of drydocking or other necessary measures to maintain the efficiency of the Vessel, deficiency of men or Owners' stores,[104] breakdown of machinery, damage to hull or other accident, either hindering or preventing the working of the Vessel and continuing for more than twenty-four consecutive hours, no hire to be paid in respect of any time lost thereby during the period in which the Vessel is unable to perform the service immediately required. Any hire paid in advance to be adjusted accordingly."

Since as we have seen, the onus is on charterers to bring themselves within the clause, it follows that the list in (A) is exhaustive, and that charterers cannot argue that any other circumstance puts the vessel off-hire, by analogy. There is also a 24-hour minimum cut-off before the clause applies. Note however that even Baltime allows adjustment to hire, though probably only retrospectively.

NYPE 93, cl. 17 has no 24-hour hurdle, and also provides:

> "... Should the vessel deviate or put back during a voyage, contrary to the orders or directions of the Charterers, for any reason other than accident to the cargo or where permitted [by the liberties clause], the hire is to be suspended from the time of her deviating or putting back until she is again in the same or equidistant position from the destination and the voyage resumed therefrom. All bunkers used by the Vessel while off hire shall be for the Owners' account. . . ."

In a similar vein we have Shelltime 4, cl. 21:

> ". . . the vessel shall be off-hire from the commencement of such loss of time until she is again ready and in an efficient state to resume her service from a position not less favourable to Charterers than that at which such loss of time commenced; provided, however, that any service given or distance made good by the vessel whilst off-hire shall be taken into account in assessing the amount to be deducted from hire. . . ."

Baltime, by contrast, has no provision regarding putting back into a position not less favourable. In *The Zanzibar*,[105] the vessel had to deviate to a repair yard for repairs to be carried out after an accident. After the repairs were finished it took a further week before she was back into the position

---

103 [1982] 2 Lloyd's Rep 140, in section [12.1.4].

104 Deficiency of men encompasses only numerical deficiency: cf. the discussion of *The Saldanha* [2011] 1 Lloyd's Rep 187, in section [12.3.6].

105 *Vogemann v Zanzibar Steamship Co Ltd (The Zanzibar)* (1902) 7 Com Cas 254.

before where the accident occurred. The charterers claimed that week as off-hire (under a clause that was in this respect similar to the Baltime clause), but the Court of Appeal held that the vessel was on hire from the moment the vessel was again in full working order – in other words, as soon as she left the repair yard. The Zanzibar was applied in The Marika M,[106] where the NYPE 46 clause covered grounding but not getting into berth once refloated.

If the charterers wish to count as off-hire the time required to put the vessel back into a position as favourable to them as it was before the off-hire event occurred, the off-hire clause must expressly so stipulate. Tanker clauses do this, however (as indeed does the NYPE 93 clause set out above).

12.3.3 Net loss of time and period off-hire

Though there are significant differences between the forms, nearly all off-hire clauses today are "net loss of time", as opposed to "period off-hire" clauses. This has not always been the case. "Period off-hire" used to predominate, but is now restricted to a small number of tanker forms.[107]

Under a "net loss of time" clause, the charterers are only entitled to the benefit of time actually lost, when the vessel is unable to perform the service immediately required. In other words, if repairs to the vessel are carried out, for example to the engines, but no delay is caused to the charterers because this happens during loading or discharge, they cannot claim off-hire. Similarly, if the speed of discharge of the vessel is reduced for any of the reasons contained in the off-hire clause, say to half speed while repairs are carried out, the charterers are entitled only to the benefit of time actually lost, or in other words half the eventual discharge period. They cannot claim off-hire for the entire discharge period.

Under a net loss of time clause, therefore, the consequences of partial inefficiency are less than those of total inefficiency.

Under a "period off-hire" clause, by contrast, once there is *any* loss of time because the vessel is off-hire, no hire is payable until she is again in a fully efficient state to resume service. In other words, there is a clear off-hire period, during which no hire at all is payable, even if the charterers have had some benefit from the vessel. Partial inefficiency has the same effect as total inefficiency.[108] If because of a breakdown in the pumps the vessel can only discharge at half speed, the charterers pay no hire at all for the discharge period, and the shipowners obtain no credit for the fact that the vessel is discharged eventually.

"Period off-hire" clauses are easier to work, and, of course, benefit charterers. They seem to have been commonly used in the past, but today are confined to a few tanker charterparties. In The Pythia it is suggested that there are "possible injustices" with period off-hire clauses.[109]

One would naturally expect the pro-shipowner Baltime to be "net loss of time", and indeed the wording is ". . . no hire to be paid *in respect of any time lost* thereby during the period in which the Vessel is unable to perform the service immediately required". NYPE 93, cl. 17 has: "the payment of hire and overtime, if any shall cease *for the time thereby lost*" – again, clearly net loss of time.[110] By contrast, Beepeetime 2, cl. 23, was worded ". . . in the event of loss of time continuing for more than 24 hours through: . . ." – and then the off-hire exceptions are set out. This is period off-hire wording. BPTIME 3 has (in cl. 19):

---

106 *Eastern Mediterranean Maritime (Liechtenstein) Ltd v Unimarine SA (The Marika M)* [1981] 2 Lloyd's Rep 622.

107 The terminology can be found (eg) in *Forestships International Ltd v Armonia Shipping and Finance Corporation (The Ira)* [1995] 1 Lloyd's Rep 103 and *The HR Macmillan* [1974] 1 Lloyd's Rep 311, and more recently in *The Athena* [2013] 2 Lloyd's Rep 673, [28]–[36], and the end of Robert Goff J's judgment in *Western Sealanes Corp v Unimarine SA (The Pythia)* [1982] 2 Lloyd's Rep 160.

108 But note that there still has to be some loss of time – that is the trigger.

109 [1982] 2 Lloyd's Rep 160, 168.

110 My emphasis in both extracts.

> "The Vessel shall be off hire on each and every occasion that there is a loss of time arising out of or in connection with the Vessel being unable to comply with Charterers' instructions (whether by way of interruption or reduction in the Vessel's services, or in any other manner) on account of:- . . .",

and then the off-hire events are set out. Although this is triggered by loss of time, once the clause is triggered, it is not a net loss of time provision. BP is an exception in providing for period off-hire today, however.

12.3.4 Cases on the types of clause

The workings of a "period off-hire" clause can be found in *The Westfalia*,[111] the clause being as follows:

> "in the event of loss of time from . . . whereby the working of the vessel was stopped . . . the payment of hire should cease until she should be again in an efficient state to resume her service".

The high pressure engine on the vessel broke down. The vessel was eventually towed to her destination by a tug, but with the assistance of her low pressure engine. At the port of discharge (Harburg), the cargo was discharged using the vessel's steam winches. The House of Lords held that no hire was payable while the vessel was being towed by the tug, although she was able to assist with her own low pressure engine.

The vessel had ceased to be off-hire on discharge, however, even though the high pressure engine had not yet been repaired, because she was then fully efficient for the service for which the charterers required her. Lord Halsbury LC noted that:[112]

> ". . . at that time [the] vessel was efficiently working: the working of the vessel was proceeding as efficiently as it could with reference to the particular employment demanded of her at the time".

The emphasis on the employment demanded of the vessel at the time can also be seen in the Court of Appeal in *The Athena*,[113] and can reduce the perceived injustice of the "period off-hire" clause, as compared with "net loss of time".

The "period" clause is obviously not generally in the interests of the shipowners, because the charterers are getting what is, in effect, a windfall; in *The Westfalia*, they did not have to pay hire although the cargo reached its destination. A "period" clause is additionally to charterers' advantage in that it makes the calculation of off-hire easier (because there is a clear off-hire period). If the charterers are entitled to deduct off-hire periods from future hire payments, it might be thought especially important for charterers to be able to calculate precisely how much they can deduct in the light of *The Mihalios Xilas*, above. Sometimes, however (as we have seen), they are entitled to make reasonable estimations of deductions, which makes *The Mihalios Xilas* less of a potential trap than it might otherwise be.[114]

---

111 Hogarth (Hugh) v Alexander Miller, Brother & Co (The Westfalia) [1891] AC 48. The Westfalia was applied in Tynedale Steam Shipping Co Ltd v Anglo-Soviet Shipping Co Ltd (The Hordern) (1936) 54 Ll L Rep 341, interpreting an old (1920) version of Baltime (even Baltime was a period clause in 1920).

112 [1891] AC 48, 57.

113 Minerva Navigation Inc v Oceana Shipping AG (The Athena) [2013] 2 Lloyd's Rep 673, in section [12.3.9].

114 Section [12.1.3].

12.3.5 Some off-hire events

This is a principles book, and in any case there is not space to consider every off-hire event. There are a number of decisions on NYPE 46, cl. 15:[115]

> "That in the event of the loss of time from deficiency [and/or default] of men or stores, fire, breakdown or damages to hull machinery or equipment, grounding, detention by average accidents to ship or cargo, dry-docking for the purpose of examination or painting bottom, or by any other cause [whatsoever] preventing the full working of the vessel, the payment of hire shall cease for the time thereby lost . . .".

We have already observed that it is for the charterers to bring themselves within the off-hire clause. Off-hire clauses are also interpreted literally (there is normally no attempt to glean a purpose), and without any predisposition to find a relationship between the off-hire clause and the remainder of the charterparty. As Staughton LJ observed in *The Berge Sund*:[116]

> "A charter-party might provide that the vessel would remain on hire *except during delay caused by a breach of contract on the part of the owner*; or it might provide that the vessel should be off hire in the event of delay, *unless caused by breach of contract on the part of the charterers.* Either solution would provide a rule that was tolerably clear and workable. *But those who make charter-parties prefer something more complicated.* They provide for a vessel to be off hire in some events which are not a breach of contract by either party for example, interference by authorities in the present case. As is fashionable nowadays, the clause is said to deal with allocation of risk. *The only general rule that can be laid down is that one must consider the wording of the off-hire clause in every case.*"

There is therefore no presumption that the off-hire clause has any relationship with breaches of contract by either party. The off-hire clause must be interpreted in its own right.

Nonetheless, the general scheme of the charterparty was used as an aid to the interpretation of the off-hire clause in *The Doric Pride*.[117] The clause covered "capture, seizure or arrest", and the issue was whether that extended to delays to a "High Interest Vessel" that was attempting, in the aftermath of September 2001, to enter a US port that (as such a vessel) might pose a high relative risk to that port. She was delayed until inspected by a USCG boarding team.[118] In holding the vessel off-hire, the Court of Appeal had regard to the basic distinction in a time charter party between matters that were the responsibility of the owners (principally vessel and crew), and those that were the responsibility of the charterers (principally the employment of the vessel). *The Berge Sund* tells us only that there is no necessary tie-in between the off-hire provision and the rest of the charterparty. It does not tell us that we must ignore the scheme of the charterparty in resolving ambiguities in the off-hire clause itself. Even if we are interpreting the clause on its own, it must be legitimate (and may well be necessary) to look more widely to resolve ambiguities.

---

115 The square bracketed words are often added; for example, both were added in *Andre & Cie SA v Orient Shipping (Rotterdam) BV (The Laconian Confidence)* [1997] 1 Lloyd's Rep 139; the first but not the second were added in *Cosco Bulk Carrier Co Ltd v Team-Up Owning Co Ltd (The Saldanha)* [2011] 1 Lloyd's Rep 187.

116 *Sig Bergesen DY & Co v Mobil Shipping and Transportation Co (The Berge Sund)* [1993] 2 Lloyd's Rep 453, 459 (my emphasis).

117 *Hyundai Merchant Marine Co Ltd v Furnace Withy (Australia) Pty (The Doric Pride)* [2006] 2 Lloyd's Rep 175, esp [28], and see section [10.4]. The principle was accepted in *NYK Bulkship (Atlantic) NV v Cargill International Sa (The Global Santosh)* [2014] 2 Lloyd's Rep 103; [2014] EWCA Civ 403, but the CA held it inapplicable to the particular clauses there under consideration.

118 United States Coast Guard.

12.3.6 Off-hire events: some cases

To attempt exhaustively to define common off-hire events is beyond the scope of this principles book, but we will briefly look at some of the recent cases.

Some of the off-hire events in NYPE 46, cl. 15 were considered in *The Saldanha*,[119] a case that involved ransom piracy, where the ship was seized, but neither ship nor cargo were damaged. She was released, and had returned to her position pre-capture after about 10 weeks. Gross J held that she was not off-hire for the period of the seizure: the loss of time was not (as argued by the charterers) caused by:

> an average accident; or
> deficiency and/or default of men; or
> "any other cause" preventing the full working of the vessel.[120]

As for the first ground, there had of course been no physical damage. Gross J rejected the charterers' argument that "average" had the same meaning as in marine insurance, meaning "loss", and did not require physical damage. In this regard he did no more than adopt the views of Kerr J, also on the NYPE form, in *The Mareva AS*.[121] Gross J emphasised the importance of certainty, and would have been prepared to depart from *The Mareva* only had he been convinced that it was clearly wrong; but, on the contrary, he thought it correct. He agreed with the arbitration tribunal that average here was used in the sense of partial rather than total loss, this conclusion being fortified by the separate inclusion of a total loss clause (cl. 16 of NYPE). On this basis, partial losses were catered for in cl. 15, and total losses in cl. 16.

(In parenthesis, one cannot help but wonder what a phrase like "average accidents" is doing in a modern charterparty. It would be tempting to scoff that though the case is recent, the form is not, but "average accidents" remains in the 1993 revision – cl. 17, and even in the 2014 proposed amendments to NYPE!)[122]

Gross J also observed that the piratical capture was not accidental. Obviously it was deliberate from the viewpoint of the pirates, but the charterers argued that it was a fortuity as far as the crew and the vessel were concerned. Gross J agreed with the view adopted by the arbitration tribunal that "accident" requires lack of intent by all protagonists:[123]

> "An obviously deliberate and violent attack is not described as an accident, no matter how unexpected it may have been to the victim. A much more specific word or phrase is put to the incident, to reflect its deliberate and violent nature."

He could not

> "imagine a master telephoning or emailing his Owners after the seizure and saying 'there has been an accident to the ship'. He would naturally say 'the ship has been seized by pirates' or 'we have been captured by pirates'."

---

119 [2011] 1 Lloyd's Rep 187; the widely-used NYPE 46 cl. 15 is set out at section [12.3.5]. On ransom piracies and construction generally, see section [22.4], and in particular the discussion of *Osmium Shipping Corp v Cargill International SA (The Captain Stefanos)* [2012] 2 Lloyd's Rep 46, another off-hire case which raises more general issues of construction.
120 "default of" was, but "whatsoever" was not added to the standard NYPE 46 cl. 15 off-hire clause.
121 *Mareva Navigation Co Ltd v Canaria Armadora SA (The Mareva AS)* [1977] 1 Lloyd's Rep 368, cited [2011] 1 Lloyd's Rep 187, [11].
122 Which can be found at https://www.bimco.org/~/media/News/2014/NYPE_93_v_NYPE_2014_comparison.ashx.
123 [2011] 1 Lloyd's Rep 187, [12].

Gross J also observed that "nobody would naturally say that President Kennedy had an accident in Dallas in 1963".[124]

Nor did the capture result from "default and/or deficiency of men". The argument was based on a factual assumption (disputed, but assumed for the purposes of the decision) that the officers and crew had failed to take recognised anti-piracy precautions, before and during the attack. If these failures were made out, the charterers argued that they would fall within the exception "default of men". There was, however, no numerical deficiency, and no refusal by the crew to perform duties. The argument was based only on the assumption that they were incompetent.

Gross J held that "default" meant refusal, not merely negligent or inadvertent performance of duties. The words "default of" are an addition to the standard NYPE 1946 clause, and he observed that it had been introduced in response to the decision in *The Ilissos*, which concerned refusal to perform.[125]

Gross J was also influenced by a realisation that the charterers' argument would significantly alter the normal risk on delay in time charters, since the vessel would be off-hire whenever officers or crew negligently or inadvertently failed to perform their duties, causing loss of time:[126]

> "If . . . Charterers' case is well-founded, it must follow that on almost every occasion when Officers or crew negligently or inadvertently fail to perform their duties causing some loss of time, then a vessel would be off-hire under this wording . . ."

Such an interpretation could, for example, even deprive the owners of the familiar exceptions in respect of errors of navigation or negligent navigation. Though both were provided for in the charterparty, because the operation of an off-hire clause did not depend on a breach by the ship-owner, they could, on this interpretation, be subverted by the wording of the off-hire clause. Gross J was not prepared to interpret the clause so as to reach so dramatic a result.[127]

As for "any other cause", there is authority that the *ejusdem generis* rule applies.[128] The piracy incident was a totally extraneous cause, falling outside the scope of the sweep-up wording, It would probably have been different had the clause been qualified by "whatsoever".[129]

12.3.7 Some general requirements: requirement of fortuity

In *The Rijn*,[130] Mustill J was also concerned to interpret the catchall provision in NYPE 46. He held that the cause must be "fortuitous, and not the natural result of the ship complying with the charterers' orders". The vessel there had been slowed by a gradual accretion of marine growth on the hull,

124 *Ibid*, another comment originating in the tribunal. Gross J was unimpressed by an analogy with *Thomas Wilson Sons & Co v Owners of Cargo per the Xantho (The Xantho)* (1887) 12 App Cas 503, where a collision was held to be a peril of the seas: "apart from all other considerations, a collision at sea is far removed from a seizure by pirates": [2011] 1 Lloyd's Rep 187, [14].

125 *Royal Greek Government v Minister of Transport (The Ilissos)* (1948–9) 82 Ll L Rep 196 (CA). In *The Laura Prima* [1982] 1 Lloyd's Rep 1, 3, Lord Roskill had cautioned against relying on the lineage of standard forms, but would have made an exception where "it is possible to detect from an alteration of clauses in standard forms an obvious intention to depart from a particular judicial decision the practical effect of which the parties wish to avoid". This might legitimately be one such situation. See further section [22.3].

126 [2011] 1 Lloyd's Rep 187, [27].

127 Though the Supreme Court case is not mentioned, such an interpretation might also flout business common sense, the importance of which was emphasised by Lord Clarke in *Rainy Sky SA v Kookmin* [2011] 1 WLR 2900 (and see section [22.2]).

128 Culminating in *The Laconian Confidence* [1997] 1 Lloyd's Rep 139, where the earlier authorities were fully discussed.

129 [2011] 1 Lloyd's Rep 187, [36] and immediately preceding discussion. Also discussed in *The Laconian Confidence* [1997] 1 Lloyd's Rep 139, culminating at 151. In *Belcore Maritime Corporation v F. Lli Moretti Cereali SpA (The Mastro Giorgis)* [1983] 2 Lloyd's Rep 66, Lloyd J held the clause, with the "whatsoever addition", wide enough to cover the arrest of the vessel in port by the receivers of the cargo.

130 *Santa Martha Baay v Scanbulk (The Rijn)* [1981] 2 Lloyd's Rep 267.

but this did not put her off-hire even on the basis of the catchall "any other cause" wording in what again appears to be the NYPE 46 off-hire clause.[131] For fouling by marine growth to put the vessel off-hire, the growth would have had to be "of a wholly extraordinary and unpredictable nature". It was not enough that it had stemmed merely from the long period the vessel had spent in the tropics, especially as it was the charterers' choice to keep the vessel there for so long.

The *Apollonius* was distinguished,[132] where fouling had been due to unexpected circumstances: it had been regarded there as an "accident", the words interpreted being the catchall, "or other accident" in Baltime.

The fortuity requirement would seem to be appropriate for any catchall wording, but presumably not necessarily for specifically enumerated events. The *Rijn* was treated as good authority on this issue, at any rate on NYPE 46, cl. 15, in *The Kitsa*.[133]

12.3.8 Some general requirements: "preventing the full working of the vessel"

In addition to being fortuitous, the cause must also affect the efficient working of the *vessel*, and not merely be referable to some condition of the *cargo*. Hence, in *The Aquacharm*,[134] the Court of Appeal held that the vessel was not off-hire where (through the fault of the master) she had too much cargo aboard to pass through the Panama Canal, and had to wait for some of the cargo to be transhipped. In the words of Griffiths LJ:[135]

> "*Aquacharm* remained at all times in herself fully efficient in all respects. She could not pass through the Canal because the canal authorities decided she was carrying too much cargo, but that decision in no way reflected upon the *Aquacharm*'s efficiency as a ship."

The case is also interesting in that the problem had arisen through the fault (bad stowage) of the master, but, as we have seen, off-hire is not necessarily tied into breach by one party or the other.

12.3.9 Full working for what?

A different issue arose in the in *The Athena*,[136] where the Court of Appeal held that the full working of the vessel referred to her ability to do that which she was immediately required to do. She had been ordered to proceed to Benghazi, but the master drifted. Though the vessel could not have discharged, even had she proceeded there directly, she was off-hire for the period of the drifting (through "default of master", typed words added to those of the printed NYPE form).

A consequence of the emphasis on the service immediately required is to reduce the effect of the distinction between period and net loss of time clauses. In *The Ira*,[137] the charterers under a NYPE 46 (hence net loss of time) form argued to include as off-hire the time taken getting into drydock. Tuckey J rejected the argument, on the ground that the drydock was *en route* to the next

---

131 The *Rijn* was said to have been chartered on the unamended 1946 form in *The Kitsa* [2005] 1 Lloyd's Rep 432, [43].

132 *Cosmos Bulk Transport Inc v China National Foreign Trade Transportation (The Apollonius)* [1978] 1 Lloyd's Rep 53.

133 *Action Navigation Inc v Bottigliere di Navigazione SpA (The Kitsa)* [2005] 1 Lloyd's Rep 432. (Leave to appeal had been given only on cl. 15, and whether bottom-fouling triggered any other off-hire provision was not decided.)

134 *Actis Co Ltd v Sanko Steamship Co Ltd (The Aquacharm)* [1982] 1 WLR 119, also in section [4.2.3].

135 [1982] 1 WLR 119, 124.

136 *Minerva Navigation Inc v Oceana Shipping AG (The Athena)* [2013] 2 Lloyd's Rep 673.

137 [1995] 1 Lloyd's Rep 103.

port, and therefore no time was lost (though she was off-hire during the drydocking event itself). In *The Athena*, Tomlinson LJ did not doubt the decision in *The Ira*, but thought the reasoning wrong. The service immediately required was not proceeding to the next port, but proceeding on the drydock (to which it was *en route*, and to which the charterers had agreed with the owners that the vessel should proceed); consequently to proceed to the drydock could not put the vessel off-hire. Tomlinson LJ observed that the position would have been exactly the same, even had the off-hire clause been in period off-hire form.[138] Conversely, in *The Athena* itself, the vessel was off-hire under a net loss of time clause, even though there was no loss of useful time to the charterers. The decision muddies the distinction between the two types of clause.

12.3.10 Additional to other remedies

Off-hire is, as we have seen, not necessarily related to breaches of contract as such, and can therefore be additional to other remedies. Whether or not the vessel is off-hire, the shipowner might be in breach of contract,[139] or, if she is off-hire because of a charterer breach, the shipowner might, in principle, be entitled to damages to recover the amount deducted.[140]

12.4 Questions

Question 12.1

A time charterer on a long-term charter fails to make one single punctual payment of hire, being one day late. Though the market is depressed, he withdraws the vessel, and claims damages, based on the difference between contract and market hire rates, for the remainder of the charterparty. Advise the parties.

Would it make any difference, if there were an anti-technicality clause in the charterparty, and the charterers paid one day after the expiry of the grace period?

Comment

This question is obviously based on *The Astra*,[141] and the later decision of Popplewell J in *Spar Shipping v Grand China Logistics Holding (Group) Co Ltd*,[142] except that here there is just one breach, and it is trivial. Of course this does not matter, if it amounts to a breach of condition.

(By way of aside, you might think the facts as they are stated here seem rather ridiculous, for why would a shipowner withdraw and repudiate, on an unfavourable market, on the basis of one trivial breach? Normally, withdrawal on such a market would be a remedy of last resort, as it was in the two cases mentioned, and if there had been numerous breaches, as there had been in those cases, there would probably be renunciation anyway. So the practical consequences of the categorisation of the punctual payment obligation may not, in reality, be all that great.)

From the discussion in section [12.1.6], you know that there are two recent first instance decisions, considered *dicta* in each of which points in a different direction. (Why are they *dicta*, by the way, not part of the *ratio* in either case?) Indeed, the views of Popplewell and Flaux JJ are

---

138 [2013] 2 Lloyd's Rep 673, [35]–[37].
139 As in, eg *Whistler International Ltd v Kawasaki Kisen Kaisha Ltd (The Hill Harmony)* [2001] 1 AC 638, in section [13.3].
140 Argued (but unsuccessfully) in *The Berge Sund* [1993] 2 Lloyd's Rep 453, 462–463, also in section [12.3.5].
141 [2013] 2 Lloyd's Rep 69.
142 [2015] EWHC 718 (Comm). See section [12.1.6].

diametrically opposed to each other. There are also other authorities, including at the level of the House of Lords or Supreme Court, which can be used to support either view, but none of which is conclusive. It may be that a later High Court would feel constrained to follow Popplewell J's views, as being later in time,[143] but the matter certainly remains open at a higher level.

Where there is no clear authority, or (as here) conflicting authority, you can only argue on principle. Flaux J emphasises certainty, and has authority, in particular Lord Diplock's views in The Afovos,[144] on his side. He also emphasises that time terms are usually conditions. Popplewell J dismisses the certainty arguments as being on a different issue.[145] He does not really deal with The Afovos, other than to observe that it is countered by other authority. He observes that though time terms are often conditions, this is not true of payment terms. Both Flaux and Popplewell JJ adopt the test for a condition from Hongkong Fir,[146] but come to different conclusions.[147] They take different views on the validity of Brandon J's dicta in The Brimnes, in the light of the overruling of The Georgios C, a case on which those dicta to some extent depended, in The Laconia.[148]

Neither Flaux J nor Popplewell J regard the existence of an anti-technicality clause as crucial, though Flaux J thought it strengthened the view that time was of the essence for punctual payment of hire. Popplewell J was unimpressed, and it would be odd if a provision intended to protect charterers had the opposite effect, in this situation.

The only way to be really confident about a question such as this is to be thoroughly conversant with the arguments addressed by Flaux and Popplewell JJ, which of course requires a close reading of both cases.

Question 12.2

Alan has time-chartered The Jumpy to Beth. The time charter lists the following off-hire events: ". . . loss of time from default and/or deficiency of men, detention by average accidents to ship or cargo, capture, or by any other cause (similar or otherwise) preventing the full working of the vessel . . .".

Beth sub-charters the vessel to Carol for a trip from Southampton to Mombasa (Kenya). The off-hire clause is the same as in the head charter, except that "seizure" is added as an additional off-hire event.

Beth orders the vessel to proceed via the coast of Somalia. Just before arriving at Mombasa, the vessel is attacked by pirates, and detained for three months, before being released unharmed, on payment of a £10 million ransom.

Advise the parties as to whether the vessel is off-hire during her detention, under head and sub-charterparties.

Would your view be different if, in the head charter, "whatsoever" had been added to the off-hire clause, after the words "any other cause"?

---

143 [2015] EWHC 718 (Comm), [92]–[95], though Popplewell J himself declined to follow Flaux J in preference to Brandon J in The Brimnes [1973] 1 WLR 386, on the same principle.

144 [1983] 1 WLR 195, that the effect of the withdrawal clause was to render the punctual payment obligation a condition.

145 Eg, The Laconia [1977] AC 850, on the question of withdrawal rather than repudiation; Bunge Corp, New York v Tradax Export SA, Panama [1981] 1 WLR 711, a decision used to support Flaux J, was distinguished on the grounds that it was an obligation upon which others depended: "performance of the nomination by the buyers was necessary in order to enable the sellers to fulfil their obligation to nominate the loading port and ship the goods" [2015] EWHC 718 (Comm), [166].

146 Hongkong Fir Shipping Co Ltd v Kawasaki Kisen Kaisha Ltd [1962] 2 QB 26, and see section [2.6.2].

147 This is a very quick summary of two very detailed judgments. Popplewell J's conclusions are at [2015] EWHC 718 (Comm), [188]–[207], his entire argument on this point running to no fewer than 165 paragraphs.

148 Refer back generally to section [12.1.6].

Comment

You should read at least *The Saldanha* (on whether the NYPE off-hire clause applies to the head charterparty),[149] and *The Captain Stefanos* (on a modified version of the NYPE off-hire clause, and on the definition of "capture and seizure").[150] You might also (without great cost) obtain a copy of my small book, *Charterparties and piracy today*, either in the Kindle version, or as a paperback. This book was written in 2014, and is therefore reasonably up to date. You can obtain it from Amazon's website.

The question is all about meaning of words, but off-hire questions generally are, off-hire clauses being interpreted literally, to a greater extent than other terms of the charterparty.

---

149 [2011] 1 Lloyd's Rep 187.
150 *Osmium Shipping Corp v Cargill International SA (The Captain Stefanos)* [2012] 2 Lloyd's Rep 46, discussed in section [22.4].

Chapter 13

Time charters: employment and indemnity

Chapter Contents

13.1 General principles

Though the coverage in this chapter might appear, at first sight, to be quite disparate, the fact situations have in common that they are about orders by charterers, which (when complied with) cause loss to shipowners. There are two basic questions:

1. Are the charterers entitled to give the order (and hence, are the shipowners required to obey)?
2. If the owners comply with the order, and loss is occasioned, are they entitled to damages or an indemnity?

The first question is of interest in its own right, but also because, if the owners are not required to comply with the order, it can be argued that any loss is occasioned by their compliance, rather than by the charterers giving the order.

If the owners comply and suffer loss, there are two possible actions to consider. If the charterers' order is a breach of contract,[1] then (subject to causation issues) damages will be for breach of contract, and ordinary principles of contractual damages will apply. Since it would be most unusual for the order to cause the loss directly, in the absence of owners' compliance with it, there will nearly always be causation issues, where the charterers' order is given in breach of charterparty.

If there is no breach by the charterers, the owners may be required to comply, but there may also be orders (the giving of which does not necessarily put the charterers in breach) with which the owners do not have to comply. In other words, there are two types of legitimate order. We see instances of the second type in *The Nogar Marin* and *The Sagona*, below.[2]

In either case, compliance with the order (whether or not required) can give the owners a right to be indemnified. Very occasionally, the order might cause loss directly. An example from *The Island Archon* is:[3]

> ". . . loss arising directly from a bill of lading which the charterer was entitled to require the master to sign but which imposed on the shipowner a different liability from that marked out, as between shipowner and charterer, by the charter-party itself".

Another possibility is where charterers who have responsibility for loading give orders directly to stevedores. Normally, however, no loss would be caused without the owners' compliance. It follows that the second situation (where the owners are not required to comply) gives rise to causation issues that are similar to those where there is a contractual breach. There is also a question whether an indemnity should be granted in principle; the charterers are not, after all, the owners' insurers, and there are some risks that are properly the owners', even if the loss is occasioned by charterers' orders (for example, to order the vessel to an allowed port, or to load allowed cargo). Consideration of which risks are properly borne by owners, and which by charterers, forms a major part of this chapter.

We also see in this chapter the relationship (and the contrasts) between indemnity, and damages for breach of contract.

Let us now see how this applies to the general scheme of time charters.

---

1 Eg, the safe port clauses in section [13.9].

2 Respectively *Naviera Mogor SA v Societe Metallurgique de Normandie (The Nogar Marin)* [1988] 1 Lloyd's Rep 412; *A/S Hansen-Tangens Rederi III v Total Transport Corp (The Sagona)* [1984] 1 Lloyd's Rep 194, respectively in sections [13.2], and esp [13.8].

3 *Triad Shipping Co v Stellar Chartering & Brokerage Inc (The Island Archon)* [1994] 2 Lloyd's Rep 227, 238 (Sir Donald Nicholls V-C). *The Island Archon* is discussed extensively in section [13.4].

13.2 Time charters, employment and indemnity

We have already seen the general division of responsibilities in time charters.[4] To the extent that the charterparty does not provide to the contrary, time charterers can direct the master as to the employment of the vessel, to carry any safe cargo to any safe port.[5] Shipowners remain responsible for the safety of the vessel, however, and generally for navigation. Time charterers can direct masters to sign bills of lading, but generally the contracts on the terms of (or at least evidenced by) those bills bind the shipowners, not the charterers, and representations made in the bill of lading can incur shipowners in liability.[6] Charterers' orders, not only in respect of bills of lading, but also as to employment generally, can cause loss to the owners. This chapter examines further this relatively complex division of roles, unique (as far as carriage by sea is concerned) to time charters. It also considers the principles upon which shipowners are entitled to indemnity against the consequences of charterers' orders.

It is usual in time charterparties for the master to be subject to directions of the charterers as to the employment of the vessel, and to sign bills of lading, or other documentation, such as waybills in NYPE 93. The NYPE requirement (which is fairly usual) is for bills of lading to be signed "as presented in conformity with mates or tally clerk's receipts". In Shelltime 4, it is "as Charterers or their agents may direct . . . without prejudice to this charter". Whatever the precise formulation, charterers have considerable leeway as to the form and content of the bills. Charterparties may provide owners with an indemnity against some or all consequences of their orders. Baltime is particularly comprehensive:[7]

> ". . . The Master shall be under the orders of the Charterers as regards employment, agency, or other arrangements. The Charterers shall indemnify the Owners against all consequences or liabilities arising from the Master, officers or Agents signing Bills of Lading or other documents or otherwise complying with such orders, as well as from any irregularity in the Vessel's papers or for overcarrying goods . . . ."

Indemnities are not always this comprehensive. That in NYPE 93 is only ". . . against all consequences or liabilities which may arise from any inconsistency between this Charter Party and any bills of lading or waybills signed by the Charterers or their agents or by the Master at their request . . .", not in other words generally against consequences of employment, and bill of lading and indemnity (as opposed to employment and indemnity) clauses are also common in tanker time charters.[8]

Even where no indemnity is expressed, an indemnity against the consequences of compliance with charterers' orders is well-established. The principle is as follows:[9]

> ". . . if [the owner] is to surrender his freedom of choice and put his master under the orders of the charterer, there is nothing unreasonable in his stipulating for a complete indemnity in return".

---

4 Chapter 10, esp sections [10.1]; [10.5].
5 On dangerous cargoes see section [4.6]. On safe ports see section [13.9].
6 See further section [17.2].
7 Baltime 2001, cl. 9.
8 See, eg, *The Sagona* [1984] 1 Lloyd's Rep 194, in section [13.8], where there was an express (Beepeetime 2) bills of lading and indemnity clause – which did not however apply to the misdelivery that had occurred.
9 *Royal Greek Government v Minister of Transport (The Ann Stathatos)* (1949) 83 Ll L Rep 228, 234 (Devlin J), cited in *Petroleo Brasileiro SA v ENE Kos (The Kos)* [2012] 2 AC 164, [9] (Lord Sumption JSC).

In *The Nogar Marin*, Mustill LJ observed that:[10]

"[the] authorities on implied indemnities in general, and on the charterer's indemnity in particular, assume that a request to act in a particular way as involving a tacit offer to indemnify. By responding as he is asked, the [shipowner] is regarded as having accepted the offer."

The implication of indemnity arises, then, from the charterers' order, and the shipowners' compliance with it. There are, however, two important limits to the principle to indemnify.

First, the order must be the proximate cause of the owners' loss. This will not normally be a problem, unless it can be argued that the master should not have complied with the order.[11]

Secondly, the right to indemnity cannot follow simply from following charterers' orders. As we will see later in this chapter, charterers are not entitled to order the vessel to an unsafe port, or (as we have seen already) to ship dangerous cargo.[12] If they do so, and the shipowners suffer loss, then of course the charterers are required to compensate (though by way of damages for breach of contract, rather than indemnity). But if an indemnity obligation followed from any order to any port, or from the loading of any cargo, where damage later followed, there would be no need to enquire whether a port was safe or not, nor whether cargo was dangerous or not, a point made by Evans LJ in *The Island Archon*.[13] In that case, the Court of Appeal held that there would be an indemnity only against risks that, on the proper interpretation of the charterparty, the shipowner had not agreed to bear. In particular, the shipowner takes the risks of navigation, as opposed to employment, and the distinction between the two is the subject of the next section. We will also need to examine further which risks the shipowner is taken to have agreed to bear.[14]

We might also observe that, if loss flows from an order that the charterers are not entitled to give, they may be liable for damages for breach of contract, as with the safe port cases considered below. There will now most certainly be a causation issue, because it might be argued that the master should not have complied with the order, and by doing so has broken the chain of causation.

13.3 What is employment?

Generally then, the owners are required to obey, and (whether the indemnity be express or implied) the charterers to indemnify, only against the consequences of obeying, orders as regards employment, agency, or other arrangements. The charterers are not therefore required to indemnify the owners against the consequences of every order given to the master. Employment does not include directions as to the navigation of the vessel, and a clause such as the Baltime employment and indemnity clause (in the last section) does not give the owners an indemnity against the consequences of such orders. Owners should exercise their own discretion regarding navigation.

In *The Ramon de Larrinaga*, Lord Porter took the view that:[15]

"an order to sail from port A to port B is in common parlance an order as to employment, but an order that a ship shall sail at a particular time is not an order as to employment because

---

10 [1988] 1 Lloyd's Rep 412, 422 (indemnity argued against the consequences of signing a bill of lading).

11 As in *The Nogar Marin* itself, where the master should have claused the bill, rather than simply signed it as presented. Also *The Sagona* [1984] 1 Lloyd's Rep 194, in section [13.8].

12 See section [4.6].

13 [1994] 2 Lloyd's Rep 227, 235.

14 See section [13.4].

15 *Larrinaga Steamship Co Ltd v The King (The Ramon de Larrinaga)* [1945] AC 246, 261.

its object is not to direct how the ship shall be employed, but how she shall act in the course of that employment".

There, the Crown as charterers ordered the vessel out at night in dangerous navigation conditions, at a time when the weather was worsening (in order to join a convoy in wartime), as a consequence of which the vessel was blown on to a sandbank in a gale, and damaged. The Crown were held by the House of Lords not liable to indemnify the shipowners, despite an express indemnity in the charterparty, because the direction related to the navigation of the vessel, not her employment.

In *The Hill Harmony*,[16] the charterparty required the master to follow "orders and directions of the charterers as regards employment and agency", and the issue was whether the charterers were entitled to order the master to follow a particular route. He had decided to follow the Rhumb Line across the Pacific, from Vancouver to Japan. This was considerably further than the direct (Great Circle) route, and his decision accordingly cost the charterers increased hire, which they claimed to recover.

(*Aside*: Some readers might remember the Lockerbie disaster in Scotland in 1988 and have been surprised that a flight from London to New York should go so far north. Surely New York is to the West of London? The Rhumb Line route (constant bearing) would indeed go slightly south of west, as you can see from looking at any atlas. But if you look at a globe, you can see that the shortest route goes much further north (try stretching a string between the two cities, so as to be as tight as possible). That is the Great Circle route. Two things are apparent from this. One is that the Rhumb Line is easier to navigate, because you simply take the same bearing for the entire route, whereas the Great Circle starts in a north-westerly direction and ends up almost south-west, with continuous changes of bearing *en route*. The second is that at these latitudes, the Great Circle route goes a lot further north, which in *The Hill Harmony* would have meant into very much colder waters.)

In the House of Lords, the decision was that the shipowners (by taking the Rhumb Line route) were in breach of their obligation to make reasonable despatch,[17] but the definition of navigation was still relevant, to a Hague Rules defence (see below).

The charterers' argument had been rejected in the lower courts, decisions as to the route being regarded as for the owners. However, this view was criticised by the late Brian Davenport, QC,[18] principally on the grounds that it allowed the owners to choose any route they liked, however long. Clearly the master should not be given a free discretion to go wherever he pleases, given the cost implications of his decision for the charterers. The lower court decisions were reversed in the House of Lords, where the charterers were held entitled to deduct hire. At the arbitration proceedings, there had been no evidence that the master's decision as to the route was taken for reasons of safety, or for any other good maritime reason. Had they been, then they would have been orders as to navigation. But subject to the safety concerns, route instructions are matters of employment.

The decision having been made that the route orders were not orders as to the navigation of the vessel, the charterers also succeeded in their claim that the owners had failed to prosecute the voyages with the utmost despatch. In the lower courts, the shipowners had been held protected by Art. IV(2)(a) of the Hague Rules, which were incorporated into the charterparty, and which protect shipowners against "loss or damage arising or resulting from . . . act, neglect, or default of the master . . . in the navigation . . . of the ship".[19]

---

16 *Whistler International Ltd v Kawasaki Kisen Kaisha Ltd (The Hill Harmony)* [2001] 1 AC 638, the charterparty being on an amended NYPE 1946 form.

17 As discussed in section [4.5].

18 Davenport [1998] LMCLQ 502.

19 The so-called nautical fault exception, discussed in sections [18.3]; [21.4].

Clarke J had observed that "the charterparty did not contain a clause requiring the owners to follow the routing advice of Ocean Routes, although it is as I understand it common ground that such clauses are readily available in the market".[20] The incorporation of such a clause would have resolved this particular dispute, and such clauses can be found in the standard forms.

Voyage charters differ in this respect from time; even where the charterer has a choice of loading and/or discharge ports, all operational details are probably left to the owners. In *The Eurus*,[21] the voyage charterers wanted the shipowners to delay loading, for reasons that were local to the particular trade in Nigeria. Staughton LJ doubted whether voyage, as opposed to time, charterers were entitled to give such orders, and though the case is not a very strong authority, it points to a possible difference as to legitimate orders, between voyage and time charters.

13.4 Limits to indemnity: risk and causation

So even where there is no express indemnity, an indemnity can be implied. But what is to be implied? Whether the indemnity is express or implied, it should not apply to every order that leads to loss, otherwise whenever loss occurs because the vessel has been ordered to a port, there would be a right to indemnity, whether or not the port was unsafe, or outside the allowed trading limits.

In *The Island Archon*,[22] the Court of Appeal held a time charterer liable for the consequences of ordering a vessel to discharge at Basrah during the Gulf War. It seems that, at that time, Iraqi courts operated a system, described by the arbitrators as the "Iraqi system", which was unique to Iraq, and which was particularly unfavourable to shipowners.[23] The shipowners claimed that they were required to make payments:[24]

> "first as security for cargo claims and then in order to satisfy the order of the Iraqi Courts even though no shortage or damage to cargo in fact had occurred, was a direct consequence of the charterers' order to the vessel to proceed to Basrah and deliver the cargo there".

The "Iraqi system" also gave rise to delay. The shipowners successfully argued an indemnity, although it was accepted that Basrah was within the worldwide trading limits in the charterparty, and was not an unsafe port. A term was implied, requiring the charterers to indemnify the shipowners against the consequences of giving the order, notwithstanding that there were no express terms preventing them from ordering the vessel to Iraq.

Whether the indemnity be express or implied, there must be limits, if charterers are not to be liable to indemnify shipowners for losses caused by any of their orders. In *The Island Archon*, the Court of Appeal held that the issue was what risks the shipowner had agreed to bear, and that this must depend on the true construction of the charter.[25] We have already seen that owners are not entitled to ordinary expenses incurred in the course of navigation, and this generalises into a principle that owners are not entitled to recover from the charterers under their indemnity the ordinary expenses and losses of trading. As Lord Sumption JSC observed in *The Kos*:[26]

---

20 [1999] QB 72, 79. His decision, and that of the CA: [1999] 3 WLR 724, were reversed in the HL.

21 *Total Transport Corp v Arcadia Petroleum Ltd (The Eurus)* [1998] 1 Lloyd's Rep 351.

22 [1994] 2 Lloyd's Rep 227. The case reached the Court of Appeal almost 15 years after the events occurred.

23 Described [1994] 2 Lloyd's Rep 227, 229.

24 [1994] 2 Lloyd's Rep 227, 230 (Evans LJ).

25 See generally section [3.6].

26 *The Kos* [2012] 2 AC 164, [11] (Sumption). See also *The Island Archon* [1994] 2 Lloyd's Rep 227, 235, Evans LJ citing Wilford's Time Charters, 3rd ed (1989), 241 (see now 7th ed (2014)), and Lloyd J in *Actis Co Ltd v Sanko Steamship Co Ltd (The Aquacharm)* [1980] 2 Lloyd's Rep 237, 245 (affd CA [1982] 1 WLR 119).

"The owners are not entitled to an indemnity against things for which they are being remuner-
ated by the payment of hire. There is therefore no indemnity in respect of the ordinary risks and
costs associated with the performance of the chartered service. The purpose of the indemnity
is to protect them against losses arising from risks or costs which they have not expressly or
implicitly agreed in the charterparty to bear."

The ordinary risks and costs associated with the performance of the chartered service are also risks
the owners have agreed to bear, but in The Kos the owners were entitled to be indemnified in respect
of delay occasioned through the unloading of charterers' cargo, following a lawful withdrawal of the
vessel from service.

Apart from that, an important factor is the shipowner's knowledge of the situation when the
charter was entered into. In The Island Archon, the "Iraqi system" was unknown at that time, and
therefore it could be said that the shipowner had not accepted the additional risks involved in discharging in Basrah. By contrast, he may be taken to have agreed to bear the risks of anything that
was known or foreseeable when the charterparty was concluded. The doctrine is not unlike that in
The Athanasia Comninos,[27] where the knowledge of the shipowner at the time the charter was entered
into was of paramount importance. In The Darya Tara,[28] the Court of Appeal felt that, in principle,
and in the absence of any provision to the contrary,[29] the shipowners had taken the risks associated
with carriage of cargo on deck when the charterers exercised their option, given by the terms of the
charterparty, so to load it. The vessel had had to put into port to restow the cargo, which had shifted
in heavy weather, and the owners attempted unsuccessfully to claim the losses caused by her thereby
being off-hire. Crucial to the decision was an arbitrators' finding that the owners were well aware
of the risks of carrying deck cargo.[30] (Indeed, the charterers were taking advantage of an express
option to load a deck cargo.)

In The Kitsa[31] the owners were held unable to recover the costs of defouling the bottom of the
vessel. She had been ordered to Visak in India, during which time her hull became seriously fouled
by barnacles, exacerbated by the warmth of the water, and by the fact that she was delayed, awaiting
discharge. Aikens J observed that the order to Visak was legitimate, and that the arbitrators had found
that "the amount of time actually spent did not exceed 'any reasonable expectation on the part of
an owner of a vessel similar to Kitsa as to how long his vessel might be required to spend there in
the course of entirely ordinary employment to the sub-continent'"[32], and "the time the vessel spent
at Visak was within the reasonable expectations of owners of vessels like Kitsa". Consequently, the
fouling was the "result of a legitimate order of the charterers as to the employment of the vessel
was something that was foreseeable and foreseen by both sides at the time the charter-party was
made".[33] The shipowners were not entitled to indemnity in respect of the cost of de-fouling the
vessel. Conversely, had "the occurrence and type of loss or expense to the shipowner flowing from
the order as to employment of the vessel [been] unforeseen, then that [would have been] a potent
factor in deciding that the loss or expense will fall within the scope of the implied indemnity".[34]

---

27 The Athanasia Comninos and The Georges Chr Lemos [1990] 1 Lloyd's Rep 277; see section [4.6].

28 L.D. Seals NV v Mitsui OSK Lines Ltd (The Darya Tara) [1997] 1 Lloyd's Rep 42.

29 At any rate this was the position under the standard NYPE employment clause (cl. 8). There was also contrary provision, which to
some extent altered this position.

30 [1997] 1 Lloyd's Rep 42, 46.

31 Action Navigation Inc v Bottigliere di Navigazione SpA (The Kitsa) [2005] 1 Lloyd's Rep 432, alluded to in section [3.6].

32 Action Navigation Inc v Bottigliere di Navigazione SpA (The Kitsa) [2005] 1 Lloyd's Rep 432, [22], Aikens J quoting the reasoning of the
arbitrators.

33 [2005] 1 Lloyd's Rep 432, [23].

34 [2005] 1 Lloyd's Rep 432, [24].

Though foreseeability was accepted as not being conclusive, probably the knowledge of the parties when the charterparty was made is the most important single factor.

It is also necessary, in order to claim indemnity, for the owners to show a causal relationship between the order and the loss. In *The White Rose*[35] a longshoreman fell through a 'tween deck hatch during loading, leading to the shipowners eventually settling a damages claim from him in Minnesota. The shipowners claimed an indemnity from the charterers, under the Baltime employment and indemnity clause set out above,[36] it being the duty of the charterers to arrange and pay for the loading, trimming and stowing of the cargo. Donaldson J held, in the Commercial Court, that the loss to the owners had not been caused by the shipowners' complying with the charterers' orders to load the vessel. The chain of causation was broken, possibly by the lack of fencing (for which the charterers were not responsible), possibly by the activities of the longshoreman himself, and possibly by the law of Minnesota. Since they were unable to establish a causal link between the charterers' orders and their own loss, the owners therefore failed.

13.5 Relationship between express and implied terms

The implied indemnities here are a specific application of the principles of terms implied generally, which were considered in chapter 22.[37] We saw there that, where a situation is covered by an express term, that negates the possibility of implying a term, whose effect is different. In the present context, in *The Berge Sund*[38] the shipowners argued an implied indemnity against the consequences of the charterers ordering a contaminated cargo to be carried, their loss being that the vessel had gone off-hire while the tanks were cleaned. The Court of Appeal refused to imply a term for something that had been expressly provided for in the charterparty. Since the off-hire clause dealt with the circumstances in which conduct by the charterers would prevent the vessel being off hire, that excluded any implied term that the charterers would indemnify the owners against loss of hire caused by compliance with the charterers' orders, if there has not been charterers' fault.

13.6 Relationship between damages and indemnity

Damages and indemnities both perform compensatory roles, but do not operate identically. Causation operates differently as between indemnities and damages for breach of contract. For breach of contract, the normal contractual rules of remoteness and causation apply; as we saw in chapter 2, the effect of these is to ensure full disclosure of the possibility of unusual losses, before the contract is finalised.[39] Remoteness is essentially foreseeability-based.

For an indemnity, by contrast, there may be no breach, in which case the issue is the risks the parties have agreed to bear. Once that has been determined, Lord Sumption in *The Kos* observed that the issue is the construction of the indemnity. Commenting on *The Island Archon*, he also observed that:[40]

> ". . . the more foreseeable the owners' loss, the more likely it is to be an ordinary incident of the chartered service and therefore outside the scope of the indemnity. The real question is

---

35 *A/B Helsingfors Steamship Co Ltd v Rederiaktiebolaget Rex (The White Rose)* [1969] 1 WLR 1098.

36 Section [13.2].

37 Section [22.2].

38 *Sig Bergesen DY & Co v Mobil Shipping and Transportation Co (The Berge Sund)* [1993] 2 Lloyd's Rep 453, considered in another context in section [12.3.5].

39 See section [2.9.1].

40 [2012] 2 AC 164, [17], Lord Sumption JSC citing *The Island Archon* [1994] 2 Lloyd's Rep 227, 238 (Sir Donald Nicholls V-C).

> whether the charterers' order was an effective cause of the owner having to bear a risk or cost of a kind which he had not contractually agreed to bear."

So foreseeability is definitely not the test for consequences, when considering indemnities.

When considering the consequences of an indemnity, the Supreme Court looked for an effective cause.[41] This is almost certainly a narrower test than in the normal rules of contractual remoteness. However, in *The Kos* itself, the charterers ordered the vessel to load, and then the owners withdrew the vessel for non-payment of hire. Allowing recovery (under the employment and indemnity clause) of hire to cover the period needed to unload the cargo, and bunker fuel used for the same period, the court held the order to load a proximate cause.[42] Lord Mance dissented, taking a narrower view of proximate cause, and also that the quest should be for *the* proximate cause, rather than *a* proximate cause. The majority view seems to have been that there can be more than one proximate cause.

13.7 Bills of lading

Time charterparties typically require masters to sign bills of lading as presented. This is central to the operation of a time chaterparty. In *The Nanfri*, the shipowners instructed the masters of three ships, in respect of which hire was claimed to be outstanding, "to withdraw all direct or implied authority to charterer or its agents to sign bills of lading", and not to sign any freight pre-paid bill. This was held by the House of Lords to amount to a renunciation of the time charter, since it would have substantially deprived the charterers of virtually the whole benefit of the charterparty.[43] Not to sign bills of lading may well therefore amount to a repudiatory breach.

There may be limits on the bills of lading the charterers are permitted to present. Moreover, if the terms of the bill of lading are more onerous than charterparty terms, the shipowners can incur a loss to the bill of lading holders. This section is concerned with possibilities of recovering in respect of that loss.

13.7.1 Presentation in breach of contract

Suppose first that the charterer presents a bill of lading that he is, by virtue of an express provision in the charterparty, not entitled to present. By presenting the bill of lading for signature, the charterer will be acting in breach of contract, and will (subject to the causation and remoteness principles discussed below) be liable to compensate the shipowner for any losses caused.

Obviously, this can occur where the charterer does not present the bill in the correct format; for example, the latest revision of Gencon requires the use of a Congenbill bill of lading, and if the charterer presents anything else he will be acting in breach of contract. Even where bills of lading have to be signed as presented, however, it might also, as in the latest revision of NYPE, be provided that "All bills of lading shall be without prejudice to this Charter Party . . .". In *The Nogar Marin*, considered further below, Mustill LJ observed that:[44]

> "where the contract stipulates that the act is to be without prejudice to the charter, the charterer's right to issue bills to suit his own convenience must be constrained by the need not to make the terms of the new contract which he thus imposes on the shipowner more

---

41 [2012] 2 AC 164, [12]. This is similar to proximate cause in marine insurance (Marine Insurance Act 1906, s. 55). Lord Mance, dissenting on this issue, thought there was only one effective cause.

42 See further section [12.1.2].

43 *Federal Commerce and Navigation Co Ltd v Molena Alpha Inc (The Nanfri)*, in sections [2.7]; [12.1.5].

44 *Naviera Mogor SA v Société Metallurgique de Normandie (The Nogar Marin)* [1988] 1 Lloyd's Rep 412, 421.

burdensome than those which the owner originally contracted to assume in exchange for the freight".

A breach of this term can also require the charterer to compensate the shipowner for any losses so caused, whether or not there is also (as in NYPE) an express indemnity provided in the charterparty.

Whatever the express terms of the charterparty, terms can be implied into charterparties, on the principles discussed in chapter 22.[45] In the present context a term might be implied, for example, that charterers will not present a bill of lading for signature whose terms impose obligations on the shipowner more onerous than those of the charterparty itself. In principle, such a term may be implied even though, by the express terms of the charterparty, the master is required to sign bills "as presented", the charterer therefore having a discretion as to the form of the bill.

This is probably the best explanation of the House of Lords decision in *Krüger & Co Ltd v Moel Tryvan Ship Co Ltd*.[46] The charterparty exempted the shipowners from liability for stranding and other accidents of navigation, even when occasioned by the negligence of the master, and the master signed bills of lading as presented, which did not give the owners that exemption. The requirement was for the master to sign bills of lading "without prejudice to this charter", however. The owners were liable to indorsees of the bill of lading, and successfully sued the charterers, the reasoning (at any rate in the House of Lords) being that they were under a duty to present bills that would not expose the shipowners to risks from which, by contract, they were to be exempt.

Where the presentation amounts to a breach of contract, it is necessary to show that the shipowner's loss has been caused by the charterer's presentation. Since it is not an order that the charterers are entitled to give, the master should arguably not have complied with it, in which case compliance broke the chain of causation. An argument based on an implied term was unsuccessful in *The Nogar Marin*, where the charterers (under an old version of the Gencon dry-cargo voyage form) shipped coils of wire rods, some of which were rusty when shipped. The ship's agents mistakenly signed two bills of lading, as presented by the charterers, which were not claused, and stated that the goods were in apparent good order and condition when loaded. It seems that the reason for the mistake was that the mate's receipt, which was signed by the master, bore the typewritten notation "clean on board", and the ship's agents were presented with this, along with two bills of lading presented for signature by the charterers.

When the goods arrived at their destination, the receivers, who had taken up the bills of lading in good faith, discovered the true condition of the goods, and arrested the vessel.[47] The shipowners were forced to settle, and attempted to claim the costs of the settlement from the charterers, either on the basis that the charterers were in breach of contract in presenting inaccurate documents for signature, or alternatively on the basis of an implied indemnity.

Mustill LJ, delivering the judgment of the Court of Appeal, held the charterers not liable. His reasoning was based in part on causation. The ship's agents were not obliged simply to sign the bills of lading as presented, without further enquiry; the master should have claused the mate's receipts, and claused bills should have been issued. The shipowners' loss was caused not by the presentation by the charterers of inaccurate documents for signature, therefore, but the chain of causation was broken by the error of judgment of the master.[48]

The Nogar Marin can be contrasted with *Krüger & Co Ltd v Moel Tryvan Ship Co Ltd* (above): the master was apparently unaware that the bill of lading presented did not, unlike the charterparty, exempt the

---

45 Section [22.2].

46 [1907] AC 272.

47 They would have had an action on the basis of the estoppel principles in section [19.4].

48 For another application of causation principles, see the discussion of *The Sagona*, at section [13.8].

shipowners from liability for stranding and other accidents of navigation, even when occasioned by the negligence of the master. He thought he was obliged to sign the bills, and his error of law did not break the chain of causation.

The claim in *The Nogar Marin* did not fail on causation alone, as Mustill LJ thought that the charterers were not in breach of contract, in any event. In rejecting the owners' argument that the charterers were in breach of an implied term, Mustill LJ said that it was not a breach of the charterparty for them to tender a clean mate's receipt. The mate's receipt is simply an acknowledgment to the shippers that the ship has taken delivery of the goods. It does not need to be signed as presented, or indeed at all, and the master can choose for himself how to act. Mustill LJ also thought that the charterers were under no duty to present accurate bills of lading, where the inaccuracy related only to statements of fact which the shipowners' servants could check. Even though a term may generally be implied that the charterers must not present bills under which the legal obligations of the shipowners towards the cargo-owners are greater than under the charterparty itself, it does not follow that they must also make accurate factual representations, especially where the master is in a position to check the facts. The issue, according to Mustill LJ, was "whether the term of which the charterers are said to have been in breach must necessarily be implied into the charter so that it shall work properly in practice",[49] and concluded that it was not.

13.7.2 Express indemnity

It is always open to the parties to put an express indemnity into the charterparty, and an interesting example is in the latest version of Gencon, the 1994 revision. As in all versions of Gencon, cl. 2 limits severely the owners' responsibility for care of the cargo:

> "The Owners are to be responsible . . . only . . . [where] caused by personal want of due diligence on the part of the Owners . . . to make the Vessel in all respects seaworthy . . .
>
> And the Owners are not responsible for . . . any other cause whatsoever, even from the neglect or default of the Master or crew or some other person employed by the Owners . . ., or from unseaworthiness of the Vessel on loading or commencement of the voyage or at any time whatsoever."

This is far more generous to the owners than Arts III(1) and III(2) of the Hague or Hague-Visby Rules,[50] but any bill of lading will almost certainly be governed by the Rules, at any rate if it is in the hands of someone other than the original shipper.[51] So it is almost certain that the owners' liability under the bill of lading will be greater than that under the charterparty. In order to resolve this issue, an express indemnity is provided by cl. 10 of Gencon:

> ". . . The Charterers shall indemnify the Owners against all consequences or liabilities that may arise from the signing of bills of lading as presented to the extent that such bills of lading impose or result in the imposition of more onerous liabilities upon the Owners than those assumed by the Owners under the Charter Party."

Thus, if the owners are sued under the bill of lading, the owners can recover from the charterers, in so far that their liability exceeds that under the charterparty. Diagrammatically:

---

49 [1988] 1 Lloyd's Rep 412, 421.
50 See section [18.3].
51 On an interpretation of *Leduc & Co v Ward* (1888) 20 QBD 475, in section [15.1.4].

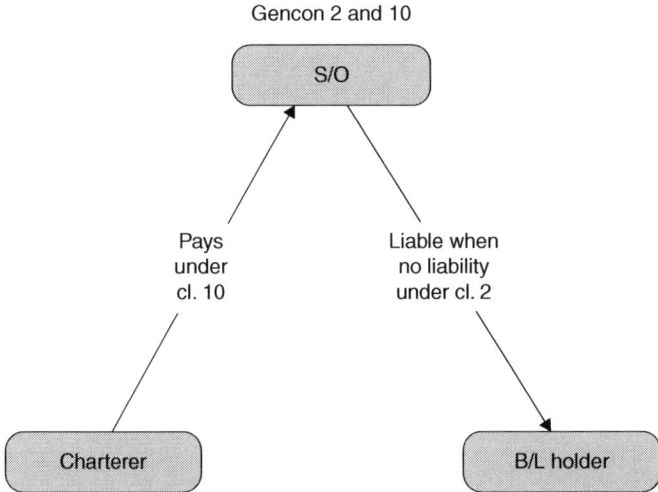

Gencon 2 and 10

To the extent that shipowners are liable under Hague or Hague-Visby, the charterers compensate them under cl. 10, in so far as that liability exceeds that under the charterparty.

13.7.3 Implied indemnity

Whether or not a presentation is in breach of contract, and even if the master signs voluntarily, the shipowners may succeed on the basis of an implied indemnity. This is an implied contract to indemnify, the charterer's tender of the bill of lading for signature constituting the offer to indemnify, and the signature of the master constituting the acceptance. The principle was stated by Mustill LJ in *The Nogar Marin* as follows:[52]

> "When an act is done by one person at the request of another which act is not manifestly tortious to the knowledge of the person doing it, and such act turns out to be injurious to the rights of a third party, the person doing it is entitled to an indemnity from him who requested that it should be done."

The principle was based on a quote from *Stanley Yeung Kai Yung v Hong Kong and Shanghai Banking Corporation*.[53] It does not matter that the master was not obliged to sign the bill of lading – indeed, it is precisely because the signature is voluntary that it acts as an acceptance of an offer of indemnity. On this reasoning, if the master is obliged to sign the bill presented, liability to indemnify arises by implied term, if not, then by implied indemnity.

In *The Nogar Marin* itself, by contrast, the implied indemnity argument failed on its facts, Mustill LJ observing that:[54]

> "The first step is always to indemnify the express or implied request by the person called upon to indemnify. Here, if the request is to be understood as meaning: 'Kindly sign this bill,

---

52 [1988] 1 Lloyd's Rep 412, 418.
53 [1981] AC 787.
54 [1988] 1 Lloyd's Rep 412, 422.

just as it stands, with its acknowledgement of receipt in apparent good order and condition', the claim for an indemnity must be sound, for the agents did precisely what they were asked; and the defence based on an intervening act must fail, since no act intervened, or ever could intervene, in such a situation. In the present case, we do not regard this as the correct reading of what happened. Everyone in the shipping trade knows that the master need not sign a clean bill of lading just because one is tendered; everyone knows that it is the master's task to verify the condition of the goods before he signs. This being so, we cannot understand the request implicit in the tender as being more than this: 'The charter requires you to bind your owners to the contract of carriage contained in the bill of lading, and please do so. The bill of lading also constitutes a receipt, and please sign it as such, with whatever qualification you may think fit.' If this is a right account of the transaction, as we believe it to be, the claim for an indemnity must fail."

In effect, then, the master was not being asked to acknowledge that the goods had been received in apparent good order and condition, because everyone knows that it is his duty to check that, and if necessary clause the bills. It would be different if the master (or ship's agent) were unable to check the true position, as in *Elder, Dempster & Co v C G Dunn & Co*,[55] where the owners had no opportunity to check the marks in the bill of lading against the marks on the goods. The shipowners were liable to the cargo-owners on the basis of the marks, and successfully claimed indemnity from the charterers. In such a case, the master was effectively being asked to acknowledge the accuracy of the facts represented, simply because he had no means of checking or contradicting them. The master should always be able to check the apparent condition of the cargo shipped.

In any case, the implied indemnity argument, like that founded on the implied term, or indeed express indemnity, requires the owners to show a causal relationship between the charterers' wrong-ful act and the loss. In *The Nogar Marin*, even had there been a cause of action, the owners would still have failed: the action of the master broke the chain of causation, because he should have verified the condition of the goods before signing the bill, and should have claused it.[56]

As with the indemnities considered in the previous section, an express entitlement will make more difficult the implication of a term, or an indemnity. In *The C Joyce*,[57] under an amended ver-sion of the Gencon voyage charterparty, the charterers were entitled – indeed required (by virtue of an express typed clause) – to present bills of lading incorporating the Hague Rules by clause paramount, even though that exposed the owners to a greater liability to subsequent holders than the very limited liability under the (unamended) cl. 2 of the Gencon form.[58] Clause 9 of Gencon (the indemnity provision) was entirely deleted,[59] and the clause replacing it gave the owners no express indemnity for the consequences of signing bills of lading as presented. The cargo owners having sued the shipowners under the Hague Rules for damage to the cargo and short delivery, where there was no personal want of due diligence on the part of the shipowners as required by cl. 2, the shipowners claimed indemnity from the charterers. Bingham J did not see how an indem-nity could be implied from the presentation for signature of bills of lading that the charterers were entitled under the charterparty to present, observing that crucial to both breach of contract and the implied indemnity, considered below, is a disparity between the bills that the charterers were under

---

55 (1909) 15 Com Cas 49 (a case considered in detail by Mustill LJ in *The Nogar Marin* [1988] 1 Lloyd's Rep 412, 418).

56 It does not necessarily follow from *The Nogar Marin* that the master is in breach of the charter by failing to clause a mate's receipt, or bill of lading: *Trade Star Line Corporation v Mitsui & Co Ltd (The Arctic Trader)* [1996] 2 Lloyd's Rep 449, a case involving a time charterparty.

57 *Ben Shipping Co (Pte) v An Bord Bainne (The C Joyce)* [1986] 2 Lloyd's Rep 285.

58 On which see section [4.2.7].

59 This would have been the 1976 revision: cf. the express indemnity covering this situation in cl. 10 of the 1994 revision: section [13.7.2].

the charterparty *entitled* to present, and the bills that they *did* present.[60] This passage was quoted with approval by Mustill LJ in *The Nogar Marin*.[61] However, in the light of cases such as *The Island Archon* and *The Berge Sund*,[62] *The C Joyce* must now be explained on the basis that an additional typed clause of the charterparty *expressly required* the charterers to present bills of lading including a paramount clause (ie, incorporating the Hague Rules); the charterers should not, on any basis, be liable for complying with an express requirement of the charterparty.[63]

13.8 Indemnities on delivery

In chapter 20 we will see that shipowners can incur liability for delivery without production of an original bill of lading, yet they may be so instructed by charterers. The charterparty may or may not entitle charterers to give such an instruction, and may or may not provide for an indemnity.

The courts will not imply the right to give the order from the existence of an express indemnity. In *The Houda*,[64] under an amended Shelltime 4 form, there was an express indemnity covering delivery without presentation of bills of lading:

> "Charterers hereby indemnify Owners against all consequences or liabilities that may arise from . . . (. . . delivery of cargo without presentation of Bills of Lading . . .) . . . Letter of Indemnity to Owners' P & I Club wording to be incorporated in this Charter-Party."

There was, however, no entitlement to require the owners so to deliver. The owners had delayed complying with an order by the charterers to deliver without production, eventually discharging only against a without prejudice agreement.[65] The time charterers claimed that they lost the services of *Houda* for the period of the delay, seeking a declaration that she was off-hire for this period, or alternatively damages for breach of contract. The Court of Appeal held that merely because the owners were indemnified against the consequences of delivering without production of bills of lading did not imply that the charterers were entitled to require this. Moreover, the charterers were not entitled lawfully to make such an order in the absence of any provision. The owners were entitled to refuse to obey the charterers' order, and the vessel was not off-hire for the period. There is the hint of a suggestion (not really any more) in Millett LJ's judgment that the charterers would have been able to rely on an express provision requiring the shipowners to deliver without production, had the charterparty so provided.[66]

If an indemnity is not expressed, the courts might be prepared to imply one, on principles similar to those discussed earlier in the chapter.[67] Such indemnities are in principle enforceable, subject to two potential difficulties. First, there is a public policy argument, but this is likely to apply only where there is something about the request that would alert the shipowner to the possibility that he is being asked to deliver to someone not entitled.[68] Secondly, there is a causation

---

60 [1986] 2 Lloyd's Rep 285, 290.

61 [1988] 1 Lloyd's Rep 412, 420.

62 Respectively [1994] 2 Lloyd's Rep 227; [1993] 2 Lloyd's Rep 453.

63 So explained in *The Island Archon* [1994] 2 Lloyd's Rep 227, 232 (Evans LJ).

64 *Kuwait Petroleum Corp v I. & D. Oil Carriers Ltd (The Houda)* [1994] 2 Lloyd's Rep 541.

65 These were extraordinary times. Kuwait had just been invaded by Iraq, and there seems to have been real doubt as to who had authority to give orders.

66 [1994] 2 Lloyd's Rep 541, 557. It is risky for shipowners to agree to such clauses unless the charterers were required to ensure that similar provision were made in the bills of lading themselves, since otherwise the shipowners would be laying themselves open to potential liability extending to the full value of the goods to the true owner of the cargo, in the event of a misdelivery.

67 See section [13.2].

68 The public policy argument would be a development of *Brown Jenkinson & Co Ltd v Percy Dalton (London) Ltd* [1957] 2 QB 621, discussed in section [19.7]. See further generally section [20.6].

argument, if the master should not have complied with the charterers' request. Causation was discussed in *The Sagona*,[69] where, in the event, the shipowners were protected by a common law implied indemnity. The shipowners delivered without production of a bill of lading, evidently at that time a common practice with oil cargoes. In *The Sagona*, time charterers (or rather, agents acting on their behalf) instructed the shipowners to deliver the cargo, although the bill of lading had not yet arrived (because a bank had refused to pay against the documents on a documentary credit, on the ground of alleged discrepancies).

The shipowners delivered the cargo as instructed, although since the bank had refused to pay on the credit, the receivers had not paid the shippers for it. Staughton J commented that if the shippers (who were still therefore the owners of the cargo) had sued them for the value of the cargo, "it is hard to see what defence the owners had to such a claim".[70] The shippers did not do so, although the vessel was arrested, because they eventually recovered money from other sources. Nevertheless the shipowners lost freight while the vessel was under arrest, and also suffered various other expenses as a result.

They sued the charterers to recover these losses, on the basis of an implied term or implied indemnity. It had to be an implied indemnity, because the Beepeetime 2 bills of lading and indemnity clause was similar to the NYPE 93 clause set out at the start of the chapter,[71] and did not extend to delivery without production. (Nor was Staughton J prepared to imply a term into the charterparty that the charterers should ensure that the persons whom they designated as receivers were in fact entitled to receive the cargo.[72]) The owners nevertheless succeeded, on the alternative basis that they were entitled to an indemnity implied at common law. The principles are the same as those discussed earlier in this chapter.[73] Staughton J adopted the following statement from *Dugdale v Lovering*:[74]

"When an act has been done by the plaintiff under the express directions of the defendant which occasions an injury to the rights of third persons, yet if such an act is not apparently illegal in itself, but is done honestly and *bona fide* in compliance with the defendant's directions, he shall be bound to indemnify the plaintiff against the consequences thereof."

The act done by the plaintiff was delivery of the cargo to the wrong person, under the charterers' express directions. Injury was thereby occasioned to the true owner of the cargo, and the charterers were bound to indemnify the plaintiff shipowners against the consequences.

The decision in *The Sagona* depends on the particular facts found, and it is much safer to deal expressly with delivery without production of a bill of lading. *The Sagona* does not accord any general protection to shipowners. There was, in Staughton J's view, a general practice of masters in the oil trade at that time to deliver without requiring production themselves of an original bill of lading, perhaps relying on the charterers' agent to check. Nothing in the charterers' request aroused their suspicion, therefore.[75] However, had the request been clearly unlawful ("manifestly illegal in itself"), for example had the charterers made clear that delivery was to be to someone other than the holder of a valid bill, then the shipowners should have refused, and had they not done so they would have broken the chain of causation. In other words, the cause of their loss would have been

---

69 [1984] 1 Lloyd's Rep 194.
70 [1984] 1 Lloyd's Rep. 194, 196.
71 See section [13.2]. BPTIME 3, cl. 11, is also directed towards liabilities arising from signing, rather than from delivery.
72 [1984] 1 Lloyd's Rep 194, 204.
73 Section [13.2].
74 (1875) LR 10 CP 196, 200, adopted by Staughton J, [1984] 1 Lloyd's Rep 194, 205.
75 [1984] 1 Lloyd's Rep 194, 206.

their own obedience to the manifestly illegal order, rather than the issue of the order itself.[76] In Staughton J's view, in the case itself, though the charterers' order was one that neither the owners were bound to obey nor the charterers entitled to give, it was not something manifestly illegal in itself. Indeed, the charterers were not in breach of contract in giving it.

It will probably be rare for an indemnity to be unenforceable on either of these principles, which of course apply both to express and implied indemnities. There are indeed a number of cases where an indemnity taken on delivery was assumed to be enforceable.[77]

In summary, then, if charterers want to be able to direct the owners to deliver without production of an original bill of lading, express provision to that effect needs to be made in the charterparty. Ideally, the bills of lading should also contain a clause exempting the carrier from liability, but, in a number of cases,[78] such clauses have always been interpreted *contra proferentem*, and nearly always fail to protect the carrier. If the carrier is liable, then indemnities, both express and implied, are in principle enforceable, but subject to the qualifications discussed above.

13.9 Safe ports

The law as to safe ports can be seen as a particular instance of the principles in the earlier part of this chapter. However, not to order the vessel to an unsafe port is a contractual obligation, and so for breach of the obligation we are considering primarily breach of contract, rather than other types of indemnity.

13.9.1 Charterparty clauses

Safe port and/or safe berth clauses are universal in dry-cargo time charterparties, where the obligation is usually strict. Thus, for example, cl. 2 of Baltime provides:[79]

> "The Vessel to be employed in lawful trades for the carriage of lawful merchandise only between good and safe ports or places where she can safely lie always afloat within the limits stated in Box 17."

The justification for the safe port obligation is probably that the risks are more easily known to the charterers than to the owners. Obligations imposed by the tanker forms are considerably less onerous than those imposed by dry-cargo charters; there may be no obligation at all, or the obligation may be qualified by a due diligence requirement.[80] This is from Shelltime 3:[81]

> "Charterers shall exercise due diligence to ensure that the vessel is only employed between and at safe ports . . . anchorages . . . where she can lie safely afloat . . . but charterers shall not be deemed to warrant the safety of any port . . . anchorage . . . and shall be under no liability except for loss or damage caused by their failure to exercise due diligence."

---

76 [1984] 1 Lloyd's Rep 194, 205. The reasoning is entirely in causation terms; the conduct of the master in obeying the without further enquiry was not a *novus actus interveniens: ibid*, 206.

77 Eg, *The Stone Gemini* [1999] 2 Lloyd's Rep 255; *The Laemthong Glory (No. 2)* [2005] 1 Lloyds Rep 688 (privity and remedies issues); *The Bremen Max* [2008] EWHC 2755 (Comm) (interpretation issue). See further section [20.8].

78 Culminating in *Motis Exports Ltd v Dampskibsselskabet AF 1912, Aktieselskab* [2000] 1 Lloyd's Rep 211, and all considered in section [20.5].

79 Box 17 has trade limits and cargo exclusions specially agreed, both to be filled in by the parties.

80 See generally for a comparison between tanker and dry-cargo forms section [22.5].

81 Chosen because litigated in *K/S Penta Shipping A/S v Ethiopian Shipping Lines Corp (The Saga Cob)* [1992] 2 Lloyd's Rep 545 and *Pearl Carriers Inc v Japan Line Ltd (The Chemical Venture)* [1993] 1 Lloyd's Rep 508. See further section [13.9.3]. Shelltime 4, cl. 4(c) is in the same terms.

Where there is no express term, the courts are cautious about implying one.[82]

The consequences of breach are that the owners can refuse to comply with the non-contractual order. If they comply, and suffer loss, then damages can be recovered for breach of contract. There are two issues about compliance. One is that the owners may be taken to have waived the breach. Secondly, there are causation issues, because the owners were not required to comply with the order, but the charterers' local knowledge will often be better than that of the owners, and the owners will often be relying on the charterers' warranty of safety. Owners are therefore treated favourably in this regard, and it is rare for a claim to be unsuccessful on these grounds. These issues are dealt with more fully, later in the chapter.[83] First, however, we should consider the definition of an unsafe port.

13.9.2 What is an unsafe port?

The classic definition of a safe port, which has been universally accepted, is that of Sellers LJ in The Eastern City:[84]

"If it were said that a port will not be safe unless, in the relevant period of time, the particular ship can reach it, use it and return from it without, in the absence of some abnormal occurrence, being exposed to danger which cannot be avoided by good navigation and seamanship, it would probably meet all circumstances as a broad statement of the law."

Obviously this definition covers the physical characteristics of the port (or, where appropriate, berth), for example its depth, searoom to manoeuvre, tides, etc., and also the characteristics of its fairways and approaches. From the cases can be gleaned examples of what can render a port unsafe.

Sometimes it can be a physical matter aspect of the port itself. In The Carnival,[85] an underwater fender that penetrated the hull was held to render the berth unsafe. But Sellers LJ's definition covers not merely the port itself: the vessel must be able to reach the port, use it and return from it. Therefore, dangers some distance from the port can put the charterers in breach of their safe port obligation. Sellers LJ went on:[86]

"Most, if not all, navigable rivers, channels, ports, harbours and berths have some dangers from tides, currents, swells, banks, bars or revetments. Such dangers are frequently minimised by lights, buoys, signals, warnings and other aids to navigation and can normally be met and overcome by proper navigation and handling of a vessel in accordance with good seamanship . . . ."

In The Sussex Oak,[87] Devlin J held that Hamburg was an unsafe port in January 1947, which was one of the coldest months this century. The vessel was damaged by ice, not in the port of Hamburg, but on the approaches through the River Elbe, and the charterers were held liable for breach of the safe port obligation in a dry-cargo charterparty:[88]

"It is immaterial in point of law where the danger is located, though it is obvious in point of fact that the more remote it is from the port, the less likely it is to interfere with the safety of the

---

82 See [13.9.11].
83 Section [13.9.7].
84 Leeds Shipping Co Ltd v Societe Francaise Bunge (The Eastern City) [1958] 2 Lloyd's Rep 127, 131.
85 Prekookeanska Plovidba v Felstar Shipping Corporation (The Carnival) [1994] 2 Lloyd's Rep 14.
86 [1958] 2 Lloyd's Rep 127, 131.
87 G.W. Grace & Co Ltd v General Steam Navigation Co Ltd (The Sussex Oak) [1950] 2 KB 383.
88 [1950] 2 KB 383, 391.

voyage. The charterer does not guarantee that the most direct route or any particular route to the port is safe, but the voyage he orders must be one which an ordinarily prudent and skillful master can find a way of making in safety."

The definition is also wide enough to cover a safe set-up, as Lord Denning MR said in the Court of Appeal in *The Evia* (No. 2).[89] Thus, a safe port/safe berth clause encompasses navigation lights and aids, provision of tugs and pilots, and meteorological stations (to ensure that if bad weather is anticipated, masters can be warned to leave port). *The Eastern City* itself was such a case, in that "high winds could arise so suddenly and unexpectedly that frequently a vessel might not have time . . . to go out in safety from her anchorage before the gale was upon her".[90] Factors mentioned by the Court of Appeal in *The Khian Sea*, where a wharf was unsafe in bad weather, were whether there following were adequate:[91]

- weather forecasting system,
- availability of pilots,
- searoom to manoeuvre, and
- a system for ensuring that the sea-room was always available.

The undertaking relates to the particular ship, so that a port that is safe for a small vessel may well not be for a larger one. (In *The Khian Sea* itself, the last two requirements had not been satisfied, and the vessel collided with a pier structure, when forced by bad weather to leave berth.)

13.9.3 Abnormal occurrence

Sellers LJ's definition does not include the situation where a port is rendered unsafe by an abnormal occurrence. Although a port can be rendered temporarily unsafe, as in *The Sussex Oak*, if the danger is caused by an abnormal occurrence the charterers are not liable for breach of the clause. What is abnormal will vary depending on the particular port. On the other hand, some occurrences may be abnormal in any port, if they are unrelated to the characteristics of that port. A vessel sinking in the fairway, and thereby reducing its depth, or the available searoom, would probably be abnormal in almost any port, and (unless itself caused by a dangerous characteristic of the port) would absolve the charterers from any liability, should the vessel suffer damage from striking the obstruction.

The safe port obligation covers not only the physical characteristics of the port, but also nomination of a port that is unsafe for political reasons. As explained above, if the danger is caused by an abnormal occurrence the charterers are not liable for breach of the clause, and some forms of political unsafety would fall into this category (for example, a sudden and unexpected coup d'etat, or revolution). However, if political upheaval is a normal feature of the port, it will be unsafe within Sellers LJ's definition.

For example, in *The Concordia Fjord*,[92] the arbitrator (whose findings in this regard were not challenged) had held the charterers liable under a NYPE safe port clause when the vessel was hit by a napalm rocket in an attack in Beirut, because such attacks were an inherent feature of that port at

89 [1982] 1 Lloyd's Rep 334, a case which was eventually appealed to the House of Lords [1983] 1 AC 736 (see section [13.9.5]).
90 [1958] 2 Lloyd's Rep 127, 133 (Sellers LJ).
91 *Islander Shipping Enterprises SA v Empresa Maritima del Estado SA (The Khian Sea)* [1979] 1 Lloyd's Rep 545, 547 (Lord Denning MR, but accepted by both counsel).
92 *Idaho D/S A/S v Colussus Maritime SA (The Concordia Fjord)* [1984] 1 Lloyd's Rep 385. The charterers appealed against the award, though the finding of liability was not challenged. On the grounds upon which the case was appealed to the High Court, see below, section [13.7.5].

that time. Another case where charterers were held liable for political unsafety was *The Lucille*,[93] where the vessel became entrapped in Basrah early in the Iran–Iraq war.

It would also follow that the charterers may not necessarily escape liability if, for example, the vessel is damaged at a port because of a revolution, or the outbreak of war, if such occurrences are not abnormal at the port in question.

In *The Saga Cob*,[94] the Court of Appeal refused to hold Massawa prospectively unsafe when all that could be said was that since a guerilla attack might take place anywhere at any time and by any means, it was foreseeable that there could be a seaborne attack either *en route* to the port or in the anchorage. Delivering the judgment of the court, Parker LJ said that a port:[95]

> "... will not, in circumstances such as the present, be regarded as unsafe unless the 'political' risk is sufficient for a reasonable shipowner or master to decline to send or sail his vessel there".

The court held that Massawa was not unsafe. However, in *The Chemical Venture*, Gatehouse J doubted the validity of this test, preferring simply to apply *The Eastern City*, and observing that Sellers LJ's test had House of Lords approval.[96] He saw no reason to add Parker LJ's gloss, and held the Kuwaiti terminal at Mina Al Ahmadi unsafe during the Iran–Iraq war. The attacks in *The Chemical Venture* were somewhat less sporadic than those in *The Saga Cob*, so there is no conflict between the actual decisions, simply on whether a gloss should be added to Sellers LJ's test.

In *The Eastern City*, high winds were common, especially in winter, and the anchorage too small for a large vessel such as *Eastern City* to manoeuvre safely. *The Ocean Victory*[97] concerned far more unusual weather conditions (a combination of long waves and very high winds). The long waves forced the vessel to leave port in very high winds, and with little sea-room, and the vessel foundered and broke up. At first instance, Teare J had held the port unsafe, and that neither the long waves nor the high winds could be regarded as abnormal occurrences.[98] The Court of Appeal took the view that Teare J had been wrong to consider separately the long waves and the high winds, but should instead have considered the "unitary" question, whether the simultaneous coincidence of the two critical features was an abnormal occurrence or a normal characteristic of the port.[99] The combination was, of course, very rare, and could not be regarded as a normal characteristic of the port.

13.9.4 When does the obligation attach?

The leading authority on the safe port obligation is the House of Lords decision in *The Evia* (No. 2).[100] The vessel was trapped (indefinitely) in Basrah, in September 1980, as a result of Iran–Iraq hostilities, but this was not a claim for damages for delay caused by breach of the safe port clause.[101] Rather, the owners claimed (among other things) time charterparty hire. The charterers claimed that the charterparty was frustrated by the entrapment of the vessel in the Shatt-al-Arab waterway,

---

93 Uni-Ocean Lines Pte Ltd v C-Trade SA (The Lucille) [1984] 1 Lloyd's Rep 244 (see further below).

94 K/S Penta Shipping A/S v Ethiopian Shipping Lines Corporation (The Saga Cob) [1992] 2 Lloyd's Rep 545. The case is noted by Brian Davenport: [1993] LMCLQ 150. On test of prospective unsafety, see further the following section.

95 [1992] 2 Lloyd's Rep 545, 551.

96 [1993] 1 Lloyd's Rep 508, 520, HL approval of the test being given in The Evia (No. 2) [1983] AC 736, 749; 750; 760. On The Evia (No. 2) see further section [13.9.5].

97 Gard Marine & Energy Ltd v China National Chartering Co Ltd (The Ocean Victory) [2015] 1 Lloyd's Rep 381.

98 [2014] 1 Lloyd's Rep 14.

99 [2015] 1 Lloyd's Rep 381, [44]; [55]–[56].

100 Kodros Shipping Corp v Empresa Cubana de Fletes (The Evia) (No. 2) [1983] 1 AC 736.

101 On delay, see section [13.9.10].

so the question arose whether (and, if so, when) the 18-month time charterparty was frustrated. The reason that any question arose over the safe port obligation was that the owners claimed that the (Baltime) charterparty could not be frustrated, because the entrapment in Basrah was due (they claimed) to the breach by the charterers of cl. 2 (the Baltime safe port clause).[102] Therefore, they argued, hire remained payable.

The House held that the charterers were not in breach of the safe port clause. It is possible to draw a number of conclusions from the case.

First, the charterers can be put into breach of the safe port undertaking by an outbreak of hostilities. It is not necessarily an abnormal occurrence within Sellers LJ's definition.

Secondly, in the case itself, Basrah was safe when nominated (in March 1980, some six months before Evia went). It had previously been thought that, unless the safe port clause was qualified (eg, by a due diligence requirement, as in many tanker time charterparties), it imposed an absolute obligation on the charterers, which continued for as long as the vessel was at the port. The Evia (No. 2) makes clear that this is incorrect. It is not a continuing obligation. The question of whether a port is safe is determined *at the date of nomination*, but the charterers undertake that it is not merely safe at the time of nomination, but also "prospectively safe for the vessel to get to it, stay at it, so far as necessary, and in due course leave it".[103] In the case itself it was, because the events of September 1980 were unexpected at the time of nomination.

In The Lucille,[104] the Court of Appeal applied The Evia (No. 2), and upheld a decision of Bingham J that Basrah had become an unsafe port, by the time the charterers ordered the vessel there, but in The Lucille the nomination was not until September 1980. By that date (which was the relevant date for the prospective safety test) there was a foreseeable risk of entrapment. In this case also, the charterers had purported to "cancel" the (NYPE) charterparty, apparently on the grounds of frustration, and the question arose whether they were in breach of the safe port clause.

The effect of The Evia test is not only that charterers will not be liable for unforeseen events, but prospective unsafety also allows them to nominate a port that is unsafe at the time of nomination, as long as it is expected to be safe by the time the vessel arrives, for example where the port is iced up at the time of the order but where the ice is likely to melt, or where a sunken vessel is likely to be removed.

Thirdly, though the obligation is not a continuing one, cl. 2 of Baltime (and, by inference, any other time charterparty safe port clause) imposed an additional *secondary obligation* on the charterers, to leave the port if possible if it became unsafe while the vessel was there. This was not possible in The Evia, so the charterers were not in breach of this secondary obligation either.

13.9.5 *Evia* second *ratio*

There was also a second *ratio* in The Evia: the charterers were not in breach of cl. 2 of Baltime (the safe port clause), because the war clause (21) constituted a "complete code" for war risks, and therefore overrode cl. 2. The extent to which this argument might apply generally, to any war clause, is considered below.[105]

13.9.6 *Evia* – other points

There are three final points to consider. First, had the charterers been held to be in breach in The Evia, the charterparty would not have been frustrated, and the shipowners would have succeeded in their

---

102 On frustration generally, and its relationship with breach by one of the parties, see further [2.12].
103 The Evia (No. 2) [1983] 1 AC 736, this being taken from the headnote.
104 Uni-Ocean Lines Pte Ltd v C-Trade SA (The Lucille) [1984] 1 Lloyd's Rep 244.
105 Section [13.8.1].

hire claim. A vessel in such a situation could be detained for a very long time, or, in the worst case, not released at all. In such a case the question arises as to how long hire remains payable, especially if it is impossible to redeliver the vessel at the end of the charterparty period. The issues are essentially the same as with early redelivery in chapter 11, and reference should be made to the cases there.[106] At latest once the redelivery date passes, I suggest that it would be difficult for owners to continue to assert a continuing interest in claiming hire (they would presumably be entitled, in the situation postulated, to her market value, as a free ship).

Secondly, it has been argued that charterers may be liable under the employment and indemnity clause, even if the safe port clause does not apply.[107] Many dry-cargo employment clauses may well be wide enough, on a literal interpretation, to indemnify the owners against the consequences of an order to an unsafe port, and though the consequences of such an order would not fall within the bills of lading and indemnity clause of the main tanker charterparties, you could argue for an implied indemnity. However, it is hard to see why the employment and indemnity provision should be construed more widely than the safe port clause, given that the safe port clause itself makes clear the risks undertaken by each of the parties; the shipowners have surely undertaken to bear the risks of going to a port that is safe.[108] In any case, in a war situation it is difficult to see why the second *ratio* of *The Evia* (No. 2) should not be equally applicable to an employment and indemnity clause as it is to a safe port clause.

Thirdly, if the charterers order the vessel to an alternative port in compliance with a safe port clause, cargo-owners may be able to sue on the bill of lading contracts. These actions will usually be against the shipowners,[109] but they may then claim indemnity from the charterers under the employment and indemnity (or in tanker charterparties bills of lading and indemnity) clause. Ideally, therefore, bills of lading presented to the master for signature should include a deviation clause, sufficiently wide in scope to cover this situation.

13.9.7 Causation and consent issues

Given that an order to an unsafe port is not an order the charterers are entitled to give, it follows that (in principle at least) the owners can refuse to comply. Inferences might therefore be drawn from their voluntary compliance, for example waiver of the breach, estoppel, or that they are *volenti non fit iniuria*.[110] There are also causation issues, which are similar to those for breaches of contract and indemnity generally, whether any loss was occasioned by the charterers' order, or by the owners' compliance with it. (Since the owners were not obliged to follow the order, they may be regarded as causing their own loss, rather as in *The Nogar Marin*, considered earlier in the chapter.[111])

However, though for the owners to comply with a non-contractual order may preclude them from later rejecting the order, that does not necessarily amount to a waiver of the breach. In *The Kanchenjunga*, the charterers nominated Kharg Island, which at the time was unsafe. The owners having initially complied and proceeded there, were later alarmed by a subsequent Iraqi air-raid and left the port, refusing to return. The charterers refused to nominate an alternative port (though the owners could require this by an express term of the charterparty), and (unlike many safe port cases, where the vessel suffers damage) the only issue was which of the two parties had wrongly repudiated

---

106 See section [11.3.1]; also [2.8] for the general principle.
107 Eg, Baker and David, *The politically unsafe port* [1986] LMCLQ 112.
108 See further the discussion in section [13.4].
109 See further section [17.2].
110 Ie, that they have consented.
111 Section [13.7].

the charterparty. The House of Lords held that the owners had waived their right to reject the nomination, but it did not follow that they had waived the breach. Lord Brandon observed that:[112]

> "... the only right which the owners waived was the right to reject the nomination ... as uncontractual; and that, if the ship had loaded there and been lost or damaged in a further air raid, the charterers would, despite that waiver, have been liable to the owners for such loss or damage on the ground of their breach of contract in ordering the ship to load at an unsafe port".

Similar sentiments can be found in Lord Goff's speech.[113] An additional unconditional representation would be needed for an inference that the owners had waived the breach itself, and the same principles would apply if the owners had complied with a non-contractual order to enter a piracy zone. The necessary additional factors were found by Gatehouse J to exist in *The Chemical Venture*,[114] where the crew had initially refused to enter an area where there was a danger of air attacks, but where the owners had co-operated with the charterers to the extent of arranging for the payment (ultimately by the charterers) of a war bonus. On Gatehouse J holding that the owners had thereby waived what he held to be a breach of the safe port obligation, the owners were also precluded from suing in respect of damage caused to the vessel by an Iranian missile.[115]

Assuming a breach in respect of charterers' orders has not been waived by the owners, that the master has complied with it and loss has been occasioned, it still does not follow that there is an automatic right to recover. The safe port authorities suggest that the owners will not normally (simply by virtue of complying with the order) be regarded as *volenti* in respect of any damage that occurs, nor as having brought about their own loss. In *The Stork*, both Singleton and Morris LJJ emphasised that (as will often be the case with a safe port warranty) the master was relying on the charterers' warranty of safety,[116] and Hodson and Morris LJJ also observed that the ship is under no obligation to doubt the validity of the order.[117] In other words, it is not easy for the master to refuse to comply, and therefore little inference should be drawn from his compliance. His compliance will rarely therefore amount to a *novus actus interveniens*.[118] His conduct would have to be unreasonable for it to break the chain, and the usual inference will be that the damages flow naturally from the charterers' breach of contract, and are recoverable on the ordinary principles of remoteness of damage in contract.[119] Of course there are limits:[120]

> "Though there would have been a breach of contract in giving the order to go to an unsafe place, this would not justify the deliberate act of allowing the ship to suffer damage. The owners must not throw their ship away."

It might also be different if the owners were as aware of the risk as the charterers, for example if the charterers ordered the vessel to a port in a piracy hotspot.[121] The justification for safe port

---

112 *Motor Oil Hellas (Corinth) Refineries SA v Shipping Corp of India (The Kanchenjunga)* [1990] 1 Lloyd's Rep 391, 392. (This issue did not however arise for decision; the owners had waived their right to reject the Khard Island nomination.)

113 [1990] 1 Lloyd's Rep 391, 393.

114 [1993] 1 Lloyd's Rep 508, discussion of this aspect beginning at 520.

115 The case reasons entirely in contract, the possibility of an implied indemnity perhaps not having being fully appreciated prior to *The Island Archon* [1994] 2 Lloyd's Rep 227.

116 *Compania Naviera Maropan S/A v Bowater's Lloyd Pulp and Paper Mills Ltd (The Stork)* [1955] 1 Lloyd's Rep 349, 365 (Singleton LJ); 373 (Morris LJ).

117 [1955] 1 Lloyd's Rep 349, 373 (Hodson LJ); 373 (Morris LJ).

118 Ie, as breaking the chain of causation.

119 [1955] 1 Lloyd's Rep 349, 365–6, Singleton LJ citing "the well-known words of Baron Alderson in *Hadley v Baxendale* (1854) 9 Ex 341 at 354".

120 [1955] 1 Lloyd's Rep 349, 373 (Morris LJ).

121 On piracy and carriage, see further section [22.5].

clauses, and for the causation principles in *The Stork*, is that the master is relying on the charterers' warranty of safety; charterers are more likely to have local knowledge of the port in question. If owners and charterers have the same knowledge, it is difficult to see why the same principles should apply.

13.9.8 Standard of seamanship required

On Sellers LJ's test a port will not be unsafe if danger can "be avoided by good navigation and seamanship". If the master makes a mistake, the port will not therefore necessarily be unsafe if damage is caused by his own poor seamanship, rather than by the characteristics of the port. Even if the port were also held to be unsafe, there is a causation issue, similar to that in the previous section. However, a heat of the moment mistake will probably not break the chain of causation. In *The Ocean Victory*, the master was forced by weather conditions to leave port in very high winds, and with little searoom. Teare J accepted that he might have over-used the rudder, and hence slowed the vessel so that she lost steerage way, but the alternative, an attempt

> "to proceed out to sea . . . with such speed as could have been mustered . . . would not merely require 'correct, prompt and resolute action' . . . but would also have required a particularly bold mariner (because the action had its own risks) and would have required a very high degree of skill [and luck] to bring it off".[122]

In these circumstances, Teare J was "unable to hold that the master's conduct . . . was negligent". Regard was had to this being, like *The Polyglory*,[123] an "agony of the moment" case, and the master could not be adjudged negligent, just because another master might have acted differently: "even the best of masters may be negligent from time to time".[124]

This aspect of *The Ocean Victory* was neither approved nor disapproved when the case went to the Court of Appeal.[125]

13.9.9 Due diligence

We have seen that the tanker forms commonly temper the safe port obligation with a due diligence requirement. In *The Saga Cob*,[126] it was suggested that if a charterer (on the Shelltime 3 form) was uncertain whether a port was unsafe and enquired of a number of owners, all of whom replied that they regarded it as safe, it would be hard to accept that the charterer had not exercised reasonable care. In *The Chemical Venture*,[127] the charterers (also on Shelltime 3) were aware of all the relevant facts and for this reason, held to be in breach of due diligence requirement. While Gatehouse J accepted the proposition stated in the Court of Appeal in *The Saga Cob*, he also said that the case would be one of *res ipsa loquitur* unless the charterer adduced evidence to justify his order.[128] In other words, the onus is on the charterers to show why the thing does not speak for itself. Whether they have satisfied the

---

122 [2014] 1 Lloyd's Rep 14, [162], citing *The Polyglory* [1977] 2 Lloyd's Rep 353, 365–6, where "correct, prompt and resolute action" would also have been required. (In *The Polyglory*, the consequence was that navigation was very difficult and hence the port unsafe.)

123 [1977] 2 Lloyd's Rep 353.

124 *Kristiandsands Tankrederi A/S v Standard Tankers (Bahamas) Ltd (The Polyglory)* [1977] 2 Lloyd's Rep 353, 364.

125 [2015] 1 Lloyd's Rep 381, [65].

126 *K/S Penta Shipping A/S v Ethiopian Shipping Lines Corp (The Saga Cob)* [1992] 2 Lloyd's Rep 545. (There was no decision on due diligence.)

127 [1993] 1 Lloyd's Rep 508.

128 [1993] 1 Lloyd's Rep 508, 519. In *The Chemical Venture*, the charterer had failed to show why it was not *res ipsa loquitur* (the thing speaks for itself).

due diligence requirement will depend on the extent of the charterer's knowledge, and his appreciation of the risks.

You should be reminded that there is no due diligence requirement in most of the dry-cargo forms.

13.9.10 Delay

There is nothing about Sellers LJ's definition of safe ports to suggest that danger extends beyond physical peril, but physical damage can itself occasion delay, and delay may be incurred in avoiding danger, so there is a good argument, in principle, for danger to include risk of delay. The Evia (No. 2) and other cases on detention in Iraq during the first Gulf War suggest that risk of detention alone can render a port unsafe. Sellers LJ's definition also covers access to, and egress from, the port, as well as the use of the port itself, and so would cover delays in grounding in the approaches, etc.

On the hand, there is a lot to be said for excluding temporary obstacles, and the definition cannot have been intended to encompass any small delay avoiding obstructions, or other dangers. In a time charterparty in any case, the charterers bear the risk of delay in any event, and so the cases where the issue has arisen have involved voyage charters.

Where the port is not otherwise unsafe, so that the only danger is delay, the Court of Appeal held in The Hermine that only a frustrating delay would render the charterers in breach.[129] The Court of Appeal held that the loading port of Destrehan, on the Mississippi some 140 miles from the open sea, was not unsafe merely because the vessel was delayed, being unable to reach the sea after leaving, even though the delay (caused ultimately by siltation) was of several weeks. It was accepted that the warranty of safety, an express term in the charterparty in that case, covered not only the port itself, but also access to and egress from it. The delay was not caused by an abnormal circumstance, but Geoffrey Lane LJ observed that "if the hazard is merely a temporary one then it will not constitute lack of safety, nor make the port unsafe".[130] The question, in essence, was whether the delay was temporary. The Court of Appeal, adopting the test whether it was sufficient to frustrate the adventure, held that it was – and therefore Destrehan was not an unsafe port. (Frustration of the adventure seems an unusual test to establish initial liability, as opposed to whether there has been a repudiation.)

Suppose, on the other hand, it is clear that there is a breach of a safe port or berth obligation. Perhaps there is a physical danger to the ship, or the port is politically unsafe, but in the event, the only consequence is delay. There is authority that damages can be recovered in these circumstances, for breach of the safety obligation. In The Count[131] the vessel was delayed only after discharge, by the grounding of another vessel (Pongola) in the channel. The shipowners sued, this time successfully, for breach of a safe berth warranty in the charterparty. The Hermine was distinguished, on the basis that in The Count there was a finding that the port was unsafe, at the time of nomination, quite apart from the temporary hazard caused by the grounding of Pongola.[132] (There were permanent physical characteristics of the port, such as the placing of the buoys and the system for monitoring the channel.) It was not necessary, unlike in The Hermine, to use the delay to establish initial breach of the obligation. There was a breach of the safe port clause in any event, and the only issue was as to damages. The shipowners were held entitled to claim the amount of their loss resulting from the delay. The effect of the decision is that where the only risk is of delay there will not normally be a breach of a safety

---

129 Unitramp v Garnac Grain Co Inc (The Hermine) [1979] 1 Lloyd's Rep 212 (a case concerning a voyage charterparty).

130 [1979] 1 Lloyd's Rep 212, 220. Donaldson J had held Destrehan unsafe on the test of a "commercially unreasonable delay": [1978] 2 Lloyd's Rep 37, 48. The CA's view was that this was insufficient.

131 Independent Petroleum Group Ltd v Seacarriers Count Pte Ltd (The Count) [2008] 1 Lloyd's Rep 72.

132 [2008] 1 Lloyd's Rep 72, [30].

warranty, but if the port or berth is unsafe in other respects the shipowners will be entitled to claim, even where the only loss occasioned is delay.[133] In *The Count*, there would have been no question of laytime or demurrage provisions applying, since the vessel had completed discharging. Unlike in *The Hermine*, there is no attempt in *The Count* to exclude temporary delays (but nor was it an issue in the case).

13.9.11 Implied safe port terms

There is no doubt that, where a term is included in a charterparty (or bill of lading contract), the courts will fill it out, possibly to include matters that the parties have not expressly included. Sellers LJ's definition of a safe port in *The Eastern City*, for example, covers use of the port, as well as the ability of the vessel to reach it and return from it.[134] This carries with it the implication that the berth also must be safe:[135]

> "where there [is] an express warranty of safety of the port but not the berth but the charterers [are] left to nominate the berth, if the port to be nominated [has] to be safe, it [follows] that the berth impliedly [has] to be safe".

This is perhaps best regarded not so much an implied safe berth obligation, as a recognition that a safe port obligation includes an obligation to nominate a safe berth also, since use of the port necessarily involves use of the loading berth.

Though (as we will see in chapter 22) in *Attorney General of Belize v Belize Telecom Ltd*, requirements for implication of terms were relaxed,[136] nonetheless there is a recognition that, especially for a well-considered form, an omission to address something may well be deliberate, and there is a good case for saying that the loss should lie where it falls.

We can see a reluctance to imply a term in *The APJ Priti*,[137] where the converse presumption to that above was not made. The Court of Appeal refused to imply a safe port from a safe berth obligation; the obligation to nominate a berth would not have arisen until the voyage to the port had been concluded. (She never reached the port, Bandar Khomeini, being severely damaged *en route* by a hostile missile, and hence towed to an alternative port.)

The sentiment in *Belize* (about an omission to address something) directly influenced the Court of Appeal in *The Reborn*. In *The Reborn*, under the (Gencon) voyage charterparty, the loading port was agreed as Chekka and any warranty of safety was struck out. Nor was there an express safe berth warranty, and the owners were unsuccessful in implying a term. It seems that there were only two available berths at Chekka, but the decision of the Court of Appeal did not depend on this. Lord Clarke MR referred extensively to Lord Hoffmann's judgment in *Belize*, but noted in particular that where there is no express provision the loss should normally lie where it falls,[138] that Lord Hoffmann is "is not in any way resiling from the often stated proposition that it must be necessary to imply the proposed term", and that it is never sufficient merely that a term be reasonable.[139] Quoting Sir Thomas Bingham MR from an earlier case, Lord Clarke MR also agreed that "it is much more

---

133 See also *Emeraldian Limited Partnership v Wellmix Shipping Ltd (The Vine)* [2011] 1 Lloyd's Rep 301; as to why laytime was not interrupted, see section [9.5].

134 See chapter 15.

135 *Mediterranean Salvage & Towage Ltd v Seamar Trading & Commerce Inc (The Reborn)* [2009] 2 Lloyd's Rep 639, [33].

136 *Attorney General of Belize v Belize Telecom Ltd* [2009] 1 WLR 1988, discussed in section [22.2].

137 *Atkins International HA v Islamic Republic of Iran Shipping Lines (The APJ Priti)* [1987] 2 Lloyd's Rep 37.

138 [2009] 2 Lloyd's Rep 639, [10]; also Carnworth LJ at [63].

139 [2009] 2 Lloyd's Rep 639, [15], citing in respect of the latter proposition Lord Wilberforce in *Liverpool City Council v Irwin* [1977] AC 239, 253–4 (HL).

difficult to infer with confidence what the parties must have intended when they have entered into a lengthy and carefully-drafted contract [such as a charterparty] but have omitted to make provision for the matter in issue",[140] from which it may be inferred that it also much more difficult to justify implying a term.

Though the Court of Appeal in *The Reborn* is demonstrating a clear reluctance to imply a term into a charterparty, it is fair to observe that the case was not a strong one for implication. The choice of port was not the charterer's, but was agreed at the time of the contract, and the number of berths was not large.[141] The word "safely" had actually been struck out of the printed Gencon term requiring the vessel to proceed to the loading port(s) or place(s).[142] Nonetheless, the Court of Appeal in *The Reborn* shows no enthusiasm for extending the implication of terms in charterparties.

13.10 War clauses

Like voyage charters, time charters usually have war clauses, but additional clauses are required for time charterparties because of the longer term nature of the commitment, and because the charterer has greater freedom to trade than under a voyage charterparty.

An outbreak of war in various parts of the world may frustrate the commercial purpose of the adventure, and there is typically a cancelling clause to cover this eventuality.[143]

Apart from that, the way in which war clauses usually work is that the owner is entitled to refuse to proceed to areas covered by the clause (which will typically be an area of increased risk), or, if consent is given and he does proceed, to claim from the charterers the cost of increased war risk insurance and other additional war expenses (for example, additional wages for the crew).[144] There are differences between the forms, but essentially this is the way they work.

The trigger for the operation of the clauses is typically that the master, in his discretion, considers it impossible or dangerous to proceed. If so, he can refuse to proceed. This discretion was considered in *The Product Star* (No. 2),[145] a case that involved trading in the Arabian Gulf during the Iran–Iraq war. The Court of Appeal took the view that the discretion of the owners had to be exercised honestly and in good faith and, having regard to the provisions of the contract by which it was conferred, and that it was not to be exercised arbitrarily, capriciously or unreasonably.[146] The charter presupposed trading in the Arabian Gulf, which had long been considered an area that was exposed to war risks. The common intention that the vessel should trade to UAE ports was relevant to the reasonableness of refusal by the owners to proceed there, and it was relevant that, at the time when the charter was made, the whole of the Gulf including UAE waters constituted a war risk zone. The court took the view that since no additional danger had been shown, the owners' refusal was arbitrary.

---

140 [2009] 2 Lloyd's Rep 639, [18], quoting Sir Thomas Bingham MR in *Philips Electronique Grand Public SA v British Sky Broadcasting Ltd* [1995] EMLR 472.

141 The position was contrasted with "a vast port such as Rotterdam", upon which there was no need to decide, and time charters, where the discretion allowed to charterers is usually greater, may well be different: [2009] 2 Lloyd's Rep 639 at [62] and [30] respectively.

142 Gencon, cl. 1 (the report does not make clear which edition of Gencon).

143 Eg, Shelltime, cl. 33; BPTIME 3, cl. 29.

144 As in, eg, *The Chemical Venture* [1993] 1 Lloyd's Rep 508, in sections [13.9.3]; [13.9.9].

145 *Abu Dhabi National Tanker Co v Product Star Shipping Ltd (The Product Star) (No. 2)* [1993] 1 Lloyd's Rep 397. The charterparty was on the Beepeetime 2 form, and the case is noted by Brian Davenport: [1993] LMCLQ 150.

146 On this aspect of the case, see further section [3.5].

We should not necessarily assume that an escalation in risk is always required. We will return to this issue, in a piracy context, in chapter 22.[147] However, *The Product Star* (No. 2) remains an authority that the master's discretion must not be exercised arbitrarily, capriciously or unreasonably.

13.10.1 *Evia* second *ratio* again

In *The Evia* (No. 2),[148] as we have seen, the House of Lords held (as a second *ratio*) that the charterers were not in breach of cl. 2 of Baltime (the safe port clause), because the war clause (cl. 21) constituted a "complete code" for war risks, and therefore overrode cl. 2. Clearly, if war clauses were *generally* taken to constitute a complete code, then safe port clauses would cease to apply at all to political unsafety. Indeed, questions of political safety are arguably better dealt with by war clauses, and the provision of war risk or extra blocking and trapping cover, rather than through the operation of safe port clauses. The reasoning has not met with universal acclaim. With one recent exception, there has been a reluctance to extend the second *ratio* beyond the facts of *The Evia* (No. 2), and the Baltime charter, itself. However, with that recent exception, we may expect to see a revival of the second ratio of *The Evia* (No. 2).

Lord Roskill's reasoning, however, is clearly not limited to cl. 21 of Baltime alone. The important points of the Baltime clause are that the owner's consent is required before a war zone is entered. Further, if a war zone is entered, the owners may increase their insurance to cover the increased risk, *to charterers' account*. It was this second point that most persuaded Lord Roskill that cl. 21 was intended to operate as a complete code. The charterers are required to pay the cost of any extra war risk insurance taken out by the owners, but unless cl. 21 is a complete code, not only do they obtain no benefit from this, but can actually be sued on the safe port clause if damage results to the vessel caused by the very risks for protection against which they have contributed the additional premiums. Furthermore, to quote Lord Roskill:[149]

> "The time charterers are to repay to the owners the premiums for the extra insurance, including extra war risk insurance premiums. But if the dangers, against the risks on which they have paid those premiums materialize and cause loss or damage to the ship, then war risk insurers, upon payment [to the owners] of the relevant claim, become subrogated to the owners' rights against the time charterers for the assumed breach of cl. 2 [safe port clause]. My Lords, this result would no doubt be highly attractive to war risk insurers but the less fortunate time charterers would have paid the premiums not only for no benefit for themselves but also without shedding any of the liabilities which cl. 2 would, apart from cl. 21 [war clause], impose on them."

Lord Roskill thought such a result would be "very remarkable". It is difficult to disagree with this conclusion.

If the decisive factor were the contribution by the charterers of any extra war risk premiums, then nearly all time charterparty war clauses ought also to be regarded as a complete code, overriding the safe port clause in cases of war and political unsafety. There has, however, at any rate in the war clause cases, not been acceptance of the view that the mere payment of premiums for the risks that have materialised relieves the charterers of liability in respect of that risk. In *The Concordia Fjord*,[150] for example, where the vessel was hit in a rocket attack in Beirut, Bingham J agreed with the arbitrators that there is no "principle exempting the Charterers from liability for their breaches of

---

147 See section [22.5].

148 [1983] 1 AC 736.

149 [1983] 1 AC 736, 767.

150 [1984] 1 Lloyd's Rep 385, 387.

contract merely on the ground that they have directly or indirectly provided the funds whereby the Owners insured themselves against such damages".

The (NYPE) charterparty in *The Concordia Fjord* differed from that in Baltime in *The Evia* (No. 2), principally in that it did not permit the owners to refuse to proceed. *The Concordia Fjord* suggests that the construction of each charter must turn on consideration of its own detailed terms. The differences between the *Evia* (No. 2) and *Concordia Fjord* clauses were enumerated as follows:

1.   The charterers in the later case did not have to pay all war risk insurance, but only any increase due to trading in the relevant area. This provision could not therefore, in the opinion of Bingham J, operate appropriately as a complete code, for a breach of the safe port clause may not necessarily lead to an increase in such premiums.
2.   The owners did not have the unqualified right, as in Baltime, to refuse to allow the vessel to trade in a war zone.
3.   There was no provision, as in Baltime, that the vessel was to remain on hire despite loss of time caused by exposure to war risks.
4.   The charterparty rubrics were different.

Many of the forms share one or more, but not all these differences from Baltime. Which, if any, of the differences is crucial is still unclear, but Gatehouse J followed *The Concordia Fjord* in *The Chemical Venture*, in effect taking account of the first three of the differences.[151]

Much more recently, in *The Ocean Victory*,[152] the Court of Appeal applied the second *ratio*, not to a war clause, but to a provision in a demise charterparty, requiring the charterers to take out hull insurance.[153] The main action in the case was brought by the demise charterers against their sub-time-charterers, but they were successfully met with the argument that, because they incurred no liability themselves, under the head (ie, demise) charterparty, they had suffered no loss. There was little in *The Ocean Victory*, other than the requirement for charterers to insure. Moreover, the effect of applying the second *ratio* was to render the safe port clause entirely nugatory, at any rate where damage was caused to the hull or machinery. So this is a very wide application of the second *ratio*.

In summary, though the second *ratio* of *The Evia* (No. 2) has not generally been enthusiastically received, it will apply when the war clause is sufficiently similar to Baltime, and it may be that attitudes to it are changing, if *The Ocean Victory* is correct. I suggest that Lord Roskill's reasoning in *The Evia* (No. 2) is fairly convincing.

13.11 Ice clauses

Whereas war clauses are usually more complex in time charterparties than in their voyage counterparts, the opposite is true of ice clauses. Most time and voyage forms contain a general ice clause, and an ice clause is essential if the vessel is trading in the Baltic or White Seas.

In a voyage charterparty the ice clause fulfils a function somewhat similar to the voyage charterparty war clause. It typically allows the vessel to proceed to another port if ice affects the port of loading or discharge, and also state who is to bear any extra expense. Usually the extra expense is borne by the charterers.

---

151 [1993] 1 Lloyd's Rep 508. On their construction, the clauses were held not to be formulated in such a way as to suggest an intention that they should constitute a comprehensive code dealing with the parties' rights in the event that any aspect of performance became affected by war. The reasoning probably does not apply beyond the particular clauses under consideration.
152 [2015] 1 Lloyd's Rep 381.
153 Not uncommon in a demise charter: see section [10.5]. Barecon (the form used in *The Ocean Victory*) allows a choice, and the option chosen was for charterers to insure.

With time charterparties, by contrast, there may be no more than a simple prohibition on forcing ice. In the now superseded Beepeetime 2, for example, the trading limit clause (10) ended: "The vessel shall not be obliged to force ice." Maybe no need was seen to protect the shipowners against entrapment of the vessel by ice, because hire remains payable whether or not the charterer is able to make use of the vessel. Voyage charterparties differ in this respect, of course, where the risk of delay is upon the shipowners.

On the other hand, a clause such as Beepeetime 2 might be thought to give inadequate protection to the shipowners against damage to the vessel by ice, compared for example with the ice clause (6) of Intertanktime. As well as stating that the vessel be not obliged to force ice, or follow ice-breakers, the Intertanktime ice clause allows the master to leave if he is afraid of the vessel being frozen in or damaged, and expressly provides (probably unnecessarily) that all time lost as a result, or if the vessel is actually frozen in, is for charterers' account.

Shelltime 4 is different, and the ice provision (which is included in the trading limits cl. (4)) has more in common with the war risks clauses considered in the earlier sections of this chapter. It does not categorically prohibit the charterers from obliging the vessel to force ice, or ordering the vessel to ice-bound waters, unless the owners' consent be reasonably withheld, as long as the charterers agree to pay any extra insurance premium required. BPTIME 3, cl. 27, allow the vessel to follow ice-breakers with owners' consent, but also allows the master to refuse to enter, or to leave a port, if he fears being frozen in.

13.12 Question

A vessel is chartered on a Gencon (1976) form. Cargo is damaged by unseaworthiness, such that the shipowner would be liable on the principles in *The Muncaster Castle*,[154] but not on the principles in *The Gundulic*.[155]

Gencon (1976) cl. 2 provides:

> "Owners are to be responsible for loss of or damage to the goods or for delay in delivery of the goods only in case the loss, damage or delay has been caused by . . . personal want of due diligence on the part of the Owners or their Manager to make the vessel in all respects seaworthy and to secure that she is properly manned, equipped and supplied or by the personal act or default of the Owners or their Manager . . . ."

(i) Consider the liability of the shipowner to an indorsee of a bill of lading for the damaged cargo, to which (being an outward voyage from the UK) the Hague-Visby Rules apply, which incorporates "all terms and conditions of the charterparty".

(ii) If the shipowner is liable, can he recover an indemnity from the charterer? Would your view be different if the 1994 version of Gencon had been used instead of the 1976 form?

Comment

On liability, you may also need to look at chapters 15 and 18. Liability to an indorsee is likely to be on the terms of the bill of lading, not the charterparty, and we are told that the Hague-Visby Rules apply to the bill of lading. Liability will therefore be on the principles of *The Muncaster Castle*.[156] This is, however, probably more onerous than charterparty liability, an authority on the interpretation of

---

154 *Riverstone Meat Co Pty Ltd v Lancashire Shipping Co Ltd (The Muncaster Castle)* [1961] AC 807, discussed in section [18.3.3].

155 *Itoh & Co Ltd v Atlantska Plovidba (The Gundulic)* [1981] 2 Lloyd's Rep 418.

156 [1961] AC 807, in section [18.3.3].

cl. 2 being *The Gundulic*, which you might have a look at. (The facts are generally similar to those in *The Muncaster Castle*, but it is an interpretation of cl. 2, rather than the Hague Rules, and the result is accordingly different.)

On the indemnity point, Gencon, cl. 2 is the same in both 1976 and 1994 versions of Gencon. The 1994 form added cl. 10, the express indemnity clause discussed at [13.7.2], but there was no indemnity in the 1976 form. If there is to be an indemnity, it must therefore be implied. Implication is discussed in this chapter, but you might consider in particular *The C Joyce* and *The Island Archon*.[157]

157 Respectively [1986] 2 Lloyd's Rep 285; [1994] 2 Lloyd's Rep 227.

Part 4

Carriage (other than charterparties)

Chapter 14

Introduction: bills of lading and similar documents

Chapter Contents

14.1 Introduction

This part of the book is mostly about bills of lading. Bills of lading relate to goods on board a ship, rather than to the ship itself, but bills of lading are less ubiquitous than once they were. They do not work satisfactorily for all types of trade, and nowadays other documents are often used instead. At the end of the chapter we consider some of the shortcomings (or perceived shortcomings) of bills of lading, and the growing use of alternative documentation. (It is worth noting that the alternative documentation can be far from ideal, and that there are security compromises in departing from the traditional documentation.)

We begin, however, with the bill of lading. A bill of lading is issued, initially as a receipt, for goods shipped (or received for shipment) on board the vessel. But it has developed to do a lot more than this.

Unlike a charterparty, the bill of lading is intended to be transferred, when the goods to which it relates are sold or pledged. Thus, even a charterer who has filled an entire ship with a single cargo (eg, crude oil) will take a bill of lading as well, in order to sell it, or to pledge it under a documentary credit. Some of the problems this causes (where, for example, bill of lading and charterparty terms differ) are dealt with in the next chapter.[1]

As a document of title, the bill of lading is sometimes said to represent the goods, to allow dealings in the goods when they are at sea. Thus (at any rate as long as it remains a document of title, and has not become spent),[2] the bill of lading needs to be presented for its holder to take delivery of the goods (and hence the bill of lading transfers – or, to be more accurate, usually transfers – "constructive", or "symbolic", possession of the goods it represents). The right to possess carries with it title to sue in conversion.[3]

Transfer of the bill of lading may also (depending on the terms of the contract of sale) transfer property from seller to buyer.[4]

Whereas a charterparty is (nearly always) a contract for the use of an entire vessel,[5] bills of lading are issued in respect of the particular goods they represent. So there can be many bills of lading issued for cargo on board a ship. Of course, if a charterer owns all the cargo on board, and sells it as a single parcel (quite common with bulk oil cargoes) there will be a single bill of lading issued for all the cargo on board the ship. (The question then arises – since the shipper has both a charterparty and a bill of lading – which prevails, if they are different? This is one of the issues considered in the next chapter.)[6]

Another observation that will be relevant to the discussion in chapter 15 is that whereas many voyage charter terms fit quite well into bills of lading, this is not true of time charter terms.

14.2 Outline of bill of lading functions

In summary, the bill of lading has the following functions:

(1)   It evidences that goods of the stated description have been received for shipment, or loaded on board the vessel. If the statements are incorrect, then the carrier will usually be liable to anybody who suffers loss through relying on them.[7]

---

1 Section [15.1].
2 On spent (sometimes described as stale) bills, see further section [16.7.3].
3 See generally section [20.4].
4 When property is transferred from seller to buyer depends ultimately on the intention of the parties to the sale contract, though there are a number of presumptions that fill this out: Sale of Goods Act 1979, ss. 16–20A. Retention of title where a bill of lading (or other document of title) is retained is readily inferred: eg, in particular s. 19(2).
5 Section [1.2].
6 Section [15.1].
7 The liability regime is not perfect, and we will consider it in detail in chapter 19.

(2)   As a document of title it allows the lawful holder, on presentation of the original bill (and nobody else), to claim delivery of the goods when they arrive. This also allows the carrier safely to identify the person entitled, since he is protected from action if he delivers to someone not entitled, as long as he has delivered against production of an original bill.[8]

(3)   The bill of lading evidences a contract of carriage. Unlike a charterparty, however, it is not of itself a contract of carriage.[9]

(4)   Transfer of the bill of lading can also transfer to the holder rights and duties under the carriage contract. Unlike a charterparty, therefore, a bill of lading contract can bind persons other than the original parties to it. This is usually accomplished by the Carriage of Goods by Sea Act 1992.[10]

(5)   Depending on the terms (usually implied) of the sale contract, transfer of a bill of lading can transfer property in the goods.

A negotiable bill of lading can be transferred many times, either to effect a sale or pledge; many commodities are traded many times, bills of lading being passed to successive purchasers and pledgees.

14.3   Negotiable and non-negotiable bills

It is of the essence of a bill of lading that it is a transferable document that can be used to transfer the right to take delivery of the goods, and often also the property in the goods. However, bills of lading are of various types. In particular, they can be "negotiable" or "non-negotiable".[11] (But even a non-negotiable bill can be transferred once, to a named consignee.)

14.4   Negotiable bills of lading

The traditional bill of lading is a transferable document, but it has to be made "negotiable" expressly, the choice usually being made by the shipper when drawing up the draft bill. This is usually done be making it out to order, in which case the bill of lading passes by delivery and indorsement. It may be made out to the order of the shipper or the consignee, or indeed sometimes someone else altogether. But, for example, bills made "to consignee or order" are commonly used.[12] Much rarer is the bearer bill, which passes by simple delivery, without the need for indorsement. (I found no examples of these when writing this book.)

An authority that the bill of lading must be made negotiable is the old case of *CP Henderson v Comptoire d'Escompte de Paris*.[13] The formulation suggested there was "or order or assigns", but there is no magic formula for determining whether shipper and carrier intend to create a negotiable bill. In *The Chitral*,[14] the bill of lading was of a hybrid type,[15] and to make it "negotiable" the shippers had specifically to fill in the notify party. They had not done so, and the fact that otherwise it was made out to consignee or assigns did not make it negotiable. David Steel J said:[16]

---

8   This regime is also not watertight. We will consider the role of the bill of lading as a document of title in chapter 20.

9   Ibid.

10   See chapter 16.

11   They are not technically "negotiable instruments" – the term "negotiable" is used inaccurately for "transferable". (Hence the quotation marks.)

12   Eg, *East West Corpn v DKBS AF 1912 A/S* [2003] QB 1509, in chapter 16.

13   (1873) LR 5 PC 253.

14   *International Air and Sea Cargo GmbH v Owners of the ship Chitral (The Chitral)* [2000] 1 Lloyd's Rep 529. The issue was who had title to sue under the Carriage of Goods by Sea Act 1992, in respect of damage to cargo. The case is complicated by there being two bills of lading for the same cargo, but only the bill of lading issued by the carrier was relevant. As it was not a negotiable bill only the named consignee could sue (apart from the original shipper), and he was time-barred."

15   That is to say, it could be used as either a negotiable or non-negotiable bill, depending on what the parties filled in.

16   [2000] 1 Lloyd's Rep 529, [19]. The defendants were carriers, and took issue with the claimants' title to sue, the cargo having been damaged on the voyage.

"19. The defendants . . . rely on the phrase within the printed section of the bill to the effect that delivery was to be 'unto the above-mentioned consignee or to his or their assigns'. This was said to have the impact of rendering the box for inserting the name of the consignee as if the words 'or order' had been added. I am unable to accept that submission:

(a.) The printed box for naming of the consignee specifically provides 'if order state notify party' (and no such notify party was so stated).
. . ."

In other words, the form of the bill of lading itself made clear how it was to be made negotiable. If that method was not used then it was reasonable to infer an intention not to make it negotiable.

It is right that it should depend on the parties' intention, because it has contractual consequences. The contractual effect of an order bill was considered by the Court of Appeal in The Houda, where Leggatt LJ observed that:[17]

"It is necessarily implicit in the power to order the issue of bills of lading which make the goods deliverable 'to order' that the obligation is accepted [by the carrier] to deliver to the holder upon production of the bill of lading. It is an incident of the bill of lading contract that delivery is to be effected only against the bill of lading. . . ."

In other words, the carrier has agreed to whom to make delivery, as part of the carriage contract. Similar statements can be found in Millett LJ's judgment.[18] The holder here would be the person currently in possession of the bill of lading, to whom it has been delivered and indorsed.[19]

The holder of a straight bill of lading is also contractually entitled to delivery upon presentation, this also being implicit in the issue of such a bill.[20]

The holder of an order bill of lading is also entitled to sue the carrier on the carriage contract, even if not an original party: s. 2(1)(a) of the Carriage of Goods by Sea Act 1992. If he triggers the conditions in s. 3 of the same Act he will also become liable on the carriage contract.[21]

14.4.1 Bearer bills, indorsement in blank and personal indorsements

A negotiable bill can be made out to bearer, in which case it can be passed from hand to hand like cash (to judge from the cases, this is very rare). More commonly, it can be indorsed in blank,[22] in which case the bill becomes a bearer bill after the indorsement. This may differ in some respects from a bill that bears a personal indorsement. In Sewell v Burdick, Lord Selborne quoted from the custom found in the earlier case of Lickbarrow v Mason that:[23]

"indorsements of bills of lading in blank may be filled up by the person to whom they are delivered or transmitted, with words ordering the delivery of goods to be made to such person; and, according to the practice of merchants, the same when filled up have the same operation as if it had been done by the shipper".

---

17 Kuwait Petroleum Corporation v I & D Oil Carriers Ltd (The Houda) [1994] 2 Lloyd's Rep 541, 553.

18 [1994] 2 Lloyd's Rep 541, 556.

19 The definition of holder is not however straightforward – see below and also section [16.7].

20 Depending on your interpretation of JI MacWilliam Company Inc v Mediterranean Shipping Co SA (The Rafaela S) [2005] 2 AC 423, in section [14.6].

21 See section [16.7].

22 Eg, Sewell v Burdick (1884) 10 App Cas 74; The Future Express [1993] 2 Lloyd's Rep 542.

23 (1884) 10 App Cas 74, 83, quoting from Lickbarrow v Mason (1787) 2 Term Rep 63.

This custom implies that something more has to be done than simply presenting the bill for delivery (though of course these are old cases, and customs can change).[24] Once the blank has been filled in, for example on a subsequent transfer, the bill thereafter becomes an order bill. Thus, in the Singapore case of *Keppel Tatlee Bank Ltd v Bandung Shipping Pte Ltd*,[25] two bills of lading had been indorsed to Keppel in blank. (Keppel was a collecting bank involved in financing a sale.) Keppel then filled in the name of the "State Bank of Saurashtra in India" (another bank involved in the sale), and transferred the bills to them. There were no further indorsements, but the bills were transferred to Lanyard, the purchaser of the cargo. Lanyard neither paid, nor came forward to collect the cargo, and the bills were transferred back to Keppel. The holder was held to be the State Bank, because, once their name had been filled in, the bills ceased to be bearer bills, and could only be transferred thereafter by delivery and indorsement (and no further indorsements occurred).[26]

Here is the order of events in *Keppel Tatlee*.

(1)   Indorsement to Keppel in blank
(2)   Keppel fills in name of State Bank, and transfers bills to them. (No longer bearer bill.)
(3)   Bills transferred but not indorsed to Lanyard purchaser and thence back to Keppel.

The holder was held to be State Bank, transaction (3) having no effect without indorsement, the bill no longer being a bearer bill at this point.

As we will see when we examine the Carriage of Goods by Sea Act 1992 in chapter 16, there are a number of cases where the person with physical custody of the bill of lading has been regarded (or argued) as having custody on behalf of another person – hence the person with physical custody has been different from the person in possession, and from the holder. One situation is where a bank has bills of lading to collect payment, or perhaps as security for payment, where the bank is not the only party with an interest.[27] Another is where documents have been sent to an insurer.[28] In the bank context, it was suggested in *East West Corpn v DKBS AF 1912 A/S*,[29] that, whereas an indorsee under a personal indorsement will become holder for the purposes of the Carriage of Goods by Sea Act 1992, even if he is holding the bill only as agent, the principal (rather than the agent in possession) may be the holder where the bill of lading is indorsed in blank. So the form of the bill can have substantive consequences.[30]

14.5 Sea waybills

The sea waybill is not a bill of lading, but is an alternative document, that is used particularly for container and multimodal transport.[31] It also shares characteristics with the straight bill of lading, so we need to introduce it, so that we can contrast the straight bill with it.[32]

---

24 It was however also the way in which BOLERO, the electronic bill of lading trialled in the late 1990s, would have worked. See section [21.2].

25 [2003] 1 Lloyd's Rep 619. The issue was who had title to sue under Singapore's equivalent of our Carriage of Goods by Sea Act 1992.

26 It followed that Keppel had no action against the carriers under the Singapore incarnation of the Carriage of Goods by Sea Act 1992: see further chapter 16.

27 Eg, *Standard Chartered Bank v Dorchester LNG (2) Ltd (The Erin Schulte)* [2015] 1 Lloyd's Rep 97, in section [16.7].

28 Argued successfully in *Primetrade AG v Ythan Ltd (The Ythan)* [2006] 1 Lloyd's Rep 457 (where, as we will see in section [16.7], nobody appears to have been holder).

29 [2003] QB 1509.

30 At any rate the view taken at first instance in *The Erin Schulte* [2013] 2 Lloyd's Rep 338, but the point was not taken in the CA: [2015] 1 Lloyd's Rep 97

31 See section [21.3].

32 See next section: [14.6].

As we have seen, the shipowner who issues a negotiable bill of lading is undertaking to deliver only to the person who physically presents that bill of lading, and (as we will see at the end of the chapter) this can be problematic if the bill of lading does not arrive in time. One situation where this can occur is with container cargoes on short routes, where the speed of the ship can out-pace that of the documentation. If the cargo is unlikely to be resold (and many container cargoes are not), and finance by documentary credit is not required, non-negotiable sea waybills are often used instead of bills of lading, to avoid the problem. Delivery has to be made to the consignee named in the waybill, but there is no requirement for the document to be presented. (The shipper may have a right to redirect, but, if so, it would be by notification to the carrier.)

The transfer of a waybill is unlikely to transfer any rights at all, though the consignee may acquire contractual rights (under the carriage contract – which can include the right to take delivery) simply by being named as consignee,[33] and property may pass to the consignee (often at shipment, but NOT usually depending on transfer of the waybill).[34]

Carriers often prefer to carry cargoes under waybills because they wish to discharge before the documentation catches up.[35] However, the requirement that a bill of lading be presented does at least ensure that the carrier knows to whom he should deliver, and he delivers against production of an original bill he is protected from action.[36] This is a good reason for continuing to use bills of lading for cargoes that are likely to be resold (eg, bulk dry-cargo and oil),[37] since otherwise the carrier might not know to whom to deliver.

14.6 Straight bills of lading

Bills of lading can themselves alternatively be made out to a named consignee (rather than to consignee or order – which would be an order bill). Old American terminology of "straight" bills is often used to describe this practice,[38] which seems to be as old, or almost as old, as using negotiable bills. The possibility of identifying a named consignee was provided for as early as the (now repealed) Bills of Lading Act 1855.[39] The straight bill was, however, less commonly used than an order bill, at least until recently.

Non-negotiable, or "straight" bills of lading are commonly used today where a negotiable document is not required, for example where the identity of the consignee is known from the outset, and the goods are not of a type that are likely to be resold. It may be supposed that the risks to carriers are lessened where a straight bill is used, since only the consignee is entitled to claim delivery. On the other hand, the presentation requirement provides proof of title, whereas a waybill (not needing to be presented) does not.

Such bills are "non-negotiable", or, to be more accurate, "negotiable" once, from shipper to consignee. They do not need to be indorsed in the consignee's favour, merely transferred to him, though they often are indorsed as well. However in The Chitral, Steel J commented that:[40]

---

33 See section [16.5] (Carriage of Goods by Sea Act 1992). It is not clear how this works, where there is a right of redirection. Presumably the right of redirection cannot itself be transferred by the Act.

34 For an instance where property passed on shipment to a consignee named in a non-negotiable document, see Kum v Wah Tat Bank Ltd [1971] 1 Lloyd's Rep 439. (The result depended on payment having been made and on no document of title being issued at any stage. Note also that the document itself transferred nothing – this is true of any non-negotiable document.)

35 Eg, Sir Anthony Lloyd, The bill of lading: do we really need it? [1989] LMCLQ 47. The shipowner is, however, still unprotected if he delivers to someone not entitled, so it is not entirely clear that carriers benefit from this practice.

36 Section [20.2.1].

37 See section [21.2], where the rather different problems for such cargoes are examined.

38 See Carver on Bills of Lading, 3rd ed (2012), Sweet & Maxwell, [1–014]–[1–015]. Curiously, the terminology seems no longer to be used in the US.

39 See also CP Henderson & Co v Comptoir d'Escompte de Paris (1873) LR 5 PC 253.

40 [2000] 1 Lloyd's Rep 529, [20].

"20. . . . an 'endorsement' of a non-negotiable bill must, by definition, be ineffective."

Only the named consignee can claim delivery of the goods, and the carrier is undertaking to deliver only to him.[41]

In *The Chitral*, the relevant (straight) bill of lading (for semi-trailers, storage tanks and pumps) named a consignee who, having obtained the bill, had later indorsed it to somebody else. The indorsement was held ineffective, so that (apart from the original shipper) only the original consignee had title to sue the carrier.[42] (It was not a negotiable bill.) However, the claim of original consignee was time-barred, and the carrier effectively evaded liability.

Obviously a straight bill of lading looks very like a waybill, and it was long thought that it was indeed a species of waybill, rather than bill of lading. Indeed, the Law Commission, whose report led to the enactment of the Carriage of Goods by Sea Act 1992, treated it as a waybill, and consequently it is so treated in the Carriage of Goods by Sea Act 1992 itself.[43] On this classification, we have the negotiable bill, which needs to be presented on delivery, and the waybill, which does not. It is not immediately apparent that we need a third type of document, which is non-negotiable but that needs to be presented. However (though the case is open to interpretation) in 2005 the House of Lords in *The Rafaela S* held that this perception is incorrect, and that the straight bill is genuinely a species of bill of lading.[44] Certainly it is a document of title, and (unlike a waybill) almost certainly has to be presented for the consignee to take delivery of the goods.

Another difference between waybills and straight bills, in practice, is that there is normally no right to redirect in straight bills.[45]

14.6.1 *The Rafaela S*

The issue in *The Rafaela S* was whether a straight bill of lading was a bill of lading or other document of title for the purposes of the Hague-Visby Rules. The bill of lading was of a hybrid type.[46] It had a box allowing the shipper to name a consignee or to make the bill out to order:

"Consignee: (B/L not negotiable unless 'ORDER OF')".

The shipper either fills in the name of the consignee (as in the case itself), or writes

"order of . . ."

to make the bill negotiable. In the case itself the named consignee route had been chosen, so this was a straight bill of lading.

The House of Lords held that this straight bill of lading was nonetheless a bill of lading or other document of title to trigger application of the Hague-Visby Rules.[47] The decision is not directly on the delivery consequences of issuing a straight bill of lading, and, in any case, the bill of lading in *The Rafaela S* had an express attestation clause, requiring presentation for delivery. However, Lord

---

41 Depending on an interpretation of *The Rafaela S* [2005] 2 AC 423, in the next section.

42 This would have been under the Carriage of Goods by Sea Act 1992, discussed in chapter 16. The original shipper could also sue, his cause of action not having been divested by s. 2(5), this being a straight bill: see sections [16.4]–[16.5].

43 We will look at how this works when we consider that legislation in detail, in section [16.5].

44 [2005] 2 AC 423. (I noted this case up at [2005] JBL 762. There is also a useful – but rather difficult – note on the CA decision, which was upheld in the HL, by Professor Treitel, *Legal status of straight bills of lading* (2003) 119 LQR 608.) See also section [20.3].

45 Liang Zhao, *Control of goods carried by sea and practice in e-commerce* [2013] JBL 585.

46 See the description at [4]. In this respect the bill of lading is similar to that in *The Chitral* [2000] 1 Lloyd's Rep 529, in section [14.4].

47 See further section [18.6.4].

Bingham in particular would have decided the case the same way, even had there been no attestation clause,[48] and Lord Rodger explicitly described the document as a bill of lading.[49] From the case it is probably reasonable to infer, therefore, that presentation is required of a straight bill of lading, though not of a waybill. Lord Steyn said in *The Rafaela S*:[50]

> "In my view the decision of the Court of Appeal of Singapore in *Voss v APL Co Pte Ltd* that presentation of a straight bill of lading is a requirement for the delivery of the cargo is right. . . .
>   . . . In the hands of the named consignee the straight bill of lading is his document of title. On the other hand, a sea waybill is never a document of title. No trader, insurer or banker would assimilate the two. . . ."

A consequence of this is that retention of a straight bill, unlike a waybill, can provide real security for sellers, because the buyer needs it to obtain delivery; the point is also made that the seller may wish to retain the bill of lading to secure payment.[51]

The Rafaela S came as a surprise because, until then, straight bills of lading had been equated with waybills, which do not have to be presented. Indeed, they are treated as waybills in the Carriage of Goods by Sea Act 1992.[52]

14.6.2 How do you distinguish a straight bill from a waybill?

As has been observed, the document in *The Rafaela S* was a hybrid. It was, however, headed "Original bill of lading" (so it described itself as a bill of lading, not a waybill). There was an attestation clause, which said:[53]

> ". . . One of the Bills of Lading must be surrendered duly endorsed in exchange for the goods or delivery order."

Thus, the bill expressly provided that one original of the set had to be surrendered in exchange for the goods.[54] The bills of lading were issued in a set of three originals issued in a set of three originals, "one of which being accomplished, the others to stand void". (This would have made no sense, unless it had been necessary to present one in order to take delivery of the goods.) So it was easy to conclude that, in the particular case, the document had to be presented, for the consignee to take delivery.

The case does not seem to be limited to these rather narrow facts, and hence raises the question: how do you distinguish a straight bill from a waybill? Is the test simply one of form, what it says? Lord Rodger had no problems with this. In his view, it was described as a bill of lading by the

---

48 [2005] 2 AC 423, [20], but he does not go so far as to decide that the straight bill is a document of title at common law (at [22]).

49 [2005] 2 AC 423, [58].

50 [2005] 2 AC 423, [45], citing *Voss v APL Co Pte Ltd* [2002] 2 Lloyd's Rep 707, 722.

51 [2005] 2 AC 423, [15] (Lord Bingham).

52 See section [16.5].

53 The bill of lading, including the attestation clause, is described by Lord Bingham: [2005] 2 AC 423, [4] (referring back to a longer description by Rix LJ in the Court of Appeal, [2004] QB 702, [11]–[17]), and by Lord Steyn at [32]. It could have been (but was not) filled in as an order bill. See also Lord Rodger, at [53].

54 The carrier's argument that this clause did not apply unless the bill was made out to order, because of the inapplicability of the phrase "duly endorsed", was rejected: see, eg, [45] (Lord Steyn).

carriers (MSC) who issued it, and they should not be allowed to go behind this.[55] Lord Steyn also noted differences of form:[56]

> "[a waybill] incorporates the standard terms of the carrier on its face. However, unlike a bill of lading, these terms are not detailed on the reverse of the waybill which is blank. A waybill is usually issued in the 'received for shipment' form but may, like a bill of lading, be notated once the goods have been loaded."

No doubt, there is a good argument that what commercial people call a document should be given great weight. Lord Bingham said that:[57]

> "It is always the task of the court to determine the true nature and effect of a legal document, and in performing that task the court is not bound by the label which the parties have chosen to apply to it. Where, however, the court is considering a *bona fide* mercantile document, issued in the ordinary course of trade, it will ordinarily be slow to reject the description which the document bears, particularly where the document has been issued by the party seeking to reject the description. This document called itself a bill of lading. It was not a bill transferable by endorsement, and so was not 'negotiable' in the somewhat inaccurate sense in which that term is used in this context . . . ."

So what the document calls itself may well be decisive.

14.7 Through bills of lading

Where cargo is brought on a long ocean route, for example from south-east Asia to various destinations in Europe, it often makes sense to tranship it on to smaller vessels once it reaches Europe, rather than take the large ocean-going ship around a number of ports, part-full of cargo. Transhipment is a deviation unless provided for in the carriage contract,[58] but it is also important to ensure that the cargo-owner has a carrier against whom he can take action, in respect of the entire voyage, and not just that part that the carrier has actually performed. This is achieved by one of the carriers undertaking (by contract) the entirety of the voyage, but sub-contracting part of it to (actual) carriers.

For example, suppose we are shipping a large cargo from south-east Asia to various ports in Europe, including Southampton.

It might make sense for the vessel to call at Rotterdam, and there tranship on to smaller vessels for (eg) Hamburg, Hull and Southampton. If a through bill of lading is used, the ocean carrier might undertake to perform the entire voyage from (eg) south-east Asia to Southampton, but delegating the stage from Rotterdam to Southampton to a (non-contracting) actual carrier. If anything happens between Rotterdam and Southampton, or there is misdelivery in Southampton, the holder of the

---

55 [2005] 2 AC 423, [58].

56 [2005] 2 AC 423, [46] quoting the then-current edition of *Schmitthoff's Export Trade: The Law and Practice of International Trade*, 10th ed (2000); see now Murray, Holloway and Timson-Hunt, Thomson (eds), *Schmitthoff's Export Trade: The Law and Practice of International Trade*, 12th ed (2012).

57 [2005] 2 AC 423, [5], citing *Kum v Wah Tat Bank Ltd* [1971] 1 Lloyd's Rep 439, 446, where a mate's receipt that was otherwise a document of title was held to be non-negotiable on the basis of stamped words on the front, which were almost certainly not considered by anybody. See further chapters 21 and 20 (on bills of lading and alternative documents, as documents of title).

58 The problem in *The Berkshire* [1974] 1 Lloyd's Rep 185, in section [17.1.7].

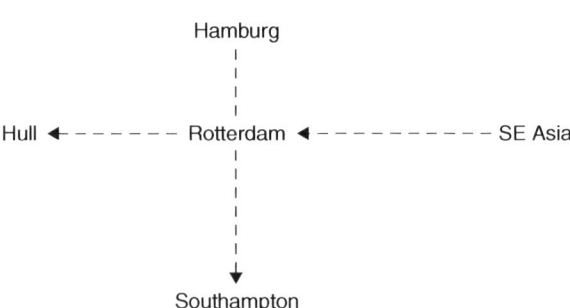

through bill sues the ocean carrier, even though the ocean carrier is not the actual carrier for that stage of the voyage.

The concept of the through bill of lading has been extended to multimodal operations, where there is typically a land, a sea and a second land leg, for which a multimodal transport document is used, essentially similar in concept to the through bill of lading.[59]

There can be problems where the actual carrier is sued in tort, rather than the contracting carrier being sued in contract. We consider these in chapter 17.[60]

14.8 Some problems with bills of lading

In recent years the bill of lading has not been universally used and, even where it still is, it does not always perform its traditional role. We look at the whole issue of alternative documentation in chapter 21. There is, however, no alternative document that gives the parties to the transaction (including banks under documentary credit), security that is as good as the shipped bill of lading (at any rate if used in the manner intended).

The main reason for moving away from the traditional bill of lading is that nowadays it frequently arrives only after the goods. Obviously this can create problems, if delivery is to be made against it.

If the goods are unlikely to be resold, a non-negotiable waybill may well be the answer – but it cannot give the seller the security of holding on to a bill of lading. The seller must be able to trust the buyer for payment, if a waybill is to be used. The carrier must also have some means of identifying the person entitled to delivery (especially as use of a waybill does nothing to protect the carrier if he delivers to someone not entitled). Nor does a waybill work as well as a bill of lading for banks under documentary credits. Nonetheless, waybills are the answer in some trades.

But in the bulk trade, the documents are delayed by a long string of sale contracts, financed by documentary credits. Now a document of title has to be used. A waybill is no use. In this latter situation, however, the bill of lading is not used in its traditional manner. Delivery of cargo is often made against an indemnity, rather than against production of the bill. This is not really problematic unless anyone goes bankrupt – but the alternatives do not offer security equivalent to use of bills of lading in a traditional manner.

This whole issue is examined in greater detail in chapter 21.

---

59 See section [21.3].
60 Esp. sections [17.3] and [17.4].

14.9 Question

Explain, with appropriate authorities, who is the holder in the following circumstances: a bill of lading made out to consignee or order is delivered to the consignee, but not indorsed, then indorsed by the consignee in blank and delivered to Alan, who fills in the blank with Betty's name and delivers it to her. Betty has delivered it to Charles but not indorsed it.

Comment

An easy question based on the material in chapter 14. If you read the chapter closely, you can answer it.

Chapter 15

Bill of lading contract terms

Chapter Contents

15.1 Relationship between bill of lading and carriage contract terms

This chapter is about the terms bill of lading contracts. Later chapters deal with identifying the parties to bill of lading contracts, and privity of contract issues.[1]

A lot of the interest in carriage of goods by sea comes from the inter-relationship between contracts between the various parties to an international trade, where carriage is by sea. This chapter, and to some extent also chapters 16 and 17, examine this inter-relationship. It is central to an understanding of the subject.

In chapter 18, we consider terms that are compulsorily written in by the Hague or Hague-Visby Rules, but this chapter is concerned instead with where the terms agreed by the parties come from. We look at the relationship between the contract and the bill of lading itself, and incorporation of terms from charterparties (or other contracts or documents). Where a bill of lading holder is also charterer, we need to know which prevails. To do this, we need again first to compare contractual aspects of charterparties and bills of lading.

15.1.1 Charterparties and bills of lading

A charterparty is a contract of carriage between shipowner and charterer.[2] There will often be sub-charterparties; these are separate contracts, in their own right, between the "disponent owner" and the charterer. Unlike bills of lading, charterparties create contracts only between the immediate parties to them. They are not transferred, a sub-charter being a separate contract between new parties.

For the purposes of this chapter you also need to know that, whereas a charterparty is itself a contract, bills of lading, at any rate if they evidence shipment, can be issued only after shipment. The contract of carriage must have been made by shipment at the latest, and so the bill of lading is evidence of a contract that has already been made. In other words, whereas the charterparty is a contract, the bill of lading will not necessarily be, though there are situations where the bill of lading terms can properly be regarded as determining the relationship between cargo-owner and shipowner.[3]

In chapter 18 we will examine the Hague-Visby Rules, which are a regime (mainly) protecting cargo-owners apply compulsorily to bills of lading, but not to charterparties (though charterparties often incorporate them, or articles from them, either by reference or by writing in the incorporated articles directly). It follows that bills of lading are, but charterparties may not be, governed by Hague-Visby under UK law, and hence that bills of lading will often be more favourable towards cargo-owners than charterparties are (where the charterers are also cargo-owners).[4] There can also be other differences between the terms of bills of lading and charterparties.

Bills of lading can (but need not) incorporate terms from a charterparty, but a ship may be subject to a number of charterparties (which the bill of lading may not identify). This creates issues over the bill of lading terms, which we consider later in the chapter.[5]

---

1 Chapters 16 and 17.
2 Sections [1.2]; [14.1].
3 Sections [15.1.3]–[15.1.5].
4 For a well-known instance of this, see section [13.7.2].
5 Section [15.2.3].

15.1.2 Transfer of contracts

A bill of lading is issued to the shipper of goods, and there will be a contract of carriage between the carrier (usually the shipowner) and the shipper. The terms of the bill of lading will be evidence of the terms of the carriage contract.[6]

As we will see in the next chapter, contractual rights and liabilities can be transferred to consignees and indorsees by the Carriage of Goods by Sea Act 1992. There is therefore nearly always a contractual relationship between the carrier and the current holder of the bill of lading. The terms of the transferred contract may not be the same as the original contract between carrier and shipper. However, where a bill of lading contract is successively transferred under a string, the transferred contract remains with the original carrier, and, at least after the first transfer, the terms will not change.[7]

Sometimes where under the sale contract the buyer is required to provide the vessel, a buyer who comes in later in the chain will simply sub-charter from his immediate seller.[8] If there is a long chain there may be quite a long string of sub-charters. But though a purchaser's relationship with his immediate seller, in such a situation, will be on the terms of the sub-charterparty between them, his relationship with the shipowner will be on bill of lading terms, which may of course be quite different.

In this chapter we will consider the terms of these various contracts, and how they interrelate with each other. The charterer of a ship may also (by virtue of shipping goods on board the ship) have a bill of lading issued to him. Or maybe the purchaser of goods, especially if on FOB terms, may have chartered the vessel, and subsequently become holder of the bill of lading. The terms of the bill of lading and charterparty may differ? So which governs? Or maybe the shipper has agreed additional oral terms with the carrier, which are not reflected in the bill of lading, and are unknown to later holders. The position may be further complicated by bills of lading incorporating charterparty terms.

15.1.3 The bill of lading and the carriage contract

While a charterparty is itself a contract of carriage, a *shipped* bill of lading should be issued only after the goods have been loaded on board the ship, by which stage the carriage contract will already have been concluded.

Any terms in the bill of lading are therefore necessarily post-contractual. They are a statement by the carrier of his view of the terms of the carriage contract, but the contract has already been made. They can be strong evidence of the terms of that contract, especially if there is no other evidence, or if the shipper had regularly contracted with the same carrier on the same bill of lading terms. It may be possible to infer from the issue of a bill of lading, and its acceptance without demur by the shipper, that the parties are content (whatever may have been the position before its issue) to contract on its terms. In other words (assuming the shipper is not also charterer, in which case he already has a contract of carriage), it may well be usual for the terms of the bill of lading to match those of the carriage contract.

It will not always be so, however. Where fairly clear terms have already been agreed, it may take more than the mere issue of a bill of lading to displace those terms. Moreover, in *Heskell v Continental*

---

6 See further sections [15.1.3]–[15.1.5].
7 Ibid.
8 Eg, R. Pagnan & Fratelli v N.G.J. Schouten NV (*The Filipinas I*) [1973] 1 Lloyd's Rep 349, in Todd, *Cases and Materials on International Trade Law* (2002), Sweet & Maxwell, [1–020]; K/S A/S Seateam & Co v Iraq National Oil Co (*The Sevonia Team*) [1983] 2 Lloyd's Rep 640.

Express Ltd (where all the goods, three bales of poplin, were left behind),[9] the bill of lading did not evidence even the existence of a carriage contract. In *Heskell*, the carriage contract would have been made on loading. Because no goods were shipped no carriage contract was made. The issue of a bill of lading could not bring a non-existent contract into existence.

15.1.4 Orally agreed terms (or otherwise agreed outside the bill of lading) between carrier and bill of lading holder

In *The Ardennes*,[10] the shipowner had made promises prior to shipment, which were important to the shipper, but were not incorporated into the bill of lading. Lord Goddard CJ held that the pre-shipment promises were nevertheless incorporated into the carriage contract, so that the terms of the carriage contract differed from those of the bill of lading.

The case concerned the shipment of mandarin oranges from Cartagena (in Spain) to London. The shippers were the exporters, and it mattered to them that the goods would arrive on or before 30 November 1947, to avoid an increase in import duty. The shipowner orally agreed to proceed directly to London, but when the bill of lading was issued, a clause in it allowed the shipowners to deviate, including carrying the goods beyond their destination. The agreement to proceed direct was held to be part of the contract, despite the liberty to deviate in the bill of lading. The carrier went first to Antwerp, increasing the voyage time beyond the 30th, and was held liable in damages, to compensate for the additional import duty, and for a drop in the market price of the oranges.[11]

At the start of his judgment, Lord Goddard CJ found "that there was a promise made to the shippers' representative that the ship should go direct to London, and that they shipped in reliance on that promise".[12] The question was therefore whether the issue of the bill of lading negated a clear promise that had earlier been made. Lord Goddard was unimpressed by this argument:[13]

> "The contract has come into existence before the bill of lading is signed; the latter is signed by one party only, and handed by him to the shipper usually after the goods have been put on board. No doubt if the shipper finds that the bill contains terms with which he is not content, or does not contain some term for which he has stipulated, he might, if there were time, demand his goods back; but he is not, in my opinion, for that reason, prevented from giving evidence that there was in fact a contract entered into before the bill of lading was signed different from that which is found in the bill of lading or containing some additional term. He is no party to the preparation of the bill of lading; nor does he sign it."

This was a case where the promise was clear, and mattered to the shippers to the extent that they shipped in reliance upon it. Not surprisingly, the fact that they did not remove the goods from the ship, once the bill of lading had been issued, did not preclude them from enforcing it.

Lord Goddard CJ distinguished the nineteenth century Court of Appeal authority of *Leduc & Co v Ward*.[14] There the shipowner, carrying cargo from what was then called Fiume (in what is now Croatia) to Dunkirk in northern France, proceeded on a very substantial deviation (some 1,200 miles) via Glasgow. The ship was lost at the mouth of the River Clyde (near Glasgow), and the shipowner

---

9 (1950) 83 Ll L Rep 438. See further section [19.9], where we also examine the consequences of there being no carriage contract there.

10 *Ardennes (cargo owners) v Ardennes (owners) (The Ardennes)* [1951] 1 KB 55.

11 From the case it is also clear that there can be damages to compensate for delay, whether or not the contract so provides. This is relevant to sections [21.4]; [21.5].

12 [1951] 1 KB 55, 59.

13 [1951] 1 KB 55, 59–60.

14 (1888) 20 QBD 475.

(in an action brought by an indorsee of the bill of lading) claimed the perils of the seas exception that was standard in bills of lading of that period. The issue was whether the substantial deviation denied him that right.[15]

Though there was a wide liberty to deviate in the bill of lading, it was held not to permit the very substantial deviation the shipowner made.[16] The shipowner could not therefore rely on the bill of lading, and additionally claimed that the shippers knew of, and agreed to, the longer route, which was not therefore an unlawful deviation. The Court of Appeal held that the bill of lading alone governed the relationship between shipowner and indorsee, and the shipowner could not rely on an oral arrangement made with the shippers.

The basis upon which *Leduc v Ward* was distinguished in *The Ardennes* was that the earlier case was between shipowner and indorsee (to whom contractual rights had passed under the Bills of Lading Act 1855, s. 1, precursor to the Carriage of Goods by Sea Act 1992 considered in chapter 16). There is certainly much to be said for the view that a subsequent holder, who will not generally know of oral pre-shipment arrangements, should take on bill of lading terms alone, though this policy is not clearly stated in either case. However, in *Leduc v Ward*, Fry LJ made much of the wording of the Bills of Lading Act 1855, which transferred "the contract contained in the bill of lading":[17]

> "Here is a plain declaration of the legislature that there is a contract contained in the bill of lading, and that the benefit of it is to pass to the indorsee under such circumstances as exist in the present case. It seems to me impossible therefore now to contend that there is no contract contained in the bill of lading, whatever might have been the case before the statute."

This was also, as observed above, the basis upon which the case was distinguished in *The Ardennes* (where of course, the 1855 Act had no application).[18] The problem is that, if this were the only basis for *Leduc v Ward*, it would not survive the replacement of the 1855 Act with the Carriage of Goods by Sea Act 1992, s. 5 of which provides that contract of carriage "means the contract contained in or evidenced by that bill . . .".[19] So statute no longer provides that the contract is "contained in" the bill of lading, and the bill of lading could be merely evidence in the hands of an indorsee, just as it was in *The Ardennes*, in the hands of a shipper.

In *Leduc v Ward*, Lord Esher MR relied on the parol evidence rule:[20]

> ". . . by which, where the contract has been reduced into a writing which is intended to constitute the contract, parol evidence to alter or qualify the effect of such writing is not admissible, and the writing is the only evidence of the contract . . .".

But then, why would that rule not also apply to *The Ardennes*? Perhaps the explanation is that the parol evidence rule does not apply where the written document is not intended to be the contract, but merely a receipt or memorandum.[21] If that is the correct explanation, it of course limits *The Ardennes* to situations where the bill of lading is intended to be merely a receipt. However, that is far more likely to be the case, where the shipper has already agreed other terms, as in *The Ardennes*, than

---

15 On the principles in section [4.4.2].

16 In this respect *Leduc v Ward* is a CA precursor to the HL decision five years later, in *Glynn v Margetson & Co* [1893] AC 351, on which see section [4.4.4]; also [22.2].

17 (1888) 20 QBD 475, 483.

18 [1951] 1 KB 55, 60.

19 Waybills come within the 1992 Act, but were not within the 1855: see further section [16.5].

20 (1888) 20 QBD 475, 480.

21 The explanation favoured by Carver on *Bills of Lading*, 3rd ed (2012), Sweet & Maxwell/Thomson Reuters, British Shipping Laws Series, [3–006].

where the bill is sent to an indorsee who knows nothing of any other dealings. Perhaps this best explains the two cases.

Another possible explanation of *Leduc v Ward* is that the shipowner, by issuing the bill of lading in the terms that he did, represented that he was content to carry the cargo under its terms. If the indorsee relied on its terms in taking up the bill, then the shipowner could be estopped from later asserting different terms. As we will see further in chapter 19, however, estoppel is not a very dependable doctrine.[22] The sale contract may require the purchaser to take up the bill, whether or not the carriage contract contains the oral terms,[23] and of course estoppel can only work against the shipowner, not in his favour, where the bill of lading terms are more favourable (as they were in *The Ardennes*).

Two final observations. First, unlike its 1855 precursor, the Carriage of Goods by Sea Act 1992 applies to documents other than bills of lading.[24] There seems no obvious reason why the reasoning in *Leduc v Ward* should not apply with equal force to these other documents. Secondly, if instead there is an implied contract, under the *Brandt v Liverpool* doctrine discussed in the next chapter,[25] it would be natural to infer that the implied contract was on the terms of the bill of lading, or other document. In other words, *Leduc v Ward* should apply in this situation also.

15.1.5 Where charterer also has bill of lading

Where the shipper is also charterer of the vessel, it follows from the preceding discussion that the charterparty will be the carriage contract and the bill of lading merely a receipt. Even if the charterparty is only oral (most plausibly, where it has not yet been reduced to writing), the position is at least as strong as in *The Ardennes*, since the charterparty is indubitably a contract, which is intended to govern the relationship between the parties. If, moreover, the charterparty is in writing (the more usual situation), there would be no possibility of using the parol evidence rule (as in *Leduc v Ward*), to argue that the bill of lading should govern.

We will see in chapter 18 that the terms of bill of lading contracts are usually subject to either the Hague or the Hague-Visby Rules, both of which provide cargo-owners with a minimum degree of protection. Charterparties are not (unless expressly made so) subject to the Rules, and it is therefore open for the parties to agree terms more favourable to the owners. Once bills of lading are negotiated, however, *Leduc v Ward* tells us that the relationship between owners and bill of lading holders will generally be governed by the Rules,[26] so there may be little point in agreeing in the charterparty terms more favourable to the owners.[27]

There is authority that the charterparty prevails (at any rate as a starting point), even if the charterer later obtains a bill of lading as subsequent holder, as opposed to being the original shipper. Unlike the situation in *Leduc v Ward*, of course, there is now a pre-existing relationship between shipowner and indorsee, and therefore a greater basis for treating the bill of lading as merely a receipt. Moreover, if the charterparty is itself in writing there will be two inconsistent documents, so that the parol evidence rule will not apply, as it did in *Leduc v Ward*. In *The Dunelmia*,[28] the action was between

---

22 See section [19.4].

23 Carriage terms must not be inconsistent with sale terms, for example where the sale contract requires a direct ship, but the carriage contract allows calling at intermediate ports, but unless the bill of lading correctly states the carriage contract terms it can probably not be rejected anyway: *Gill & Duffus SA v Berger & Co Inc* [1984] AC 382. Carriage terms must also be reasonable: Sale of Goods Act 1979, s. 32(2).

24 Section [16.5]; [16.6].

25 See section [16.9].

26 Section [15.1.4].

27 See an example of how this problem is dealt with in section [13.7.2].

28 *President of India v Metcalfe Shipping Co Ltd (The Dunelmia)* [1970] 1 QB 289.

the shipowners and FOB purchasers, who were both charterers and indorsees. The charterparty contained an arbitration clause but, on the principles discussed in the following section, the bill of lading did not incorporate this clause.[29] Thus bill of lading and charterparty terms differed. The Court of Appeal held that the charterparty prevailed, that the charterparty was *prima facie* the contract that governed relations between shipowners and charterers, and that it was not (in the absence of contrary evidence) superseded by the bill of lading in the hands of the indorsee.

We can see who the parties were in *The Dunelmia* as follows:

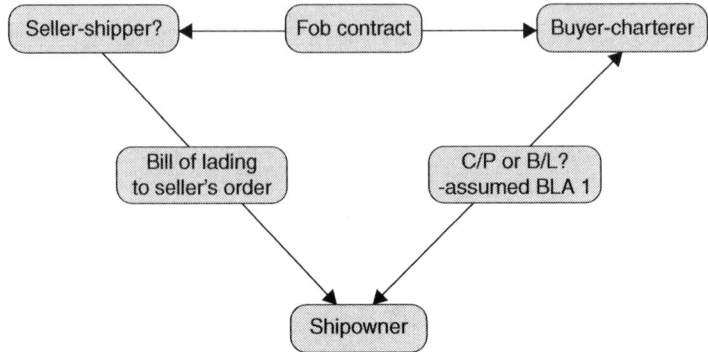

The issue was the relationship between the buyer and the shipowner; the buyer was charterer, but had also had rights transferred to him under the Bills of Lading Act 1855, s. 1, precursor to the Carriage of Goods by Sea Act 1992.

In the case itself the master had authority only to sign and issue bills of lading "without prejudice" to the terms of the charterparty, and there is an argument that *The Dunelmia* depends on this, but statements in the case itself suggest that the argument is incorrect.[30] The view was taken that *The Dunelmia* is of *general* application in *The El Amria and The El Minia*,[31] although as things turned out in the later case, the FOB purchasers there were not party to any contract other than the bill of lading. Consequently the views on *The Dunelmia* are not part of the *ratio* in the later case.

Nonetheless, *The Dumelmia* is only a starting point, since the courts are engaged ultimately in interpreting the intentions of the parties. In *The Jocelyne*,[32] Brandon J accepted that in principle the parties could agree that the bill of lading to be issued would supersede the charterparty provisions. Had this happened then of course the bill of lading, rather than the charterparty, would have governed the contract. In the case itself there was a supersession clause in the charterparty, but it required the bill of lading to be in a specified form, and to contain specified clauses. In the event, the bill of lading did not satisfy the terms of the supersession clause, and the charterparty remained therefore the applicable instrument.

---

29 The bill of lading made "Freight payable by the charterers as per charterparty", and incorporated "All conditions and exceptions as per charterparty", but these general words of incorporation would have been insufficient to incorporate the arbitration clause: see section [15.2].

30 Eg, [1970] 1 QB 289, 306, where Lord Denning MR suggests that the reasoning is general, and not so limited.

31 [1982] 2 Lloyd's Rep 28.

32 *Moscow V/O Exportkhleb v Helmville Ltd (The Jocelyne)* [1977] 2 Lloyd's Rep 121.

Even where the charterparty constitutes the contract of carriage, bills of lading retain their other functions, as documents of title, and as a receipt for the goods and evidence of quantity loaded.

15.1.6 Where the only relationship is on the terms of the bill of lading

In *The El Amria and The El Minia*,[33] the issue was the relationship between FOB purchasers and shipowners. The FOB sellers had entered into a contract of affreightment, and obtained bills of lading that were indorsed in the purchasers' favour. The Court of Appeal held that, despite being FOB sellers, they had entered into the contract of affreightment as principals, so that the only contract between the purchasers and shipowners was the bill of lading (transferred under the 1855 Act). Hence only the bill of lading, and not the contract of affreightment, governed their relationship, just as the bill of lading had governed in *Leduc v Ward*. (It contained an exclusive jurisdiction clause, which the contract of affreightment did not.) Here is a diagrammatic representation of the relationships:

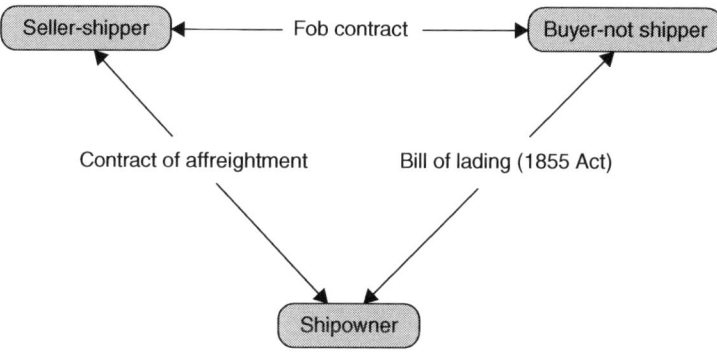

The bill of lading would also govern, were the issue the relationship between sub-charterers and shipowners, if the sub-charterers were holders of a bill of lading. There would be no binding charterparty between sub-charterers and shipowners, although obviously the sub-charterparty would determine the holders' relationship with the head charterers.

Where the relationship between cargo-owners and shipowners is on bill of lading terms, what happens to the charterparty is irrelevant to the bill of lading contract. In *Hain SS Co Ltd v Tate & Lyle Ltd*,[34] the charterers had waived a breach (deviation) by the shipowners. This did not affect the cargo-owners, whose only contract with the shipowners was on the terms of the bill of lading.

15.2 Incorporation of charterparty terms into bills of lading

It is common for bills of lading not to set out all the terms of the carriage contract, but instead to incorporate terms from a charterparty. While this makes a great deal of sense from the

---

33 [1982] 2 Lloyd's Rep 28.
34 (1936) 55 LL L Rep 159. See section [4.4].

shipowner's viewpoint, it can be problematic for holders. Purchasers and banks taking up such bills will not necessarily have had sight of the charterparty, and there is authority that a CIF seller may tender a charterparty bill of lading, whether or not the charterparty is also tendered.[35] Though this right is arguably restricted to charterparties that are on a commonly used standard form and not heavily amended,[36] the CIF buyer would still need to know the charterparty terms in order safely to reject the tendered documents, and of course the problem is precisely that he has not seen them.

Nonetheless, charterparty bills are sufficiently common that, since 1993, explicit provision has been made for them in the UCP (for documentary credits). Also, for example, BIMCO's 1994 revision of the Gencon voyage charterparty is specifically intended to be used with the 1994 revision of the Congenbill bill of lading.

There are three main issues for us to consider when looking at charterparty bills:

. from which charterparty terms are incorporated, where there is more than one;
    . which terms are incorporated, in particular where general words of incorporation are used (such as "all conditions and exceptions" or "all terms, conditions and exceptions" as per charterparty); and
    . whether the incorporated terms are directly set out in the bill of lading or adapted ("manipulated") to suit the different context of the bill of lading contract (because clauses drafted for a charterparty may not fit directly into a bill of lading).

15.2.1 Why incorporate charterparty terms into bills of lading?

The earliest cases on incorporation date from the nineteenth century. This might look like ancient history, but the justification in *The San Nicholas*[37] for incorporating head rather than sub-charter terms (where the charterparty was unidentified) hark back to the early use of charterparty bills. Also, the fact that use of such bills started at a time when arbitration clauses were widely distrusted might explain the courts' very narrow views on incorporation of arbitration clauses into bills of lading.[38]

The concern in the nineteenth century seems always to have been to bind purchasers, or eventual receivers, to pay freight and (eg) demurrage due on discharge, even if they were not party to the charterparty. The charterparty would often have a cesser clause, which would typically require the shipowner to proceed against the receivers, rather than the charterers, for (eg) freight and demurrage at discharge.[39] The objective could be achieved by incorporating freight and demurrage terms from the charterparty into the bill of lading, as it made sense for freight and demurrage terms and rates to be the same as those from the charterparty. In the early cases the bill of lading incorporated "freight as per charterparty",[40] or sometimes added demurrage.

To make provision in the bill of lading can also give the shipowner a lien enforceable against the receiver of the cargo (protection of the lien is often referred to in the cases).[41]

---

35 *Finska Cellulosaforeningen v Westfield Paper Co Ltd* (1940) 68 Ll L Rep 75.

36 *SIAT Di Del Ferro v Tradax Overseas SA* [1978] 2 Lloyd's Rep 470, 492 (Donaldson J). There was no comment on this in the Court of Appeal (upholding Donaldson J's decision: [1980] 1 Lloyd's Rep 53), where it was instead observed that even had the charterparty been tendered, it would have shown that the discharge ports were not in accordance with the CIF contract.

37 *Pacific Molasses Co v Entre Rios Compania Naviera SA (The San Nicholas)* [1976] 1 Lloyd's Rep 8.

38 In *Federal Bulk Carriers Inc v C. Itoh & Co Ltd (The Federal Bulker)* [1989] 1 Lloyd's Rep 103, 107, Bingham LJ observed that "arbitration clauses were in 1911 viewed with less favour than they are today", but that was not a ground for distinguishing a 1911 decision.

39 See section [7.9].

40 Eg, *Hamilton & Co v Mackie & Sons* (1889) 5 TLR 677.

41 Also in section [7.9].

Such usage (protection of shipowner lien) continues today, for example in *The San Nicholas* and *The Sevonia Team*,[42] but trade practices are now more flexible.[43] Cesser clauses are rare today, freight is more often payable in advance, and there are other ways of binding receivers to demurrage terms. However, much of the case law developed around early practices.

15.2.2 Widening general words of incorporation

Later, shipowners wished to widen incorporation, to (eg) "freight and other conditions". "Conditions" was interpreted "*ejusdem generis* with that for the payment of freight",[44] to mean "such of the charterparty conditions as were to be performed by the consignee", and therefore mainly concerned with freight, laytime and demurrage. This interpretation of conditions continues to this day. It is not the same as the general contractual meaning of conditions (as opposed to warranties), described in chapter 2.[45] Later still the formulation widened to "all conditions and exceptions", and then (the common formulation today) "all terms conditions and exceptions". ("Conditions and exceptions" did not alter the definition of "conditions" but simply added charterparty exceptions. "Terms" appears to have been interpreted to have added nothing.)[46]

Today, the purpose of incorporation of charterparty terms is a lot more than simply binding receivers to freight and demurrage provisions. An area of particular concern is over cargo-handling provisions, the incorporation of which can leave cargo-owners with inadequate protection where cargo is damaged during stowage, or in the loading or unloading process.

15.2.3 From which charterparty

A bill of lading can incorporate clauses from any charterparty, or indeed any document. In *The Heidberg*,[47] however, His Honour Judge Diamond QC thought that the charterparty itself must have been concluded and reduced to writing before the bill of lading was issued. One rationale for this view was that, in the hands of anyone other than the original shipper, oral terms do not form part of the bill of lading contract. This was important to ensure that the bill of lading terms were readily ascertainable:[48]

> "This rule facilitates the use of bills of lading in international commerce since it enables a prospective transferee of a bill of lading to see, merely by inspecting the bill, whether it conforms to his contract (whether it be a sale contract or a letter of credit) and what rights and obligations will be transferred to him if he takes up the bill."

His Honour thought that the same principle should apply where the bill of lading incorporates a charterparty, "save that the rights and obligations which will be or have been transferred to the consignee or indorsee are now set out in two documents, the bill of lading and the charterparty. Once again the transferee should not be affected by oral terms not contained in the two documents." One can certainly appreciate the logic of this approach, particularly at a time when, under the Bills of Lading Act 1855, the bill of lading in the hands of an indorsee contained the contract. In reality,

---

42 Respectively [1976] 1 Lloyd's Rep 8; [1983] 2 Lloyds Rep 640.

43 Eg, *Partenreederei M/S Heidberg v Grosvenor Grain and Feed Company Ltd (The Heidberg)* [1994] 2 Lloyd's Rep 287, in section [15.2.3].

44 *T.W. Thomas & Co Ltd v Portsea SS Co Ltd (The Portsmouth)* [1912] AC 1, 10 (Lord Robson).

45 Section [2.6].

46 The historical development is described (eg) in *The Varenna* [1984] 1 QB 599, 604 (Hobhouse J). Authorities from the time include *Gray v Carr* (1871) LR 6 QB 522, *Serraino & Sons v Campbell* [1891] 1 QB 283, and *Diederichsen v Farquharson Brothers* [1898] 1 QB 150.

47 [1994] 2 Lloyd's Rep 287, also discussed in section [2.2].

48 [1994] 2 Lloyd's Rep 287, 310, citing *Leduc v Ward* (1888) 20 QBD 475 and *The Ardennes* [1951] 1 KB 55, above, section [15.1.4].

however, given that it is common for charterparties to be orally fixed long in advance of being reduced to writing, this view would place a very substantial restriction on incorporation of charterparty terms. The policy objective is also less clear, once the bill of lading incorporates terms from a document the indorsee may not have seen, whether written or not. Fortunately, there are other grounds for the decision in *The Heidberg*, which go less far.

A narrower basis for *The Heidberg* is simply that, where the issue is incorporation of an arbitration clause, which must be itself be in writing, the charterparty from which it is incorporated must be in writing.[49] This rationale applies only to incorporation of arbitration clauses (the actual issue in *The Heidberg*).

In *The Heidberg* itself a recap telex was held insufficient, but this aspect of *The Heidberg* has been limited by the Court of Appeal in *The Epsilon Rosa*.[50] Tuckey LJ did not think the earlier case wrong, but emphasised that in *The Epsilon Rosa*:[51]

> "[both] the bill of lading and the charterparty relate to the same voyage by the same carrier. It is obvious that the shipowner will want to ensure, so far as possible, that his rights and obligations as carrier as against the original and any later holder of the bill of lading are the same as his rights and obligations as against the charterer . . . It should be apparent to any holder of the bill that all the terms of the contract are not contained in that document and that the other terms are to be found in the related charterparty."

Because the holder is expecting this, this presumably justifies relaxing the formality requirements. The argument will normally apply to the traditional situation, where the charterers of the vessel sell the cargo to indorsees, using bills of lading that incorporate the terms of their own charter. The argument would not have applied in *The Heidberg*, where the charterparty at issue was entered into late, with shipowners who were unknown to either of the trading parties, where additional temporary tonnage was needed to perform a by then longstanding contract of affreightment. It is therefore possible for both cases to be correct. At first instance in *The Epsilon Rosa*, David Steel J had taken a stronger view, that to argue that the recap telex was not writing was "wholly inconsistent with commercial realities".[52] This implies that *The Heidberg* is incorrect, at least on this issue.

However, the unusual circumstance of *The Heidberg* makes an altogether different explanation more appropriate.[53]

15.2.3.1 Charterparty not identified

The charterparty is not always identified. There is clear authority that, even where there is more than one charterparty, this does not render the incorporation clause void for uncertainty.[54]

The general principle (based on the decision of the Court of Appeal in *The San Nicholas*)[55] is that the courts presume incorporation from the head charter, to which the shipowner is party. This again makes perfect sense, if we consider the traditional nineteenth century incorporation, where the owner is anxious to protect his right to freight and demurrage, there being a cesser clause in

---

49 Now provided by Arbitration Act 1996, s. 5.

50 *Welex AG v Rosa Maritime Ltd (The Epsilon Rosa)* [2003] 2 Lloyd's Rep 509.

51 [2003] 2 Lloyd's Rep 509, [25].

52 [2002] 2 Lloyd's Rep 81, [29].

53 See below, section [15.2.3.1].

54 Many authorities, but recently *National Navigation Co v Endesa Generacion SA (The Wadi Sudr)* [2009] 1 Lloyd's Rep 666, reversed on other grounds by the CA: [2010] 1 Lloyd's Rep 193.

55 *Pacific Molasses Co v Entre Rios Compania Naviera SA (The San Nicholas)* [1976] 1 Lloyd's Rep 8.

the head charterparty. However, it is merely a presumption, which can be displaced by a number of factors, eg:

1. where the head charter is a time charter;[56]
2. where the sub, but not the head charter, has been reduced to writing;[57]
3. arguably where the charterer is the contracting carrier, when the justification for The San Nicholas does not apply.

Let us begin with an examination of The San Nicholas. This case is authority for the general position: that the incorporation is not rendered uncertain, and that the head charterparty is incorporated. The head charter was governed by English law, the sub-charter by the flag of the vessel. The incorporation clause in the bill of lading provided that:

> "This shipment is carried under and pursuant to the terms of the Charter dated [– the date is left blank with nothing filled in –] at [– blank –] between [– blank –] and [– blank –] as Charterer, and all the terms whatsoever of the said Charter except for the rate and payment of freight specified therein apply to and govern the rights of the parties concerned . . .".

Lord Denning MR said that the blanks (which should have been, but were not, filled in) did not render this clause uncertain, and that:[58]

> "The head charter was the only charter to which the shipowners were parties: and they must, in the bill of lading, be taken to be referring to that head charter."

He agreed with Scrutton on Charterparties that a general reference will normally incorporate terms from the head charter.[59] Roskill LJ agreed.

The San Nicholas adopts a normal presumption, but it is displaceable, and it was displaced a few years later in The SLS Everest, also in the Court of Appeal.[60] In this case, buyers of cargo voyage chartered a vessel to carry the cargo, but the vessel was already on time charter. This time the bill of lading stated:

> "Freight and other conditions as per [then there is a blank] . . .".

The issue was which charter was incorporated, also in order to decide the governing law of the bill of lading.[61] This time the Court of Appeal held that the sub-charter was incorporated. The San Nicholas was distinguished, and will not normally apply where the head charter is a time charter. The reason is that time and demise charterparty terms differ fundamentally from voyage terms. Bill of lading terms will be more similar to voyage terms. It follows that voyage terms will generally be better suited for incorporation into bills of lading than time or demise terms (and especially given the actual incorporation clause in The SLS Everest).

---

56 *Bangladesh Chemical Industries Corp v Henry Stephens Shipping Co Ltd (The SLS Everest)* [1981] 2 Lloyd's Rep 389; *The Wadi Sudr* [2009] 1 Lloyd's Rep 666.

57 *The Heidberg* (above), if this is the true basis for this decision.

58 [1976] 1 Lloyd's Rep 8, 11.

59 *Ibid*, citing the then-current *Scrutton on Charterparties*, 18th ed (1974), 63. See also *The Sevonia Team* [1983] 2 Lloyd's Rep 640.

60 *The SLS Everest* [1981] 2 Lloyd's Rep 389.

61 Only the sub-charter was governed by English law – necessary for a *Mareva* injunction remedy (nowadays called a freezing order).

We know that, though long-period consecutive voyage charterparties bear some similarities to time charters, they remain voyage charters in their fundamentals.[62] It is therefore not surprising that The San Nicholas, and not The SLS Everest, was applied in The Nai Matteini, where the head charter was a very long-term consecutive voyage charter.[63]

We need now to return to The Heidberg, where I suggest the true basis of the decision was that The San Nicholas should not be applied to the particular situation. We start with a contract of affreightment (COA) between disponent owners and shippers, for a number of shipments of bulk maize. Apparently after a number of shipments had been made, the disponent owners needed extra tonnage, so (some nine months after entering into the COA) chartered in Heidberg under a voyage charter. It was this (head) charter that was still oral when the bill of lading was issued. Neither the shippers nor the claimants (who were CIF purchasers of the maize) had anything to do with it. The bill provided for the arbitration clause of an unidentified charterparty to be incorporated in the bill, and the issue was whether that from the head charter should be incorporated. In holding that it should not, His Honour Judge Diamond QC doubted the generality of The San Nicholas:[64]

"There may indeed be reasons for adopting this approach as, for example, if it appears that the words of incorporation were designed to give the owners a lien on the cargo for freight or demurrage. A bill of lading, however, is a bilateral contract and while weight should be given to the presumed intention of the master who signed and issued the bill, equal weight must be given to the intention of the shipper who normally draws up the bill and presents it to the master for signature. In some cases, as in the present, he also signs it, though this is less common."

It is perfectly reasonable to apply The San Nicholas in the traditional situation, where the shipowner's objective (as everyone knows) is to protect his freight and demurrage claims, but that is no reason to apply it in the very different circumstances of The Heidberg, where neither shipper not subsequent holder knew anything of the head charter. This is certainly a forceful argument, but this seems to be the only time the generality of The San Nicholas has been doubted.

The rationale of The San Nicholas breaks down where the charterer is the contracting carrier, and there are suggestions in The Wadi Sudr that this is a ground for incorporating from the sub-charter.[65] However, the head charter also was also in time form there, so the same result would have been reached, whoever had been the contracting carrier.

15.2.4 Which terms incorporated?

We have seen how early incorporation was about freight and demurrage, how the courts interpreted "conditions" so as not to go far beyond this, and in particular that the word "conditions" has a narrower meaning than in the general law of contract. "Exceptions" has a well-known (narrow) definition. Even with wider terminology, such as "all the terms, conditions, clauses and exceptions contained in the said charterparty", the courts have nevertheless continued to construe even general words narrowly.

There are good reasons for caution. Remember that the bill of lading holder will typically not be the charterer, and will often never have seen the charterparty. In The Jordan II, Lord Steyn observed that:[66]

---

62 Section [5.5].

63 Navigazione Alta Italia SpA v Svenska Petroleum AB (The Nai Matteini) [1988] 1 Lloyd's Rep 452, not followed, but not on this issue, in The Nerano: section [15.2.5].

64 [1994] 2 Lloyd's Rep 287, 311.

65 National Navigation Co v Endesa Generacion SA (The Wadi Sudr) [2009] 1 Lloyd's Rep 666, rvsd (other grounds) [2010] 1 Lloyd's Rep 193.

66 Jindal Iron and Steel Co Ltd v Islamic Solidarity Shipping Co Jordan Inc (The Jordan II) [2005] 1 WLR 1363, [25].

". . . third party bill of lading holders will in practice often not have seen the charter-party or had advance notice of relevant charter-party clauses. This is . . ., however, an inevitable risk of international trade . . .".

This consideration influenced their Lordships in *The Portsmouth* to hold that general words of incorporation will not incorporate an arbitration clause from a charterparty.[67] The courts have also been concerned to protect the negotiability of bills of lading (probably this is another way of looking at the same problem).

As to which clauses are incorporated by general words, in *The Portsmouth*[68] a germaneness test found favour: general words incorporate into a bill of lading only terms that are germane to it (ie, to the receipt, carriage or delivery of the cargo or the payment of the freight). This would obviously include freight and demurrage, and the shipowner exemptions and limitations of liability that were commonly found in charterparties of this period. (Of course, other clauses can be incorporated, if referred to expressly in the bill of lading.)

There are two main areas of contention. First, what is the effect of the charterparty placing cargo-handling duties on the charterer? Can the shipowner avoid liability if damage is caused to the cargo during these processes, bearing in mind that the charterparty does not have to be tendered with the bill of lading, so that the indorsee may be unaware of its terms? Secondly, what about clauses that (clearly or arguably) do not relate directly to the receipt, carriage or delivery of the cargo or the payment of the freight? Most of the litigation has been on arbitration clauses, but we also need to consider jurisdiction and applicable law clauses, where the law remains somewhat inconclusive (and arguably lacking in clear principle).

15.2.4.1 Cargo-handling

In *The Garbis*[69] the bill of lading incorporated "all terms whatsoever" of the charterparty (except rate and payment of freight). Goff J thought this phrase sufficiently wide to encompass terms relating not only to the carriage itself, but also to loading and discharge. In *The Eems Solar*[70] a FIOST clause was incorporated by general words,[71] it being assumed to be germane.

If the charterparty places responsibility for loading and discharge on the charterers, but it is a shipowner's bill, and if the charterparty division of responsibilities is incorporated into the bill of lading, the cargo-owner will be unable to sue the shipowner for damage during this period, nor will he be able to sue the charterer, at any rate in contract, since the charterer is not party (at any rate expressly) to the bill of lading contract. Refer to diagram overleaf:

A FIOST problem

There are, in principle, two ways of avoiding this conclusion, both of which were discussed in the Court of Appeal in *The Coral*.[72] First, the shipowners could perform the stowage obligation through

---

67 The courts do not appear to have distinguished between particular general words – in *TW Thomas & Co Ltd v Portsea SS Co Ltd (The Portsmouth)* [1912] AC 1, "terms" added nothing – nor indeed in *The Federal Bulker*, below, section [15.2.4].

68 [1912] AC 1, eg, the emphasis on the bill of lading being a "negotiable instrument": 6 (Lord Atkinson); 9 (Lord Gorell); 11 (Lord Robson), though there it was actually the holder, not the shipowner, who (unsuccessfully) argued to incorporate the arbitration clause from the charterparty.

69 *Garbis Maritime Corporation v Philippine National Oil Co (The Garbis)* [1982] 2 Lloyd's Rep 283.

70 *Yuzhny Zaavod Metall Profil LLC v Eems Beheerder BV (The Eems Solar)* [2013] 2 Lloyd's Rep 487.

71 Free in and out stowed trimmed. See further section [5.3].

72 *Balli Trading Ltd v Afalona Shipping Co Ltd (The Coral)* [1993] 1 Lloyds Rep 1, 7 (Beldam LJ).

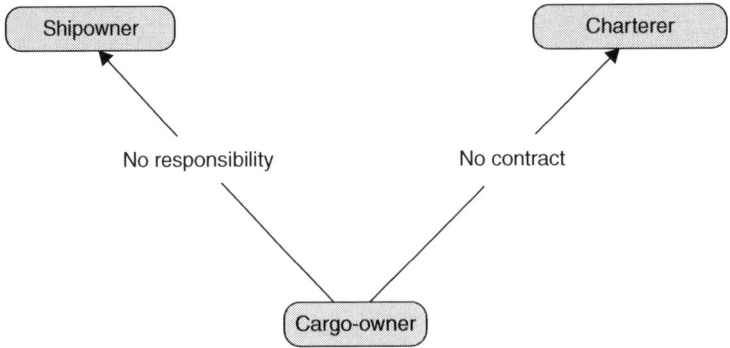

the agency of another party, while remaining ultimately responsible for it. In the event that they were sued, they would be able to claim an indemnity from the person who had actually performed the operation, much as contracting carriers can claim indemnities from performing carriers if they do not themselves perform the entire carriage operation.[73] The courts have not, however, developed the agency concept in this context. Secondly, the cargo owners could bring an action directly against the person performing the operation. The problem is that there will be an express contract only with the contracting carrier (assumed to be the shipowner in this case), and the suggestion in *The Coral* that an implied contract (with the charterers) may arise, similar to that between the FOB sellers and the shipowners in *Pyrene Co Ltd v Scindia Navigation Co Ltd*,[74] is subject to later House of Lords criticism of that aspect of *Pyrene*, and to later decisions limiting the utility of implied contracts as a device.[75] (At best it can be said that there may be an implied contract, but that it would be necessary to look closely at the relationship between the charterers, shippers and bill of lading holders.) The potential for lack of liability on anyone's part remains a real one, I suggest.

In chapter 18, we will see that avoidance by owners of liability, by placing responsibility for stowage elsewhere, does not trigger Art. III(8) of the Hague or Hague-Visby Rules, which renders void any term "lessening [the carrier's] liability otherwise than as provided in these Rules".[76]

15.2.4.2 Arbitration and other ancillary clauses

Arbitration clauses are not generally incorporated by general words. In *The Portsmouth*, Lord Atkinson gave as his reason for refusing to incorporate the arbitration clause that general words incorporate into a bill of lading only terms that are germane, and that the arbitration clause was not germane. (The House was unanimous in holding the arbitration clause not incorporated, but the germaneness test, which is the one that has gained widespread favour, is Lord Atkinson's alone.)[77] There is authority that arbitration clauses will not (normally) be incorporated by general words, however wide.[78]

---

73 Eg, where through bills of lading or multimodal transport documents are used. See sections [14.7]; [21.3].

74 [1954] 2 QB 402.

75 This aspect of *Pyrene* was criticised in *Scruttons Ltd v Midland Silicones Ltd* [1962] AC 446, 471 (Viscount Simonds) (cf. 490, Lord Denning, dissenting), and more general limits were placed on the implied contract device in *The Aramis* [1989] 1 Lloyd's Rep 213; *Mitsui & Co Ltd v Novorossiysk Shipping Co (The Gudermes)* [1993] 1 Lloyd's Rep 311 (both discussed in section [16.8]).

76 See section [18.4].

77 See generally Todd, *Incorporation of charterparty terms by general words* [2014] JBL 407.

78 *The Portsmouth* applied *Hamilton & Co v Mackie & Sons* (1889) 5 TLR 677, and subsequent authorities include *The Annefield* [1971] P 168; *The Varenna* [1984] 1 QB 599; *The Federal Bulker* [1989] 1 Lloyd's Rep 103.

It is true that what is germane might require analysis of the particular charterparty clause,[79] so that a very wide arbitration clause (covering any dispute arising out of the charter or any bill of lading "issued hereunder") was held incorporated by general words in *The Merak*.[80] However, it is now clear that the primary document to be interpreted is the bill of lading, and that unless the bill of lading on its terms incorporates, the charterparty will not be considered at all.[81] *The Merak* has been received without enthusiasm, and seems either to be limited to its unusual facts, or to be wrong.[82]

15.2.4.3 What is germane?

We need to consider what is germane. Are there other clauses that are not germane, or is it just arbitration clauses that are singled out for special treatment? Until recently the second seemed likely. Thus, in *The Njegos*,[83] it was held that the clauses that were incorporated could not be isolated from their context, and hence incorporation also included the proper law of the charterparty. In effect, therefore, a choice of law clause will be incorporated. *The Njegos* was applied in *The San Nicholas* and in *The Dolphina*,[84] in both of which a choice of law clause was incorporated by general words.

The Portsmouth was also distinguished in *The Pioneer Container*,[85] where the issue concerned an exclusive jurisdiction clause. If choice of law and exclusive jurisdiction clauses were not subject to *The Portsmouth* principle, it looked, by about 20 years ago, as though *The Portsmouth* might be confined to arbitration clauses. There are in any case good reasons for according arbitration clauses special treatment:[86]

"In particular, first, an arbitration agreement may preclude the parties to it from bringing a dispute before a court of law; secondly, an arbitration agreement has to be 'a written agreement'; thirdly, the arbitration clause differs from other types of clause because it constitutes a 'self-contained contract collateral or ancillary to' the substantive contract."

However, more recent cases cast doubt on confinement of the germaneness principle to arbitration clauses. The test in *OK Petroleum AB v Vitol Energy SA* and in *Siboti K/S v BP France SA* was whether the clause to be incorporated was ancillary.[87] If so, it is not germane. In *Vitol*, a time bar was not incorporated by general words, Colman J observing that the reason that arbitration clauses are not germane is that they are:[88]

---

79 Which, of course, the holder of the bill of lading may never have seen.

80 *The Merak* [1965] P 223. There was some support for this approach in *The Portsmouth* itself. *The Merak* had unusual features, however, and should not be seen as a general authority: see further [2014] JBL 407, 419.

81 *The Varenna* [1984] 1 QB 599, and see also the explanation in *Siboti K/S v BP France SA* [2003] 2 Lloyd's Rep 364, [26].

82 *The Merak* was explained in *The Varenna* as depending on a very wide bill of lading incorporation clause: all "terms, conditions, clauses and exceptions" whereas *The Varenna* incorporated only "conditions and exceptions". In *The Federal Bulker* all "terms, conditions, and exceptions" were incorporated, but *The Varenna* was followed, suggesting that if *The Merak* is correct, the distinguishing feature is the word "clauses". For another (probably preferable) explanation of *The Merak*, see *Caresse Navigation Ltd v Office National de l'Electricité (The Channel Ranger)* [2015] QB 366, [32]–[39].

83 [1936] P 90.

84 Respectively [1976] 1 Lloyd's Rep 8; [2012] 1 Lloyd's Rep 304.

85 *KH Enterprise (cargo owners) v Pioneer Container (owners) (The Pioneer Container)* [1994] 2 AC 324. (The case should perhaps be treated with caution, as the issues were not quite the same as for incorporation of charterparty terms into a bill of lading; that in *The Pioneer Container* was instead the scope of authority to sub-contract the carriage "on any terms": see section [17.4].)

86 *Aughton Ltd v MF Kent Services Ltd* (1991) 57 Build LR 1 (Sir John Megaw, but note that Ralph Gibson LJ did not single out arbitration clauses for special treatment).

87 Respectively [1995] 2 Lloyd's Rep 160; [2003] 2 Lloyd's Rep 364.

88 [1995] 2 Lloyd's Rep 160, 165, Colman J here applying the germaneness test to an international sale contract, rather than a bill of lading.

"no more than a contractual facility for dispute resolution and therefore merely ancillary to the carriage and delivery of the goods under the charter-party".

That reasoning would also apply to a time bar, and an exclusive jurisdiction clause. In *Siboti*, an exclusive jurisdiction clause was not regarded as germane.[89]

The San Nicholas was however followed in respect of a proper law clause in *The Dolphina*,[90] where (as Ang Saw Ean J observed), the charterparty and bill of lading:

". . . related to the same voyage by the same carrier also meant that it made good commercial sense for its rights and obligations as carrier against the original and any later holder of the bill of lading to be, as far as possible, the same as its rights and obligations against the charterer".

Interestingly, this is essentially the same distinction as that made in *The Epsilon Rosa*,[91] and this may perhaps become a fruitful distinction in future cases.[92]

In summary, the authorities suggest that choice of law is treated differently from arbitration.[93] For exclusive jurisdiction clauses and time bars, whether *Siboti* is correct, and whether *Vitol* would apply in a bill of lading context, are issues on which the authority is not weighty, though, for the time being, we should probably regard neither as germane.

For completeness, we should remember that any clause, including an arbitration clause, can be incorporated by express words of incorporation.[94] The germaneness test applies only to general words.

15.2.5 Manipulation

If the charterparty terms are written directly into the bill of lading, they may not fit exactly, talking about rights and duties of charterers, for example, rather than cargo-owners. To what extent is it permissible for the courts to "manipulate" the incorporated clauses to fit into the bill of lading?

For incorporation generally, the courts will manipulate the incorporated clause. In *Adamastos Shipping Co Ltd v Anglo-Saxon Petroleum Co Ltd*,[95] the House of Lords had held that where the Hague Rules from US COGSA 1936 were incorporated into a consecutive voyage charter, references to "This bill of lading . . ." should be read as if they were "This charterparty . . ."; and that the words in US COGSA, "The provisions of the Act shall not be applicable to charterparties", must be rejected as being meaningless. As Viscount Simonds said:[96]

"I cannot attribute to either party an intention to incorporate a provision which would nullify the total incorporation."

---

89 If correct, this casts doubt on the applicability in this context of *The Pioneer Container*.

90 [2012] 1 Lloyd's Rep 304.

91 See section [15.2.3].

92 It has however been argued (with some force, in this context) that there is no obvious principle behind the distinction drawn in *The Dolphina*: [2012] LMCLQ 481.

93 Also *Caresse Navigation Ltd v Office National de l'Electricite (The Channel Ranger)* [2014] 1 Lloyd's Rep 337, affd other grounds [2015] QB 366, applying *The Njegos* and *The San Nicholas*.

94 Eg, *Golden Endurance Shipping SA v RMA Watanya SA (The Golden Endurance)* [2015] 1 Lloyd's Rep 266; *The Channel Ranger* [2015] QB 366, in the latter of which express incorporation of the "law and arbitration clause" was held apposite to incorporate the law and jurisdiction clause, there being no law and arbitration clause in the charterparty.

95 [1959] AC 133. See also section [18.9].

96 [1959] AC 133, 154.

It made no sense to incorporate the Hague Rules, but then to interpret them so as to deny them any effect in the charterparty.

In *The Annefield*, Lord Denning MR would not have been prepared to manipulate an arbitration clause, incorporated from a charterparty into a bill of lading, so that it applied to disputes under the bill of lading, though the issue did not arise directly; the clause (not being germane) would not have been incorporated in any event, by general words of incorporation. However, he also said that:[97]

". . . a clause which is directly germane to the subject-matter of the bill of lading (that is, to the shipment, carriage and delivery of goods) can and should be incorporated into the bill of lading contract, even though it may involve a degree of manipulation of the words in order to fit exactly the bill of lading".

On this basis, for example, a demurrage provision, incorporated into a bill of lading by general words, can and should be manipulated to fit. Of course this is *obiter dicta*, since *The Annefield* was not concerned with such a clause.

Caution was sounded in the House of Lords in *The Miramar*,[98] though the decision itself is relatively narrow in its scope. Charterparty terms were incorporated into the bill of lading by general words of incorporation, which of course, were effective to incorporate the demurrage clause. However, the charterparty clause imposed obligations only on the "charterer", and the issue was whether, when incorporated into the bill of lading, the words "consignee of the cargo" or "bill of lading holder" could be substituted – since obviously otherwise the clause would be ineffective in the bill of lading contract.

The House considered that, as a matter of construction, only the charterers were intended to be liable. It would have been absurd to extend liability to consignees or bills of lading holders, and therefore this cannot have been intended. Laytime was combined for loading and discharge, and the bill of lading related only to part of the cargo on the vessel. Liability for demurrage could however continue until all the cargo had been discharged, not just the cargo described in the bill of lading; in other words, it could continue to accrue, even after all the consignee's cargo had been discharged. As Lord Diplock observed, if the clause were to be manipulated as the shipowners contended:[99]

". . . every consignee to whom a bill of lading covering any part of the cargo is negotiated, is . . . accepting blindfold a potential liability to pay an unknown and wholly unpredictable sum for demurrage which may, unknown to him, already have accrued or may subsequently accrue without any ability on his own part to prevent it, even though that sum may actually exceed the delivered value of the goods to which the bill of lading gives title".

He continued:

"My Lords, I venture to assert that no business man who had not taken leave of his senses would intentionally enter into a contract which exposed him to a potential liability of this kind; and this, in itself, I find to be an overwhelming reason for not indulging in verbal manipulation of the actual contractual words used in the charter-party so as to give to them this effect when they are treated as incorporated in the bill of lading."

---

97 [1971] 1 Lloyd's Rep 1, 4.

98 *Miramar Maritime Corporation v Holborn Oil Trading Ltd* [1984] AC 676.

99 [1984] AC 676, 685.

It is difficult to disagree with this observation, but of course it applies only to the particular situation under consideration. On manipulation generally, Lord Diplock said only that:[100]

> "I regard it [as] important that this House should take this opportunity of stating unequivocally that, where in a bill of lading there is included a clause which purports to incorporate the terms of a specified charter-party, there is not any rule of construction that clauses in that charter-party which are directly germane to the shipment, carriage or delivery of goods and impose obligations upon the 'charterer' under that designation, are presumed to be incorporated in the bill of lading with the substitution of (where there is a cesser clause), or inclusion in (where there is no cesser clause), the designation 'charterer,' the designation 'consignee of the cargo' or "bill of lading holder'."

Notice the negative form of this rule, that there is no rule requiring manipulation. *The Miramar* is not really authority for the proposition that there should never be manipulation, even where incorporation is by general words. However, it has been treated as such. For example, Evans J (at first instance) in *The Federal Bulker* said that:[101]

> "... the scope for what has been called manipulation of the wording of the charterparty clause, if and when it is found to be incorporated in the bill of lading, is extremely limited if it exists at all. In *The Miramar* the House of Lords said, in terms, that no manipulation is possible."

This is not an accurate description of what Lord Diplock said in *The Miramar*, and, when *The Federal Bulker* reached the Court of Appeal,[102] there was no direct mention of *The Miramar*. The "manipulation" issue did not arise directly because, of course, an arbitration clause cannot be incorporated by general words, and *The Federal Bulker* concerned general words of incorporation.

However, a wide view of *The Miramar* has found less favour recently. In *The Eems Solar*, a FIOST clause in a charterparty relieving the shipowner from responsibility for cargo-handling was held not to require manipulation in a bill of lading context, even though it imposed liability only on the charterers, not shippers or consignees. (The only issue was whether the owners were relieved of responsibility, and the clause did that, without any need for manipulation.) In *The Dolphina*, the charterparty clause stated:[103]

"THIS CP TO BE GOVERNED BY ENGLISH LAW"

Nevertheless it was held to govern the bill of lading into which it had been incorporated by general words of incorporation, *The Miramar* being distinguished (since clearly the clause required manipulation). A much more restrictive view was taken of *The Miramar*, than had been taken at first instance in *The Federal Bulker*:[104]

> "... the House of Lords [in *The Miramar*] refused to 'verbally manipulate' the term 'charterer' so as to substitute or include the term 'bill of lading holder' because to do so would result in a change in pre-existing and agreed contractual liabilities, by transferring the obligation to

100 [1984] AC 676, 688.

101 QBD, 18 Dec 1987.

102 [1989] 1 Lloyd's Rep 103.

103 Of ancillary clauses the issue is only likely to arise with choice of law, since other ancillary clauses are probably not incorporated by general words anyway. By contrast, in *The San Nicholas*, the clause stated: "[t]his Contract shall be governed by the laws of England". Arguably, therefore, no manipulation was required – though see the above remarks on *The Federal Bulker*.

104 [2012] 1 Lloyd's Rep 304, [130].

pay demurrage from the charterer to the consignee when the obligation to pay demurrage was, on the facts of *The Miramar*, the charterer's alone."

By contrast, manipulating the proper law clause in *The Dolphina*:[105]

"... would result in no such alteration of the parties' pre-existing contractual obligations; it simply enabled those obligations to be understood and given effect to".

This is another possible limit to *The Miramar*, which would, however, seem to apply to any ancillary clause. But remember that in the earlier case Lord Diplock said only that:

"... there is not any rule of construction that clauses in that charterparty which are directly germane to the shipment, carriage or delivery of goods ...".

and which are incorporated by general words should be manipulated. He did not necessarily adopt the reverse rule of construction.

By contrast, if an arbitration clause covering disputes under the charterparty is expressly incorporated, the words will be "manipulated" so as to cover disputes under the bill of lading. There was a conflict of first instance authority, which was resolved by the Court of Appeal in *The Nerano*.[106]

15.3 Question

Apollo purchases 30,000 tons of coffee from Darius, on FOB terms, under which he (Apollo) undertakes to make the carriage contract. In fact, Apollo has already chartered *The Aroma* for the voyage (from South America to London). Demurrage rate is £20,000 per day, "payable by the charterer".

The Aroma is already on charter, however, so Apollo's charter is a sub-charter. The head charter (for the same voyage) is oral (though contemplating a Gencon standard form), and freight, laytime and demurrage have been orally agreed. Under the head charter, the demurrage rate is £30,000 per day, also "payable by the charterer".

Darius ships the coffee, and takes a bill of lading to his own order. The bill of lading (which the master has signed on behalf of the owner under the head charter) provides:

"demurrage as per charterparty between ... and ... dated ..." (the blanks are not filled in).

Darius agrees that the ship can call *en route* to Portugal, but the liberty to deviate is not included in the bill of lading, or in either of the two charterparties. The bill of lading is later delivered to Apollo, and indorsed in his favour.

Advise Apollo as to his demurrage liability, if any.

Would your view have been different had the sale contract been on CIF terms, with Darius, rather than Apollo, chartering the vessel for the voyage?

Would your view have been different, had the bill of lading incorporated "all terms and conditions as per charterparty between ... and ... dated ..."?

---

105 Ibid.

106 *Daval Aciers D'Usinor et de Sacilor v Armare SRL (The Nerano)* [1996] 1 Lloyd's Rep 1, applying *The Rena K* [1978] 1 Lloyd's Rep 545 and not following *The Nai Matteini* [1988] 1 Lloyd's Rep 452.

Comment

This question covers quite a bit of the material in this chapter, but I think you will be able to form a view, by reading the chapter closely. For each of the alternative facts situations, you will need to consider at least:

whether the contract is on bill of lading or charterparty terms;
if on bill of lading terms, which charterparty terms are incorporated;
whether the terms can be "manipulated";
the relevance (if any) of the oral agreement.

Chapter 16

Carriage of Goods by Sea
Act 1992 (and related issues)

This chapter and the next deal with privity of contract issues, that is to say who are the parties to a bill of lading contract, and the extent to which non-parties can be affected. This chapter is devoted to the Carriage of Goods by Sea Act 1992,[1] the smooth operation of which is essential to the viability of a bill of lading as a negotiable document. In the next chapter we consider the identity of the contracting carrier, Himalaya clauses and related devices, and other privity aspects, unrelated to the 1992 Act.

Time charterparty privity issues have already been dealt with in chapter 10.[2]

16.1 Background

The Carriage of Goods by Sea Act 1992 transfers the benefits, and sometimes the burdens, of carriage contracts when the bill of lading, or occasionally other document, is transferred. It is essential to the operation of modern international trade, in the sense that the transactions would have to be quite different, if it did not exist.

The 1992 Act is Parliament's second attempt to effect this transfer, as it replaced the Bills of Lading Act of almost 140 years before. That Act, of 1855, was prompted by changes in the nature of international trade, with which the common law had not kept pace.

By 1855, maritime trade had evolved to the stage when transferring carriage contracts had become necessary. While in the early days of international trade communication difficulties usually demanded that the buyer take responsibility for carriage, by the middle of the nineteenth century sellers desired to make carriage contracts, as principals and not merely as agents for the buyers. If the seller is not the contractual shipper, he cannot demand a bill of lading in his own right, to use as security against payment, even if he has the mate's receipt.[3] The ultimate consequence of this development was the CIF (cost insurance freight) contract by which, today, the majority of the world's tonnage is still shipped.[4] (The CIF contract also allows for the possibility of sales of goods afloat.[5] Today, it is common to see very long chains of sales of the same goods while they are at sea, and some of the problems of this will be examined in chapter 22.)[6]

The problem with the CIF contract, in particular, is that if the buyer is required (as a CIF buyer is) to pay against tender of a bill of lading, in order to take delivery, and to bear the risk of loss or damage after shipment, then if anything happens to the goods on the voyage, it is the buyer, rather than the seller, who will wish to sue the shipowner. But on what basis, if the carriage contract has been made by the seller, and the buyer has no contract with the carrier? This is the problem that was addressed, ultimately, by the Carriage of Goods by Sea Act 1992,[7] which can transfer rights of action in the circumstances set out in this section.

This is a diagrammatic representation of the Carriage of Goods by Sea Act 1992. You can see that the only express carriage contract is with the seller as shipper. Any carriage contract with the buyer is on the basis of the 1992 Act. Indeed, the whole purpose of the 1992 Act is to create this contractual relationship.

---

1 Other than s. 4, on representations, which is covered in section [19.9].

2 Section [10.6].

3 Eg, *Cowas-Jee v Thompson* (1845) 3 Moore Ind App 422; cf. *Ruck v Hatfield* (1822) 5 B & A 632, an unusual case that was distinguished in *Cowas-Jee*.

4 The first reported CIF case was *Tregelles v Sewell* (1862) 7 H & N 574, shortly after the 1855 Act. Probably the CIF contract, at any rate in its present form, depended on the legislation.

5 Eg, *Vantol v Fairclough* [1955] 1 WLR 642, 646, appealed [1957] 1 WLR 136; *Pyke v Cornelius* [1955] 2 Lloyd's Rep 747, 751; *Zijden v Tucker* [1975] 2 Lloyd's Rep 240, 242; *Tradax v Andre* [1976] 1 Lloyd's Rep 416, 423. These cases revolve around whether the contract was impossible to perform, if the CIF seller could have purchased afloat.

6 Section [22.2].

7 Replacing the earlier Bills of Lading Act 1855, s. 1.

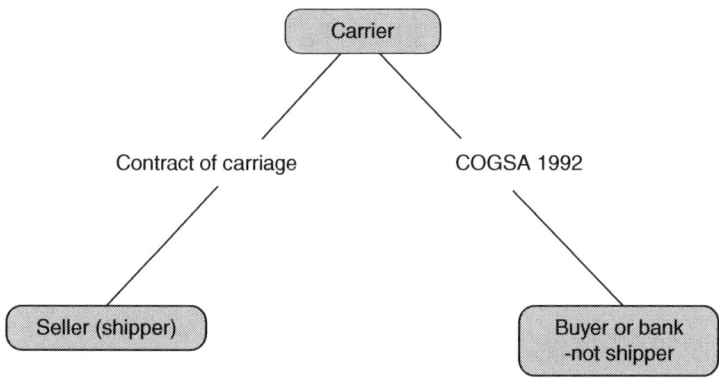

A further twist came, historically, with the use of bills of lading to create pledges, and ultimately with the development of the modern documentary credit about 100 years ago.[8] The bank takes the bill of lading as security for an advance, or, in the case of documentary credit, for payment. Clearly his security will be affected by the loss of, or damage to the goods while they are at sea. But just like a CIF buyer, the bank has no contract with the ship, and would also wish to rely on a statutory contract. Banks can also acquire rights to sue under the Carriage of Goods by Sea Act 1992.

Nor by any means are carriers necessarily opposed to the imposition of a statutory contract. If the carriage contract provides for freight on delivery, or demurrage is incurred at discharge, it is often more convenient for the receiver to pay it. It may even be that a CIF (or possibly FOB) seller has chartered the vessel,[9] and that there is a cesser clause in the charterparty, requiring the ship-owner to proceed against the receiver, rather than the charterer.[10] But, in such a case, the receiver is not expressly party to a contract of carriage. Again, the Carriage of Goods by Sea Act 1992 helps, this time by imposing liabilities on receivers.[11] Moreover, carriers would not willingly carry cargo if they thought that the excepted perils, package limitation and time bar in the bill of lading would not protect them. Since the Hague or Hague-Visby Rules operate only by incorporation into contracts of carriage, their time limits, limits to liability and excepted perils only protect the carrier, if there is a contractual relationship between himself and the cargo-owner.[12] It follows that if a CIF buyer can sue in tort, he will avoid the bill of lading exceptions unless there is contract between buyer and carrier.[13] The 1992 Act provides such a contract, and buyers are therefore prevented from avoiding the Hague or Hague-Visby Rules by suing in tort.[14]

---

8 Eg, Todd, *Bills of Lading and Bankers' Documentary Credits*, 4th ed (2007), Informa, ch. 1.

9 It is probably more usual for FOB buyers, rather than sellers, to be contractual shippers, but for the flexibility of the FOB term see *Scottish & Newcastle International Ltd v Othon Ghalanos Ltd* [2008] 1 Lloyd's Rep 462, [34] (Lord Mance).

10 The cesser clause, which was commonly used in the nineteenth century, appears to be uncommon today, and is to be found in none of the major standard form charterparties. Presumably shipowners are unwilling to agree to them. See further on cesser section [7.9].

11 For instances of cases where the shipowner claimed freight other than from the original shipper, see (eg) *K/S A/S Seateam & Co v Iraq National Oil Co (The Sevonia Team)* [1983] 2 Lloyd's Rep 640 (where the action was successful) and *Sewell v Burdick* (1884) 10 App Cas 74 (where it was not). Both these cases are on the earlier legislation, the Bills of Lading Act 1855, s. 1, which was replaced by the Carriage of Goods by Sea Act 1992.

12 Ratio of *Compania Portorafti Commerciale SA v Ultramar Panama Inc (The Captain Gregos)* [1990] 1 Lloyd's Rep 310.

13 See further section [16.10] for tort actions.

14 *The Captain Gregos* [1990] 1 Lloyd's Rep 310 involved avoidance of a time bar. The reasoning would apply equally to excepted perils, package limitation, etc. Conversely, the (other) claimant who had a contract with the carrier was bound. See further sections [16.9] and [16.10] below.

16.2 Was legislation really necessary?

Accepting that sellers often wish, or in the case of resales need, to contact with the carrier as principal, it would still have been possible to resolve the privity issue, without the intervention of Parliament, by a term requiring sellers to sue on the buyers' behalf,[15] or by requiring sellers to assign contractual actions to buyers.[16] A document assigning contractual rights could perhaps have become a required shipping document, much as is the case anyway, with an assignable policy of marine insurance. Assignments work only for rights, though, not liabilities, but even in the nineteenth century, carriers were able to some extent to use implied contracts to resolve this issue, at any rate where the cargo was delivered.[17] As it turned out, none of these devices was necessary, as s. 1 of the Bills of Lading Act 1855 transferred rights of suit, and liabilities, to consignees and indorsees along with property. This allowed for the development of the CIF contract in its modern form[18] but, even in the absence of legislation, it should have been possible, though inconvenient, to develop something functionally similar.

By 1992, the 1855 Act had become seriously outdated. Much of the problem revolved around its dependence on the passing of property,[19] the complexities of which had not become apparent by 1855.

16.3 History prior to 1992

In chapter 20 we will see that, even before the nineteenth century began, the shipped bill of lading was recognised as a document of title at common law, and it had been held that transfer of the bill of lading might, by custom of merchants, also transfer the property in the goods.[20] This development was a major part of the process culminating in giving the bill of lading the delivery function it enjoys today.[21] The courts could perhaps have developed this idea further, to hold that transfer of the bill of lading could also transfer contractual rights and liabilities, but in the Exchequer decision of Thompson v Dominy,[22] the plaintiff indorsees for value of a bill of lading failed in an action against the carrier for alleged short delivery, on the grounds that the transfer of a bill of lading does not enable the transferee to bring an action in his own name on the carriage contract, at any rate as a matter of law. Thompson v Dominy decided, in effect, that just because the transfer of the bill of lading could transfer property, it did not follow that it could also transfer the contract.

Even in the early nineteenth century, it was possible for contracts on the terms of the bill of lading to be inferred, as a matter of fact, from the presentation by the consignee of the bill of lading and the delivery of the goods to him by the carrier.[23] This is still the position at common law. But such contracts could not (and cannot) always be inferred,[24] and it was to avoid this problem that the 1855 legislation (precursor to the current 1992 Act) was enacted. The effect of s. 1 was to reverse Thompson v Dominy: prior to 1855, it did not follow that because a bill of lading transferred property

---

15 The House of Lords having allowed the possibility of substantial damages in Dunlop v Lambert (1839) 6 Cl & F 600, discussed in section [16.11].

16 As suggested in Leigh and Sillivan Ltd v Aliakmon Shipping Co Ltd (The Aliakmon) [1986] AC 785, 819 (Lord Brandon).

17 Eg, Stindt v Roberts (1848) 5 D & L 460; Allen v Coltart & Co (1883) 11 QBD 782. This development later matured into the Brandt v Liverpool doctrine considered in section [16.9].

18 The first reported CIF case was Tregelles v Sewell (1862) 7 H & N 574, shortly after the 1855 Act.

19 Eg, Enichem Anic SpA v Ampelos Shipping Co Ltd (The Delfini) [1990] 1 Lloyd's Rep 252.

20 Lickbarrow v Mason (1787) 5 TR 63; see also section [20.3].

21 See generally chapter 20.

22 (1845) 14 M and W 403. See also Sewell v Burdick (1884) 10 App Cas 74, 91 (Lord Blackburn).

23 Eg, Stindt v Roberts (1848) 5 D & L 460. On new implied contracts, depending on factual inferences, see below, section [16.9].

24 See in particular The Aramis [1989] 1 Lloyd's Rep 213, discussed in section [16.9].

it also transferred the contract; after 1855, it did. But that is all the Act did. It depended on property passing, and on a literal interpretation, also on the timing of its passing, and on the causal connection between the passing of property and either consignment or indorsement.

On the understanding of the passing of property in 1855, the Act no doubt did what was intended. It must have been assumed that where a consignee was named, or a negotiable bill was made out to the order of the consignee, property would pass upon or by reason of consignment, but that where the bill of lading was taken out to the seller's order, it would pass upon or by reason of indorsement. Parliament had not foreseen, in 1855, sales of parts of undivided bulk cargoes, where risk still passed though property did not.[25] Nor could it have foreseen the increased use of bills of lading to pledge property to banks, and the eventual widespread use of documentary credits, where the bank's special property as pledgee was not sufficient to trigger the operation of the Act.[26] Equally unforeseen was the use of waybills and other documentation to which the custom of merchants in 1855 did not apply,[27] and the lengthy chain sales leading to bills of lading being delivered and indorsed long after rather cargo had been delivered, paid for, and perhaps consumed.[28] In short, through no fault of Parliament in 1855, by 1992 the 1855 Act no longer performed its original function very well. Following a joint report of the English and Scottish Law Commissions,[29] it was replaced by the Carriage of Goods by Sea Act 1992.

The 1855 Act is now of historical interest only, but, since the 1992 Act was a reaction to its perceived defects, we should note that there were three main problems with the 1855 Act:

1.   the documentation was limited to the shipped bill of lading;
2.   property did not pass at all, or it passed at the wrong time, or for the wrong reason, to trigger the section;
3.   the law required to determine (2) was very complex.

The Carriage of Goods by Sea Act 1992 dealt with the first by increasing the range of documents covered, in s. 1, to include:[30]

-    received for shipment bills;
-    ship's delivery orders;
-    straight bills and waybills (these are treated as the same);
-    electronic documentation possibilities (in s. 1(5)).

The other main problem with the 1855 Act was its dependence on the passing of property. In later years, moreover, it became clear that the issue was not just whether property had passed, but also the timing of and reasons for its passing. The courts in later years interpreted the Act literally: if the bill of lading named a consignee property had to pass upon or by reason of consignment;

---

25 Eg, *Inglis v Stock* (1885) 10 App Cas 263, where property in unascertained goods (part of an undivided bulk) could not pass. The rule regarding property in unascertained goods was later codified in s. 16 of the Sale of Goods Act 1893 and 1979, which remained good law until the changes made by the Sale of Goods (Amendment) Act 1995. See further generally Todd, *Cases and Materials on International Trade Law* (2002), Sweet & Maxwell, [5–080].

26 *Sewell v Burdick* (1884) 10 App Cas 74 (bank incurred no liability as pledgee).

27 It probably applied only to the shipped bill of lading: *Diamond Alkali Export Corp v Fl Bourgeois* [1921] 3 KB 443. For a fuller discussion on waybills and other alternative documentation, see section [21.2].

28 Eg, *The Delfini* [1990] 1 Lloyd's Rep 252.

29 *Rights of Suit in Respect of Carriage of Goods by Sea* (Law Com No. 196; Scot Law Com No. 130 (1991)). A helpful consequence of this being a report also of the Scottish Law Commission is that, despite its age, it can be freely obtained from the Internet: www.scotlawcom.gov.uk/download_file/view/267/.

30 The statute is set out in its entirety in Appendix B.

if it was taken out to seller's order it had to pass upon or by reason of indorsement.[31] Quite apart from the fact that this did not always happen, another issue was the related complexity. As the Law Commission and Scottish Law Commission commented in their joint report, precisely when property passed was by no means an easy issue to determine.[32] To the objection that the law was overly complex, the response should be to enable whoever "has acquired a right of delivery against the carrier" to sue.[33] The objective addressed here is simplicity, and it was met by extending rights to sue to "lawful holders" under s. 2(1) of the 1992 Act – regardless of the passing of property. Thus the intricacies of passing of property are no longer an issue. However, whether the simplicity objective has been met is debatable, for (though the issues were probably unforeseen in 1992) recent cases suggest that the identity of "lawful holders" is far from self-evident.[34]

16.4 1992 Act in outline

The documentary requirements have already been outlined. A point to note, however, is that the definition of a "bill of lading" in s. 1(2):

> "(a) [does] not include references to a document which is incapable of transfer either by indorsement or, as a bearer bill, by delivery without indorsement; but
> (b) subject to that, [does] include references to a received for shipment bill of lading."

Thus, s. 1(2)(b) explicitly includes the received for shipment bill.

The effect of s. 1(2)(a) is to exclude straight bills of lading, since they are not transferred by indorsement or delivery alone. The straight bill would, however, fall within the definition of a waybill in s. 1(3). Waybills are brought within the 1992 Act, but because the transfer of a waybill has no legal consequence, the Act works differently for waybills than for bills of lading.[35]

Continuing in outline, rights and liabilities are passed, separately, under ss. 2 and 3 of the 1992 Act. We will examine the operation of s. 2 below.[36] In essence, though, it transfers rights of suit to:

(a)   lawful holders of negotiable bills of lading;
(b)   named consignees in waybills and straight bills of lading, whether they become holders or not;
(c)   persons to whom delivery is to be made under a ship's delivery order, again whether they become holders or not.[37]

In none of these cases does the passing of property any longer have any role to play; the key (for negotiable bills) is to be the lawful holder. As we will see, the lawful holder is defined in s. 5(2). It was probably thought, in 1992, to be a straightforward definition, but we will see that recent cases cast doubt on what has turned out to be a complacent assumption.[38]

---

31   The high point of literalism was *The Delfini* [1990] 1 Lloyd's Rep 252, but see also *Hispanica de Petroleos SA v West of England Ship Owners Mutual P & I Association (Luxembourg) (The Kapetan Markos NL) (No. 2)* [1987] 2 Lloyd's Rep 321. In both cases property passed too early. Cf. the cases cited in section [16.8], where the courts adopted a purposive construction. But it is the cases here that eventually prevailed.

32   Law Com No. 196, [2.9].

33   Law Com No. 196, [2.22].

34   See section [16.7.2].

35   See further section [16.7].

36   Section [16.7].

37   For delivery orders, see section [21.2].

38   See section [16.7.2].

We will examine liabilities in detail below, but one of the problems with the 1855 Act was that whenever rights were transferred, so were liabilities. The 1992 legislation recognises that it is not always fair to transfer liabilities, whenever rights of suit are transferred. By way of example, it is possible to acquire rights merely by being named as consignee in a waybill or straight bill of lading.[39] It was felt unreasonable to impose liabilities on someone who may have acquired rights without any choice on his part. It is another matter, of course, if he has taken advantage of the rights conferred by the document, or of the rights conferred by the 1992 Act. In those cases it is reasonable also to impose liabilities. Liabilities are imposed by s. 3 of the 1992 Act.[40]

Section 2(5) (at least for a negotiable bill) divests the rights under the carriage contract, of shippers and intermediate holders, once the rights have been transferred, though of course there is nothing to stop shippers and intermediate holders acquiring rights subsequently, for example if they are later purchasers in a chain,[41] or if the goods are rejected by their purchaser, and the bill of lading returned (and reindorsed) to them.[42] In respect of liabilities, however, there is no equivalent of s. 2(5). The shipper retains his original liability (rightly because the solvency of a later holder may be an issue). It has been held that intermediate holders are divested of liabilities on redelivery and/or reindorsement, whether or not the subsequent holder himself becomes liable under s. 3.[43]

We also need to consider the transfer of bills after they have become spent (in other words, where they are transferred after the goods have been delivered or destroyed).[44] This can be quite a problem with long chains and short voyages. The position under the 1855 Act was never clarified, though in *The Delfini* Phillips J (at first instance) regarded as a main ground for not applying the 1855 Act, that on completion of discharge "the contract of carriage was discharged and the bill of lading ceased to be effective as a transferable document of title".[45] When the case reached the Court of Appeal, it was decided solely on property issues, so Phillips J's view was not tested. The Law Commissions were keen not to exclude transfers simply on the grounds that the bills were spent when negotiated, but also wished to discourage "trafficking in bills of lading simply as pieces of paper which give causes of action against sea carriers".[46] The resulting provisions, which might also be thought to be quite straightforward, have given rise to a greater degree of complexity than was probably expected.[47]

16.5 Negotiable bills and waybills

One of the problems of the 1855 Act was the limited range of documents to which it applied, perhaps reflecting the documents that were in use at that time. By 1992, for the reasons considered in chapter 21, waybills and multimodal transport documents were in common use.[48] Waybills are explicitly provided for in s. 1(3). A multimodal transport document, if negotiable, might

---

39 Section 2(1)(b).

40 See generally section [16.8].

41 Thereby converting the chain into a circle, as in (eg) *Concordia Trading BV v Richco International Ltd* [1991] 1 Lloyd's Rep 475.

42 Section 2(5) does not apply in the same way to waybills: section [16.5]. Note also that charterparty rights are not divested: see further section [16.11].

43 See the discussion of *The Berge Sisar* in section [16.8], below.

44 The terms "stale" and "exhausted" are also used. Each of the three terms appears to have the same meaning.

45 *The Delfini* [1988] 2 Lloyd's Rep 599, 609; affd on other grounds [1990] 1 Lloyd's Rep 252.

46 Law Com No. 196, [2.43].

47 *The Ythan* [2006] 1 Lloyd's Rep 457 and *Standard Chartered Bank v Dorchester LNG (2) Ltd (The Erin Schulte)* [2015] 1 Lloyd's Rep 97 both concerned interpretations (among other things) of s. 2(2)(a). Both these cases are discussed in detail in sections [16.7.2] and [16.7.3].

48 Section [21.2].

(depending on the circumstances of its issue) come within the Act as a received for shipment bill of lading;[49] if not, it might be regarded as a species of waybill. Straight bills of lading are not provided for as such. They are outside the definition of a bill of lading, but for the purposes of the Act are treated as waybills.

For a negotiable bill of lading it makes sense to transfer rights to lawful holders, and indeed this is precisely what s. 2(1)(a) does. Transfer of a waybill has no legal consequences, however, and so rights are transferred to the consignee, simply by virtue of his being named as consignee. Thus, rights under s. 2(1)(b) are transferred to:

> "(b) the person who (without being an original party to the contract of carriage) is the person to whom delivery of the goods to which the sea waybill relates is to be made by the carrier in accordance with the contract . . . ".

There is no need for a physical transfer, or for the consignee to become lawful holder.[50] However, while this makes perfect sense for a waybill, it makes less sense for a straight bill of lading, at any rate if The Rafaela S is authority for the proposition that the consignee needs to present the bill to obtain delivery.[51] If that interpretation is correct, transfer of a straight bill of lading does have legal consequences, and it would have been better for them not to come within s. 2(1)(b).

Another difference is in the application of s. 2(5), which divests shippers of their contractual rights.[52] This would not be appropriate for a waybill, where a shipper would expect to have a right of redirection, and so s. 2(5) only operates:[53]

> " . . . without prejudice to any rights which derive from a person's having been an original party to the contract contained in, or evidenced by, a sea waybill . . . ".

16.6 Delivery orders

Where cargo is sold in bulk, there will often be a number of buyers. If the identity of all buyers is known from the outset, then bills of lading can be issued for the amounts due to each buyer. If there are later sub-sales, this is not possible, and the best that can be issued is a delivery order, ordering the carrier to deliver the specified amount to the holder of the document.

A delivery order issued by a seller of part of a bulk, to a carrier, where the carrier himself has neither attorned, nor otherwise undertaken to deliver the cargo to the holder of the document, gives no rights against the carrier, and that has not been altered by COGSA 92. If, however, the carrier undertakes to deliver to the holder of the document, this becomes a ship's delivery order. Before 1992, even a ship's delivery order, falling as it did outside the 1855 Act, gave the purchaser virtually nothing of value, but now ship's delivery order is brought within the 1992 Act, and can transfer contractual rights to buyers in this situation. The ship's delivery order is defined in s. 2(4), the important point being that the carrier undertakes to deliver the cargo to which the document relates, to the person identified in the document.

---

49 For which provision is made in s. 1(2)(b) of the 1992 Act.

50 Cf. for a "consignee or order" bill, where he must become holder, requiring only possession, by virtue of s. 5(2)(a).

51 JI MacWilliam Company Inc v Mediterranean Shipping Co SA (The Rafaela S) [2005] 2 AC 423, in section [14.6.1].

52 See section [16.4].

53 A waybill names a consignee and is not made out to order. In East West Corpn v DKBS AF 1912 A/S [2003] QB 1509 the goods were consigned to the order of named consignees. These were not waybills, and shippers' contractual rights were divested by s. 2(5): see further section [16.7.1].

Section 2(1)(c) of the 1992 Act transfers rights, where there is a delivery order to:

> "(c) the person to whom delivery of the goods to which a ship's delivery order relates is to be made in accordance with the undertaking contained in the order."

As with a waybill, there is no requirement that the person becomes holder, the assumption being that the delivery order need not necessarily be transferred for it to be effective. By s. 2(3), rights transferred are confined to "the goods to which the order relates", and s. 3(2) does the same in respect of liabilities. This is because the document will usually mention the bulk as a whole, whereas rights and liabilities should obviously be confined to that part of the bulk to which the document relates.

Partly because of the 1992 Act,[54] a ship's delivery order can provide the person identified in it security that is really as good as a traditional bill of lading.[55]

16.7 Holders, possession and spent bills

Whatever the position for waybills, straight bills and ship's delivery orders, for a negotiable bill of lading s. 2(1)(a) transfers rights only to lawful holders. It follows that identification of the lawful holder is key to the operation s. 2, and, since (as we will see) liabilities are imposed by s. 3, only where the cargo-owner comes within s. 2, it is key to the operation of s. 3 also, at any rate where a negotiable bill of lading is used. Identification of holder turns out to be an issue of some complexity.

16.7.1 Definition of holder: requirement for possession

The holder, and lawful holder, are defined in s. 5(2), and for normal use of a negotiable bill we should begin with s. 5(2)(b):

> "(2) References in this Act to the holder of a bill of lading are references to any of the following persons, that is to say —
>
> . . .
>
> (b) a person with possession of the bill as a result of the completion, by delivery of the bill, of any indorsement of the bill or, in the case of a bearer bill, of any other transfer of the bill;
>
> . . . ".

We can observe that the holder must, at the very least, be in possession of the bill. This might be thought to be a relatively simple concept, but merely to have physical custody is not necessarily to be in possession. Usually it will be, but one person can have custody on behalf of someone else. So it is not enough to enquire simply where the bill of lading is, physically.

We will see in chapter 20 that, at common law, the courts have apparently been prepared to accept that custody can be on behalf of someone else. In *The Aliakmon*,[56] C & F purchasers of a cargo of steel, which had been damaged on the voyage, sued the shipowners in contract.[57] The sale contract was rather unusual. It was renegotiated when the buyers failed to pay on tender of documents. Under the renegotiated contract, the buyers were allowed to retain the bills of lading, but the contract also

---

54 Also the changes to passing of property in undivided bulks made by the Sale of Goods (Amendment) Act 1995.
55 See further chapter 20 in respect of delivery.
56 *Leigh and Sillavan Ltd v Aliakmon Shipping Co Ltd (The Aliakmon)* [1986] AC 785.
57 The contract claim went as high only as the CA: [1985] QB 350. The HL considered only a tort action: see section [16.10].

contained an express reservation of title clause. By the time the cargo was damaged, the buyers had still not paid for it, and because property had therefore not passed, there was no possibility of a claim under the 1855 Act. Up as far as the Court of Appeal, the buyers alternatively argued an implied contract, arising on their presentation of the bill of lading to take delivery of the goods.[58] The problem was that, in the unusual circumstances, they were held to be presenting the bill, not on their own behalf, but on that of the C & F sellers. It seems likely that they were not holders, despite having physical custody of the bill. In the House of Lords, Lord Brandon observed that:[59]

> " . . . the buyers were to present the bill of lading to the ship at Immingham and take delivery of the goods there, they were to do so, not as principals on their own account, but solely as agents for the sellers".

This is at any rate consistent with the view that the buyers, though being custodians physically of the bill of lading, were not holder. In *The Berge Sisar*, Lord Hobhouse postulated that an FOB seller might take a bill of lading evidencing a bailment not to himself, but to his purchaser.[60] This is also consistent with that view. The principle seems to have been accepted, therefore, that a person can have physical custody, but on behalf of someone else, and in *The Aliakmon* it was the someone else who had contractual rights under the bill of lading.[61]

It can be argued, however, that, whatever the position at common law, the logic of the 1992 Act is to exclude fine distinctions, such as this. This was the sentiment that was strongly adopted by Thomas J at first instance, and in a more muted manner in the Court of Appeal in *East West Corpn v DKBS AF 1912 A/S*.[62] There, the shipper had transferred (and indorsed) bills of lading to various banks whose role was to collect payment. The buyers never paid, and the banks redelivered the bills to the shipper, but without reindorsement. In the meantime, the carrier had delivered the goods anyway, to the buyers who had not paid, without production of bills of lading. The shippers sued the carriers for misdelivery.

One issue was the shipper's title to sue in contract.[63] The Court of Appeal accepted that the shipper's original contractual title had been divested by s. 2(5) of the 1992 Act, and held that, in the absence of any indorsement back, the claimant shippers had not reacquired rights of suit by virtue of the return of the bills to them. The court rejected the shipper's argument that the banks were never holders, despite having custody of the bills – that they had custody, simply as shipper's agents to collect payment. (In other words, on this argument, the shippers remained holders all along.) Mance LJ thought this argument unsustainable in the light of a personal indorsement in favour of the banks,[64] which leaves open the possibility that the argument might have succeeded, had the bills been blank indorsed. This distinction had been drawn in the then edition of *Carver on Bills of Lading*,[65] but if it is correct it introduces a very technical distinction into the operation of the 1992 Act. At first instance, Thomas J had also rejected an argument that the holders of a bill of lading might be

---

58 On the basis of the principles in section [16.8].

59 [1986] AC 785, 808.

60 *Borealis AB v Stargas Ltd (The Berge Sisar)* [2002] 2 AC 205, [18]. *The Berge Sisar* is a decision on the 1992 Act, discussed at section but [16.8], the comments at [18] relate to the common law.

61 The CA held ([1985] QB 350) that the buyers took delivery of the goods as agents for the sellers, and consequently no contract could be implied with the buyers on the principles in section [16.9] below. There was no appeal against this aspect of the decision.

62 [2002] 2 Lloyd's Rep 182 (Thomas J), affd [2003] QB 1509 (CA).

63 In the event, he succeeded in bailment, and so it did not matter that there was no contract action: see further section [20.4].

64 [2003] QB 1509, [16].

65 Now *Carver on Bills of Lading*, 3rd ed (2012), Sweet & Maxwell, [5–023].

other than the persons with actual custody, observing that the 1992 Act was intended to simplify the law, whereas:[66]

> " . . . if the claimants were correct, there would need to be an enquiry into the question as to whether the consignee named on the face of the bill of lading had, as between the shipper and the person named as consignee, an entitlement to delivery. It would in another guise re-open the enquiry into the contractual arrangements that the reform brought about by the 1992 Act sought to remove."

This is a somewhat stronger sentiment than that expressed in the Court of Appeal.

East West does not rule out the possibility of a divorce between custody and possession, at least where a bearer bill is used, as in *The Ythan*,[67] where Aikens J did not think the person with custody was either the "owner" of the bill, or the lawful holder. We will consider *The Ythan* further below;[68] but, briefly, a cargo (of metallic HBI fines), which had been purchased (FOB) by Primetrade, exploded at sea, causing the total loss of both cargo and ship – regrettably, there was also loss of life. The shipowners sued Primetrade for shipment of a dangerous cargo. Primetrade were not the shippers, but were (the shipowners argued) holders of the bills of lading, and came within s. 3 of the 1992 Act.[69] However, Primetrade at no stage had physical custody of the bills. After the explosion, they were sent by UBS, a bank that was financing the sale, to Marsh, the insurers, who made an *ex gratia* payment to Primetrade. Aikens J did not think that Marsh were holders, since they had custody of the bills only on behalf of Primetrade. In principle at least, Primetrade could have possession, though Marsh had custody.[70]

The bills in *The Ythan* were indorsed in blank, whereas those in *East West* were personally indorsed. For bills indorsed in blank, any presumption that the person with custody also has possession would seem to be weaker. So we end up with a situation where the form of the bill may well be crucial.

16.7.2 Holdership and validity of indorsement chain

To become a holder it is not enough to have possession of the bill – possession is a necessary but not a sufficient requirement. If it is a negotiable bill, s. 5(2)(b) requires the person with possession of the bill to have obtained possession "as a result of the completion, by delivery of the bill, of any indorsement of the bill or, in the case of a bearer bill, of any other transfer of the bill". So in the case of an order bill, we need to be assured that possession is derived from delivery and indorsement.[71]

For these purposes, indorsement means valid indorsement. In *The Aegean Sea*[72] bills of lading had been transferred (and indorsed) to the wrong person in error, and Thomas J held that the recipients did not become holders. The result was the transferee did not become liable for the shipment of dangerous goods. The reasoning was adopted by the Court of Appeal in *The Erin Schulte*,[73] where a bank that had rejected tender of documents, but retained the bill of lading, was held not at that time to be holder, because both delivery and indorsement depended on the intention of both transferor

---

66 [2002] 2 Lloyd's Rep 182, [22].
67 *The Ythan* [2006] 1 Lloyd's Rep 457. The bills were indorsed in blank, and hence became bearer bills, on the principles discussed in section [14.4.1].
68 Section [16.6.2].
69 On the principles of section [16.8].
70 Nor, however, in his view, were Primetrade holders: see below, section [16.7.3]. This does not affect the present discussion.
71 By contrast, under s. 5(2)(a), possession is enough for a consignee under a "consignee or order bill".
72 *Aegean Sea Traders Corp v Repsol Petroleo SA (The Aegean Sea)* [1998] 2 Lloyd's Rep 39, a decision on COGSA 92, s. 3.
73 [2015] 1 Lloyd's Rep 97.

and recipient, and the recipient had chosen to reject. Moore-Bick LJ commented that " . . . a person cannot be forced to accept a transfer of property or rights against his will",[74] sentiments with which it is difficult to disagree.

A more controversial case, perhaps, is The Dolphina, a decision of the High Court of Singapore.[75] Singapore cases are, of course, only of persuasive authority in England, but the court was applying English law and, in any case, Singapore (like many other jurisdictions) has adopted legislation exactly equivalent to our own Carriage of Goods Act 1992. Belinda Ang Saw Ean J's judgment is closely reasoned, and so the case has considerable weight, as persuasive authority. In essence, a seller of a cargo of palm oil (apparently fraudulently) tendered to Maybank, a correspondent bank under a documentary credit, a bill of lading which, he knew, covered cargo that had already been delivered under an earlier contract. Maybank then (innocently) indorsed it in favour of the plaintiffs (Bank of Communications, or BOC), who were the issuing bank. When the purchaser failed to reimburse BOC, BOC sued the shipowners in respect of the earlier misdelivery, but were met with the claim that they had no title to sue.

Belinda Ang Saw Ean J held that BOC were not holders, and so had no title to sue under the Carriage of Goods by Sea Act 1992 (recall that English law applied). A fraudulent indorsement was not a valid indorsement, and consequently neither Maybank, nor any subsequent transferee, became lawful holder. Though this may well be a perfectly valid (though very literal) interpretation of the Carriage of Goods by Sea Act 1992, the decision looks very unfair on BOC, which failed to become a lawful holder through no fault of their own. (Fortunately they succeeded in an alternative tort claim for conspiracy, but a tort claim will by no means always be available.)

To come within s. 2 of COGSA 1992 a claimant must also be a lawful holder, which means (in s. 5(2)) that he has become the holder of the bill in good faith. This addresses the good faith of the *recipient*. But where the *transferor* is in bad faith, as in The Dolphina, the recipient may never become holder at all, whether the recipient has acted in good faith or not.

16.7.3 Spent bills

We have seen that the legislature in 1992 were keen not to exclude transfers simply on the grounds that the bills were spent when negotiated, but also wished to discourage a trade in spent bills as such. This requires us to look at ss. 5(2)(c) and 2(2)(a). Section 5(2)(c) makes provision for spent bills, by providing that a lawful holder can be:

> "(c) a person with possession of the bill as a result of any transaction by virtue of which he would have become a holder falling within paragraph . . . (b) above had not the transaction been effected at a time when possession of the bill no longer gave a right (as against the carrier) to possession of the goods to which the bill relates . . . ".

In other words, it does not matter that the bill is no longer a valid document of title, at the time when possession is transferred. Holders do not automatically acquire rights under s. 2, however, s. 2(2) excluding the holders of a spent bill:

> " . . . unless he becomes the holder of the bill —
> (a) by virtue of a transaction effected in pursuance of any contractual or other arrangements made before the time when such a right to possession ceased to attach to possession of the bill; or

---

74 [2015] 1 Lloyd's Rep 97, [17]. The bank later became holder: see section [16.7.3].
75 [2012] 1 Lloyd's Rep 304.

(b) as a result of the rejection to that person by another person of goods or documents delivered to the other person in pursuance of any such arrangements."

It is this provision that discourages the trade in spent bills as such.

Returning to *The Ythan*, it may be remembered that the shipowners sued Primetrade as FOB purchasers, who were not the original shippers, for shipment of a dangerous cargo. They therefore had to show that both:

1. Primetrade became lawful holders, and acquired rights under s. 2; *and*
2. the requirements of s. 3 were satisfied.

In the event they failed to show either. For the moment we are concerned only with the first. Primetrade could not have become holders until, at the very earliest, the bills were sent to Marsh, their insurers. Since this was not until after the destruction of the cargo, the owners would also have had to show that they came within s. 5(2)(c), and were not excluded by s. 2(2)(a).[76]

In the event, Aikens J did not think Primetrade became holders at all,[77] but, if he were wrong about this interpretation of s. 5(2), and Primetrade did become holders when the bills of lading were sent to Marsh, this was not "by virtue of a transaction effected in pursuance of" a contract made before the goods were lost, as required by s. 2(2)(a). He adopted a proximate cause test, and, in his view, "the immediate reason and proximate cause of the transfer of the bills to Marsh" was the agreement leading to Marsh making the *ex gratia* payment to Primetrade.[78] This of course came after the loss. (The other main contender was the original taking out of the open cargo cover, a transaction that clearly took place before the cargo was lost, but Aikens J rejected this as a proximate cause.[79]) Yet this was not trading in spent bills as such, and therefore not within the mischief that bothered the joint Law Commissions. In *The Ythan*, the proximate cause was the last in time, and of course, the later the effective cause, the less likely it is that s. 2(2) will apply.

Here is a timeline of events in *The Ythan* (the relevant transaction being marked with the arrows):

Timeline in The Ythan

. Open cover taken out **(before B/L spent)** – too distant

. Cargo destroyed in explosion – goods lost – **B/L becomes spent**

. B/L sent to Marsh **(after B/L spent)** <--

---

76 At any rate, given that Aikens J held that s. 2(2)(a) was triggered by the destruction, as well as the delivery, of the goods: [2006] 1 Lloyd's Rep 457, [70].

77 [2006] 1 Lloyd's Rep 457, [80] (because the transfer to Marsh, the insurers, was not a transaction "in the normal course of trading"); this looks wrong, because there is no requirement in the section for the transaction to be in "the normal course of trading". See generally, Treitel & Reynolds, *Carver on Bills of Lading*, 3rd ed (2012), Sweet & Maxwell/Thomson Reuters, British Shipping Laws Series, [5–059]–[5–063].

78 [2006] 1 Lloyd's Rep 457, [85].

79 Other possible contenders were the original sale contract, and the "Master Credit Agreement" (ie, the setting up of the documentary credit), both of which preceded the loss – but these were causally too remote.

Because the shipowners were unable to show that Primetrade became holders, or that, if they did, they did so in circumstances that triggered s. 2, there was no prospect of Primetrade becoming liable under s. 3. In any event, Aikens J thought that the requirements of s. 3 were not met.[80]

Issues of a similar type arose in *The Erin Schulte*,[81] the essential facts of which were that Standard Chartered Bank (SCB) were confirming bank under a documentary credit, the ultimate beneficiary of which was Gunvor (in whose favour the benefit of the credit had been transferred); Gunvor was a CIF supplier of gasoil for an onward contract, in respect of which the credit had been originally opened. Serious concerns were voiced, as to the quality of the gasoil, by the ultimate buyers, who were prepared to accept only part of the cargo, at a reduced price. SCB informed United Bank of Africa (UBA, the issuing bank), that Gunvor had accepted an amendment to the credit to reflect these concerns, but this was incorrect; in reality, Gunvor rejected the requested amendment. The consequence was that, while SCB remained liable to Gunvor under the original credit, they had limited their recourse to reimbursement from UBA.

Gunvor, of course, tendered under the original letter of credit, negotiable bills of lading that SCB (wrongly) rejected. SCB did not, however, return the bills to Gunvor. In the meantime, alternative buyers had been found for the *Erin Schulte* cargo, and Gunvor instructed the shipowners to deliver the *Erin Schulte* gasoil to the alternative buyers against an indemnity (since, of course, SCB still had the bills of lading). Only later did SCB finally agree to settle Gunvor's claim for the price.

We have seen that the Court of Appeal did not think that SCB became holders from the time of initial tender, since they did not intend, at that stage, to accept the bill.[82] They became holders when they agreed to settle Gunvor's claim, but, by then, the cargo had been delivered.[83] However, the Court of Appeal saw no need for a proximate cause test at all in the operation of s. 2(2)(a) (and there is nothing in the wording of the section to require it); the bank became holders because they had settled the claim under the credit, and so, of course, they had become holders by virtue of the credit.

Here is a timeline of events in *The Erin Schulte* (the relevant transaction being marked with the arrows):

Timeline in The Erin Schulte

. Credit transferred to Gunvor **(B/L not spent)** <--

. Misdelivery – **B/L becomes spent**

. SCB settled action with Gunvor and paid

(SCB clearly became holders) **(B/L spent)**

----

80 See section [16.8].
81 [2015] 1 Lloyd's Rep 97.
82 See section [16.7.2].
83 See generally [2015] 1 Lloyd's Rep 97, [53]–[57]. Moore-Bick LJ thought that "the right to obtain delivery of the goods from the carrier, did not cease when the goods were discharged against the letter of indemnity. They remained in existence and were capable of forming the basis of a claim against Dorchester for misdelivery": [2015] 1 Lloyd's Rep 97, [53]. However, the action was fought on the basis that s. 2(2) applied. If Moore-Bick LJ is right, it is hard to think of any situations where the section will be triggered.

Just as in *The Ythan*, there is nothing about *The Erin Schulte* that looks like trading in spent bills as such. On the wording of the statute, and on the issues of policy, the approach in *The Erin Schulte* is surely far to be preferred to that in *The Ythan*.

16.8 Liabilities

The 1855 Act transferred rights and liabilities together, so that anyone who obtained contractual rights was also subject to contractual liability. The effect of the decision in *Sewell v Burdick* was to prevent banks as pledgees from becoming automatically liable for bill of lading freight,[84] but it also, as a necessary consequence, deprived them of any right to sue under the Act. In that case, a bank had taken bills of lading, indorsed in blank, as security for an advance, but when their owner disappeared the goods had been seized, and sold to pay Russian custom-house duty and charges. Consequently the bank were unable to claim delivery of the cargo, and obtained no benefit from the pledge. The House of Lords held that the shipowners were unable to claim freight from the bank, on the basis of the 1855 Act, because the general property in the goods had not passed to the bank. To have decided the case the other way would arguably have been unfair on the bank, but a corollary of the decision was that a bank as pledgee could not rely on the Act either. The consequence of this was that banks who advanced payment under documentary credits could never use the provisions of the 1855 Act.

The view taken by the joint Law Commissions was that a bank as pledgee should not thereby become automatically liable under the carriage contract. The potential unfairness of this would be all the greater, if (as in *Sewell*) it were sought to impose liability on the holder of a bearer bill, which can be transferred from hand to hand.[85] But the bank as pledgee should be able to sue on the bill of lading, as lawful holder.[86] However, if the bank did sue, or demanded delivery of the goods, it would also (quite fairly) become subject to liabilities. Another situation, which might not be regarded as fair, would be to make a named consignee liable, just because he has been named in a bill of lading (and hence came within s. 2(1)(b)). Again, it would be another matter if he took delivery, or took advantage of the rights conferred by the 1992 Act.

An important feature of the new legislation, then, is that liability is now dealt with separately from rights. Liabilities are transferred under s. 3, not automatically, but only if s. 2 applies and the following additional criteria are satisfied (under s. 3(1)), that the person in whom rights are vested under s. 2 either:[87]

"(a) takes or demands delivery from the carrier of any of the goods to which the document relates; [or]
(b) makes a claim under the contract of carriage against the carrier in respect of any of those goods; . . . "
(c) is a person who, at a time before those rights were vested in him, took or demanded delivery from the carrier of any of those goods . . . ".

Only those who come within s. 2 can be subjected to liabilities under s. 3. In the case of a bill of lading, this requires the person in possession of the bill also to be the holder. We have seen that not everyone with custody of a bill of lading will necessarily be a holder.[88]

---

84 (1884) 10 App Cas 74.
85 The bill had been indorsed in blank, and was hence a bearer bill: see section [14.4.1].
86 Law Com No. 196, Part III(e).
87 There is also s. 3(1)(c), which makes provision where a spent bill is transferred.
88 Eg, not in *The Aegean Sea* or *The Ythan*, earlier in this section, in both of which claims based on s. 3 failed, wholly or partly for this reason.

The additional criteria in s. 3(1)(a) and (b) have been considered, twice, by the courts. The idea of the necessity for a voluntary election was emphasised in *The Berge Sisar*, Lord Hobouse observing that:[89]

> "Each of (a) and (b) involves a choice by the endorsee to take a positive step in relation to the contract of carriage and the rights against the carrier transferred to him by s. 2(1). It has the character of an election to avail himself of those contractual rights against the carrier.
>
> . . .
>
> . . . it is clear that s. 3 must be understood in a way which reflects the potentially important consequences of the choice or election which the bill of lading holder is making."

There was no voluntary election in *The Berge Sisar* itself, where the House of Lords held that merely taking samples for testing did not bring a holder within s. 3(1)(a). Buyers (who were not the original shippers) requested samples of the cargo for testing. After testing, the buyers rejected delivery of the cargo and sold it on. They received bills of lading, which they immediately forwarded to their purchasers. (In other words, these buyers were in fact only intermediate purchasers, not the eventual receivers of the cargo.) The shipowners claimed that these intermediate purchasers were liable for the corrosion caused by the cargo (propane) to their ship. The House held that they were not liable. They had not demanded delivery to fall within s. 3. Moreover, even if they had become liable, their liability ceased upon their reindorsement of the bills of lading to their purchasers.[90]

The second case on s. 3 was *The Ythan*. We have already seen that Aikens J did not think that Primetrade, who were sued for shipment of a dangerous cargo, were holders or came within s. 2,[91] but, even if they did, s. 3 was not triggered. Loss adjusters for Marsh (the insurers) had demanded the provision of a letter of undertaking (LOU) from the shipowners' P & I Club, to provide security for the cargo claim, and the shipowners argued that this triggered s. 3(1)(b). Aikens J held that the demand for an LOU did not amount to a claim, there not being a sufficient commitment. The need for a voluntary election, from *The Berge Sisar*, was adopted directly in *The Ythan*.

16.9 Implied contracts

Even where (before 1992) the Bills of Lading Act 1855 did not apply, it was sometimes possible to imply a contract between the carrier and the receiver of the cargo at common law. Prior to the Court of Appeal decision in *Brandt v Liverpool, Brazil & River Plate SN Co*,[92] the implied contract had always been used to enable the carrier to sue the receiver of cargo for freight or demurrage; by delivering the cargo, the carrier released his lien for freight, and it was reasonable to infer that he would only do this on the basis that he would be paid freight or demurrage by the receiver of the cargo.[93] These cases remain good law.

In *Brandt v Liverpool*, a contract was successfully implied in favour of a receiver of cargo, a bank that had realised the security of its pledge, but was unable to rely on the 1855 Act.[94] The receiver having paid the freight was able to sue the carrier for damages for delay, and for the return of a

---

89 [2002] 2 AC 205, [32]–[33], elaborated on [33]–[36].

90 The Court of Appeal had held ([1999] QB 863) that liabilities were divested on reindorsement, a view approved in the House of Lords. Note that this could leave *lacuna* in liabilities, since the subsequent holder would not necessarily himself become liable under s. 3: see further Reynolds, *Bills of Lading: Liabilities of Transferee (The Berge Sisar)* [2001] LMCLQ 344, 350.

91 Above, section [16.7].

92 [1924] 1 KB 575.

93 Eg, *Allen v Coltart* (1883) 11 QBD 782.

94 Because of *Sewell v Burdick* (1884) 10 App Cas 74.

reconditioning cost of the cargo (which they had paid to the carrier under protest), where a clean bill of lading had been issued for defective cargo.[95] The Court of Appeal was prepared to imply a new contract between receiver and carrier: on delivery of the cargo against tender of a bill of lading, a contract was implied that delivery would be on the terms of the bill of lading.[96]

Brandt v Liverpool contracts, then, are contracts implied between the receiver of cargo and the carrier. Diagrammatically we have:

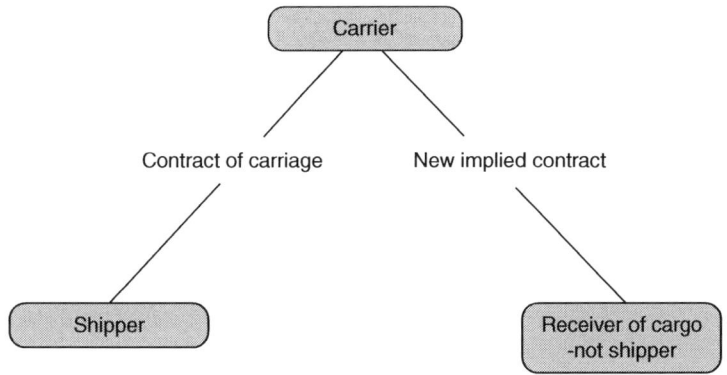

The implied contract in *Brandt v Liverpool* did not depend on the passing of property, and therefore (as in the case itself) could be used in circumstances where the 1855 Act could not. Indeed, for a time it looked as though this device might be extended and used to plug the gaps in the 1855 legislation, especially as, at the same time, the courts were being freer in their interpretation of s. 1 itself.[97] In *The Dona Mari*,[98] delivery was held (on the basis of *Brandt v Liverpool*) to be on the terms of a ship's delivery order (which of course, did not come within the 1855 Act). In *The Elli 2*,[99] the receiver was successfully sued for demurrage, despite delivery not being made against bills of lading at all, merely a guarantee that the receiver would produce them later, and despite freight not having been paid by the receiver. The inference was nonetheless made that delivery was on the terms of the bills of lading, yet to be produced. The doctrine was taking on the appearance of a device, in the sense that the courts were not looking for a genuine contract between the parties (though it still depended on cargo being delivered).

Though the cases themselves remain good authority, these hopes were to be dashed. The wide interpretation of s. 1 died at the latest with *The Aramis* and *The Delfini*,[100] and *The Aramis* took with it any

95 The basis of the liability for this type of misrepresentation is discussed in chapter 19.

96 In *Brandt v Liverpool* itself, the shipowner delivered the goods against presentation of the bill of lading, and the receiver (a bank as pledgee) paid the freight. The Court of Appeal was prepared to imply a fresh contract between receiver and carrier, on the terms of the bill of lading.

97 The high point probably being *K/S A/S Seateam & Co v Iraq National Oil Co (The Sevonia Team)* [1983] 2 Lloyd's Rep 640; also *Pacific Molasses Co v Entre Rios Compania Naviera SA (The San Nicholas)* [1976] 1 Lloyd's Rep 8 (Roskill LJ); *Karlshamns Olje Fabriker v Eastport Navigation Corp (The Elafi)* [1981] 2 Lloyd's Rep 679 (dicta of Mustill J). Cf. the cases cited in section [16.7], where the courts adopted a literal construction. It was the literal construction that eventually came to predominate.

98 *Cremer v General Carriers SA (The Dona Mari)* [1974] 1 WLR 341. The ship's delivery order there did not come within the 1855 Act, though it is within 1992: see section [16.6].

99 *Ilyssia Compania Naviera SA v Ahmed Abdul Oawi Bamadoa (The Elli 2)* [1985] 1 Lloyd's Rep 107.

100 [1989] 1 Lloyd's Rep 213; [1990] 1 Lloyd's Rep 252.

hopes based on an extension of *Brandt v Liverpool*. In order to be able to imply a contract, it is necessary to be able to infer offer, acceptance and consideration. In *The Aramis*, Bingham LJ said:[101]

> "It must, surely, be necessary to identify conduct referable to the contract contended for or, at the very least, conduct inconsistent with there being no contract made between the parties to the effect contended for. Put another way, I think it must be fatal to the implication of a contract if the parties would or might have acted exactly as they did in the absence of a contract."

He continued:[102] "One cannot cast principle aside, and simply opt for a commercially convenient solution." You cannot reason, in other words, from the convenience of an implied contract, that the requirements for a contract must therefore be satisfied. If the requirements for a contract are not satisfied, there is no contract, however commercially convenient it would be. A contract needs offer, acceptance, and consideration. In *Brandt v Liverpool* itself the payment of freight (and other charges)[103] constituted the consideration, moving from the receiver of the cargo.[104] The consideration moving from the carrier was delivery of the cargo, on the terms of the bill of lading, but it is not always possible to find acceptance by the shipowner of an obligation to deliver on bill of lading terms, and consideration moving from the receiver. In *The Aramis* itself, freight and other charges had been prepaid by the shipper,[105] so it was difficult to find any consideration moving from the receiver. When the ship arrived, two bills of lading were presented (by different receivers), each for 200 tonnes, but for reasons that were not entirely clear from the evidence, only about 11 tonnes of cargo remained on board the vessel. Consequently, one of the bill of lading holders received no cargo at all. To the other was delivered such cargo as remained on board, but no freight or other charges were paid, and the shipowner did no more than he was obliged to do anyway, in delivering up the remainder of the cargo. There was no material here from which a contract could be inferred, and the court refused to imply a fictitious one. Similar (indeed stronger) statements can be found a few years later, also in the Court of Appeal, in *The Gudermes*.[106]

It was really the combination of *The Aramis* and *The Delfini* that made clear the necessity for the legislation that shortly afterwards became the Carriage of Goods Act 1992. The cases were decided within just under a year of each other, the later case making clear that the 1855 Act would be literally interpreted, and the earlier that *Brandt v Liverpool* could not be used to plug the gap. After these decisions, it was clear that the sticking-plaster approach would not do. There had to be the root and branch reform of a new statute.

As we know, that happened with the 1992 Act, and, with the narrow view taken of *Brandt v Liverpool* in *The Aramis* and *The Gudermes*, it might be thought that there is no room for the implied contract doctrine today. That, however, is too gloomy an assessment. In the first place, the 1992 Act is not universally applicable. Despite the extension in documentary coverage described earlier in the chapter,[107] it does not apply to all forms of documentation, excluding for example mate's receipts, delivery orders that are not ship's delivery orders, and combined transport documents (unless they fall within the definition of a received for shipment bill of lading), but in principle, the *Brandt v Liverpool* doctrine can apply to any document, as long as the inference can be drawn that delivery was to be on the basis of its terms.

---

101 [1989] 1 Lloyd's Rep 213, 244.

102 *Ibid*, 225.

103 Including a reconditioning cost, which they had paid under protest.

104 There would also have been no consideration problem in either *The Dona Mari* or *The Elli II*.

105 Freight is commonly prepaid for dry-cargo shipments, but not for tankers: see section [7.5].

106 *Mitsui & Co Ltd v Novorossiysk Shipping Co (The Gudermes)* [1993] 1 Lloyd's Rep 311.

107 See section [16.4].

In the second place, *Brandt v Liverpool* has enjoyed a resurgence. It was applied, after *The Aramis*, in *The Captain Gregos* (No. 2),[108] in which a cargo of oil was allegedly short-delivered, and the receiver (BP) sued in conversion.[109] The shipowner claimed the benefit of the time bar in the Hague-Visby Rules, but BP became lawful holder (and probably obtained property) only long after delivery, so there was no argument for a statutory contract under the Bills of Lading Act 1855, s. 1, still at that time in force. Delivery was made against a letter of indemnity, and BP never even undertook to present bills of lading; but, even so, a contract was implied (on *Brandt v Liverpool* principles) that delivery was to be made on bill of lading terms (or at least on the terms of the Hague-Visby Rules, to which BP were taken to have consented). This entitled the shipowner to rely on the Hague-Visby time bar in the bill of lading.

What is clear is that, for a contract to be implied, the parties must change their position, in a way that is only consistent with the implication of a contract. In *The Gudermes*, Staughton LJ thought that this was not particularly problematic where, as in *Brandt v Liverpool* itself, or *The Dona Mari*, the receiver paid the freight, or as in the earlier cases, the carrier had, by delivering, released his lien for freight. In *The Elli 2*, the shipowners were under no obligation to deliver without production of the bills of lading and, by so doing, also released their lien for demurrage (which was payable by the receiver of the cargo), so again it was not unreasonable to infer a contract. In *The Captain Gregos* (No. 2), we have seen that delivery was made against an indemnity. The shipowners were under no obligation to deliver to BP without production of the bills of lading, although it was to their advantage to do so, and BP were under no obligation either to provide an indemnity, or to co-operate with the carrier by allowing the cargo to be discharged into their tanks. Again, therefore, though BP neither paid freight nor undertook to pay it, the parties had altered their position, consistently with the implication of a new contract.

More generally, assuming a document of title has been issued, the carrier is under no obligation to deliver except against its production, and changes his position by so doing. Consideration thus moves from the carrier, and a receiver who provides an indemnity also changes his position, and provides consideration. *Brandt v Liverpool* also continues to have relevance, even after the 1992 Act, where even if a bill of lading is issued, it never reaches the holder (since the 1992 Act will not then apply). It is, however, difficult to envisage many other situations where *Brandt v Liverpool* continues to have relevance today, where the 1992 Act would not in any event apply.

Another limit on the *Brandt v Liverpool* principle was suggested by Mustill J in *The Athanasia Comninos*, where the doctrine was argued to impose liability for a dangerous cargo. Mustill J took the view that:[110]

> " . . . the consignee, by taking delivery of the goods under the bill of lading, assumes only those rights and liabilities created by the contract of carriage which concern the carriage and delivery of the goods, and the payment therefor . . . I can, however, see no ground for extending this implication to embrace a warranty by the consignee as to the fitness of the goods for carriage."

In other words, not all terms of the bill of lading will necessarily be imported into the implied contract. The consignee was there held not to be liable for a breach by the shipper of the obligation not to ship dangerous cargo. The situation is not all or nothing; we have to consider precisely which bill of lading terms it is appropriate to imply.

---

108 *Compania Portorafti Commerciale SA v Ultramar Panama Inc (The Captain Gregos) (No 2)* [1990] 2 Lloyd's Rep 395. An intermediate purchaser (PEAG) also sued, and was held not to be party to any contract with the shipowner. See below, section [16.9], where there is also a diagrammatic representation of the case.

109 Action was also brought by an intermediate purchaser (PEAG), in respect of whom no contract could be implied. See further on this aspect of the case the following section.

110 [1990] 1 Lloyd's Rep 277, 281.

16.10 Actions other than in contract

In 1992 the legislature provided for a comprehensive contractual regime, filling nearly all the gaps that had become apparent in the previous regime. There was really no need for the continued existence, alongside the new regime, of actions in tort or bailment, whether the issue was loss of or damage to the goods, as considered in this chapter, or misdelivery, considered in chapter 20. But the 1992 Act left entirely alone the law outside contract. For the most part this does not matter. The comprehensiveness of the contractual regime renders tort and bailment actions largely unnecessary. Nonetheless, there continue to be problems, on the margins, where tort or bailment actions continue to exist, in the absence of a contract, with all the attendant problems that we see with *The Captain Gregos*, later in the section. It is probably regrettable that the legislature did not decide, when it enacted the Carriage of Goods by Sea Act 1992, to provide a regime that was exclusively contractual, and to curtail tort and bailment in this area of activity.[111]

We will leave conversion and bailment until chapter 20, but we do need to look at negligence in this chapter. If the carrier negligently damages the cargo-owner's goods, then there can be liability in negligence, whether or not there is also liability in contract. (If the carrier misdelivers the goods, the cargo-owner can sue him in conversion, as we will see in chapter 20.) Like *Brandt v Liverpool*, the negligence action was seen for a time as a potential plug for some of the gaps in the 1855 contractual coverage, but the House of Lords decision in *The Aliakmon* removed any hope there might have been in this regard. Today, there will usually be an action in contract, in which case there is no need to sue in tort, and where there is a contract between the parties, the tort action cannot be used to avoid contractual exemptions and limitations.[112] Tort actions today are likely to be of relevance only where there is no contract between the parties, in which case the action will also be unconstrained by any limitations or exemptions in the contract of carriage.[113]

In *The Aliakmon*[114] the House of Lords held that, in order to sue in negligence, it is necessary for the claimant to have property in the goods at the time that they were damaged. (The buyers in *The Aliakmon* did not, and failed in both contract and tort.) The House of Lords went further in *The Starsin*, holding that a duty of care in negligence is owed only to the owner of the cargo, or person with an immediate right of possession, at the time of the breach.[115] In *The Starsin*, the cargo had been negligently stowed, at the beginning of the voyage, causing progressive damage during the voyage. Property passed at some time during the voyage, but the House held the buyer had no title to sue in tort, not having had property at the time of the breach.

Since one of the main problems with the 1855 Act arose when property had not passed,[116] clearly the tort action did not resolve this.

One of the reasons for the refusal of the House of Lords to extend recovery in *The Aliakmon* was that, precisely because there was no contract between the buyers and the carrier,[117] to allow the tort action would have been to deprive the carrier of the benefit of any exemption clauses, time bars or limitation clauses in the bill of lading. The contract of carriage incorporated the Hague Rules, which

---

111 One of the problems of the divorce in 1992 between property and contract is that there might now be double liability, to property-owners in tort, and to holders in contract, where these are different people. There are no authorities providing guidance as to how the courts would deal with this problem: see further section [16.11].

112 Eg, *Henderson v Merrett Syndicates Ltd* [1995] 2 AC 145, 191 (Lord Goff), approving Oliver J in *Midland Bank Trust Co Ltd v Hett, Stubbs & Kemp* [1979] Ch 384, 522.

113 As in *The Captain Gregos* (No 2) considered below.

114 [1986] AC 785. C & F purchasers failed in a negligence action against the carrier, property not having passed to them by the time the damages occurred. As we have already seen, they also failed in contract: see section [16.7].

115 *Homburg Houtimport BV v Agrosin Private Ltd* (*The Starsin*) [2004] 1 AC 715. See in particular Lord Bingham at [39], approving Rix LJ in the CA: [2001] 1 Lloyd's Rep 437, [96].

116 See section [16.2].

117 Because property had not passed, the 1855 Act did not apply, and on the facts there was no *Brandt v Liverpool* contract (because the buyer with custody of the bill of lading took delivery on the seller's behalf): see section [16.7].

give the carrier the benefit of excepted perils, package limitation and a one-year time bar.[118] There was no sound policy, in Lord Brandon's view, in extending recovery in tort if the effect would be to deprive the carrier of the benefits he would have under the Hague Rules, on the basis of which he had undertaken to carry the cargo. The buyers argued that, in principle, the duty of care in tort could be limited by reference to the Hague Rules, but the House of Lords held that the duty of care in tort could not be limited by clauses contained in a contract to which the plaintiffs were not party.[119] The Hague-Visby Rules are drafted differently, but arguments that they are sufficiently different to enable the carrier to rely on their provisions, even where the plaintiff is not party to the contract of carriage, were dispelled by the Court of Appeal in The Captain Gregos (see below).

Actions in bailment and conversion for the most part concern misdelivery, and are better dealt with in chapter 20. There are, however, two matters worth noting for this chapter. First, though the shipper in East West was deprived by the 1992 Act of his contract action,[120] he succeeded in bailment, thus showing that the old common law regime continues to operate alongside the new Act. Secondly, we will finish the substantive part of the chapter with a more detailed look at the two Captain Gregos cases, since they bring together a number of points considered earlier in the chapter.[121]

In The Captain Gregos, a cargo of oil was sold to an intermediate purchaser (PEAG), to whom property had passed on shipment, and thence to BP, who were the final receivers. It was alleged that part of the cargo had been stolen by the shipowner, and that therefore the carriers were liable in conversion. Both BP and PEAG sued, PEAG unusually having an interest, despite having sold the cargo on, because they had a "processing deal", giving them an optional buy-back on the cargo. At the time of the alleged theft, PEAG were still the owners of the cargo, the bills of lading being negotiated to BP only some time later. The shipowners relied on the one-year time bar in Art. III(6) of the Hague-Visby Rules, but, in the first Captain Gregos case, the Court of Appeal held that they could only do this if the claimants were party to a carriage contract. The court in the first Captain Gregos case did not determine this, that being the issue when the case came back, as The Captain Gregos (No. 2). There, the Court of Appeal held that BP were party to a Brandt v Liverpool contract, and hence bound by the time bar.[122] PEAG, however, not having taken delivery of the cargo, were not party to any carriage contract, and by suing in conversion were able to avoid Art. III(6). Diagrammatically, the case looks like this.

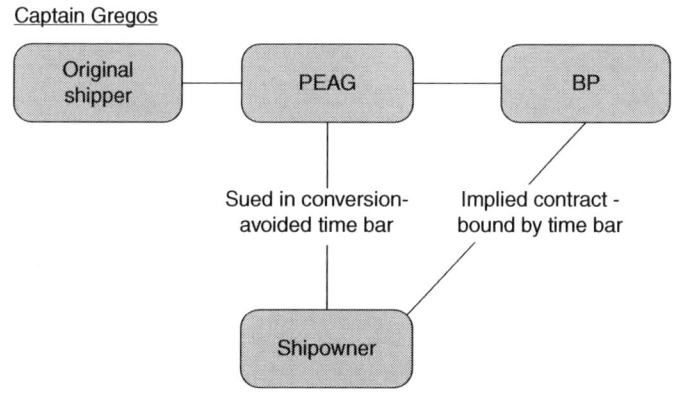

Captain Gregos

---

118 See generally on Hague and Hague-Visby chapter 18.
119 [1986] AC 785, 817–8.
120 See section [16.7.1].
121 *Compania Portorafti Commerciale SA v Ultramar Panama Inc (The Captain Gregos)* [1990] 1 Lloyd's Rep 310; *Compania Portorafti Commerciale SA v Ultramar Panama Inc (The Captain Gregos) (No 2)* [1990] 2 Lloyd's Rep 395.
122 See section [16.9].

The decision is important for the *Brandt v Liverpool* reasoning discussed in the last section, but also for showing how contractual exceptions, including those in the Hague-Visby Rules, can be avoided by a tort action (in this case conversion), where there is no contract between the cargo-owner and the carrier.

16.11 Double liability possibilities

When new contract actions are granted by statute, there is always the possibility of the carrier being liable to more than one person, unless the contracting shipper, and any intermediate holders, are divested of their actions. We have seen that s. 2(5) effects this divestment, at any rate for negotiable bills of lading. There are contractual rights, however, that will not be divested, for example where a shipper or intermediate holder is also a charterer.[123] Also, especially now that contractual actions are divorced from the whereabouts of property, there is no doubt that the holder, with title to sue in contract, can be a different person from the person with property, with a right to sue in tort.[124]

In *The Albazero*,[125] CIF sellers of goods were also time charterers of *The Albacruz*, sister ship to *The Albazero*. A bill of lading was issued to them, as shippers, pursuant to the charterparty. During the voyage *The Albacruz* and her goods sank and were totally lost, due to a breach of the charterparty, and also of the bill of lading contract, by the shipowners. The Court of Appeal held that property had passed to the buyers,[126] who therefore could, in principle, have sued on the bill of lading (relying on the 1855 Act, still then in force). They could not do so in reality, however, because they were time-barred by the Hague Rules.[127]

However, the shippers (who were themselves FOB purchasers) were a company in the same group as the indorsees, and they therefore decided to sue, in their own right but on behalf of the buyers, on the charterparty. The Hague Rules did not apply to charterparties (nor do the amended Hague-Visby Rules today),[128] and they were not incorporated into this charterparty, so effectively this was an action to avoid the time bar. *The Albazero*, belonging as it did to the same owners as *The Albacruz*, was arrested for the action. The shippers claimed substantial damages to be held in trust for the indorsee, on the basis of the old House of Lords authority of *Dunlop v Lambert*.[129]

Here is a diagrammatic representation (the action being brought by B):

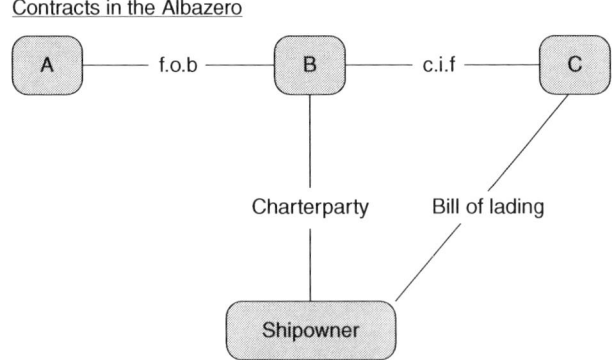

Contracts in the Albazero

A — f.o.b — B — c.i.f — C

Charterparty   Bill of lading

Shipowner

---

123 Section 2(5) is set out in Appendix B, and at the very least applies only to bills of lading and other documents to which the Act applies (which are defined in s. 1).

124 We need only consider *The Captain Gregos* (No. 2), in the previous section, where BP had a contract action, and PEAG were able to sue in tort. This could be expected to be more common under the 1992 Act.

125 [1977] AC 774.

126 Also reported [1977] AC 774. There was no appeal from this aspect of the decision.

127 Art. III(6). On the Hague Rules, see generally chapter 18.

128 Art. V.

129 (1839) 6 Cl & F 600.

When the case reached the House of Lords, it was held that, property in the goods having passed to the indorsees, the shippers were entitled to recover only nominal damages on the charter-party. Lord Diplock took the view that:

"With the passing of the Bills of Lading Act 1855 the rationale of *Dunlop v Lambert* could no longer apply in cases where the only contract of carriage into which the shipowner had entered was that contained in a bill of lading, and the property in the goods passed to the consignee or indorsee named in the bill of lading by reason of the consignment or indorsement. Upon that happening the right of suit against the shipowner in respect of obligations arising under the contract of carriage passes to him from the consignor. . . .

The rationale of the rule is in my view also incapable of justifying its extension to contracts for carriage of goods which contemplate that the carrier will also enter into separate contracts of carriage with whoever may become the owner of goods carried pursuant to the original contract."

With no significant extension of this reasoning, one would expect only nominal damages to be available to any shipper or intermediate holder whose rights had not been divested, whenever either the 1992 Act or the *Brandt v Liverpool* doctrine applied. The spectre of double liability to that extent recedes.

However, in *The Sanix Ace*,[130] Hobhouse J distinguished *The Albazero*, in a case where the property in the goods remained in the original shipper (who was also charterer of the vessel). He rejected the carrier's argument that the plaintiffs had suffered no recoverable loss and hence were limited to nominal damages alone:[131]

"It has long been settled law that the owner of goods is entitled to sue and recover damages in respect of loss or damage to those goods."

Though the action was brought in contract, he clearly thought that the same position would apply in tort. If *The Sanix Ace* is correct, it would have significant double liability ramifications for the 1992 Act, where holder and property owner were different persons. It is not known how the courts would resolve these issues.

16.12 Critique of 1992 Act

One effect of the 1992 Act is considerably to improve the value of shipping documents, whether traditional bill of lading or otherwise. Its most obvious impact is where there is a loss of, or damage to, goods at sea. Yet though only contractual issues are resolved by the new Act, and there is no change, for example, to the definition of a document of title, the misdelivery actions in chapter 20 can also be contract-based, and probably have to be, where the holder of the document does not also have property in the goods. For the same reason, the 1992 Act can significantly increase the usefulness of, for example, a waybill or ship's delivery order, which come within the new legislation, but were not within the old.

The Bills of Lading Act 1855 was seriously dated by 1992, and the 1992 Act has had the beneficial effects of removing the property link, and (perhaps) of simplifying the law. From the discussion in this chapter it can be seen, however, that it is far from perfect.[132] It is also perhaps regrettable that

---

130 *Obestain Inc v National Mineral Development Corporation Ltd (The Sanix Ace)* [1987] 1 Lloyd's Rep 465.

131 [1987] 1 Lloyd's Rep 465, 468.

132 Esp. section [16.7].

the legislation reformed only the law of contract, leaving the old tort and bailment actions alone. *The Captain Gregos* (No. 2) shows us one of the pitfalls of this omission.

16.13 Questions

Question 16.1
Who is the lawful holder in the following circumstances:

(a)   a bill of lading is indorsed in blank to a bank under a documentary credit; does it make any difference whether the bank accepts the documents and pays the seller for the goods (assume that if the bank has paid, it has yet to be reimbursed by the buyer)?
(b)   same as (a) but the bill of lading bears a personal indorsement in favour of the bank?
(c)   a bill of lading is indorsed in blank to a bank which has agreed to collect payment on behalf of the CIF seller; the buyers do not pay and the bill of lading is returned to the seller, but not reindorsed?
(d)   same as (c) but the bill of lading bears a personal indorsement in favour of the bank?

Comment
You should be able to work this out from the cases in section [16.7], but the distinction between a personal indorsement and indorsement in blank has not been categorically established, and was not taken by the Court of Appeal in *The Erin Schulte*.[133]

Question 16.2
Charles is the purchaser (from Adam) of a fire engine, of which he takes delivery when it arrives. On inspection, he discovers that it has been damaged, because of a breach of carriage contract by the shipowner. Advise him in the following circumstances:

(a)   A straight bill of lading was issued to Adam (who was responsible for putting the fire engine physically on board the vessel), naming Charles as consignee. Charles paid for the fire engine before shipment, and Adam has not sent the bill of lading to Charles. Delivery was made to Charles, without its presentation.
(b)   The same as (a), but the bill of lading was made out to "consignee or order".
(c)   The same as (b), but freight has not been prepaid, and, in order to obtain delivery, Charles promised the shipowner to present the bill of lading and pay the freight when the bill of lading arrives. As yet the bill of lading has not arrived, and Charles has not paid any freight.

Comment
In (a) you might think COGSA 92 applies, but it looks unlikely in (b) or (c), at least unless Charles becomes holder (why does it not matter in (a)?). You might, however, consider whether *Brandt v Liverpool* does (section [16.9]).

---

133 [2015] 1 Lloyd's Rep 97.

Chapter 17

Other privity of contract issues

This chapter is about privity of contract issues, apart from the Carriage of Goods by Sea Act 1992. Privity of contract is very much a feature of English law, and a similar jurisdiction is not apparent outside the Commonwealth. It has to be taken into account in sea carriage, and can create problems with international conventions, unless they have been drafted to take the doctrine into account.

17.1 Identity of carrier

The master or other person signing the bill of lading will do so, ultimately as agent for the shipowner or a charterer, who will therefore be the contracting carrier. This is the person with whom the cargo-owner contracts, and this section is about the identity of that carrier.

17.1.1 Identity of carrier: why it matters

A bill of lading may be signed on behalf of a shipowner or a charterer (or, for that matter, sub-charterer etc). There are a number of reasons why it is important to identify who the contracting carrier is.

. The cargo-owner needs to know who to sue, either as shipper, or under the Carriage of Goods by Sea Act 1992.
. Either the shipowner or the charterer might be bankrupt. In *The Nea Tyhi*, the charterers were bankrupt.[1] In *Manchester Trust v Furness, Withy & Co Ltd*,[2] the charterers, who had persuaded the master to deliver the cargo to themselves, without production of a bill of lading, had disappeared.[3] In each case, if they had been contracting carriers the cargo-owner would have been left with no effective remedy, at any rate in contract.[4] In *The Starsin*,[5] the charterers were bankrupt and were not the contracting carriers. The consequence was that the cargo-owners had no contractual remedy against anyone, and, as we have seen, only one of the claimants had a useful tort action against the shipowner.

If a carrier is sued in tort, he will need to establish a contract between himself and the cargo-owner if he wishes to rely on excepted perils, time bar or limit of liability.[6] In The *Starsin*, the shipowner, who was not the contracting carrier, was sued in negligence, and was able to rely on the Hague Rules package limitation only because of a Himalaya clause in the carriage contract between the cargo-owner and the charterers.[7]

17.1.2 How the law works

In *The Rewia*,[8] the Court of Appeal accepted that the issue is for whom does the person signing the bill of lading actually or ostensibly act. This is based on ordinary principles of agency: actual or ostensible authority. In *The Starsin*[9] the House of Lords, while recognising that the issue was not exactly the same, treated the issue essentially as one of contractual interpretation of the bill of lading. Lord Bingham made the comparison as follows:[10]

---

1 [1982] 1 Lloyd's Rep 606.

2 [1895] 2 QB 282.

3 At first instance, Mathew J commented that "There seems to be no doubt at all upon the evidence that a fraud was intended to be committed, and that the captain (whose good faith was not questioned) was deliberately imposed upon": [1895] 2 QB 282, 285.

4 As we saw above, in *The Nea Tyhi* the cargo-owners also succeeded in tort, but that aspect of the decision can no longer be regarded as correct: section [16.10].

5 *Homburg Houtimport BV v Agrosin Private Ltd (The Starsin)* [2004] 1 AC 715.

6 Consequence of *Compania Portorafti Commerciale SA v Ultramar Panama Inc (The Captain Gregos)* [1990] 1 Lloyd's Rep 310, in section [16.10]. Cf. the bailment on terms doctrine, in section [17.4].

7 Himalaya clauses are in section [17.2].

8 [1991] 2 Lloyds Rep 325.

9 [2004] 1 AC 715.

10 [2004] 1 AC 715, [9].

"When construing a commercial document in the ordinary way the task of the court is to ascertain and give effect to the intentions of the contracting parties. Here, the task is to ascertain who, on one side, the contracting party was. But a similar approach is appropriate."

This may have been true in the context of *The Starsin*, but it will not always be so. If the person signing the bill has not even the general authority of (eg) the shipowner to contract on his behalf, nothing in the bill of lading can create that authority.[11] It therefore cannot always follow that identifying the contracting party is the same question as interpreting the substance of the contract, once the identity of the contracting parties is clear.

In *The Starsin* itself, there were a number of factors, and, in principle, the person signing could have had the authority of either party. That being so, it was reasonable to resolve the identity issue by construing the bill of lading contract. However, the courts often start with presumptions, as in *The Starsin* itself, at least at first instance. Colman J, whose judgment on this issue was affirmed in the House of Lords, put it this way:[12]

"If the shipper were to ask the question what is the identity of the carrier in this case, that is to say the person undertaking the obligation of carriage, the answer would surely be: the shipowner, unless the bill of lading stated that some other person was to be treated as the carrier."

In other words, Colman J's initial presumption was that the shipowner was the carrier.[13] The carriage contract was then considered, to see if that presumption should be rebutted. Whereas the demise and identity of carrier clauses in the printed part of the bill of lading supported the initial presumption, there were other factors weakening it. The bills were not signed by the master; they made provision for signature other than by the master, and were actually signed by port agents, purportedly for the charterers.[14] They were also on the time charterer's forms. The initial presumption was ultimately displaced by the words in the signature box, stating that the bills were signed for the charterers.

In a case like *The Starsin*, where there are many factors at work, initial presumptions may make very little difference (and, indeed, the House of Lords did not use them, as clearly as Colman J had), but most cases are simpler. Then, the presumptions not only are the starting point, but in the absence of something in the bill of lading to displace them (for example, if the bill of lading is silent as to identity of carrier), also the end point. So we should begin by considering the presumptions, before moving to construction of express provisions, such as demise and identity of carrier clauses, and signature boxes.

17.1.3 Demise charterer: charterer contracting carrier

In *Baumwoll Manufactur von Carl Scheiber v Furness*,[15] the House of Lords held that where the ship is chartered by demise, the charterer is the contracting carrier. In *Baumwoll* the master was employed by the charterer, and (the charterparty being by demise) had no authority to act for the owners. Nothing in the bill of lading could give him that authority, and therefore the owners were liable neither in contract nor in tort for loss of the cargo (allegedly due to unseaworthiness). No special principles

---

11 *Armagas Ltd v Mundogas SA (The Ocean Frost)* [1986] AC 717, cited in *The Starsin* at first instance (on the *Grant v Norway* issue): [2000] 1 Lloyd's Rep 85, and see section [19.8]. This is also the explanation for *Baumwoll Manufactur von Carl Scheiber v Furness* [1893] AC 8, in section [17.1.3], where (the charterparty being by demise) the master had no authority from the owners at all.

12 [2000] 1 Lloyd's Rep 85, 93. *The Starsin* is considered in detail in section [17.1.8].

13 See section [17.1.4] (the charter not being by demise).

14 On the relevance of this, see section [17.1.5].

15 [1893] AC 8.

were being applied to carriage contracts, and Lord Herschell observed that: "A contract of affreightment is only like any other contract."[16]

17.1.4 Charterparty other than by demise: master signs as agents for owners

Manchester Trust v Furness, Withy & Co Ltd applies the reverse presumption where the ship is chartered otherwise than by demise, and the bill of lading is signed by the master.[17] The presumption now is that the owners are the contracting carriers.

This was a voyage charterparty, where the master was therefore hired by the owners, and the Court of Appeal held that there is a presumption that the captain acts for the owners. The then recent decision of *Baumwoll v Furness* was distinguished on the basis that that was a charterparty by demise.

The master had discharged the goods (a cargo of coal) *en route*, having been persuaded to do so by the charterers, for fraudulent purposes of their own. The charterers were obviously not worth suing, but the purchasers of the coal successfully sued the shipowners, in contract. The main issue was the effect of a demise clause in the charterparty, which stated that that charterer was the contracting party:

> "The captain and crew, although paid by the owners, shall be agents and servants of the charterers for all purposes, whether of navigation or otherwise, under the charter. In signing bills of lading it is especially agreed that the captain shall only do so as agent for the charterers; and the charterers hereby agree to indemnify the owners from all consequences or liabilities (if any) that may arise from the captain signing bills of lading, or in otherwise complying with the same."

The bill of lading said:

> ". . . and other conditions as per charterparty".

However, the charterparty clause set out was not seen by cargo-owner, and the court refused to extend the notion of constructive notice from land transactions into the general field of commerce. In respect of the reluctance to extend equitable principles into commercial transactions, the case has been cited with approval many times.[18]

Note also the indemnity provision in the charterparty clause, set out above. This was regarded by Lindley LJ as:[19]

> ". . . extremely significant. It seems as if these parties felt that, notwithstanding this clause, the owners might be held liable for the acts of the master; and they stipulated in that event, notwithstanding the previous bargain that the captain is to be the agent and servant of the charterer – the charterer shall indemnify the shipowner".

The point is that the owners had provided for the possibility that they would, notwithstanding the demise clause, be the contracting carrier.

---

16 [1893] AC 8, 19 (Lord Herschell).
17 [1895] 2 QB 539.
18 See section [3.4.3], where there is also a diagrammatic representation of the parties involved.
19 [1895] 2 QB 539, 544.

Though *Manchester Trust* creates no more than a presumption, it is a very strong presumption, at any rate where the master signs the bill of lading.[20]

17.1.5 Does it matter who signs the bill of lading?

As noted, there is a strong presumption that a bill of lading signed by the master is an owners' bill unless the charter is by demise. What if the bill is signed by charterers or sub-charterers? This may make a difference, but is by no means conclusive, because they may be signing for the master, as in *The Nea Tyhi*. Sheen J adopted the following passage from *Time Charters* by Wilford, Coughlin and Healey:[21]

> "The practice of owners whose ships are time chartered to leave it to the charterers or their agents to prepare and sign bills of lading 'for the master' is now widespread. It may be that now even in the absence of express provision, owners who time charter their ships and put them on the charterers' berths without taking positive steps to indicate the contrary must be taken to have held out the charterers and their agents as having authority to make bill of lading contracts on their behalf. The charterers and their agents would thus have ostensible authority to bind the owners irrespective of any actual authority."

Of course, if the owners incur liability because of the terms of bills presented by the charterers, the charterers may be liable to indemnify the owners.[22]

17.1.6 Liner operator chartering in additional temporary tonnage

It sometimes happens that a large liner operator charters in temporarily additional tonnage, on a time or voyage basis. If the liner operator is a substantial and well-known concern, the shippers may well think they are contracting with the liner, rather than (perhaps a small) shipowner. Though this has been considered, in some of the cases, a factor for reversing the *Manchester Trust* presumption, we need also to consider the identity of the signatory, and perhaps other factors.[23]

We start with the decision of the Court of Appeal in *The Okehampton*.[24] There, a sub-charterer was adding to his fleet, and was held to be the contracting carrier, but the bill of lading was signed by the sub-charterers and not by the master, and the decision was that they had been signed by them in their own capacity. Of this case Leggatt LJ observed in *The Rewia*:[25]

> "The case merely shows that even if the signatory had authority to bind the shipowner, he did not in fact purport to do so, and the charterers alone were made parties to the contract. The bill of lading was signed by the charterers not on account of the ship but on their own account. They were signing for themselves as principals, and the shipowners were not parties to the contract of carriage. It is important to note that although the sample bills bore the words 'el capitan', the charterers did not purport to sign for him."

The case turned, in other words, on whether the charterers signed for themselves or the master: "In short, in that case, as in this, the question is one of construction."

---

20 *The Rewia* [1991] 2 Lloyds Rep 325, in section [17.1.6].
21 [1982] 1 Lloyd's Rep 606, 610. The current edition is Coghlin, Baker, Kenny, Kimball and Belknap, *Time Charters*, 7th ed (2014), Taylor & Francis.
22 On the principles in section [13.7].
23 As in *The Starsin* [2004] 1 AC 715, in section [17.1.8].
24 [1913] P 137.
25 [1991] 2 Lloyd's Rep 325, 332.

A case where the charterers were treated as contracting carrier though they did not sign the bill was *Elder Dempster & Co v Paterson, Zochonis & Co.*[26] There is very little discussion in the House of Lords, but at first instance Rowlatt J (whose view on this issue was accepted with little elaboration when the case went higher) said:[27]

> ". . . it seems to me that there is a contract with the [charterers] on this bill of lading. This is a case where a well-known line of ships found it necessary to supplement its fleet by getting in another upon a time-charter; and people in the commercial world who use the line know nothing at all about that. They think they are shipping by this line; and unless it is clear to the contrary the contract should be regarded as being made with the line. In this case the mate's receipt – as the bill of lading itself which goes just as far – it is the more material document – proclaims to the people who took the bill of lading that those who are going to carry the goods are the [charterers]; and there is the signature at the bottom which may be the signature of the master without qualification. Therefore, I think, in these circumstances it is a bill of lading with the [charterers]."

As in *The Okehampton*, the charterers had chartered in just one additional ship, about which "people in the commercial world who use the line know nothing at all". But that is not the only consideration, for we are also told that the bill of lading "proclaims to the people who took the bill of lading that those who are going to carry the goods are the [charterers]".

Both these cases were regarded as exceptional (and not followed) in *The Rewia*.[28] *Elder Dempster* was distinguished on the grounds that in the later case *all* the tonnage was chartered in. *The Okehampton* was regarded as an unusual case where the issue was whether the sub-chaterers, as bailors of the goods, had title to sue in tort. The bill of lading had been signed by the master in *The Rewia*, and Leggatt LJ took the view that the cases:[29]

> ". . . support the conclusion that a bill of lading signed for the Master cannot be a charterers' bill unless the contract was made with the charterers alone, and the person signing has authority to sign, and does sign, on behalf of the charterers and not the owners. Accordingly, the bills of lading in this case were owners' bills."

In other words, where the ship is not chartered by demise, and the bill of lading is signed by the master, the presumption that the owners are the contracting carrier is very strong.

The strong presumption in *Manchester Trust* and *The Rewia* explains the need for employment and indemnity, and similar clauses, in charterparties.[30] Conversely, in *Manchester Trust*, the existence of such an indemnity supported the conclusion that the owners were the contracting carrier.[31]

17.1.7 Demise clauses

Demise, and identity of carrier, clauses state who is carrier, and therefore remove the need for presumptions – assuming the clause applies.

---

26 [1924] AC 522. This was not, however, the main issue in the case, and the decision did not turn on it; the owners were entitled to claim the benefit of bill of lading exceptions, though it was a charterers' bill. On this aspect of the case, see section [17.4].
27 (1922) 12 Ll L Rep 69, 71–2, affd on this issue [1924] AC 522.
28 [1991] 2 Lloyds Rep 325.
29 [1991] 2 Lloyds Rep 325, 333.
30 See section [13.2].
31 Section [17.1.4].

In *Manchester Trust* a demise clause in a charterparty made no difference, notice of the clause not being imputed to the bill of lading holder.[32] More modern times have seen the introduction of demise, and identity of carrier clauses, into bills of lading. These are generally used in situations where (on the principles in the previous paragraphs) the charterers might otherwise be regarded as the contracting carrier. Their combined purpose is to make the shipowner, and only the shipowner, contracting carrier.[33] In *The Starsin* at first instance, Colman J observed of the history of such clauses:[34]

> "The [demise clause] has survived from the era when a time charterer who was party to a bill of lading contract as carrier was not entitled to limit his liability under the Merchant Shipping Act. It was therefore necessary, particularly for liner companies who issued bills, to avoid being held liable as carriers."

The owners, of course, could rely on the Act, and it made sense to direct liability through them.

There is no need for notice when the clause is explicitly set out in the bill of lading, and so the problems in *Manchester Trust* do not arise. There is no doubt that a demise clause is in the bill of lading can be effective. In *The Berkshire*,[35] damage was occasioned to a cargo of cotton after they had been transhipped in breach of contract, and the cargo-owners sued the shipowners. The bill of lading had been signed by charterers' agents,[36] with charterers' agents' heading on the bill of lading, but from the signature box it was not clear for whom they were signing.[37] Quite possibly, on the principles in the previous sections, this would have been held to have been a charterer's bill, had not a demise clause resolved the issue in favour of the shipowner being contracting carrier. Brandon J said that:[38]

> "Despite arguments to the contrary put forward for the shipowners, I see no reason not to give effect to the demise clause in accordance with its terms."

Ocean Wide (the charterers' agents) were therefore held to be signing as agents only, for the shipowners.

In *The Berkshire* the effect of the demise clause was to impose liability on the shipowners. What if it is intended to relieve from liability the person who would otherwise be regarded as the contracting carrier? In *The Mica*[39] Heald J held that a demise clause was rendered void by Art. III(8) of the Hague Rules, as purporting to relieve the carriers from responsibility. Whether this is correct depends on the relationship between Arts. III(2) and III(8) of Hague and Hague-Visby, and in particular the scope of the House of Lords decisions in *G.H. Renton & Co Ltd v Palmyra Trading Corp of Panama* and *The Jordan II*.[40] This is discussed in chapter 18.[41] It may be that Art. III(8) could apply in principle, but the clause would have to shift liability away from a party who would otherwise clearly be the carrier, on the basis of the presumptions or other factors.

---

32 Section [3.4.3].
33 In *The Starsin*, the identity of carrier clause identified the contacting party, and the demise clause provided that the only contract of carriage would be with that party identified.
34 [2000] 1 Lloyd's Rep 85, 89.
35 [1974] 1 Lloyd's Rep 185.
36 Or to be more accurate, by their agents, on their behalf.
37 In this respect, the case differs from *The Starsin* in the next section.
38 [1974] 1 Lloyd's Rep 185, 188.
39 [1973] 2 Lloyd's Rep 478 (Canada Federal Court), concerning a cargo of steel bars.
40 Respectively [1957] AC 149; *Jindal Iron and Steel Co Ltd v Islamic Solidarity Shipping Co Jordan Inc (The Jordan II)* [2005] 1 WLR 1363.
41 Section [18.4].

17.1.8 *The Starsin*

The House of Lords decision in *The Starsin* is the leading recent case on the identity of the carrier.[42] It is ultimately a construction case, however. The bill of lading contained a demise clause (in the standard printed conditions), which stated that the owners were the contracting party. However, the signature box stated (typed) that the signatory was acting "as agent for [CPS or charterers] (the carrier)",[43] and there was also the rubber stamp of the charterers' port agents (and two actual signatures). The issue was which prevailed. The House held that these were charterers' bills, thereby according priority to the signature box.

The case was treated simply as a matter of construction of the bill of lading, though regard was also paid to the fact that the bill of lading would be negotiated; it is addressed to parties other than just the original shipper, and third parties may typically inspect no more than the front of the bill of lading.[44] Ultimately, however, the case is an application of the principles of interpretation in *Glynn v Margetson & Co*:[45] greater weight should attach to terms of a contract specially chosen by the parties than to standard printed conditions. The signature box was filled in, whereas the demise clause was just one of the printed clauses.

The case arose from damage caused to timber, at various stages of the voyage, from condensation because the timber was badly stowed. The charterers were bankrupt, and therefore action was brought (by various cargo-owners) against the shipowners for negligent stowage, alternatively in contract or tort. Because these were held to be charterers' bills the only action was in tort. The owners attempted to rely on a Himalaya clause in the bills of lading affording complete protection to "every independent contractor from time to time employed by the carrier",[46] the charterers being the carriers and the owners themselves being the independent contractors.

Only one of the claimants succeeded in tort, having property in the cargo at the time of the breach.[47] In respect of this one claim, in principle the Himalaya clause protected the owners,[48] but only to the extent that it did not reduce liability below that provided by the Hague Rules, which were incorporated by paramount clause into the bill of lading. This was an application of Art. III(8) of the Hague Rules.[49]

17.2 Himalaya clauses and circular indemnities

17.2.1 *Midland Silicones Ltd v Scruttons Ltd*

Himalaya clauses and circular indemnities are devices that were used to obviate the effects of the decision of the House of Lords in *Midland Silicones Ltd v Scruttons Ltd*.[50] The problems with the Himalaya clause have been largely resolved in England by the Contract (Rights of Third Parties) Act 1999, but we will nonetheless begin with *Midland Silicones*, because it has also impacted on the drafting of the Hague-Visby Rules and later international conventions.[51]

---

42 [2004] 1 AC 715.

43 The case differed from *The Berkshire* [1974] 1 Lloyd's Rep 185, in the previous section, in that the bills clearly stated that the signature was "as agent for [CPS or charterers] (the carrier)" – the actual signature appeared to be that of the port agents. In *The Berkshire*, it was not clear for whom the agents were signing.

44 [2004] 1 AC 715, [74] (Lord Hoffmann).

45 [1893] AC 351, and see sections [4.4]; [22.2].

46 On Himalaya clauses, see section [17.2].

47 See further section [16.10].

48 See further section [17.2] on Himalaya clauses generally.

49 See further section [18.4].

50 [1962] AC 446.

51 See section [17.5].

In *Midland Silicones*, the claimants were consignees of a drum of chemicals. The defendants were a stevedoring company engaged by the carrier to unload his vessels in London. They negligently dropped the drum, thereby causing damage to the value of £593. The contract of carriage, to which only shippers and consignees were party, incorporated the Hague Rules (incorporated by virtue of the United States Carriage of Goods by Sea Act 1936, on an outward voyage from the United States to London). These limited the liability of the carrier for damage to $500 (then a significantly lesser sum). The consignees sued the stevedores in tort, for negligence, and successfully recovered the whole of the £593 (ie, substantially more than $500). The House of Lords, restating the privity of contract doctrine, held that the stevedores could not rely on a clause in a contract to which they were not party. Here is a somewhat simplified diagram, showing the relationships:[52]

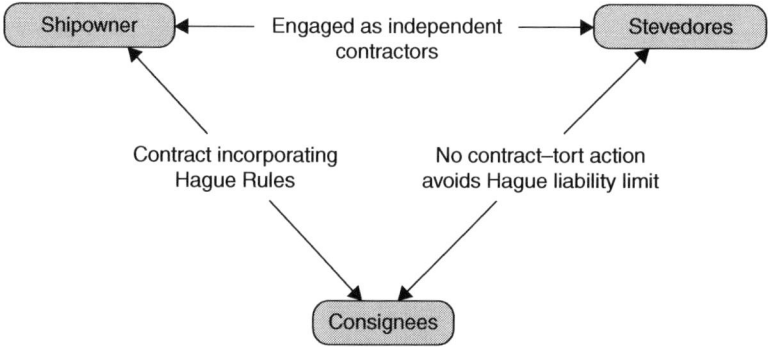

By suing the stevedores in tort, rather than the shipowners in contract, the consignees were able to avoid the liability limits in the US incarnation of the Hague Rules, incorporated into the bill of lading.

One of the motivations for the Visby amendments to the Hague Rules was to reverse the effects of this decision.[53] Accordingly, Art. IV *bis*, added by the Visby amendments, provides for the defences and limits of liability to apply to tort actions, as well as contract, and extends the benefit of such limits to servants and agents of the carrier (but not to independent contractors).[54] Because Hague-Visby works by incorporation into carriage contracts,[55] it is possible that this amendment achieved nothing, the problem being precisely the lack of such contract between the cargo-owners and the "servant or agent of the carrier". In so far as that was a problem, however, it has been resolved by the Contract (Rights of Third Parties) Act 1999, of which we should set out parts of ss. 1 and 6:

"1.   (1) Subject to the provisions of this Act, a person who is not a party to a contract (a "third party") may in his own right enforce a term of the contract if –

(a)   the contract expressly provides that he may, or

(b)   . . . the term purports to confer a benefit on him.

. . .

---

52 It is slightly simplified because the consignees would also not have been directly party to the carriage contract, but would have been affected by it on the principles in chapter 16.

53 See section [18.1].

54 The full text can be found in Appendix A.

55 See section [16.10].

(3)   The third party must be expressly identified in the contract by name, as a member of a class or as answering a particular description but need not be in existence when the contract is entered into.

6.   (5) Section 1 confers no rights on a third party in the case of —

(a)   a contract for the carriage of goods by sea, or

(b)   a contract for the carriage of goods by rail or road, or for the carriage of cargo by air, which is subject to the rules of the appropriate international transport convention,

except that a third party may in reliance on that section avail himself of an exclusion or limitation of liability in such a contract.

It can be seen that s. 1(3) allows the benefits of a contract to be extended to third parties, "as a member of a class or as answering a particular description", a phrase that would presumably include the "servant or agent of the carrier". The Hague-Visby term purports to confer a benefit on them as required by s. 1(1)(b), and it cannot be said that "on a proper construction of the contract it appears that the parties did not intend the term to be enforceable by the third party", which would lead to disapplication of the Act under s. 1(2). Section 6(5) expressly allows third parties to be protected in respect of exclusions or limitation of liability (though not of any other type of clause). So a combination of Hague-Visby and the 1999 Act protects servants and agents. It does not extend protection to independent contractors, a proposal to do so having been defeated in the CMI,[56] and therefore will not normally protect performing (but non-contracting) carriers. Nor of course, will it actually have any effect on the decision in *Midland Silicones* itself! However, an appropriate clause in the bill of lading, combined with the 1999 Act, should achieve the desired purpose.

There are similar provisions in Art. 7(1) of the Hamburg Rules and Art. 4(1) of the Rotterdam Convention, both of which use the phrase, "whether founded in contract, in tort, or otherwise". Hamburg is otherwise similar to Hague-Visby, protecting servants and agents of the carrier, but Rotterdam extends protection to "all performing carriers", which should (if ever enacted) avoid cargo-owners avoiding limits by suing performing carriers in tort.[57]

Note, however, that only benefits can be conferred on third parties by the 1999 Act. A clause that is equivocal, in the sense that it could be either a benefit or a detriment, such as a jurisdiction or arbitration clause, probably falls outside its scope.

17.2.2 Himalaya clauses

The Himalaya clause was drafted by the commercial parties to avoid the result in *Midland Silicones*. It was named after *The Himalaya*,[58] a Court of Appeal decision that can be seen as a precursor to *Midland Silicones*. Typically, it provides for exemptions and limitations to be extended to servants and agents, and independent contractors engaged by the carrier. It would therefore protect not only stevedores, but also performing carriers, for example where a through bill of lading is used, or in a multimodal transport operation.[59]

Before the 1999 Act, Himalaya clauses were the main means of extending carriage contract protection to non-parties. They use the device of the implied unilateral offer to extend the benefits, to be accepted by the servant, agent or independent contractor performing his contractual duties. To

---

56 Treitel and Reynolds, *Carver on Bills of Lading*, 3rd ed (2012), [9–295]–[9–303].

57 See generally sections [21.3]; [21.4]. There will be performing, but non-contracting carriers, whenever a through bill of lading or multimodal transport document is used. On through bills, see section [14.7].

58 *Adler v Dickson (The Himalaya)* [1955] 1 QB 158.

59 See sections [14.6]; [21.2].

refer back to the *Midland Silicones* diagram, the effect of a Himalaya clause would be to imply a contract between the consignees and the stevedores, thereby avoiding the privity problem. That they were generally successful was established in a number of cases culminating with the decision of the House of Lords in *The Starsin*, where a shipowner as performing but not actual carrier was protected.[60] However, a contract could not always be implied, and so there was always uncertainty about the application of any Himalaya clause.[61] Perhaps more fundamentally, in *The Mahkutai*[62] the Privy Council took the view that a Himalaya clause worked only for provisions for the carrier's benefit and protection, and not to a mutual agreement such as the exclusive jurisdiction clause in that case; such clauses, it would seem, cannot bind third parties under the Himalaya clause technique.

After the 1999 Act it is no longer necessary to invoke the contractual fiction of the implied contract, so the difficulties in a case such as *Raymond Burke Motors Ltd v The Mersey Docks and Harbour Co* probably no longer apply. There remain problems, however, with any clause that is not unequivocally for the benefit of the carrier.

17.3 Circular indemnities

Possibly because Himalaya clauses could not (at least prior to 1999) be guaranteed to work, it became common, especially in through bills and those intended for multimodal transport, to incorporate a circular indemnity (or variation thereon). This can be made always to work, and the classic form of circular indemnity was indeed another of the devices to avoid the privity doctrine discussed by Lord Reid in *Midland Silicones* itself.[63] It is usually used to protect from tort actions performing carriers, who have no contract with the cargo-owner.

The point of circular indemnities is to deprive the cargo-owner from obtaining any benefit from suing the third party (usually, but not necessarily, a performing carrier). Typically, the cargo-owner will undertake (by an express clause in the bill of lading) not to bring any action against servants, agents and independent contractors engaged by the carrier, or at any rate not to sue on terms more favourable than those available against the carrier. This differs from an exemption clause in that a positive obligation is imposed on the shipper, or those claiming through him, so that the cargo-owner will be in breach of the carriage contract if he brings an action against the third party. In a true circular indemnity, the carrier also, in his contract with the third party (ie, his servants, agents and independent contractors), agrees to indemnify the third party against any claim brought by the cargo-owner. The terms of this indemnity are made known to the cargo-owner.

Suppose then, the cargo-owner has undertaken not to sue a third party (let us suppose a performing carrier) at all. If the cargo-owner sues the performing carrier in tort, the contracting carrier has contracted to indemnify the third party. The amount of the indemnity will be the same as the amount of damages recovered by the cargo-owner. The carrier can now sue the cargo-owner for breach of the carriage contract, and (assuming the cargo-owner is aware of the indemnity) the damages will be the loss the carrier has suffered as a result of the breach. This will be the amount of the indemnity he has paid, or become liable to pay, to the performing carrier, which will itself be the sum that the performing carrier paid in damages to the cargo-owner. The result, of course, is that any action by the cargo-owner against the performing carrier achieves nothing: the damages

60 *New Zealand Shipping Co Ltd v AM Satterthwaite & Co Ltd (The Eurymedon)* [1975] AC 154 (stevedores); *Port Jackson Stevedoring Pty Ltd v Salmond and Spraggon (Australia) Pty Ltd (The New York Star)* [1981] 1 WLR 138 (stevedores); *The Starsin* [2004] 1 AC 715 (see section [17.1.8]).

61 Eg, *Raymond Burke Motors Ltd v The Mersey Docks and Harbour Co* [1986] 1 Lloyd's Rep 155, where the stevedores damaged the claimants' cargo before they had even started to load it, and therefore could not be said to have accepted a unilateral offer. See further Todd, *Cases and Materials on International Trade Law* (2002), Sweet & Maxwell, [11–038].

62 [1996] AC 650.

63 [1962] AC 446, 473.

successfully obtained by the cargo-owner in his action against the performing carrier will have to be paid back by him to the carrier. The carrier will reimburse the performing carrier on the indemnity, and the net result of all the actions will be to benefit the cargo-owner nothing. Nor will the performing carrier suffer. This is illustrated here diagrammatically.

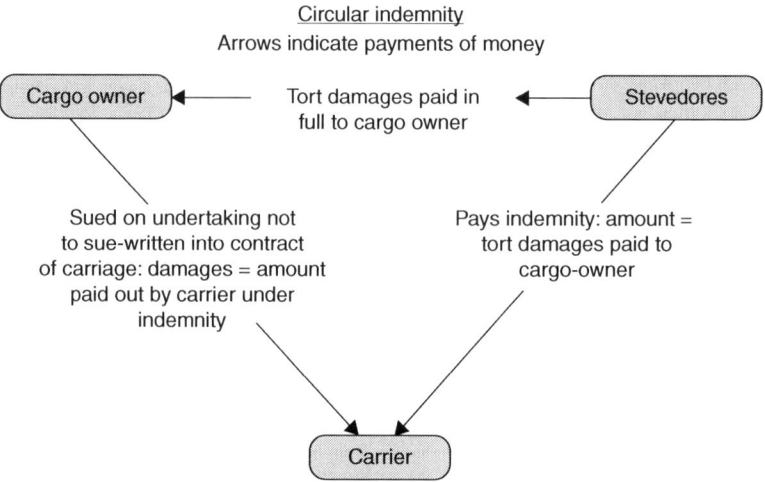

If the cargo-owner attempts to sue the performing carrier in spite of the clause, the carrier can go further and ask the court to restrain the original action against the third party, under the provisions of s. 49(3) of the Senior Courts Act 1981 (replacing an earlier provision, but without altering the law). The court has a discretion to grant a stay of action, if the action would be a fraud on the carrier.

In reality, contracting carriers generally prefer not to use proper circular indemnities, and the use of any kind of circular indemnity is largely confined to through bills and combined transport documents, where there will be a number of performing carriers involved in the operation. Moreover, circular indemnities, when incorporated, usually complement, rather than replace Himalaya clauses. But if the contracting carrier has undertaken to indemnify the performing carrier, and the performing carrier claims on the indemnity, this leaves the contracting carrier to pursue his claim against the cargo-owner, with whom he has possibly had no previous relations, who may reside in a foreign jurisdiction, and whose solvency may be in doubt. There is no good reason why contracting carriers should agree to be exposed to such hazards. True circular indemnities are therefore uncommon, and, even where they are incorporated, they are additional to the Himalaya clause, and do not replace it.

More usually, the cargo-owner is subject, in the bill of lading, to a contractual undertaking not to sue, but the contracting carrier does not undertake to indemnify the third party (though of course he may do so in reality).[64] Another possibility is for the bill of lading contract expressly to allow the carrier to recover from the cargo-owner any moneys recovered in any action against third parties. Clauses of this nature are often incorporated, whether or not there is a true circular indemnity.[65]

These clauses are intended to give the carrier the benefits of the circular indemnity without the risks. Of course, they are less satisfactory from the point of view of the performing carrier than

---

64 Eg, BIMCO's Multidoc 95, cl. 15: https://www.bimco.org/~/media/Chartering/Document_Samples/Bill_of_Ladings/Sample_Copy_MULTIDOC_95.ashx.

65 BIMCO's Conlinebill 2000, cl. 15: https://www.bimco.org/~/media/Chartering/Document_Samples/Bill_of_Ladings/Sample_Copy_CONLINEBILL_2000.ashx.

is a true circular indemnity, since the performing carrier must rely on the goodwill of the carrier to protect him. Further, unless he has also agreed to indemnify the performing carrier the carrier may not always be able to invoke the stay of action under s. 49(3), since he must show that the action of the cargo-owner would be a fraud on him. The carrier must have a sufficient interest in restraining the action. He will certainly have sufficient interest if, as in the true circular indemnity, he has agreed to indemnify the performing carrier against the consequences of any action brought by the cargo-owner. In such a case the carrier stands to lose financially because of a breach by the cargo-owner of the contract of carriage, and if the cargo-owner knows this, the carrier will have no difficulty in obtaining a stay. The action would be a clear fraud.

If the carrier has not undertaken to indemnify the performing carrier, however, the cargo-owner's breach of undertaking may be insufficient to give the contracting carrier sufficient interest to obtain a stay. This was the issue in *The Elbe Maru*, a decision of Ackner J.[66] The contracting carrier succeeded in obtaining a stay of action under s. 41 of the Supreme Court of Judicature Act 1925, the precursor to s. 49(3) of the Senior Courts Act 1981, but only because he established "a real possibility, if the [merchant's] claim is allowed to proceed, of . . . suffering financial loss".[67] Ackner J continued:

> "If it was to be established, however, that it was basically an academic exercise, that the breach of agreement [by the merchant] not to sue would involve [the contracting carrier] in no form of possible prejudice, then I think a court would be reluctant to exercise its discretion and allow such [carriers] to interfere with a pending action."

It may therefore be possible to establish prejudice without establishing a formal requirement that the carrier indemnify the performing carrier. But if the carrier cannot establish prejudice, he cannot stay the action.

In *The Elbe Maru* itself, the cargo-owner argued that the carrier could not be prejudiced precisely because the cargo-owner had agreed to indemnify the contracting carrier against any consequences of his breach in suing the performing carrier. Ackner J did not think that the inclusion of this indemnity was itself a ground for taking away the contracting carrier's right to apply for a stay.

Now that enforcement of Himalaya clauses has been made less uncertain by the 1999 Act, there is less need for the indemnity provisions than was previously the case.

17.4 Bailment on terms

This jurisdiction originated in *Elder, Dempster & Co Ltd v Paterson, Zochonis & Co Ltd*,[68] and was resurrected by the Privy Council in *The Pioneer Container*.[69] It can be used to protect sub-carriers, for example in a multimodal transport operation, such as described in the previous section.[70] There will be a bailment from the shipper to the contracting carrier, but it will also be envisaged that the contracting carrier will sub-bail the cargo to the actual carriers, and the shipper will typically agree the terms of the sub-bailments with the contracting carrier, or allow the contracting carrier to a discretion as to those terms.

In *The Pioneer Container*, the contracting carrier was expressly allowed, by the terms of the head-carriage contract to sub-contract on any terms whatever, and he sub-bailed the goods (to a

---

66 *Nippon Yusen Kaisha v International Import and Export Co Ltd (The Elbe Maru)* [1978] 1 Lloyd's Rep 206.
67 [1978] 1 Lloyd's Rep 206, 210.
68 [1924] AC 522, also in section [17.1.6].
69 [1994] 2 AC 324.
70 Or in unimodal sea transit, where it is envisaged that the cargo will be transhipped for some of the voyage, a through bill of lading being issued, as described in section [14.7].

shipowner). The sub-bailment was on the terms of feeder bills, which contained an exclusive jurisdiction clause, to which the cargo-owner was held impliedly to have consented, and that could be relied on by the sub-contractor (the shipowner). Though the effect can be to allow the sub-bailee (ie, actual carrier) to enjoy the terms agreed between shipper and head bailor, this is not how it works conceptually, and bailment on terms is in that respect quite different from the Himalaya clause considered earlier.[71] In *The Pioneer Container*, the cargo-owner was *burdened* by the terms of the feeder bill, whereas in (eg) *The Starsin*, the shipowner (using a Himalaya clause) was *benefited* by the charterer's bill. But though it is *conceptually* quite different, it allows clauses such as exclusive jurisdiction clauses *in fact* to apply between parties other than cargo-owner and contracting carrier.

The doctrine depends on the existence of a sub-bailment. It depends on the *authority* given by head-bailor (usually the cargo-owner) to the terms of any sub-bailment, so that the sub-bailment terms *bind* the head-bailor. It does not allow sub-bailees to claim the *benefit* of the terms of the head-bailment. The doctrine did not operate in *The Mahkutai*.[72] There, as we saw earlier in the chapter, a Himalaya clause did not (on its terms) extend the protection of an exclusive jurisdiction clause, and this also precluded general authority needed for bailment on terms argument. It would have been better had there been no Himalaya clause in the head contract.

17.5 Binding non-contracting cargo-owners: *The Captain Gregos*

This is more of a problem. It can allow cargo-owners to avoid Hague-Visby exceptions, limits and time-bars entirely, though it is arguable that it would not affect Hamburg or Rotterdam in the same way.

In *The Captain Gregos*[73] a shipowner was sued in conversion (for non-delivery of part of the cargo) by PEAG, an intermediate purchaser with whom (under the regime of the Bills of Lading Act 1855) he had no contract. The shipowner claimed the benefit of the time bar in Art. III(6) of the Hague-Visby Rules, which governed the bill of lading contract. The Court of Appeal held, as part of the *ratio*, that the Hague-Visby Rules operated by incorporation into carriage contracts, and therefore by any cargo-owner who was not party to such a contract. In this diagram, we are looking at PEAG's action. BP had a contract, and would have been unable to avoid the time bar.

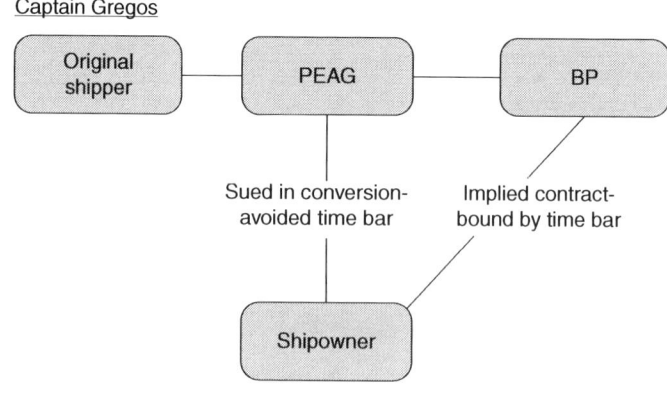

Captain Gregos

Original shipper — PEAG — BP

Sued in conversion-avoided time bar

Implied contract-bound by time bar

Shipowner

---

71 In section [17.2].
72 [1996] AC 650.
73 [1990] 1 Lloyd's Rep 310. The issue of who were in fact parties to the carriage contract was determined later, in *The Captain Gregos* (No 2) [1990] 2 Lloyd's Rep 395; see further section [16.9].

We have seen that Art. IV bis of Hague-Visby applies the "defences and limits of liability provided for in these Rules . . . in any action against the carrier . . . whether the action be founded in contract or in tort".[74] Moreover, s. 1(2) of the Carriage of Goods by Sea Act 1971 gives the provisions "the force of law". In the context of another provision where similar wording was used, *Sidhu v British Airways plc* concerned an (unsuccessful) attempt by air passengers to avoid the Warsaw Convention time bar by suing at common law, in tort.[75] Like Hague-Visby, the Convention was given "force of law" by the Carriage by Air Act 1961, s. 1(2) and Sch. 1. In holding that the common law tort action was excluded, Lord Hope adopted a purposive construction to the legislation:[76]

> "To permit exceptions, whereby a passenger could sue outwith the convention for losses sustained in the course of international carriage by air, would distort the whole system, . . . Thus, the purpose is to ensure that, in all questions relating to the carrier's liability, it is the provisions of the convention which apply and that the passenger does not have access to any other remedies, whether under the common law or otherwise . . . The carrier does not need to make provision for the risk of being subjected to such remedies, because the whole matter is regulated by the convention."

The issues were not the same as here, because the claims were brought by one contracting party against another, and there were not the additional privity issues that can arise where the action is brought by a non-contracting party. However, Lord Hope's sentiments lend support to the view that avoidance of the liability limits and time bar by the passenger should not be possible, even in principle.

To return to *The Captain Gregos*, one of two purchasers was able, by suing the carrier in the tort of conversion, to avoid the Hague-Visby time bar (Art. III(6)). The purchaser in question (though owner of the goods) was not party to any carriage contract, and the Court of Appeal held that Hague-Visby operated only through incorporation into the carriage contract. However, Bingham LJ's reasoning in *The Captain Gregos* is based on the detailed drafting of Hague-Visby, and, in particular, its treatment of the bill of lading as "the bedrock on which this mandatory code is founded".[77] The bill of lading is well-known as a contractual document, and (to continue with Bingham LJ's judgment) there was no reason "why the code should treat the existence of a bill of lading as a matter of such central and overriding importance if the code is to apply with equal force as between those who are not parties to the contract which the bill contains or evidences".[78] Moreover "[much] of the language in the [Carriage of Goods by Sea Act 1971] and the [Hague-Visby Rules] suggests that the code is intended to govern the relations between the parties to the bill of lading contract".

It is probably fair to say that the bill of lading features less centrally in both the Hamburg and the Rotterdam Rules, and that the reasoning in *The Captain Gregos* may therefore not apply to them.

17.6 Question

Bob has contracted to ship his two fire engines, each of which is worth £100,000, aboard Charles's ship. Each is to be shipped under a separate carriage contract (each of whose terms are common in the trade), each of which contains a Himalaya clause to the effect, *inter alia*, that no independent contractor engaged by the carrier is to be under any liability whatsoever to the shipper, consignee or owner, that any exemption, limitation or other clause in the carriage contract shall extend to

---

74 Section [17.2].
75 [1997] AC 430.
76 [1997] AC 430, 447.
77 [1990] 1 Lloyd's Rep 310, 318 (Bingham LJ).
78 Ibid.

protect every such independent contractor engaged by the carrier. The carriage contract also limits the liability of the carrier to £10,000 per fire engine, and requires that all disputes be submitted to arbitration in London.

(Assume that neither the Hague nor Hague-Visby Rules apply to the carriage contract.)

Doddle Co is a company of stevedores, which is engaged, for the first time, as an independent contractor by Charles. Doddle does not know the exact terms of the contract of carriage. Before loading the fire engine it is necessary to unload other goods from Charles' ship, and, in doing so, the stevedores negligently drop a large drum containing sulphuric acid on top of one of the fire engines, which completely destroys it. The second fire engine is negligently dropped into the sea during the loading process, also destroying it.

Bob brings an action in negligence against Doddle, in the High Court, claiming £200,000 damages.

Discuss.

Comment

Carriage contract benefits can be extended to third parties either by the Contract (Rights of Third Parties) Act 1999 or by a Himalaya clause, as discussed in The Eurymedon.[79] Probably the £10,000 limit would come under the 1999 Act, but the arbitration clause would not (because it is not an exclusion or limitation of liability). The arbitration clause might present problems under the Himalaya clause as well, partly on the basis of The Mahkutai,[80] and partly because the analysis in The Eurymedon depends on a unilateral implied contract, accepted by performance. Here, Doddle does not know the terms of the contract he is apparently accepting, and, in any case, it must be questionable whether he has accepted it; certainly he cannot be said to have fully performed. Himalaya clauses usually work, but remember their juridical basis: if there is no implied contract, the clause is ineffective.

---

79 *New Zealand Shipping Co Ltd v A.M. Satterthwaite & Co Ltd (The Eurymedon)* [1975] AC 154.
80 [1996] AC 650, in section [17.2.2].

Chapter 18

Hague and Hague-Visby Rules

Chapter Contents

18.1 Introduction

Whereas charterparties are generally free of regulatory control,[1] that is not true of bills of lading. In fact, either the Hague or the Hague-Visby Rules (which generally protect cargo-owners) apply to almost every bill of lading issue anywhere in the world. A very small number might be governed by the Hamburg Rules,[2] and occasionally the common law applies, but in this last case it is either because of a mistake, or because there is a gap in the coverage of the law.[3]

This chapter covers the Hague and Hague-Visby Rules, but it is not complete coverage, because some parts of the regime are (or have been) more conveniently covered as part of the substantive coverage of an area. Examples are deviation, seaworthiness, privity issues, and misrepresentations in bills of lading.[4] This chapter is best seen as an outline of the backbone and principles of the Rules.

By way of a brief introduction, by about the end of the nineteenth century carriers were able to incorporate wide exceptions into carriage contracts, reducing the value of bills of lading.[5] This was the age of freedom of contract, and carriers must have enjoyed strong bargaining power, but a feature of bills of lading is that they are transferable.[6] Consequently their terms affect third parties, who will generally have had no say in those terms. The value of bills of lading as negotiable documents was being reduced.[7] This was widely thought to justify an international convention, and UK legislation, implementing a pro-cargo-owner regime.

The original Hague Rules were drafted in 1922, and implemented in the UK in 1924 (in the US not until 1936).[8] They were very successful at harmonising the law, probably applying at one time to most of the world's international carriage. They offered essentially fault-based liability, with seaworthiness remaining paramount, but otherwise subject to excepted perils (these being based on the exceptions used in contracts in 1922), and also subject to limitation of liability and a time bar. But carriers were not permitted to lower their liability below that provided by the Rules.[9]

By the 1960s the Hague Rules were becoming dated in some respects (mostly financial), and there were issues with some of the English decisions. The Visby amendments were a response to this, and were evolutionary in nature, by which I mean that they made no radical alterations to the structure. The Visby amendments were agreed as the Brussels Protocol of 1968 and brought into force in the UK by the Carriage of Goods by Sea Act 1971, which came into force (in the UK and internationally, on adoption then by 20 nations) in 1977. The Hague-Visby Rules are set out in the Schedule to the 1971 Act, and are set out in full in Appendix A.

Briefly, the motivations for the Visby amendments were as follows:

(1)   Most importantly (probably) from a practical viewpoint, the package limitation was regarded as too low.

---

1 See sections [1.3]; [1.8].
2 On which see section [21.4].
3 See *Vita Food Products Inc v Unus Shipping Co Ltd* [1939] AC 277 and (at least for the relevant time) *Trafigura Beheer BV v Mediterranean Shipping Company SA (The MSC Amsterdam)* [2007] 2 Lloyd's Rep 622, respectively in sections [18.6.1]; [18.6.3].
4 See respectively sections [4.4], [4.2] and chapter 19 (sections [19.2]; [19.5]).
5 See further generally Todd, *Cases and Materials on International Trade Law* (2002), Sweet & Maxwell, ch. 11. On the process of agreeing Hague, see (eg) *The Bunga Seroja* [1999] 1 Lloyd's Rep 512, [10] *et seq* (High Court of Australia). On the Visby amendments see generally Diamond, *The Hague-Visby Rules* [1978] LMCLQ 225.
6 On the principles in chapter 14. Transferable but not (technically) negotiable.
7 [1978] LMCLQ 225, 227. This is also a justification for not applying the Rules to charterparties. Another possible justification was that shipowners were seen as abusing a monopoly position (using a Conference system): eg, Goff, *Commercial contracts and the Commercial Court* [1984] LMCLQ 382, 392.
8 The US already had its own legislation, the Harter Act 1893, which was really a precursor to Hague; it is probably correct to regard Hague as a development of Harter. UK implementation was the Carriage of Goods by Sea Act 1924.
9 See generally section [18.2].

(2) The package limitation also did not work well with large undivided bulk cargoes, or with cargoes that were consolidated, for example by being packed into a container.

(3) There was dissatisfaction with the House of Lords decision in *The Muncaster Castle*, on the due diligence standard for provision of a seaworthy vessel. However, agreement could not be reached on what to do about it, and *The Muncaster Castle* remains unchanged by the amendments.[10]

(4) There was also dissatisfaction with *Midland Silicones Ltd v Scruttons Ltd*, considered in the last chapter.[11] I explained that the amendments may not have effected a useful change, but that matters have been to some extent overtaken by the Contract (Rights of Third Parties) Act 1999.

(5) The rule in *Grant v Norway*, the subject of the next chapter, was altered but not entirely abolished. This has also been overtaken, this time by the Carriage of Goods by Sea Act 1992.[12]

(6) Article X, on the application of the Rules, considered later in this chapter, is new, and was a reaction to the Privy Council decision in *Vita Food*.[13]

Even at the time of Visby, there was dissatisfaction with it in some quarters. Excepted perils were seen as too wide, the seaworthiness obligation too narrow, and limits of liability too low. Moreover, Hague-Visby does not deal well with multimodal transport (which creates quite difficult issues). These issues were, to some extent, addressed by the Hamburg Rules, and later by the Rotterdam Rules, the latter of which were agreed in 2009. Rotterdam goes far further than was necessary, though, and covers a great deal of ground over which there was no general dissatisfaction, and which would be more appropriate in a Maritime Law code. Whether or not for this reason, Rotterdam has not yet been widely adopted, at any rate as a whole.[14]

The chapter will now move on to consider the general scheme of the Rules. We will then consider some problems in detail, as to their application and, finally, criticisms of the regime.

18.2 General scheme of the Rules

In this section we deal with the main principles of the Rules, the principles behind Arts. III and IV. Later, we will consider when they apply, and examine aspects of the regime in greater detail.

The Hague-Visby Rules are set out, almost *verbatim*, in the Schedule to the Carriage of Goods by Sea Act 1971, the text of which can be found in Appendix A.

The general principles are that liability should be fault-based (essentially, for lack of care or due diligence). The carrier should not be liable for the excepted perils that are defined in Art. IV, and that are based on the excepted perils that were in use in bills of lading in 1922. There are statutory limitations on damage per unit or package, and time for bringing actions. Beyond that, the carrier is not permitted to reduce the extent of his liability further (Art. III(8)).[15] Cargo-owners therefore gain because they can bring actions where they could not before. On the other hand, exemptions and limitations on carrier liability are also written into the Rules. The Rules can properly be seen as a package. They are not entirely pro-cargo-owner, and cargo-owners should not be entitled to take the benefits without the burdens (for example by suing in tort).[16]

---

10 *Riverstone Meat Co Pty Ltd v Lancashire Shipping Co Ltd (The Muncaster Castle)* [1961] AC 807.
11 [1962] AC 446, in section [17.2].
12 See generally sections [19.8]–[19.10].
13 See section [18.6.1].
14 See generally sections [21.4]; [21.5].
15 Also in section [18.4].
16 See sections [16.10]; [17.3].

Filling out, the common law duties, whose origins as we have seen derive from the law of bailment,[17] are set out in Art. III(1) and (2), the former of which requires the carrier "before and at the beginning of the voyage to exercise due diligence to" make the ship seaworthy. Note that the requirement is one of due diligence only, not the strict liability of the common law.[18] By contrast with Art. III(1), Art. III(2) applies throughout the voyage, requiring the carrier "properly and carefully [to] load, handle, stow, carry, keep, care for, and discharge the goods carried". Note again that it does not provide for strict liability, nor even the common law bailee liability, requiring the bailee to disprove fault.

Art. IV of the Rules set out the excepted perils (in Art. IV(2)). Art. III(2) is subject to Art. IV, whereas Art. III(1) is not; we will see that Art. III(1) mirrors the common law, in that the seaworthiness obligation remains paramount, in the sense that once loss is shown to have been caused wholly or partly by a breach of Art. III(1), the carrier will be unable to rely on the excepted perils in Art. IV.[19]

The Rules provide a floor of rights for cargo-owners, in that carriers are prevented from reducing their obligations below that provided by the Rules. Thus, Art. III(8) provides that any term "lessening [carrier] liability otherwise than as provided in these Rules, shall be null and void and of no effect". Conversely, carriers are free to increase their responsibilities, this being provided by Art. V.[20]

18.2.1 The Visby amendments

By the 1960s the Hague Rules were showing their age, and there was a trio of House of Lords and Privy Council decisions that caused dissatisfaction. In the end, however, Hague-Visby represents only a minor update and clean-up.

18.2.2 The Visby changes in outline

The most important change perhaps was the package limitation (Art. IV(5)). Under the original Rules it was £100 sterling, a figure that seemed very low by the 1960s.[21] It is now 666.67 units of account per package or unit or 2 units of account per kilogramme of gross weight of the goods lost or damaged, whichever is the higher.[22] A point to note, however, now that multi-modal operations are much more common than they were 50 years ago, is that the Hague-Visby weight limit is much lower than for other unimodal conventions.[23] This can lead to obvious problems, where it is not known where the damage has occurred (for example, if the goods are in a sealed container).

Other changes include to the value of statements in bills of lading when the bill has been negotiated (Art. III(4), covered in the next chapter),[24] and to protecting carriers, servants and agents when the action is brought in tort, rather than contract.[25]

---

17 See section [3.2].

18 This is strengthened by Art. IV(1), which negates liability ". . . for loss or damage arising or resulting from unseaworthiness unless caused by want of due diligence on the part of the carrier . . .". It also provides that ". . . the burden of proving the exercise of due diligence shall be on the carrier . . .".

19 Section [18.3.2].

20 The full text can be found in Appendix A. On Art. III(8), see also section [18.4].

21 It had already been raised to £200 in UK by Gold Clause Convention 1950; for example, the limit was £200 in *Pyrene Co Ltd v Scindia Steam Navigation Co Ltd* [1954] 2 QB 402, in section [18.4]. It was raised again, to £400, in 1977, and the agreement ceased to have effect in 1988. See http://www.pomorci.com/Skole/Recnici/Glossary%20of%20Maritime%20Law.pdf, at 25. On Art. III(6), see sections [18.6.3]; [7.6].

22 By Art. IV(5)(d), as amended by the Merchant Shipping Act 1995, s. 314(2), the unit of account is the special drawing right as defined by the International Monetary Fund. Its value varies, but it is usually around 80p.

23 Section [21.3].

24 Sections [19.8]–[19.10].

25 Art. IV bis, a reaction to *Midland Silicones Ltd v Scruttons Ltd* [1962] AC 446, in section [17.2].

There is also Art. X, considered below (a reaction to *Vita Food Products Inc v Unus Shipping Co*).[26]

I observed earlier that the trigger for the Visby amendment process was *The Muncaster Castle*,[27] with which there was much dissatisfaction. Ironically, no agreement could be reached, and *The Muncaster Castle* remains good law, untouched by the Visby amendments.

The Visby amendments attracted widespread, but by no means universal, support, so now both Hague and Hague-Visby are in force, in various parts of the world.

In summary:

Seaworthiness and due diligence were unchanged by the amendments;
Art. IV *bis* was added, to deal with privity issues;[28]
Art. X was added to deal with the *Vita Food* decision;[29]
Changes were made to the rule in *Grant v Norway*;[30]
The package limitation was changed.[31]

18.2.3 Evaluation and subsequent history

Hague was a remarkably successful harmonisation of the law, but 90 years on we see fragmentation into two or more regimes.

Hague was based on a model of sea transport in 1922, which is no longer universal today. It is very pro-carrier by today's standards, and applies only to unimodal, rather than multimodal transport.[32]

It has been suggested that Hague-Visby remains too favourable towards carriers (with its wide excepted perils, low liability limits, lack of explicit liability for delay, and seaworthiness only "before and at the beginning of the voyage"), and it remains unsuited to multimodal operations. Criticisms have been levelled primarily at the liner rather than the tramp trade, and hence less at the bulk cargo trade.

Very soon after Hague-Visby, cargo-owning nations proposed the Hamburg Rules, which were adopted by UNCITRAL in 1978.[33] These have achieved limited international success, but have not been adopted in the UK. They favour cargo-owners significantly more than Hague-Visby. More recently we have the Rotterdam Rules, finalised and adopted by an UNCITRAL Convention at the end of 2009. These are not quite so favourable towards cargo-owners, but can extend to multimodal operations. Hamburg and Rotterdam are briefly discussed in chapter 21.[34]

We now consider Hague and Hague-Visby in more detail.

18.3 Arts. III(1), III(2) and IV

Central to the operation of the regime are the basic duties of the carrier, and the excepted perils, and this section considers the interplay between these.

Article III(1) provides a seaworthiness obligation, and Art. III(2) other responsibilities caring for the cargo. They need to be considered alongside Art. IV(1), all these provisions being identical

---

26 [1939] AC 277, in section [18.6.1].
27 [1961] AC 807, in section [18.3.3].
28 See section [17.2].
29 See section [18.6.1].
30 See sections [19.8]–[19.10].
31 See section [18.5].
32 See further section [21.3].
33 The Hamburg Rules are set out in Appendix C, and discussed in sections [21.4]; [21.5].
34 Section [21.5].

in Hague and Hague-Visby. They are set out in full in Appendix A. Article III(1) requires the carrier, before and at the beginning of the voyage, to exercise due diligence to make the ship seaworthy.[35] Article III(2) provides:

> "Subject to the provisions of Art. IV,[36] the carrier shall properly and carefully load, handle, stow, carry, keep, care for, and discharge the goods carried."

The effect of Art. IV(1) is (in summary) to prevent liability arising from unseaworthiness, unless caused by want of due diligence on the part of the carrier. It also provides that the burden of proving the exercise of due diligence shall be on the carrier.

A number of points can quickly be made about these provisions:

(1) The Art. III(1) standard is the exercise of due diligence. This is lower than the common law strict liability, and is part of the package (the provision is not all pro-cargo-owner). Strict liability might be thought inappropriate, given the complexity of modern ships.

(2) Art. IV(1) is the other side of the coin. It precludes liability under Art. III(1), unless there is a want of diligence, and provides for the burden of proving due diligence to be on the carrier.

(3) The Art. III(1) duty operates only "before and at the beginning of the voyage"; this is similar (but as we will see not identical) to the position at common law.[37] Article III(2) is not so limited temporally, and applies up to and including discharge of the goods.

(4) The Art. III(2) standard is to act "properly and carefully". This has been interpreted as meaning acting in accordance with a sound system, "properly" relating to the conception and "carefully" to the implementation.[38] It is akin to a negligence standard, rather than strict liability.

(5) Article III(2) is, but Art. III(1) is not, made "[subject] to the provisions of Article IV". Article IV(2) sets out the excepted perils.[39] This reflects the common law, to the extent that the seaworthiness obligation is paramount, but Art. III(2) is not paramount, in the same way. By contrast, the duty not to be negligent, in the care of the cargo, was treated as a paramount obligation.[40]

(6) The excepted perils mirror those that were commonly used in bills of lading in 1922. Note however Art. IV(2)(q):

> "Any other cause arising without the actual fault or privity of the carrier, or without the fault or neglect of the agents or servants of the carrier, but the burden of proof shall be on the person claiming the benefit of this exception to show that neither the actual fault or privity of the carrier nor the fault or neglect of the agents or servants of the carrier contributed to the loss or damage."

This is consistent with the general fault basis for liability. However, the carrier is not always liable even if at fault, since Art. IV(2)(a) provides as an excepted peril:

---

35 The duty is filled out by Art. III(1)(b) and (c).

36 Art. IV(2) sets out the excepted perils, and so there is no liability under Art. III(2) if the loss is caused by an excepted peril.

37 Section [18.3.1].

38 *Albacora SRL v Westcott & Laurance Line Ltd* [1966] 2 Lloyds Rep 58, in section [18.3.4] (where a sound system was adopted), and see the observations in *Volcafe Ltd v Compania Sud Americana de Vapores SA* [2015] EWHC 516 (Comm), [15] (where it was not).

39 I will not discuss each individual excepted peril. Art. IV is set out fully in Appendix A.

40 Compare sections [18.3.2] and [4.2.9].

"Act, neglect, or default of the master, mariner, pilot, or the servants of the carrier in the nav-igation or in the management of the ship."

As we will see in chapter 21, Hague and Hague-Visby have come under criticism for their inclusion of this excepted peril, and it does seem to run counter to the general fault-based liability of the regime.

18.3.1 Seaworthiness before and at the beginning of the voyage

Though the seaworthiness obligation mirrors that at common law, at least in applying only at the start of the voyage, in *Maxine Footwear Co Ltd v Canadian Government Merchant Marine Ltd*,[41] the Privy Council took the view that under the Hague Rules the obligation was of a continuing nature (up until the vessel sailed), rather than applying only at specified points. The Privy Council did not apply the common law doctrine of stages.[42]

In *Maxine*, the cargo was damaged by fire, caused by an acetylene torch used to thaw out frozen scupper pipes. The person using the torch was an employee of an independent contractor, acting on the authority of the master of the ship, but since the fire was not caused "by the actual fault or privity of the carrier", the carrier attempted to rely on Art. IV(2)(a) and (b) (the bill of lading incorporating the Hague Rules):

"(a)   Act, neglect, or default of the master, mariner, pilot, or the servants of the carrier in the navi-gation or in the management of the ship.
(b)   Fire, unless caused by the actual fault or privity of the carrier."

However, the Privy Council took the view that the fire resulted in the vessel becoming unseaworthy (she had to be scuttled, along with the cargo). She certainly became unseaworthy before she sailed, but perhaps not before loading. However, this did not matter, Lord Somervell saying of the doctrine of stages:[43]

"In their Lordships' opinion, 'before and at the beginning of the voyage' means the period from at least the beginning of the loading until the vessel starts on her voyage. The word 'before' cannot, in their opinion, be read as meaning 'at the commencement of the loading'. If this had been intended it would have been said. The question when precisely the period begins does not arise in this case, hence the insertion above of the words 'at least'. On that view the obligation to exercise due diligence to make the ship seaworthy continued over the whole of the period from the beginning of loading until the ship sank. There was a failure to exercise due diligence during that period. As a result the ship became unseaworthy and this unseaworthiness caused the damage to, and loss of, the appellants' goods. The appellants are, therefore, entitled to succeed."

He continued:[44]

"When the warranty was absolute [as at common law] it seems at any rate intelligible to restrict it to certain points of time. It would be surprising if a duty to exercise due diligence ceased as soon as loading began only to reappear later shortly before the beginning of the voyage."

---

41 [1959] AC 589.
42 On which see section [4.2.4].
43 [1959] AC 589, 603.
44 [1959] AC 589, 604.

So the case is authority that there is no doctrine of stages under the Hague or Hague-Visby regimes, whether or not there is at common law.

Though there was no "actual fault or privity of the carrier", the carrier nonetheless lacked due diligence; this is consistent with the decision in *The Muncaster Castle*, which we look at below.[45] We will also see below that, because Art. III(1) is paramount, the carrier in breach of Art. III(1) was disentitled from relying on Art. IV.[46]

On the issue of unseaworthiness (but not on the application of the doctrine of stages), *Maxine Footwear* was distinguished in *The Apostolis*.[47] *The Apostolis* also concerned fire on board a ship, but the cargo-owners failed to prove the cause of the fire, and that it had been caused by unseaworthiness (the burden of proof being on them at this stage).[48] But did the fire itself make the ship unseaworthy? The Court of Appeal thought not, in spite of *Maxine Footwear*. In *Maxine* the fire was in the fabric of the vessel (the cork lining of the hold). In *The Apostolis* the court rejected the notion that fire in one cargo might render the ship unseaworthy in respect of another. Unseaworthiness was (in the view of the Court of Appeal) about the state of the ship. If *The Apostolis* is right then it also impacts on the definition of unseaworthiness, considered in chapter 4.[49]

As we will see in chapter 21, the Rotterdam Rules, should they ever become part of English law, would alter everything.[50] The seaworthiness obligation in Art. 14 of Rotterdam continues throughout the voyage. The effect of Rotterdam, Art. 17(5) would be to retain the paramount nature of the seaworthiness obligation, so the main effect of this change would probably be to preclude carriers relying on excepted perils, where Art. 14 was breached, even after the start of the voyage.

18.3.2 Paramount obligations

We saw in chapter 4 how, at common law, the obligation to provide a seaworthy vessel, and not to damage the cargo negligently, are regarded as paramount obligations.[51]

Under the Hague and Hague-Visby Rules, Art. III(2) begins: "Subject to the provisions of Article IV, . . ." (Art. IV containing the list of excepted perils). Clearly, therefore, Art. III(2) is not paramount. There are no similar words in Art. III(1), though nor does the Rules explicitly state that if there is a breach of Art. III(1), the carrier cannot rely on Art. IV.

This issue was resolved in *Maxine Footwear*, where the Privy Council held that Art. III(1) is overriding (this mirrors the common law).[52] In *Maxine* the vessel was rendered unseaworthy by fire during loading (fire being an excepted peril under Art. IV(2)(b), unless caused with actual fault or privity of the carrier). Because the carriers were in breach of Art. III(1), they were held unable to rely on Art. IV(2). Lord Somervell observed that:[53]

> "Article III (1) is an overriding obligation. If it is not fulfilled and the non-fulfilment causes the damage the immunities of Art. IV (2) cannot be relied on."

---

45 See section [18.3.3].

46 Section [18.3.2].

47 *A Meredith Jones & Co v Angemar Shipping Co Ltd (The Apostolis)* [1997] 2 Lloyd's Rep 241. Of Maxine Footwear, Phillips LJ said that he had "always found that a difficult decision": [1997] 2 Lloyd's Rep 241, 257.

48 See section [18.3.4] on burden of proof.

49 See section [4.2.3], and note also there the contrast between this case and *Northern Shipping Co v Deutsche Seereederei GmbH (The Kapitan Sakharov)* [2000] 2 Lloyd's Rep 255, where there was a breach of Art. III(1).

50 See section [21.5].

51 Section [4.2.6].

52 For the common law see section [4.2.6].

53 [1959] AC 589, 603.

We saw in chapter 4 how, when the shipowner is in breach of Art. III(1), he cannot rely on Art. IV(6), the dangerous cargo indemnity.[54] All of this is, of course, consistent with the paramount nature of the Art. III(1) obligation. However a different view has been taken of the relationship between Arts. III(1) and IV(5), the package limitation. The package limitation (Art. IV(5)) applies even if the carrier is in breach of Art. III(1).[55] We will consider the relationship between Art. IV(5) and serious breaches of contract in a later chapter.[56]

By contrast, Art. III(2) (care of the cargo) is expressly subject to Art. IV, and so a breach of Art. III(2) does not preclude the carrier from relying on any of the excepted perils.

18.3.3 Due diligence

Article III(1) is qualified by a due diligence standard. Strict liability would arguably be a very harsh regime, at a time when ships have become sufficiently complex that a shipowner has to contract out maintenance, and trust the contractors. However, in *The Muncaster Castle*[57] the House of Lords held that the carrier could be liable under the Hague Rules for any negligent work done on the ship prior to the voyage, including that of contractors whose fault the shipowner could not readily detect. A fitter in a ship repair yard had failed to harden up nuts on some inspection covers, with the result that seawater got into the hold, damaging the cargo of ox-hides. The House held the carrier liable, although he was not personally at fault. In reality the decision was not unexpected and was probably legally uncontroversial; the House simply applied earlier case law.[58] Nonetheless, it was this decision, perhaps above all, that prompted the revision process culminating in the Hague-Visby Rules. It was proposed, for example, that a carrier should be protected who engaged an independent contractor of repute,[59] but agreement could not be reached, and *The Muncaster Castle* was unchanged.

Due diligence involves a weighing up of risks, and very small risks can be ignored. In *The Amstelslot*[60] cargo suffered a general average loss because of a breakdown caused by a failure in the reduction gearing. The issue was whether cracks in the gearbox should have been spotted by surveyors before loading. No doubt there were tests the surveyors could have performed, but did not, which would have led to the discovery of the cracks. But for a gearbox suddenly to crack was most unlikely, and just because more tests could have been performed did not put the owners in lack of due diligence. The fact that the burden of proof was on the carriers did not affect the standard of care.

18.3.4 Burden of proof

We have seen that rules on burden of proof can be important where there is no other evidence. We have also seen that the Hague(-Visby) regime (in Art. IV(1)) qualifies the seaworthiness obligation with a due diligence standard, but then places the burden of proving due diligence on the carrier. In other respects, it does not change the common law, and so one might expect the shifts in the common law burdens of proof to remain otherwise unchanged. However, the interplay between the provisions may lead to changes in practice.

---

54 On which see further section [4.6.2].

55 *The Happy Ranger* [2002] 2 Lloyd's Rep 357.

56 See section [20.5].

57 *Riverstone Meat Co Pty Ltd v Lancashire Shipping Co Ltd (The Muncaster Castle)* [1961] AC 807.

58 Eg, *Dobell & Co v SS Rossmore Co* [1895] 2 QB 408, a decision on the US Harter Act 1893, a precursor to the Hague Rules.

59 Eg, the suggestions of the Sub-Committee on *Bills of Lading Clauses* of the International Maritime Committee, cited Sandström [1962] JBL 340, 349; Colinvaux, *Revision of the Hague Rules Relating to Bills of Lading* [1963] JBL 341.

60 *Union of India v NV Reederij Amsterdam (The Amstelslot)* [1963] 2 Lloyd's Rep 223.

This is essentially what Lloyd J held in *The Hellenic Dolphin*.[61] This is a summary of the way in which he saw the burden of proof shifting:

(1)   Cargo owner proves loss;
(2)   Carrier proves peril of the seas (or other Art. IV excepted peril);
(3)   Cargo owner proves a breach of Art. III(1) – note that it is no good to show a breach of Art. III(2);
(4)   Carrier proves no lack of due diligence (Arts. III(1) and IV(1)).

Lloyd J said in respect of (2) that the "position in that respect is exactly the same whether the Hague Rules are incorporated or not". He also thought that (3) was unaffected: "The cargo-owner can then seek to displace the exception by proving that the vessel was unseaworthy at commencement of the voyage and that the unseaworthiness was the cause of the loss. The burden in relation to seaworthiness does not shift."[62] Lloyd J seemed to take the view that only the last stage (4) had been altered by the Hague(-Visby) regime.[63]

In *The Hellenic Dolphin*, water had undoubtedly entered the ship through a leaking seam, causing damage to the cargo of asbestos. The issue was timing: if the seam was leaking at the commencement of the voyage there was potentially a breach of Art. III(1); otherwise not. The claimants failed to prove that the vessel was unseaworthy before the commencement of the voyage, and the burden of course was on them to do so: "if at the end of the day, having heard all the evidence and drawn all the proper inferences, the Court is left on the razor's edge, the cargo-owner fails on unseaworthiness and the shipowners are left with their defence of perils of the sea". (Even if Lloyd J was wrong about this, the carrier had acted with due diligence.)[64]

That the burden is on the carrier at stage (2), where the carrier claims an excepted peril, is fairly clear, and, for example, the carrier failed to show negligence in navigation and management in *The Canadian Highlander*.[65] But for stage (2), the carrier is protected if he proves the loss was caused by an Art. IV(2) excepted peril, as Lloyd J observed, but alternatively, he can directly refute the claim that he failed to act properly and carefully under Art. III(2). The burden is not explicitly on the carrier under Art. III(2), but if the goods arrive lost or damaged an explanation is called for (or *res ipsa loquitur*: the thing speaks for itself). So the burden is in reality on the carrier at stage (2), whether he seeks to refute Art. III(2) directly, or to rely on an excepted peril defence.

While on the relationship between Arts. III(2) and IV(2), the carrier does not need to show absence of negligence to claim the benefit of an excepted peril, though he must have acted properly and carefully, if he is to defend an Art. III(2) claim directly.[66] For some of the excepted perils, however, proof of the peril and rebuttal of Art. III(2) can amount to the same thing. For example, if the carrier shows that the loss was caused by inherent vice, that will also necessarily negate a breach of Art. III(2).[67] The same would be true of the catchall Art. IV(2)(q) (the general lack of fault exception).

---

61 [1978] 2 Lloyd's Rep 336.
62 [1978] 2 Lloyd's Rep 336, 339.
63 Note that there is an argument for a contrary burden of proof at stage 3: Ezeoke: *Allocating onus of proof in sea cargo claims: the contest of conflicting principles* [2001] LMCLQ 261.
64 [1978] 2 Lloyd's Rep 336, 341–3.
65 *Gosse Millerd Ltd v Canadian Government Merchant Marine Ltd (The Canadian Highlander)* [1929] AC 223.
66 *Albacora SRL v Westcott & Lawrence Line Ltd* [1966] 2 Lloyd's Rep 53, 64 (Lord Pearson). Of course, Art. IV(2)(a) protects even a negligent carrier, though the carrier must prove that the negligence was in the navigation or management of the ship: *The Canadian Highlander* [1929] AC 223 (where the carrier failed).
67 *Volcafe Ltd v Compania Sud Americana de Vapores SA* [2015] EWHC 516 (Comm), [17].

There can also be a link between stages (2) and (3). Indeed, this may well be more common than the situation in *The Hellenic Dolphin*, where it was either perils of the seas or unseaworthiness, stages (2) and (3) being clearly distinct. Where there is a link, the practical effect may be to put the onus on the carrier to disprove unseaworthiness. In *The Torenia*[68] there was incursion of seawater into the ship, and, as in *The Hellenic Dolphin*, the shipowners claimed the protection of Art. IV(2)(c) (perils of the seas). In Hobhouse J's view, they had to show that the *only* cause was a peril of the seas and, therefore, the onus was on the shipowners to show that unseaworthiness was not also a concurrent cause. In effect, therefore, the burden was on the owners at the seaworthiness stage. By contrast, in *The Hellenic Dolphin*, there was no question of concurrent causes. The cause was either a peril of the seas or unseaworthiness. It was not both. If *The Torenia* is correct, it has significant ramifications where concurrent causes are claimed. Probably *The Torenia* is more likely to represent the normal situation than *The Hellenic Dolphin*.

18.4 Art. III(2) and (8)

Any legislation that protects a weaker party against a stronger must also render void contractual terms reducing the liability of the stronger party, since otherwise the stronger party could simply use his superior bargaining strength to avoid the regime. To the extent that the Hague Rules are intended to protect cargo-owners as the weaker party, this is the logic of Art. III(8):

> "Any clause, covenant or agreement in a contract of carriage relieving the carrier or the ship from liability for loss or damage to or in connection with goods arising from negligence, fault or failure in the duties and obligations provided in this article or lessening such liability otherwise than as provided in these Rules, shall be null and void and of no effect. . . ."

We have seen that Art. III(2) requires the carrier properly and carefully to perform the various tasks enumerated therein. Consequently, a contractual term that purported to substitute a lower standard would be void and of no effect – similarly a term purporting to add excepted perils, lower liability limits, and so on, compared with the provision of the Hague(-Visby) regime.

However, the effect of Art. III(8) has been weakened by a line of a line of cases culminating with *The Eems Solar*.[69] As long ago as *Pyrene Co Ltd v Scindia Steam Navigation Co Ltd*,[70] Devlin J had thought that Art. III(2) defines not the scope of the contract service but the terms on which that service is to be performed. Suppose, for example, under the carriage contract the shipowner did not undertake to engage at all in the loading or discharge processes, or perhaps the charterparty placed the responsibility on the charterers, and these terms were incorporated into the bill of lading.[71] It might be thought that this is precisely the sort of term that should be caught by Art. III(8), but it defines the scope of the contract service (to exclude cargo-handling), and, according to Devlin J, is therefore outside the ambit of the provision.

The reason Devlin J had to face the issue was because he held, in *Pyrene v Scindia*, that the Hague Rules covered the entirety of the loading process, both before and after the goods crossed the ship's

---

68 *Aktieselskabet de Danske Sukkerfabrikker v Bajamar Compania Naviera SA (The Torenia)* [1983] 2 Lloyd's Rep 210.

69 *Yuzhny Zaavod Metall Profil LLC v Eems Beheerder BV (The Eems Solar)* [2013] 2 Lloyd's Rep 487, noted [2014] LMCLQ 140.

70 [1954] 2 QB 402, 418, adopting the then current edition of *Carver's Carriage of Goods by Sea*, 9th ed (1952), 186.

71 There is authority that cargo-handling terms are germane, and hence incorporated by general words of incorporation: section [15.2.4.1]. This can present cargo-owners with real problems, as they may be left without recourse against anyone, and may have no awareness of the charterparty terms that deny them this recourse.

rail. He therefore had to address the argument:[72] "If 'load' includes both stages, does [Art. III(2)] oblige the shipowner, whether he wants to or not, to undertake the whole of the loading?" His answer:[73]

> "The phrase 'shall properly and carefully load' [in Art. III(2)] may mean that the carrier shall load and that he shall do it properly and carefully: or that he shall do whatever loading he does properly and carefully. The former interpretation perhaps fits the language more closely, but the latter may be more consistent with the object of the rules."

It was in this context that he took the view set out above. While, clearly, to take the opposite view would have impacted heavily on the operation of FIO clauses in charterparties,[74] the consequence of allowing carriers to determine the extent of the contract service might be to allow them an easy way out of the Rules.

Devlin J's views were affirmed by a majority of their Lordships in *G.H. Renton & Co Ltd v Palmyra Trading Corp of Panama*.[75] The issue was whether a clause in the bill of lading:

> "should it appear that . . . strikes . . . would prevent the vessel from . . . entering the port of discharge or there discharging in the usual manner and leaving again . . . safely and without delay, the master may discharge the cargo at port of loading or any other safe and conven-ient port . . .".

allowed the shipowner to discharge in Hamburg when London was strike-bound. One issue was whether the clause was struck down by Art. III(8), but the majority view (Lords Morton of Henryton, Cohen, and Somervell of Harrow) was that Devlin J had been right, and that a clause merely defining the scope of the contract did not come within Art. III(8). (Viscount Kilmuir LC and Lord Tucker reached the same result, but only on the basis that the obligation in Art. III(2) "properly to carry and discharge the goods carried" had no geographical significance; in other words it did not require discharge in any particular place.)

The correctness of *Renton v Palmyra*, and its rationale, came again before the House of Lords in *The Jordan II*,[76] which categorically reaffirmed the majority view in the earlier case. The issue there was precisely whether any agreement purporting to transfer responsibility for loading, stowage and discharge from the carrier to the shippers, charterers and consignees was invalid under the Hague Rules. The House held that, if the carrier performs the stowage operation, he must do it properly and carefully, but there is no reason why the Rules should not leave the parties free to determine by their own contract the part that each has to play, whether, in other words, the ship-owner undertakes stowage at all. The correctness of the majority view in *Renton* was the main issue in *The Jordan II*.

Renton and *The Jordan II* were (of course) followed at first instance in *The Eems Solar*.[77] The case concerned a cargo of steel sheets that had shifted and been damaged in bad weather, because they were not properly constrained by locking coils (which should look something like this – they are intended to prevent the rolls from moving):

---

72 [1954] 2 QB 402, 417, and see further on this issue, section [18.6.3].

73 [1957] AC 149. Lord Morton thought that "not only is the construction approved by Devlin J more consistent with the object of the rules, but it is also the more natural construction of the language used": [1957] AC 149, 170.

74 See section [5.3].

75 [1957] AC 149, and see also section [4.4.4].

76 *Jindal Iron and Steel Co Ltd v Islamic Solidarity Shipping Co Jordan Inc (The Jordan II)* [2005] 1 WLR 1363.

77 [2013] 2 Lloyd's Rep 487, noted [2014] LMCLQ 140.

Locking coils in bold

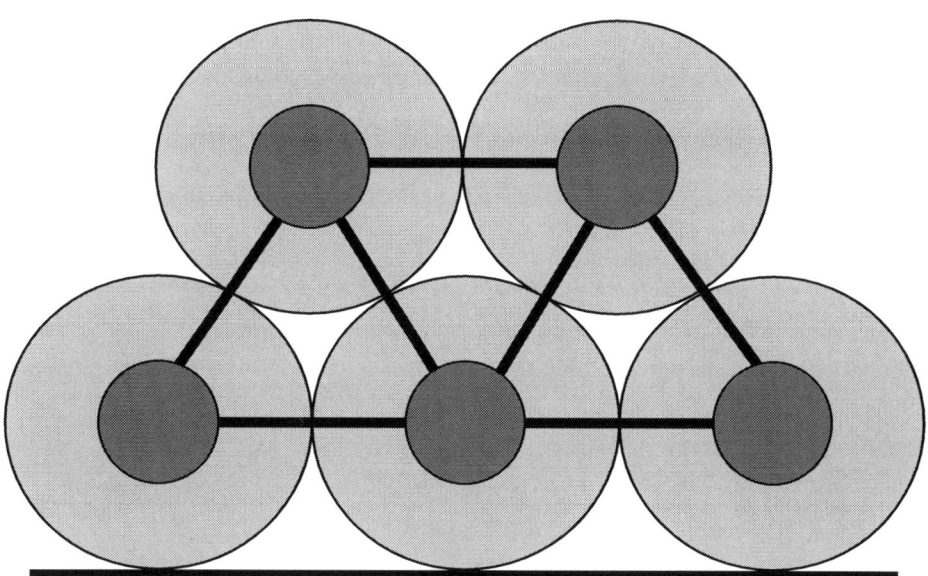

The cause was held to be bad stowage and not unseaworthiness, and a term in the charterparty (incorporated into the bill of lading by general words of incorporation) relieved the shipowner of stowage obligations.[78] The bill of lading holders attempted, without success, to advance an argument based on Art. III(8). There was, however, an additional argument in The Eems Solar. In Pyrene v Scindia itself, Devlin J had made the point that the "carrier is practically bound to play some part in the loading and discharging",[79] and Lord Wright observed in Court Line Ltd v Canadian Transport Co Ltd "that to the extent that the master exercises supervision and limits the charterers' control of the stowage, the charterers' liability will be limited in a corresponding degree".[80] In The Eems Solar, Jervis Kay QC (Admiralty Registrar) thought that, had the stowage plan made by the master and the mate (which failed to provide for the necessary locking coils to be placed on three rows of cargo) been relied on by the stevedores, the shipowners would not have been able to avoid liability for bad stowage. In reality, however, the position was that there "is no evidence that the stevedores paid any attention to the stowage plan provided or that they felt obliged to follow it or that their own responsibilities for proper stowage were inhibited".[81] Consequently, the position was covered by The Jordan II, and there was no liability.

There is the issue to which of the carrier's obligations these principles apply. Is it just stowage? Lord Steyn in The Jordan II observed that in Pyrene, "Devlin J certainly did not suggest that the owner may by agreement under [Art. III(2)], transfer responsibility for caring for the cargo during the voyage."[82] Renton is less guarded however, Lord Morton observing that Art. III(2) "does not place

---

78 There was a Miramar issue: see section [15.2.5].

79 [1954] 2 QB 402, 418.

80 [1940] AC 934, 944.

81 [2013] 2 Lloyd's Rep 487, [102].

82 [2005] 1 WLR 1363, 1370.

any obligation on the carrier to transport the goods at all, unless the contract says he is to transport them".[83]

Under the Rotterdam Rules, should they ever become part of UK law, Art. 13(2) would explicitly allow Art. 13(1) (the Rotterdam equivalent of Art. III(2) of Hague or Hague-Visby) to be qualified, providing that: "the carrier and the shipper may agree that the loading, handling, stowing or unloading of the goods is to be performed by the shipper, the documentary shipper or the consignee". The carrier is then relieved of liability under Art. 17(3)(i). There is, however, no more general provision in Rotterdam, just the provisions to do with cargo-handling.[84]

18.5 Package limitation

One of the motivations for the Visby amendments was to raise the package limitation, the original £100 limit looking rather low by the 1960s.[85] There were also problems in applying the package to bulk cargoes, or to cargoes that were consolidated, for example, into containers. So, the current Art. IV(5) provides:[86]

> "(a) Unless the nature and value of such goods have been declared by the shipper before shipment and inserted in the bill of lading, neither the carrier nor the ship shall in any event be or become liable for any loss or damage to or in connection with the goods in an amount exceeding the equivalent of 666.67 units of account per package or unit or 2 units of account per kilogramme of gross weight of the goods lost or damaged, whichever is the higher.
> . . ."

Thus it can be seen that, for cargo that is above a third of a tonne in weight, the weight limitation will be higher, Art. IV(5) thereby making provision for bulk cargoes.

The units of account in Art. IV(5)(a), defined as IMF special drawing rights (SDRs) in Art. IV(5)(d), though protected against currency fluctuation, are not inflation-proofed (unlike the gold units under Hague-Visby as originally implemented).[87] The value of course varies, but an approximate figure would be £500 per package. We should also observe Art. IV(5)(e), providing for breaking of the limits for intentional or reckless damage.

The Visby amendments were intended to improve the position of cargo-owners, but the cases now suggest that, in some respects, the Hague Rules were actually better.

18.5.1 Amount

Undoubtedly the Visby amendments were intended to improve the position of cargo-owners, but SDRs are not protected against inflation (indeed, their value has already been significantly eroded since Hague-Visby was adopted internationally). It is interesting to compare the position under

---

83 [1957] AC 149, 171. This debate is also relevant to discussion of *The Mica* [1973] 2 Lloyd's Rep 478, in section [17.1.7].

84 The Rotterdam Rules are considered in section [21.5].

85 Though increased to £200 in the UK by British Maritime Association's Gold Clause Agreement 1950. It has always been $500 in the US, under US COGSA 1936.

86 As amended, originally by the Merchant Shipping Act 1981, s. 2(3), now by the Merchant Shipping Act 1995, s. 314(2), the limit originally having been defined in terms of gold value. Units of account are defined in Art. IV(5)(d), and the limit is disapplied "if it is proved that the damage resulted from an act or omission of the carrier done with intent to cause damage, or recklessly and with knowledge that damage would probably result": Art. IV(5)(e).

87 This was the change made, originally by the Merchant Shipping Act 1981, presumably to give shipowners a clear figure to work with.

the original Hague Rules, which in some respects are considerably better for cargo-owners than Hague-Visby.[88]

We start with *The Rosa S*,[89] where the bill of lading simply incorporated the Hague Rules by paramount clause. We should observe that, though there was an English law and jurisdiction clause, the case concerned a shipment from Italy to Kenya, which does not trigger the compulsory application of Hague-Visby.[90] The £100 limit was interpreted as meaning £100, tied into the sterling gold value in 1924, in other words, the value of gold that could have been purchased with £100 then. This is much higher than the non-inflation-proofed Visby package, and indeed was £6,491.25, even in 1989! *The Rosa S* is an interpretation of Art. IX of the unamended Rules:

> "The monetary units mentioned in this Convention are to be taken to be gold value.
>
> Those contracting States in which the pound sterling is not a monetary unit reserve to themselves the right of translating the sums indicated in this Convention in terms of pound sterling into terms of their own monetary system in round figures.
> . . ."

The court simply interpreted this provision at face value, being unimpressed by arguments advanced to cut down its scope.[91] The *Rosa S* interpretation would not, however, apply to all implementations of Hague. For example, the limit in US COGSA 1936 is clearly $500, and there is no question of it being tied into a gold value.[92] Where the Hague Rules are incorporated by paramount clause, Art. IX (the gold clause) might be excluded.[93]

18.5.2 Containers

In order to deal with containers, Art. IV(5)(c) of Hague-Visby provides:

> "(c) Where a container, pallet or similar article of transport is used to consolidate goods, the number of packages or units enumerated in the bill of lading as packed in such article of transport shall be deemed the number of packages as far as these packages or units are concerned. Except as aforesaid such article of transport shall be considered the package or unit."

For containers, then, the container itself is not the package, as long as the number of packages are enumerated in the bill of lading. This is probably a compromise, enumeration allowing the shipowner accurately to be able to calculate his maximum liability, useful of course for insurance purposes.

This is another respect in which the original Hague Rules may be more generous. In *The River Gurara*,[94] action was brought by the cargo-owners, after ship and cargo were lost. This was another case where the Hague and not the Hague-Visby Rules were applicable (West African ports of loading,

---

88 Also *Yemgas FZCO v Superior Pescadores SA Panama (The Superior Pescadores)* [2014] 1 Lloyd's Rep 660, where however, on the facts, Males J held the bill of lading to be governed by the lower Hague-Visby limits.

89 [1989] 1 QB 419.

90 See section [18.6.2]. It is important to appreciate that, though Hague-Visby has been adopted in the UK, even where English law applies, there can be circumstances where the Hague Rules can remain applicable (or for that matter the common law).

91 See also *The Nadezhda Krupskaya* [1989] 1 Lloyd's Rep 518 (Australia Supreme Court of New South Wales Court of Appeal), also an interpretation of the unamended Hague Rules.

92 See also *The Tasman Discoverer* [2004] 2 Lloyd's Rep 647; it all depends on the particular implementation of the Rules (this was a contractual incorporation that was interpreted not to incorporate Art. IX).

93 As in *Trafigura Beheer BV v Mediterranean Shipping Company SA (The MSC Amsterdam)* [2007] 2 Lloyd's Rep 622, in section [18.6], where the bill of lading expressly excluded Art. IX, and also expressly provided that the container was to be package (cl. 22). So the limit on 18 containers was just £1,800, on a cargo of copper worth about a thousand times that amount.

94 *River Gurara (Owners of Cargo Lately Laden on Board) v Nigerian National Shipping Line Ltd (The River Gurara)* [1998] QB 610.

and Hague Rules incorporated in accordance with the law of the places of shipment).[95] The bills of lading also stated, in cl. 9(B):

> ". . . notwithstanding any provision of law to the contrary the Container shall be considered a package or unit even though it has been used to consolidate the Goods, the number of packages or units constituting which have been enumerated on the face hereof as having been packed therein by . . . the Merchant and the liability of the Carrier . . . shall be calculated accordingly."

In other words, they provided for the container to be the package, and the limit therefore to be correspondingly lower. The bills of lading also stated that each container was "said to contain" a number of packages. The cargo-owners successfully claimed cl. 9 of the bill of lading to be void under Art. III(8) of the Hague Rules (a provision that is identical to its counterpart in Hague-Visby).[96] At first instance,[97] Colman J thought that Hague Rules should be interpreted similarly to Hague-Visby, and that "said to contain" did not negate enumeration for liability limit purposes (a point that, if correct, is therefore of importance for Hague-Visby as well). The Court of Appeal went further, with Phillips LJ (with whom Mummery LJ agreed) taking the view that the units inside, not the containers, were the packages, *whether enumerated or not*. The *travaux* were referred to,[98] and also the object of Rules and their interpretation in other countries, none of which, in Phillips LJ's view, supported the shipowner's argument that he must be able to verify his liability (the point being, of course, that he does not know the number of packages). Moreover, Phillips LJ was unwilling to allow the shipowner effectively to contract out of liability by inserting "said to contain" into the bills of lading. If Phillips LJ's view is correct, then the original Hague Rules are also more favourable to cargo-owners (on enumeration) than their Visby successors.

18.5.3 Other container issues

Containers are often carried multimodally, and often under documents other than bills of lading. The problems to which this gives rise are considered later.[99]

18.6 Application of the Hague-Visby Rules

Now that we have examined the general principles of Hague and Hague-Visby, we need to consider when they apply. There are three aspects to this enquiry:

> Article X (this provision, which is only in the Visby amendments, is a reaction to gaps in coverage in the original Hague Rules);
> > temporal application; and
> > documentary requirements.

18.6.1 Trigger for application: Art. X

We should remind ourselves that international conventions have no force, whether the UK signs them or not, unless they are enacted into law UK. The Hague Rules were brought into force by the

---

95 On the application of the original Hague Rules, and their incorporation by paramount clause, see below, section [18.6].

96 There was another issue, on the effect of "stc" on a statement of quantity. We return to this aspect of the case in section [19.11].

97 [1996] 2 Lloyd's Rep 53.

98 See further section [18.7].

99 See section [21.3].

Carriage of Goods by Sea Act 1924 (COGSA 1924), Hague-Visby by the Carriage of Goods by Sea Act 1971 (COGSA 1971). In each case the Schedule sets out the Convention, and the (short) main part of the Act sets out implementation provisions.[100]

Article X of Hague-Visby was a reaction to gaps in the original Hague coverage, so we need to start with the position under COGSA 1924. This applied to bills of lading issued in Great Britain and Northern Ireland, and (hence) outward voyages from Great Britain and Northern Ireland.[101] Similar provision was made in the legislation in other contracting states, the idea being that the Hague Rules would thereby apply to outward voyages from all contracting states.

Unfortunately, this legislative technique did not work in all circumstances. Section 1 of the 1924 Act (which brought into effect the original Hague Rules in Great Britain and Northern Ireland) provided that:[102]

"... the Rules shall have effect in relation to and in connection with the carriage of goods by sea in ships from any port in Great Britain or Northern Ireland to any other port whether in or outside Great Britain or Northern Ireland".

Section 3 of the 1924 Act provided:

"Every bill of lading or similar document of title issued in Great Britain or Northern Ireland which contains or is evidence of any contract to which the Rules apply shall contain an express statement that it is to have effect subject to the provisions of the said Rules as applied by this Act."

Note that this covers outward voyages only (but there would have been similar provision in all contracting states, and the idea, therefore, was obviously to apply the Rules to outward voyages from all contracting states). However, the *Vita Food* case tells us that there was a gap in the coverage.[103]

In *Vita Food Products Inc v Unus Shipping Co Ltd*, the carriage was from Newfoundland to New York, on the *Hurry On*, a vessel that was registered in Nova Scotia. Newfoundland was a Hague Rules signatory, and had enacted legislation similar to our own COGSA 1924.[104] Consequently, the bill of lading should have contained a statement that the Rules were to apply. An old bill of lading was accidentally used, which did not contain the required statement. This would not have mattered, had the bill of lading been governed by Newfoundland law, but it was made expressly subject to English law. English law also, of course, applied the Hague Rules, but only for bills of lading issued in Great Britain or Northern Ireland, and hence outward voyages from Great Britain or Northern Ireland, not to outward voyages from Newfoundland. The Privy Council (to which the case came from the Supreme Court of Nova Scotia) held that the English choice of law clause was valid, despite there being no connection between the carriage contract and England; the only requirement was that the intention expressed was *bona fide* and legal, and that there was no reason for avoiding the choice on the ground of public policy. Since English law did not apply the Hague Rules to an outward voyage from Newfoundland, it followed the Hague Rules did not apply.

In the event this made no difference to the decision. The cargo of herring was damaged when the ship grounded in a gale, and the carrier wished to rely on an exception. He could rely on either the Hague Rules negligence in navigation excepted peril, or on an express clause in the bills of

---

100 See Appendix A.
101 Hence excluding the Irish Free State.
102 Finding repealed legislation is not always easy, but COGSA 24 is set out in Appendix II of *Carver on Bills of Lading*, 3rd ed (2012).
103 [1939] AC 277.
104 Though (obviously) with "any port in this Dominion" substituted for "any port in Great Britain or Northern Ireland", etc.

lading, exempting him from liability for negligence of servants. Though he failed on the Hague Rules, he was able to rely on the clause in the bill of lading, the Privy Council having also held that the carriage contract was not illegal.

The conclusion in *Vita Food* seemed absurd. Here was a carriage from a contracting state, where the bill of lading was governed by the law of a contracting state, yet the Rules did not apply. The problem in *Vita Food* arose because old bills of lading were used by mistake. This was certainly not a case where the carrier was attempting to avoid the application of the Rules; indeed he argued for their application, but the decision opened up the possibility of deliberate evasion. Thus, Colinvaux observed:[105]

> "The fact is that a carrier, provided he makes his bill of lading subject to English law, may contract on what terms he pleases, in the case of shipments to the United Kingdom. This loophole has been of assistance to shipowners importing fruit and other perishable cargoes, particularly from the Mediterranean, and it might be a matter for consideration whether carriers of such cargoes should not be entitled to contract on special terms."

The current Art. X is a reaction to *Vita Food*. During the amendment process, a proposal to apply the Rules to inward voyages was not adopted,[106] but Art. X compulsorily applies the Rules (which under the implementation provisions are given the "force of law")[107] where:

> "(a) the bill of lading is issued in a contracting State, or
> (b) the carriage is from a port in a contracting State, or
> (c) the contract contained in or evidenced by the bill of lading provides that these Rules or legislation of any State giving effect to them are to govern the contract
> . . . .".

In other words, the Hague-Visby Rules (by Art. X) apply compulsorily to bill of lading contracts, not only where shipment is from the UK (or the bill of lading issued in the UK), but also where it is from other contracting states (or the bill of lading issued there). Article X(c) was intended to cover proper law clauses choosing the law of a contracting state. The *Vita Food* scenario is therefore comprehensively covered by Art. X, and had the Hague Rules had Art. X, each of the sub-provisions would have applied. As we will see, however, there are still gaps, reminiscent of *Vita Food*, even under the Hague-Visby regime.[108]

It became clear that the legislative changes were generally effective in *The Hollandia*.[109] There the House of Lords held that Art. X creates a mandatory rule, which cannot be avoided by (in that case) a choice of law and forum clause. The case concerned an outward voyage from Scotland, and the House held that Art. X applied Hague-Visby, whatever forum was chosen (in this case Amsterdam, which would have applied the lower limits of the Hague Rules).[110]

The action came to the English courts because of the arrest of *Hollandia*, and the shipowner applied for a stay, on the basis of the jurisdiction clause. The application failed because the Amsterdam court would apply lower Hague Rules limits, and the jurisdiction clause was rendered void by

---

105 Colinvaux, *Revision of the Hague Rules Relating to Bills of Lading* [1963] JBL 341.

106 Eg, [1963] JBL 341. This would not, on its own, have solved the problem in Vita Food itself, though it would have addressed the problem with which Colinvaux was particularly concerned.

107 COGSA 71, s. 1(2).

108 Section [18.6.2].

109 [1983] 1 AC 565 (also referred to as The Morviken).

110 The cargo, a large machine, weighed 9,906 kg, and the Amsterdam court would have limited liability by reference to their local currency (D.fl. 1,250, or about £250), so the gold clause considerations in the previous section would not have applied. The Visby (weight-based) limit was about £11,000.

Art. III(8) of Hague-Visby. One issue in *The Hollandia* was whether Art. III(8) could be triggered by a procedural clause, such as choice of forum, which did not *ex facie* deal with liability at all. Moreover, it is not possible to tell in advance of litigation whether a choice of forum clause will trigger Art. III(8), since it will depend on the dispute. Lord Diplock said that:[111]

> ". . . the time at which to ascertain whether a choice of forum clause will have an effect that is proscribed by Art. III(8) should be when . . . the carrier seeks to bring the clause into operation and to rely upon it . . .".

The carriers in *The Benarty* also claimed the benefit of an exclusive jurisdiction clause,[112] this time for Indonesia, in respect of a voyage from London, when Indonesia applied the Hague Rules. However, during the proceedings (after the writ was issued), the carriers disclaimed any reliance on the Hague Rules at all, and indeed undertook not to use a package limit below that provided by Hague-Visby. They were intending to rely on a tonnage limit, but their ability to invoke the tonnage limit was expressly preserved by Art. VIII of Hague-Visby. The Court of Appeal held the carrier entitled to rely on the Indonesian choice of forum clause, *The Hollandia* being distinguished. Given their disclaimer, this is entirely consistent with Lord Diplock's statement on timing, set out above.

18.6.2 Limits to Art. X

Article X does, however, depend on the concept of the contracting state. In *The MSC Amsterdam*,[113] the bill of lading was issued in South Africa. Though South Africa had enacted domestic legislation giving effect to the Hague-Visby Rules, it was not a signatory state. Had the bill of lading been governed by the law of South Africa, there is no doubt that Hague-Visby would have applied, but it was subject to English law, and incorporated the original Hague Rules (not Hague-Visby) by paramount clause. The particular implementation of Hague would have led to a package limit of £1,800 for 18 containers, whereas the Visby limits (based on weight) were significantly higher.[114] The Court of Appeal, however, held that neither Art. X(a) or (b) applied (as clearly they do not, on a literal interpretation), and that Art. X(c) was circular: English law would apply the Hague-Visby Rules if English law would apply the Hague-Visby Rules. Hence the limit was that of Hague not Hague-Visby.[115]

The decision is in many respects reminiscent of *Vita Food*. England and South Africa apply Hague-Visby; the bill of lading was issued in South Africa and subject to English law, yet Hague-Visby did not apply. Had it not been incorporated by paramount clause, even Hague would not have applied, since there was no compulsory regime. Of course, the practical implications of this aspect of *The MSC Amsterdam* are limited to those states that have enacted HVR but are not contracting states. There are not many, but there are some.[116] The case therefore demonstrates a potential problem with the present drafting of Art. X.

The lower limit did not avail the carrier in the end, since, as we will see in the next section, he could not rely on it in any event.

---

111 [1983] 1 AC 565, 574.

112 [1985] QB 325. The carriers were charterers, and there was also other cargo, from other European ports.

113 [2007] 2 Lloyd's Rep 622.

114 On Hague, see section [18.5]. The Visby limit would have been SDR 720k, or about £500k, more than 250 times Hague.

115 [2007] 2 Lloyd's Rep 622, [4]–[16].

116 Eg, China "has devised its own rules using some features of Hague-Visby and Hamburg": http://www.admiraltylaw.com/papers/countrytable.pdf, but is not a signatory to Hague-Visby (or for that matter, Hamburg).

18.6.3 Temporal application of Hague and Hague-Visby

Another issue in *The MSC Amsterdam*[117] was when coverage starts and stops under the Rules. This was first considered in *Pyrene Co Ld v Scindia Navigation Co Ld*.[118] The cargo (a fire engine) was damaged (by being dropped) during loading, before crossing the ship's rail, and the carrier wished to rely on the Hague Rules package limitation.[119] Devlin J, interpreting Art. 1(e), concluded that it included the loading and discharge process:

> "(e) 'Carriage of goods' covers the period from the time when the goods are loaded to the time they are discharged from the ship."

Thus the Hague Rules applied to the time in question. The cargo-owners (FOB sellers of the goods) argued that they were a ship's rail to ship's rail provision. Rejecting this contention, Devlin J said:[120]

> "In my judgment this argument is fallacious, the cause of the fallacy perhaps lying in the supposition inherent in it that the rights and liabilities under the rules attach to a period of time. I think that they attach to a contract or part of a contract. . . . Even if 'carriage of goods by sea' were given by definition the most restricted meaning possible, for example, the period of the voyage, the loading of the goods (by which I mean the whole operation of loading in both its stages and whichever side of the ship's rail) would still *relate* to the carriage on the voyage and so be within the 'contract of carriage'."

Later in his judgment he famously commented that:[121]

> "Only the most enthusiastic lawyer could watch with satisfaction the spectacle of liabilities shifting uneasily as the cargo sways at the end of a derrick across a notional perpendicular projecting from the ship's rail."

So the whole of the loading process is covered. In *Volcafe Ltd v Compania Sud Americana de Vapores SA*,[122] the Hague Rules were incorporated (by paramount clause) into a multimodal contract under which the carrier undertook responsibility for the whole of the intermodal transport. Terms were LCL/FCL,[123] which meant that the containers were provided and "stuffed" by the carrier but "unstuffed" by the consignee after arrival at their destination. David Donaldson QC applied *Pyrene v Scindia*, holding that the Rules applied to the stuffing. He observed that "the parties are free to agree on what for the purpose of Art. I(e) constitutes loading . . .", and that "[where], as here, the obligation to stuff its own containers is assumed by the carrier, I . . . have little difficulty in interpreting the contract of carriage as including that as part of the loading".[124] He also observed, however, that, unlike *Pyrene v Scindia*, there was no damage caused during the stuffing process as such, but that poor stuffing led to later damage (by condensation): "The breach alleged is thus of a duty at the heart of the carriage."[125]

---

117 [2007] 2 Lloyd's Rep 622, noted [2007] JIML 356; [2008] LMCLQ 214.
118 [1954] 2 QB 402.
119 Then £200 in England. See section [18.5].
120 [1954] 2 QB 402, 415.
121 [1954] 2 QB 402, 419.
122 [2015] 1 Lloyd's Rep 639, a test case (where coffee was damaged by condensation) on a relatively small claim.
123 Less container load/full container load. See [2015] EWHC 516 (Comm), [5]. On multimodal issues generally, see section [21.3].
124 [2015] EWHC 516 (Comm), [9].
125 [2015] EWHC 516 (Comm), [10].

At the other end of the operation, it may be presumed that the whole of the discharge process is also covered. But container cargoes in particular are often stored after discharge, before being delivered. Post-discharge breaches were considered in *The MSC Amsterdam*;[126] they are generally outside the regime, though the courts will readily accept extension of the regime by contract to cover this period.

The MSC Amsterdam concerned a misdelivery of cargo from a container depot, after it had been discharged from the ship, the issue being whether the shipowner could limit his liability in respect of the misdelivery. As well as Art. I(e), the Court of Appeal also had regard to Art. II:

> "Subject to the provisions of Article VI, under every contract of carriage of goods by sea the carrier, in relation to the loading, handling, stowage, carriage, custody, care and *discharge* of such goods, shall be subject to the responsibilities and liabilities, and entitled to the rights and immunities hereinafter set forth."

It referred to Art. III(2):[127]

> ". . . the carrier shall properly and carefully load, handle, stow, carry, keep, care for and *discharge* the goods carried".

In each case the words used are "discharge", not "deliver", and on this basis the Court of Appeal concluded that the regime was intended to run only as far as discharge.

There are contrary arguments. Devlin J had observed in *Pyrene v Scindia Navigation* that some obligations, for example, that under Art. III(1),[128] to use due diligence to make the ship seaworthy and man and equip her properly "are independent of time". It is also true that the time bar in Art. III(6) refers expressly to *delivery*, not *discharge*. However, these arguments did not persuade the Court of Appeal in respect of the package limitation in Art. IV(5).

Suppose, then, that as in *The MSC Amsterdam*, the Hague(-Visby) regime does not apply. During the post-discharge period, however, common law bailment and conversion obligations continue, and indeed the misdelivering shipowners were held liable for conversion in *The MSC Amsterdam* itself.[129] If the Rules do not apply, a consequence will be that the carrier will be unable to rely on the package limitation, again as in *The MSC Amsterdam* itself. However, a continuation on Hague(-Visby) terms will easily be implied.[130] It was not in the case itself, because of another clause in the contract purporting expressly to exclude liability. Though it failed because it was not sufficiently visible,[131] its mere presence precluded an argument that the shipowner intended to contract on Hague Rules terms. Ironically, the shipowner would have been better off not including the exemption clause at all!

18.6.4 Need for document of title

The Hague-Visby Rules were brought into force in the UK by the Carriage of Goods by Sea Act 1971, s. 1(4) of which provides:[132]

---

126 [2007] 2 Lloyd's Rep 622.
127 See section [18.3].
128 *Ibid.*
129 On bailment, see section [3.2].
130 [2007] 2 Lloyd's Rep 622, starting at [28] (Longmore LJ).
131 See section [20.5.2].
132 This is not quite the end of the matter, because we need also to consider s. 1(6) (in section [18.6.6]) – but s. 1(6) is not relevant for present purposes.

"(4) Subject to subsection (6) below, nothing in this section shall be taken as applying anything in the Rules to any contract for the carriage of goods by sea, unless the contract expressly or by implication provides for the issue of a bill of lading or any similar document of title."

The Rules themselves are set out in the Schedule to the Act, and we also need to note Art. I(b):

"(b) 'Contract of carriage' applies only to contracts of carriage covered by a bill of lading or any similar document of title, in so far as such document relates to the carriage of goods by sea, including any bill of lading or any similar document as aforesaid issued under or pursuant to a charter-party from the moment at which such bill of lading or similar document of title regulates the relations between a carrier and a holder of the same."

As explained in chapter 14, in *The Rafaela S* the House of Lords held that "a bill of lading or any similar document of title" included a straight bill of lading. However, a waybill is not covered, making it necessary to find tests for distinguishing between the two types of document.[133]

We have seen that Hague(-Visby) was never intended to have any application to charterparties, and indeed Art. V provides that:

". . . [the] provisions of these Rules shall not be applicable to charter-parties, but if bills of lading are issued in the case of a ship under a charter-party they shall comply with the terms of these Rules. . . ."

It is argued that the rationales for the Rules do not apply to charterparties, since there is no issue about protection of third parties, as with bills of lading.[134] However, it can also argued that this is not a good reason today for limiting application to bills of lading and other documents of title. Third parties could have been provided for directly, rather than relying on the document of title trigger. This is more of an issue today, with the proliferation of documentation, than it was when Hague was originally agreed in 1922.

18.6.5 Bill of lading not yet issued

A consequence of the damage in *Pyrene v Scindia Navigation* occurring when it did was that the goods were never loaded, and no bill of lading was ever issued. Nor was a bill of lading ever issued in *The Happy Ranger*,[135] again because the damage occurred earlier. However, the wording of Art. 1(b) is "contracts of carriage *covered by* a bill of lading or any similar document of title", and as Tuckey LJ observed in the latter case:[136] "Provided it was contemplated that a bill of lading would be issued which would contain the terms of the contract it was *covered by* a bill." The contemplation, rather than the issue of the bill, is therefore what is crucial, and so it does not matter that no bill of lading is eventually issued.

---

133 Section [14.6.2].

134 Protection of third parties, rather than inequality of bargaining power on its own, was one of the main justifications for the original Hague Rules: eg, *JI MacWilliam Company Inc v Mediterranean Shipping Co SA (The Rafaela S)* [2005] 2 AC 423, [18] (Lord Bingham).

135 *Parsons Corp v CV Scheepvaartonderneming (The Happy Ranger)* [2002] 2 Lloyd's Rep 357.

136 [2002] 2 Lloyd's Rep 357, [21].

18.6.6 No bill of lading issued

What if there is no intention to issue a bill of lading at all? We have already seen that COGSA 1971, s. 1(4) requires a document of title,[137] but it is subject to s. 1(6):

"(6) Without prejudice to Article X (c) of the Rules, the Rules shall have the force of law in relation to-

(a) any bill of lading if the contract contained in or evidenced by it expressly provides that the Rules shall govern the contract, and

(b) any receipt which is a non-negotiable document marked as such if the contract contained in or evidenced by it is a contract for the carriage of goods by sea which expressly provides that the Rules are to govern the contract as if the receipt were a bill of lading,

but subject, where paragraph (b) applies, to any necessary modifications and in particular with the omission in Article III of the Rules of the second sentence of paragraph 4 and of paragraph 7."[138]

Thus, in principle at least, non-negotiable documentation can be included.

These provisions have been considered twice, in *The Vechscroon* and in *The European Enterprise*.[139] The issue has been what exactly is required to trigger s. 1(6)(b)? In *The Vechscroon*,[140] Lloyd J refused to distinguish between a document that said "this non-negotiable receipt shall be governed by the Hague-Visby Rules" and a document that said "this non-negotiable receipt shall be governed by the Hague-Visby Rules as if it were a bill of lading". He therefore applied the Rules to a document containing the former wording. *The Vechscroon* was not followed in *The European Enterprise*. There, the document (a consignment note) did not expressly provide that "the Rules are to govern the contract as if the receipt were a bill of lading", and Steyn J held that the words used: "as if the receipt were a bill of lading", did not suffice. On one view this is simply a very literal interpretation of a statute, but, even on a strict interpretation, s. 1(6) allows carriers easily to avoid the Hague-Visby Rules, in trades where a non-negotiable document could reasonably be used. Indeed, Steyn J observed that:[141]

"It follows that shipowners, if they are in a strong enough bargaining position, can escape the application of the rules by issuing a notice to shippers that no bills of lading will be issued by them in a particular trade. Subject to the limited restriction introduced by the Unfair Contract Terms Act, 1977 in favour of carriage for consumers . . ., the position is that freedom of contract prevails. Section 1(6)(b) can only be activated by contracting into the statutory regime in the appropriate contractual form."

If the rationale for the Rules is to protect weaker parties then this is obviously a problem. If it is to protect third parties it is probably not, since documents of this type are less likely to be used where the goods are resold (though of course, the original consignee can be affected by a contract that has been negotiated by the shipper).

---

137 Section [18.6.4].
138 Art. III(4) applies to quantity statements and is discussed in section [19.9]. Art. III(7) deals with provision of a shipped bill of lading, where one is issued.
139 Respectively *McCarren & Co Ltd v Humber International Transport Ltd (The Vechscroon)* [1982] 1 Lloyd's Rep 301; *Browner International Ltd v Monarch Shipping Co Ltd (The European Enterprise)* [1989] 2 Lloyd's Rep 182.
140 [1982] 1 Lloyd's Rep 301.
141 [1989] 2 Lloyd's Rep 182, 188.

18.6.7 Deck cargo and live animals

Article I(c) of Hague-Visby provides:

> "(c) 'Goods' includes goods, wares, merchandise, and articles of every kind whatsoever except live animals and cargo which by the contract of carriage is stated as being carried on deck and is so carried."

However, COGSA 71, s. 1(7) provides:

> "(7) If and so far as the contract contained in or evidenced by a bill of lading or receipt within paragraph (a) or (b) of subsection (6) above applies to deck cargo or live animals, the Rules as given the force of law by that subsection shall have effect as if Article I(c) did not exclude deck cargo and live animals.
>
> In this subsection 'deck cargo' means cargo which by the contract of carriage is stated as being carried on deck and is so carried."

In the UK at least, therefore, deck cargo and live animals can fall within the Hague-Visby Rules.

18.7 Interpretation of Rules

The Hague-Visby Rules, like the Hague Rules before them, are brought into force by an English statute. It would be possible to interpret them just like any other English statute, and, for example, in *The Canadian Highlander*, Lord Hailsham said of negligence in navigation or management of the ship, interpreting Art. IV(2)(a):[142]

> "I am unable to find any reason for supposing that the words as used by the Legislature in the Act of 1924 have any different meaning from that which has been judicially assigned to them when used in contracts for the carriage of goods by sea before that date . . . ."

He then proceeded to analyse the pre-1924 English case law. This might be acceptable for an excepted peril that reflected English bills of lading that had been in use prior to 1924, but part of the justification for the Rules was to harmonise the law throughout the world. The question is how far an English statute can be interpreted to achieve this objective.

Stag Line v Foscolo, Mango & Co differs from *The Canadian Highlander* in that it is concerned not with a commonly-used bill of lading exception, but with a longstanding principle of English law. The case involved a deviation to drop off engineers,[143] and one of the issues was whether this was a reasonable deviation within Art. IV(4) of the Hague Rules. By the time of the case there was, of course, a body of English law on permitted deviation, but the House of Lords took the view that COGSA 1924 (implementing Hague) should not be assumed to be simply a codification provision, and that the old common law deviation authorities were irrelevant. Courts should look at plain language rather than adopt the construction of earlier English courts; international uniformity was important, and the Act should be construed by reference to "broad principles of general acceptance" appropriate to

---

142 *Gosse Millerd Ltd v Canadian Government Merchant Marine Ltd (The Canadian Highlander)* [1929] AC 223, 230.
143 [1932] AC 328. See section [4.4.3].

the international mercantile subject matter.[144] Even on that interpretation, the deviation was held not reasonable, and consequently the carrier was unable to rely on the perils of the seas excepted peril.

Promotion of international conformity implies a purposive rather than a literalist approach, and this has been confirmed by later decisions of the House of Lords.[145]

Stag Line was silent on the issue whether it was permissible to take account of the published *travaux préparatoires*, explaining the reasons for the provisions forming part of the Rules.[146] Had the Rules come into force later, the Vienna Convention on Treaties 1969, Art. 31(1) would have provided that a "treaty shall be interpreted in good faith in accordance with the ordinary meaning to be given to the terms of the treaty in their context and in the light of its object and purpose", and Art. 32 allows "the preparatory work of the treaty" to be taken into account to resolve ambiguities. The Vienna Convention came into force only after 1977, however, so cannot assist in the interpretation of the Hague or Hague-Visby Rules.

No doubt the use of *travaux préparatoires* may tend to promote uniformity of approach, but purposive interpretations raise constitutional issues in the UK, arguably allowing the courts too much influence over what should be matters for Parliament. Aside from the Vienna Convention, therefore, their use is only allowed in UK law to resolve ambiguity.[147] The limits on the cautious use of *travaux* were set out by Lord Wilberforce in *Fothergill v Monarch Airlines Limited*:[148]

> "first, . . . the material involved is public and accessible; secondly, . . . it clearly and indisputably points to a definite legislative intention . . .".

In *Fothergill* itself, the House would have allowed their cautious use in the interpretation of the Warsaw Convention (on air carriage), but in the event they were unnecessary; the language alone resolved the issue, on a purposive construction.

Travaux préparatoires have been referred to in UK cases, but have usually been found to be unhelpful, and have rarely been decisive. For example, they were referred to in *The Rafaela S*, but found unhelpful, principally because the issue to be resolved had not been considered in 1922, and hence the *travaux* were silent.[149] Given that international conventions are nearly always borne of compromise, one might also suppose that *travaux* would not point to a definite legislative intention, where a Convention is a compromise of conflicting views (as indeed was the case with Hague).

The *travaux* were referred to in *The Captain Gregos* (on the application of the Hague-Visby Rules time bar, but were of limited help, discussing a different issue).[150] They were referred to in *The River Gurara*,[151] where the Court of Appeal differed from the international law consensus (which the *travaux* did not support). In other words, the *travaux* and the international consensus were not at one, and so neither can be said decisively to have influenced the court. In *J.J. Silber Ltd v Islander Trucking Ltd*,[152] Mustill J observed that "the foreign cases do not establish any coherent body of authority". In summary, it

---

144 [1932] AC 328, 350.

145 *The Hollandia* [1983] 1 AC 565 (section [18.6.1]); *James Buchanan & Co Ltd v Babco Forwarding and Shipping (UK) Ltd* [1978] AC 141 (CMR – measure of damages – excise duty on whisky).

146 There is a CMI publication setting out the *travaux*, at http://www.comitemaritime.org/Uploads/Publications/Travaux%20 Preparatoires%20of%20the%20Hague%20Rules%20and%20of%20the%20Hague-Visby%20Rules.pdf.

147 *Fothergill v Monarch Airlines Inc* [1981] AC 251 (Diplock, Fraser and Scarman). The Vienna Convention also allows use to avoid absurdity.

148 [1981] AC 251, 252.

149 [2005] 2 AC 423, [19]; [43].

150 *Compania Portorafti Commerciale SA v Ultramar Panama Inc (The Captain Gregos)* [1990] 1 Lloyd's Rep 310, the *travaux* addressing misdelivery without production of bill of lading, rather than theft of cargo.

151 [1998] QB 610, in section [18.5.2].

152 [1985] 2 Lloyd's Rep 243, 246 (CMR duty of care).

is difficult to find cases, at any rate in this area of law, where either the *travaux* or the international consensus have been decisive.

There are also problems about what to do with foreign precedents, which may be summarised as follows:

Can UK courts understand them?
Do they speak with one voice?
Are they consistent with *travaux*?
Different ideas of precedent.
Do we allow bad foreign decisions to govern our law, just because first in time?

The idea of achieving international conformity is very attractive, but difficulties lie in the way of achieving it, and it cannot be said that the issues have been properly resolved.

18.8 Incorporation into charterparties

The problems of incorporating into charterparties rules intended for bills of lading (and definitely not for charterparties) are the converse of those considered at the end of chapter 15.[153] However, we saw there that in *Adamastos Shipping Co Ltd v Anglo-Saxon Petroleum Co Ltd*[154] the House of Lords was prepared to manipulate the words to fit their new context. In that case, the US Hague Rules were incorporated by paramount clause. The House was also prepared to delete any part of the provision that was "insensible", such as s. 5 of US COGSA 1936, which (mirroring Art. V) provides, "The provisions of the Act shall not be applicable to charterparties." In effect, the courts will strive to make Hague or Hague-Visby work, in a charterparty context.

One difficulty is in determining how the time bar in Art. III(6), which provides that the carrier and the ship shall be discharged from all liability whatsoever in respect of the goods, unless suit is brought within one year of their delivery or of the date when they should have been delivered, operates where the charterer complains of continuing breaches of the charterparty, which prevent the cargo being loaded on board the vessel. In *The Marinor*[155] Colman J saw no reason in principle why the protection provided to the shipowners by Art. III(6) should not apply in such cases, provided that it was possible to identify a date when goods sufficiently relevant to the claim were delivered or should have been delivered. The charterers had claimed market losses caused by delays in shipping cargoes of sulphuric acid, which were eventually shipped on board other vessels, and the shipowners successfully claimed the benefit of the time bar.

18.9 Summary and conclusions

On one level, the Hague Rules were an astonishingly successful harmonisation initiative, and the Hague-Visby Rules have been widely used, in both bills of lading and charterparties, for almost 40 years. However, the Visby amendments do not by any means solve all the problems of carriage under bills of lading; privity, the package limitation, and the due diligence requirement for the seaworthiness obligation, have all be argued as unsatisfactory. They are also arguably dated, being unduly favourable to carriers (both in terms of the package limits and the excepted perils), and being

---

153 Section [15.2.5].
154 [1959] AC 133.
155 *Noranda Inc v Barton (Time Charter) Ltd (The Marinor)* [1996] 1 Lloyd's Rep 301.

unsuited to multimodal transport. We consider criticisms, and possible ways forward, in chapter 21. I suggest, however, that Hague and Hague-Visby will be around for a time yet.

18.10 Questions

Question 18.1

Alan's cargo of sugar reaches the end of the voyage, and is discovered to be damaged by seawater. The sugar was on board a vessel chartered from Yvonne for the voyage, the charterparty incorporating the Hague-Visby Rules. The vessel is old, and the welding of some of the hull plates has failed, allowing seawater to get into the cargo holds. Heavy weather has been encountered on the voyage, and it is not known if the plates were still holding when the vessel sailed.

Advise Alan as to any claim he may have against Yvonne, what will need to be shown and on which party the burden of proof will lie.

Comment

An easy question based on *The Hellenic Dolphin*,[156] but remember that most real-life fact situations will be more complex than the issues in that case.[157]

Question 18.2

Are there any circumstances where the Hague Rules are more onerous on carriers than the later Hague-Visby Rules?

Comment

Hague-Visby was meant to offer more protection to cargo-owners, but have a look at section [18.5].

Question 18.3

A B/L incorporates the Hague Rules with the exception of Art. IX, and there is a clause that a container is to constitute one package. What, if anything, is the effect of Art. III(8), and what is the package limitation? Would your view be different if it said "whether enumerated or not"?

Comment

The Art. IX point is the same as in *The MSC Amsterdam*,[158] and there seems to be no question of Art. III(8) applying, where only part of the Hague Rules are incorporated in the first place. There was also a clause in *The MSC Amsterdam* that a container is to constitute one package. There is no decision in the case on whether this was valid, or would have been caught by Art. III(8) (had the Hague Rules ultimately applied).[159] The alternative part ("whether enumerated or not") is on all fours with *The River Gurara*.[160] Whether the original container clause in the problem is caught by Art. III(8) might

---

156 [1978] 2 Lloyds Rep 336.
157 See section [18.3.4], in section [18.6].
158 [2007] 2 Lloyd's Rep 622.
159 Though probably assumed valid: [2007] 2 Lloyd's Rep 622, [35].
160 [1998] QB 610.

depend on whether Phillips or Hirst LJJ's view, or on the need for enumeration in *The River Gurara*, is correct. If Phillips LJ is correct, then that clause should surely be rendered void also.

Question 18.4

The Cargoworthy is chartered on terms that state that the charterers shall load and stow the cargo at their expense, the charterparty also placing all responsibility for loading and stowing on the charterers. Puffer is the owner of a large box of cigars loaded on board *The Cargoworthy*. A bill of lading is issued, in Southampton, in respect of the box of cigars, signed by the master, incorporating "all terms and conditions as per charterparty".

Puffer's box of cigars is badly damaged during stowage. The charterers have gone into liquidation.

Advise Puffer. Does your answer depend on whether the shipowners have intervened in the loading process, and, if so, what type of intervention would suffice?

Would your answer be different in any of the following scenarios:

(i) The bill of lading (which is expressly subject to English law) is issued, not in Southampton, but in a state that, though it has enacted legislation in similar terms to the Hague-Visby Rules, is not a signatory to the Rules?
(ii) The bill of lading (issued in Southampton) also stated that "the contract evidenced by this bill of lading is between the merchant and the charterer of the vessel and it is therefore agreed that said charterer only shall be liable for any damage or loss due to any breach or non-performance of any obligation arising out of the contract of carriage". The boxes are damaged not during stowage, but when seawater comes through an open hold while the vessel is at sea?

Comment

The main part of this question is similar to the problem question at the end of chapter 5. The bill of lading here is, however, subject to the Hague-Visby Rules, and there is an intervention point here, which there was not there. Have a look, in particular, at *The Eems Solar*.[161]

Alternative (i) invites you to consider whether Hague-Visby applies, in the light of *The MSC Amsterdam*.[162]

Alternative (ii) is a demise clause such as examined in chapter 17.[163] Are they affected by Art. III(8)? Have a look at the discussion of *Renton v Palmyra* and *The Jordan II*.[164]

Question 18.5

Suppose that in *The River Gurara*[165] the shipment had been from the UK, rather than Africa. On what basis would the package limitation have been calculated: what would have been the package, and what would have been the amount per package?

Comment

An easy question, because Hague-Visby now applies, but is your answer here also relevant to question 18.2? (This depends on whether Phillips LJ or Hirst LJ is correct in *The River Gurara*.)

---

161 [2013] 2 Lloyd's Rep 487, in section [18.4].
162 [2007] 2 Lloyd's Rep 622, in section [18.6.1].
163 Section [17.1.7].
164 [1957] AC 149 and [2005] 1 WLR 1363, in section [18.4].
165 [1998] QB 610.

Chapter 19

Representations in bills of lading

Chapter Contents

19.1 Value of representations in bills of lading

In many international sales contracts, for example the CIF contract under which a large percentage of the world's cargo is shipped, the buyer is required to pay against tender of documents. This will typically occur before the goods arrive, giving the buyer the opportunity to inspect them.[1] If payment is by documentary credit, the bank will pay against tender of documents, and, again, the bank will have had no opportunity to inspect the goods. In the first case the buyer, and in the second the bank, rely heavily for an assurance that the seller has performed his obligation to ship conforming goods, on statements in the bill of lading. If any of these statements is incorrect, he may be induced to take up and pay against documents when, had they stated the truth, he would have rejected them. In the worst case, where for example the goods described have never been shipped, he may end up paying for documents that are worthless. If he is unable to sue the person who made the incorrect statement, then not only will he have suffered a grave injustice, but much of the value of the bill of lading as a negotiable document will have been lost. It is no answer to say the buyer can sue the seller on the contract of sale. The seller may be financially insecure, and the bill of lading is used precisely to guard against that possibility.

The bill of lading contains representations about the goods, typically including a description, quantity loaded, statement as their apparent order and condition, shipment date, etc. It is signed by the ship's master (or perhaps a loading broker or charterer's agent, acting in his stead). The master (or other person signing) will be acting as agent for the carrier; whether this is shipowner or charterer was considered in chapter 17.[2] For most non-liner shipping, it will be the owner. Moreover, although the bill of lading is issued to the shipper, the master knows that it will be transferred, and hence that the representations will be relied upon by subsequent holders, for example in deciding whether to take up and pay against the documents.

If we assume, for the moment, that master is acting for the shipowner, in an ideal world the shipowner should be liable for incorrect representations, to anyone who relies upon them. For example, there are Colman J's observations in *The Starsin*:[3]

> ". . . if an innocent shipper, indorsee or consignee could not rely on statements on the face of a bill of lading . . . and was obliged to verify [their] accuracy . . . each time he took a bill of lading, that would represent a most serious impediment to international trade which depends so heavily on the accuracy of bills of lading as negotiable instruments".

We can see a similar statement in *The Saudi Crown*, this time made by Sheen J:[4]

> ". . . great injustice may be done to the innocent third party if he is left to pursue whatever remedy he may have against a person of unknown financial means in some distant land".

For a purchaser to be restricted to an action against the immediate seller alone negates much of value of the bill of lading, the whole point of which is to assure the purchaser that he will not need to sue the foreign seller.[5]

---

1 *E. Clemens Horst Co v Biddell Bros* [1912] AC 18 (CIF buyer not entitled to delay payment until delivery).
2 Section [17.1].
3 *Homburg Houtimport BV v Agrosin Private Ltd (The Starsin)* [2000] 1 Lloyd's Rep 85, 97. The case eventually went to the House of Lords ([2004] 1 AC 715), but on this issue it went no higher than first instance. See section [17.1.8].
4 [1986] 1 Lloyd's Rep 261, 265.
5 For an action against a seller, see, eg, *Hindley & Co Ltd v East Indian Produce Co Ltd* [1973] 2 Lloyd's Rep 515 (where no goods were shipped). The action was presumably of value there, but of course would not be, if the seller were bankrupt.

For the most part, the law works moderately well, and shipowners generally are liable to sub-sequent holders (if not to the shippers to whom the bills are issued), if there are misstatements in them. The legal devices are not always intuitive, however, and (though matters have been improved by legislation) there remain significant gaps in the regime. Also, even though the master typically acts as agent for the shipowner, as we will see later in the chapter, not all statements in bills of lad-ing can be attributed to him.[6] We also need to consider the status of the statements, whether mere statements of fact, contractual promises, etc.[7]

19.2 Signing and clausing process

We need to consider how the statements in bills of lading come to be there, from whom they ema-nate, and the master's duty to clause, or not to clause, a bill of lading.

We should remember that, in the first instance, the bill of lading is issued to the shipper.[8] The shipper is already aware of much of the information in a bill of lading, and indeed much of it emanates from him. Thus, it is the shipper who draws up the mate's receipt, and later presents the bill of lading for signature. It is the shipper himself who provides the description of the goods. However, the master is not required simply to sign the shipper's statements, but is expected to clause the bill of lading as appropriate. Ultimately, therefore, the statements in the bill are those of the master, to the extent that he does not qualify them by clausing the bill of lading, and to the extent that they are within the master's authority, the statements are also those of the carrier.

In the bulk cargo trade the traditional mate's receipt is still used. The cargo is described in the mate's receipt by the shipper, and, unless the master insists on clausing, this description will be carried over to bills of lading. Masters have their principal's authority to describe the apparent con-dition of the goods loaded.[9] Unless the master clauses the bill it will state that the goods as described were loaded in "apparent good order and condition". This would be a clean bill, which (assuming it was not otherwise defective) a purchaser or bank would be required to accept.

Under both the Hague and Hague-Visby Rules, Art. III(3), the shippers are entitled to demand a bill of lading showing the apparent order and condition of the goods. However, masters are not obliged to accept the shipper's statement as to condition without more, and are entitled to clause bills of lading if it is appropriate so to do. The consequences of failing to do so were considered by the Court of Appeal in The Nogar Marin.[10] Rusty steel had been shipped, but the master had been guilty of an error of judgment in failing to clause the mate's receipts, and consequently the ship's agents had issued clean (unclaused) bills of lading. The shipowners settled a claim made by receivers of the cargo, presumably on the principles discussed later in this chapter, and were unsuccessful in claim-ing an indemnity from the (voyage) charterers, who had presented clean mate's receipts, and later clean bills of lading for signature. Central to the decision were the following passages:[11]

"The charterers tender the document. The master has a free choice whether or not to clause it. He chooses not to do so. Later, those acting for the owners have the opportunity to clause the bill of lading, so as to protect the owners. Again they let the opportunity pass. . . .

---

6 Section [19.8].

7 Sections [19.3]; [19.4].

8 There is a useful, if perhaps slightly dated, description of the process, in Devlin J's judgment in *Heskell v Continental Express Ltd* (1950) 83 LL L Rep 438; see also Dockray, *Cases and Materials on the Carriage of Goods by Sea*, 3rd ed (2004), Cavendish, 12–13. Also Todd, *Cases and Materials on International Trade Law* (2002), Sweet & Maxwell, beginning at [14–007].

9 But not the actual condition: *Cox v Bruce* (1886) 18 QBD 147.

10 *Naviera Mogor SA v Societe Metallurgique de Normandie (The Nogar Marin)* [1988] 1 Lloyd's Rep 412. See further sections [13.1]; [13.7].

11 [1988] 1 Lloyd's Rep 412, 421; 422.

> Everyone in the shipping trade knows that the master need not sign a clean bill just because one is tendered; everyone knows that it is the master's task to verify the condition of the goods before he signs. This being so, we cannot understand the request implicit in the tender as being more than this: 'The charter requires you to bind your owners to the contract of carriage contained in the bill of lading, and please do so. The bill of lading also constitutes a receipt, and please sign it as such, with whatever appropriate qualification you may think fit.'"

Consequently, the charterers were not in breach in tendering clean mate's receipts or bills of lading for signature, and had made no request leading to the implication of an indemnity. The shipowners would in any case have failed on causation. The master could have claused the mate's receipt, but chose not to do so. "Later, those acting for the owners have the opportunity to clause the bill of lading, so as to protect the owners. Again they let the opportunity pass."[12] The presentation by the charterers, of clean mate's receipt and (later) bill of lading for signature, was not the cause of the shipowner's loss.

It follows from all this that though statements in the bill of lading may have originated with the shipper, the master (or others acting for the owner) have the opportunity to accept these statements as they stand, or to qualify them by clausing, so in this sense the statements in the bill are shipowner's statements (assuming shipowner contracting carrier). The master is not required simply to sign the bill of lading clean, where the goods are obviously damaged.

Suppose, however, that in the light of this, masters insist on clausing bills of lading, even where the apparent condition of the goods does not justify clausing. Now the shipowners can potentially become liable to the shippers, under Art. III(3) if not at common law: *The David Agmashenebeli*,[13] Colman J there adopting a fairly low standard, amounting to little more than the honest exercise of a professional judgment, though subject to the qualification that:[14]

> ". . . the master who honestly takes an eccentric view of the apparent condition of the cargo which would not be shared by any other reasonably observant master would not be justified in issuing bills of lading which were qualified to reflect his view".

Sometimes the judgment is difficult, and there may be contractual provision to resolve this, as in RETLA clauses for steel, as interpreted in *The Saga Explorer*.[15]

19.3 Are statements in bills of lading contractual?

If the carrier's statements about the description, apparent quality, etc, were to constitute contractual promises, for example to deliver goods as described, then the bill of lading holder could sue if they were untrue. The starting point for damages would be the difference in value between the goods as described, and as shipped in their actual condition. For breach of contract there is no need to show negligence or other intent, or reliance on the statement made (though reliance could be relevant to a damages claim).

However, contract reasoning did not succeed in *Compania Naviera Vasconzada v Churchill & Sim*,[16] and no doubt has been cast on this decision. One reason is that because the seller prepares the bill of lading, it would be odd if statements in it constituted any kind of warranty of accuracy by the master to the shipper (given that the shipper has himself prepared it). However, not all statements in the bill of lading originate with the shipper; some factual statements (such as the date of shipment, whether

---

12 [1988] 1 Lloyd's Rep 412, 421.

13 [2003] 1 Lloyd's Rep 92.

14 [2003] 1 Lloyd's Rep 92, 105. The CA had suggested a higher standard in *The Arctic Trader* [1996] 2 Lloyd's Rep 449, which Colman J refused to adopt, also observing that these remarks were *obiter*.

15 *Breffka & Hehnke GMBH & Co KG v Navire Shipping Co Ltd (The Saga Explorer)* [2013] 1 Lloyd's Rep 401.

16 [1906] 1 KB 237.

the goods are loaded above or below deck) may originate with the carrier. Other examples might be quantity statements and the shipment date. Perhaps these can properly be regarded as contractual promises.[17] If so, they are enforceable, whether or not there is any reliance by the representee.

19.4 Estoppel

The estoppel doctrine prevents a representor from denying the truth of his representation, where it has been relied up by the person to whom the representation is made. Though there was no contract action in *Compania Naviera Vasconzada v Churchill & Sim*,[18] an estoppel prevented the shipowner from denying the truth of the statement he had made, of the condition of the goods on shipment. He was therefore liable since the goods were now not in the stated condition, and the shipowner was precluded (by the estoppel) from bringing evidence to explain this. This estoppel reasoning was applied in the Court of Appeal in *Silver v Ocean SS Co Ltd, Brandt v Liverpool, Brazil and River Plate SN Co Ltd and Brown Jenkinson & Co Ltd v Percy Dalton (London) Ltd*,[19] and may therefore be regarded as well-established law.

Estoppel depends on reliance. This will not be problematic if the holder takes up the bill of lading in reliance on the representations contained in it, but it is a different matter if the new holder would have accepted the bill of lading anyway, perhaps because the contract of sale so requires.[20] However, even if the new holder would have accepted anyway, for example on a generally rising market where the defects are not very bad (because it is better to accept the goods as they are, rather than go back into a now unfavourable market), the statements in the bill of lading may affect the price paid or other matters, in which case there can still be reliance.

We will see in the next section that where the Hague-Visby Rules apply, there is a statutory estoppel, whether or not reliance is shown. However, the estoppel may not be a panacea. With statements as to shipment date, for example, an estoppel would be of little use.[21] How does it help the holder for the carrier to bound to the truth of the shipment date statement? The only possibility might be to establish a breach of the reasonable despatch obligation, which will not normally be useful. Other limits to estoppels are that they will be limited by the value the goods would have had, had the statement been true (which may not provide adequate compensation on a falling market), and that the action suffers from all the limitations of suing on the carriage contract, for example the Hague-Visby limits to liability.

19.5 Hague and Hague-Visby Rules

Article III(3) was unchanged by the Visby amendments, requiring bills of lading to show, among other things:

> "(b) Either the number of packages or pieces, or the quantity, or weight, as the case may be, as furnished in writing by the shipper.
> (c) The apparent order and condition of the goods."

---

17 Eg, *The Nea Tyhi* [1982] 1 Lloyd's Rep 606 (statements goods shipped under deck contractual term).
18 [1906] 1 KB 237.
19 *Silver v Ocean SS Co Ltd* [1930] 1 KB 416; *Brandt v Liverpool, Brazil and River Plate SN Co Ltd* [1924] 1 KB 575; *Brown Jenkinson & Co Ltd v Percy Dalton (London) Ltd* [1957] 2 QB 621.
20 *The Skarp* [1935] P 134; cf. *The Dona Mari* [1974] 1 WLR 341 (where this inference was not drawn).
21 Eg, *The Saudi Crown* [1986] 1 Lloyd's Rep 261. There was no need for an estoppel there, because the statement was made fraudulently, and the holder could sue in deceit.

It goes on to provide that the carrier shall be not bound to make statements "which he has reasonable ground for suspecting not accurately to represent the goods actually received, or which he has had no reasonable means of checking". Article III(4) then continues:

> "Such a bill of lading shall be *prima facie* evidence of the receipt by the carrier of the goods as therein described in accordance with paragraph 3 (a), (b), and (c). However, proof to the contrary shall not be admissible when the bill of lading has been transferred to a third party in good faith."

Note that the second sentence was added to Art. III(4), by the Visby amendments. Finally, Art. III(5) provides for an indemnity against the shipper, where the carrier has relied on statements given to him by the shipper, and incurred liability as a result.[22]

Under the Hague Rules, the statements in Art. III(3) are no more than *prima facie* evidence, but under Hague-Visby, the second sentence of Art. III(4), added by the Visby amendments, provides for a statutory estoppel, whether or not reliance can be shown. The carrier cannot then deny the truth of the statements he makes.

19.6 Tort actions – deceit and negligence

Another possibility is an action in tort, for negligent or fraudulent misstatement. Tort damages effectively unravel the transaction (as far as money can), and would therefore be better on a falling market, if the buyer would have rejected, had he known the truth. However, a tort action may not be available. It also depends (like estoppel) on reliance.

Where there is fraud there is no issue. Fraud by the master will normally give rise to liability; even frauds by the master will not take him outside the course of his employment, and therefore the shipowner should be liable for the master's fraudulent misstatements.[23]

Where the misrepresentation is innocent,[24] there will be no action in tort. However, a statement negligently made, and relied on, by the holder, probably gives rise to liability in tort, the action being based on the well-known House of Lords authority of *Hedley Byrne & Co Ltd v Heller & Partners Ltd*.[25] The action would depend on negligence and reliance (so to that extent the limits of estoppel reasoning apply here also).

19.7 Indemnities

Sometimes masters might be persuaded to issue clean bills of lading for faulty goods, perhaps on the promise of an indemnity. On the above principles, these statement might incur the carrier in liability. But if the statements in the bills amount to deliberate lies, the indemnity will be unenforceable, as an indemnity against the consequences of deceit (in effect, fraud).

This was the situation in the well-known case of *Brown Jenkinson & Co Ltd v Percy Dalton (London) Ltd*.[26] By issuing a clean bill of lading for goods that were clearly defective, the shipowner was precluded from enforcing a contract of indemnity against the shippers, being unable to claim without relying

---

22 The full text of these provisions, paraphrased here, can be found in Appendix A. See also sections [9.10]; [9.11].

23 *Lloyd v Grace Smith & Co* [1912] AC 716; the action was for fraudulent misrepresentation in *The Saudi Crown* [1986] 1 Lloyd's Rep 261.

24 Unlikely perhaps, but this was the finding in *V/O Rasnoimport v Guthrie & Co Ltd* [1966] 1 Lloyd's Rep 1, where a bill of lading was issued for goods which were not on board the ship.

25 [1964] AC 465. Details of the scope of the negligent misstatement action are beyond the scope of this book, but it probably covers the situation here.

26 [1957] 2 QB 621.

on his deceit. The result was that the shipowner, who arguably did no worse than follow common business practice, was branded fraudulent, and failed in a claim against a far less meritorious shipper.[27]

In *Brown Jenkinson*, the master had been persuaded, at the shipper's request, to issue a clean bill of lading for goods that were obviously faulty (casks of orange juice, which were clearly leaking), taking an indemnity from the shippers against any loss occasioned to him. The shipowner did not seriously dispute the claim from the eventual receiver (or, to be more accurate, his insurer to whom his claim was subrogated).[28] The Court of Appeal (by a majority) took the view that the shipowner could not enforce the indemnity. He had committed the tort of deceit,[29] and, since he could not claim on the indemnity without disclosing his deceit, his claim was barred as arising *ex turpi causa*. Indeed, the indemnity contract had as its very object, the commission of the tort of deceit.

There might also be causation issues, if the master should clearly not have signed the bill.[30]

In *Brown Jenkinson* the master lied, stating that the goods were in apparent good order and condition when this was clearly untrue. It was this that constituted the tort of deceit. An indemnity can be recoverable, however, if there is genuine doubt about the condition, and the shipper promises to indemnify in the event that the master gets it wrong. There is no deceit in that situation.

19.8 Quantity statements in bills of lading

It might be expected that all or most of the above would apply equally to quantity statements, but this is to reckon without the decision in *Grant v Norway*.[31] This case, which pre-dates modern agency developments, holds that the master has no authority to sign bills of lading for goods not loaded on board the ship.[32]

Grant v Norway has been entrenched (albeit with some reluctance) by later cases, and must be regarded as clear law, but it appears out of line with later agency authority and hence anomalous.[33] It is based on "the authority of [the master] to perform all things usual in the line of business in which he is employed", rather than the more general test of ostensible authority or course of employment. It is almost limited to a test of actual authority. *Grant v Norway* is also a very inconvenient decision that can obviously work harshly on subsequent holders.

Though the decision in *Grant v Norway* is fairly firmly entrenched it has not been popular with the courts, and should probably be regarded as limited to its facts. It was not extended in *The Nea*

---

27 As Morris LJ observed, it was they who had requested the procedure, and that "they are prepared to condemn their own conduct in order to save their own pocket": [1957] 2 QB 621, 629.

28 At any rate, he paid under threat of legal proceedings: [1957] 2 QB 621, 632 (Morris LJ).

29 The receivers could have sued the shipowners for deceit, had the shipowners not readily paid up. To the argument that the receivers were not really defrauded, since they had a clear action against the shipowners, on the basis of the estoppel discussed in section [19.4], Morris, LJ observed ([1957] 2 QB 621, 634): "that, though there may be an estoppel against the shipowner, the holder of a clean bill of lading may still be in great difficulties if defective goods are shipped. He may have resold the goods and he may find that his purchaser will not accept, and he may sometimes experience great practical difficulties in suing the shipowner if, for example, the shipowner is a foreign shipowner. If he sues the shipowner, the latter may be entitled to rely on some clause in the bill of lading which protects him: furthermore, some time limit may prove fatal to a claim. But in any event buyers and bankers who act on the faith of clean bills of lading are not seeking law suits."

30 Discussed in *The Nogar Marin* [1988] 1 Lloyd's Rep 412, where however the context was slightly different. See also *The Sagona*, in section [13.8].

31 (1851) 10 CB 665.

32 The principle was extended to actual (though not apparent) quality in *Cox v Bruce* (1886) 18 QBD 147.

33 Eg, *Lloyd v Grace Smith & Co* [1912] AC 716, where the HL takes an apparently wider view of agency, based on the course of employment.

Tyhi (goods under deck),[34] nor in *The Saudi Crown* (backdated bills),[35] nor even if the bills were signed before the goods were loaded (and hence were not on board *at the time* the bills were signed).[36] In some circumstances it might be possible to sue master (or other person signing the bill of lading, such as a loading broker) for breach of warranty of authority.[37]

19.9 Quantity statements and legislation

A number of attempts have been made in legislation to reverse *Grant v Norway*, and the present legislation is probably reasonably effective, but the legislative attempts have a chequered history. It is important to provide conclusive evidence against the carrier, not just against the master (as was done by s. 3 of the Bills of Lading Act 1855). Where the Hague-Visby Rules apply, the second sentence of Art. III(4), set out above, does this, but provides conclusive evidence only of receipt, not shipment. The Carriage of Goods by Sea Act 1992, s. 4, extends the law to provide evidence of shipment, but the section applies only to bills of lading, as defined by the Act. As we have seen, a bill of lading under the 1992 Act must be negotiable. Straight bills remain governed by the pre-1992 law.

There is another problem with both the 1971 and 1992 Acts. Both depend on the existence of a contract of carriage, but, just because there is a bill of lading, it does not follow that there is also a carriage contract. In *Heskell v Continental Express*,[38] no goods were shipped at all, and as a consequence no carriage contract ever made. Indeed, Devlin J regarded the bill of lading as a nullity:[39]

> "It could never have been more than a bit of paper purporting to record a bargain that had never been made."

If there is no carriage contract, and hence no proper bill of lading, neither the 1971 nor 1992 Acts will have any effect.

19.10 Qualified quantity statements: Hague-Visby Rules, Art. III(3)

Where the Hague-Visby Rules apply, by Art. III(3):

> "After receiving the goods into his charge, the carrier, or the master or agent of the carrier, shall, on demand of the shipper, issue to the shipper a bill of lading showing among other things – . . . (b) either the number of packages or pieces, or the quantity, or weight, as the case may be, as furnished in writing by the shipper; . . .".

However, the provision continues:

> ". . . provided that no carrier, master or agent of the carrier, shall be bound to state or show in the bill of lading any marks, number, quantity, or weight which he has reasonable grounds

---

34 [1982] 1 Lloyd's Rep 606, Sheen J's comments on *Grant v Norway* being scathing.
35 [1986] 1 Lloyd's Rep 261.
36 *The Starsin* [2000] 1 Lloyd's Rep 85 (Colman J).
37 *V/O Rasnoimport v Guthrie & Co Ltd* [1966] 1 Lloyd's Rep 1, where a loading broker was successfully sued. The action (which is based on an implied contract, under which the loading broker warrants that he has the authority to sign the bill) is likely to be of little practical use against a master.
38 (1950) 83 Ll. L. Rep 438, also in section [15.1.3].
39 (1950) 83 Ll. L. Rep 438, 456.

for suspecting not accurately to represent the goods actually received, or which he has had no reasonable means of checking".

The original Hague Rules are the same, and the provision allows carriers to qualify quantity statements. They may also, of course, qualify statements, whether permitted by Art. III(3) or not. So how does this affect the present discussion?

19.11 Evidential value of statements

Quantity statements will be conclusive, in the absence of other evidence.[40] In *Profindo Pte Ltd v Abani Trading Pte Ltd*,[41] CFR buyers claimed short shipment of 4 tonnes of a cargo of 2,750 mt of cement. The bill of lading showed that the full contractual quantity had been shipped, and, in the absence of other evidence, their claim failed. This was a claim against their sellers, but the weight would also have been conclusive evidence, as between cargo-owner and carrier.

Otherwise quantity statements are *prima facie* evidence of truth, unless of course the Hague-Visby Rules apply, in which case they are conclusive, if the statutory estoppel applies. If, however, they are qualified, for example as permitted by Art. III(3), then the qualification may negate any statement of quantity at all.[42] If there is no quantity statement, neither the 1971 nor 1992 Acts will apply. Thus, in *The Mata K*,[43] a weight unknown qualification negated the effect of s. 4 of COGSA 1992, where the allegation was that the goods had been left behind. "Weight unknown" or "weight and quantity unknown" negates any statement of quantity loaded, so that there is no such statement at all. Such a clause removes even *prima facie* evidence of the number of packages, or weight of goods loaded.

In *The River Gurara*[44] there is discussion (incidentally) of the effect of an "stc" or "said to contain" clause. (This means said by shipper to contain.) Colman J (with whom Hirst LJ agreed) accepted that this had the same effect as "weight and quantity unknown", though it did not affect enumeration for package limitation purposes under the Hague Rules.[45] Phillips LJ was less sure, however, saying only that:[46]

> "it seems to me at least arguable that the words 'said to contain' do no more than make plain that the carrier is, as required by Art. III(3), stating on the bill the 'number of packages . . . as furnished in writing by the shipper' without dissenting from the description, so that the description can be relied upon as providing *prima facie* evidence as to what was within the containers".

The issue did not arise directly in *The River Gurara*, which ultimately concerned only the Hague Rules package limitation, and therefore we cannot say whether "said to contain" has the same meaning as "weight and quantity unknown" or not.

---

40 *Henry Smith & Co v Bedouin Steam Navigation Co Ltd* [1896] AC 70 (HL).

41 [2013] 1 Lloyd's Rep 370 (High Ct, Singapore).

42 *New Chinese Antimony Co Ltd v Ocean Steamships Co Ltd* [1917] 2 KB 664; *The Atlas* [1996] 1 Lloyd's Rep 642 (weight and quantity unknown qualification).

43 [1998] 2 Lloyd's Rep 614.

44 *River Gurara (Owners of Cargo Lately Laden on Board) v Nigerian National Shipping Line Ltd (The River Gurara)* [1998] QB 610.

45 See section [18.5.2]. Colman J's judgment is reported at [1996] 2 Lloyd's Rep 53.

46 [1998] QB 610, 626.

19.12 Questions

Question 19.1

What, if anything, is the effect of the following ALTERNATIVE qualifications to a statement in a bill of lading as to quantity loaded:

(i) "quantity unknown"
(ii) "said to contain"?

Note

In respect of (ii), have a look at observations in *The River Gurara*, noting that there is more than one view expressed.[47]

Question 19.2

An indorsee, Graham, takes delivery of a container after presenting a bill of lading governed by the Hague-Visby Rules. The bill of lading describes the container as "said to contain" 30 widgets. In fact only 20 widgets have been loaded, the remainder having been left behind.

(i)   Advise Graham as to whether he might have an action against the carrier or the master.
(ii)   Would your answer have been different had the bill of lading been governed by the Hague Rules, and the contract of sale provided that buyers were not to reject shipping documents, but to submit any disputes to arbitration?
(iii) Would your answer to either (i) or (ii) have been different had the bill of lading not been negotiable, but named Graham as consignee?
(iv)   Would your answer to either (i) or (ii) have been different had the bill of lading never reached Graham (though he had seen a copy), and Graham had taken delivery under an LOI?

In each of the above situations, consider in the alternative that the bill of lading simply described the container as "containing 30 widgets".

Comment

Leaving aside the "said to contain" issue, on which (as already observed) you need to read *The River Gurara*, (i) would appear to be governed by both Art. III(4) of Hague-Visby and COGSA 92, s. 4. (ii) will not benefit from the Visby amendment to Art. III(4), and an estoppel might be difficult to establish against the carrier. But COGSA 92 still applies, but it does not in (iii), because s. 4 applies only to negotiable bills. Nor does COGSA 92 apply in (iv), even s. 2, so there might be a cause of action problem (but *Brandt v Liverpool* might).[48]

---

47 [1998] QB 610.
48 You may need to look again at chapter 16 for this.

Chapter 20

The bill of lading as a document of title

Chapter Contents

20.1 Importance of document of title

This chapter is about delivery.[1]

Possibly the most important single feature of a bill of lading is that it is the key to the warehouse, the document that allows the holder to take delivery of the goods from the vessel. As long ago as 1883, Bowen LJ famously described the bill of lading as:[2]

> "a key which in the hands of a rightful owner is intended to unlock the door of the warehouse, floating or fixed, in which the goods may chance to be".

At that time the shipped bill of lading was probably the only document of title that could be described as the key to the warehouse, but the description might apply to a greater range of documents today.[3]

Even the shipped bill of lading is not always the key to the warehouse, however, and it is important to bear in mind the limits of the document of title concept. Merely to have a bill of lading may not give the holder anything. The value of the document lies in what it does, rather than what it is.[4] So, for example, it has long been recognised that transfer of the bill of lading may transfer property in the goods,[5] but it has also long been recognised that it does not always do so, and that the passing of property depends ultimately on the intention of the parties.[6] If the bill of lading does pass property, with that will also usually go the immediate right of possession, necessary to bring a conversion action in the event of a misdelivery.[7] Alternatively, the bill of lading may symbolically transfer possession directly, which would again give title to sue in conversion, but this has also been held to depend on intention; it will not always do so.[8] It might also transfer the contractual right to take delivery, but, as we saw in chapter 16, not necessarily.[9] In all of these cases, it is what the bill of lading does, rather than the document itself, that creates the value. This is an important point, because, even if for some reason the parties do not wish to use a bill of lading, provision can be made for any document to pass property, possession and contractual rights, as long as it is done explicitly. This is essentially what the BOLERO electronic bill of lading would have done.[10] The difference with the bill of lading is that property, possession and contractual rights are usually transferred without the need for further explicit provision.[11] With documents that are not documents of title, provision has to be made explicitly.[12]

---

1 The chapter is not very detailed, but I have written elsewhere about delivery, if you are interested in taking the subject further: Todd, *The bill of lading and delivery: the common law actions* [2006] LMCLQ 539; Todd, *Excluding and limiting liability for misdelivery* [2010] JBL 243.

2 *Sanders Bros v Maclean & Co* (1883) 11 QBD 327, 341.

3 See section [20.3].

4 Essentially the thesis advance in Bools, *The Bill of Lading: A Document of Title to Goods* (1997), LLP.

5 *Lickbarrow v Mason* (1794) 5 TR 683.

6 *Sewell v Burdick* (1884) 10 App Cas 74, where general property did not pass to a bank, to render it liable for freight under s. 1 of the Bills of Lading Act 1855: see sections [16.3]; [16.8].

7 The actions are described in section [20.4].

8 *The Future Express* [1993] 2 Lloyd's Rep 542, where possession of the bill of lading gave its holder no useful rights at all.

9 See section [16.7].

10 See section [21.2], and references therein.

11 For example, if the bill of lading is taken out to seller's order, s. 19(2) of the Sale of Goods Act 1979 creates a presumption that he retains property until payment against transfer of the bill of lading; if another document were used, s. 19(2) would not apply, but of course provision could be made explicitly.

12 See further section [20.3].

20.2   What is a document of title?

A document of title, then, is the key to the warehouse. Its presentation allows the holder to take delivery of the goods from the carrier, when they arrive at the port of discharge. If the goods have already been delivered to someone else, or the carrier refuses to make delivery against presentation, then there should be a contract, conversion or bailment action, either against the carrier, or against the person to whom delivery has been made (or both). Conversely, a carrier should be protected if he makes delivery against production of an original document of title, or refuses to deliver unless one is produced.

In summary, then, the bill of lading as a document of title should have the following features:

(a)   if the shipowner delivers other than against production of an original document, he should be liable to the holder of the original document;

(b)   the shipowner should be entitled to refuse to deliver except against production of an original document;

(c)   the shipowner should be protected if he delivers against production of an original document;

(d)   the shipowner must deliver against production of an original.

20.2.1   Authorities for (a)

If the shipowner delivers to someone not entitled, without production of an original bill of lading, he is in principle liable, in contract and conversion, to the person with the bill of lading, who is entitled. A leading modern authority is *Sze Hai Tong Ltd v Rambler Cycle Co*,[13] where a shipping company was held liable to the shipper for delivering, against an indemnity but without production of an original bill of lading, to a consignee who had not paid for the goods. Liability was in both contract and conversion, and there might also have been liability for breach of bailment.[14] A conversion action may also be brought against the person to whom delivery has been wrongly made.[15]

In *Sze Hai Tong Ltd*, the carrier was aware that he was acting unlawfully, but the principle was extended to situations where the shipowner believed that he was behaving lawfully in *The Sormovskiy* 3068, where Clarke J envisaged a simple rule:[16]

> "It makes commercial sense to have a simple rule that in the absence of an express term of the contract the master must only deliver the cargo to the holder of the bill of lading who presents it to him."

Clarke J also suggested there might be limited exceptions to the shipowner's liability, for example for a lost or stolen bill of lading. Later cases have embraced the simple rule, but not the exceptions.[17] It now appears that there are no exceptions to the liability, even for example where the bill

---

13 [1959] AC 576.

14 As in *East West Corp v DKBS AF 1912 A/S* [2003] QB 1509. Successful bailment actions are rare, there being authority that only the shipper, as original bailor, can sue, title to sue in bailment not being transferred with the bill of lading: *The Future Express* [1993] 2 Lloyd's Rep 542.

15 The result in *Barber v Meyerstein* (1870) LR 4 HL 317.

16 *SA Sucre Export v Northern River Shipping Ltd (The Sormovskiy 3068)* [1994] 2 Lloyd's Rep 266, 274. The defendants claimed that they delivered the cargo in accordance with the practice, custom and local law of the port.

17 *Kuwait Petroleum Corp v I & D Oil Carriers Ltd (The Houda)* [1994] 2 Lloyd's Rep 541; *Motis Exports Ltd v Dampskibsselskabet AF 1912, Aktieselskab* [1999] 1 Lloyd's Rep 837 (Rix J), noted [1999] LMCLQ 449, and upheld [2000] 1 Lloyd's Rep 211 (CA).

of lading has become lost and its absence satisfactorily accounted for. The carrier might, however, be protected by an express clause in the bill of lading.[18]

The principle was extended to presentation of a forged bill of lading in *Motis Exports v Dampskibssels-kabet AF 1912*,[19] where the shipowner (being fooled by the forgery) believed he was delivering to the person entitled. As with *Sze Hai Tong*, in *Motis*, liability was assumed in both contract and conversion.

It should perhaps be added that conversion is an intentional tort, involving the denial of the claimant's title. It is committed both by the person who makes, and the person who accepts, a mis-delivery (so the holder is not limited to an action against the carrier).[20] But it does not require that the denial of the claimant's title is intentional, and so it can be committed even if, as in *Motis Exports*, the carrier believed that he was delivering to the person entitled. The intentional element is satisfied by the delivery being intentional, as all misdeliveries will presumably be.

20.2.2 Authorities for (b)

The leading authority, that the carrier is entitled to refuse to deliver except against production of an original (subject to express contrary provision), is *The Houda*,[21] a Court of Appeal case, actually on whether a time charterer could order the shipowner to deliver (but the court tied the position under a time charter into that under bills of lading).

In *The Houda*, Millett LJ, reviewing earlier authorities, concluded that:[22]

> "[the authorities] clearly establish . . . that under a bill of lading contract . . . the shipowners are obliged to deliver cargo only against presentation of a bill of lading".

Leggatt LJ went further, saying that:[23]

> "Under a bill of lading contract a shipowner is obliged to deliver goods upon production of the original bill of lading. Delivery without production of the bill of lading constitutes a breach of contract even when made to the person entitled to possession. . . ."

A similar view was taken by Clarke J in *The Sormovskiy 3068*.[24] This stronger formulation implies that the carrier is not merely entitled, but also obliged to refuse to deliver, other than on production of a bill of lading, and therefore that it is wrongful so to deliver, even to a person entitled to take delivery, though as Neill LJ observed:[25]

> "Of course if such a delivery is made and the person to whom the cargo is delivered proves to be the true owner no damages would be recoverable."

The Houda reasons in contract, that it is implicit in the issue of bills of lading that make the goods deliverable "to order", that the carrier accepts the obligation to deliver to the holder upon

---

18 Assumed in *The Houda* and *Motis Exports*.

19 [2000] 1 Lloyd's Rep 211.

20 Eg, *Barber v Meyerstein* (1870) LR 4 HL 31.

21 [1994] 2 Lloyd's Rep 541. In this case also, the exceptions envisaged by Clarke J, above, were doubted.

22 *Kuwait Petroleum Corp v I & D Oil Carriers Ltd (The Houda)* [1994] 2 Lloyd's Rep 541, 556, approving Diplock J in *Barclays Bank Ltd v Commissioners of Customs and Excise* [1963] 1 Lloyd's Rep 81, 89.

23 [1994] 2 Lloyd's Rep 541, 553.

24 *SA Sucre Export v Northern River Shipping Ltd (The Sormovskiy 3068)* [1994] 2 Lloyd's Rep 266.

25 [1994] 2 Lloyd's Rep 541, 552.

production of the bill of lading.[26] If the straight bill of lading is a document of title then the carrier is undertaking a contractual obligation to deliver to the consignee only on production.[27] It is important that the carrier also has a defence if he is sued in conversion; though this has not been made explicit, is seems likely that it is not wrongful to refuse to deliver except against production of an original bill, and hence not a conversion.[28]

20.2.3 Authorities for (c)

That the carrier is protected if he delivers (even if to someone not entitled) against production of an original bill of lading was established by the House of Lords in the nineteenth century in *Glyn Mills Currie & Co v East and West India Dock Co*:[29] a shipowner, who delivered against the first original bill tendered of a set of three, would be protected against the claim of the true owner, of whose title the shipowner had no notice. (In parenthesis, we might observe that the situation, where originals in the set are negotiated separately, is unlikely to arise without fraud.) Part of the reasoning in *Glyn Mills* was that the practice of carrying three was not for the shipowner's benefit.[30]

The precise legal basis of *Glyn Mills* is not altogether clear. The best explanation, I suggest, is that conversion is a wrongful act, and to deliver against production of an original bill of lading is not wrongful.[31] If this is the correct explanation then it applies only to bills of lading and other documents of title. If other documents are used, while it is relatively easy to recreate the actions against carriers considered in this chapter, it is much more difficult explicitly to recreate the defences. The ramifications of this are considered further in the next chapter.[32]

20.3 Which documents are documents of title?

The custom of merchants, the basis of recognition of a document as a document of title from as long ago as *Lickbarrow v Mason*,[33] applied originally only to the shipped bill of lading, and not to any other document. Commenting (albeit some 65 years later) on the custom of merchants in 1855, when the Bills of Lading Act was enacted, McCardie J observed that it too was confined to the shipped bill of lading.[34] At that time, other documents were not widely used. That is no longer true, and so the question must be asked, are other documents of title today?

It is clear from *Nippon Yusen Kaisha v Ramjiban Serowgee* that a mate's receipt will not generally be regarded as a document of title at common law.[35] It is also clear from *Lickbarrow v Mason* and *Sanders v Maclean* that whether a document is a document of title is a question of fact, depending on the custom of merchants. There is also no doubt that a document can become a document of title, in

---

26 See section [14.4].

27 See section [14.6], at least on a wide reading of J.I. MacWilliam Company Inc v Mediterranean Shipping Co SA (The Rafaela S) [2005] 2 AC 423.

28 Eg, Glyn Mills Currie & Co v East and West India Dock Co (1882) 7 App Cas 591, 596 (Lord Selborne); Bools, The Bill of Lading: A Document of Title to Goods, 166.

29 (1882) 7 App Cas 591 (not actually a shipowner but principles apply to shipowners). The practice of requiring three originals continues to this day, despite the obvious fraud risks.

30 (1882) 7 App Cas 591, 599 (Lord Cairns). It is interesting to compare this case with Motis Exports, where the shipowner thought, but was not in fact, delivering against a genuine original. It is arguable that to use bills of lading at all is for the benefit of merchants rather than carriers: [1999] LMCLQ 449.

31 See the cases cited at the end of the last section.

32 See section [21.3].

33 (1794) 5 TR 683.

34 Diamond Alkali Export Corp v Fl. Bourgeois [1921] 3 KB 443, 450.

35 [1938] AC 429.

a particular trade, because of a local custom. In *Kum v Wah Tat Bank Ltd*,[36] the Privy Council could "see no reason in principle why a document of title should not be created by local custom",[37] and were prepared to accept that even a mate's receipt could be a document of title in the particular trade. The existence of a local custom is sufficient, and it is not necessary to show a worldwide custom. The evidence showed that from Sarawak to Singapore between 90 per cent and 95 per cent of the traffic was being carried on mate's receipts, without a bill of lading. That was sufficient to establish the custom. Curiously, in the opposite direction the percentage was between 75 per cent and 80 per cent, and so the custom may have been established only in one direction.

The custom was that a bill of lading was not issued at all, so that the only document that could be a document of title was the mate's receipt. It is in this respect that the case differed from *Nippon Yusen Kaisha v Ramjiban Serowgee*, where the mate's receipt was envisaged as a preliminary document only. Normally, a mate's receipt would later be given up for a bill of lading, the latter being used as a document of title. Had that been usual in *Kum v Wah Tat Bank*, probably no local custom that mate's receipts were used as documents of title could have been established.

In spite of the universality and notoriety of the custom, their Lordships in *Kum v Wah Tat Bank* refused to hold that the mate's receipt was a document of title in the particular case, because it was marked "Not Negotiable". The parties do not seem to have given much thought to the form of the document, but whether or not these words were really intended to have this effect, the parties were held to the words they had used.[38] It follows that a non-negotiable document can never be a document of title. Waybills are therefore never documents of title at common law.

What about acceptance of a global custom of merchants, without proof of a particular custom? There is some authority that a received for shipment bill is now a document of title at common law,[39] but there are quite good arguments against. A received for shipment bill of lading differs from a mate's receipt in that normally it will be the last document issued, and it may well be a reasonable inference that the carrier undertakes to deliver only against its production. Nonetheless, there is an argument for restricting the range of documents of title, since, to the extent that they give rights to their holders, they necessarily prejudice the rights of those who deal in the goods themselves.[40] This injustice cannot arise where it is impossible physically to deal with the goods, for example when they are at sea, but dealings with the goods themselves remain possible as long as they have only been received for shipment. This argues for restricting documents of title to those issued only after the goods have been shipped.[41] Apart from that, there are two other arguments against recognising the received for shipment bill as a document of title, without proof of a custom. The first is that received for shipment bills are sometimes used like mate's receipts, and exchanged for shipped bills of lading, rather than being used directly to take delivery of the goods. Secondly, there is no clear notion of what constitutes a received for shipment bill. It may state that the goods have been received for shipment aboard a particular vessel, or it may leave the carrier with a discretion as to the identity of the vessel. It may state that the carrier has received the goods personally, or it may merely state receipt by an agent. It must be more difficult to recognise a worldwide custom where the document itself can admit of so wide a variation, though of course a custom may well be established in particular trades.

---

36 [1971] 1 Lloyd's Rep 439.

37 [1971] 1 Lloyd's Rep 439, 443.

38 Arguments dependent on form rather than substance seem unsatisfactory, but there is a case for holding commercial people to what they say. See further section [14.6.2], where there is probably no alternative to a distinction based on form.

39 Eg, *The Marlborough Hill* [1921] 1 AC 444; the two Lycaon cases: *Ishag v Allied Bank International (The Lycaon)* [1981] 1 Lloyd's Rep 92 and *Elder Dempster Lines v Zaki Ishag (The Lycaon)* [1983] 2 Lloyd's Rep 548.

40 Treitel, *Legal status of straight bills of lading* (2003) 119 LQR 608, 622 (note on *The Rafaela S*).

41 Carver, *Bills of Lading*, 3rd ed (2012), [6–030] et seq.

The straight, non-negotiable, bill of lading is not made out to order but names a consignee.[42] This document can be transferred once only, to the consignee. The Carriage of Goods by Sea Act 1992 treats it as a species of waybill, not a document of title.[43] However, in 2005 the House of Lords held, in *The Rafaela S*, that a straight bill of lading was a document of title, to trigger the application of the Hague-Visby Rules.[44] Although it was not necessary for the actual decision, the House also appears to have granted it the status of a document of title at common law, because the consignee must produce it to obtain delivery of the cargo.[45] One reason was to allow the document to secure sellers against non-payment, a contrast therefore between straight bills of lading and sea waybills. By contrast, a waybill is not a document of title, and does not have to be presented to take delivery. Indeed, that is precisely why it is so commonly used.[46]

The reasoning was (essentially) that the document was a document of title because it had to be produced in order to obtain delivery of the goods. In the particular document before them, this was required by the attestation clause, and, in any case, a set of three was issued, which would have been quite unnecessary had production not been necessary to obtain delivery.[47] However, the reasoning appears to apply more generally, to any straight bill of lading. It was said that the carrier may need production of the bill to ascertain the identity of the consignee, and that the seller of goods, who obtains a straight bill of lading, may wish to hold on to the bill as security for payment of the price.[48] This justifies the requirement for production of the bill, and the conclusion that it is a document of title (at least in Lord Bingham's view, and probably also Lord Steyn's) follows from this.

The House of Lords' reasoning is essentially that a document of title has to be presented to obtain delivery of the goods, and the converse also, that a document that has to be presented to obtain delivery of the goods, is a document of title. The House did not reason explicitly on the basis of the custom of merchants, and conclusions based on evidence that shippers use such documents as security, much as they would an order bill of lading, have been criticised.[49] Nonetheless, Lord Rodger was concerned to "reflect commercial usage" in *The Rafaela S*,[50] and the custom of merchants might in reality justify the decision. It would be necessary, of course, unlike the received for shipment bill, to find reasonable uniformity of custom. It should not be sufficient that sometimes it is, and sometimes it is not, required for presentation.

If a document is a document of title, probably the courts will be prepared to make presumptions that they are not prepared to make with other documents, for example a contractual term that delivery must be made only against production, and that delivery against production is not wrongful. It may be that such presumptions are really the heart of what a document of title is today. (Another is the statutory presumption, in s. 19(2) of the Sale of Goods Act 1979, that a seller of goods who takes a bill of lading to his own order reserves title in those goods, in which case property would usually pass with the bill of lading, on tender against payment of the price.) With other documents, the presumptions are not made, and the parties must make provision explicitly.

---

42 See section [14.6].

43 See section [16.5]. These provisions are, of course, concerned with the transfer of contractual rights and duties, and not with delivery of the cargo.

44 [2005] 2 AC 423. On the application of the Hague-Visby Rules, triggered by the contract of carriage expressly or by implication providing for the issue of a bill of lading or any similar document of title, see section [18.6.4].

45 The case is not very strong on this: see section [14.6].

46 See further section [21.3].

47 Eg, [2005] 2 AC 423, [45] (Lord Steyn).

48 *Ibid*, [6] (Lord Bingham).

49 The conclusions as to customary usage (for straight bills of lading and waybills), of the Court of Appeal in *The Rafaela S* [2004] QB 702, were criticised, as factual conclusions, by Treitel, (2003) 119 LQR 608, 615 *et seq*.

50 [2005] 2 AC 423, [64], defining a bill of lading.

20.4 Liabilities and defences for misdelivery

The Houda reasons in contract,[51] and since COGSA 92 the holder of the bill of lading will normally have a contract action.[52] If he sues the carrier, the carrier will be able, again under the contract, to demand presentation of the original bill, or to defend himself, if he delivers in the Glyn Mills situation.[53]

There is also the possibility of a tort action, in conversion. This protects property, and also an immediate right of possession.[54] A holder of a bill of lading will usually have the latter, and often the former. If the shipowner is sued in tort, then he will want to establish a contract, to set up a defence or limit his liability, for example based on Arts. III(6) or IV(5) of the Hague or Hague-Visby Rules, considered later in this chapter.[55] We know from The Captain Gregos that Hague-Visby, like Hague, operates only by incorporation into a carriage contract, and, in the absence of such a contract between claimant and defendant, the carrier will be precluded from relying on any Hague-Visby terms.[56] Cases where there was no contract but the potential of a conversion action include The Captain Gregos (No. 2),[57] and The Filiatra Legacy,[58] the latter of which at least would be decided the same way even after 1992, since no bill of lading appears ever to have reached the claimants.

Bailment actions are not usually of value as the only bailment is by the shipper.[59] However, in East West Corpn v DKBS AF 1912 A/S,[60] an action could be brought only for breach of bailment (and maybe conversion). There was exceptionally no contract action, it having been divested by s. 2(5) of COGSA 1992.

Where a conversion action is brought by a claimant who (perhaps because he is holder of a bill of lading) has a contract with the carrier, the carrier should be able to rely on contractual defences, so that he will not be liable if he refuses to deliver without production of the bill, or if he has already delivered against an original bill. But the owner may not be a holder, and there may be no contract between the parties. However, the carrier should still be protected, because conversion is a wrongful act, in which case the carrier in either of these situations will simply not be liable in tort. That being so, the defences in The Houda or Glyn Mills do not depend on a contractual relationship between the parties; delivering against production of an original bill of lading or document of title, or refusing to deliver except against its production, is not a wrongful act.[61] The defences do, however, depend on the use of a bill of lading or other document of title, since it would be a wrongful act, for example, to deliver against production of any other document. For this reason, if documents other than bills of lading are used, while actions can relatively easily be given (explicitly) to holders of such documents, it is more problematic to recreate the carrier defences.[62]

---

51 Section [14.4].

52 See chapter 16.

53 Section [20.2.3].

54 Section [22.2.1].

55 Section [20.5.4].

56 Sections [16.10]; [17.3].

57 Compania Portorafti Commerciale SA v Ultramar Panama Inc (The Captain Gregos (No. 2)) [1990] 2 Lloyd's Rep 395 (conversion action on its own by intermediate holder – again there was no contract).

58 Anonima Petroli Italiana SPA and Neste OY v Marlucidez Armadora (The Filiatra Legacy) [1991] 2 Lloyd's Rep 337 (conversion though purchaser did not have bill of lading – he would not have been a holder, had the case arisen after COGSA 1992).

59 The Future Express [1993] 2 Lloyd's Rep 542, where the holder of a bill of lading failed to establish any cause of action at all. Prior to this case, an argument based on attornment in advance had been argued, under which, by issuing a bill of lading or other document of title, the carrier undertakes to surrender goods to (and become bailee for) whomever is lawful holder of the document: Goode, Proprietary Rights and Insolvency in Sales Transactions (1985), 6–7; Goode, Commercial Law (1982), 63. If The Future Express is correct, attornment in advance is not.

60 [2003] QB 1509, noted by Baughen, Misdelivery and the Boundaries of Contract and Tort [2003] LMCLQ 413. The case is described fully in section [16.7.1].

61 See the citations at the end of section [20.2.2].

62 See further section [21.3].

20.5 Exempting and limiting liability for misdelivery

In *The Houda*, and again in *Motis Exports*, there was a clearly expressed assumption that even a carrier who delivered without production of an original bill of lading would be protected by an express clause in the bill of lading.[63] In *Motis Exports* it was observed that: "[there] is no dispute that an appropriately worded clause could achieve the result for which the shipowner contends".[64] In reality, shipowners have rarely been successful in arguing for such protection, and failed in *Motis Exports* itself. The courts regard delivery without production as a very serious breach, requiring the clearest words to exempt liability.

Assuming there is a contract subsisting between the shipowner and the claimant, the enquiry might be broken down into the following stages:

(1) Is it possible to exempt liability in principle, or is there a rule of law preventing this?
(2) If there is no special law, and the ordinary law of contract applies, how does it apply to exempting liability?
(3) What about package limitations and time bars?
(4) What about Arts. III(6) and IV(5) in particular?

20.5.1 Is it possible to exempt liability in principle, or is there a rule of law preventing this?

Delivering to somebody not entitled, without production of an original bill of lading, is regarded by the courts as a very serious breach. The consequences are usually serious for the person entitled, and the breach (at any rate the delivery) is intentional.

I discussed in chapter 4 some breaches, such as deviation, for which it is arguable that special rules apply, and it remains arguable that a deviating shipowner is not entitled to rely on any bill of lading or charterparty exceptions.[65] For present purposes, let us assume that this argument is correct (though the authorities are far from being entirely convincing). The question then becomes, if deviation has that consequence, do the same principles apply also beyond deviation (to other very serious breaches)? The courts have been reluctant to extend them.[66] It seems more likely that, with the possible exception of deviation, the ordinary law of contract applies, however serious the breach.

20.5.2 If there is no special law, and the ordinary law of contract applies, how does it apply to exempting liability?

Even if exempting is possible in principle, there are no cases where an exemption has clearly worked. Thus, for example, arguments to exempt liability failed in *Sze Hai Tong Bank Ltd v Rambler Cycle Co Ltd*,[67] *Motis Exports Ltd v Dampskibsselskabet AF 1912*,[68] and *The MSC Amsterdam*.[69]

It is clear from these authorities that, at the very least, the clause must clearly cover delivery without production, and not be capable of being interpreted as covering something else. Thus, for example, misdelivery is a deliberate act, and so the clause must not be capable of being interpreted

---

63 As to the drafting of such a clause, see, eg, Wilson [1995] LMCLQ 289, 296–8.
64 [2000] 1 Lloyd's Rep 211, [5] (Mance LJ).
65 See section [4.4], where I suggest that this view of the law is not correct.
66 Eg, *Kenya Railways v Antares Co Pte Ltd (The Antares)* [1987] 1 Lloyd's Rep 424.
67 [1959] AC 576.
68 [2000] 1 Lloyd's Rep 211.
69 [2007] 2 Lloyd's Rep 622.

as covering only negligence. In *Motis* the clause was interpreted as covering theft but not misdelivery. Probably it must actually state that it covers delivery without production of an original bill of lading. It also appears, from *The MSC Amsterdam*, that the clause must also be clear and plain. In *The MSC Amsterdam*, it was hidden away in the middle of another provision, which was itself buried in the middle of the bill of lading.[70] However clearly expressed, a clause that is hidden away will not protect the shipowner.

All such terms are interpreted narrowly. The cases are all in line with the restrictive interpretation in *Glynn v Margetson and Co*,[71] whereby clauses are interpreted to be consistent with the main object and intent of contract. In respect of total exemption cases, this seems to be an almost insurmountable hurdle. However, both *Sze Hai Tong Bank Ltd v Rambler Cycle Co Ltd* and *Motis Exports Ltd v Dampskibsselskabet AF 1912* (where the clause did not protect the shipowner, and *Glynn v Margetson and Co* was expressly applied)[72] involved fairly general clauses, so it is just possible that a more specific clause would work.

Delivery without production seems to be regarded as especially serious, however, and any clause will probably need to cover it explicitly. If the clause is capable of applying to something else, it will probably be interpreted not to apply to delivery without production.

20.5.3 What about package limitations and time bars?

The courts interpret limitation clauses more generously than exemptions,[73] and it is indeed hard to see how *Glynn v Margetson* would apply to limitation of liability or a time bar, to anything, in fact, other than exclusion of liability. So owners who wish merely to limit might be in a more favourable position. It is not clear whether this generosity would apply to very low limits, though the limit in the leading case was very low.[74]

20.5.4 What about Arts. III(6) and IV(5) in particular?

There is no clear authority on whether these provisions of the Hague and Hague-Visby Rules would apply to misdelivery, though if the courts are tolerant of limitations and time bars then they might, even though they are in general terms, and do not mention misdelivery specifically. It will probably depend on the strength of the wording. Article IV(5) provides that "neither the carrier nor the ship shall in any event be or become liable for any loss or damage to or in connection with the goods in an amount exceeding . . .", and then the limits are set out. There is no material difference between the Hague and Hague-Visby provisions, at least in this respect.

The wording of Art. III(6) is arguably rather stronger: ". . . the carrier and the ship shall in any event be discharged from all liability whatsoever in respect of the goods, unless suit is brought within . . .", and then the one-year limit is set out. The word "whatsoever" was added by the Visby amendments, apparently to cover misdelivery.[75]

The question is whether, in spite of the generality of the wording in each case, either or both of these provisions is of sufficient width to cover misdelivery. None of the cases cover misdelivery as such, but in *The Happy Ranger*[76] the Court of Appeal was prepared to apply Art. IV(5) of Hague-Visby to a breach of Art. III(1) (the obligation to provide a seaworthy vessel), at least indicating that it is capable of applying to serious breaches of the carriage contract. It was observed that "[a] limitation

70 [2007] 2 Lloyd's Rep 622, [33]–[35].
71 [1893] AC 351; see further sections [4.4]; [22.2].
72 Respectively [1959] AC 576; [2000] 1 Lloyd's Rep 211.
73 *Ailsa Craig Fishing Co Ltd v Malvern Fishing Co Ltd* [1983] 1 WLR 964.
74 In *Ailsa Craig*, the limit was £1,800.
75 Diamond, *The Hague-Visby Rules* [1978] LMCLQ 225, 231.
76 *Parsons Corp v CV Scheepvaartonderneming (The Happy Ranger)* [2002] 2 Lloyd's Rep 357.

of liability is different in character from an exception".[77] In *The Kapitan Petko Voivoda*[78] Art. IV(5) of the Hague Rules protected a carrier who had deliberately and unlawfully carried cargo on deck. The result was that about a third of the cargo was washed overboard, serious consequences indeed, and directly consequential on the breach. The provision certainly applies widely, and I suggest is of sufficient width to cover misdelivery. However, the issue was deliberately left open in *The MSC Amsterdam*.[79] Delivery was made, from a container yard after discharge, against forged bills of lading. The original bills were presented the next day, but by then it was impossible to make delivery to the true owners, and the shipowners were eventually sued. There was no issue as to their liability, but they claimed the benefit of the Hague or Hague-Visby package limitation; the Hague Rules limit was just £1,800, Hague-Visby, based on weight, much higher but still well below the value of the cargo (of copper).

We know from chapter 18 that the Court of Appeal held Hague-Visby inapplicable, because Art. X was not triggered.[80] We have also seen that the Hague Rules, incorporated by paramount clause, did not apply to delivery after discharge,[81] and that an express term claimed to exempt the shipowner entirely was too buried in the contract to be effective.[82] Because they had held that the Hague Rules did not apply to delivery after discharge, the court did not need to consider whether Art. IV(5) protected the shipowner, and indeed left the point open.[83] So there remains no definitive ruling on this issue.

Article III(6), at any rate of Hague-Visby, I have suggested is wider in its scope than Art. IV(5). In *The Captain Gregos*, it was held applicable to an alleged non-delivery by theft of part of the cargo, "the acts of which the cargo-owners complain" being described by Bingham LJ as "the most obvious imaginable breaches of" Art. III(2).[84] If it is of sufficient width to cover this breach, then surely it is also sufficient to cover misdelivery. *The New York Star*,[85] a similarly worded clause, applied to delivery without production (though the contract there was of a different type to the carriage contracts considered here). Again, there is no definitive ruling, but I would tentatively suggest that Art. III(6) does apply to misdelivery.

In conclusion, exemption is probably possible in principle, but it requires a very clear clause, and a generic clause probably never suffices, if only because it can be interpreted as applying to something else. Limitation is also probably possible in principle, and even Art. IV(5) might well apply to misdelivery.

20.6 Delivering against LOI

Suppose an oil cargo with a long chain of sales. The voyage is not particularly long, financing banks will wish to inspect the documents on each sale, and, consequently, there is no reasonable prospect of the bill of lading reaching the ultimate receiver before the ship arrives. But the ship has to discharge the cargo quickly, and, unlike a container cargo, there is no prospect of discharging into a terminal first, from where it is later delivered. The only realistic option is to deliver the cargo directly into the receiver's oil tanks. But of course, the receiver has no bill of lading. The charterers might

---

77 [2002] 2 Lloyd's Rep 357, [38].

78 *Daewoo Heavy Industries Ltd v Klipriver Shipping Ltd (The Kapitan Petko Voivoda)* [2003] 2 Lloyd's Rep 1.

79 [2007] 2 Lloyd's Rep 622.

80 See section [18.6.2].

81 See section [18.6.3].

82 [2007] 2 Lloyd's Rep 622, [33]–[35].

83 [2007] 2 Lloyd's Rep 622, [27].

84 *Compania Portorafti Commerciale SA v Ultramar Panama Inc (The Captain Gregos)* [1990] 1 Lloyd's Rep 310, 315. See further (on other issues) sections [16.10]; [17.5].

85 *Port Jackson Stevedoring Pty Ltd v Salmond and Spraggon (Australia) Pty Ltd (The New York Star)* [1981] 1 WLR 138: see section [17.2].

instruct the shipowner to make delivery, and the shipowners might take a letter of indemnity (LOI) from the receivers, or the charterers, or both.[86]

The position of charterers has already been considered.[87] It is similar for consignees or other holders, in that there are two reasons why an indemnity of this type might be impugned. One is public policy and the other causation. However, whereas there is no doubt that, in an appropriate case, either or both of these might operate in principle, the authorities suggest that indemnities against delivery without production are generally enforceable.

In chapter 19, I described how, in *Brown Jenkinson & Co Ltd v Percy Dalton (London) Ltd*, the Court of Appeal held an indemnity unenforceable on public policy grounds.[88] An indemnity against the commission of a crime, or the intentional tort of deceit, will not be enforceable.[89] In the present context, however, this is likely to apply only in fairly extreme cases. An indemnity against theft of the cargo by the shipowner would clearly be unenforceable, but would also require the shipowner to know, or at least suspect, that the person to whom he delivered was not the true owner of the cargo. That will of course rarely be the case, since usually the shipowner will believe that he is delivering to the person who is entitled to the goods, but who for some reason cannot produce a bill of lading. Indemnities seem generally to be enforceable.[90]

Indemnities have been routinely used for probably around half a century, and presumably they usually work satisfactorily. Of course they can be expensive. It is also important to observe that the security they offer is personal; they do not provide good protection if there is a bankruptcy: one might consider what the situation would have been, had the charterer gone bankrupt in *The Sagona*.

20.7 Question

Alan is the holder of the bill of lading, and owner of the cargo to which it relates, on Jane's ship. The cargo is discharged into a container depot, from where it is delivered to fraudsters, against production of a forged bill of lading. The carriage contract, which is governed by the Hague-Visby Rules, incorporates the following clause:

> "The carrier shall not in any event be or become liable for any loss or damage to or in connection with the goods in an amount exceeding £50, in respect of any liability whatsoever in respect of the goods, howsoever caused, even if caused by misdelivery or a fundamental breach of contract."

Advise Jane whether she is liable, and, if so, whether she can rely on the clause, in an action by Alan for breach of contract and conversion.

Comment

Presumably, if Hague-Visby applies, the clause set out will be rendered void by Art. III(8), but does Hague-Visby apply? (Think about the temporal application issue, in section [18.6.3].) If not, is Jane protected by the clause? This is really about the material in section [20.5].

---

86 This situation is discussed in another context in section [21.2].

87 Section [13.8].

88 [1957] 2 QB 621; see section [19.7].

89 Eg, the authorities cited in *Standard Chartered Bank v Pakistan National Shipping Corporation (No. 2)* [2000] 1 Lloyd's Rep 218, noted [2000] LMCLQ 394.

90 Not clearly held, but assumed in *The Sagona* [1984] 1 Lloyd's Rep 194 (in section [13.8]; *The Stone Gemini* [1999] 2 Lloyd's Rep 255; *The Laemthong Glory (No. 2)* [2005] 1 Lloyds Rep 688 (privity and remedies issues); *The Bremen Max* [2008] EWHC 2755 (Comm) (interpretation issue); *The Jag Ravi* [2012] 1 Lloyd's Rep 637 (privity again).

Chapter 21

Carriage by sea in the modern world

21.1 Two types of problem

International trade has changed over the past few decades, and this has ramifications for the documents used, and the ideal legal regime.

A central problem is that bills of lading arrive after the cargo. We know that carriers incur significant potential liabilities if they deliver without production of an original bill of lading,[1] but they may have little choice, in reality, other than to deliver the cargo.[2]

There are two main reasons for bills of lading arriving late. First, particularly with commodities, the same cargo is often sold many times on the voyage. If the voyage is fairly short, and each sale is financed (as is typical) by two banks, each of which needs to inspect the documents, it can be seen how delays in sending the documents down the chain can rapidly build up. This is a difficult problem, because there is no room for using non-negotiable documentation. Bills of lading continue to be used, but not in the traditional way, and they do not provide the parties with the traditional security.[3]

The second problem is caused by what has been described as the container revolution, and there are a number of aspects to it. Containerised cargoes are not usually sold more than once, but the ships themselves, and the loading and discharge, can be fast, so that even though the documents do not get stuck in a chain they can still arrive late. However, precisely because the identity of the consignee is known from the start, and resales are rare, non-negotiable documents can be used in place of the traditional bill of lading. The advantage to a carrier of a non-negotiable document is that there is no point in waiting for it to arrive, since delivery can be made (though not necessarily safely), whether the document is presented or not.

Another aspect of the container revolution is that the containers are usually loaded, or stuffed, and unloaded, or unstuffed, inland, and so their carriage is not just a port-to-port operation. Typically there will be land, sea and land legs, probably with different carriers performing each. This gives rise to three main problems:

1. Different liability regimes apply to each stage of the voyage, but it may not be known where damage has occurred, nor which carrier is responsible (though development of smart containers might be able to alter this);[4]
2. There are privity problems (as discussed in chapter 17) if a performing carrier is sued in tort, if he is not also a contracting carrier;[5]
3. The use of different documents requires adjustment to the traditional Hague and Hague-Visby regimes.

21.2 Commodities, indemnities and electronic bills

Commodities are often sold many times on the same voyage. A seller may even become a buyer further down the chain, in which case we have a circle, rather than just a chain. Many of the standard form commodity sale contracts have circle clauses to deal with this eventuality, since, as long as nobody in the circle goes bankrupt, there is no point in sending the documents around the circle,

---

1 Section [20.2.1].
2 Section [20.6].
3 Eg, the standby letters of credit in *Enichem Anic SpA v Ampelos Shipping Co Ltd (The Delfini)* [1990] 1 Lloyd's Rep 252 and *Anonima Petroli Italiana SPA and Neste OY v Marlucidez Armadora (The Filiatra Legacy)* [1991] 2 Lloyd's Rep 337; the entire reason for their use is that it is not expected that sellers later in the chain will have a bill of lading to tender to the bank. The parties must be content to operate without the traditional security.
4 Eg, http://www.intermodal-events.com/files/technology_case_study_don_miller.pdf.
5 See sections [17.2]–[17.4].

for them only to end up where they started. All that needs to happen is for payments to be made between the parties, to reflect the different prices in the sale contracts.[6] I mention it in this context only to demonstrate that the situation is sufficiently common for it to be provided for in standard forms. Commodity sales involve long chains, or even circles.

A number of cases arose from sales and carriage of oil, when the markets became chaotic, following the OPEC oil embargo of 1973. Stable supply markets broke down completely, and vast numbers of middlemen appeared, as buyers and sellers of oil in the chain. Their role was entirely speculative; they had no facilities for the storage of oil, and purchased simply to resell. The large number of sales made it impossible to transfer the bills of lading down the chain until months, or even years, had passed after delivery. When the master of the *Sagona*, who had been commanding tankers for 14 years, was asked how often an original bill of lading had been presented to him prior to discharge, he answered: "I have never seen it".[7] The charterers, who would normally have known the identity of the eventual receiver, instructed the master as to delivery. In the case they were mistaken, and were held liable to indemnify the owners.[8] While this protected the owners, the charterers were probably left out of pocket, and of course indemnities work only if there are no bankruptcies. They are also expensive. Moreover, apart from giving an action against the shipowner for misdelivery, a bill of lading is likely to be of little value once the cargo has been discharged, since it will almost certainly be impossible to identify it, or to assert any property in it.

For decades it has been recognised that an electronic solution is probably the best way to deal with this problem. As long ago as the early 1980s a partial dematerialisation was piloted in the form of SeaDocs.[9] More recently, schemes for fully electronic bills of lading have been piloted, the best-known of which was BOLERO. This maintained a title register (using public–private key encryption to ensure security) to track ownership, and explicitly transferred contractual rights along with the electronic bill. BOLERO was also making moves towards more structured documentation, necessary to automate the checking process.[10] Both these schemes failed, principally because they required a central registry to maintain the title register, and there was distrust at the concentration of power. Banks also were reluctant to accept electronic documentation.[11] Though little documentation is publicly available, it seems likely that ScanDocs, the latest electronic scheme, is similar, at least in concept, to BOLERO, though it is said to be significantly easier to operate.[12]

BOLERO and ScanDocs operate on the basis that the law will not be changed to accommodate electronic bills. However, if we were to adopt the Rotterdam Rules,[13] Art. 8(a) allows "electronic transport records" to be used in place of conventional transport documents, as long as "[the] issuance, exclusive control, or transfer of an electronic transport record has the same effect as the issuance, possession, or transfer of a transport document". Article 9(1) requires that "surrender shall be subject to procedures that provide for:

"(a) The method for the issuance and the transfer of that record to an intended holder;
(b) An assurance that the negotiable electronic transport record retains its integrity;

---

6 Eg, GAFTA 100, cl. 24.

7 *A/S Hansen-Tangens Rederi III v Total Transport Corp (The Sagona)* [1984] 1 Lloyd's Rep 194, 201.

8 See section [13.8].

9 Described, eg, Kathy Love, *Seadocs: The Lessons Learned* [1992] 2 Oil and Gas Law and Taxation Review 53, 55.

10 An XML initiative: see generally http://www.bolero.net/.

11 See generally Todd, *Cases and Materials on International Trade Law* (2002), Sweet & Maxwell, ch. 16.

12 See generally Gaskell, *Bills of lading in an electronic age* [2010] LMCLQ 233. On other current developments, see Goldby, *The CMI Rules for Electronic Bills of Lading Reassessed in the Light of Current Practices* [2008] LMCLQ 56 (essentially a study of single-carrier schemes, and in particular that operated by APL).

13 See further section [21.5]. Selected articles are set out in Appendix D.

(c) The manner in which the holder or the consignee is able to demonstrate that it is the holder or the consignee;[14] and

(d) The manner of providing confirmation that delivery to the holder or the consignee has been effected . . .".

This would treat electronic bills of lading, as long as they satisfied the requirements of Art. 9, as equivalent to paper bills, for all the purposes discussed, for example, in chapters 16 and 20.[15]

21.3 Containers, multimodal transport documents and waybills

For many years now, containers have been carried under waybills or other documents that are not bills of lading. As long as a quarter of a century ago, Sir Anthony Lloyd (as he then was) observed that the sea waybill is widely used in the container business and short sea trades, estimating that perhaps 70 per cent of all liner goods were, even then, carried under sea waybills.[16] Around the same time, in *The European Enterprise*[17] Steyn J observed that: "It is the invariable practice of all English cross channel operators not to issue bills of lading for the cross channel Ro-Ro ferry trade. Instead, they issue commercial non-negotiable receipts." Containers are also deck cargo. Though the Hague-Visby Rules can be extended to non-negotiable documents and deck cargo, the regime is really intended for bills of lading, and has a pre-container view of deck cargo.[18]

Sir Anthony Lloyd also took the view that the waybill's usage would increase still further if, like the bill of lading, it could transfer rights of suit under carriage contracts. Since that article was written, this reform was of course made by the enactment of the Carriage of Goods by Sea Act 1992.[19] There is no doubt that the 1992 Act has significantly increased the security provided by the waybill, but security against the bankruptcy of another trader can still only effectively be provided by a document of title.

Containers are also usually shipped as part of a multimodal operation, for which again the Hague-Visby Rules are not ideally suited (though to which they can be extended).[20] With a multimodal operation, the contracting carrier will typically undertake responsibility for the entire voyage, but sub-contracting the parts he does not perform himself. This is very similar in concept to transhipment and the through bill of lading discussed in chapter 14,[21] except that it is in a multimodal rather than unimodal context, and we have seen some of the attendant privity problems in chapter 17.[22] There will also, as with the through bill of lading, be contracting and performing carriers.

From the viewpoint of the transport conventions, multimodal transport poses a number of issues, which can be summarised as follows:

---

14 The note in the original states that "Reference to 'the consignee' has been added to this subparagraph so as to accurately include in this provision coverage of an electronic equivalent of a non-negotiable transport document that requires surrender." This would allow for an electronic replacement of the document that was used in *JI MacWilliam Company Inc v Mediterranean Shipping Co SA (The Rafaela S)* [2005] 2 AC 423, in section [14.6.1].

15 Assuming, at least, we only adopted this. If we adopted the entirety of Rotterdam, much of the substance of chapters 16 and 20 would also be changed.

16 Sir Anthony Lloyd, *The bill of lading: do we really need it?* [1989] LMCLQ 47.

17 [1989] 2 Lloyd's Rep 185, 187.

18 Sections [18.6.4]–[18.6.7].

19 See chapter 16.

20 Eg, *Volcafe Ltd v Compania Sud Americana de Vapores SA* [2015] 1 Lloyd's Rep 639. EWHC 516 (Comm), where the Hague Rules were incorporated (by paramount clause) into a multimodal contract under which the carrier undertook responsibility for the whole of the intermodal transport. See section [18.6.3].

21 See section [14.7].

22 See sections [17.2]–[17.4].

- a document other than a bill of lading or other document of title is likely to be used;
- it may be necessary to provide for both performing and contracting carriers;
- the privity issues, where a performing carrier is sued in tort, need to be addressed;
- given that it is difficult, where containers are used, to determine when damage has occurred, and where responsibility lies, ideally a similar regime should be in place for each of the transport stages.

21.4 The Hamburg Rules

From even before their adoption in 1977, the Hague-Visby Rules came in for a great deal of criticism. The two main alternatives advanced have been the Hamburg and Rotterdam Rules,[23] neither of which have received widespread support, though it is still possible that Rotterdam might.

In general terms, Hamburg is very favourable to cargo-owners, but is otherwise not very ambitious; Rotterdam is less extreme in favour of cargo-interests but, if adopted wholesale, is a much more ambitious regime. It is probably fair to say the protection of third parties, a major part of the original justification for Hague, is not a major factor in the new regimes. These are much more nakedly cargo-protection regimes, and it is surely legitimate to ask why commercial parties are in need of protection from the law.

In general, the main problems perceived with Hague-Visby can be summarised in the following note form:

- Port to port only.
- Excepted perils pro-shipowner.
- Package limitation low.
- Deck cargo unsatisfactory in container era.
- Sensible to exclude charterparties, but why otherwise limit documentation?
- Assumes one carrier only, or at least makes no provision for actual, as opposed to contracting carriers.

Almost before the ink was dry on the Hague-Visby Rules, and because of disappointment with them, UNCITRAL began work on Hamburg as early as 1968.[24] Hamburg was agreed in 1978, and came into force internationally in 1992. By and large, the contracting states are cargo-owning but not maritime nations,[25] and Hamburg is favourable towards cargo-owners. Its principal features are:

Application (Art. 2) is to contracts of carriage by sea, apart from charterparties; there is no documentary requirement, as there is in Hague-Visby, application of the Rules being based on the nature of the contract.

Application is triggered by the port of discharge being a contracting state, not just the port of loading.

The period of responsibility in Art. 4 "covers the period during which the carrier is in charge of the goods at the port of loading, during the carriage and at the port of discharge". This would presumably include the container terminal after discharge, which was held not

---

23 The full text of Hamburg is set out in Appendix C; selected parts of Rotterdam in Appendix D. Full text can also be found, respectively at http://www.uncitral.org/pdf/english/texts/transport/hamburg/hamburg_rules_e.pdf and http://www.uncitral.org/pdf/english/texts/transport/rotterdam_rules/Rotterdam-Rules-E.pdf.

24 United Nations Commission on International Trade Law, at http://www.uncitral.org/uncitral/en/index.html.

25 See http://www.uncitral.org/uncitral/en/uncitral_texts/transport_goods/Hamburg_status.html for the current status of Hamburg.

part of the Hague Rules regime, in *The MSC Amsterdam*.[26] It also includes the stowage period. However, it is not a door-to-door regime for a multimodal operation, as Rotterdam can be.

There is a general liability (in Art. 5) for loss, damage or delay, "unless the carrier proves that he, his servants or agents took all measures that could reasonably be required to avoid the occurrence and its consequences". By contrast, there is no explicit liability for delay in Hague-Visby.[27]

There is nothing equivalent to the specific heads of liability in Art. III(1) and (2) of Hague-Visby, nor is there a list of excepted perils, though specific provision is made for fire (without fault) in Art. 5(4), and live animals (in Art. 5(5)).

In particular, the nautical fault exception in Art. IV(2)(a) of Hague-Visby was considered dated where the shipowner can communicate with ship, and can exercise control.[28]

Art. 5(6) provides that "The carrier is not liable, except in general average, where loss, damage or delay in delivery resulted from measures to save life or from reasonable measures to save property at sea". This is narrower than Hague-Visby.

Liability for loss or damage (Art. 6) is "limited to an amount equivalent to 835 units of account per package or other shipping unit or 2.5 units of account per kilogram of gross weight of the goods lost or damaged, whichever is the higher". This is 25 per cent higher than Hague-Visby, a relatively modest increase. Being based on units of account,[29] the limits are not inflation-proofed. For delay, the limit is "two and a half times the freight payable for the goods delayed, but not exceeding the total freight payable under the contract of carriage of goods by sea".

For containers, the enumeration provision in Art. 6(2) is exactly the same as in Hague-Visby. Deck cargo can be covered by agreement or usage of trade, detailed provision being made in Art. 9.[30]

Art. 7 is essentially the same as Art. IV *bis* of Hague-Visby, and subject to the same general problems. Its purpose will include protecting the actual carrier from tort claims, but since, by Art. 2, Hamburg applies to contracts of carriage, it may run into the problems described in chapter 17.

Arts. 10 and 11 deal with actual and contracting carriers (though the period of responsibility limits this to essentially a port-to-port regime), the default position being joint and several liability. However, Art. 11 allows provision to be made for the contracting carrier to be "not liable for loss, damage or delay in delivery caused by an occurrence which takes place while the goods are in the charge of the actual carrier during such part of the carriage".

There is a two-year time bar in Art. 20.

In general, Hamburg offers a regime that generally favours cargo-owners to a greater extent than Hague-Visby. While it can be used in principle to cover multimodal transport, it remains essentially a carriage by sea convention, unlike the Rotterdam Rules, considered next, which attempt to apply more generally door-to-door.

21.5 The Rotterdam Rules

This is a book on the English law of carriage of goods by sea, and the Rotterdam Rules currently form no part of this. Moreover, Rotterdam extends, at least in principle, beyond sea carriage. There

---

26 *Trafigura Beheer BV v Mediterranean Shipping Company SA (The MSC Amsterdam)* [2007] 2 Lloyd's Rep 622, in section [18.6.3].

27 But it is probably not necessary. Compensation in respect of delay was awarded in *Koufos v C. Czarnikow Ltd (The Heron II)* [1969] 1 AC 350, in section [2.9.2], and in *Ardennes (cargo owners) v Ardennes (owners) (The Ardennes)* [1951] 1 KB 55, in section [15.1.4]. In neither case did the contract explicitly provide for damages for delay. The issue is simply one of remoteness of damage, and delay losses will usually fall within the remoteness rules.

28 Hamburg Rules Explanatory Notes, [17].

29 Defined in Art. 26. Hamburg adopted units of account while Hague-Visby limits were still defined in terms of gold value: Hamburg Rules Explanatory Notes, [23].

30 See also Hamburg Rules Explanatory Notes, [18].

are excellent and detailed reviews of the Rotterdam Rules,[31] and this section will not compete with them.

However, the Hague-Visby regime has long been criticised, and Rotterdam is the culmination of that process. We are also beginning to see states (while not being signatories) nonetheless adopting some parts of Rotterdam in their domestic law. It is therefore possible that bills of lading incorporating aspects of Rotterdam will be litigated in English courts, in much the same way as currently, with the Hague Rules. In the light of that, we should at least contrast Rotterdam's sea carriage liability regime with the equivalent Hague-Visby provisions.

The Rotterdam Rules began as a maritime-only initiative, and are still principally a maritime convention. However, UNCITRAL Working Group later widened the remit to include door-to-door multimodal operations, but involving a sea leg, and that is how the Rotterdam Rules end up.[32] Such operations will typically (but not necessarily) involve a land, a sea, and a second land leg, and usually involve containers, which are both loaded and unloaded some distance from the ship.

I have observed that multimodal liability regimes present difficulties.[33] Often, particularly with container traffic, it will be difficult or impossible to know when damage has occurred, and there is therefore a lot to be said for a unified liability regime across the different legs. The problem is that there are already in place regimes for road and rail carriage,[34] and unless these are to be replaced by the new multimodal regime, the new regime must cater for them, by leaving them in place. This is essentially what Rotterdam does, but obviously this limits its efficacy as a door-to-door regime.[35] Another problem is that road and rail liability limits (at least on a weight basis) are higher than Hague-Visby,[36] and a uniform multimodal regime would almost certainly have to adopt the higher, rather than the lower, limits. This will impact on the competitiveness of sea carriers as part of a multimodal operation, as opposed to unimodal sea carriers.[37] Whether for these or other reasons, multimodal liability regimes have not enjoyed success.

Rotterdam, then:[38]

> ". . . applies to contracts of carriage in which the place of receipt and the place of delivery are in different States, and the port of loading of a sea carriage and the port of discharge of the same sea carriage are in different States, if, according to the contract of carriage, any one of the following places is located in a Contracting State:
>
> (a)   The place of receipt;
> (b)   The port of loading;
> (c)   The place of delivery; or
> (d)   The port of discharge."

(c) and (d) are of course, wider than Hague-Visby.[39] Of a contract of carriage:[40]

---

31 Eg, Diamond, *The Rotterdam Rules* [2009] LMCLQ 135 (on an earlier, but not significantly different, draft); Baatz, Debattista, Lorenzon, Serdy, Staniland, Tsimplis (eds), *The Rotterdam Rules: A Practical Annotation* (2009), Informa.

32 For a description, see (eg) Nikaki, *The Uncitral Draft Instrument on the Carriage of Goods [wholly or partly] [by Sea]: multimodal at last or still all at sea* [2005] JBL 647.

33 Sections [21.1]; [21.3].

34 Eg, CMR for international road haulage, with limits of SDR 8.33 per kilo, but no package limit; there are comparative figures at http://www.cnaeurope.com/CNADownloadsLibrary/Freight%20Liability%20Comparative%20Limits%20-%2021-05-10.pdf. For rail, the Convention concerning International Carriage by Rail (COTIF): http://www.cit-rail.org/en/rail-transport-law/cotif/.

35 As Nikaki observes: [2005] JBL 647.

36 But because of the package limitation, Hague-Visby is more generous for low-weight packages.

37 Glass, *Meddling in the multimodal muddle?* [2006] LMCLQ 307.

38 Art. 5(1).

39 Cf. Art. X of Hague-Visby, in section [18.6.1].

40 Art. 1(1).

"The contract shall provide for carriage by sea and may provide for carriage by other modes of transport in addition to the sea carriage."

To this extent, therefore, because it extends beyond sea carriage, Rotterdam can be door to door. However, it is entirely for the parties to determine whether the contract of carriage does add other modes of transport, and, in any case,[41] Arts. 26 and 82 disapply Rotterdam where it would conflict with another convention applying before loading or after discharge. To this extent, therefore, though the regime is in principle uniform, Rotterdam adopts what is often described as a "network" solution, which is to say that different regimes apply to each stage of the multimodal operation. Article 26 has been described as introducing a "limited network rule".[42]

This is, however, a book on carriage of goods by sea, and we will therefore confine ourselves to discussing Rotterdam as a sea carriage regime. There are no documentary requirements as such, but charterparties are excluded, as are:[43]

". . . contracts of carriage in non-liner transportation except when:

(a)   There is no charter party or other contract between the parties for the use of a ship or of any space thereon; and
(b)   A transport document or an electronic transport record is issued."

The effect of this will surely be to apply Rotterdam, even in the bulk trade, where the only relationship between the parties is governed by the bill of lading, just as Hague-Visby does now.[44]

21.5.1 Seaworthiness and excepted perils

Rotterdam is more conventional than Hamburg in returning to a regime that sets out heads of liability and excepted perils. To that extent, therefore, it is less radically in favour of cargo-owners, and that might be expected to widen its appeal.[45]

Article 14 is Rotterdam's equivalent of Art. III(1) of Hague-Visby, the principal difference being that it extends the seaworthiness obligation to continue "during the voyage". The due diligence requirement is the same, and the obligation also extends to "any containers supplied by the carrier in or upon which the goods are carried".

Then Art. 17(1) makes the carrier liable for loss, damage or delay if the claimant proves that it took place within his period of responsibility.[46] This is the starting point, but it is subject to a general lack of fault provision in Art. 17(2) (carrier burden of proof), and then there are excepted perils set out in Art. 17(3). Again the burden of proof is on the carrier, to prove "that one or more of the following events or circumstances caused or contributed to the loss, damage, or delay". There can be partial relief from liability. Even so, Art. 17(4) provides for liability if the claimant proves that (a) it is the carrier's fault that the excepted peril has arisen, or (b) something else has also contributed and the carrier cannot disprove fault. Under Art. 17(5), the carrier is also liable if the claimant proves

---

41 Art. 12(3), unless the carrier performs the entire operation himself. But if the contracting carrier performs just the sea leg, the parties can restrict application of Rotterdam to that one leg.
42 CMI International Working Group on the Rotterdam Rules: *Questions and Answers on The Rotterdam Rules* (2012), 7: http://www.comitemaritime.org/Uploads/Rotterdam%20Rules/RotterdamRules_QA_10102012.pdf.
43 Art. 6.
44 See also Art. 7, which would apply the Convention to subsequent holders.
45 Eg, Si and Zhang, *An Analysis and Assessment on the Rotterdam Rules in China's Marine Industry*: http://www.comitemaritime.org/Uploads/Rotterdam%20Rules/Paper%20of%20Prof.%20Si%20Yuzhuo%20and%20Dr.%20Zhang%20Jinlei.pdf.
46 While delay is not explicitly covered in Hague-Visby, it probably falls within remoteness of damage rules: section [2.9.1].

unseaworthiness and carrier cannot prove compliance with the Art. 14 due diligence standard. Thus seaworthiness remains paramount, as with Hague-Visby.

The excepted perils largely mirror Hague-Visby. However, there is no equivalent of Art. IV(2) (a), the nautical fault exception: "Act, neglect, or default of the master, mariner, pilot, or the servants of the carrier in the navigation or in the management of the ship." This has long been thought to be too favourable towards carriers. Nor is Art. IV(2)(q) replicated, the "without the actual fault or privity of the carrier" exception.[47] There is, of course, no need for it, given that the carrier is not liable anyway, in the absence of fault provision (because of Art. 17(2)). On the issue of fault, however, we need to be aware that the carrier is liable not just for his own default, but also (under Art. 18) for:

"(a) Any performing party;
(b) The master or crew of the ship;
(c) Employees of the carrier or a performing party; or
(d) Any other person that performs or undertakes to perform any of the carrier's obligations under the contract of carriage, to the extent that the person acts, either directly or indirectly, at the carrier's request or under the carrier's supervision or control."

While on the subject of performing parties, Art. 4 extends contracting carrier defences and limits of liability to:

"(a) The carrier or a maritime performing party;
(b) The master, crew or any other person that performs services on board the ship; or
(c) Employees of the carrier or a maritime performing party."

This is a somewhat more extensive provision than Art. IV *bis* of Hague-Visby, considered in chapter 17. Any privity of contract difficulties that might have created problems for this provision would have been resolved by the Contract (Rights of Third Parties) Act 1999.[48]

Of course there are detailed differences between Rotterdam and Hague-Visby, and Art. 18(a) is really required for multimodal operations. From the perspective of a carriage by sea liability regime, probably the most important single change, however, given its paramount nature, is the extension of the seaworthiness obligation so that it continues throughout the voyage.

21.5.2 Package limitation

There is a modest increase of limits of liability to:[49]

"875 units of account per package or other shipping unit, or 3 units of account per kilogram of the gross weight of the goods that are the subject of the claim or dispute, whichever amount is the higher, except when the value of the goods has been declared by the shipper and included in the contract particulars, or when a higher amount than the amount of limitation of liability set out in this article has been agreed upon between the carrier and the shipper."

Though this is slightly higher than both Hague-Visby and Hamburg, the weight limit at least is a lot lower than CMR. CMR does not, however, have a package limitation, so, for small items, Rotterdam limits will be higher.[50]

---

47 Full text is in Appendix A, and see section [18.3].
48 On which see section [17.2.1].
49 Art. 59(1).
50 CMI International Working Group on the Rotterdam Rules: *Questions and Answers on The Rotterdam Rules* (2012), 18.

Article 60 provides that "liability for economic loss due to delay is limited to an amount equivalent to two and one-half times the freight payable on the goods delayed". This is subject to total liability not exceeding the package or weight limitations in Art. 59.

21.5.3 Other provisions

Article 24 is aimed directly at the UK position on deviation,[51] and is as follows:

> "When pursuant to applicable law a deviation constitutes a breach of the carrier's obligations, such deviation of itself shall not deprive the carrier or a maritime performing party of any defence or limitation of this Convention, except to the extent provided in article 61."

Article 61 refers back to the delay limits in Art. 60, which are lost:

> "... if the claimant proves that the delay in delivery resulted from a personal act or omission of the person claiming a right to limit done with the intent to cause the loss due to delay or recklessly and with knowledge that such loss would probably result".

Obviously, this provision could operate where there is a voluntary deviation. The effect of Art. 24 is to prevent deviating carriers losing the benefit of all exemptions and limitations, which appears currently to be the position in English law:[52]

> "In some cases, the Rotterdam Rules changed the position in certain jurisdictions. For instance, the purpose of Art. 24 is to change the case law regarding the consequence of unreasonable deviation in a certain jurisdiction, which was thought problematic."

Article 25 changes the position for deck carriage, principally in allowing it where the cargo is carried in containers.

Article 13(2) provides that:

> "... the carrier and the shipper may agree that the loading, handling, stowing or unloading of the goods is to be performed by the shipper, the documentary shipper or the consignee".

This FIO provision effectively mirrors *Renton v Palmyra* and *The Jordan II*,[53] while making it clear that these are the only activities for which the carrier may divest himself of responsibility.

21.5.4 Scope of Rotterdam

Rotterdam does much more than would be expected of a sea carriage convention. It looks more like a maritime code than a liability convention.[54] Chapter 9 provides for delivery, and chapter 11 for transfer of rights, which is of course provided for by our own Carriage of Goods by Sea Act 1992.

---

51 See section [4.4].
52 CMI International Working Group on the Rotterdam Rules: *Questions and Answers on The Rotterdam Rules* (2012), 25.
53 Section [18.4].
54 It covers much the same ground, for example, as the Chinese Maritime Code 1993: http://www.lawinfochina.com/display. aspx?lib=law&id=191 (English and Chinese versions), and extracts at repub.eur.nl/pub/6943/14.pdf. This Code is quite interesting, in cherry-picking the best bits from various conventions. Perhaps this is the way forward, rather than adopting the Rotterdam or Hamburg Rules wholesale.

Perhaps the very ambition of Rotterdam is one of the reasons why it has been so slow to take on.[55] It looks unlikely to become part of English law, at least for the shelf-life of this book, and I hope I can therefore be forgiven for not examining these provisions in detail.

21.6 Question

Suppose Art. III(1) of the Hague-Visby Rules was altered to read the same as Art. 14 of the Rotterdam Rules, so that it applied "before, at the beginning of, and during the voyage by sea". What difference would this make to the law?

Comment

At present, of course, Art. III(2) covers the entire voyage, and the standard of care is similar under Art. III(1) and (2) so, in many cases, the change may make little difference. But as we saw in chapter 18, Art. III(2) is subject to the excepted perils, whereas Art. III(1) is not, and this may be the practical effect of extending the period, as Rotterdam does.

---

55 See, eg, Diamond's comments: [2009] LMCLQ 135, 139.

Part 5

Supporting material

Chapter 22

Case studies

Chapter Contents

22.1 Introduction

The substantive part of the book is now finished. There follow two chapters of supporting material, this one on case studies, and next, an additional reading chapter.

In this chapter we look at a number of issues, the first of which (terms and their construction) affects carriage of goods by sea in general. The second and third (reachable on arrival, and piracy and time charterparties) are instances of the construction of terms, but also raise issues of their own. Finally, we will look (briefly) at some of the particular difficulties surrounding carriage of oil by sea, at any rate in so far that the issues impinge on matters covered in this book.

22.2 Terms and their construction

22.2.1 Express and implied terms

Standard form charterparties typically run to 40 or more clauses, and it might be thought that almost every eventuality would be covered by an express term. Even the most complicated document can never cover everything, however, and there is room for the courts to fill out terms, or perhaps even to imply terms that are not express. The courts recognise that not even the most detailed charterparty can cover all eventualities, and that they must often fill in the details. In *The Johanna Oldendorff* Lord Diplock observed that:[1]

> "although any standard form of modern charterparty is a document of great elaboration, it still does not spell out in express words the division of responsibility between charterer and shipowner for securing that all the various things are done that must be done to carry out the adventure. It tacitly assumes that the parties have intended this to be regulated by mercantile usage to which legal sanction has been given by decisions of the courts."

The agreement there did not explicitly determine when the vessel became an "arrived ship", but it could be deduced, in the absence of contrary terms, from the categorisation of the contact as a port charterparty. In effect, the port charterparty is used as a template, from which details will be inferred, in the absence of contrary stipulation.

Sometimes, of course, the courts need do no more than fill out a definition, where the parties have left it undefined, as in *The Johanna Oldendorff* itself, where the House supplied the definition of an "arrived ship". In chapter 13 we see another instance, where the courts fill out the definition of a safe port,[2] so that it carries with it the implication that the berth also must be safe.[3]

It is one thing to deduce the commencement of laytime from the categorisation of the type of charterparty, or to hold that undertaking one obligation (eg, a safe port obligation) necessarily implies another (eg, safe berth), but to imply a duty from scratch, where none is expressed, is another matter entirely, and the courts appear justifiably cautious about implying terms to cover omissions in the charterparty. Charterparties are, after all, well thought-out commercial documents. Implication may sometimes be legitimate, but surely rarely.

Traditionally, implication of terms has been done sparingly, where the term to be implied must "go without saying", or that it must be "necessary to give business efficacy to the contract".[4] Recently, however, Lord Hoffmann said that "There is only one question: is that what the instrument, read as

---

1 [1974] AC 479, 554. The case is discussed in section [8.5].

2 From *Leeds Shipping Co Ltd v Societe Francaise Bunge (The Eastern City)* [1958] 2 Lloyd's Rep 127, in section [13.9.2].

3 See section [13.9.11].

4 Eg, *Shirlaw v Southern Foundries (1926) Ltd* [1939] 2 KB 206; *The Moorcock* (1889) LR 14 PD 64.

a whole against the relevant background, would reasonably be understood to mean?"[5] He regarded other tests as different ways of saying the same thing, rather than being different or additional tests.[6] If this approach of the Privy Council finds favour with the courts,[7] it will likely relax the test for implying a term, though in the case itself, the term implied into the articles of association of a company, that a director would vacate office when the appointing shareholder ceased to hold the requisite shares, might well have satisfied the traditional tests.[8]

In spite of *Belize*, the courts appear to remain cautious about implying obligations into charter-parties, as is demonstrated in *The Reborn* in chapter 13,[9] where the Court of Appeal refused to imply a safe berth obligation into a voyage charterparty. Safety is something that the parties might reasonably be expected to have in their contemplation, when negotiating the charterparty. An omission to address it may well be deliberate, and there is a good case for saying that the loss should lie where it falls.[10] (This was very much the view adopted in *The Reborn*.)

Nevertheless, courts will sometimes imply obligations into charterparties even where none is expressed, an interesting instance being *The Island Archon*, where an indemnity was implied against the consequences of the charterers ordering the ship to a particular port. *The Island Archon* is of particular interest because an analysis was adopted, in terms of the risk the shipowners had agreed to bear. A similar approach has now been used in other areas, and the whole issue is discussed in chapters 3, 4 and 13.[11]

The case also shows that permitted choices under a charterparty may be constrained by implied terms, whether or not those choices are limited by an express clause.

We see in chapter 3 the extent to which, if at all, choices which are excluded by no express term, might nonetheless be limited by a requirement that they be exercised in good faith.[12]

22.2.2 Construction of carriage contracts

A charterparty is a contract that is largely unregulated by the law. Both parties to a charterparty are likely to be large powerful organisations, dealing at arm's length. Bills of lading, as we will see in Part 4 of this book, are often regulated to protect cargo-owners. The way in which the protection works, however, is by writing terms into the contracts. Nonetheless, in construing bills of lading, it is sometimes necessary to be aware that some of the terms derive from statute and international convention, rather than simply agreement between the parties.[13]

With that proviso, the principles of construction of carriage contracts are the same as those of any other contract. Charterparties, in particular, however, are carefully drafted by companies who are legally advised. They are usually on standard forms (albeit often quite heavily amended) to which a great deal of thought has been given. There is no need for the courts to protect one party as against the other, and little reason to write in terms that the parties have not chosen explicitly to include.

---

5 *Attorney General of Belize v Belize Telecom Ltd* [2009] 1 WLR 1988, [21], criticised by Davies, *Recent developments in the law of implied terms* [2010] LMCLQ 140.

6 [2009] 1 WLR 1988, [21], and following discussion, esp at [27].

7 On its "not . . . wholly enthusiastic" reception to date, see [2010] LMCLQ 140, 146–9.

8 Davies suggests that it would have satisfied the *Moorcock* test: [2010] LMCLQ 140, 143, referring to the "business efficacy" test from *The Moorcock* (1889) LR 14 PD 64.

9 *Mediterranean Salvage & Towage Ltd v Seamar Trading & Commerce Inc (The Reborn)* [2009] 2 Lloyd's Rep 639, commented on by Ward, *Unsafe berths and implied terms reborn* [2010] LMCLQ 489. See in particular [2009] 2 Lloyd's Rep 639, [10] (Lord Clarke MR); [63] (Carnworth LJ). See further section [13.9].

10 The usual inference: *Attorney General of Belize v Belize Telecom Ltd* [2009] 1 WLR 1988, [17] (Lord Hoffmann).

11 *Triad Shipping Co v Stellar Chartering & Brokerage Inc (The Island Archon)* [1994] 2 Lloyd's Rep 227. See further sections [3.6]; [4.6]; [13.4].

12 Section [3.5].

13 See *Stag Line v Foscolo, Mango & Co* [1932] AC 328, in section [18.7].

The construction of contracts generally was considered in the Supreme Court in *Rainy Sky SA v Kookmin Bank*,[14] where Lord Clarke of Stone-cum-Ebony JSC, summarising the effect of earlier decisions, emphasised that:[15]

> ". . . the exercise of construction is essentially one unitary exercise in which the court must consider the language used and ascertain what a reasonable person, that is a person who has all the background knowledge which would reasonably have been available to the parties in the situation in which they were at the time of the contract, would have understood the parties to have meant . . .".

Though "[where] the parties have used unambiguous language, the court must apply it",[16] Lord Clarke continued:[17]

> "[If] there are two possible constructions, the court is entitled to prefer the construction which is consistent with business common sense and to reject the other."

In other words, he emphasised the need for a unitary exercise of construction, and the importance of business common sense.[18]

Where, as with an area of law such as carriage of goods by sea, a number of fairly well-established principles of construction have developed over a long period, the value of general statements of this type may perhaps be doubted. Lord Clarke does, however, remind us that detailed traditional rules must always be judged against "the ultimate aim of interpreting a provision in a contract".[19] To the extent that they do not, the technical rules should surely give way. Detailed technical rules are (or should be) the servants, not the masters, of the general principle.

On the other hand, detailed guidance from *Rainy Sky* is quite limited. We should look to business common sense, but only where there is genuine ambiguity, and only one interpretation that is consistent with business common sense. In *The Gaz Energy*,[20] Flaux J was concerned to interpret speed clause provisions in a time charterparty. Having resolved a conflict between two parts of the charterparty, he arrived at an unambiguous construction, and consequently did not need to consider consistency with business common sense.[21] In *The Target*, Andrew Smith J was required to resolve which should prevail, of two interpretations of charter freight rates. He found that:[22]

> "[neither party's] interpretation flouts common sense in as much as it would be a perfectly workable arrangement . . ., but, in my judgment, both interpretations produce a result that businessmen would consider unusual and would be commercially surprising".

In neither of these cases was *Rainy Sky* of any assistance, though it was cited in both.

---

14 [2011] 1 WLR 2900. *Rainy Sky* has nothing to do with charterparties, but is the leading modern authority on principles of commercial contract construction. It was cited in *Osmium Shipping Corp v Cargill International SA (The Captain Stefanos)* [2012] 2 Lloyd's Rep 46, in section [22.4].

15 [2011] 1 WLR 2900, [21], this being the judgment of the court.

16 [2011] 1 WLR 2900, [23].

17 Ibid (presumably also if there are more than two).

18 Lords Phillips, Mance, Kerr and Wilson agreed with Lord Clarke.

19 [2011] 1 WLR 2900, [14]. This might conceivably affect technical rules, such as, for example, in section [15.2.4].

20 *Hyundai Merchant Marine Co Ltd v Trafigura Beheer BV (The Gaz Energy)* [2012] 1 Lloyd's Rep 211.

21 See also *Griffon Shipping LLC v Firodi Shipping Ltd (The Griffon)* [2013] 2 Lloyd's Rep 50, [26], where in Teare J's view there was no ambiguity requiring resolution.

22 *BP Oil International Ltd v Target Shipping Ltd (The Target)* [2012] 2 Lloyd's Rep 245, [150].

Turning to the need to regard construction as essentially one unitary exercise, Cooke J, though citing *Rainy Sky* in *The Captain Stefanos*,[23] observed that this is not an easy task with a heavily amended form. While *Rainy Sky* did persuade Andrew Smith J in *The Valle di Cordoba* to adopt a unitary construction rather than look too closely at the motivation for an amendment to a standard form, there was no mention of the Supreme Court decision when *The Valle di Cordoba* was affirmed in the Court of Appeal.[24]

In summary, it is perhaps too early to say what effect, if any, *Rainy Sky* will have on construction of charterparties. Certainly, however, there are a number of construction principles, to which we should now turn.

22.2.3 Specific construction issues

Just over 30 years ago, Lord Roskill in *The Laura Prima* emphasised that charterparties must be construed as a whole, so that individual clauses are not interpreted in isolation from the remainder of the contract.[25] In that particular case, a newly-added clause (in a standard form) was interpreted in the light of (and hence affected by) another, quite different clause, elsewhere in the charterparty, a problem that had not apparently been foreseen by those responsible for the amendment. It is probably fair to say that the amendment consequently achieved nothing at all. *The Laura Prima* concerned a revision to a standard form, but we know that it is very common for charterparties to be amended by the parties themselves, often without sufficient consideration. This is affected by the same problem. If you amend a form, you have to look at the whole form.

Amendments can be problematic for other reasons, usually lack of care in drafting (that is why some standard forms are drafted to try to avoid the rider syndrome). A famous instance, where a careless amendment led to litigation right up to the House of Lords, was *The Johanna Oldendorff*, where the entirety of the problem arose from an amendment which was poorly considered, and (unlike the unamended parts of the form) did not make clear precisely when the vessel arrived.[26]

Suppose there is a conflict between two parts of a contract. The contract may itself provide for a means of resolution. If not, various principles have been used. One such principle, which could also be a trap for careless amenders, is that typed or written amendments to the standard forms prevail where there is a conflict over the standard terms themselves, because of the assumption that the parties have addressed their minds more directly to them. In *Glynn v Margetson*[27] a liberty to deviate was narrowly interpreted, so as not to defeat the "main object and intent" of the contract. It was therefore necessary to identify the main object and intent, as to carry oranges from Malaga to Liverpool. But why did that prevail over the liberty? The liberty was very important to the shipowners, who intended to collect cargo from various ports, to ensure a full vessel. This would have been fundamental to what we would nowadays call their business plan. But the liberty was simply part of the standard form, whereas the voyage details were (obviously) filled in for each voyage, and so, of course, it was the voyage details that prevailed. For the same reason, where there is a division into Parts I and II, the provisions of Part I prevail, because they have to be specifically filled in, whereas Part II is merely adopted wholesale.

Any principle addressed at resolving conflict only applies if there is a conflict. In *Pagnan SpA v Tradax Ocean Transportation SA*, Bingham LJ said:[28]

---

23 [2012] 2 Lloyd's Rep 46.
24 *Trafigura Beheer BV v Navigazione Montanari SpA (The Valle di Cordoba)* [2014] 1 Lloyd's Rep 550, affd [2015] 1 Lloyd's Rep 529.
25 *Nereide SpA di Navigazione v Bulk Oil International (The Laura Prima)* [1982] 1 Lloyd's Rep 1, 6, discussed in detail in section [22.3.4].
26 See section [8.5.2].
27 [1893] AC 351, in sections [4.6]; [17.1.8].
28 [1987] 2 Lloyd's Rep 342.

> "It would in my judgment be quite wrong to approach this question of construction with any predisposition to find inconsistency . . . On the other hand, it is wrong to approach the contract on the assumption that there is no inconsistency. . . . One should, therefore, approach the documents in a cool and objective spirit to see whether there is inconsistency or not."

Though this appears neutral, he adopted a narrow test for inconsistency:

> "It is not enough if one term qualifies or modifies the effect of another; to be inconsistent a term must contradict another term or be in conflict with it, such that effect cannot fairly be given to both clauses."

Remember that the courts try to give effect to the parties' intention, if they can. If effect can fairly be given to both clauses, then the courts will do so, even if (for example) it means that Part I does not prevail over Part II. In *The Leonidas*,[29] the issue was how to interpret an absolute speed warranty and a clause paramount incorporating exceptions from the Hague Rules. There was an absolute speed warranty in Part I of a time charterparty, but also apparently contradictory Hague Rules exceptions (incorporated by clause paramount, in Part II). Langley J held that there was no conflict: the shipowner would not be liable if the cause of speed reduction was a Hague Rules exception. This is an application of another principle, where the specific limits the general.[30]

Another principle is that the terms of the written document in the ordinary way prevail over the terms incorporated by reference. At first instance in *Indian Oil Corp v Vanol Inc*[31] Webster J was concerned to resolve a conflict between two applicable law clauses, and held that the incorporated term should give way to the one written directly in.

We have seen elsewhere in the book the great reluctance of the courts to construe terms so as to exempt liability for fundamental obligations (an application of the *contra proferentem* principle, that an ambiguous term will be construed against the party for whose benefit it is intended), and the extent to which the concepts of good faith and risk allocation are beginning to affect the construction of charterparties.[32]

The various rules and principles are not always applicable. In *The Gaz Energy*[33] Flaux J resolved a conflict between provisions without explicitly relying on any rules at all.

22.3 Reachable on arrival clauses

We look at reachable on arrival clauses, partly because there are construction issues that follow on neatly from the previous section, partly because they demonstrate the use of a damages for detention claim to avoid laytime provisions, but mostly because the saga makes an interesting story. The story itself is old, but the Asbatankvoy form, which plays a central role, is still in widespread use, and the principles of construction and damages remain with us. The story concerns the (not very successful) adaptation of a standard form charterparty to avoid an inconvenient decision of the House of

---

29 *Bayoil SA v Seawind Tankers Corp (The Leonidas)* [2001] 1 Lloyd's Rep 533.
30 Also the basis of the eventual resolution in *Pagnan*. This was an international sale contract, where a (general) clause requiring sellers to provide an export certificate was limited by a (specific) clause which applied in the event of government prohibition of exports. *Pagnan* was recently applied in *Public Company Rise v Nibulon SA* [2015] EWHC 684 (Comm).
31 [1991] 2 Lloyd's Rep 634, rvsd CA [1992] 2 Lloyd's Rep 563, but on other grounds (construction of another incorporated clause – concerning a time bar – held only applied to arbitration). No doubt was cast in the Court of Appeal on Webster J's principle.
32 The ideas are introduced at sections [3.5] and [3.6], and we can see specific applications at [4.6]; [13.4].
33 [2012] 1 Lloyd's Rep 211.

Lords, a decision that was ultimately recognised as being wrong, and overruled by a later House of Lords case.

22.3.1 Reachable on arrival clause: Exxonvoy, Exxonvoy 1969 and Asbatankvoy

This is about allocating delay risks when the vessel reaches the port to load or discharge, and concerns the American Exxonvoy tanker voyage form. It may be that Exxonvoy's original reachable on arrival clause had nothing to do with commencement of laytime, but was intended to give effect to a safe berth provision. Clause 6 (of the original – not 1969-form) was in the following terms:

> "The Vessel shall load and discharge at a place or at a dock or alongside lighters reachable on her arrival which shall be indicated by Charterers, and where she can always lie afloat . . . .".

Roskill J observed in *The President Brand* that the clause may have originated in a berth charter,[34] in which case it could have been interpreted as meaning only the berth would be reachable safely, when the vessel arrived there.

In the original Exxonvoy there was a separate notice of readiness clause (cl. 7, the precursor to the later (Asbatankvoy) cl. 6), with a berth or no berth provision:

> "The lay days shall commence from the time the Vessel is ready to receive or discharge her cargo, the Captain giving six hours' notice to the Charterers' agents, berth or no berth."

The existence of this separate NOR clause may perhaps be taken as further evidence that the reachable on arrival clause was not intended to affect notice of readiness. The berth or no berth provision was probably intended to give effect to the traditional allocation of risk, whereby the charterers take the risk of congestion whereas shipowners take the weather risk.[35]

However, the reachable on arrival clause was interpreted in such a way as to place on the charterers the entirety of the risk of delay in getting into berth. Also, because (due to then applicable *Aello* test) it fell outside voyage stages 2 or 4, damages were for detention: neither laytime nor demurrage applied.[36]

We will begin by considering Exxonvoy and the delay risk. As an aside, we will look at some of the construction issues that arose in this litigation. Later, we will look at the damages for detention issue.

22.3.2 Reachable on arrival and delay risk

After the (original) Exxonvoy clause was drafted, the test for whether a vessel had arrived under a port charterparty was moved later than commercially desirable, by the decision of the House of Lords in *The Aello*,[37] and this was the context of the early litigation on cl. 6. Nonetheless, in *The Angelos Lusis* and *The President Brand*,[38] although the vessel had not arrived within *The Aello* test, the charterers

34 *Inca Compania Naviera SA v Mofinol Inc (The President Brand)* [1967] 2 Lloyd's Rep 338, 350.

35 Like the WIBON clause in section [8.1].

36 *Sociedad Financiera de Bienes Raices SA v Agrimpex Hungarian Trading Company for Agricultural Products, et è Contra (The Aello)* [1961] AC 135, and the stages from *The Johanna Oldendorff* [1974] AC 479. To make sense of this paragraph, see sections [8.5]; [8.7].

37 [1961] AC 135.

38 Respectively *Sociédad Carga Oceanica SA v Idolinoele Vertriebsgesellschaft mbH (The Angelos Lusis)* [1964] 2 Lloyd's Rep 28; [1967] 2 Lloyd's Rep 338.

were held to be in breach of the reachable on arrival clause, it being sufficient that the vessel had arrived in a lay sense.[39]

In *The Angelos Lusis*, Megaw J said:[40]

> "The parties, in using the words 'on her arrival', did not have in mind, or at least did not have solely and exclusively in mind, the technical meaning of 'arrival' in respect of an 'arrived vessel' in a port charter-party: they had in mind her physical arrival at the point, wherever it might be, whether within or outside the fiscal or commercial limits of the port, where the indication or nomination of a particular loading place would become relevant if the vessel were to be able to proceed without being held up. At that point the charterers had to nominate a reachable place, which involves that it was the charterers' responsibility to ensure that there was at that point of time a berth which the vessel, proceeding normally, would be able to reach the occupy."

Moreover, no distinction was drawn between congestion (Constanza) in *The Angelos Lusis* and navigation delays in *The President Brand* (where delay was caused by tide – crossing the bar at Laurenco Marques). In the latter case, Roskill J said:[41]

> "'Reachable' as a matter of grammar means 'able to be reached'. There may be many reasons why a particular berth or discharging place cannot be reached. It may be because another ship is occupying it; it may be because there is an obstruction between where the ship is and where she wishes to go; it may be because there is not a sufficiency of water to enable her to get there. The existence of any of those obstacles can prevent a particular berth or dock being reachable and in my judgment a particular berth or dock is just as much not reachable if there is not enough water to enable the vessel to traverse the distance from where she is to that place as if there were a ship occupying that place at the material time. Accordingly, in my judgment, the charterers' obligation was to nominate a berth which the vessel could reach on arrival and they are in breach of that obligation if they are unable so to do."

In other words, no distinction is to be drawn between congestion and tide. The result was to place the entirety of the delay risk of getting into berth (not just the congestion risk) on the charterers. This was almost certainly not the result intended by those responsible for drafting the clause.

22.3.3 Changes in Exxonvoy 1969

Consequently, when the form was revised, Exxonvoy 69 added the following to the present Asbatankvoy cl. 6 (successor to the old NOR cl. 7), which was almost certainly intended to achieve the traditional allocation of risks:

> ". . . However where delay is caused to Vessel getting into berth after giving notice of readiness for any reason over which Charterer has no control, such delay shall not count as used laytime."

Indeed, it clearly does so, as can be seen from *The Notos*,[42] which was on an identical clause from the STB VOY charterparty (later to be renamed ASBA II). Unfortunately, the reachable on arrival

---

39 One of the problems in both these cases was that, though the clause might originally have been intended for use in a berth charter, in neither case did the charterparty fall within the test in *Stag Line Ltd v Board of Trade* [1950] 2 KB 194, in section [8.5], and therefore each charterparty was a port charter.

40 [1964] 2 Lloyd's Rep 28, 33.

41 [1967] 2 Lloyd's Rep 338, 350.

42 *Société Anonyme Marocaine de l'Industrie du Raffinage v Notos Maritime Corporation of Munrovia (The Notos)* [1987] 1 Lloyd's Rep 503.

clause was still left in Exxonvoy 69 (but was not in STB VOY), and in *The Laura Prima*[43] cl. 6 was interpreted subject to the reachable on arrival clause (now cl. 9). In other words, the berth in cl. 6 has to be a reachable on arrival berth as in cl. 9: if the berth was not reachable on arrival, cl. 6 did not bite at all. It thus became clear that the alterations to Exxonvoy had made no difference.

As was the case before the Exxonvoy 69 revisions, where no distinction had been drawn between congestion and other types of delay, so after the revisions no distinction was drawn either. This became clear in the later cases of *The Johs Stove*, *The Ugland Obo One*, *The Fjordaas*, and *The Sea Queen*.[44] Congestion and other delays were treated in just the same way.

Exxonvoy 69 was renamed Asbatankvoy in 1977.[45] However, it was not otherwise altered. Thus, Asbatankvoy does not give effect to the traditional allocation of delay risks, as between shipowner and charterer, any more than did Exxonvoy or Exxonvoy 69.

22.3.4 Construction issues

The Laura Prima concerned the construction of cl. 6 of Exxonvoy 69, but Lord Roskill held that cl. 6 could be interpreted only in the light of cl. 9. It was not permissible to divorce cl .6 from the remainder of the charterparty.[46]

There was another issue, as to the extent to which the lineage of a form should be taken into account, to ascertain the legislative intent. As we have seen, Exxonvoy 69 was the successor to Exxonvoy, and the clauses at issue in *The Laura Prima* had been drafted specifically in the light of cases on the Exxonvoy provisions, in order to alter the effect of those decisions. But a standard form charterparty is not legislation, rather an agreement between parties, one or both of whom may have no knowledge of the history. There is a good case for ignoring the lineage of the form.

The Court of Appeal (whose decision the House of Lords overruled) had considered the history, Lawton LJ observing that:[47]

> "The Exxonvoy 1969 common form clauses came into use after the decision in *The Angelos Lusis* and *The President Brand*. The inference is that alterations were made for a purpose. [They] . . . must have been inserted to make certain that which had been the cause of dispute in both *The Angelos Lusis* and *The President Brand*."

In the House of Lords Lord Roskill was not prepared to take this route. His reasoning is based less on principle, however, than utility: the lineage was ignored because it was not useful:[48]

> "Your Lordships were invited to examine the lineage of this form and other forms, some in the line of descent others not in that line, were placed before your Lordships. My Lords, sometimes it is possible to detect from an alteration of clauses in standard forms an obvious intention to depart from a particular judicial decision the practical effect of which the parties wish to avoid. But I do not find any assistance towards solving the instant problem in tracing the lineage of the Exxonvoy 1969 form. Its construction must be determined by reference to its own provisions and not to those of some of its predecessors."

---

43 Nereide SpA di Navigazione v Bulk Oil International (The Laura Prima) [1982] 1 Lloyd's Rep 1.

44 Sametiet M/T Johs Stove v Istanbul Petrol Rafinerisi A/S (The Johs Stove) [1984] 1 Lloyd's Rep 38; Aden Refinery Co Ltd v Ugland Management Co Ltd (The Ugland Obo One) [1986] 2 Lloyd's Rep 336, K/S Arnt J. Moerland v Kuwait Petroleum Corp (The Fjordaas) [1988] 1 Lloyd's Rep 336; and Palm Shipping Inc v Kuwait Petroleum Corp (The Sea Queen) [1988] 1 Lloyd's Rep 500.

45 Full text at http://shippingforum.files.wordpress.com/2012/08/asbatankvoy.pdf.

46 See section [22.2.3].

47 [1981] 2 Lloyd's Rep 24, 27.

48 [1982] 1 Lloyd's Rep 1, 3–4.

The inference is, then, that it is sometimes permissible to take account of lineage, where "it is possible to detect from an alteration of clauses in standard forms an obvious intention to depart from a particular judicial decision the practical effect of which the parties wish to avoid". We came across an instance of this in chapter 12.[49]

We should always remember, though, that the courts are concerned to interpret the intention of the contracting parties, and are not considering the purpose of "legislation".

22.3.5 Reachable on arrival and damages for detention

There is another (more fundamental) difficulty with *The Angelos Lusis* and *The President Brand*. Because in each case the vessel was not an arrived ship on the then-applicable *Aello* test, the shipowners were able to claim damages for detention, and were not limited to the demurrage clause. In the event, nothing turned on this in *The Angelos Lusis*, but by the time of *The President Brand* the shipowners had appreciated the potential. By claiming damages for detention, they successfully deprived the charterers of much of their laytime.

The essential timescale was as follows:

110 hours' laytime was allowed for discharge;
 The vessel was delayed by the tide, on her arrival (in the layman's sense), and could not proceed immediately to berth;
 The time between arrival in the layman's sense (for reachable on arrival clause purposes) and becoming an arrived ship (in the legal sense), and tendering NOR was 99 hours;
 The time between arrival in the layman's sense (for reachable on arrival clause purposes) and reaching berth was 128 hours.

The owners claimed in respect of the entirety of the delay (even after ship had become an arrived ship) as damages for detention. This would have entirely deprived the charterers of their laytime. They succeeded only until NOR was tendered (ie, 99 hours until she became an arrived ship, in the legal sense) less:[50]

"From that total period must be deducted the short period . . . during which the ship crossed the bar and moved into port . . . for this cannot be time which was lost to the ship by reason of the charterers failing to have a berth reachable on the vessel's arrival under cl. 6 [reachable on arrival clause]."

This was 2.5 hours. After this deduction, however, the owners recovered in respect of the whole of the remaining 96.5 hours. The charterers actually discharged in about 55 hours, once the ship had berthed. This was about 183 hours after the reachable on arrival clause was triggered; had they been entitled to their 110 hours' laytime from that time, certainly they would have exceeded it, but the owners would have recovered only in respect of around 73 hours. Thus, the charterers lost the benefit of much of their laytime.[51]

---

49 Eg, *Cosco Bulk Carrier Co Ltd v Team-Up Owning Co Ltd (The Saldanha)* [2011] 1 Lloyd's Rep 187, in section [12.3.6], where words had been added to an off-hire clause in a NYPE charterparty, to avoid the consequences of an earlier decision. Gross J said (at [25]) "that the mischief which the amended clause was designed to address must be a powerful factor in its construction".
50 [1967] 2 Lloyd's Rep 338, 352 (Roskill J).
51 This is borne out by the figures in the case. The shipowners' damages for detention claim was £2,800, and they were awarded £2,110. An alternative demurrage claim, which would have allowed the charterers the benefit of the entirety of their laytime, was for just £1,235.

One of the issues was why the shipowners did not get the entirety of their claim. Roskill J said that:[52]

> "... it is trite commercial law that a charterer is entitled to the laytime for which his contract provides. If he is to be deprived by one clause of that which is expressly given by another clause, very, very clear words indeed would be required to produce that startling result. I think that the charterers are entitled to the benefit of all the time from the time notice of readiness was given. To reach any other conclusion would be to deprive them of the benefit of laytime and notice time, which they are accorded by the laytime provisions of the clause."

In other words, once the ship was able to tender NOR, the charterers were entitled to their laytime.[53]

Nonetheless, this was clearly a very undesirable state of affairs, which, by the time of The Delian Spirit,[54] the shipowners had come at last to realise. This time, the vessel (also chartered on the original Exxonvoy form) had to anchor in the roads at Tuapse because of congestion, and, while there, gave notice of readiness. The shipowners originally limited their claim to demurrage only, but before the dispute was resolved The Angelos Lusis was decided, inducing them to alter their claim to a much higher one for damages for detention. Again in outline, what happened was this. The vessel was delayed for about 108 hours, but then loaded in just 22 hours, and had the charterers had the benefit of the entirety of their 120 hours' laytime from the time of anchoring, it would have covered all but about 10 hours of that (though the charterers would then have had no laytime in which to discharge). The shipowners, of course, claimed damages for detention, which would have deprived the charterers of nearly all their laytime. Donaldson J would have allowed damages for detention for the entire delay, observing also that:[55]

> "[the] argument upon this award in the form of a special case has a looking glass quality which would have delighted Lewis Carroll, for the claimant shipowners have been busily contending that the Delian Spirit was not an arrived ship before she berthed at Tuapse, whereas the charterers contend that she became an arrived ship several days earlier when she anchored in the roads. Alas, this is not a practical expression of the spirit of Christmas but a belief on the part of the shipowners that they will recover more by way of damages for the detention of the vessel than by way of demurrage ...".

In the event the Court of Appeal held the vessel to have been an "arrived ship" from the start, so the damages for detention claim failed (although the charterers clearly being in breach of the "reachable on arrival" clause, remained liable for demurrage). In The Johanna Oldendorff, however, Lord Reid commented that this conclusion (that the vessel had "arrived") was difficult to reconcile with the Aello test, which was still then the applicable test.[56]

Today, of course, the test of whether a vessel has "arrived" is wider than when the above cases were decided, so that the issues arising in the above cases are less likely to arise today. Indeed, by the time of The Laura Prima, the arrival test had been moved earlier by the House of Lords decision in The

---

52 [1967] 2 Lloyd's Rep 338, 352.
53 Roskill J applied Inverkip SS Co Ltd v Bunge & Co [1917] 2 KB 198, in section [9.5].
54 Shipping Developments Corp v V/O Sojuzneftexport (The Delian Spirit) [1972] 1 QB 103.
55 This depended on the factual assumption that the vessel would have loaded earlier had there been no delay in getting into berth – an assumption that may not always apply. It is also a spectacular refusal to apply the principle that the contract-breaker would have performed in the manner least beneficial to the other party: see section [11.4].
56 [1974] AC 479.

Johanna Oldendorff,[57] overruling *The Aello*, so that in *The Laura Prima*, the vessel had arrived, and the delay counted against laytime.

The damages for detention issue was largely resolved by *The Johanna Oldendorff*, rather than the charterparty amendments, and the saga demonstrates some of the pitfalls of amending standard form charterparties.

22.4 Piracy and construction of charterparties

Ransom piracy, of the type seen in Somalia in the 2000s, was a development unanticipated by those responsible for drafting charterparty forms.[58] This matters less with purposive than with literal construction of forms. In chapter 12 we looked at *The Saldanha*, where the issue was whether a ransom capture had put the vessel off-hire.[59] Gross J interpreted the off-hire provision absolutely literally, as one would expect of an off-hire clause. It is likely that the result, that the vessel was not off-hire, would have accorded with prevalent industry views, but that that was really a matter of chance, since the parties (not surprisingly) had given no consideration to the matter.

22.4.1 Off-hire

The effects of very literal construction are even clearer in *The Captain Stefanos*, which also concerned the application of a (heavily amended) NYPE off-hire clause to piratical capture.[60] This time the following off-hire event was added:[61]

"... capture/*seizure, or* detention or threatened detention by any authority including arrest, ...".

It is important to note where the comma is. Though Cooke J started off with discussion of *Rainy Sky* and general principle,[62] in the end he held that the clause covered piracy, *because of the placement of the comma!* Neither capture nor seizure were qualified by the words, "by any authority including arrest", and there was authority that capture does, but seizure does not, denote authority.[63] So the detention was "seizure", and hence within the clause. Cooke J rejected the shipowner's argument that the off-hire clause should be read in the light of the war clause (CONWARTIME 2004), which (the shipowner argued) placed the risks on the charterer, observing (sentiments we have already seen) that:[64]

"The difficulty about such an approach is that the off-hire provisions of a charter do not necessarily, nor indeed usually, tie in with the provisions of the charter which relate to breach of obligation by one party or the other."

He also made the point that many charters (as this one) were heavily amended, making a unitary construction more difficult. It may be that any purposive interpretation is more difficult with a

---

57 Ibid.
58 See further Todd, *Charterparties and piracy today* (2014), CreateSpace. There is a lot more detail there, than there is here.
59 [2011] 1 Lloyd's Rep 187, in section [12.3].
60 *Osmium Shipping Corp v Cargill International SA (The Captain Stefanos)* [2012] 2 Lloyd's Rep 46.
61 My emphasis. This was an additional (rider) off-hire clause (56).
62 As discussed in section [22.2.2].
63 *Cory & Sons v Burr* (1883) 8 App Cas 393.
64 [2012] 2 Lloyd's Rep 46, [10]. The owners argued that the war clause should be regarded as a complete code, an argument which has echoes of that in *Kodros Shipping Corp of Monrovia v Empresa Cubana de Fletes (The Evia) (No. 2)* [1983] 1 AC 736, in section [13.9].

heavily amended form. Anyway, in *The Captain Stefanos* a purposive argument was rejected, in favour of a very literal interpretation of the off-hire clause.[65]

It is hard to imagine the parties, when negotiating the fixture, deciding that piratical capture was to be an off-hire event, and providing for it by placing a comma after "seizure". A problem with very literal construction is that when circumstances change the parties need explicitly to reconsider clauses, to take account of the new situation. BIMCO and INTERTANKO eventually responded, producing piracy clauses that, if adopted, deal rationally with the phenomenon of ransom piracy.

22.4.2 War clauses

The Somali troubles led to litigation on time charter war clauses, and, in particular, CONWAR-TIME.[66] The effect of these, in general terms, is to allow masters to refuse to proceed to areas where there is a likelihood of attack, and to provide for indemnities in the event that they do, and suffer loss, or additional expense, as a result.[67]

One of the more interesting cases is *The Paiwan Wisdom*.[68] Teare J, interpreting CONWAR-TIME 2004, distinguished *The Product Star* (No. 2),[69] and held that there was nothing in the CONWARTIME clause requiring war risk to have escalated, as a trigger to apply the clause. In *The Paiwan Wisdom*, the owners had refused to comply with an order to proceed to Mombasa, fearing proximity to Somali piracy outbreaks. This was the first voyage under the charterparty, and there was no evidence of escalation of risk. *The Product Star* (No. 2) had required escalation to trigger a similar (Beepeetime 2) clause, but it was, in Teare J's view, a very different type of case. In the earlier case, the charterparty envisaged trading in the Arabian Gulf during the Iran–Iraq war, and provided for the payment by the charterers of war risk premium in respect of trading, in particular, to Ruwais in the UAE. It was hardly surprisingly in Teare J's view, that the Court of Appeal there held the owners not entitled to refuse to proceed to Ruwais, *the very place in respect of which provision had been made*, in the absence of any increase in risk. By contrast, in *The Paiwan Wisdom*, there was no suggestion that the owners were aware, when entering the charterparty, that the vessel was likely to be employed on one or more voyages to Kenya, or anywhere near Somalia. There was therefore no reason to suppose that they had considered and accepted the risk.[70]

If *The Paiwan Wisdom* is correct, *The Product Star* (No. 2) does not establish an invariable rule of law, that for a provision such as that in CONWARTIME or Beepeetime 2 to apply, the war risk has to have escalated.[71] Instead, a war clause must be read in the light of the charterparty as a whole, and in its factual matrix. In Teare J's view, the factual matrix in *The Paiwan Wisdom* differed sufficiently from *The Product Star* (No. 2) for the earlier case to be inapplicable in the case before him.

In 2013, BIMCO revised CONWARTIME. Under the new clause, the owners may refuse to proceed "where it appears that the Vessel, cargo, crew or other persons on board the Vessel, in the reasonable judgement of the Master and/or the Owners, may be exposed to War Risks *whether such*

---

65 A literal interpretation, without attempting to force the off-hire clause into the general scheme of the charterparty, is also consistent with the observations in *The Berge Sund*, cited in section [12.3.5].

66 In addition to those considered here, *Pacific Basin IXX Ltd v Bulkhandling Handymax A/S (The Triton Lark)* [2012] 1 Lloyd's Rep 151; [2012] 1 Lloyd's Rep 457, which are beyond the scope of this book. See further Todd, *Charterparties and piracy today* (2014), Createspace, [3.3]–[3.4].

67 See generally section [13.10].

68 *Taokas Navigation SA v Komrowski Bulk Shipping KG (GmbH & Co) (The Paiwan Wisdom)* [2012] 2 Lloyd's Rep 416.

69 *Abu Dhabi National Tanker Co v Product Star Shipping Ltd (The Product Star) (No. 2)* [1993] 1 Lloyd's Rep 397, also in section [3.5] (on the obligation to perform in good faith).

70 [2012] 2 Lloyd's Rep 416, discussion beginning at [19].

71 *The Product Star* (No. 2) was a decision on Beepeetime 2, but the war clause was essentially similar to CONWARTIME considered in *The Paiwan Wisdom*.

risk existed at the time of entering into this Charter Party or occurred thereafter."[72] Similar wording can be found in BIMCO's recent piracy clauses,[73] and for the same reason. In the light of *The Product Star (No. 2)* (considered above), BIMCO feared the need for an escalation in risk before CONWARTIME could be applied. If the new clause is accepted by the market, then this aspect of *The Product Star (No. 2)* will no longer apply.

War clauses do not demand the very literal interpretation required for off-hire clauses. *The Paiwan Wisdom* is of interest in taking account of the factual matrix of the charterparty as a whole. This is an approach that is more likely to lead to a satisfactory result, where the standard forms have not yet explicitly taken account of a situation that is novel.

22.5 Issues surrounding carriage of oil by sea

Oil cargoes differ from their dry-cargo counterparts. In some respects, the differences are quite obvious; the cargo is of a different nature, and its care and handling will obviously be different. What is less obvious is the difference between the markets. The charterers are the large refiners with the bargaining power, whereas with dry-cargo the ball is on the other boot, the market favouring ship-owners. This makes comparison of standard forms more interesting, because one can see the effect of markets on the drafting.

This section continues the theme of this chapter, by concentrating principally on construction, however.

22.5.1 Standard forms

We have contrasted pro-shipowner dry-cargo and pro-charterer oil forms throughout the book. Just by way of example, you can see the differences in cancelling clauses, speed and performance clauses (more detailed for tankers), freight (never advance freight in oil carriage), final voyage clauses (much more common for tankers), safe ports (due diligence qualification), anti-technicality clauses (usually longer period of grace), and off-hire (more comprehensive provision generally, and even sometimes period off-hire clauses). There are also a number of questions, at the start of the next chapter, which compare oil and dry-cargo forms.

Tanker clauses also sometimes have an anti-arbitration bias, providing for all disputes to be litigated in the High Court in London. The large concerns are interested in litigating to create precedents, and you cannot do that in arbitration. Dry-cargo charters, by contrast, typically have arbitration clauses.

There are differences between the tanker forms themselves, with BP generally favouring charterers to a greater extent than Shell. And there are of course INTERTANKO's forms, representing the shipowner's viewpoint (though never actually used, in a charterers' market).

There is, in short, a lot to be said for studying the oil standard forms.

22.5.2 Transportation losses

There is an inevitable loss of tanker cargoes on any voyage through evaporation, sedimentation, clingage, etc. Some of this takes place *en route*, but the greatest losses are likely to occur on loading and at discharge. If the sea buoys are some distance out from the shore, the delivered quantity ashore may differ substantially from the amount discharged from the vessel, whatever has happened on the voyage itself.

---

72 The emphasis is mine.
73 Todd, *Charterparties and piracy today*, ch. 4.

There have even been difficulties in measuring loaded and discharged quantities of oil cargoes. These practical difficulties are beyond the scope of this book, but occasionally measurement issues are litigated: should you use ship or shore figures, and so on?[74]

But we will concern ourselves with losses. The inevitable loss of cargo through evaporation, sedimentation, clingage, etc., is sometimes referred to as "transportation loss", whereas non-inevitable loss, such as damage caused by weather or collision, or war, is referred to as "marine loss".[75] Tanker voyage charterparties will always have an out-turn loss or cargo retention clause, or both, to compensate charterers in respect of transportation losses. The working is to require compensation above a margin – usually 0.3 or 0.5 per cent – in the case of an out-turn loss clause, and to penalise inefficient discharge in the case of a cargo retention clause. With cargo-retention clauses, shipowners are responsible for pumpable cargo that remains on board the vessel after discharge. Both clauses typically work by allowing deduction from freight, to compensate for the damage caused by the shortfall, and not otherwise recoverable in the light of *The Aries*.[76] They effectively provide for strict liability, but do not normally provide any remedy other than deduction from freight.

Though the cargo-retention clause is more commonly found, the litigation has mostly concerned out-turn loss clauses. In *The Olympic Brilliance* the Court of Appeal considered the following out-turn loss clause, which was a typed addition to the Exxonvoy 1969 form:[77]

"If there is a difference of more than 0.50% between B/Lading figures and delivered cargo as ascertained by Custom Authorities at discharging port, Charterers have the right to deduct from freight the C.I.F. value for the short delivered cargo. Owners have the right to appoint independent surveyor in order to check cargo figures in conjunction with Custom Authorities."

This is fairly typical of such clauses. The court held that the clause gave the charterers the right to make a permanent deduction from freight for the CIF value of the short delivered cargo, as the loss exceeded 0.5 per cent. The clause effectively provided for a form of strict liability. The charterers did not therefore need to show that the loss was not caused by an excepted peril under the Hague Rules,[78] which were incorporated into the charterparty. Further observations about the clause are that it made clear how the shortfall was to be measured, and also how it was to be valued. This is important because there are different ways of doing both of these. Here the CIF value was taken, but another common basis is the FOB (free on board) value at the loading port, plus freight to the discharge port (as with the BP clause).

The clause in *The Olympic Brilliance* provided for automatic deduction from freight, but had the charterers been left to a damages claim, for example if the value of the shortfall exceeded the total freight and the charterers were suing for the excess, the Hague Rules would have applied to that claim. Nor would the Court of Appeal necessarily have taken the same view on strict liability had the clause been drafted to apply to a damages claim as well.[79]

In *The Valle di Cordoba* the clause was wider, and, on a literal interpretation, would have provided for strict liability, for a damages claim also:[80]

---

74 Eg, *Amoco Oil Co v Parpada Shipping Co Ltd (The George S)* [1989] 1 Lloyd's Rep. 369.

75 Eg, Lightburn & Nienaber, *Out-turn clauses in c.i.f. contracts in the oil trade* [1987] 2 LMCLQ 177, 178–9.

76 *Aries Tanker Corporation v Total Transport Ltd (The Aries)* [1977] 1 WLR 185, in section [7.6].

77 *Lakeport Navigation Co Panama SA v Anonima Petroli Italiana SpA (The Olympic Brilliance)* [1982] 2 Lloyd's Rep 205.

78 There had been an unexplained loss of just over 2,500 tonnes of cargo – or about 1 per cent.

79 Eg, [1982] 2 Lloyd's Rep 205, 208 (Eveleigh LJ).

80 [2015] 1 Lloyd's Rep 529 EWCA Civ 91, on appeal from [2014] 1 Lloyd's Rep 550. The clause was an amended version of the standard Beepeevoy 3 form, the amendments being shown here by the struck-through and underlined text. See generally Todd, *Charterparties and piracy today* (2014), CreateSpace, ch. 1.

"In addition to any other rights which Charterers may have, Owners will be responsible for the full amount of any in-transit loss if in-transit loss exceeds 0.3% *0.5%* and Charterers shall have the right to ~~deduct from freight~~ *claim* an amount equal to the FOB port of loading value of such lost cargo plus freight and insurance due with respect thereto. In-transit loss is defined as the difference between net vessel volumes after loading at the loading port and before unloading at the discharge port."

This clause, which was described as an "in transit loss clause", but which is otherwise similar to the clause in *The Olympic Brilliance*, was not however limited to deduction from freight, but on its face allowed a damages action as well. The charterers contended that it should be interpreted literally (as the clause had been in *The Olympic Brilliance*). This would however have led to an extreme result, since strict liability is unheard of, for a damages claim, in modern carriage contracts, but Andrew Smith J refused so to interpret the clause, taking account of the purpose of such clauses.

The vessel was captured in 2010, by pirates off the coast of Lagos, who arranged for an STS (ship-to-ship) transfer of cargo, in order to effect a theft. They released the vessel after three days, but the pirates having stolen over 5,000 tonnes of cargo, obviously there was a shortfall on delivery, which was far greater than 0.5 per cent. The charterers claimed damages, under the clause. It seems most unlikely that the clause was intended to cover this situation, and, at first instance, Andrew Smith J held that the in-transit loss clause should be interpreted as applying only to losses "incidental to the carriage of oil products", and not the sort of fortuitous losses that might generally be expected to be covered by a marine all-risks insurance policy.[81] If this was wrong, he held that the clause should take subject to the charter exceptions (which included Hague Rules excepted perils). In reaching this conclusion, he cited observations from *Rainy Sky SA v Kookmin Bank*,[82] where Lord Clarke in the Supreme Court emphasised the need for a unitary exercise of construction, the importance of business common sense, and the avoidance of a non-commercial interpretation. Conversely, on the charterers' interpretation, this would be strict liability, but only for loss not damage. In rejecting this view, this meant that Andrew Smith J was not prepared to interpret the clause literally, as it stood.

The charterers had argued that to limit the clause in such a way was effectively to emasculate it. In rejecting this argument, Andrew Smith J observed that the clause still provides how loss is established by measurement, and provides for the FOB value to be used in calculating the compensation.[83] So there was no redundancy, a factor to which courts have regard (but even if there is redundancy, it is not necessarily fatal).

Andrew Smith J also refused the charterers' invitation to look closely at the amendment process, to try to determine what the amendments must have meant. (The charterers argued that the parties must be assumed to have been familiar with *The Olympic Brilliance*, and that the amendments were clearly intended to extend that decision to a damages claim.) He thought that it was wrong to assume that the parties started with the unamended clause and then negotiated amendments separately and, in any case, felt that to interpret the clause in this way was inconsistent with the unitary construction emphasised in the Supreme Court in *Rainy Sky*.[84]

Andrew Smith J's judgment was approved in the Court of Appeal, though without resort to (or indeed mention of) *Rainy Sky*. The Court of Appeal essentially approved the construction that had been adopted at first instance.[85] Longmore LJ made some other observations. Clearly relevant, for him, was the extreme width of the charterers' argument, providing (in a charterparty that also

---

81 [2014] 1 Lloyd's Rep 550, [16]. He accepted that insurance provides "a rough rule of thumb" as to the type of loss that should be excluded.
82 [2011] 1 WLR 2900, in section [22.2.2], and cited [2014] 1 Lloyd's Rep Plus 26, [24].
83 [2014] 1 Lloyd's Rep Plus 26, [21].
84 [2014] 1 Lloyd's Rep Plus 26, [24], the arguments being set out in the preceding paragraphs.
85 Briggs LJ *dubitante* on this issue.

incorporated the Hague Rules) for a liability that was even greater than that against a common carrier:[86]

> "At common law, even a common carrier was exempted from loss or damage caused by the act of the Queen's enemies. Not surprisingly this exemption was confirmed by international conventions. Both the Hague Rules and the Hague-Visby Rules contain an exemption in respect of loss or damage arising or resulting from 'Act of public enemies', see Article IV rule 2(f). It is an open question whether loss resulting from piracy falls within this exception but one possible view is that it does, since pirates are by international law enemies of the human race (or, as the old books put it, 'hostes humani generis') and thus, necessarily, enemies of the Queen. But if the loss does not fall within rule 2(f) it would fall either within Article IV rule 2(c) – 'perils of the sea' or within the residual provision of rule 2(q)."

This is a purposive interpretation of the clause that avoids absurdities, and is in line with its intended purpose. It is also consistent with *Rainy Sky*. It is unclear to what extent it is possible to generalise from the case, and adopt purposive interpretations more generally.

As ever, it is important to be aware that sea carriage is not carried out in isolation, and that it is part of a wider transaction. There will be bill of lading and sale contracts, not just the charterparty. Shipowners should guard against agreeing to terms which allow the charterer to deduct from freight, if the cargo owner also has a potential claim for short delivery. There can be out-turn loss and cargo retention clauses in bill of lading, and international sale contracts are often on an out-turn basis, and the parties need to ensure that the provisions are properly intermeshed. For example, if a CIF sale is on the basis that purchaser pays only for out-turned quantity, the seller should ensure that there is an out-turn loss clause in his carriage contract, whereas conversely there should not be one in the purchaser's carriage contract. In this situation (for example), if the seller is charterer, the out-turn loss clause should be in the charterparty, and not in the bill of lading to which the purchaser will become party.

22.6 Question

How do you think *The Laura Prima* would have been decided had there been no cl. 9 in the charterparty (reachable on arrival clause)?[87]

Note:

You might usefully read *The Notos*.[88] The charterparty was similar to that in *The Laura Prima*, but there was no reachable on arrival clause (the equivalent of Exxonvoy 69, cl. 9). It is clear that the reachable on arrival clause makes a difference, and that cl. 9 affects the interpretation of cl. 6.

---

86 [2015] EWCA Civ 91, [2]. The comments on shipowner liability in respect of piracy are also of interest, though they would not apply if the vessel were unfit to go to sea, in a piracy-infested area, and hence unseaworthy for the particular voyage: see further section [4.2].

87 [1982] 1 Lloyd's Rep 1.

88 [1987] 1 Lloyd's Rep 503 (though that was a demurrage rather than commencement of laytime claim).

Chapter 23

Further reading

A textbook, such as this, is a starting point only. Its aim is to provide the general structure of the subject, but, once that has been gleaned, you will want to read further. The law does not arrive, fully formed, from thin air, but has been set down in legislation and/or honed by the cases. This book is fully footnoted. The footnotes provide the authority that allows me to say what I say (for no statement of law is possible without authority). But they also tell you what I read myself, in order to write the book. If you really want to study this subject, you could do a lot worse than look up the material in the footnotes.

The law of charterparties is derived almost entirely from case law, bills of lading less so, but there are still a great number of cases. I wrote this book almost entirely from online material, and if you are at a university with access to Lexis, Westlaw and i-Law (or if you otherwise have access to these databases), you will also be able to study online, if you wish. Even if you do not have such access, legislation and recent cases are freely available on the Internet, the former through http://www.legislation.gov.uk/, and the latter through http://www.bailii.org/ (which is extending its coverage, though for the most part it is still limited to recent cases). The Hamburg and Rotterdam Rules can be found at UNCITRAL's site, at http://www.uncitral.org/uncitral/en/index.html.

Many students, especially those with a civil law background, resist reading cases, but very little understanding of the law can be gleaned without so doing. There are shortcuts. One is to read the newer cases first, since they discuss earlier authorities, whereas (obviously) the converse is not true. You miss seeing the development of the law, but it is useful if you are short of time. Cases are not like novels. They do not need to be read from start to finish. You can dip in, and return later. You will usually have some idea what the case is about, before you read it, so you can look for that first. If you are not sure what to look for, remember that nearly all cases (at least if they are decided on a point of law) advance the law in some way. Loser pays costs, and cases can always be settled, so if they go to trial it is reasonable to suppose both sides think they can win. At the very least, the case will reject the arguments of the losing side. So you should look for the way in which the case advanced the development of the law; if you cannot find it, you have almost certainly not read it properly.

There are a number of textbooks on carriage of goods by sea, but when I was a student (quite a long time ago) I used to favour cases and materials books, especially those with good commentary, and questions. There is still a value for such books, even in the Internet era, in selecting the sources, bringing them together in one place, and provoking thought about them. Dockray, *Cases and Materials on the Carriage of Goods by Sea*, 3rd ed (2004), Cavendish, is, in my view, very good, though sadly a little old now. Even older is my own book, *Cases and Materials on International Trade Law* (2002), Sweet & Maxwell. Obviously this is mostly on sale contracts, but chapters 11–14, and 16, cover some of the ground also covered in this book, though of course concentrating on the sources. Nearly all the student carriage books, including *Dockray*, are in my view much better on charterparties than bills of lading.

For international sales in a real-world context, Murray, Holloway and Timson-Hunt (eds), *Schmitthoff's Export Trade: The Law and Practice of International Trade*, 12th ed (2012), Thomson/Sweet & Maxwell, remains the classic text.

I have made occasional reference to the standard forms. I made much use of Per Gram, *Chartering Documents* (1981), LLP, and its successor, Williams, *Chartering Documents*, 4th ed (1998), LLP. The older edition remains useful for some of the earlier developments discussed in this book (eg, Jupiter clauses).

Specialist books

There are a number of good, specialist, reference books, some of which are available electronically, on i-Law or elsewhere. Sometimes these texts can legitimately be used as sources, since they are often cited in the cases (though by no means always with approval). Covering the whole subject is *Scrutton on Charterparties and Bills of Lading*, 23rd ed (2015), Sweet & Maxwell. Covering the whole of bills of lading is Treitel & Reynolds, *Carver on Bills of Lading*, 3rd ed (2012), Sweet & Maxwell/Thomson Reuters, British Shipping Laws Series, a very academic reference book (but many of the cases in this book were decided on very academic issues). Both these books are on Westlaw, if the subscription covers them (and Westlaw subscriptions vary).

For laytime, the leading reference work is Baughen, *Summerskill on Laytime*, 5th ed (2013), Sweet & Maxwell/Thomson Reuter. It is very thorough, both on laytime and demurrage (though less so on damages for detention), but is in no sense an introductory work. This is a book for people who already know about laytime. (It is also on Westlaw.) If you want to be even more specialist, there is Davies, *Commencement of Laytime*, 4th ed (2006), Taylor & Francis. On charterparties, Cooke, *Voyage Charters*, 4th ed (2014), Taylor & Francis, and Coghlin, *Time Charters*, 7th ed (2014), Taylor & Francis, are classic works, and both on i-Law.

On the Rotterdam Rules, Baatz, *Rotterdam Rules: A Practical Annotation* (2009), Taylor & Francis, is comprehensive, and also on i-Law.

Since you are unlikely to consult one of the large reference books as the starting point for your study, the easiest way to find your way around them might be the table of contents, but it is more likely to be the tables of cases and legislation. The index might also help, though these are of variable quality.

I have written a small specialist book, of relevance to the discussion in section [22.4]: Todd, *Charterparties and piracy today* (2014), CreateSpace. Details can be found on Amazon.

Websites

I provided links to legislation and recent cases above, and to the Rotterdam and Hamburg Rules.

> Links to charterparties and other documents: https://www.bimco.org/en/Chartering/Claus
> es_and_Documents/Documents/
> Links to tanker charterparties: https://shippingforum.wordpress.com/new_page_1/

I have referred mostly to the main standard forms in this book, Gencon, Baltime and NYPE for dry cargo, and the Shell and BP forms for tankers. But INTERTANKO's forms are worth a look. They are really an academic exercise, though, being pro-shipowner forms in a charterer market, so you rarely if ever see them in the cases. You can link to Tankervoy 87 and Intertanktime 80 from BIMCO's site (above).

Appendices

Appendix A

Carriage of Goods by Sea Act 1971 (Hague-Visby Rules)

Author's note

The Carriage of Goods by Sea Act 1971 (as amended by the Merchant Shipping Acts 1981 and 1995) implements the Hague-Visby Rules as part of UK domestic legislation. We discuss them in detail in chapter 18, and in that chapter can be found many references to this appendix. The Rules themselves are in the schedule, but there are a few sections bringing them into force.

The full text of the statute can be found at http://www.legislation.gov.uk/ukpga/1971/19/contents, and also in Westlaw or Lexis, should you have access to those databases.

The Act

Be it enacted by the Queen's most Excellent Majesty, by and with the advice and consent of the Lords Spiritual and Temporal, and Commons, in this present Parliament assembled, and by the authority of the same, as follows:-

1. Application of Hague Rules as amended.

(1) In this Act, 'the Rules' means the International Convention for the unification of certain rules of law relating to bills of lading signed at Brussels on 25th August 1924, as amended by the Protocol signed at Brussels on 23rd February 1968 and [inserted by the Merchant Shipping Act 1981, s. 2(1) and by the Merchant Shipping Act 1995, s. 314(2)] by the Protocol signed at Brussels on 21st December 1979.

(2) The provisions of the Rules, as set out in the Schedule to this Act, shall have the force of law.

(3) Without prejudice to subsection (2) above, the said provisions shall have effect (and have the force of law) in relation to and in connection with the carriage of goods by sea in ships where the port of shipment is a port in the United Kingdom, whether or not the carriage is between ports in two different States within the meaning of Article X of the Rules.

(4) Subject to subsection (6) below, nothing in this section shall be taken as applying anything in the Rules to any contract for the carriage of goods by sea, unless the contract expressly or by implication provides for the issue of a bill of lading or any similar document of title.

(5) The Secretary of State may from time to time by order made by statutory instrument specify the respective amounts which for the purposes of paragraph 5 of Article IV of the Rules and of Article IV bis of the Rules are to be taken as equivalent to the sums expressed in francs which are mentioned in subparagraph (a) of that paragraph. [Note: this subsection has now been repealed.]

(6) Without prejudice to Article X(c) of the Rules, the Rules shall have the force of law in relation to—

(a) any bill of lading if the contract contained in or evidenced by it expressly provides that the Rules shall govern the contract, and

(b) any receipt which is a non-negotiable document marked as such if the contract contained in or evidenced by it is a contract for the carriage of goods by sea which expressly provides that the Rules are to govern the contract as if the receipt were a bill of lading,

but subject, where paragraph (b) applies, to any necessary modifications and in particular with the omission in Article III of the Rules of the second sentence of paragraph 4 and of paragraph 7.

(7) If and so far as the contract contained in or evidenced by a bill of lading or receipt within paragraph (a) or (b) of subsection (6) above applies to deck cargo or live animals, the Rules as given the force of law by that subsection shall have effect as if Article I(c) did not exclude deck cargo and live animals.

In this subsection 'deck cargo' means cargo which by the contract of carriage is stated as being carried on deck and is so carried.

[Note: The next section was added by the Merchant Shipping Act 1995, s. 314(2). Originally, liability limits were fixed in terms of gold value, rather than SDRs.]

1A. Conversion of special drawing rights into sterling

(1) For the purposes of Article IV of the Rules the value on a particular day of one special drawing right shall be treated as equal to such a sum in sterling as the International Monetary Fund have fixed as being the equivalent of one special drawing right—

(a) for that day; or

(b) if no sum has been so fixed for that day, for the last day before that day for which a sum has been so fixed.

(2) A certificate given by or on behalf of the Treasury stating—

(a) that a particular sum in sterling has been fixed as aforesaid for a particular day; or

(b) that no sum has been so fixed for a particular day and that a particular sum in sterling has been so fixed for a day which is the last day for which a sum has been so fixed before the particular day,

shall be conclusive evidence of those matters for the purposes of subsection (1) above; and a document purporting to be such a certificate shall in any proceedings be received in evidence and, unless the contrary is proved, be deemed to be such a certificate.

(3) The Treasury may charge a reasonable fee for any certificate given in pursuance of subsection (2) above, and any fee received by the Treasury by virtue of this subsection shall be paid into the Consolidated Fund.

2.   Contracting states, etc.

(1)   If Her Majesty by Order in Council certifies to the following effect, that is to say, that for the purposes of the Rules–

(a)   a State specified in the Order is a contracting State, or is a contracting State in respect of any place or territory so specified; or

(b)   any place or territory specified in the Order forms part of a State so specified (whether a contracting State or not), the Order shall, except so far as it has been superseded by a subsequent Order, be conclusive evidence of the matters so certified.

(2)   An Order in Council under this section may be varied or revoked by a subsequent Order in Council.

3.   Absolute warranty of seaworthiness not to be implied in contracts to which Rules apply

There shall not be implied in any contract for the carriage of goods by sea to which the Rules apply by virtue of this Act any absolute undertaking by the carrier of the goods to provide a seaworthy ship.

4.   Application of Act to British possessions, etc.

(1)   Her Majesty may by Order in Council direct that this Act shall extend, subject to such exceptions, adaptations and modifications as may be specified in the Order, to all or any of the following territories, that is–

(a)   any colony (not being a colony for whose external relations a country other than the United Kingdom is responsible),

(b)   any country outside Her Majesty's dominions in which Her Majesty has jurisdiction in right of Her Majesty's Government of the United Kingdom.

(2)   An Order in Council under this section may contain such transitional and other consequential provisions as appear to her Majesty to be expedient, including provisions amending or repealing any legislation about the carriage of goods by sea forming part of the law of any of the territories mentioned in paragraphs (a) and (b) above.

(3)   An Order in Council under this section may be varied or revoked by a subsequent Order in Council.

5.   Extension of application of Rules to carriage from ports in British possessions, etc.

(1)   Her Majesty may by Order in Council provide that section 1 (3) of this Act shall have effect as if the reference therein to the United Kingdom included a reference to all or any of the following territories, that is–

(a)   the Isle of Man;

(b)   any of the Channel Islands specified in the Order;

(c)   any colony specified in the Order (not being a colony for whose external relations a country other than the United Kingdom is responsible);

(d)   any associated state (as defined by section 1(3) of the West Indies Act 1967) specified in the Order;

(e)   any country specified in the Order, being a country outside Her majesty's dominions in which Her Majesty has jurisdiction in right of Her Majesty's Government of the United Kingdom.

(2)   An Order in Council under this section may be varied or revoked by a subsequent Order in Council.

6.   Supplemental

(1)   This Act may be cited as the Carriage of Goods by Sea Act 1971.

(2)   It is hereby declared that this Act extends to Northern Ireland.

(3)   The following enactments shall be repealed, that is–

(a)   the Carriage of Goods by Sea Act 1924,

(b)   section 12(4)(a) of the Nuclear Installations Act 1965, and without prejudice to section 38(1) of the Interpretation Act 1889, the reference to the said Act of 1924 in section 1 (1) (i) (ii) of the Hovercraft Act 1968 shall include a reference to this Act.

[Note: This subsection was substituted by the Merchant Shipping Act 1995, s. 314(2).]

(4)   It is hereby declared that for the purposes of Article VIII of the Rules section 186 of the Merchant Shipping Act 1995 (which entirely exempts shipowners and others in certain circumstances for loss of, or damage to, goods) is a provision relating to limitation of liability.

(5)   This Act shall come into force on such day as Her Majesty may by Order in Council appoint, and, for the purposes of the transition from the law in force immediately before the day appointed under this subsection to the provisions of this Act, the Order appointing the day may provide that those provisions shall have effect subject to such transitional provisions as may be contained in the Order.

Schedule

The Hague Rules as amended by the Brussels Protocol 1968.

Article I

In these Rules the following words are employed, with the meanings set out below:

(a)   'Carrier' includes the owner or the charterer who enters into a contract of carriage with the shipper.

(b)   'Contract of carriage' applies only to contracts of carriage covered by a bill of lading or any similar document of title, in so far as such document relates to the carriage of goods by sea, including any bill of lading or any similar document as aforesaid issued under or pursuant to a charter-party from the moment at which such bill of lading or similar document of title regulates the relations between a carrier and a holder of the same.

(c)   'Goods' includes goods, wares, merchandise, and articles of every kind whatsoever except live animals and cargo which by the contract of carriage is stated as being carried on deck and is so carried.

(d)   'Ship' means any vessel used for the carriage of goods by sea.

(e)   'Carriage of goods' covers the period from the time when the goods are loaded to the time they are discharged from the ship.

Article II

Subject to the provisions of Article VI, under every contract of carriage of goods by sea the carrier, in relation to the loading, handling, stowage, carriage, custody, care and discharge of such goods, shall be subject to the responsibilities and liabilities, and entitled to the rights and immunities hereinafter set forth.

Article III

(1)   The carrier shall be bound before and at the beginning of the voyage[1] to exercise due diligence to-

  (a)   Make the ship seaworthy.
  (b)   Properly man, equip and supply the ship.
  (c)   Make the holds, refrigerating and cool chambers, and all other parts of the ship in which the goods are carried, fit and safe for their reception, carriage and preservation.

(2)   Subject to the provisions of Article IV,[2] the carrier shall properly and carefully load, handle, stow, carry, keep, care for, and discharge the goods carried.

(3)   After receiving the goods into his charge the carrier or the master or agent of the carrier shall, on demand of the shipper, issue to the shipper a bill of lading showing among other things–

  (a)   The leading marks necessary for identification of the goods as the same are furnished in writing by the shipper before the loading of such goods starts, provided such marks are stamped or otherwise shown clearly upon the goods if uncovered, or on the cases or coverings in which such goods are contained, in such a manner as should ordinarily remain legible until the end of the voyage.
  (b)   Either the number of packages or pieces, or the quantity, or weight, as the case may be, as furnished in writing by the shipper.
  (c)   The apparent order and condition of the goods.

Provided that no carrier, master or agent of the carrier shall be bound to state or show in the bill of lading any marks, number, quantity or weight which he has reasonable ground for suspecting not accurately to represent the goods actually received, or which he has had no reasonable means of checking.

(4)   Such a bill of lading shall be *prima facie* evidence of the receipt by the carrier of the goods as therein described in accordance with paragraph 3 (a), (b), and (c). However, proof to the contrary shall not be admissible when the bill of lading has been transferred to a third party in good faith.[3]

---

1 Hague-Visby has been criticised for limiting this obligation to the start of the voyage.
2 Art III(2) is, but III(1) is not, subject to the excepted perils in Art. IV.
3 Second sentence added by the Visby amendments.

(5) The shipper shall be deemed to have guaranteed to the carrier the accuracy at the time of shipment of the marks, number, quantity and weight, as furnished by him, and the shipper shall identify the carrier against all loss, damages and expenses arising or resulting from inaccuracies in such particulars. The right of the carrier to such indemnity shall in no way limit his responsibility and liability under the contract of carriage to any person other than the shipper.

(6) Unless notice of loss or damage and the general nature of such loss or damage be given in writing to the carrier or his agent at the port of discharge before or at the time of the removal of the goods into the custody of the person entitled to delivery thereof under the contract of carriage, or, if the loss or damage be not apparent, within three days, such removal shall be *prima facie* evidence of the delivery by the carrier of the goods as described in the bill of lading.

The notice in writing need not be given if the state of the goods has, at the time of their receipt, been the subject of joint survey or inspection.

Subject to paragraph 6 *bis* the carrier and the ship shall in any event be discharged from all liability whatsoever in respect of the goods,[4] unless suit is brought within one year of their delivery or of the date when they should have been delivered. This period may, however, be extended if the parties so agree after the cause of action has arisen.

In the case of any actual or apprehended loss or damage the carrier and the receiver shall give all reasonable facilities to each other for inspecting and tallying the goods.

(6) *bis.* An action for an indemnity against a third person may be brought even after the expiration of the year provided for in the preceding paragraph if brought within the time allowed by the law of the Court seized of the case. However, the time allowed shall be not less than three months, commencing from the day when the person bringing such action for indemnity has settled the claim or has been served with process in the action against himself.

(7) After the goods are loaded the bill of lading to be issued by the carrier, master, or agent of the carrier, to the shipper shall, if the shipper so demands, be a 'shipped' bill of lading, provided that if the shipper shall previously have taken up any document of title to such goods, he shall surrender the same as against the issue of the 'shipped' bill of lading, but at the option of the carrier such document of title may be noted at the port of shipment by the carrier, master, or agent with the name or names of the ship or ships upon which the goods have been shipped and the date or dates of shipment, and when so noted, if it shows the particulars mentioned in paragraph 3 of Article III, shall for the purpose of this article be deemed to constitute a 'shipped' bill of lading.

(8) Any clause, covenant or agreement in a contract of carriage relieving the carrier or the ship from liability for loss or damage to or in connection with goods arising from negligence, fault or failure in the duties and obligations provided in this article or lessening such liability otherwise than as provided in these Rules, shall be null and void and of no effect. A benefit of insurance in favour of the carrier or similar clause shall be deemed to be a clause relieving the carrier from liability.

Article IV

(1) Neither the carrier nor the ship shall be liable for loss or damage arising or resulting from unseaworthiness unless caused by want of due diligence on the part of the carrier to make the ship seaworthy, or to secure that the ship is properly manned, equipped and supplied, and

---

4 The word "whatsoever" added by the Visby amendments, probably to cover misdelivery.

to make the holds, refrigerating and cool chambers and all other parts of the ship in which the goods are carried fit and safe for their reception, carriage and preservation in accordance with paragraph 1 of Article III. Whenever loss or damage has resulted from unseaworthiness the burden of proving the exercise of due diligence shall be on the carrier or other person claiming exemption under this article.

(2)   Neither the carrier nor the ship shall be responsible for loss or damage arising or resulting from—

    (a)   Act, neglect, or default of the master, mariner, pilot, or the servants of the carrier in the navigation or in the management of the ship.[5]

    (b)   Fire, unless caused by the actual fault or privity of the carrier.

    (c)   Perils, dangers and accidents of the sea or other navigable waters.

    (d)   Act of God.

    (e)   Act of war.

    (f)   Act of public enemies.

    (g)   Arrest or restraint of princes, rulers or people, or seizure under legal process.

    (h)   Quarantine restrictions.

    (i)   Act or omission of the shipper or owner of the goods, his agent or representative.

    (j)   Strikes or lockouts or stoppage or restraint of labour from whatever cause, whether partial or general.

    (k)   Riots and civil commotions.

    (l)   Saving or attempting to save life or property at sea.

    (m)   Wastage in bulk or weight or any other loss or damage arising from inherent defect, quality or vice of the goods.

    (n)   Insufficiency of packing.

    (o)   Insufficiency or inadequacy of marks.

    (p)   Latent defects not discoverable by due diligence.

    (q)   Any other cause arising without the actual fault or privity of the carrier, or without the fault or neglect of the agents or servants of the carrier, but the burden of proof shall be on the person claiming the benefit of this exception to show that neither the actual fault or privity of the carrier nor the fault or neglect of the agents or servants of the carrier contributed to the loss or damage.

(3)   The shipper shall not be responsible for loss or damage sustained by the carrier or the ship arising or resulting from any cause without the act, fault or neglect of the shipper, his agents or his servants.

(4)   Any deviation in saving or attempting to save life or property at sea or any reasonable deviation shall not be deemed to be an infringement or breach of these Rules or of the contract of carriage, and the carrier shall not be liable for any loss or damage resulting therefrom.

(5)   (a)   [as amended by Merchant Shipping Act 1981, s. 2(3), and by the Merchant Shipping Act 1995, s. 314(2)] Unless the nature and value of such goods have been declared by the shipper before shipment and inserted in the bill of lading, neither the carrier nor the ship shall in any event be or become liable for any loss or damage to or in connection with the goods in an amount exceeding the equivalent of 666.67 units of account per package or unit or 2 units of account per kilogramme of gross weight of the goods lost or damaged, whichever is the higher.[6]

---

5 Heavily criticised, and no counterpart in Rotterdam.

6 Amounts changed by the Visby amendments.

(b) The total amount recoverable shall be calculated by reference to the value of such goods at the place and time at which the goods are discharged from the ship in accordance with the contract or should have been so discharged.

The value of the goods shall be fixed according to the commodity exchange price, or, if there is no such price, according to the current market price, or, if there be no commodity exchange price or current market price, by reference to the normal value of goods of the same kind and quality.

(c) Where a container, pallet or similar article of transport is used to consolidate goods, the number of packages or units enumerated in the bill of lading as packed in such article of transport shall be deemed the number of packages as far as these packages or units are concerned. Except as aforesaid such article of transport shall be considered the package or unit.[7]

(d) [as amended by Merchant Shipping Act 1981, s. 2(4), and by the Merchant Shipping Act 1995, s. 314(2)] The unit of account mentioned in this Article is the special drawing right as defined by the International Monetary Fund. The amounts mentioned in sub-paragraph (a) of this paragraph shall be converted into national currency on the basis of the value of that currency on a date to be determined by the law of the Court seized of the case [at the date of the judgment in question: Merchant Shipping Act 1981, section 2(5)].

(e) Neither the carrier nor the ship shall be entitled to the benefit of the limitation of liability provided for in this paragraph if it is proved that the damage resulted from an act or omission of the carrier done with intent to cause damage, or recklessly and with knowledge that damage would probably result.

(f) The declaration mentioned in sub-paragraph (a) of this paragraph, if embodied in the bill of lading, shall be *prima facie* evidence, but shall not be binding or conclusive on the carrier.

(g) By agreement between the carrier, master or agent of the carrier and the shipper other maximum amounts than those mentioned in sub-paragraph (a) of this paragraph may be fixed, provided that no maximum amount so fixed shall be less than the appropriate maximum mentioned in that sub-paragraph.

(h) Neither the carrier nor the ship shall be responsible in any event for loss or damage to, or in connection with, goods if the nature or value thereof has been knowingly mis-stated by the shipper in the bill of lading.

(6) Goods of an inflammable, explosive or dangerous nature to the shipment whereof the carrier, master or agent of the carrier has not consented with knowledge of their nature and character, may at any time before discharge be landed at any place, or destroyed or rendered innocuous by the carrier without compensation and the shipper of such goods shall be liable for all damages directly or indirectly arising out of or resulting from such shipment. If any goods shipped with such knowledge and consent shall become a danger to the ship or cargo, they may in like manner be landed at any place, or destroyed or rendered innocuous by the carrier without liability on the part of the carrier except to general average, if any.

Article IV bis[8]

(1) The defences and limits of liability provided for in these Rules shall apply in any action against the carrier in respect of loss or damage to goods covered by a contract of carriage whether the action be founded in contract or in tort.

(2) If such an action is brought against a servant or agent of the carrier (such servant or agent not being an independent contractor), such servant or agent shall be entitled to avail himself of the defences and limits of liability which the carrier is entitled to invoke under these Rules.

---

7   Provision added by the Visby amendments.
8   Added by the Visby amendments.

(3)   The aggregate of the amounts recoverable from the carrier, and such servants and agents, shall in no case exceed the limit provided for in these Rules.

(4)   Nevertheless, a servant or agent of the carrier shall not be entitled to avail himself of the provisions of this article, if it is proved that the damage resulted from an act or omission of the servant or agent done with intent to cause damage or recklessly and with knowledge that damage would probably result.

Article V

A carrier shall be at liberty to surrender in whole or in part all or any of his rights and immunities or to increase any of his responsibilities and liabilities under these Rules, provided such surrender or increase shall be embodied in the bill of lading issued to the shipper. The provisions of these Rules shall not be applicable to charter-parties, but if bills of lading are issued in the case of a ship under a charter-party they shall comply with the terms of these Rules. Nothing in these Rules shall be held to prevent the insertion in a bill of lading of any lawful provision regarding general average.

Article VI

Notwithstanding the provisions of the preceding articles, a carrier, master or agent of the carrier and the shipper shall in regard to any particular goods be at liberty to enter any agreement in any terms as to the responsibility and liability of the carrier in respect of such goods, or his obligation as to seaworthiness, so far as this stipulation is not contrary to public policy, or the care or diligence of his servants or agents in regard to the loading, handling, stowage, carriage, custody, care and discharge of the goods carried by sea, provided that in this case no bill of lading has been or shall be issued and that the terms agreed shall be embodied in a receipt which shall be a non-negotiable document and shall be marked as such.

Any agreement so entered into shall have full legal effect.

Provided that this article shall not apply to ordinary commercial shipments made in the ordinary course of trade, but only to other shipments where the character or condition of the property to be carried or the circumstances, terms and conditions under which the carriage is to be performed are such as reasonably to justify a special agreement.

Article VII

Nothing herein contained shall prevent a carrier or a shipper from entering into any agreement, stipulation, condition, reservation or exemption as to the responsibility and liability of the carrier or the ship for the loss or damage to, or in connection with, the custody and care and handling of the goods prior to the loading on, and subsequent to the discharge from, the ship on which the goods are carried by sea.

Article VIII

The provisions of these Rules shall not affect the rights and obligations of the carrier under any statute for the time being in force relating to the limitation of the liability of owners of sea-going vessels.

Article IX

These Rules shall not affect the provisions of any international Convention or national law governing liability for nuclear damage.

Article X[9]

The provisions of these Rules shall apply to every bill of lading relating to the carriage of goods between ports in two different States if:

(a) the bill of lading is issued in a contracting State, or
(b) the carriage is from a port in a contracting State, or
(c) the contract contained in or evidenced by the bill of lading provides that these Rules or legislation of any States giving effect to them are to govern the contract,

whatever may be the nationality of the ship, the carrier, the shipper, the consignee, or any other interested person.

[Articles 11 to 16 deal with the coming into force of the Convention, procedure for ratification, accession and denunciation, and the right to call for a fresh conference to consider amendments to the Rules contained in the Convention.]

---

9 Added by the Visby amendments.

Appendix B

Carriage of Goods by Sea Act 1992

Author's note

This Act replaced the Bills of Lading Act 1855, and is covered in chapter 16. Sections 2 and 3 are on transfer of (respectively) rights and liabilities, and replace ss. 1 and 2 of the 1855 Act. Section 4 is on representations in bills of lading, covered in chapter 19, and replaces s. 3 of the 1855 Act.

This provision can be found at http://www.legislation.gov.uk/ukpga/1992/50/contents, or in Westlaw or Lexis, should you have access.

The Act

An Act to replace the Bills of Lading Act 1855 with new provision with respect to bills of lading and certain other shipping documents. [16th July 1992]

Be it enacted by the Queen's most Excellent Majesty, by and with the advice and consent of the Lords Spiritual and Temporal, and Commons, in this present Parliament assembled, and by the authority of the same, as follows:–

1. Shipping documents etc. to which Act applies.

(1) This Act applies to the following documents, that is to say–

    (a)   any bill of lading;

    (b)   any sea waybill; and

    (c)   any ship's delivery order.

(2) References in this Act to a bill of lading–

    (a)   do not include references to a document which is incapable of transfer either by indorsement or, as a bearer bill, by delivery without indorsement;[1] but

    (b)   subject to that, do include references to a received for shipment bill of lading.

(3) References in this Act to a sea waybill are references to any document which is not a bill of lading but–

    (a)   is such a receipt for goods as contains or evidences a contract for the carriage of goods by sea; and

    (b)   identifies the person to whom delivery of the goods is to be made by the carrier in accordance with that contract.

---

1 So straight bills are excluded, but fall within the definition of waybills, for the purposes of this Act.

(4) References in this Act to a ship's delivery order are references to any document which is neither a bill of lading nor a sea waybill but contains an undertaking which–

(a) is given under or for the purposes of a contract for the carriage of goods to which the document relates, or to goods which include those goods; and

(b) is an undertaking by the carrier to a person identified in the document to deliver the goods to which the document relates to that person.

(5) The Secretary of State may by regulations make provision for the application of this Act to cases where a telecommunication system or any other information technology is used for effecting transactions corresponding to–

(a) the issue of a document to which this Act applies;

(b) the indorsement, delivery or other transfer of such a document; or

(c) the doing of anything else in relation to such a document.

(6) Regulations under subsection (5) above may–

(a) make any such modifications of the following provisions of this Act as the Secretary of State considers appropriate in connection with the application of this Act to any case mentioned in that subsection; and

(b) contain supplemental, incidental, consequential and transitional provision;

and the power to make regulations under that subsection shall be exercisable by statutory instrument subject to annulment in pursuance of a resolution of either House of Parliament.[2]

2. Rights under shipping documents.

(1) Subject to the following provisions of this section, a person who becomes–

(a) the lawful holder of a bill of lading;

(b) the person who (without being an original party to the contract of carriage) is the person to whom delivery of the goods to which the sea waybill relates is to be made by the carrier in accordance with the contract;[3] or

(c) the person to whom delivery of the goods to which a ship's delivery order relates is to be made in accordance with the undertaking contained in the order,

shall (by virtue of becoming the holder of the bill, or, as the case may be, the person to whom delivery is to be made) have transferred to him and vested in him all rights of suit under the contract of carriage as if he had been a party to that contract.

(2) Where, when a person becomes the lawful holder of a bill of lading, possession of the bill no longer gives a right (as against the carrier) to possession of the goods to which the bill relates, that person shall not have any rights transferred to him by virtue of subsection (1) above unless he becomes the holder of the bill–

(a) by virtue of a transaction effected in pursuance of any contractual or other arrangements made before the time when such a right of possession ceased to attach to possession of the bill; or

---

2 No regulations have been made.
3 No need to become holder.

(b)   as a result of the rejection to that person by another person of goods or documents delivered to the other person in pursuance of any such arrangements.

(3)   The rights vested in any person by virtue of the operation of subsection (1) above in relation to a ship's delivery order–

(a)   shall be so vested subject to the terms of the order; and

(b)   where the goods to which the order relates form a part only of the goods to which the contract of carriage relates, shall be confined to rights in respect of the goods to which the order relates.

(4)   Where, in the case of any document to which this Act applies–

(a)   a person with any interest or right in or in relation to goods to which the document relates sustains loss or damage in consequence of a breach of the contract of carriage; but

(b)   subsection (1) above operates in relation to that document so the rights of suit in respect of that breach are vested in another person,

the other person shall be entitled to exercise those rights for the benefit of the person who sustained the loss or damage to the same extent as they could have been exercised if they had been vested in the person for whose benefit they are exercised.

(5)   Where rights are transferred by virtue of the operation of subsection (1) above in relation to any document, the transfer for which that subsection provides shall extinguish any entitlement to those rights which derives-

(a)   where that document is a bill of lading, from a person's having been an original party to the contract of carriage; or

(b)   in the case of any document to which this Act applies, from the previous operation of that subsection in relation to that document;

but the operation of that subsection shall be without prejudice to any rights which derive from a person's having been an original party to the contract contained in, or evidenced by, a sea waybill and, in relation to a ship's delivery order, shall be without prejudice to any rights deriving otherwise than from the previous operation of that subsection in relation to that order.

3. Liabilities under shipping documents.

(1)   Where subsection (1) of section 2 of this act operates in relation to any document to which this act applies and the person in whom rights are vested by virtue of that subsection–

(a)   takes or demands delivery from the carrier of any goods to which the document relates;

(b)   makes a claim under the contract of carriage against the carrier in respect of any of those goods; or

(c)   is a person who, at a time before those rights were vested in him, took or demanded delivery from the carrier of any of these goods,

that person shall (by virtue of taking or demanding delivery or making the claim or, in a case falling within paragraph (c) above, of having the rights vested in him) become subject to the same liabilities under that contract as if he had been party to that contract.

(2)   Where the goods to which a ship's delivery order relates form a part only of the goods to which the contract of carriage relates, the liabilities to which any person is subject by virtue of the operation of this section in relation to that order shall exclude liabilities in respect of any goods to which the order does not relate.

(3)   This section, so far as it imposes liabilities under any contract on any person, shall be without prejudice to the liabilities under the contract of any person as an original party to the contract.

[Note: Unlike ss. 2 and 3, s. 4 is not about transferring rights and liabilities, but is another attempt to reverse *Grant v Norway* (1851) 10 CB 665, in section [19.8].]

4. Representations in bills of lading.

A bill of lading which[4]

   (a)   represents goods to have been shipped on board a vessel or to have been received for shipment on board a vessel; and

   (b)   has been signed by the master of the vessel or by a person who was not the master but had the express, implied or apparent authority of the carrier to sign bills of lading,

shall, in favour of a person who had become the lawful holder of the bill, be conclusive evidence against the carrier of the shipment of the goods or, as the case may be, of their receipt for shipment.

5. Interpretation etc.

(1)   In this Act–
"bill of lading", "sea waybill" and "ship's delivery order" shall be construed in accordance with section 1 above;
      "the contract of carriage"–

   (a)   in relation to a bill of lading or sea waybill, means the contract contained in or evidenced by that bill or waybill;[5] and

   (b)   in relation to a ship's delivery order, means the contract under or for the purposes of which the undertaking contained in the order is given;

      "holder", in relation to a bill of lading, shall be construed in accordance with subsection (2) below;
      "information technology" includes any computer or other technology by means of which information or other matter may be recorded or communicated without being reduced to documentary form; and
      "telecommunication system" has the same meaning as in the Telecommunications Act 1984.

(2)   References in this Act to the holder of a bill of lading are references to any of the following persons, that is to say–

   (a)   a person with possession of the bill who, by virtue of being the person identified in the bill, is the consignee of the goods to which the bill relates;[6]

---

4 This section applies only to bills of lading, which as seen above, does not include straight bills.
5 A change since 1855, which had only "contained in".
6 Must be a consignee or order bill – otherwise it would be a waybill, not a bill of lading.

(b)   a person with possession of the bill as a result of the completion, by delivery of the bill, of any indorsement of the bill or, in the case of a bearer bill, of any other transfer of the bill;

(c)   a person with possession of the bill as a result of any transaction by virtue of which he would have become a holder falling within paragraph (a) or (b) above had not the transaction been effected at a time when possession of the bill no longer gave a right (as against the carrier) to possession of the goods to which the bill relates;

and a person shall be regarded for the purposes of this Act as having become the lawful holder of a bill of lading wherever he has become the holder of the bill in good faith.

(3)   References in this Act to a person's being identified in a document include references to his being identified by a description which allows for the identity of the person in question to be varied, in accordance with the terms of the document, after its issue; and the reference to section 1(3)(b) of this Act to a document's identifying a person shall be construed accordingly.

(4)   Without prejudice to sections 2(2) and 4 above, nothing in this Act shall preclude its operation in relation to a case where the goods to which a document relates–

(a)   cease to exist after the issue of the document; or

(b)   cannot be identified (whether because they are mixed with other goods or for any other reason);

and references in this Act to the goods to which a document relates shall be construed accordingly.

(5)   The preceding provisions of this Act shall have effect without prejudice to the application, in relation to any case, of the rules (the Hague-Visby Rules) which for the time being have the force of law by virtue of section 1 of the Carriage of Goods by Sea Act 1971.

6. Short title, repeal, commencement and extent.

(1)   This Act may be cited as the Carriage of Goods by Sea Act 1992.

(2)   The Bills of Lading Act 1855 is hereby repealed.

(3)   This Act shall come into force at the end of the period of two months beginning with the day on which it is passed, but nothing in the Act shall have effect in relation to any document issued before the coming into force of this Act.

(4)   This Act shall not extend to Northern Ireland.

Appendix C

Hamburg Rules

Author's note

This text, and also explanatory notes, can be found at UNCITRAL's website: http://www.uncitral.org/pdf/english/texts/transport/hamburg/hamburg_rules_e.pdf. Only the general liability regime provisions are set out here, as a contrast with Hague-Visby. See further the coverage in chapter 21.

Part I. General provisions

Article 1. Definitions

In this Convention:

(1) "Carrier" means any person by whom or in whose name a contract of carriage of goods by sea has been concluded with a shipper.

(2) "Actual carrier" means any person to whom the performance of the carriage of the goods, or of part of the carriage, has been entrusted by the carrier, and includes any other person to whom such performance has been entrusted.

(3) "Shipper" means any person by whom or in whose name or on whose behalf a contract of carriage of goods by sea has been concluded with a carrier, or any person by whom or in whose name or on whose behalf the goods are actually delivered to the carrier in relation to the contract of carriage by sea.

(4) "Consignee" means the person entitled to take delivery of the goods.

(5) "Goods" includes live animals; where the goods are consolidated in a container, pallet or similar article of transport or where they are packed, goods includes such article of transport or packaging if supplied by the shipper.

(6) "Contract of carriage by sea" means any contract whereby the carrier undertakes against payment of freight to carry goods by sea from one port to another; however, a contract which involves carriage by sea and also carriage by some other means is deemed to be a contract of carriage by sea for the purposes of this Convention only in so far as it relates to the carriage by sea.

(7) "Bill of lading" means a document which evidences a contract of carriage by sea and the taking over or loading of the goods by the carrier, and by which the carrier undertakes to deliver the goods against surrender of the document. A provision in the document that the goods are

to be delivered to the order of a named person, or to order, or to bearer, constitutes such an undertaking.

(8)   "Writing" includes, *inter alia*, telegram and telex.

Article 2. Scope of application

(1)   The provisions of this Convention are applicable to all contracts of carriage by sea between two different States, if:

   (a)   the port of loading as provided for in the contract of carriage by sea is located in a Contracting State, or

   (b)   the port of discharge as provided for in the contract of carriage by sea is located in a Contracting State,[1] or

   (c)   one of the optional ports of discharge provided for in the contract of carriage by sea is the actual port of discharge and such port is located in a Contracting State, or

   (d)   the bill of lading or other document evidencing the contract of carriage by sea is issued in a Contracting State, or

   (e)   the bill of lading or other document evidencing the contract of carriage by sea provides that the provisions of this Convention or the legislation of any State giving effect to them are to govern the contract.

(2)   The provisions of this Convention are applicable without regard to the nationality of the ship, the carrier, the actual carrier, the shipper, the consignee or any other interested person.

(3)   The provisions of this Convention are not applicable to charter-parties. However, where a bill of lading is issued pursuant to a charter-party, the provisions of the Convention apply to such a bill of lading if it governs the relation between the carrier and the holder of the bill of lading, not being the charterer.

(4)   If a contract provides for future carriage of goods in a series of shipments during an agreed period, the provisions of this Convention apply to each shipment. However, where a shipment is made under a charter-party, the provisions of paragraph 3 of this article apply.

Article 3. Interpretation of the Convention

In the interpretation and application of the provisions of this Convention regard shall be had to its international character and to the need to promote uniformity.

Part II. Liability of the carrier

Article 4. Period of responsibility

(1)   The responsibility of the carrier for the goods under this Convention covers the period during which the carrier is in charge of the goods at the port of loading, during the carriage and at the port of discharge.

---

1   No equivalent in Hague-Visby.

(2)　For the purpose of paragraph 1 of this article, the carrier is deemed to be in charge of the goods

    (a)　from the time he has taken over the goods from:

        (i)　the shipper, or a person acting on his behalf; or

        (ii)　an authority or other third party to whom, pursuant to law or regulations applicable at the port of loading, the goods must be handed over for shipment;

    (b)　until the time he has delivered the goods:

        (i)　by handing over the goods to the consignee; or

        (ii)　in cases where the consignee does not receive the goods from the carrier, by placing them at the disposal of the consignee in accordance with the contract or with the law or with the usage of the particular trade, applicable at the port of discharge; or

        (iii)　by handing over the goods to an authority or other third party to whom, pursuant to law or regulations applicable at the port of discharge, the goods must be handed over.

(3)　In paragraphs 1 and 2 of this article, reference to the carrier or to the consignee means, in addition to the carrier or the consignee, the servants or agents, respectively of the carrier or the consignee.

Article 5. Basis of liability[2]

(1)　The carrier is liable for loss resulting from loss of or damage to the goods, as well as from delay in delivery,[3] if the occurrence which caused the loss, damage or delay took place while the goods were in his charge as defined in article 4, unless the carrier proves that he, his servants or agents took all measures that could reasonably be required to avoid the occurrence and its consequences.

(2)　Delay in delivery occurs when the goods have not been delivered at the port of discharge provided for in the contract of carriage by sea within the time expressly agreed upon or, in the absence of such agreement, within the time which it would be reasonable to require of a diligent carrier, having regard to the circumstances of the case.

(3)　The person entitled to make a claim for the loss of goods may treat the goods as lost if they have not been delivered as required by article 4 within 60 consecutive days following the expiry of the time for delivery according to paragraph 2 of this article.

(4)　(a) The carrier is liable

        (i)　for loss of or damage to the goods or delay in delivery caused by fire, if the claimant proves that the fire arose from fault or neglect on the part of the carrier, his servants or agents;

        (ii)　for such loss, damage or delay in delivery which is proved by the claimant to have resulted from the fault or neglect of the carrier, his servants or agents in taking all measures that could reasonably be required to put out the fire and avoid or mitigate its consequences.

    (b)　In case of fire on board the ship affecting the goods, if the claimant or the carrier so

---

2　Note no excepted perils.

3　No explicit delay liability in Hague-Visby.

desires, a survey in accordance with shipping practices must be held into the cause and circumstances of the fire, and a copy of the surveyors report shall be made available on demand to the carrier and the claimant.

(5) With respect to live animals, the carrier is not liable for loss, damage or delay in delivery resulting from any special risks inherent in that kind of carriage. If the carrier proves that he has complied with any special instructions given to him by the shipper respecting the animals and that, in the circumstances of the case, the loss, damage or delay in delivery could be attributed to such risks, it is presumed that the loss, damage or delay in delivery was so caused, unless there is proof that all or a part of the loss, damage or delay in delivery resulted from fault or neglect on the part of the carrier, his servants or agents.

(6) The carrier is not liable, except in general average, where loss, damage or delay in delivery resulted from measures to save life or from reasonable measures to save property at sea.

(7) Where fault or neglect on the part of the carrier, his servants or agents combines with another cause to produce loss, damage or delay in delivery, the carrier is liable only to the extent that the loss, damage or delay in delivery is attributable to such fault or neglect, provided that the carrier proves the amount of the loss, damage or delay in delivery not attributable thereto.

Article 6. Limits of liability

(1) (a) The liability of the carrier for loss resulting from loss of or damage to goods according to the provisions of article 5 is limited to an amount equivalent to 835 units of account per package or other shipping unit or 2.5 units of account per kilogram of gross weight of the goods lost or damaged, whichever is the higher.[4]

(b) The liability of the carrier for delay in delivery according to the provisions of article 5 is limited to an amount equivalent to two and a half times the freight payable for the goods delayed, but not exceeding the total freight payable under the contract of carriage of goods by sea.

(c) In no case shall the aggregate liability of the carrier, under both subparagraphs (a) and (b) of this paragraph, exceed the limitation which would be established under subparagraph (a) of this paragraph for total loss of the goods with respect to which such liability was incurred.

(2) For the purpose of calculating which amount is the higher in accordance with paragraph 1 (*a*) of this article, the following rules apply:

(a) Where a container, pallet or similar article of transport is used to consolidate goods, the package or other shipping units enumerated in the bill of lading, if issued, or otherwise in any other document evidencing the contract of carriage by sea, as packed in such article of transport are deemed packages or shipping units. Except as aforesaid the goods in such article of transport are deemed one shipping unit.

(b) In cases where the article of transport itself has been lost or damaged, that article of transport, if not owned or otherwise supplied by the carrier, is considered one separate shipping unit.

(3) Unit of account means the unit of account mentioned in article 26.

---

4 25 per cent higher than Hague-Visby but, like Hague-Visby, not inflation-proofed.

(4)   By agreement between the carrier and the shipper, limits of liability exceeding those provided for in paragraph 1 may be fixed.

Article 7. Application to non-contractual claims[5]

(1)   The defences and limits of liability provided for in this Convention apply in any action against the carrier in respect of loss of or damage to the goods covered by the contract of carriage by sea, as well as of delay in delivery whether the action is founded in contract, in tort or otherwise.

(2)   If such an action is brought against a servant or agent of the carrier, such servant or agent, if he proves that he acted within the scope of his employment, is entitled to avail himself of the defences and limits of liability which the carrier is entitled to invoke under this Convention.

(3)   Except as provided in article 8, the aggregate of the amounts recoverable from the carrier and from any persons referred to in paragraph 2 of this article shall not exceed the limits of liability provided for in this Convention.

Article 8. Loss of right to limit responsibility

(1)   The carrier is not entitled to the benefit of the limitation of liability provided for in article 6 if it is proved that the loss, damage or delay in delivery resulted from an act or omission of the carrier done with the intent to cause such loss, damage or delay, or recklessly and with knowledge that such loss, damage or delay would probably result.

(2)   Notwithstanding the provisions of paragraph 2 of article 7, a servant or agent of the carrier is not entitled to the benefit of the limitation of liability provided for in article 6 if it is proved that the loss, damage or delay in delivery resulted from an act or omission of such servant or agent, done with the intent to cause such loss, damage or delay, or recklessly and with knowledge that such loss, damage or delay would probably result.

Article 9. Deck cargo

(1)   The carrier is entitled to carry the goods on deck only if such carriage is in accordance with an agreement with the shipper or with the usage of the particular trade or is required by statutory rules or regulations.

(2)   If the carrier and the shipper have agreed that the goods shall or may be carried on deck, the carrier must insert in the bill of lading or other document evidencing the contract of carriage by sea a statement to that effect. In the absence of such a statement the carrier has the burden of proving that an agreement for carriage on deck has been entered into; however, the carrier is not entitled to invoke such an agreement against a third party, including a consignee, who has acquired the bill of lading in good faith.

(3)   Where the goods have been carried on deck contrary to the provisions of paragraph 1 of this article or where the carrier may not under paragraph 2 of this article invoke an agreement for carriage on deck, the carrier, notwithstanding the provisions of paragraph 1 of article 5, is liable for loss of or damage to the goods, as well as for delay in delivery, resulting solely from

---

5 A rather more extensive equivalent of Art. IV bis of Hague-Visby.

the carriage on deck, and the extent of his liability is to be determined in accordance with the provisions of article 6 or article 8 of this Convention, as the case may be.

(4) Carriage of goods on deck contrary to express agreement for carriage under deck is deemed to be an act or omission of the carrier within the meaning of article 8.

Article 10. Liability of the carrier and actual carrier[6]

(1) Where the performance of the carriage or part thereof has been entrusted to an actual carrier, whether or not in pursuance of a liberty under the contract of carriage by sea to do so, the carrier nevertheless remains responsible for the entire carriage according to the provisions of this Convention. The carrier is responsible, in relation to the carriage performed by the actual carrier, for the acts and omissions of the actual carrier and of his servants and agents acting within the scope of their employment.

(2) All the provisions of this Convention governing the responsibility of the carrier also apply to the responsibility of the actual carrier for the carriage performed by him. The provisions of paragraphs 2 and 3 of article 7 and of paragraph 2 of article 8 apply if an action is brought against a servant or agent of the actual carrier.

(3) Any special agreement under which the carrier assumes obligations not imposed by this Convention or waives rights conferred by this Convention affects the actual carrier only if agreed to by him expressly and in writing. Whether or not the actual carrier has so agreed, the carrier nevertheless remains bound by the obligations or waivers resulting from such special agreement.

(4) Where and to the extent that both the carrier and the actual carrier are liable, their liability is joint and several.

(5) The aggregate of the amounts recoverable from the carrier, the actual carrier and their servants and agents shall not exceed the limits of liability provided for in this Convention.

(6) Nothing in this article shall prejudice any right of recourse as between the carrier and the actual carrier.

Article 11. Through carriage

(1) Notwithstanding the provisions of paragraph 1 of article 10, where a contract of carriage by sea provides explicitly that a specified part of the carriage covered by the said contract is to be performed by a named person other than the carrier, the contract may also provide that the carrier is not liable for loss, damage or delay in delivery caused by an occurrence which takes place while the goods are in the charge of the actual carrier during such part of the carriage. Nevertheless, any stipulation limiting or excluding such liability is without effect if no judicial proceedings can be instituted against the actual carrier in a court competent under paragraph 1 or 2 of article 21. The burden of proving that any loss, damage or delay in delivery has been caused by such an occurrence rests upon the carrier.

(2) The actual carrier is responsible in accordance with the provisions of paragraph 2 of article 10 for loss, damage or delay in delivery caused by an occurrence which takes place while the goods are in his charge.

---

6 Applicable to through bills of lading, where there is transhipment.

Part III. Liability of the shippers

Article 12. General rule

The shipper is not liable for loss sustained by the carrier or the actual carrier, or for damage sustained by the ship, unless such loss or damage was caused by the fault or neglect of the shipper, his servants or agents. Nor is any servant or agent of the shipper liable for such loss or damage unless the loss or damage was caused by fault or neglect on his part.

Article 13. Special rules on dangerous goods

(1) The shipper must mark or label in a suitable manner dangerous goods as dangerous.

(2) Where the shipper hands over dangerous goods to the carrier or an actual carrier, as the case may be, the shipper must inform him of the dangerous character of the goods and, if necessary, of the precautions to be taken. If the shipper fails to do so and such carrier or actual carrier does not otherwise have knowledge of their dangerous character:

   (a) the shipper is liable to the carrier and any actual carrier for the loss resulting from the shipment of such goods, and

   (b) the goods may at any time be unloaded, destroyed or rendered innocuous, as the circumstances may require, without payment of compensation.

(3) The provisions of paragraph 2 of this article may not be invoked by any person if during the carriage he has taken the goods in his charge with knowledge of their dangerous character.

(4) If, in cases where the provisions of paragraph 2, subparagraph (b), of this article do not apply or may not be invoked, dangerous goods become an actual danger to life or property, they may be unloaded, destroyed or rendered innocuous, as the circumstances may require, without payment of compensation except where there is an obligation to contribute in general average or where the carrier is liable in accordance with the provisions of article 5.

Part IV. Transport documents

Article 14. Issue of bill of lading

(1) When the carrier or the actual carrier takes the goods in his charge, the carrier must, on demand of the shipper, issue to the shipper a bill of lading.

(2) The bill of lading may be signed by a person having authority from the carrier. A bill of lading signed by the master of the ship carrying the goods is deemed to have been signed on behalf of the carrier.

(3) The signature on the bill of lading may be in handwriting, printed in facsimile, perforated, stamped, in symbols, or made by any other mechanical or electronic means, if not inconsistent with the law of the country where the bill of lading is issued.

Article 15. Contents of bill of lading

(1) The bill of lading must include, *inter alia*, the following particulars:

   (a) the general nature of the goods, the leading marks necessary for identification of the goods, an express statement, if applicable, as to the dangerous character of the goods, the number of packages or pieces, and the weight of the goods or their quantity otherwise expressed, all such particulars as furnished by the shipper;

(b)   the apparent condition of the goods;

(c)   the name and principal place of business of the carrier;

(d)   the name of the shipper;

(e)   the consignee if named by the shipper;

(f)   the port of loading under the contract of carriage by sea and the date on which the goods were taken over by the carrier at the port of loading;

(g)   the port of discharge under the contract of carriage by sea;

(h)   the number of originals of the bill of lading, if more than one;

(i)   the place of issuance of the bill of lading;

(j)   the signature of the carrier or a person acting on his behalf;

(k)   the freight to the extent payable by the consignee or other indication that freight is payable by him;

(l)   the statement referred to in paragraph 3 of article 23;

(m)   the statement, if applicable, that the goods shall or may be carried on deck;

(n)   the date or the period of delivery of the goods at the port of discharge if expressly agreed upon between the parties; and

(o)   any increased limit or limits of liability where agreed in accordance with paragraph 4 of article 6.

(2)   After the goods have been loaded on board, if the shipper so demands, the carrier must issue to the shipper a "shipped" bill of lading which, in addition to the particulars required under paragraph 1 of this article, must state that the goods are on board a named ship or ships, and the date or dates of loading. If the carrier has previously issued to the shipper a bill of lading or other document of title with respect to any of such goods, on request of the carrier the shipper must surrender such document in exchange for a "shipped" bill of lading. The carrier may amend any previously issued document in order to meet the shippers demand for a "shipped" bill of lading if, as amended, such document includes all the information required to be contained in a "shipped" bill of lading.

(3)   The absence in the bill of lading of one or more particulars referred to in this article does not affect the legal character of the document as a bill of lading provided that it nevertheless meets the requirements set out in paragraph 7 of article 1.

Article 16. Bills of lading: reservations and evidentiary effect

(1)   If the bill of lading contains particulars concerning the general nature, leading marks, number of packages of pieces, weight or quantity of the goods which the carrier or other person issuing the bill of lading on his behalf knows or has reasonable grounds to suspect do not accurately represent the goods actually taken over or, where a "shipped" bill of lading is issued, loaded, or if he had no reasonable means of checking such particulars, the carrier or such other person must insert in the bill of lading a reservation specifying these inaccuracies, grounds of suspicion or the absence of reasonable means of checking.

(2)   If the carrier or other person issuing the bill of lading on his behalf fails to note on the bill of lading the apparent condition of the goods, he is deemed to have noted on the bill of lading that the goods were in apparent good condition.

(3)   Except for particulars in respect of which and to the extent to which a reservation permitted under paragraph 1 of this article has been entered:

(a)   the bill of lading is *prima facie* evidence of the taking over or, where a "shipped" bill of lading is issued, loading, by the carrier of the goods as described in the bill of lading; and

(b)   proof to the contrary by the carrier is not admissible if the bill of lading has been transferred to a third party, including a consignee, who in good faith has acted in reliance on the description of the goods therein.

(4)   A bill of lading which does not, as provided in paragraph 1, subparagraph (k), of article 15, set forth the freight or otherwise indicate that freight is payable by the consignee or does not set forth demurrage incurred at the port of loading payable by the consignee, is *prima facie* evidence that no freight or such demurrage is payable by him. However, proof to the contrary by the carrier is not admissible when the bill of lading has been transferred to a third party, including a consignee, who in good faith has acted in reliance on the absence in the bill of lading of any such indication.

Article 17. Guarantees by the shipper

(1)   The shipper is deemed to have guaranteed to the carrier the accuracy of particulars relating to the general nature of the goods, their marks, number, weight and quantity as furnished by him for insertion in the bill of lading. The shipper must indemnify the carrier against the loss resulting from inaccuracies in such particulars. The shipper remains liable even if the bill of lading has been transferred by him. The right of the carrier to such indemnity in no way limits his liability under the contract of carriage by sea to any person other than the shipper.

(2)   Any letter of guarantee or agreement by which the shipper undertakes to indemnify the carrier against loss resulting from the issuance of the bill of lading by the carrier, or by a person acting on his behalf, without entering a reservation relating to particulars furnished by the shipper for insertion in the bill of lading, or to the apparent condition of the goods, is void and of no effect as against any third party, including a consignee, to whom the bill of lading has been transferred.

(3)   Such a letter of guarantee or agreement is valid as against the shipper unless the carrier or the person acting on his behalf, by omitting the reservation referred to in paragraph 2 of this article, intends to defraud a third party, including a consignee, who acts in reliance on the description of the goods in the bill of lading. In the latter case, if the reservation omitted relates to particulars furnished by the shipper for insertion in the bill of lading, the carrier has no right of indemnity from the shipper pursuant to paragraph 1 of this article.

(4)   In the case of intended fraud referred to in paragraph 3 of this article, the carrier is liable, without the benefit of the limitation of liability provided for in this Convention, for the loss incurred by a third party, including a consignee, because he has acted in reliance on the description of the goods in the bill of lading.

Article 18. Documents other than bills of lading

Where a carrier issues a document other than a bill of lading to evidence the receipt of the goods to be carried, such a document is *prima facie* evidence of the conclusion of the contract of carriage by sea and the taking over by the carrier of the goods as therein described.

Part V. Claims and actions

Article 19. Notice of loss, damage or delay

[This Article is not reproduced.]

Article 20. Limitation of actions

(1) Any action relating to carriage of goods under this Convention is time-barred if judicial or arbitral proceedings have not been instituted within a period of two years.
(2) The limitation period commences on the day on which the carrier has delivered the goods or part thereof or, in cases where no goods have been delivered, on the last day on which the goods should have been delivered.
(3) The day on which the limitation period commences is not included in the period.
(4) The person against whom a claim is made may at any time during the running of the limitation period extend that period by a declaration in writing to the claimant. This period may be further extended by another declaration or declarations.
(5) An action for indemnity by a person held liable may be instituted even after the expiration of the limitation period provided for in the preceding paragraphs if instituted within the time allowed by the law of the State where proceedings are instituted. However, the time allowed shall not be less than 90 days commencing from the day when the person instituting such action for indemnity has settled the claim or has been served with process in the action against himself.

[Jurisdiction and arbitration provisions are not reproduced.]

Part VI. Supplementary provisions

Article 23. Contractual stipulations

(1) Any stipulation in a contract of carriage by sea, in a bill of lading, or in any other document evidencing the contract of carriage by sea is null and void to the extent that it derogates, directly or indirectly, from the provisions of this Convention. The nullity of such a stipulation does not affect the validity of the other provisions of the contract or document of which it forms a part. A clause assigning benefit of insurance of goods in favour of the carrier, or any similar clause, is null and void.
(2) Notwithstanding the provisions of paragraph 1 of this article, a carrier may increase his responsibilities and obligations under this Convention.
(3) Where a bill of lading or any other document evidencing the contract of carriage by sea is issued, it must contain a statement that the carriage is subject to the provisions of this Convention which nullify any stipulation derogating therefrom to the detriment of the shipper or the consignee.
(4) Where the claimant in respect of the goods has incurred loss as a result of a stipulation which is null and void by virtue of the present article, or as a result of the omission of the statement referred to in paragraph 3 of this article, the carrier must pay compensation to the extent required in order to give the claimant compensation in accordance with the provisions of this Convention for any loss of or damage to the goods as well as for delay in delivery. The carrier must, in

addition, pay compensation for costs incurred by the claimant for the purpose of exercising his right, provided that costs incurred in the action where the foregoing provision is invoked are to be determined in accordance with the law of the State where proceedings are instituted.

Article 24. General average

(1)   Nothing in this Convention shall prevent the application of provisions in the contract of carriage by sea or national law regarding the adjustment of general average.

(2)   With the exception of article 20, the provisions of this Convention relating to the liability of the carrier for loss of or damage to the goods also determine whether the consignee may refuse contribution in general average and the liability of the carrier to indemnify the consignee in respect of any such contribution made or any salvage paid.

Article 25. Other conventions

(1)   This Convention does not modify the rights or duties of the carrier, the actual carrier and their servants and agents provided for in international conventions or national law relating to the limitation of liability of owners of seagoing ships.

(2)   The provisions of articles 21 and 22 of this Convention do not prevent the application of the mandatory provisions of any other multilateral convention already in force at the date of this Convention relating to matters dealt with in the said articles, provided that the dispute arises exclusively between parties having their principal place of business in States members of such other convention. However, this paragraph does not affect the application of paragraph 4 of article 22 of this Convention.

(3)   No liability shall arise under the provisions of this Convention for damage caused by a nuclear incident if the operator of a nuclear installation is liable for such damage:

(a)   under either the Paris Convention of 29 July 1960 on Third Party Liability in the Field of Nuclear Energy as amended by the Additional Protocol of 28 January 1964, or the Vienna Convention of 21 May 1963 on Civil Liability for Nuclear Damage, or

(b)   by virtue of national law governing the liability for such damage, provided that such law is in all respects as favourable to persons who may suffer damage as is either the Paris Convention or the Vienna Convention.

(4)   No liability shall arise under the provisions of this Convention for any loss of or damage to or delay in delivery of luggage for which the carrier is responsible under any international convention or national law relating to the carriage of passengers and their luggage by sea.

(5)   Nothing contained in this Convention prevents a Contracting State from applying any other international convention which is already in force at the date of this Convention and which applies mandatorily to contracts of carriage of goods primarily by a mode of transport other than transport by sea. This provision also applies to any subsequent revision or amendment of such international convention.

Article 26. Unit of account

(1)   The unit of account referred to in article 6 of this Convention is the special drawing right as defined by the International Monetary Fund. The amounts mentioned in article 6 are to be

converted into the national currency of a State according to the value of such currency at the date of judgement or the date agreed upon by the parties. The value of a national currency, in terms of the special drawing right, of a Contracting State which is a member of the International Monetary Fund is to be calculated in accordance with the method of valuation applied by the International Monetary Fund in effect at the date in question for its operations and transactions. The value of a national currency, in terms of the special drawing right, of a Contracting State which is not a member of the International Monetary Fund is to be calculated in a manner determined by that State.

(2)   Nevertheless, those States which are not members of the International Monetary Fund and whose law does not permit the application of the provisions of paragraph 1 of this article may, at the time of signature, or at the time of ratification, acceptance, approval or accession or at any time thereafter, declare that the limits of liability provided for in this Convention to be applied in their territories shall be fixed as 12,500 monetary units per package or other shipping unit or 37.5 monetary units per kilogram of gross weight of the goods.

(3)   The monetary unit referred to in paragraph 2 of this article corresponds to sixty-five and a half milligrams of gold of millesimal fineness nine hundred. The conversion of the amounts referred to in paragraph 2 into the national currency is to be made according to the law of the State concerned.

(4)   The calculation mentioned in the last sentence of paragraph 1 and the conversion mentioned in paragraph 3 of this article is to be made in such a manner as to express in the national currency of the Contracting State as far as possible the same real value for the amounts in article 6 as is expressed there in units of account. Contracting States must communicate to the depositary the manner of calculation pursuant to paragraph 1 of this article, or the result of the conversion mentioned in paragraph 3 of this article, as the case may be, at the time of signature or when depositing their instruments of ratification, acceptance, approval or accession, or when availing themselves of the option provided for in paragraph 2 of this article and whenever there is a change in the manner of such calculation or in the result of such conversion.

[Part VII, Final Clauses, is not set out.]

Appendix D

Rotterdam Rules (selected Articles)

Author's note

The full text of the Rotterdam Rules (United Nations Convention on Contracts for the International Carriage of Goods Wholly or Partly by Sea) can be found on UNCITRAL's site, at http://www.unci tral.org/pdf/english/texts/transport/rotterdam_rules/Rotterdam-Rules-E.pdf. This appendix sets out those parts which relate to carrier liability, so that these can be contrasted with the Hague-Visby and Hamburg Rules. See further the coverage in chapter 21.

Chapter 1: General provisions

Article 1: Definitions
For the purposes of this Convention:

(1) "Contract of carriage" means a contract in which a carrier, against the payment of freight, undertakes to carry goods from one place to another. The contract shall provide for carriage by sea and may provide for carriage by other modes of transport in addition to the sea carriage.

(2) "Volume contract" means a contract of carriage that provides for the carriage of a specified quantity of goods in a series of shipments during an agreed period of time. The specification of the quantity may include a minimum, a maximum or a certain range.

(3) "Liner transportation" means a transportation service that is offered to the public through publication or similar means and includes transportation by ships operating on a regular schedule between specified ports in accordance with publicly available timetables of sailing dates.

(4) "Non-liner transportation" means any transportation that is not liner transportation.

(5) "Carrier" means a person that enters into a contract of carriage with a shipper.

(6) (a) "Performing party" means a person other than the carrier that performs or undertakes to perform any of the carrier's obligations under a contract of carriage with respect to the receipt, loading, handling, stowage, carriage, care, unloading or delivery of the goods, to the extent that such person acts, either directly or indirectly, at the carrier's request or under the carrier's supervision or control.

(b) "Performing party" does not include any person that is retained, directly or indirectly, by a shipper, by a documentary shipper, by the controlling party or by the consignee instead of by the carrier.

(7) "Maritime performing party" means a performing party to the extent that it performs or undertakes to perform any of the carrier's obligations during the period between the arrival of the goods at the port of loading of a ship and their departure from the port of discharge of a ship. An inland carrier is a maritime performing party only if it performs or undertakes to perform its services exclusively within a port area.

(8) "Shipper" means a person that enters into a contract of carriage with a carrier.

(9) "Documentary shipper" means a person, other than the shipper, that accepts to be named as "shipper" in the transport document or electronic transport record.

(10) "Holder" means:

  (a) A person that is in possession of a negotiable transport document; and (i) if the document is an order document, is identified in it as the shipper or the consignee, or is the person to which the document is duly endorsed; or (ii) if the document is a blank endorsed order document or bearer document, is the bearer thereof; or

  (b) The person to which a negotiable electronic transport record has been issued or transferred in accordance with the procedures referred to in article 9, paragraph 1.

(11) "Consignee" means a person entitled to delivery of the goods under a contract of carriage or a transport document or electronic transport record.

  . . .

(14) "Transport document" means a document issued under a contract of carriage by the carrier that:

  (a) Evidences the carrier's or a performing party's receipt of goods under a contract of carriage; and

  (b) Evidences or contains a contract of carriage.

(15) "Negotiable transport document" means a transport document that indicates, by wording such as "to order" or "negotiable" or other appropriate wording recognized as having the same effect by the law applicable to the document, that the goods have been consigned to the order of the shipper, to the order of the consignee, or to bearer, and is not explicitly stated as being "non-negotiable" or "not negotiable".

(16) "Non-negotiable transport document" means a transport document that is not a negotiable transport document.

(17) "Electronic communication" means information generated, sent, received or stored by electronic, optical, digital or similar means with the result that the information communicated is accessible so as to be usable for subsequent reference.

(18) "Electronic transport record" means information in one or more messages issued by electronic communication under a contract of carriage by a carrier, including information logically associated with the electronic transport record by attachments or otherwise linked to the electronic transport record contemporaneously with or subsequent to its issue by the carrier, so as to become part of the electronic transport record, that:

  (a) Evidences the carrier's or a performing party's receipt of goods under a contract of carriage; and

  (b) Evidences or contains a contract of carriage.

(19) "Negotiable electronic transport record" means an electronic transport record:

  (a) That indicates, by wording such as "to order", or "negotiable", or other appropriate wording recognized as having the same effect by the law applicable to the record, that

the goods have been consigned to the order of the shipper or to the order of the consignee, and is not explicitly stated as being "non-negotiable" or "not negotiable"; and

(b) The use of which meets the requirements of article 9, paragraph 1.

(20) "Non-negotiable electronic transport record" means an electronic transport record that is not a negotiable electronic transport record.

(21) The "issuance" of a negotiable electronic transport record means the issuance of the record in accordance with procedures that ensure that the record is subject to exclusive control from its creation until it ceases to have any effect or validity.

(22) The "transfer" of a negotiable electronic transport record means the transfer of exclusive control over the record.

(23) "Contract particulars" means any information relating to the contract of carriage or to the goods (including terms, notations, signatures and endorsements) that is in a transport document or an electronic transport record.

(24) "Goods" means the wares, merchandise, and articles of every kind whatsoever that a carrier undertakes to carry under a contract of carriage and includes the packing and any equipment and container not supplied by or on behalf of the carrier.

(25) "Ship" means any vessel used to carry goods by sea.

(26) "Container" means any type of container, transportable tank or flat, swapbody, or any similar unit load used to consolidate goods, and any equipment ancillary to such unit load.

(27) "Vehicle" means a road or railroad cargo vehicle.

(28) "Freight" means the remuneration payable to the carrier for the carriage of goods under a contract of carriage.

. . .

Article 2: Interpretation of this Convention

In the interpretation of this Convention, regard is to be had to its international character and to the need to promote uniformity in its application and the observance of good faith in international trade.

[Article 3 sets out form requirements.]

Article 4: Applicability of defences and limits of liability[1]

(1) Any provision of this Convention that may provide a defence for, or limit the liability of, the carrier applies in any judicial or arbitral proceeding, whether founded in contract, in tort, or otherwise, that is instituted in respect of loss of, damage to, or delay in delivery of goods covered by a contract of carriage or for the breach of any other obligation under this Convention against:

(a) The carrier or a maritime performing party;

(b) The master, crew or any other person that performs services on board the ship; or

(c) Employees of the carrier or a maritime performing party.

(2) Any provision of this Convention that may provide a defence for the shipper or the documentary shipper applies in any judicial or arbitral proceeding, whether founded in contract, in tort, or otherwise, that is instituted against the shipper, the documentary shipper, or their subcontractors, agents or employees.

---

1 The equivalent of Hague-Visby, Art. IV bis, but somewhat more extensive.

Chapter 2: Scope of application

[Note that there is no documentary requirement, unlike Hague-Visby.]

Article 5: General scope of application

(1)   Subject to article 6, this Convention applies to contracts of carriage in which the place of receipt and the place of delivery are in different States, and the port of loading of a sea carriage and the port of discharge of the same sea carriage are in different States, if, according to the contract of carriage, any one of the following places is located in a Contracting State:

    (a)   The place of receipt;
    (b)   The port of loading;
    (c)   The place of delivery; or
    (d)   The port of discharge.

(2)   This Convention applies without regard to the nationality of the vessel, the carrier, the performing parties, the shipper, the consignee, or any other interested parties.

Article 6: Specific exclusions

(1)   This Convention does not apply to the following contracts in liner transportation:

    (a)   Charter parties; and
    (b)   Other contracts for the use of a ship or of any space thereon.

(2)   This Convention does not apply to contracts of carriage in non-liner transportation except when:

    (a)   There is no charter party or other contract between the parties for the use of a ship or of any space thereon; and
    (b)   A transport document or an electronic transport record is issued.

Article 7: Application to certain parties

Notwithstanding article 6, this Convention applies as between the carrier and the consignee, controlling party or holder that is not an original party to the charter party or other contract of carriage excluded from the application of this Convention. However, this Convention does not apply as between the original parties to a contract of carriage excluded pursuant to article 6.

Chapter 3: Electronic transport records

Article 8: Use and effect of electronic transport records

Subject to the requirements set out in this Convention:

    (a)   Anything that is to be in or on a transport document under this Convention may be recorded in an electronic transport record, provided the issuance and subsequent use of an electronic transport record is with the consent of the carrier and the shipper; and
    (b)   The issuance, exclusive control, or transfer of an electronic transport record has the same effect as the issuance, possession, or transfer of a transport document.

Article 9: Procedures for use of negotiable electronic transport records

(1) The use of a negotiable electronic transport record shall be subject to procedures that provide for:

   (a) The method for the issuance and the transfer of that record to an intended holder;
   (b) An assurance that the negotiable electronic transport record retains its integrity;
   (c) The manner in which the holder is able to demonstrate that it is the holder; and
   (d) The manner of providing confirmation that delivery to the holder has been effected, or that, pursuant to articles 10, paragraph 2, or 47, subparagraphs 1 (a) (ii) and (c), the electronic transport record has ceased to have any effect or validity.

(2) The procedures in paragraph 1 of this article shall be referred to in the contract particulars and be readily ascertainable.[2]

Article 10: Replacement of negotiable transport document or negotiable electronic transport record

(1) If a negotiable transport document has been issued and the carrier and the holder agree to replace that document by a negotiable electronic transport record:

   (a) The holder shall surrender the negotiable transport document, or all of them if more than one has been issued, to the carrier;
   (b) The carrier shall issue to the holder a negotiable electronic transport record that includes a statement that it replaces the negotiable transport document; and
   (c) The negotiable transport document ceases thereafter to have any effect or validity.

(2) If a negotiable electronic transport record has been issued and the carrier and the holder agree to replace that electronic transport record by a negotiable transport document:

   (a) The carrier shall issue to the holder, in place of the electronic transport record, a negotiable transport document that includes a statement that it replaces the negotiable electronic transport record; and
   (b) The electronic transport record ceases thereafter to have any effect or validity.

Chapter 4: Obligations of the carrier

Article 11: Carriage and delivery of the goods

The carrier shall, subject to this Convention and in accordance with the terms of the contract of carriage, carry the goods to the place of destination and deliver them to the consignee.

Article 12: Period of responsibility of the carrier

(1) The period of responsibility of the carrier for the goods under this Convention begins when the carrier or a performing party receives the goods for carriage and ends when the goods are delivered.

---

2 No objective criteria for how good these procedures must be.

(2) (a) If the law or regulations of the place of receipt require the goods to be handed over to an authority or other third party from which the carrier may collect them, the period of responsibility of the carrier begins when the carrier collects the goods from the authority or other third party.

(b) If the law or regulations of the place of delivery require the carrier to hand over the goods to an authority or other third party from which the consignee may collect them, the period of responsibility of the carrier ends when the carrier hands the goods over to the authority or other third party.

(3) For the purpose of determining the carrier's period of responsibility, the parties may agree on the time and location of receipt and delivery of the goods, but a provision in a contract of carriage is void to the extent that it provides that:

(a) The time of receipt of the goods is subsequent to the beginning of their initial loading under the contract of carriage; or

(b) The time of delivery of the goods is prior to the completion of their final unloading under the contract of carriage.

Article 13: Specific obligations

(1) The carrier shall during the period of its responsibility as defined in article 12, and subject to article 26, properly and carefully receive, load, handle, stow, carry, keep, care for, unload and deliver the goods.

(2) Notwithstanding paragraph 1 of this article, and without prejudice to the other provisions in chapter 4 and to chapters 5 to 7, the carrier and the shipper may agree that the loading, handling, stowing or unloading of the goods is to be performed by the shipper, the documentary shipper or the consignee. Such an agreement shall be referred to in the contract particulars.

Article 14: Specific obligations applicable to the voyage by sea

The carrier is bound before, at the beginning of, and during the voyage by sea to exercise due diligence to:[3]

(a) Make and keep the ship seaworthy;

(b) Properly crew, equip and supply the ship and keep the ship so crewed, equipped and supplied throughout the voyage; and

(c) Make and keep the holds and all other parts of the ship in which the goods are carried, and any containers supplied by the carrier in or upon which the goods are carried, fit and safe for their reception, carriage and preservation.

Article 15: Goods that may become a danger

Notwithstanding articles 11 and 13, the carrier or a performing party may decline to receive or to load, and may take such other measures as are reasonable, including unloading, destroying, or rendering goods harmless, if the goods are, or reasonably appear likely to become during the carrier's period of responsibility, an actual danger to persons, property or the environment.

---

3 Note inclusion of "during the voyage", and note the general due diligence standard.

Article 16: Sacrifice of the goods during the voyage by sea

Notwithstanding articles 11, 13, and 14, the carrier or a performing party may sacrifice goods at sea when the sacrifice is reasonably made for the common safety or for the purpose of preserving from peril human life or other property involved in the common adventure.

Chapter 5: Liability of the carrier for loss, damage or delay

Article 17: Basis of liability

(1)   The carrier is liable for loss of or damage to the goods, as well as for delay in delivery, if the claimant proves that the loss, damage, or delay, or the event or circumstance that caused or contributed to it took place during the period of the carrier's responsibility as defined in chapter 4.

(2)   The carrier is relieved of all or part of its liability pursuant to paragraph 1 of this article if it proves that the cause or one of the causes of the loss, damage, or delay is not attributable to its fault or to the fault of any person referred to in article 18.

(3)   The carrier is also relieved of all or part of its liability pursuant to paragraph 1 of this article if, alternatively to proving the absence of fault as provided in paragraph 2 of this article, it proves that one or more of the following events or circumstances caused or contributed to the loss, damage, or delay:[4]

(a)   Act of God;

(b)   Perils, dangers, and accidents of the sea or other navigable waters;

(c)   War, hostilities, armed conflict, piracy, terrorism, riots, and civil commotions;

(d)   Quarantine restrictions; interference by or impediments created by governments, public authorities, rulers, or people including detention, arrest, or seizure not attributable to the carrier or any person referred to in article 18;

(e)   Strikes, lockouts, stoppages, or restraints of labour;

(f)   Fire on the ship;

(g)   Latent defects not discoverable by due diligence;

(h)   Act or omission of the shipper, the documentary shipper, the controlling party, or any other person for whose acts the shipper or the documentary shipper is liable pursuant to article 33 or 34;

(i)   Loading, handling, stowing, or unloading of the goods performed pursuant to an agreement in accordance with article 13, paragraph 2, unless the carrier or a performing party performs such activity on behalf of the shipper, the documentary shipper or the consignee;

(j)   Wastage in bulk or weight or any other loss or damage arising from inherent defect, quality, or vice of the goods;

(k)   Insufficiency or defective condition of packing or marking not performed by or on behalf of the carrier;

(l)   Saving or attempting to save life at sea;

(m)   Reasonable measures to save or attempt to save property at sea;

(n)   Reasonable measures to avoid or attempt to avoid damage to the environment; or

(o)   Acts of the carrier in pursuance of the powers conferred by articles 15 and 16.

---

4 Unlike Hamburg, there are excepted perils, but no equivalent of Art. IV(2)(a) of Hague-Visby.

(4)   Notwithstanding paragraph 3 of this article, the carrier is liable for all or part of the loss, damage, or delay:

   (a)   If the claimant proves that the fault of the carrier or of a person referred to in article 18 caused or contributed to the event or circumstance on which the carrier relies; or

   (b)   If the claimant proves that an event or circumstance not listed in paragraph 3 of this article contributed to the loss, damage, or delay, and the carrier cannot prove that this event or circumstance is not attributable to its fault or to the fault of any person referred to in article 18.

(5)   The carrier is also liable, notwithstanding paragraph 3 of this article, for all or part of the loss, damage, or delay if:

   (a)   The claimant proves that the loss, damage, or delay was or was probably caused by or contributed to by (i) the unseaworthiness of the ship; (ii) the improper crewing, equipping, and supplying of the ship; or (iii) the fact that the holds or other parts of the ship in which the goods are carried, or any containers supplied by the carrier in or upon which the goods are carried, were not fit and safe for reception, carriage, and preservation of the goods; and

   (b)   The carrier is unable to prove either that: (i) none of the events or circumstances referred to in subparagraph 5 (a) of this article caused the loss, damage, or delay; or (ii) it complied with its obligation to exercise due diligence pursuant to article 14.

(6)   When the carrier is relieved of part of its liability pursuant to this article, the carrier is liable only for that part of the loss, damage or delay that is attributable to the event or circumstance for which it is liable pursuant to this article.

Article 18: Liability of the carrier for other persons

The carrier is liable for the breach of its obligations under this Convention caused by the acts or omissions of:

   (a)   Any performing party;[5]
   (b)   The master or crew of the ship;
   (c)   Employees of the carrier or a performing party; or
   (d)   Any other person that performs or undertakes to perform any of the carrier's obligations under the contract of carriage, to the extent that the person acts, either directly or indirectly, at the carrier's request or under the carrier's supervision or control.

Article 19: Liability of maritime performing parties[6]

(1)   A maritime performing party is subject to the obligations and liabilities imposed on the carrier under this Convention and is entitled to the carrier's defences and limits of liability as provided for in this Convention if:

   (a)   The maritime performing party received the goods for carriage in a Contracting State, or delivered them in a Contracting State, or performed its activities with respect to the goods in a port in a Contracting State; and

---

5   Assuming a through bill, or multimodal transport.
6   Again, assuming non-contracting carriers.

(b)　The occurrence that caused the loss, damage or delay took place: (i) during the period between the arrival of the goods at the port of loading of the ship and their departure from the port of discharge from the ship; (ii) while the maritime performing party had custody of the goods; or (iii) at any other time to the extent that it was participating in the performance of any of the activities contemplated by the contract of carriage.

(2)　If the carrier agrees to assume obligations other than those imposed on the carrier under this Convention, or agrees that the limits of its liability are higher than the limits specified under this Convention, a maritime performing party is not bound by this agreement unless it expressly agrees to accept such obligations or such higher limits.

(3)　A maritime performing party is liable for the breach of its obligations under this Convention caused by the acts or omissions of any person to which it has entrusted the performance of any of the carrier's obligations under the contract of carriage under the conditions set out in paragraph 1 of this article.

(4)　Nothing in this Convention imposes liability on the master or crew of the ship or on an employee of the carrier or of a maritime performing party.

Article 20: Joint and several liability

(1)　If the carrier and one or more maritime performing parties are liable for the loss of, damage to, or delay in delivery of the goods, their liability is joint and several but only up to the limits provided for under this Convention.

(2)　Without prejudice to article 61, the aggregate liability of all such persons shall not exceed the overall limits of liability under this Convention.

Article 21: Delay[7]

Delay in delivery occurs when the goods are not delivered at the place of destination provided for in the contract of carriage within the time agreed.

Article 22: Calculation of compensation

(1)　Subject to article 59, the compensation payable by the carrier for loss of or damage to the goods is calculated by reference to the value of such goods at the place and time of delivery established in accordance with article 43.

(2)　The value of the goods is fixed according to the commodity exchange price or, if there is no such price, according to their market price or, if there is no commodity exchange price or market price, by reference to the normal value of the goods of the same kind and quality at the place of delivery.

(3)　In case of loss of or damage to the goods, the carrier is not liable for payment of any compensation beyond what is provided for in paragraphs 1 and 2 of this article except when the carrier and the shipper have agreed to calculate compensation in a different manner within the limits of chapter 16.

---

7 Not explicitly provided for in Hague-Visby.

Article 23: Notice in case of loss, damage or delay

(1) The carrier is presumed, in absence of proof to the contrary, to have delivered the goods according to their description in the contract particulars unless notice of loss of or damage to the goods, indicating the general nature of such loss or damage, was given to the carrier or the performing party that delivered the goods before or at the time of the delivery, or, if the loss or damage is not apparent, within seven working days at the place of delivery after the delivery of the goods.

(2) Failure to provide the notice referred to in this article to the carrier or the performing party shall not affect the right to claim compensation for loss of or damage to the goods under this Convention, nor shall it affect the allocation of the burden of proof set out in article 17.

(3) The notice referred to in this article is not required in respect of loss or damage that is ascertained in a joint inspection of the goods by the person to which they have been delivered and the carrier or the maritime performing party against which liability is being asserted.

(4) No compensation in respect of delay is payable unless notice of loss due to delay was given to the carrier within twenty-one consecutive days of delivery of the goods.

(5) When the notice referred to in this article is given to the performing party that delivered the goods, it has the same effect as if that notice was given to the carrier, and notice given to the carrier has the same effect as a notice given to a maritime performing party.

(6) In the case of any actual or apprehended loss or damage, the parties to the dispute shall give all reasonable facilities to each other for inspecting and tallying the goods and shall provide access to records and documents relevant to the carriage of the goods.

Chapter 6: Additional provisions relating to particular stages of carriage

Article 24: Deviation

When pursuant to applicable law a deviation constitutes a breach of the carrier's obligations, such deviation of itself shall not deprive the carrier or a maritime performing party of any defence or limitation of this Convention,[8] except to the extent provided in article 61.

Article 25: Deck cargo on ships[9]

(1) Goods may be carried on the deck of a ship only if:

(a) Such carriage is required by law;

(b) They are carried in or on containers or vehicles that are fit for deck carriage, and the decks are specially fitted to carry such containers or vehicles;

or

(c) The carriage on deck is in accordance with the contract of carriage, or the customs, usages or practices of the trade in question.

(2) The provisions of this Convention relating to the liability of the carrier apply to the loss of, damage to or delay in the delivery of goods carried on deck pursuant to paragraph 1 of this

---

8 Almost certainly intended to change English law in this regard.

9 More up to date than Hague-Visby.

article, but the carrier is not liable for loss of or damage to such goods, or delay in their delivery, caused by the special risks involved in their carriage on deck when the goods are carried in accordance with subparagraphs 1 (a) or (c) of this article.

(3) If the goods have been carried on deck in cases other than those permitted pursuant to paragraph 1 of this article, the carrier is liable for loss of or damage to the goods or delay in their delivery that is exclusively caused by their carriage on deck, and is not entitled to the defences provided for in article 17.

(4) The carrier is not entitled to invoke subparagraph 1 (c) of this article against a third party that has acquired a negotiable transport document or a negotiable electronic transport record in good faith, unless the contract particulars state that the goods may be carried on deck.

(5) If the carrier and shipper expressly agreed that the goods would be carried under deck, the carrier is not entitled to the benefit of the limitation of liability for any loss of, damage to or delay in the delivery of the goods to the extent that such loss, damage, or delay resulted from their carriage on deck.

Article 26: Carriage preceding or subsequent to sea carriage[10]

When loss of or damage to goods, or an event or circumstance causing a delay in their delivery, occurs during the carrier's period of responsibility but solely before their loading onto the ship or solely after their discharge from the ship, the provisions of this Convention do not prevail over those provisions of another international instrument that, at the time of such loss, damage or event or circumstance causing delay:

(a) Pursuant to the provisions of such international instrument would have applied to all or any of the carrier's activities if the shipper had made a separate and direct contract with the carrier in respect of the particular stage of carriage where the loss of, or damage to goods, or an event or circumstance causing delay in their delivery occurred;

(b) Specifically provide for the carrier's liability, limitation of liability, or time for suit; and

(c) Cannot be departed from by contract either at all or to the detriment of the shipper under that instrument.

[Chapter 7 is about the obligations of shippers. We need only note Art. 32.]

Chapter 7: Obligations of the shipper to the carrier

Article 32: Special rules on dangerous goods

When goods by their nature or character are, or reasonably appear likely to become, a danger to persons, property or the environment:[11]

(a) The shipper shall inform the carrier of the dangerous nature or character of the goods in a timely manner before they are delivered to the carrier or a performing party. If the shipper fails to do so and the carrier or performing party does not otherwise have knowledge of their dangerous nature or character, the shipper is liable to the carrier for loss or damage resulting from such failure to inform; and

(b) The shipper shall mark or label dangerous goods in accordance with any law, regulations or other requirements of public authorities that apply during any stage of the intended

---

10 Necessary to avoid conflict with liability conventions applicable other than to sea carriage.

11 Note inclusion of environment.

carriage of the goods. If the shipper fails to do so, it is liable to the carrier for loss or damage resulting from such failure.

Chapter 8: Transport documents and electronic transport records

Article 35: Issuance of the transport document or the electronic transport record

Unless the shipper and the carrier have agreed not to use a transport document or an electronic transport record, or it is the custom, usage or practice of the trade not to use one, upon delivery of the goods for carriage to the carrier or performing party, the shipper or, if the shipper consents, the documentary shipper, is entitled to obtain from the carrier, at the shipper's option:

(a)   A non-negotiable transport document or, subject to article 8, subparagraph (a), a non-negotiable electronic transport record; or

(b)   An appropriate negotiable transport document or, subject to article 8, subparagraph (a), a negotiable electronic transport record, unless the shipper and the carrier have agreed not to use a negotiable transport document or negotiable electronic transport record, or it is the custom, usage or practice of the trade not to use one.

Article 36: Contract particulars

(1)   The contract particulars in the transport document or electronic transport record referred to in article 35 shall include the following information, as furnished by the shipper:

(a)   A description of the goods as appropriate for the transport;

(b)   The leading marks necessary for identification of the goods;

(c)   The number of packages or pieces, or the quantity of goods; and

(d)   The weight of the goods, if furnished by the shipper.

(2)   The contract particulars in the transport document or electronic transport record referred to in article 35 shall also include:

(a)   A statement of the apparent order and condition of the goods at the time the carrier or a performing party receives them for carriage;

(b)   The name and address of the carrier;

(c)   The date on which the carrier or a performing party received the goods, or on which the goods were loaded on board the ship, or on which the transport document or electronic transport record was issued; and

(d)   If the transport document is negotiable, the number of originals of the negotiable transport document, when more than one original is issued.

(3)   The contract particulars in the transport document or electronic transport record referred to in article 35 shall further include:

(a)   The name and address of the consignee, if named by the shipper;

(b)   The name of a ship, if specified in the contract of carriage;

(c)   The place of receipt and, if known to the carrier, the place of delivery;

and

(d)   The port of loading and the port of discharge, if specified in the contract of carriage.

(4)   For the purposes of this article, the phrase "apparent order and condition of the goods" in subparagraph 2 (a) of this article refers to the order and condition of the goods based on:

(a)   A reasonable external inspection of the goods as packaged at the time the shipper delivers them to the carrier or a performing party; and

(b)   Any additional inspection that the carrier or a performing party actually performs before issuing the transport document or electronic transport record.

[Article 37 is on identity of the carrier.]

Article 41: Evidentiary effect of the contract particulars

Except to the extent that the contract particulars have been qualified . . . :

(a)   A transport document or an electronic transport record is prima facie evidence of the carrier's receipt of the goods as stated in the contract particulars;

(b)   Proof to the contrary by the carrier in respect of any contract particulars shall not be admissible, when such contract particulars are included in:

(i)   A negotiable transport document or a negotiable electronic transport record that is transferred to a third party acting in good faith; or

(ii)   A non-negotiable transport document that indicates that it must be surrendered in order to obtain delivery of the goods and is transferred to the consignee acting in good faith;

(c)   Proof to the contrary by the carrier shall not be admissible against a consignee that in good faith has acted in reliance on any of the following contract particulars included in a non-negotiable transport document or a non negotiable electronic transport record:

(i)   The contract particulars referred to in article 36, paragraph 1, when such contract particulars are furnished by the carrier;

(ii)   The number, type and identifying numbers of the containers, but not the identifying numbers of the container seals; and

(iii)   The contract particulars referred to in article 36, paragraph 2.

[Chapter 9 is on delivery of the goods, Chapter 10 on rights of the controlling party (a concept with no English law equivalent), and Chapter 11 on transfer of rights, which of course we deal with in the Carriage of Goods by Sea Act 1992.]

Chapter 12: Limits of liability

Article 59: Limits of liability

(1)   Subject to articles 60 and 61, paragraph 1, the carrier's liability for breaches of its obligations under this Convention is limited to 875 units of account per package or other shipping unit,[12] or 3 units of account per kilogram of the gross weight of the goods that are the subject of the

---

12 A little higher than Hamburg.

claim or dispute, whichever amount is the higher, except when the value of the goods has been declared by the shipper and included in the contract particulars, or when a higher amount than the amount of limitation of liability set out in this article has been agreed upon between the carrier and the shipper.

(2)   When goods are carried in or on a container, pallet or similar article of transport used to consolidate goods, or in or on a vehicle, the packages or shipping units enumerated in the contract particulars as packed in or on such article of transport or vehicle are deemed packages or shipping units. If not so enumerated, the goods in or on such article of transport or vehicle are deemed one shipping unit.

(3)   The unit of account referred to in this article is the Special Drawing Right as defined by the International Monetary Fund. The amounts referred to in this article are to be converted into the national currency of a State according to the value of such currency at the date of judgement or award or the date agreed upon by the parties. The value of a national currency, in terms of the Special Drawing Right, of a Contracting State that is a member of the International Monetary Fund is to be calculated in accordance with the method of valuation applied by the International Monetary Fund in effect at the date in question for its operations and transactions. The value of a national currency, in terms of the Special Drawing Right, of a Contracting State that is not a member of the International Monetary Fund is to be calculated in a manner to be determined by that State.

Article 60: Limits of liability for loss caused by delay

Subject to article 61, paragraph 2, compensation for loss of or damage to the goods due to delay shall be calculated in accordance with article 22 and liability for economic loss due to delay is limited to an amount equivalent to two and one-half times the freight payable on the goods delayed. The total amount payable pursuant to this article and article 59, paragraph 1, may not exceed the limit that would be established pursuant to article 59, paragraph 1, in respect of the total loss of the goods concerned.

Article 61: Loss of the benefit of limitation of liability

(1)   Neither the carrier nor any of the persons referred to in article 18 is entitled to the benefit of the limitation of liability as provided in article 59, or as provided in the contract of carriage, if the claimant proves that the loss resulting from the breach of the carrier's obligation under this Convention was attributable to a personal act or omission of the person claiming a right to limit done with the intent to cause such loss or recklessly and with knowledge that such loss would probably result.

(2)   Neither the carrier nor any of the persons mentioned in article 18 is entitled to the benefit of the limitation of liability as provided in article 60 if the claimant proves that the delay in delivery resulted from a personal act or omission of the person claiming a right to limit done with the intent to cause the loss due to delay or recklessly and with knowledge that such loss would probably result.

[Chapters 13–15 are not reproduced.]

Chapter 16: Validity of contractual terms

Article 79: General provisions[13]

(1) Unless otherwise provided in this Convention, any term in a contract of carriage is void to the extent that it:

(a) Directly or indirectly excludes or limits the obligations of the carrier or a maritime performing party under this Convention;

(b) Directly or indirectly excludes or limits the liability of the carrier or a maritime performing party for breach of an obligation under this Convention;

or

(c) Assigns a benefit of insurance of the goods in favour of the carrier or a person referred to in article 18.

(2) Unless otherwise provided in this Convention, any term in a contract of carriage is void to the extent that it:

(a) Directly or indirectly excludes, limits or increases the obligations under this Convention of the shipper, consignee, controlling party, holder or documentary shipper; or

(b) Directly or indirectly excludes, limits or increases the liability of the shipper, consignee, controlling party, holder or documentary shipper for breach of any of its obligations under this Convention.

[Article 80 provides special rules for "volume contracts", and 81 for live animals and certain other goods.]

Chapter 17: Matters not governed by this Convention

Article 82: International conventions governing the carriage of goods by other modes of transport[14]

Nothing in this Convention affects the application of any of the following international conventions in force at the time this Convention enters into force, including any future amendment to such conventions, that regulate the liability of the carrier for loss of or damage to the goods:

(a) Any convention governing the carriage of goods by air to the extent that such convention according to its provisions applies to any part of the contract of carriage;

(b) Any convention governing the carriage of goods by road to the extent that such convention according to its provisions applies to the carriage of goods that remain loaded on a road cargo vehicle carried on board a ship;

(c) Any convention governing the carriage of goods by rail to the extent that such convention according to its provisions applies to carriage of goods by sea as a supplement to the carriage by rail; or

---

13 The Art. III(8) (of Hague-Visby) equivalent.
14 An avoidance of conflict provision that should be read alongside Art. 26.

(d)   Any convention governing the carriage of goods by inland waterways to the extent that such convention according to its provisions applies to a carriage of goods without trans-shipment both by inland waterways and sea.

Article 83: Global limitation of liability

Nothing in this Convention affects the application of any international convention or national law regulating the global limitation of liability of vessel owners.

Article 84: General average

Nothing in this Convention affects the application of terms in the contract of carriage or provisions of national law regarding the adjustment of general average.

Article 85: Passengers and luggage

This Convention does not apply to a contract of carriage for passengers and their luggage.

[Article 86 deals with damage caused by nuclear incident. Then there are final clauses in Chapter 18.]

Index